THE ROCK YEARBOOK

EDITED BY IAN CRANNA

St. Martin's Press
New York

In-house editor
CAT LEDGER

Editor's assistant
ALISON TAYLOR

Cover by
KEN ANSELL and **DAVE DRAGON, THE DESIGN CLINIC**

Design by
DAVID BOSTOCK

Assisted by
MARCUS LYNCH

THE ROCK YEARBOOK 1988
Copyright © 1987 Virgin
Library of Congress Catalog Number 81-640382

ISBN 0-312-01082-6

Black and white printing by Anchor Brendon Ltd, Tiptree, Essex

Colour printing by Scot Print, Musselburgh, Scotland

Bound by Anchor Brendon Ltd, Tiptree, Essex

Typeset by Keyline Graphics, London, NW6

CONTRIBUTORS

● **LLOYD BRADLEY** was lured back to music journalism by such outrageous assurances as how endless discussions about food and "having a bloody good laugh" are adequate compensation for financial ruin. He now combines screen and stage writing with gruelling days working for *Q* magazine. So far, the highlight of 1987 has been donning that coveted garment the *Smash Hits* football shirt and making a fool of himself on Clapham Common. He sincerely hopes his one-year-old son, Georgie, will have more sense in both of the above areas.

● **GEOFF BROWN** has written books on Michael Jackson and Diana Ross, and commentated on all aspects of black music, theatre and film in numerous papers and films. Currently the Sports Editor at *Time Out*, he still gets on the good foot at least once a day.

● **JULIE BURCHILL** has been a journalist since she was 16. She has been called "the cleverest woman of all time" (by Peter York) and the BBC has described her as "more influential than Kim Wilde, Vanessa Redgrave and the Princess of Wales rolled into one". She is a contributor to *New Society*, *Elle*, *The Tatler* and *The Mail On Sunday*.

● **MARK COLEMAN** is a writer on youth culture whose articles have appeared in *Rolling Stone*, *Village Voice* and *Star Hits*. He is currently considering not writing another book.

● **RICHARD COOK** is the editor of *Wire*, Britain's jazz and new music magazine. Sometimes he thinks he's heard every record ever made but is convinced there's a few more to go yet. He also broadcasts and does other stuff. This year his very good friend the milkman said he should get married, so he did.

● **SIR IAN "JOCKY" CRANNA** remains the UK's most enduringly celebrated Scotsperson. He was knighted in '79 for his contribution to the exports of Skids and Simple Minds records and was awarded the DSO (and bar) two years later for his contributions to *NME* and his work as pioneering editor of *Smash Hits*. These days he writes for *Q*, *Smash Hits* and *Star Hits*, and edits projects like this one. In his spare time he is a major shareholder in the *Spud-U-Like* fast food chain. "Try the turnip," he says. "Yum!"

● **PAUL ELLIOTT** has been a freelance for *Sounds* for just over two years (fresh from A Level re-takes), covering the loudest and most objectionable thrash/speed/death metal rackets he can find. Somebody has to do it. Packing 12 months of incident and excitement into 2,000 words proved pretty difficult and so, for the exact opposite reasons, did this potted autobiography. Not to mention downright embarrassing.

● **DESSA FOX** is video editor of *NME* and contributes to *Time Out*.

● **PETE FRAME** lives in remotest Buckinghamshire, isolated from reality. There he continues to convince himself that the world of rock is still exciting enough to write about and, when not building a house in his own back garden, is *still*

bashing together a third volume of *Rock Family Trees*.

● **SIMON FRITH** teaches sociology at Warwick University when not being a rock critic for *The Observer* and a columnist for *Village Voice*.

● **SIMON GARFIELD** is a former *Guardian* Student Journalist Of The Year and author of the highly acclaimed music industry exposé, *Expensive Habits*. He is currently music editor of *Time Out*.

● **JOHN GILL** is books editor of *Time Out*. Prior to that he was their music editor and had earlier misspent his early twenties as house pseud on *Sounds*. He has also contributed to, amongst others, *The Times*, *Times Education Supplement* and *Smash Hits*.

● **ANDREW HARRISON** is a 20-year-old freelance pop pundit from Maghull on Merseyside. He has worked for the *City Press* agency, the *Daily Post* and *Liverpool Echo*, *Smash Hits* and the *Yorkshire Evening Post's Splash* paper. He likes comics, Volkswagen Beetles and hip-hop, and he lives in Leeds with two vegetarians, a Dire Straits fan and lots of records.

● **CHRIS HEATH, 24,** square-jawed and softly spoken, when not constructing the longest and most complex sentences this side of Zambesi (and probably the other side as well) and saying "y'know" more often than is strictly necessary, is Deputy Editor of *Smash Hits*; his hobbies include pro/celebrity kite-flying and he is currently sponsoring a Micro-Lite aircraft service to ferry people to Smiths concerts.

● **DAVID HEPWORTH**, when not reporting from remote foreign outposts for *Q* (where, as at *Smash Hits*, *Just Seventeen* and *Looks*) he is Editorial Director), divides his time between globe-shrinking TV journalism for the BBC and buffing up his priceless collection of Bruce Springsteen promotional hubcaps. It's a tough, demanding job but someone's got to do it. "While there are mountains left unclimbed," he begins . . .

● **TOM HIBBERT** of *Smash Hits*, *Q* and other "fine" titles is an English person with a pathetic devotion to Jack Palance, the bloke in *Man In A Suitcase* and other poor actors. His wife is far more impressive, having once kissed Elvis Presley on the lips and having been born just around the corner from Eric Brann of Iron Butterfly. (Eats toast.)

● **COLIN IRWIN** adores: Prince, pussycats, Irish folk music, avocado, cricket, living in Long Ditton, presenting programmes called *Acoustic Roots* for BBC Radio 2, being editor of *No. 1*, spending holidays in Alderney to be near the great John Arlott, and contributing to the *Virgin Rock Yearbook*. Ha, ha, ha.

● **DAVID A. KEEPS**, editor of *Star Hits* and contributor to only the best glossy magazines the world over, is a handsome, irrepressible rogue and "a birrova scamp" who loves blue skies above his head and white sand between his toes. He lives and works in New York City, natch, and is longing for the day

when he can introduce Madonna to the man with "the most beautiful eyelashes I've ever seen on a mammal".

● **VICI MacDONALD** spent a "memorable" 1986 as *Smash Hits'* mad dictator/genius design editor, during which she (a) single-handedly kept British Telecom in business by throwing at least 475 telephones a day into the waste paper basket, (b) nearly got sued by the Bank of England for a front cover consisting entirely of £5 notes and (c) earned about 50p (a snip!). She has now traded in her wonky typescale and grungy paintbrushes for the more serene (and lucrative) occupation of writing for the likes of *Smash Hits*, *Just Seventeen* and *The Face* – but when no one's looking, a lone tear moistens her cheek and out come those grungy paintbrushes again . . .

● **JIM McFARLIN**, 34, has covered rock and r'n'b music in the ancestral home of Motown since 1979. As entertainment critic of the *Detroit News*, this Michigan native has been writing on popular music and culture for over 13 years. His work has appeared in *USA Today*, *People*, *Life* and *Hit Parader*. He was also voted Michigan's best rock critic in 1981 and was the only Mid West rock critic to appear on the national media panel at the 1986 New Music Seminar. He is single, drives a rusting Ford Escort and knows Bob Seger personally.

● **MARK MOORE** started life early when he decided to become a club mega-star and sex symbol at the tender age of 13. By chance, he started DJing at the legendary Mud Club in London in 1983 when all the other DJs died in a mysterious shooting incident which still baffles police. The 22-ish-year-old DJ is currently helming the decks at the Mud, Pyramid and Sacrosanct clubs, has started producing and remixing records for the Rhythm King label and is a contributor to *Buzz* magazine.

● **CHARLES SHAAR MURRAY** was born in 1831 in Bad Ass, Texas. The eldest of 27 children, he spent his first 120 years in a state of edgy anticipation waiting for Johnny Guitar Watson to make his first record. When this failed to go platinum, Murray decided in a fit of pique to opt for reincarnation as a British pop-culture pundit. He resides in London with his wife, two Stratocasters and a word processor, and lives in hope that Simon Garfield will be able to read his forthcoming book on Jimi Hendrix before qualifying for an old-age pension.

● **FRANK OWEN** is a regular contributor to *i-D* and *Melody Maker* on rap and black music, and is currently working with Fred and Judy Vermorel on 'A Short History of Desire' (a book about post-Live Aid pop) to be published in 1988. With his new haircut, both Run DMC and Mantronix think he looks like Eddie Munster, though he can't see it himself.

● **BETTY PAGE** is currently Editrix of *Record Mirror*, but started off as secretary to the editor of *Sounds*, "looking for the ladder", as

Prince once said. Ten years later, after serving time as a writer on *Sounds* and as features editor on sadly short-lived popzine *Noise!*, she is still an enthusiastic observer of the pop circus and does not regret giving up a nice civil service pension for the joys of writing about pop groups.

● **TONY PARSONS** first received money for his writing when he was ten. Educated at Nick Logan's *New Musical Express*, he left the music business to write his bestseller, *Platinum Logic*, recently reprinted by Virgin Books. He is a regular contributor to *Arena*, *The Face* and *Elle*. He lives in Highbury – "The Home Of Football" – with his wife and his son. His latest novel is the infamous *Baby Love*.

● **PENNY REEL** has been writing about reggae for some sixteen years, and for *Echoes* for ten. Previously with the *NME*, he can now be found in the company of *Sounds*.

● **WILLIAM SHAW** was born in Newton Abbot in Devon and has been a music so-called journalist for four years, working on titles as diverse as *ZigZag* and *Smash Hits*. His local tax office have just found out about it and now he's in deep water. He doesn't like living in London one little bit.

● **DAVID SINCLAIR** is rock critic of *The Times* and a contributor to *Q*. His book *Tres Hombres – The Story of ZZ Top* was published last autumn.

● **MAT SNOW** fell victim to the *New Musical Express's* Night Of The Short Trousers in Spring 1987 and has since attached himself like a leech to the backside of the entertainment industry. His journeyman effusions have appeared in a growing list of publications including *Sounds*, *Q*, *The Guardian* and *Time Out*, and his ambition is to be a Yuppie by the time he's 30.

● **PHIL SUTCLIFFE**, in the circumstances, following free and frank discussions, weighing up the pros and cons, feels that, in the light of recent events, all things considered, it's probably six of one and half a dozen of the other – and will *nuke* anyone who challenges his right to say so! Meanwhile, hopes to continue gainful employment for *Q* and *Time Out*.

● **ALLYCE TESSIER** is a researching phenomenon who once kissed Elvis Presley on the lips before he was dead and who was born just around the corner from Eric Brann of Iron Butterfly. "Digs" Al Nipper of the Boston Red Sox and once bought an oscillating fan in a hardware store with her mother's credit card. (Perfect ankles.)

● **JOHN TOBLER** sets the questions for Radio One's *Rock Brain Of The Universe* and contributes to *Music Week*, *Billboard*, *Folk Roots* and *Which Compact Disc?* His office resembles a second hand shop, and he is unsure whether to boast about having become a grandfather. Nearly all the over twenty books on rock which he has written are now out of print. He is rather partial to asparagus.

ACKNOWLEDGEMENTS

Strange as it may seem, books like this *eighth* volume of opinion, information and sheer malice aforethought do not mysteriously assemble themselves on the eve of publication and, as so often happens, many of the unsung hero(in)es doing the most important backstage jobs never see their names in lights. They know who they are but so should you:

Heroine of the year is undoubtedly Alison Taylor in the Virgin office who photocopied, cut up, typed out, toted, fetched and was generally the meat in everyone's sandwich with unfailing good grace and ne'er so much as a dirty look whatever the lateness or ludicrousness of the task. Bravo Ma'am!

As ever, our thanks go out to those in the press and publicity offices of record companies and publishers great and small without whom there would be no pictures in this book. Well, almost no pictures – special thanks are due to Andrew Catlin for his photo of Bo Diddley, to Andre Csillag for his photo of the boy on his bike, to Chris Balcombe for his photo of the Boy George puppet, and especially to Drew Carolan in New York for his photo of the Black Rock Coalition. May their telephones never be silent.

The "Erm, Could We Have It Tomorrow?" Special Awards for emergency rescue services go to those tender-hearted souls who don't like to see a grown man beg: Charles Shaar Murray, John Tobler, Brian Harrigan, Mark Ellen (whose biographical skills were also much appreciated) and to Drew Carolan in New York. Friends in deed indeed.

The "Look This Really Is The Last Bit" Award for long-suffering typesetters goes this year to Geoff, Jim and Julie.

Gratitude in no small measure is also due to Derrin Schlesinger and Sue Miles at *Smash Hits* for allowing their brains (and their files) to be picked, and to Bill Rainbow of Regency for emergency transportation when it counted. Thanks, pop chums.

The Design Editor would also like to thank Chris Dart and Graham Street, sure of scalpel and wizard with wax, for their lay-out assistance during unsocial hours.

The Editor would also like to personally thank the Design Editor for unfailingly rising to the bait of the Editor's teasing and thereby preserving what little is left of his sanity. And for remaining calm when he got kranky. Scoff, you're a toff.

That's it – over and out.

I.C.

This book is dedicated to Johnnie Ray Rousseau of *Eight Days A Week* and to Larry Duplechan, his creator.

CONTENTS

AUGUST 1986

THE

1 Liverpool's 47 "rate rebel" councillors lose their appeal against surcharging and disqualification from office for failing to get a proper rate in 1985. "It was obvious the Tory judges were only intent on doing Thatcher's dirty work for her," quoth Derek Hatton, Mr Jobs-and-Services himself.

3 Sarm West Studios, where 'Feed The World' was made, records 'This Is My World', a benefit single for sickle cell anaemia research. Participants include Dee C Lee, Paul Weller, Paul Hardcastle and a couple of *EastEnders*.

5 Panic on the streets of Jo'burg as Britain goes for "teeny weeny" sanctions against South Africa. Mrs Thatcher tells the Nassau summit that Britain will only stop importing coal, steel, iron and krugerrands from the Land of the Rand.

● "Reagan is a fool and a madman. I am sorry that the power of a great nation is in the hands of an irresponsible man." Col. Muammar Gadafy, opening his campaign for the US presidency.

● Ozzy Osbourne is "elated, relieved and over the moon" when the Los Angeles Supreme Court decides his song 'Suicide Solution' was not responsible for a young American's death. John McCollum's father claimed that Ozzy's music had incited his son to commit suicide but Judge Cole, presiding, pronounced that "Ozzy's music may be totally objectionable to many but it can be given First Amendment protection too."

● Keyboards player Michael Rudetski, 27, dies of respiratory failure at Boy George's Hampstead home. An in-demand session man and expert with Ye Olde Fairlighte, he had worked with Man Parrish, and was in London to help make George's first solo album. An inquest detects heroin and methadone in his blood.

● The heady days of the seventies etc are revived in Channel 4's spittle-encrusted punk anniversary special *The Way They Were*, in which Tony Wilson introduces brilliant vintage footage of The Sex Pistols, The Clash, Elvis Costello and . . . er . . . Sham 69. Among the gems on show are The Fall's epic 'Industrial Estate' (lyrics: "Yeah, yeah! / Industrial estate!") and Pete Shelley telling an unruly crowd "Don't gob at me . . ."

9 A 21-year-old man is stabbed to death during Queen's set at the 120,000-capacity Knebworth Festival.

● Over 250 Gary Numan fans protest outside Radio One's offices – it seems Gazz is not getting enough airplay. Well, well.

13 Prince and the Revolution play Wembley – the Purple Perv's first appearance in the UK in five years and his first date here as a fully paid-up member of the popocracy. The diminutive genius rents out London clubs for three nights' intensive paaaaaartyin' after the shows.

15 The British Government's attempts to keep Peter Wright's MI5 revelations quiet by banning their publication in Australia become farcical as it is forced to admit that yes, the allegations of infiltration are true. To an extent, anyway.

● Record jobless figures: 3,279,594. The trend has been upwards for eight months now.

19 The Smiths' new videos – oops, film clips – are previewed at the Edinburgh Film Festival. Directed by Derek *Sebastiane* Jarman, the films for 'Panic', 'The Queen Is Dead' and 'There Is A Light That Never Goes Out' are a far cry indeed from standard visual brain-candy and accordingly get short shrift from our pop programmers.

20 The Band Aid trustees are sued for £700,000 by a West German firm which alleges that they failed to fulfil an oral contract to buy 28 trucks for use in Africa.

● Marilyn is freed on charges of heroin possession after the prosecution offers no evidence. He was arrested in the Operation Culture investigation which led to Boy George's arrest and had pleaded not guilty under his real name Peter Anthony Robinson. "I feel ecstatic," he chirrups later. "It wasn't what I had expected." The rumour that ZTT are after Maz's signature is not what *anybody* expected.

21 A post office worker and Vietnam vet kills 14 people and then shoots himself at his Oklahoma workplace after he's warned that he might lose his job unless his performance improves.

22 Channel 4 announces a new experiment; the "Special Discretion Required" triangle in the corner of the screen, denoting material which may be unsuitable for impressionable young minds and all that. The first late-night scorcher, *Themroc*, proves to be a tedious arty French job, leaving the lager-and-curry crew severely disappointed.

ALSO . . .

● Sigue Sigue Sputnik announce plans to flog advertising space between the tracks of their "long-awaited" debut album, originally *Buy The World* but now called *Flaunt It!* Among those who take space are *i-D* magazine, a hair gel manufacturer, EMI and of course the Sputnik Corporation.

● Band Aid tops the UK league of charities with £56.5 million donated in 1984/5.

● Assorted Radio One worthies – notably Mike Smith – complain that The Jesus And Mary Chain single 'Some Candy Talking' is about heroin. They miss the fact that it is A Brilliant Record.

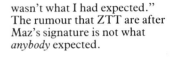

YEAR

2 Britain's first academic course in pop music opens at West Lothian College of Further Education. Essay titles include "Describe the main problems a new band must overcome before gigging . . ."

4 The Mission hit the independent number one spot with the ageing Neil Young song 'Like A Hurricane'.

5 Life begins for Freddie Mercury – he's 40 today.

8 The Human League release their first album in two years, the Jimmy Jam-Terry Lewis produced *Crash*. The single 'Human' makes number one in America.

10 Space Services Ltd. of the USA are granted permission to launch an orbiting mausoleum for the cremated remains of 10,000 people. Book early. . .

14 The tabloids go crazy apeshit as Alan Bleasdale's BBC series *The Monocled Mutineer* is accused by MP's of "distorting history". The series shows mutiny and rape by British soldiers stationed at Etaples in 1917 and according to the *Daily Mail* it is "evidence of the BBC's left-wing bias".

15 Ron 'n' Nancy make their first joint production since *Hellcats Of The Navy* in 1955 – a prime-time anti-drugs TV special. Nancy earlier admitted that her children may have smoked "a

17 Pat Phoenix, *Coronation Street*'s Elsie Tanner for 23 years, dies of cancer aged 62 at the Alexandra Hospital, Cheadle. Britain's one and only real queen of soap until the advent of the horrible *EastEnders*, she left the Street in 1983 for media immortality and a spot on a Smiths cover – 'Shakespeare's Sister'.

little dope" at college – the rascals!

● Naughty Wayne Hussey of The Mission is banned from Leeds' Warehouse club for having it off in the Ladies.

22 The Smiths announce their signing to EMI for a fee rumoured to be close to a million nicker. Behind-the-scenes wrangles which delayed *The Queen Is Dead* are said to be to blame. Though they ought to be used to losing their top acts to the majors by now, Rough Trade are bemused as they still have Mozzer and his chums under contract. Videos, new guitarists. . . where will it all end?

23 Health Minister Edwina Currie berates spotty northerners for eating too many chips and other unhealthy eating habits, to everyone's scorn. Apparently Britain gets through £900m worth of crisps each year.

24 Disneyland is hit by a $3m lawsuit from a woman who claims a drunken man in a Mickey Mouse outfit attacked her son while they were on holiday there.

28 The storm breaks over Harvey Proctor MP (Con, Billericay) as the *Sunday People* publishes allegations of spanking sessions.

● Eight Liverpool Militants fail to appeal against their expulsions to the Labour Party conference in Blackpool. "We were not prepared to give credibility to a farce," rants their chief self-publicist Derek Hatton.

30 The nation weeps as Michelle jilts Lofty at the alter in *EastEnders*. The final heart-rending scene in which the bespectacled goon collapses in tears on his bed proves the final straw for 60 inmates of Dartmoor Prison 'B' wing, who have put up with bad TV reception all week. They trash the telly room.

● Trouble for the pioneering ex-independent label Stiff. The ailing empire of Dave Robinson has debts of £3.5 million, including £750,000 to ex-partners Island Records. Eventually they are bought out by none other than 1984's money-spinners ZTT.

● Madness announce that they are splitting just when we need them most, bringing to an end seven years of effortlessly brilliant pop which yielded 23 Top 40 singles.

They had grown from a septet of "do-what-john" chirpy cockney types into the Double Deckers of *Top Of The Pops* and beyond, and that was their charm. Dependable to a fault, they wrote songs and made videos which made a far more permanent soundtrack to growing up in the 1980's than any preening pop dullard, because they lived in the same world as the rest of us not in some Campari-ad designer universe. Everybody – whether they admitted it or not – liked Madness.

But even pop institutions cannot last for ever and comedy's a melancholy business at heart. Fittingly, it was sadness that ended Madness. The departure in 1984 of keyboards player Mike Barson, who had held the fledgling Madness steady in the early days, cast a shadow on the house of fun. Their last album proper, the pensive, poignant *Mad Not Mad*, found the erstwhile Nutty Boys not in Benny Hill territory as the public still half expected, but swapping wry, despondent cracks at the graveside of the easygoing England that we thought would last for ever. They left a parting single 'Waiting For The Ghost Train' and a final compilation *Utter Madness*, each one inducing a lump in the throat as the eighties finest pop moments slip by. Madness is over and pop is poorer for it. Suddenly, a lot of people feel very old.

OCTOBER
1986

1 "Duke" Hussey is appointed chairman of the BBC – it's seen as a move to silence Conservative claims of political bias in the Corporation.

● Chernobyl No.1 reactor is working again, according to *Isvestia*. Five months previously, it burnt out in the world's worst nuclear accident.

7 *The Independent*, Britain's first new quality newspaper in 131 years, is launched. It sells 650,000 copies, and wins the 1986 Newspaper of the Year award early in 1987.

9 The British Medical Council stuns the nation with the news that "there is a clear link between illegal drug use and unemployment."

14 St Bob Geldof doesn't get the Nobel Peace Prize for his Band Aid efforts but does get an unprecedented special mention from the organizers who deem him "worthy of all possible praise and honour." The prize goes instead to historian Elie Wiesel who survived Buchenwald to document the Holocaust. Bob's comment? "As I said to my dad, there are only two hopes – Bob Hope and fuck all hope." Meanwhile Bob's autobiography *Is That It?* becomes Sidgwick & Jackson's biggest selling autobiography ever, shifting 100,000 copies but his first solo single, the remarkably unremarkable, 'This Is The World Calling', is a flop.

12 Ronald Reagan and Mikhail Gorbachev's summit meeting in Reykjavik fails when the USA refuses to discuss Star Wars. According to George Schultz, they arrive at "extremely important potential agreements" – whatever that means.

13 The Queen goes to China. During the trip, fun-loving royal consort Prince Philip warns a British student that "If you stay here much longer, you'll get slitty eyes." Flunkies scurry to cover up the gaffe.

14 Happy birthday, Lord Cliff Richard – the Dorian Gray of pop is 46 today!

15 Terry Waite hands a cheque for £1.25 million to Sport Aid organizer St Bob on behalf of the YMCA's Youth Care International charity.

19 Six arrests as The Smiths' concert in Newport turns nasty. Morrissey is pulled offstage and receives a black eye and sound engineer Grant Showbiz is hit on the head by a bottle.

20 The BBC settles out of court in the *Panorama* "Maggie's Militant Tendency" case which alleged that two Tory MPs had extreme right-wing links. With its new chairman, the BBC appears increasingly open to political pressure.

25 Half Man Half Biscuit take the indie number one position with 'Dickie Davies' Eyes'.

26 Best-selling novelist Jeffrey Archer resigns as Tory Party chairman after the *News Of The World* allegedly set him up with Monica Coghlan, a prostitute he says he has never met. She claims to need £2,000 to leave the country and Archer gives it to her, thinking it will prevent their names being linked. But the *NOTW* blows the gaffe and Archer returns to political wilderness like one of his own fictional characters with the words "I have been very silly, very foolish . . . what else can I say?"

27 The Big Bang happens and nobody notices, except exasperated Stock Exchange people whose new computerized exchange goes off-line for an hour on its first day of operation.

● More trouble for The Smiths. Morrissey is hit by a coin at their Preston Guildhall show and it is called off. The press have a field day portraying Smiths concerts as a cross between the Heysel disaster and a Roman Arena.

28 The last great "up and under" for the legendary Eddie Waring who dies aged 76 after a long illness. The Rugby League commentator extraordinaire and *It's A Knockout* presenter will be sorely missed by those in the rugby world.

● *The News Of The World* (again) runs an exposé on Sarah-Jane Morris, singer with "left-wing gay duo" The Communards, and her "seedy past that would shock her trendy teenage fans." It seems Sarah used to sing rude blues songs. And, er, that's it.

30 Norman Tebbit claims that Kate Adie's BBC report on the American bombing of Libya was "uncritical carriage of Libyan propaganda." The piece later wins the Royal Television Society's award for best news item.

ALSO . . .

● Codpiece-sportin' Larry Blackmon of Cameo nails the world's problems in one fell blow: "I reckon the world is going crazy because of bad diet habits." Word!

● The British Gas flotation is heralded by the "Tell Sid" campaign. For weeks and weeks the nation is pestered into buying shares with one of the biggest, most annoying ad campaigns ever staged.

● Marc Almond is the latest victim of the new pop puritanism as his video for 'Ruby Red', which features "romping devils and lots of choreography," is censored not by the TV authorities but by Virgin Records. "Men's buttocks have been around for a long time and we must learn to live with them," Almond declares.

● Next year's naughty nerds the bouncing Beastie Boys run into trouble with Michael Jackson, who refuses them permission to release their Bestial version of The Beatles' 'I'm Down'. Jacko owns the lovable mop-tops' back catalogue, much to the annoyance of his chum Paul McCartney.

● UB40 go on the biggest tour of the USSR ever by a British band. They play to 120,000 people at 12 dates in Moscow, Minsk and Leningrad. They shoot a video and record a live album especially for the State Melodia label.

NOVEMBER 1986

1 Billy Bragg is arrested and charged with criminal damage after a CND wire-cutting demonstration at Baw Bargh military base near Norwich.

5 Headmistress Maureen McGoldrick, suspended by Brent Council pending an investigation into a racist remark she allegedly made at school, returns to work.

6 Ron Atkinson sacked as manager of Manchester United after a dismal run of results.

● Bassist Cait O'Riordan leaves The Pogues to take further education classes and be with her feller, Elvis Costello. Pogue-roadie Darryl Hunt takes over the bass chores.

● Ringo Starr's son Jason Starkey, aged 19, is fined £125 by Marylebone magistrates for stealing a radio cassette from a car.

● A two-year suspended sentence for the Marquess of Blandford, for possession of cocaine. The heir to the £60 million Blenheim Palace estate is said to have spent £20,000 on nose candy between October and December 1985.

12 Go! Mansions, seat of the mighty Go! Discs empire, is burgled. Gold discs, a computer, an ansaphone, teabags and a unique Billy Bragg woolly disc (especially knitted by the man himself) are among the items to "walk". Some of the stuff is returned but The Housemartins' *London O, Hull 4* gold disc is still missing.

13 The Irangate scandal breaks as Ronald Reagan admits the Americans sold "small amounts of arms to Iran." The Reagan administration is eventually revealed to have made the sales via the shady National Security Council in return for freed hostages, and they sent the money to the Nicaraguan Contras without telling anyone. It may have run to $50 million.

Reagan claims he "was not fully informed of the nature of one of the activities undertaken in connection with this initiative" and sacks NSC boss Admiral John Poindexter and Colonel Oliver North as a damage-limitation exercise.

15 Unemployed hod carrier Michael Lush, 25, falls 120ft to his death while rehearsing a stunt for the BBC's *Late Late Breakfast Show*. Presenter Noel says he "doesn't have the heart to carry on" and the show is scrapped.

● Shares plummet on the Stock Exchange as Ivan Boesky's multi-million dollar insider dealing scam breaks.

Hindley, now 43 and in her 22nd year of a life sentence for five child murders, passed on new information to the police. Ian Brady, 46, is in Park Lane high security mental hospital on Merseyside and refuses to co-operate.

● Two armed robbers shoot dead Terrance and Mary Duffy, the parents of actor Patrick Duffy who plays Bobby Ewing in *Dallas*, at their bar in Boulder, Montana.

24 Barclays Bank sells its interests in South Africa after 17 years of boycotting by the Anti-Apartheid movement.

27 The organizer of the arms-for-Iran operation Col. Oliver North admits he destroyed potentially incriminating evidence when he was dismissed from President Reagan's National Security Council.

17 The heftiest live album ever, Bruce Springsteen's 40-track box set *Live 1975-1985* comes out to the anguish of bootleggers. At 30 nicker, aficionados judge it a bargain.

19 Police return to the Pennine Moors to search for the bodies of two more suspected victims of the Moors Murderers. Myra

28 Independent distributors Making Waves go under leaving the indie scene minus another useful asset.

ALSO...

● Run DMC collaborate with Michael Jackson on an anti-crack track for Jacko's new album.

● The Government's "Don't Die Of Ignorance" AIDS campaign begins with 23 million leaflets distributed and prime-time TV adverts. The DHSS will not issue free needles to drug injectors, nor lift the IBA's ban on condom advertising, in case they are seen to condone drug-taking and promiscuity.

But the medical establishment widely criticizes the campaign as too little, too late. The TV adverts in particular are very peculiar, with sombre voice-overs and sober black-and-white camera-work, depicting large tombstones. Little practical information is included apart from advice to use a condom.

The Communicable Disease Surveillance Centre estimates that AIDS deaths will double every year. It expects 3,000 in 1988.

● The Revolution stops at closing time . . . Prince splits his band after four years together, and puts together a new version. He records the *Sign 'O' The Times* album solo, while former Revolutionaries Wendy Melvoin and Lisa Coleman plan an album together. Drummer Bobby Z returns to producing.

● Publishing magnate Robert Maxwell wins £250,000 damages from *Private Eye*. The satirical magazine had claimed that Cap'n Bob had financed Neil Kinnock's foreign trips in the hope of gaining a peerage from a future Labour government . . .

● Ex-Birthday Party bassist Tracy Pew dies aged 28 in Melbourne of an epileptic fit. He had made a guest appearance on Nick Cave's *Kicking Against The Pricks* album but had otherwise given music up for a politics and philosophy course at Monash University.

DECEMBER 1986

1 Guinness shares go through a very iffy patch as DTI inspectors probe their £2.5 billion takeover of Distillers. Links with inside-dealer Ivan Boesky are revealed.

● The 119 assorted hippies and ne'er-do-wells yet to be charged after their arrest at the 1985 Battle of Stonehenge have their cases dropped – the courts can't be bothered to follow them up.

2 Hoorah! – 'The Skye Boat Song' by Roger Whittaker and Des O'Connor brings some decorum back to a riff-raffy chart.

5 Mark E. Smith's first play *Hey! Luciani* opens at London's Riverside Theatre. Based around the life and death of Pope John Paul I, it is universally agreed to be crap.

7 Run DMC's scratch DJ Jam Master Jay livens up a phone-in held by New York's Radio WGCI on the teenage gang problem. After an hour of old fogies holding forth, Jay rings in and tells them that The Kids will never quit the gangs until people like him tell them it's cool. Immediately The Kids ring up in droves . . .

8 An instant killing for anyone who bought British Gas shares – they go up 17p on their first day on the Stock Market.

9 Czech police disperse 400 peace demonstrators who gather in Prague to mark the fifth anniversary of John Lennon's murder.

11 In a jolly Christmas address to an AIDS and hepatitis conference in Manchester, Chief Constable James Anderton announces: "Everywhere I go I see increasing evidence of people swirling about in a human cesspit of their own making . . ."

15 The Dead Kennedys get into yet another censorship row when HMV are rumbled for removing a 12-page paper detailing their American court case from inside the *Bedroom For Democracy* album. Their company Alternative Tentacles stops sending any records to the chain.

In the States they face possible imprisonment for distributing the poster "Penis Landscape" (depicting lots of private parts) by H.R Giger with their *Frankenchrist* album. Proscutors claim it is "obscene" and that the Kennedys are "distributing disturbing harmful matter to minors."

16 One-time Wings member Denny Laine goes bust to the tune of £76, 035. He blames bad financial advice.

● Actor Douglas Lambert, star of *Bonanza*, *Inside Story* and *Rawhide*, dies aged 50 of AIDS.

20 Hard-drinkin', rock 'n' roll rascal guitarist Craig Gannon, 20, "leaves" The Smiths after just eight months. Gannon was blamed for the Whalley Range wonders' strange mutation into a Mancunian Rolling Stones but it seems he had less involvement than met the eye. The Smiths claim he often didn't turn up for rehearsals and could "put it away a bit." He vanishes to form The Cradle and The Smiths soldier on.

21 The Curse of George strikes again as unemployed Mark Golding, 20, collapses and dies at the Boy's Paddington flat. An inquest examines his blood and finds methadone and heroin.

16 Their acapella version of the Isley Brothers 'Caravan Of Love' is the Housemartins' first number one. The group have a bet on that it'll be the Christmas chart-topper and they intend to give the cash to Anti-Apartheid, but 'tis not to be . . . Jackie Wilson's 'Reet Petite' becomes the first posthumous Christmas number one since John Lennon's 'Starting Over' in 1981 (which doesn't really count).

The jolly tinsel-encrusted indie Christmas number one is Age Of Chance's brutally lacerated version of Prince's 'Kiss'. Half-a-dozen remixes later it earns them a fat contract with Virgin.

ALSO...

● Alison Moyet splits up from her husband Malcolm, taking son Joe with her.

● US National Archives reveal that Elvis Presley had an audience with tricky Dicky Nixon in 1970 and denounced the lovable Beatles as anti-American and pro-drugs! He wanted to be part of a law-and-order campaign "to restore some respect for the flag," and eventually they gave him a specially-made Bureau of Narcotics badge. His death in 1977 was largely due to prolonged drug abuse . . .

● Super dynamite socialist soul men The Redskins split up.

● The first British concerts by a-ha provoke incredible scenes of screaming young ladies reminiscent of Beatlemania etc.

● St Cliff Richard objects to the rude contents of the Comic Relief *Utterly*, *Utterly Live Video* and it is replaced by an edited version which is utterly, utterly Cliff-less.

● AIDS-mania reaches epidemic proportions and everybody wants a condom for Christmas. Radio One launches a "Play Safe" campaign which Monsignor Vincent Nicholas, the General Secretary of the Roman Catholic Bishops' Conference condemns as encouraging promiscuity.

There isn't much else to do during the winter months in Iceland so the government there issues a free condom to the island's 15,000 young people as a gentle hint. Back home, pilot schemes for free needles are opened in London, Edinburgh, Glasgow and Dundee.

Condoms get the inevitable designer treatment for the fashion-conscious, with *Jiffi* putting them in cigarette-style packs and Katherine Hamnett launching boxer shorts with a condom-pouch (just in case). Even Filofax release an optional condom-container for their "personal organizers" and the London Rubber Company reports record sales. Truly, in the words of Boy George, we are becoming a Condom Nation.

JANUARY 1987

2 Miki Zone, keyboards players with Man 2 Man, dies aged 25 in New York of spinal meningitis. After the death of Michael Rudetsky in 1986, this leaves Miki's brother Paul as the only surviving band member. The Man Parrish meets Man 2 Man single 'Male Stripper' is a hit later this month.

● God calls on American televangelist Oral Roberts at his Tulsa home and tells him that, unless he raises $4.5 million in donations by March, God will "call him home . . ." At least that's what millionaire pentecostalist Oral says. "I am asking you to help extend my life," pleads the 69 year old. "You are building an account with God." Donations of $100 and more flood in.

5 The nation weeps as Aled Jones announces his retirement from the top of the rock 'n' roll tree at the age of 16. He wants to concentrate on his 'O' levels.

● Elton John goes into St Vincent's Hospital in Sydney, Australia for exploratory throat surgery.

● Self-confessed "punk rocker" Brian Ralph, 20, from Cheltenham, is admitted to train for the priesthood. "I'll keep my hair spiky," the future padre says, "but only because it looks stupid flat."

7 Prince Edward leaves the Royal Marine barracks to "consider the future." Eventually he quits.

11 Frankie Goes To Hollywood open what proves to be their farewell tour at Manchester's G-Mex Centre. Their second album *Liverpool*

struggles to shift 60,000 copies against *Welcome To The Pleasure Dome's* million-plus sales but to everyone's amazement the final shows are stunning spectacles. They'd been pocket-scally Springsteens all along and nobody had noticed . . .

12 Michael Jackson is rumoured to want to buy Motown Records (est. 1959). Berry Gordy's reported asking price for the soul empire is a mere $75 million.

15 Inspector Douglas Lovelock is cleared of maliciously wounding Cherry Grace in the shooting which caused the September 1985 Brixton riots.

16 The panic button is well and truly pushed at Tyne Tees and Channel 4 when *Tube* presenter Jools Holland drops a classic clanger during a trailer for the ailing pop prog. Speaking in the commercial break during Bob Holness's *Blockbusters* kids quiz, Jolly Jools advises "all the groovy fuckers" to tune into *The Tube* later. His face registers mute horror even as the offending word leaves his lips, but not even an apology on that very self-same *Tube* can save him from a six-week suspension.

But it's a good month for Paula Yates rumour-fans. She is said to be "carrying on" not only with superfly hardest-working-man-in-showbusiness Dr Robert of The Blow Monkeys but also with Ben Volpeliere-Pierrot of Curiosity Killed The Cat and also velvet-voiced beanpole Terence Trent D'Arby. And all unbeknownst to husband St Bob. What a busy life she must lead.

18 More words of wisdom from Chief Constable James Anderton, this time on Radio 4: "God moves in mysterious ways. Given my love of God and my belief in God and Jesus Christ, I have to accept that I may well be used by God."

● The BBC's planned then banned *Secret Society* series exposes the Zircon project – a £500 million spy satellite for Britain.

21 Terry Waite fails to return to his Beirut hotel after meeting two US hostages and representatives of the Islamic Jihad.

24 There are 300 injuries, including 167 policemen, in a night of picketline violence outside News International's Wapping plant. The police claim that the trouble was organized; the pickets claim police brutality.

25 Two new Levi 501 ads make their debut on TV, mixing great music of the sixties with slick nostalgic presentation to exploit the mood of a country that's run out of optimism for the future. Ben E. King's 'Stand By Me' is the soundtrack for the nightclub ad featuring former motorbike stuntman Eddie Kidd, while 14-year-old "model" Rachel Roberts waves a tearful farewell to her GI to the tune of Percy Sledge's 'When A Man Loves A Woman' in the other. Barnett and Lyons' productions of the two exceed Levi's £400,000 budget and stand head and shoulders over the rest of the TV advertising.

● The Zircon row gets nastier as Special Branch raid the offices of the New Statesman and journalist Duncan Campbell in a search for naughty materials.

29 BBC Director-General Alistair Milne resigns "for personal reasons." Did he fall or was he pushed and was it anything to do with the BBC's wanting to regain the Government's favour?

ALSO...

● A cache of previously unknown Jim Morrison material is found in San Francisco, in a box marked "127 Fascination". Poems, song lyrics and postcards are among the final thingies put together by the Lizard King in Paris just proir to his death in 1971, and which are still owned by The Doors.

● **The Cure find their 1979 song 'Killing An Arab' on the compilation *Standing On The Beach* is being used by right-wing American DJs to whip up anti-Arab feelings in the wake of the Tripoli bombing. They offer to play a concert in the States and donate the proceeds to American and Palestinian/Lebanese orphanages.**
Robert Smith condemns the hijacking of the song and future copies of the album and its accompanying video *Staring At The Sea* carry a sticker saying so.

FEBRUARY 1987

1 Special Branch raids the Glasgow offices of BBC Scotland, confiscating all episodes of the *Secret Society* series and any connecting material they fancy. Opposition spokesmen go crazy apeshit – it's "a major menace to civil liberties and freedom of speech in Britain."

● Ridiculous sentences are handed out to the guilty in the Ealing Vicarage rapes and burglary case. One man found guilty of aggravated burglary and assault gets 14 years imprisonment while the two who also raped a woman get just three and five years.

● Veteran broadcaster Fyfe Robertson – he of the deerstalker and refined Scots accent – dies at 84.

5 Fearing bankruptcy, Brenda Dean's SOGAT calls off the Wapping dispute after a troubled year. News International re-opens its compensation fund for 5,000 printers sacked by Rupert Murdoch, and drops the pending legal action which had threatened to destroy SOGAT.

6 Morgan Khan's Streetsounds empire hits trouble. Built on the riches of his definitive hip-hop and dance compilation albums which brought expensive imports within The Kids' reach, it loses on Khan's Streetwave label and the accompanying magazine.

● Gary Numan's label Numa also goes down the tubes.

9 Go! Discs sue *The Sun* over a ridiculous "Housemartins are gay and rich too!" story.

● Auditors discover that hundreds of fraudulent British Gas share applications were passed without action.

11 'Shoplifters Of The World Unite' by the Smiths is the new indie number one. Top album is *Pictures Of Starving Children Sell Records* by Chumbawamba.

● Cynthia Payne is cleared of controlling prostitutes at her Streatham home. Weeks of lurid coverage had revealed tales of lesbianism in the lounge, and bondage in the bathroom and the testimony of an undercover policeman who had to attend a Payne sex party as a transvestite called "Amanda".

15 The Crufts' Supreme Champion is Champion Viscount Grant – a pedigree afghan hound bred by Chris Amoo of Liverpool funksters The Real Thing.

23 A 23-year-old Oxford student launches a court fight to prevent his 21-year-old ex-girlfriend from having "his" baby aborted. It fails.

24 Robert Maxwell's *London Daily News* is launched and to everyone's surprise it is not crap. Not to be outdone, Lord Rothermere exhumes the *Evening News* after seven years' absence and Maxwell halves the price of the *LDN* to compete. A good old-fashioned newspaper war ensues.

25 Stevie Winwood wins the Best Vocalist Award and Single Of The Year for 'Higher Love', his first Grammies in 20 years of trying.

26 CD bores have a field day as the first four Fab Four albums are remastered by

9 The BPI awards are given out at London's Grosvenor Hotel, and the major label popocrats of our fine pop-exporting nation slap each other's backs until they get sore hands. All-round creep Jonathan King compères to the horror of the ordinary viewer. 'West End Girls' by the Pet Shop Boys gets Best British Single and Peter Gabriel gets Best British Singer and Best Video for the fruitcake 'Sledgehammer' vid. Best International Artist is Paul Simon . . .

original producer George Martin and released in shiny, silver, over-priced format. *Please Please Me*, *With The Beatles*, *A Hard Day's Night* and *Beatles For Sale* arouse a nostalgia-wallowing session among yuppies, fogies, bogies and all and sundry as the march of CD engulfs us all. "If it's round and it's analogue, it's a diminishing configuration," trumpets Russ Back of WEA. Tony Wilson of Factory agrees: "I've always hated vinyl because it's so temperamental and there's so much shit on the records."

27 Fine Yong Cannibal David Steele is hit by a car and suffers a broken arm, just as FYC return to the charts with their questionable cover of Pete Shelley's 'Ever Fallen In Love?' from the soundtrack of the movie *Something Wild*.

ALSO ...

● Blue Note's Alfred Lion dies aged 78. He founded the label, which handled Thelonious Monk and Art Blakey's Jazz Messengers among many others, in 1939.

● American immigration officials plan to tighten up the regulations for obtaining work permits for foreign entertainers. It could mean no US tours for British acts unless they're in the Dire Straits bracket.

● AIDS is still public enemy number one and everyone has their own little snippet to add. Health Minister Edwina Currie leads the crusade: "Good Christian people who would not dream of misbehaving will not catch AIDS," she reveals. And her advice to the businessmen of Great Britain? "There is one thing above all they can take with them to stop them catching AIDS – and that is the wife." So there you have it.

The Government allocates an extra £4 million to AIDS treatment – some £9 million short of what doctors say they need – and decide not to back research into a cure.

But who needs a cure when Mike Smith has told you how to use a condom? All the TV channels fling themselves into the crisis with the sort of enthusiasm usually reserved for Royal Weddings and the World Cup, with AIDS Specials littering the schedules.

In the States, the three major networks drop their ban on condom ads. Time to burn rubber!

MARCH 1987

1 Two tracks from the forthcoming Michael Jackson album – possibly called *Bad* – are previewed at a music business bash. 'Pyramid Girl' and 'Bad' are reportedly in the can, along with a duet with Barbra Streisand, the Run DMC anti-crack collaboration and one called 'Smooth Criminal'. Rumours abound, however, that the album requires "substantial re-writes" and producer Quincy Jones is said to be nearing the end of his tether after nearly four years of off-and-on work. Jackson keeps diverting himself – most recently to shoot a video for 'Bad' with Martin Scorcese – and another for 'Smooth Criminal'. Stevie Wonder was never like this.

Meanwhile, true to his Wacko Jacko label, the Peter Pan of Pop launches a range of fluffy toys based on himself and his menagerie of llamas, chimps and snakes.

4 Wrist-slapping for Big Audio Dynamite when they show video nasties at their London Astoria show. The punters feel queasy.

5 New at number nine in the charts – 'The Great Pretender' by the now-moustacheless Freddie Mercury. The muzzie starts its own career as bassist with Zodiac Mindwarp.

6 The Townsend Thoreson ferry *Herald Of Free Enterprise* sails out of Zeebrugge harbour with its bow doors open. It sinks, trapping hundreds of people inside. The bodies of 173 people are entombed in the ferry which lies on its side outside Zeebrugge harbour for

weeks before it can be righted.

The horror of the accident is undeniable but there is something distasteful about *The Sun's* Ferry Aid fund-raising record. Though it makes number one at the end of the month, *The Sun* and the other tabloids wallow deeply in the ferry story's "human interest".

And what Boy George, as much a victim of the self-righteous Street of Shame as anyone, is doing singing on the record is anyone's guess. Nevertheless, the rehabilitation of George is complete as the troubled Culture Clubber has his own number one single with the old Ken Boothe hit 'Everything I Own'. Buddhism seems to be the secret of the Boy's recovery, but he says he won't become a monk. At least he's kicked that habit.

● Dennis Potter's provocative series *The Singing Detective* wins the Broadcasting Press Guild Award for Best Television Drama and its star Michael Gambon gets the Best Actor Award. Potter himself receives a special award for his "imaginative and pioneering use of the medium as a writer." The awards are a vindication for *The Singing Detective*, which attracted a lot of flak for having the temerity to show human bottoms and other things during prime-time viewing.

17 *The Tube* is killed off. Its current fifth series, marred by Jools Holland's faux pas and the departure of its driving force producer Malcolm Gerrie, will be its last, and TV pop will be a little

blander for its demise.

● The Budget is best described as "cautious" and the pundits detect a General Election on the horizon.

● U2's fifth album *The Joshua Tree* sprouts up at number one in the album chart. A London record shop opens at midnight on the release day so that eager buyers don't have to wait until 9 am.

Meanwhile the shadow of Beastiedom falls over our innocent pop kids as '(You Gotta) Fight For Your Right (To Party)' lurches into the British chart. The custard pie infested video is eventually banned – sorry, given low rotation – by the BBC as it encourages all kinds of unruliness.

19 Three men are given life sentences for the murder of PC Keith Blakelock during the Broadwater Farm riots. He was hacked to death by a mob of 60 rioters in the 1985 disturbances.

● Mrs Thatcher refuses an inquiry into allegations that members of MI5 who believed Harold Wilson was a Soviet agent tried to bring down his government in the late 1970's.

● Praise the Lord, Oral Roberts is not taken up to Glory when he reaches his collection target as "God's" deadline expires. But what's this? It seems that the final $870,000 is not going to a medical mission at all but to maintaining his PTL (Praise The Lord) TV Church empire

and Heritage USA theme park which have inexplicably fallen on hard times. God is not mocked . . .

Meanwhile the gaff is blown on another dodgy American God-slot merchant. Rev Jim Bakker has to resign his ministry for failing to obey the twelfth commandment – thou shalt not covet thy neighbour's secretary – and he too is in financial trouble. Wags that they are, the US press nickname the whole mess "Pearlygate".

23 South African President P.W. Botha receives his first gold disc, for 40,000 sales of his first single 'Why You Should Vote NP' – an electioneering double A-side in English and Afrikaans. It does not become a dancefloor fave anywhere.

30 The Oscars are doled out. Oliver Stone's Vietnam guilt-purger *Platoon* scoops four, including Best Film and Best Director, while deaf actress Marlee Matlin gets Best Actress for her first major role, opposite William Hurt in *Children Of A Lesser God*. 'Take My Breath Away' by Berlin from *Top Gun* is the Best Original Song while Herbie Hancock's score for the jazz movie *Round Midnight* wins the Best Score award. Woody Allen's *Hannah And Her Sisters*, and *A Room With A View* with Helena Bonham-Carter each get three awards, and Micheal Caine's Best Supporting Actor prize is his very first Oscar.

ALSO...
● Sean Penn belts a Los Angeles musician who said hello to his spouse and gets a $1,200 fine for the privilege.

● The *Sun* launches its nasty "Elton John in cocaine and rent boys shock" "exposé" and Elton sues for libel. He later withdraws a writ blocking the publication of personal photographs.

16 So, farewell then Frankie Goes To Hollywood . . . After months of in-fighting, it's finally revealed that, yes, Frankie do hate each other and they split at the end of a European tour. What a sad way for it all to end.

APRIL 1987

1 International AIDS Day is marked by concerts across the nation including The Party at Wembley Arena which raises £125,000. Many thousands of condoms are given away.

3 Keith Best MP (Ynys Mon, Con.) is rumbled for having made multiple applications for British Telecom shares. The naughty honourable member for Anglesey put in for no fewer than six sets of shares; he resigns as the Election and criminal proceedings loom.

5 Paul Simon's *Graceland* tour comes to Britain. Anti-Apartheid campaigners picket the shows, which feature black South African band Ladysmith Black Mambazo and seasoned AA Campaigner Hugh Masekela.
The ubiquitous Jerry Dammers of Artists Against Apartheid says: "To say that you like Paul Simon's music is irrelevant. That's like saying we shouldn't boycott South African fruit because it tastes nice. The boycott has to be total and consistent if it's to be effective."

6 Two first cousins of the Queen are found to have spent 40 years in a Surrey mental hospital while Burke's Peerage listed them as dead. Their family deny a cover-up and say there was an "oversight" in filling out the Burke's forms.

8 The noose tightens around Harvey Proctor MP as he is charged with four acts of gross indecency with young boys . . .

13 Extradition proceedings against 26 Liverpool "fans" in connection with the Heysel Disaster collapse. DPP lawyers are accused of incompetence in compiling the case.

20 The Jesus And Mary Chain make their comeback with the 'April Skies' single – a surprise Top Ten hit

for the spotty Scots who were the bane of the universe this time last year.

23 It's revealed that the former MI5 officer Sir Maurice Oldfield was gay and would have been considered a security risk had he not kept his sex life a secret. It was later discovered and Oldfield was placed under surveillance.

24 The very last ever *Tube* sails off down the Tyne. Duran Duran are the last big act but Godfather of Soul James Brown – who was scheduled to appear – can't make it.

26 The *News On Sunday*, Britain's first left-wing tabloid Sunday paper, launches. Touting itself as "Britain's Brightest and Bravest", it's also non-sexist and non-racist with a unique charter intended to keep the paper sound. Unfortunately, the punters are not attracted in any great numbers and within weeks the paper is in trouble. It is bailed out by property millionaire Owen Oyston.

28 Hang out the bunting – the boyo himself Tom Jones is back in the charts with the gruesome single 'The Boy From Nowhere'. This heralds something of a Jones renaissance as his appearance on Channel 4's *The Last Resort* chat-prog reveals a Jonesy on finer form than ever, performing a cover of Prince's 'Kiss' which contains more throbbing sexuality than is humanly imaginable. Jonathan Ross is lost for words, Dawn French – also a guest of Ross – is reduced to inarticulate slobbering and Age Of Chance find their iron-foundry treatment suddenly sounding extremely unsexy. A Great Moment In Pop to be sure.

● Morgan Khan resurrects his business dealings with new labels Westside – for new domestic talent – and Hardcore, which will license def imports as did the late-lamented Streetsounds.

29 Lew Lewis is jailed for seven years for robbing a sub-post office with a fake pistol near his Westcliff home. The one-time Stiff Records artist and pub-rock hero got away with five grand. Judge John Taylor told Southend

Crown Court that it was his duty to impose "a stiff sentence."

30 Matt Johnson, utterly knackered after the exertions of the *Infected* merry-go-round, announces he's retiring from music for three years to recharge his batteries and work on film soundtracks. On no you aren't, says Fate which quickly brings him back into the limelight as part of Red Wedge's pre-Election tour and his first live dates for five years.

● Five law lords sanction the sterilization of a 17-year-old mentally handicapped girl "Jeanette" despite public disquiet.

ALSO...

● Jerry Lee Lewis, The Killer, shows he's still a mean rock 'n' roll dude by wrecking the stage during his show at Northampton Derngate Centre. He smashes a piano stool, stomps all over the keyboard of a £19,000 Steinway in 'Great Balls Of Fire', and pours water into the said Joanna while defiantly rendering 'I Am What I Am' – presumably acapella. The dazed venue managers ban him for ever and ever amen.

● Queen win an Ivor Novello award for "their continued success and innovative style of music over their 15-year career." Hoorah!

● Soul-baldies The Christians from Liverpool are refused entry into East Germany because their name is "too religious." They change it to The Zoroastrans.

● Prince rehearses the lavish *Sign 'O' The Times* show at Birmingham NEC in preparation for his summer tour. The mammoth set – a replica of the album sleeve – is already finished and the Royal Perv decrees that purple is out, peach and black are in.

● **Dub poet Benjamin Zephaniah is nominated for the post of "Visiting Fellow" to Cambridge's Trinity College by students who want a bit less wandering lonely as a cloud and a bit more Dis Policeman Is Kicking Me To Death. Sadly the boreaway *Sun* latches onto this novel idea and lambasts Benny, basically because he's black. "Would you let this man near your daughter?" *The Sun* says. Erm, no, reply those with the power of appointing the Visiting Fellow and lo! Cambridge does not get its first black rastafarian academic. It's their loss.**

MAY
1 9 8 7

● George Michael's mega-erotic, orgasm-inducing single 'I Want Your Sex' is banned by the BBC – surprise, surprise – but still goes Top Five. Liberally sprinkled with gasps and moans, the Prince-ish record is said by Radio One controller Johnny Beerling to be " too sexually explicit for the massive Radio One airplay which a George Michael single would normally receive." The video is also banned – it features George writing on his girlfriend Kathy Yeung with lipstick, as is George's bum. Eeurgh.

Radio One also ban The Blow Monkeys' anti-Thatcher single '(Celebrate) The Day After You', recorded with superfly Curtis Mayfield. It's taken off air until after the election in case it influences anyone's vote. In the event, the record proves hopelessly optimistic.

5 Curiosity Killed The Cat manage to beat the Beatles' faint-rate at Liverpool's Royal Court theatre when 135 adulation-crazed young girls pass out – more than when the Fab Four played at the height of their gearness.

8 Gary Hart withdraws from the Democrat nomination race for next year's Presidential elections after his relationship with Donna Rice, a 29-year-old model and former star of *Miami Vice*, becomes a public embarrassment.

● The Smiths are at number one in the indie single and album charts with 'Sheila Take A Bow' and *The World Won't Listen*. Life goes on . . .

11 The balloon goes up. After weeks and weeks of prophecy, polls and punditry the Prime Minister announces that the General Election will be held on 11 June. The Conservatives begin the election with a commanding

12 After years of providing the engine-room sounds for Grace Jones, Black Uhuru, Bob Dylan and others, Sly and Robbie's first big hit in their own name is 'Boops (Here To Go)' from the *Rhythm Killers* album.

lead in the polls and, no matter what the opposition parties do, nothing seems to seriously dent it in the month's campaign.

● The so-called butcher of Lyons Klaus Barbie, 73, goes on trial in the city accused of war crimes against humanity.

● The happy medium Doris Stokes dies aged 67 of cancer – or as she would have it, "passes on to the next room." Best selling books and many live (?) shows convinced thousands that she really could contact the afterworld – now she knows the truth herself. One knock for yes, two for no, Doris.

12 Denis Healey enters the General Election campaign with his foot firmly in his mouth. He tells reporters that "the Russians are praying for a Labour victory." A bad move, considering that the Tories have targeted Labour's non-nuclear defence policy as the party's prime weak spot.

16 The end of the political line for Harvey Proctor who resigns as parliamentary candidate for Billericay. He is later fined £1,450 when found guilty of four charges of gross indecency with rent boys. Billericay choose a brand spanking new candidate for the Election.

17 The campaign starts to show its real character as the Sunday papers smear David Steel – he issues a writ for libel.

● Johnny Cash is taken to hospital in Iowa with heart trouble.

19 The Advertising Standards Authority puts the blocks on an advert for the *Today* newspaper which depicts the party leaders dangling from nooses with the caption "Would Britain be better off with a hung parliament?" They say they've never had so many complaints against one advert.

22 Eurythmics pay out a sum said to be close to $300,000 to their former US

record company Transatlantic for failing to pay agreed back royalties.

24 Famous next-to-last words from David Owen: "I'm really beginning to enjoy this Election . . . "

30 Weeks of shock-horror press coverage of the Run DMC/Beastie Boys British tour culminates in a near-riot at the Beasties solo date at the Royal Court Theatre, Liverpool. Drunken scallies hurl cans at the stage, hitting DJ Hurricane's turntable. AdRock Beastie (allegedly) retaliates by throwing some back, and hitting the missiles with a baseball bat. The show collapses into chaos after 12 minutes when teargas floods the hall – though no one knows who threw it.

The Beasties flee Liverpool while some "fans" – chanting "Scousers have beaten the Beastie Boys" – remain to wreck the mixing desk, pull out seats and lights from the auditorium and topple the PA. There are five arrests after the show. AdRock himself is arrested at his London hotel and charged in Liverpool with causing grievous bodily harm to a 20-year-old girl fan, who claims she was hit by one of the cans thrown by AdRock who is bailed for £10,000 under real name, Adam Horowitz.

AdRock Senior, the distinguished playwright Israel Horowitz, flies out to the 'Pool for the hearing and is asked whether his son's image is inaccurate: "That is one of the great understatements of Western man," waffles DadRock.

The Beasties Riot Horror tale is the latest episode in a long line of self-righteous tabloid tub-thumping concerning MCA, Mike D and naughty AdRock. The *Mirror*'s faultlessly accurate Gill Pringle claims that the spotty Def Jam trio said "Go away you fucking cripples" to a group of terminally-ill kids brought to see them at the Montreux festival by the Dreams Come True charity. POP IDOLS SNEER AT DYING KIDS trumpets the headline but in fact a Dream Comes True organizer tells Channel 4's *Network 7* prog that they were actually quite nice to the kids in question. Not that this stops Mike Smith and the TV-am team from pontificating on the evils of Beastiedom.

1 It was 20 years ago today, yeah yeah yeah, etc. A multi-media nostalgia-gorging session ensues on the twentieth anniversary of the release of *Sgt. Pepper's Lonely Hearts Club Band*, which comes out on the inevitable CD today. It hauls the LP a massive 94 places up the chart to number 4.

More pertinently, a Beatles fan club in Liverpool inform the world that John Lennon would have voted Labour. So there you go.

4 The BPI's counterfeit squad swoop on the bootlegger's paradise Camden Market and confiscate £20,000 worth of illegal tapes. More than 4,500 live and rare studio recordings are nabbed.

● While Eurythmics play on the West side of the Berlin Wall, a thousand youths gather in the East chanting "the Wall must go." Riot police disperse them.

11 General election day. Mrs Thatcher is returned to power with a majority of 101.

The Alliance is routed with just 21 per cent and almost immediately talks on a merger begin. David Owen seems likely to split that Alliance rather than join the Liberals.

Labour scrapes 30.5 per cent of the vote, their second worst percentage since the war, but the first black MPs Bernie Grant, Keith Vas and Diane Abbott are all Labour. Sheffield City Council leader David Blunkett too wins a seat and his guide dog Ted becomes the first canine allowed in the House, unless you count Clement Freud (who loses his seat).

16 Princes Andrew and Edward and Fergie, Duchess of York, make complete prats of themselves at a charity *It's A Knockout* tournament at Alton Towers, eternally besmirching the Royal Family's proud name.

● The *News On Sunday* calls in the receiver and makes plans for 45 per cent redundancies. It has never sold more than

250,000 copies (it needed 800,000 to break even).

● Pop Will Eat Itself munch up to the indie number one spot with their 'Covers' EP. It includes Poppified versions of Sigue Sigue Sputnik's 'Love Missile F1-11' and 'Orgone Accumulator' by Hawkwind. Top LP is *Dawnrazor* by Fields of the Nephilim.

19 The umpteenth Glastonbury festival includes Trouble Funk, New Order, the condom-scatterin' Communards, the new squeaky-clean St Julian Cope, a fine 'n' fuzzy That Petrol Emotion and a vintage set from Elvis Costello and his collaborators. New faces of note include Michelle Shocked and the bespectacled Proclaimers. With 55,000 festival-goers, the weekend makes £100,000 for CND.

Mendip Council's ruling Conservatives have tried to stop the festival for years but this time they reap their bad karma: in the June local elections they lose overall control, clearing the path for next year's event.

22 Prince cancels his two outdoor shows at Wembley Stadium, citing fears about the rainy weather. He reschedules for Earls Court but then pulls these four replacement dates too. Rumours of poor ticket sales abound but the villains of the piece, it emerges, are Kensington council who refuse a short-notice licence for the shows.

23 Completely sane Michael Jackson gets a hearty rebuff from the London Medical College when he offers $1 million for the remains of the Elephant Man, John Merrick, who died in 1900. They say any sale would be morally wrong but Jackson is said to be fascinated by the bones' "ethical, medical and historical significance." Meanwhile in a Hollywood studio, Quincy Jones tears what's left of his hair out in silent frustration.

On a lighter note, Jacko is said to have left the Jehovah's Witnesses, much to his family's annoyance. Pretending to be a satanic demon, hot lady-lover and everything else on *Thriller* is one thing . . . but wanting to call your album *Bad*? Disgraceful!

30 Rupert Murdoch buys out *Today*, the paper that changes hands quicker than Vince Clarke changes singers. The Monopolies Commission seems to have no objection, despite the Dirty Digger owning four other national titles. Once you've got 20 million or so readers sewn up, another couple of hundred thousand won't make any odds.

ALSO . . .

● Tyne Tees launch *The Roxy*, an independent *Top Of The Pops*. Up against *EastEnders*, it doesn't stand much chance of doing very well but Tyne Tees claim "encouraging" figures.

● Genesis play a record-breaking four consecutive dates at Wembley Stadium (that's around 320,000 punters, fact fans) as well as dates in Leeds and Glasgow on their *Invisible Touch* tour. U2's *Joshua Tree* outing takes in Wembley, Elland Road in Leeds and Murrayfield in Edinburgh. Poor old David Bowie's *Glass Spider* tour looks a bit cheesy in comparison.

● Is the cover of the Bee Gees' 'Jive Talkin' ' by Boogie Box High a secret George Michael job? No, say some. Yes, say others. "Erm, I can't say," says George.

● Evil wicked Beastie AdRock and Molly Ringwald – star of *Pretty In Pink* – get engaged. All say "Aaah." It seems that the King AdRock may want to split the Beastie Boys, tired as he is of their on-the-road lifestyle. Picture it: No Sleep 'til Dunbeastin – Mr & Mrs AdRock's love-nest.

● **Los Lobos decide not to sue Paul Simon for not crediting them on the 'Myth Of Fingerprints' track on *Graceland*. They decide to let him come to them: "We're not gonna sue," says one Lobo, Cesar Rojas. "But we are really pissed off."**

JULY

1987

2 The body of Moors Murder victim Pauline Reade, who disappeared aged 16 in 1962, is finally recovered with the help of information from Myra Hindley.

● Goodbye to *Crossroads*. The 23-year-old lowest common denominator of Soapdom will be put out of its (and our) misery in early 1988, Central TV decides.

Headbanging blood-gargling psycho Blackie Lawless of W.A.S.P. announces plans to sue Tipper Gore of the right-wing Parents' Music Resource Centre. He claims that the P.M.R.C. infringed W.A.S.P.'s copyright to the lyrics of their 'Animal (Fuck Like A Beast)' single by reproducing it as an example of the evils of rock etc.

3 Tricky Dicky Branson's Virgin company signs a deal to buy 23 million condoms from Aussie firm Ansell International, purveyors of the world's most popular prophylactic.

But disaster strikes Branson's record-breaking Atlantic crossing by hot air balloon. His 195-ft tall airborne condom *Atlantic Flyer* ditches into the Irish Sea, plunging him and partner Per Lindstrand into icy waters.

● A Lyons assize court sentences former Nazi Klaus Barbie to life imprisonment for war crimes.

6 Way out and up we go . . . Echo And The Bunnymen indulge their periodic Beatles fantasy by playing an open-air set atop the London HMV Shop in Oxford Street *à la Let It Be*. True to form, the Bunnies include 'Twist And Shout' in their four-song alfresco sesh.

● Sean Penn's 60-day prison sentence for punching a film

extra is delayed so that he can finish film projects in New York and West Germany.

7 Starting as he means to go on, Ken Livingstone MP (Brent East, Lab) uses his Commons maiden speech to air allegations of dirty tricks in Northern Ireland from two former intelligence officers. He says there's evidence that murders were engineered by rogue MI5 officers – including Captain Robert Nairac, murdered SAS officer – with the connivance of murdered Tory MP Airey Neave.

● The Irangate circus begins in earnest as "American Hero" Colonel Oliver North takes the stand at the Washington hearings and its ratings rocket. His evidence appears to satisfy the inquiry that Col. North, his boss Admiral John Poindexter and the late CIA boss William Casey had acted without Reagan's full knowledge.

8 Sonic Youth's *Sister* is the indie number one album and the Soup Dragons are at the top in the singles chart with 'Can't Take It No More'.

9 The Government sets up an inquiry into the Cleveland child sex abuse controversy; 113 children have been taken into care after diagnosis which some fear might have been over-enthusiastic.

11 A man drowns while trying to swim across the River Boyne and get into David Bowie's Slane Castle concert free.

20 Yo! The Beastie terror continues. Marylebone magistrate Barrington Black fines a 17-year-old junior Beastie £100 for the theft of a Volkswagen logo (as worn by Mike D) with these stern words: "The cannibalization of motor vehicles has become something of a fun thing, caused seemingly by the antics of a pop group. I don't think it

is a fun thing at all."

Nor do Volkswagen themselves who find dealers' shelves stripped bare of the coveted metal badges. So they start giving them away free to stop the Beastie Beetle Badge Carnage . . .

30 The Law Lords ban all reproduction of "Spycatcher" material, and even reports on the Australian court battle. The press flies into apoplexy and almost unanimously calls for a Bill of Rights to protect its freedom – and even Lord Hailsham says the decision is ludicrous. Meanwhile Tony Benn does his bit by reading out the best bits of the book in Hyde Park.

31 Rioting in Mecca during the Islamic Hajj festival leaves 402 people dead, including 295 Iranian Shi'ite pilgrims. Saudi Arabia blames the Iranians – Iran blames the Saudis and who else but the Great Satan USA, promising blood in the Gulf as vengeance.

ALSO...

● The long-awaited Jeffrey Archer libel action against *The Star* newspaper ends in a £500,000 damages award to the top novelist and erstwhile Tory party top nob, plus costs said to be near £750,000. Archer says he will donate the money to charity after *The Star*'s appeal, and that he will proceed with a similar action against the *News Of The World*. *The Star* and the *News Of The World* had claimed that Archer had had sex with prostitute Monica Coghlan and then tried to bribe her to keep quiet.

● Radio One's "Our Tune" feature faces cancellation but the nauseating slot, in which Simon Bates relates a tale of woe over weepy music, is saved after 16,000 angry punters ring in to protest.

News Editor:
Andrew Harrison

"I get letters from people who say 'When The Smiths break up I will die, I will make a reservation for the next world.' But to me that's not extreme. I don't leap back with shock because I understand that form of expression, that form of drama."
(Morrissey)

That joke isn't funny any more. Within weeks of Morrissey's latest snippet of wisdom, the unthinkable happens. A brief flurry of speculation is followed by the announcement that Johnny Marr is leaving The Smiths before the release of their fourth album proper, *Strangeways Here We Come* in September.

Marr claims there is no rancour between himself and young Steven Patrick M. and that he simply wants to do musical things "that there is just not scope for in The Smiths".

Morrissey, Rourke and Joyce's decision to continue with "the concept of The Smiths" is a hollow joke; no matter who "replaces" Johnny Marr, the fact is that Morrissey's solo career begins here.

In September 1986 the first edition of **Q** magazine was published. "We don't presume to know what you like but we hope you like this" ran the journal's first and only editorial. With its pragmatic, open-ended approach, **Q** turned out to be a success. In-depth features on **Paul McCartney**, **Elton John**, **Rod Stewart**, **Fleetwood Mac** and **Eric Clapton** catered for, among others, the neglected music fan , closer to middle-age than their teens, whose flagging interest in rock had been revived, in part, by the rapidly expanding catalogue of CD releases.

In this 12-month period the same theoretical customer would also have been tempted by the blandishments of a new fashion magazine for upwardly mobile men, **Arena**, and have heard the comforting voice of old-timer **Johnnie Walker** presiding for hours on end over a weekly event on Radio 1 called the "Stereo Sequence", which incorporated, for no very good reason, retrospectives on the likes of **T Rex** and **The Rolling Stones**, and discussions with savants like **John Peel** on what it was like to

Queen: Released in 1981, their *Greatest Hits* spent another 52 weeks in the LP chart.

have been around in the sixties and seventies.

As if this wasn't worrying enough, **Jackie Wilson**'s 'Reet Petite', first released in 1957, became a surprise Christmas No.1, and shortly afterwards **Ben E King**'s 'Stand By Me' (from 1961) reached the top with **Percy Sledge**'s 'When A Man Loves A Woman' (1966) hard on its heels at No.2. Jackie Wilson scored a "follow up" success with 'I Get The Sweetest Feeling' (1968) while **Freddie Mercury** captured the mood and enjoyed a preposterous hit with 'The Great Pretender' (a **Platter**'s song from 1956), and a rehabilitated **Boy George** hit the top with his lovers' rock version of **Bread**'s 1972 hit 'Everything I Own'.

While the music industry could shrug off responsibility for such a string of aberrations with talk of a fallow period in rock and the rogue effects of a series of

jeans' commercials, there were few innocents when it came to the nostalgic meltdown that occurred with the anniversary of the release of **Sergeant Pepper's Lonely Hearts Club Band**.

"It was twenty years ago today" trumpeted the headlines of a legion of dozy newspaper and colour supplement sub-editors, while on the day in question, June 1, a party held at Abbey Road studios to celebrate the "event" was reported on the *Six O'Clock News*, and a two-hour Granada documentary, entitled *It Was Twenty Years Ago Today*, was networked round the country.

This programme made decidedly uncomfortable viewing, as a succession of daft old buffers like Robert Jasper Grootveld, the former non-leader of a Dutch anarchist group, and Tom McGrath, ex-editor of the *International*

The shackles of hip conformity had been abandoned. The notions of "in" or "out", "cool" or "uncool", "bad" or "ba-a-ad" still held sway, but nobody agreed on what was which any more

Times, explained in largely incomprehensible terms what the Summer Of Love was supposed to have been about. A prominent participant was hippie "guru" Dr Timothy Leary, whose memorable slogan was paraphrased by *Private Eye* to read "Turn up, talk crap, go home," which summed it all up rather neatly.

Such a readiness to embrace the past may lead to easy theorizing about the supposedly parlous state of rock in the present. After all, imagine the lukewarm response to anyone foolish enough to have suggested celebrating the ten-year anniversary of *Sergeant Pepper* during the excitements of 1977. But I'll bet that by the time you read this, in the absence of any genuine musical developments there will have been a tediously repetitive barrage of retrospectives to mark the tenth anniversary of the death of Elvis Presley in August. Can you imagine what it will be like when it gets to be ten years since Live Aid?

The fact is that there *was* a tremendous spirit abroad during the eras of punk and flower power, a sense of unity and purpose that was entirely absent during 1986/7. This is partly explained by the very different fragmented nature of rock in the eighties.

Ask any ten people in 1977 or 1967 what was the happening thing and you would get roughly the same answer ten

times. Ask ten people in 1987, and the vastly different answers, ranging from Def Jam to New Age, would have in common only an underlying assumption that at the end of the day nothing very notable was happening at all. No wonder editors and newscasters, hacks and CD owners alike were all so eager to look back to a time when everything was that much clearer, when everyone could make their statement by listening to the same record.

Television's continuing inability to harness a "rock" audience for anything other than these retrospectives, and the ever-popular *Rock 'n' Roll Years*,

The Beatles: Nostalgic meltdown occurred with the anniversary of *Sergeant Pepper*.

18

provided a stark reflection of the lack of a clearly defined youth music movement. Somebody at last noticed that, apart from Mary Whitehouse's National Viewers' and Listeners' Association, nobody watched *The Tube* any more and the ailing show finally went off the air amid a welter of accusations aimed by producer Malcolm Gerrie at the Tyne-Tees TV management of heavy-handed smothering of creative freedom. Even with the coast thus cleared the BBC chose not to re-promote *Whistle Test*, which was relegated to a status of permanent stand-by.

The odd chart shows that turned up to challenge *Top Of The Pops* were strictly pop as family fare and, ironically, the most successful and palatable "youth programme" of the year turned out to be Jonathan Ross's *The Last Resort*, which succeeded by presuming nothing about the likely demographics of its audience, nor their musical preferences, but simply by aiming to produce an entertaining show.

Which brings us back to *Q*'s apparent presumption not to know what their readers wanted, a philosophy further summed up in their style sheet's admonition to contributors that "reviews should be informative first and opinionated second" followed by a general warning to "steer clear of sweeping dismissals of entire fields of music."

Writers at *NME*, *Melody Maker*, *Record Mirror* et al would have stood aghast at either suggestion, but in essence these requirements were simply a recognition of the fundamental revolution in rock that had been completed by 1986. The shackles of hip conformity had been abandoned. The notions of "in" or "out", "cool" or "uncool", "bad" or "ba-a-ad" still held sway, as they always will, but nobody agreed on what was which any more, and the old axiomatic dogmas reluctantly gave way to a more widely informed musical liberalism.

U2: Towering above them all, the latest "greatest rock 'n' roll band in the world".

The fans, as ever, knew who their favourites were. **Bruce Springsteen** released a five live albums boxed set that began cluttering up overstocked shops after its initial "hardcore" sales of roughly three million copies, while in Britain, **Simple Minds**' *Live In The City Of Light* became the fastest-selling live album of all time.

Queen's *Greatest Hits*, which was released in 1981, also spent another 52 straight weeks in the album chart. **Dire Strait**'s *Brothers In Arms* did the same, and Mark Knopfler looked decidedly sheepish when receiving the BPI award for Best Album of 1986, pointing out that the record had been in circulation since May 1985.

Genesis became the first act ever to play four successive nights at the 72,000 capacity Wembley Stadium while the previous week **Peter Gabriel** had had to make do with four nights at the 18,000 capacity Earls Court Exhibition Centre. **David Bowie**, whose *Never Let Me Down* album had garnered absolutely the worst reviews in his career, staged his spectacular "Glass Spider" show at Wembley Stadium.

Madonna enjoyed another incredible run of hits including three No.1s since June '86 – 'Papa Don't Preach', 'True Blue' and 'La Isla Bonita' – while **Tina Turner** embarked on the most ambitious world tour ever undertaken by a solo female performer, scheduled to finish either in Bangkok or Rio sometime in May 1988. Her partner for the European dates was **Robert Cray** who had enjoyed a stunning year with both a single, 'Smoking Gun', and an album, *Strong Persuader*, in the US Top 20.

Former blues guitarist **Eric Clapton**'s *August* received a panning in the papers, but after his London Albert Hall residency in January and with the aid of a hit single, 'Behind The Mask', it

became his biggest-selling solo album to date.

In October, **ZZ Top** turned in an epic if rather battle-weary show at Wembley, towards the end of their marathon *Afterburner* world tour. They had started the year before (1985) in Canada and still had Australia and Japan to go.

Thus, in the teeth of the usual recurring complaints that rock music had become subject to bland formulae and an overall creative ennui, the rock *business* boomed like never before. Among the acts to do brisk trade on the arena circuit in the face of implacable critical indifference were **Whitney Houston**, **George Benson**, **Lionel Richie**, **Meat Loaf**, **Eurythmics**, **Spandau Ballet**, **The Pretenders**, **Duran Duran**, **Big Country**, **Status Quo** and **The Stranglers**.

And towering above them all was **U2**, now tacitly understood to be the latest "greatest rock 'n' roll band in the world". With the release of *The Joshua Tree* and the start of an 18-month world tour, a critical and commercial consensus contrived to put the quartet from Dublin on the cover of *Time* magazine, and at the top of the charts in both Britain and America. Bruce Springsteen, it must be said, suddenly looked very much like last year's pan-global thing.

Eric Clapton: *August* received a panning in the papers but became his biggest solo LP.

The closest we got to a punk or hippie movement in '86/7 was in the emergence of the previously marginalized music of **hip-hop** as a sizeable crossover phenomenon. For the first time since the beat boom of the early sixties the British market took its lead from America, where **Run DMC** and **The Beastie Boys** each sold three million copies of their albums *Raising Hell* and *Licensed To Ill*, thus becoming the genre's equivalent to the legendary Pistols/Clash or Beatles/Stones pairings of earlier generations.

Although the bands had played in

19

Britain, without incident, at the time of Run DMC's Top Ten hit 'Walk This Way' in September '86, their subsequent visit in May '87 prompted a series of hysterical outbursts led by a *Daily Mirror* story by Gill Pringle, with the Headline "*Pop idols sneer at dying kids – shame of rampaging stars*".

The incident, said to have happened in Montreux, was both uncorroborated and swiftly denied on all sides except La Pringle's. As a thoroughly depressed Mike D put it, "There's a certain virtue in negative publicity, and a lot of it has come from us just being ourselves, particularly on stage. But there's a world of difference between that and beating up on cripples."

Nevertheless the Capitol Radio DJ "moderate" John Sachs engaged in a ritual smashing of 'Fight For Your Right (To Party)' on the air, *The Mirror* penned an editorial insisting CBS should drop the act rather than "climb down further into the filth with the Beastie Boys" and that stalwart self-publicist and now ex-MP Peter Bruinvels made it his business to raise the matter during question time at the House of Commons.

While most of this was predictable, antipathy to the Beasties didn't end

Dire Straits: Released in 1985, *Brothers In Arms* was the BPI's Best Album of 1986.

there, and it was especially interesting to see how the Establishment critics were joined by the equally intolerant puritans of the left in this urgent matter of upholding public morals. As part of their campaign against the sexist middle-class boors, the caring *NME* ran a plainly anti-Semitic cartoon of the Beastie Boys, prompting a reader's complaint which was printed on the letters page. Far from being abashed, Don Watson explained in his riposte that "homophobe misogynists are fair game, even for the cheapest shots."

Hardly a week went by when some rap or hip-hop star wasn't getting his wrist smacked by these new moralists. **LL Cool J** was constantly in deep shit for his uncomplimentary references to women, and **Schoolly D**, a desperately feeble performer who died the death when he toured here as support to Big Audio Dynamite, was repeatedly criticised for his "macho" raps and stated fondness for guns. The old "us and them" days were well and truly finished,

The Jesus And Mary Chain: They went Top Ten with 'April Skies'.

and an eighties rebel drop-out must now expect flak from all quarters.

Sigue Sigue Sputnik, incidentally, released their album, *Flaunt It*, in August and then announced a multi-media extravaganza to be held in October at London's Albert Hall. "We've sold it out," Tony James boasted on Radio 4's *Start The Week* on the morning of the gig, which in fact turned out to be less than half full. What a storm in a teacup that turned out to be.

One curious side effect of hip-hop's ascendency was the seemingly impossible feat of conferring a new and vigorous credibility on **heavy metal**. This was largely due to **Rick Rubin**, the Def Jam producer, who in addition to Run DMC, The Beastie Boys and LL Cool J, also produced a grim thrash metal group called **Slayer**, with a regulation Sabbath guitar sound and a slick line in neo-Nazi lyrics. Suddenly everyone was hip not only to Slayer but also to **Metallica**, **Anthrax**, **Megadeth**, and others, all bands that had not changed their music or personae one whit since the very recent days when they were routinely reviled as power-mad, devil-worshipping chumps.

While a plethora of pop bands with an eye on the main chance – **Simply Red**, **Wet Wet Wet**, **The Communards**, **Deacon Blue**, **Danny Wilson**, **Curiosity Killed The Cat** – were careful to locate their roots, however implausibly, in the "soul" camp and so distance themselves as far as possible from the discredited norms of rock, another of Rick Rubin's clients, **The Cult**, revelled in a new discovery: seventies roots. "We ain't funky dudes," said a relieved-sounding Billy Duffy. "Finally, I'm just totally proud of the music I listen to – of not going through life embarrassed and really wishing I'd listened to James Brown records when I was 14. I'm very happy I used to listen to Led Zeppelin."

Both 'Love Removal Machine' and 'Lil' Devil' were Top 20 hits for The Cult, while **The Mission** tapped a similar vein with their hits 'Severina' and 'Wasteland', and even **Zodiac** "I only have a bath when there's a bird coming round" **Mindwarp** made chart inroads with his piece of biker comedy 'Prime Mover'.

More serious issues were at stake when **Paul Simon**'s much-discussed *Graceland* tour came to Britain in April. The album, partly recorded in South Africa with South African musicians, and thus technically in contravention of the United Nations-sponsored cultural boycott, had already sold four million copies, and Simon had mustered a touring party comprising **Ladysmith Black Mambazo**, the township acapella group, together with exiled SA trumpeter **Hugh Masekela** and singer **Miriam Makeba**.

"God sent Paul Simon to do this," said Joseph Shabalala, Ladysmith's leader. But anti-apartheid campaigners picketed the British concerts anyway in a farcical act of misguided idealism. John Peel, who turned up to see the show, asked of no one in particular whether he was allowed to play South African music on his radio show, but got no certain answer either way.

Whatever the politics, there is no doubt that the *Graceland* album and tour elevated township music to a far more prominent degree than could have been dreamed of previously. Only last year this very publication bemoaned the diminishing interest in African rhythms, and commented pessimistically that "it is doubtful that African music will ever rise beyond its present status in British record shops." Yet the **Bhundu Boys** have become regulars on the UK club scene, **Gaspar Lawal**, **Jonah Moyo**, **The Real Sounds** and

Tom Verlaine: Evidence to contradict the claim that rock music has run its course.

Johnny Clegg have all toured here this year, while Ladysmith's *Shaka Lu* album made an impressive dent in the national Top 40 no less.

Red Wedge threw themselves with unremitting vigour into the hopeless task of attempting to get the Labour Party elected to government. While their efforts were hardly reflected in the eventual outcome of the contest, they could take comfort from the enormous shift in the pattern of voting behaviour among the 18-24 age group. This went from the 1983 figures of Conservative – 42%; Labour – 33%; Alliance – 23% to a

1987 result of Conservative – 33%; Labour – 40%; Alliance – 21%, an extraordinary swing by any standards and perhaps a moral victory for the Wedge. A decent record from **The Style Council** would have been a bonus, but the insipid *The Cost Of Loving* was certainly not it.

Rock's charity drive slackened off comparative to the wide range of causes that its heroes had championed immediately after Live Aid. **Amnesty International** became the card-carrying mega-star's preferred organization, with **U2** and **Simple Minds** the most visible supporters, while a series of Amnesty concerts in America in June '86 marked the last time **The Police** played together in public.

International Aids Week in April prompted an encouraging grass-roots response around the country, but the Wembley condom party was generally

Bob Geldof: After penning an extraordinarily racy autobiography, released a dire album.

felt to be a little light on bona fide superstars. **George** "I Want Your (Safe) Sex" **Michael** was a notable exception. Hardy perennials **The Prince's Trust** and **The Secret Policeman's (Third) Ball** were joined by the **Ferry Aid** drive, which spawned yet another of those ghastly all-star No.1s 'Let It Be'.

After penning his extraordinarily racy biography, *Is That It?*, and releasing a dire album, *Deep In The Heart Of Nowhere*, **Bob Geldof KBE** was put out to grass, and could be seen from time to time on television, advertising razor blades with somewhat less conviction than that mustered by Victor "I bought the company" Kiam. Other demises this year included **Wham!, Frankie Goes To Hollywood, Madness** and **Culture Club**, not to mention **The Boomtown Rats**.

etting aside the comically disastrous **Womack & Womack** extended family gathering at the Albert Hall in January, there was a string of visits by outstanding **American soul acts** who have

increasingly made their presence felt within the rock milieu: **Freddie Jackson, Luther Vandross, The Gap Band, Phyllis Hyman** and **Maze** all had that touch of class that modern groups like Simply Red and Swing Out Sister aspire towards, while **Cameo**, who toured in September '86, wrapped up the whole business – funk, soul, rap and rock – in one super-bad, codpieced package. "Word Up" was word.

A new **New Country** campaign also gave rock critics yet another chance to practice their recently-acquired techniques of informed liberalism. **The Judds**' British debut at The London Palladium was bristling with hardline music journalists, many of them former scourges of the punk era, who now sat attentively while mother and daughter trilled their way through sweet Kentucky lullabies and mellifluous country honks. The reports which followed were unanimously complimentary.

Although the pundits continued to decry the genus "rock" in 1986/7 as a decrepit and backward-looking dilution of the splendid ideals of earlier generations, such carping simply did not accord with the evidence of so much diverse excellence on offer to the rock audience.

Elvis Costello's "Wheel Of Fortune" shows at the London Royalty were strikingly original presentations,

George Michael: A bona fide superstar at the International Aids Week concert in April.

Skies'.

Head, a band from Bristol, released a superb debut, *A Snog On The Rocks* on Demon Records, a record that more than any other this year spotlighted the vibrant strength of rock in its continuing ability to copy, absorb and mutate the numerous influences now available. By adopting hip-hop's "we'll use anything" approach to their songwriting and casting their punky abrasiveness within a mould of crude and sensual sleaze, they contributed more than most to the process of setting new wheels in motion on the enormous, sprawling Heath Robinson-like structure of inter-connected musical mechanisms

For the first time since the beat boom of the early sixties the British market took its lead from America, where Run DMC and The Beastie Boys each sold three million copies of their albums thus becoming the genre's equivalent to the legendary Pistols/Clash or Beatles/Stones pairings

Ted Hawkins was a one-in-a-million-soul-singers find, and the magnificent **Tom Jones** rarely got a bad review on his "Boy From Nowhere" comeback tour. **Steve Earle**'s *Guitar Town* married rock and country, **Sly & Robbie**'s *Rhythm Killers* married rap and reggae, and **Richard Thompson** and **Suzanne Vega** kept the folk traditions in mind, both of them playing electric band and solo shows.

What the detractors really meant was that rock *music*, as distinct from soul, country, hip-hop and so forth, had run its course, but here again the evidence was contradictory. **Killing Joke, Spear Of Destiny, Julian Cope, The Psychedelic Furs, Tom Verlaine, The Del Fuegos, Hüsker Dü** and many others had a good year. **The Smiths** and **That Petrol Emotion** both signed to major record labels and **The Jesus And Mary Chain** went Top Ten with 'April

that rock has now become.

But if ever a group demonstrated the ability to hang on to the essence of the rock dream in their music, then it was the much-maligned **New Model Army**, whose album *The Ghost Of Cain* was a great personal favourite. It has the unerring quality that used to distinguish the work of groups when rock still had an undisputed sense of direction, and the album owes much to the production work of **Glyn Johns**, whose previous clients include The Rolling Stones, The Who, Led Zeppelin and The Clash.

Perhaps that makes New Model Army as dated as rock itself, which ironically seems to be one reason why the media have been reluctant to take up their cause. Everyone is much too busy remembering the good old days to fall for a new band who emphasize those kind of passé rock 'n' roll values.

DAVID SINCLAIR

Terence Trent D'Arby: Only an honorary member of the British soul scene.

Reviewing any given year in soul it is inevitable that one's thoughts turn, like a homing pigeon, to the USA. The past 12 months, however, have for once given us a valid excuse to contemplate matters more parochial. Two excuses actually.

While the emergence of a large number of diverse acts under the convenient umbrella "Brit Soul" is now into its second, if not third, generation there has until this year been one big problem. None of the acts gathered together under that generic title could muster a convincing lead vocalist between them. Then in a matter of months, two appeared.

It is, perhaps, stretching the bounds of licence to their utmost to dub **Terence Trent D'Arby** anything more than an honorary member of the British soul scene. He was, after all, born in New York, raised in New Jersey, Chicago and Florida and even did a term of service in the US Army. Like James Brown, Berry Gordy, Jackie Wilson and others before him he also fought with some success in the ring there – but his professional career in music has at least been nurtured to fruition here.

Paul Johnson is definitely more British, although even he spent two years living in New York with a grandmother, a period in which the seeds of his musical ambitions were sown. By the time he returned to London to be encouraged to sing in local churches, Johnson had been exposed to enough American influences to give his interpretations a mid-Atlantic authority as he grew. Having a voice which, at the age of 25, still had not

broken is a bonus of nature that will turn out to have been the making of his career.

To date, D'Arby and Johnson have barely a handful of singles between them, though the latter has just released a very impressive debut LP. In the next 12 months we will undoubtedly hear a great deal more of them, and memorably so I suspect.

Turning from the particular to the general soul year, it has been one in which black music has continued to hijack more than its fair share of the pop charts, in which the well-established "megastar" (yes, I hate that word too) acts continued their noisy gallop towards rock styles, and in which the multi-faceted nature of contemporary black music proved itself hugely, rewardingly and satisfyingly broad based.

There has been the continued resurgence of ballad singers, the establishment of Go-Go and House, and after a period in which its limitations

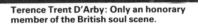

Having done his very best to scupper his film career once and for all with the stupefyingly dire *Under The Cherry Moon*, the shows proved conclusively that Prince is unique

Luther Vandross: The ballad revival, with its kernel in his debut album, continued apace.

seemed cruelly exposed and insurmountable, hip-hop finally gave us a record or two to cherish. Further, the various artists who attempt fusions of funk, soul, rock and more did so with quite staggering diversity of success.

Prime among these in the past 12 months has been **Prince**. Having done his very best to scupper his film career once and for all with the stupefyingly dire *Under The Cherry Moon*, he toured with **The Revolution** and used much of *Parade*, the film's soundtrack, in his set. With the memory of the movie still haunting one, the shows were approached with trepidation. They proved conclusively that Prince is unique – a bandleader and organizer of music on a par with James Brown and Sly Stone, a musician as naturally gifted and comfortable on as wide a range of

UL

Sunshine' and several songs which, contrary to his stage image as flighty gadabout and insatiable stud, are essentially very moral tracts about committed relationships. Very AIDS conscious, in fact.

Unexpectedly, he took this music out on the road almost immediately with a largely new band. On the road, Prince's excursions into pop and rock become a lot funkier, a lot blacker. This was diametrically opposed to recent trends as highlighted by two other major artists on the road at the same time – Lionel Richie and Tina Turner.

It was ironic in the extreme that **Lionel Richie**'s tour should be subtitled "Outrageous" and Turner's "Break Every Rule", for in fact they were and did exactly the opposite. Richie rigorously conformed to the precepts of a rock band's show and his dabblings in

Tina Turner: Surrounded herself with a deafeningly loud white rock band.

But **Trouble Funk** of Washington and Go-Go's godfather **Chuck Brown** have shown that that music has staying power outside DC while newer acts at the popular end of the market like **Club Nouveau** have kept it in the charts.

Importantly, the people who are producing this music seem to realize the dangers inherent in its assumed limitations. For example, the **Def Jam** label – whose rise in the mid-eighties had been almost entirely due to unmelodic hip-hop and rap records – suddenly sprouted a quietly impressive tributary of solo singers – **Oran "Juice" Jones**, **Tashan** and **Chuck Stanley**. On *Juice*, *Chasin' A Dream* and *The Finer Things In Life*, respectively their three Def debuts, there are more than enough indications that these three can carry a tune and interpret a lyric as well as most of their peers.

The implied acknowledgement in Def's move is that of the ballad revival of the past six years, assuming that one accepts its kernel was the debut album of **Luther Vandross**. It has continued apace in the past year with Vandross's reappearance in a slimmed down physique – the loss in weight being inversely proportional to his improvement as a live performer which, almost unbelievably, was very considerable.

(A sad footnote: his wonderful drummer, **Yogi Horton**, committed suicide in June '87, apparently because he felt his contributions as a musician were underappreciated; considering the Press he usually received in Britain, at least, both for his work on stage and on record, it sounds as though someone was

● Paul Johnson: An unbroken voice at 25 – a bonus of nature and the making of his career.

instruments as Brown, Stevie Wonder or the late Marvin Gaye and a live performer of great energy, athleticism and humour.

Prince has also become remarkably prolific these past couple of years. Disbanding the Revolution and returning to his previous *modus operandi* of recording – writing, arranging, producing and performing the whole damn shebang himself, Prince assembled a new double LP. *Sign 'O' The Times* drew together not only the previous strands of his own music – hard funk to quasi-psychedelia – but incorporated a dazzling spectrum of pop and rock styles past and present filtered through Prince's particular appreciation and perception of what makes the music work.

There was the rap-funk of 'Housequake' (musically accurate, lyrically a lampoon) to the "white" rock of 'The Cross', fluff such as 'Play In The

various musical styles were precisely that – he appeared like a man changing hats in front of a mirror: "Here's my reggae hat, here's my samba hat, here's my rock 'n' roll hat, oh yes, and here's my tatty old funk hat . . ." **Tina Turner**'s was, alas, even crasser than her *Break Every Rule* album had forewarned, surrounding herself with a deafeningly loud white rock band of astonishingly unsubtle touch.

F or some while it had seemed as though the various types of music spawned in the streets or drawn from the clubs of the US – the rap of New York, Go-Go of Washington, House of Chicago – were destined to be little more than the Emperor's new clothes.

Club Nouveau: Keeping music from the clubs of the US in the charts.

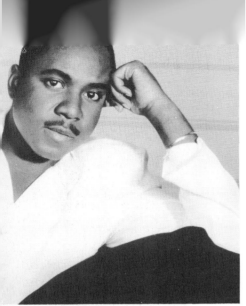

Freddie Jackson: *Rock Me Tonight* reprised in slightly different clothing.

keeping his cuttings from him. The great drummer's sure, unfussy, emphatic touch will be missed.)

The classy ease with which Vandross sings on stage and record has rather thrown into sharp contrast the work of others who would work in his milieu – basically that of romantic soul ballads. **Freddie Jackson**'s *Just Like The First Time*, an album which reprised much of *Rock Me Tonight* in slightly different clothing, was somewhat overshadowed by Vandross while few others could sustain material. One of the more potent shots was **Gregory Abbot**'s single 'Shake You Down'.

I t has also been a year in which "veterans" have enjoyed an unprecedented resurgence in the wake of the ad-man's success with the music of late **Sam Cooke** as the aural accompaniment to their visual blandishments. **Percy Sledge** and

Percy Sledge: Renewed interest after an old hit was used to sell modern products.

Ben E King both found renewed interest in their voices after old hits had been used to sell modern products, which said much about the enduring qualities of the soul music of the early and mid-sixties, of the songs themselves ('When A Man Loves A Woman' and 'Stand By Me' respectively) and of the singers' natural ability to bring a believable passion to all that they sang.

This type of soul singer will always find an audience, no matter how far from the public gaze they appeared to have strayed. **Clarence Carter** is still best known for 'Patches' and had been off the specialist charts for at least seven years when *Dr C C*, his self-produced set on the independent Ichiban label proved yet again that there was a market for his music which is still imbued with

Prince: An organizer of music on a par with James Brown and Sly Stone.

traditional R&B values.

The shift back towards this type of singer – rougher than Vandross, inevitably less widely-appealing than Prince – has been underway for some years, since the signing by Malaco of the late **Z Z Hill**, and has continued apace in its own underground way with the likes of **Luther Ingram** resurfacing on Profile and **Prince Philip Mitchell** also on Ichiban.

One of the higher profile "rescue" missions was that of **Bobby Womack** by Beverly Glen, which revived his career artistically at the turn of the decade. Although he had to spend a certain time getting out of that contract – label owner Otis Smith has been involved in several similar litigations recently – his move to a major company proved no block to his rejuvenation.

Until, that is, his most recent album *Womagic*, a set that sounds like the work of a man who has simply produced too much in the past two years. Bobby

Womack has said he'd like to remix the album. Remixing would not, I fear, do too much to rescue *Starbright*, the third album by **Womack & Womack** (Cecil and Linda, Bob's brother and sister-in-law) who since '83's 'Love Wars' have done everything in their power to douse one's enthusiasm for their music.

The other, younger, dynasty of black popular music (yes, we are at last talking **Jacksons**) has had a comparatively quiet time of it, their heads well below the parapets and only the occasional, ever-extraordinary rumour concerning **Michael** and the pictures of **Janet** collecting yet another award for *Control* to remind one that they are still around.

Janet was fortunate in that her album caught the busy production bees **Jimmy Jam** and **Terry Lewis** at the peak of their creative curve – subsequent collaborations, as with Herb Alpert or the Human League, have been profoundly less than gratifying. The waning of inspiration by overkill, and proliferating copyists flooding the market with inept imitations of an easily identifiable sound is no new phenomenon. Ask Nile Rodgers and Bernard Edwards, late of Chic. Expect, however, Jam-Lewis to rise again, assuming they choose their projects with greater care.

A lthough Janet Jackson, Tina Turner and the year's other awards scooper, **Whitney Houston**, have been the most prominent among the women who might commonly be found in any round-up of "soul" music, their connection with that music

Anita Baker: Made of determined stuff and taking charge of her own career.

has become increasingly spurious. Janet is a pop star; Tina seems happy in her noisy affiliation with stadium rock; Whitney, aside from infrequent moments on stage when a gospel singer peeks out from the Vegas-here-I-come "safe soul" in *haute couture* rags, has her career too well mapped out for that impression to be mistaken.

Beneath these three vastly successful

that has enabled **Anita Baker** to take charge of her own career to such good effect.

Speaking of a woman who has found it necessary to assume control of her own career in the generally white and male-dominated music business, the inimitable **Millie Jackson** staged something of a roaring comeback with her *Imitation Of Love* album, which was rather less raunchy lyrically than many of her past records but proved slightly more appealing commercially. Yes, the two things probably are linked but live Millie Jackson remains the supreme sexual iconoclast and an outstanding soul singer to boot. Bet she still doesn't wash no one's funky drawers but her own.

Has **Diana Ross** ever washed anyone's funky drawers? We do not discover this in **Mary Wilson**'s book *Dreamgirl: My Life As A Supreme* but we do discover and have confirmed more than a few of the suspicions based on hearsay of Ross's insatiable desire to succeed at all costs no matter whom she had to use, whom she had to tread underfoot.

Dreamgirl was one of several books in the past year which are commended to soul fans – **James Brown**'s autobiography *The Godfather Of Soul*, in which he casts himself in an heroic role, is well worth reading as is *I, Tina*, Turner's account of a hard, hard life

Whitney Houston: Vegas-here-I-come "safe soul" in *haute couture* rags.

which makes her recent marriage to lucrative hard rock almost totally forgivable.

But back with Ross. She has had an ill-defined, misguided time of it in the recording studio in recent years. In such a context her *Red Hot Rhythm & Blues* was most interesting in that on several tracks she was quite audibly using material which attempted to recreate the song structures of Holland-Dozier-Holland and Ashford & Simpson, the two teams at Motown which knew best how to write for her. But that was then and this is now . . . One Motown vet of the sixties who's still on the label and still going strong is **Smokey Robinson** – his *One Heartbeat* was his best LP in a good while.

Finally, just to prove that life goes on, the year saw *Smooth Sailin'* from the remaining elder **Isley Brothers** Ronnie and Rudolph, while the younger **Isley Jasper Isley** team followed '85's excellent *Caravan Of Love* with another good set, *Different Drummer*. Oh, and did you hear **Norwood**? The guy's got a great voice . . . and how about **Sly & Robbie**'s fusion with the **Clinton/ Bootsy** funksters on *Rhythm Killers*? And on and on and on it goes, where it'll end nobody knows . . .

GEOFF BROWN

The Jacksons had a comparatively quiet time of it, only the occasional, ever-extraordinary rumour concerning Michael and pictures of Janet collecting yet another award for *Control* to remind one that they are still around

women singers whose divergent styles have found favour with, largely, the same audience, there is a mighty and, it seems, incredibly fast-growing host of very fine women soul singers whose only fault is that they can't find a compatible producer or suitable material. These range from writers themselves (the aptly named **La La**, for one) through gospel graduates (**Vesta Williams**) to those who've been around for a while but always as somebody's vocal helper (**Regina Belle**, **Peggi Blu**) to those who come from nowhere, or so it seems (**Donna Allen**).

All have released albums in the past 12 months which reveal promise, moments in which genuine soulful interpretation or an aptitude for the natural reading of a pop song spell out a bright future. There are also tracks on which one's initial impressions begin to seem like a trick of the ear. But I strongly suspect that one, possibly two, of the aforementioned singers will prosper, particularly if they are made of the same determined stuff

Diana Ross: Audibly using material which attempted to re-create the song structures of Motown.

HEAVY

Thrash, slam, speed, death, mosh . . .

Over the last half decade, heavy metal has gained not only a new lease of life but a new vocabulary too. Simplistic and unsubtle words reflecting the basic, frenzied thrust of the music.

Yet thrash metal isn't all kill-crazy aggression. There's depth, humour, variety and colour in there too, qualities which, throughout the past 12 months, have proved this new metal sensation to be no mere thrash in the pan.

But to sum up first the older way of life, it's been business as usual for the older, established acts like **Iron Maiden**, **Judas Priest** and the revived (but desperately wrinkled) **Deep Purple**, with **Whitesnake** even getting a new lease of chart life after

David Coverdale: A new lease of chart life for Whitesnake after a lengthy absence.

a lengthy absence. In America, most of the many new tack 'n' roll acts (**Poison**, **Faster Pussycat**, **Cinderella**, **Guns 'n' Roses**) simply recharged a few old Kiss and Aerosmith riffs, while **David Lee Roth** remained metal's great humorist, egotist and exhibitionist. **Queensryche** mixed the ambitious with the exotic, while **Bon Jovi** and the saccharine **Europe** successfully conquered the pop charts. **The Cult** and **Zodiac Mindwarp** too staked their claim with some heady riff rock, but it was thrash that redefined our whole concept of metal.

The impact thrash has had in shaking up the rather staid and rusty old ways of mainstream metal has been akin to rap's effect on black music. Both thrash and rap are essentially youthful and streetwise; embracing a spirit of pushy,

inventive rebellion. Thus, in the same way that, Prince aside, the ground-breaking black artists of the day aren't traditional perfectionists like Whitney Houston or View From The Hill but Run DMC, LL Cool J and Mantronix, so the major influences in metal recently have been Slayer, Metallica, Anthrax, Celtic Frost, etc.

And the similarities don't end there. Although Run DMC, LL Cool J and the Beastie Boys' pirating of HM clout hasn't gone as far as to borrow thrash traits, there have been tentative crossovers; Slayer's signing to rap's hippest label, Def Jam; Celtic Frost's oddball experimentation with processed drum patterns; and Anthrax's goofy yet remarkably sussed rap pastiche, 'I'm The Man'.

It's probably **Anthrax** who've succeeded most in popularizing thrash outside of underground metal circles. If Metallica were the first jab to bloody the nose of public consciousness around 1983, then Anthrax in the first half of '87 provided a

swift haymaker that smashed clean through the music industry's tough old guard and got in right where it hurts – the singles Top 40.

'I Am The Law', backed by 'I'm The Man' and banned from the radio by dint of its salty language, sneaked thrash in through the backdoor of the charts. Although its success was primarily due to grassroots support, it surely can't have

Faster Pussycat: One of many new tack 'n' roll acts recharging old Kiss riffs.

gone all the way to the lower thirties without beating a few non-metal fans into submission too.

Sounding for the most part like some brutal form of rhythmic, psyched-up tribal war-dance, thrash's first and only hit single offered no hand of compromise

Anthrax: Sounding like some brutal form of rhythmic, psyched-up tribal war dance.

METAL

Slayer: Branded idiotic, disgusting and perverted (par for the course for most thrash acts).

death/My face you will not see/I'll rip your flesh till there's no breath/Dismembered destiny" ('Piece By Piece'). Worse still is 'Angel Of Death', awesome, exhausting and chilling, which openly glories in the bloody details of Nazi butcher Josef Mengele's wartime death camp atrocities.

It's hardly surprising therefore that *Reign In Blood* spent seven months following its American release on Def Jam skulking in British import racks before London Records quit stalling, did the indecent thing and let it have its evil way in Britain. So far, at least, there's been no real trouble, no calls for censorship. They've even released 'Criminally Insane', a touching boy-meets-girl-meets-homicidal-maniac tale, as a single without so much as a ripple of protest.

Slayer have been branded idiotic, disgusting and perverted (par for the course for most thrash acts); yet, as Joe Walsh once put it, you can't argue with a sick mind. *Reign In Blood* has brilliance and breathtaking power to compensate for its gratuitous gore and, as the most intimidating record I've ever heard, it overshadows every other speed metal release from this year and all others before it.

With drummer Dave Lombardo now permanently (?) back with the band after a brief bust-up over his right to bring his dear wife on tour, Slayer will no doubt continue to lead thrash further and further into the deep unknown.

to chart format and convention. Likewise, the album that houses 'Law', *Among The Living*, was further proof of Anthrax's spunky determination to keep their lovable rough edges from being sandpapered down by a meddling big buck major label mentality.

Fortunately, Island Records, who for a while after signing the band seemed to have absolutely no idea of how to market or what to do with them, have been sympathetic towards their scruffy little New York investment and have wisely kept their sticky hands to themselves. Anthrax haven't mellowed or been smothered in lavish over-production. They still clown and thrash like they did five years ago, albeit with a whole lot more punch and surety.

Anthrax have spread the disease far and wide, but it's Californian crackpots **Slayer** who push the purest, meanest speed fix. Their *Reign In Blood* album is extremism incarnate; fast or slow, the intensity never wavers. Drums rattle every last bone in your body, guitars slice around like meat cleavers in Rick Rubin's incredibly toothsome mix, and over it all, Tom Araya's vocals are a rabid, nightmarish snarl.

The lyrics don't tread lightly either. Most cast a cruel, unflinching eye over a stomach-churning catalogue of obscene violence: "*You have no choice of life or*

The *original* thrash band – not Discharge or Venom or Motorhead or any such seminal forerunners but the band who first took up the reins of what suddenly became a noisy, sloganeering thrash bandwagon – was **Metallica**. "Thrash" is a description they've long since outgrown and nowadays just shrug off with a frown and a laugh, but as the band who opened up the gates for a flood of bullet-headed speed brats, any assessment of thrash seems incomplete without them.

Metallica: A bittersweet year but once again the feeling is good and strong.

The kids won't want to go back to crusty, pedestrian trad metal now that they've tasted the thrill of speed. Everywhere, new speed combos are springing up like the reborn in a zombie flick

Megadeth: Combining anger and articulacy, bludgeon and complexity, pace and accuracy.

Metallica's year was a bittersweet one. Near the end of 1986, while on tour in Sweden promoting the phenomenal *Master Of Puppets* LP, they were stopped in their tracks by a road accident which killed bass player Cliff Burton. Split rumours were rife, but by the time of Cliff's funeral the future of the band was already decided. As drummer Lars Ulrich explained: "Cliff would be the first one to get pissed off if we just sat around and cried. I know that he'd come round and kick us in the ass and tell us to get back out on the road and continue where we left off."

So a new bassist was found – Jason Newsted, ex of Arizona act Flotsam & Jetsam – and the "Master" tour was finally wound up. Once again, the feeling in the band is good and strong – James, Lars and Kirk know they chose the right man one legless night in San Francisco, and Jason simply couldn't have got himself a better gig.

This year also saw Metallica sign to Phonogram, marking the end of their contract with Britain's foremost independent metal label, Music For

Iron Maiden: It's been business as usual for older, established acts.

Nations. Realistically, the move to a major label was inevitable, as was the case with Anthrax before them, and Megadeth too.

Megadeth (the name derives from a phrase originally coined by a US politician when describing the effect that a nuclear fall-out would have on the world's population) peddle a calculated kind of violence: dense, intricate, twisted, off the wall.

It's exactly the kind of raw yet chiselled sound you'd expect from a sharp, hard-nosed and unpredictable

labels were continuing to accept and fund speed metal on its own terms.

One track on the album was of particular interest; a curt bastardization of Willie Dixon's 'I Ain't Superstitious' which brought the blues influence on heavy metal full circle; blues to heavy rock to metal to thrash and then back to blues via Megadeth's scarred and blackened approximation of the form.

Megadeth's punishing music is given extra flexibility by a couple of band members' jazz backgrounds, while Mustaine's hot-headed temperament adds further venom to the sneering, streetwise lyrics. Admittedly, Mustaine is full of brusque and uncompromising arrogance, but it's this fire that makes Megadeth's lithe and biting speed metal so unique.

The snowballing of speed metal has had a knock-on effect on hardcore too. Hardcore (like thrash, American-dominated, and the ultimate street vibe) is currently in such a good state of health that one of the leading bands, US skatecore fiends **Suicidal Tendencies**, have even managed to wriggle their way onto a major label, Virgin.

The upshot, Suicidal's *Join The Army* LP, isn't just an accessible, fun, hardcore party record. It's also a first, a breakthrough that's established a certain credibility for hardcore in big money circles. In Rocky George, Suicidal have a truly gifted high-speed guitarist, and with their loopy 'board anthem, 'Possessed To Skate', they *almost* chalked up a minor hit. Maybe if skating breaks big again . . .

However, Suicidal *are* an exception.

The impact thrash has had in shaking up the rather staid and rusty old ways of mainstream metal has been akin to rap's effect on black music. Both thrash and rap are essentially youthful and streetwise

chap like Dave Mustaine, the man who jumped (or was pushed) from Metallica back in '82 due to his and James Hetfield's ego problems. Mustaine struck out on his own, and as '86 neared its close, Megadeth's second album *Peace Sells . . . But Who's Buying?*, was put out by their new label, Capitol.

Peace Sells . . . combines anger and articulacy, bludgeon and complexity, pace and accuracy. Again, it was proof that Mustaine was as much the architect of Metallica as Hetfield or Ulrich. And it also acted as proof that the major record

It's unlikely that a whole bunch of big companies will be rushing to sign up, say, Cryptic Slaughter for an eight-album deal. Pure hardcore is simply too unpalatably rough and noisy to appeal to anything but a limited audience. And naturally, there's no such thing as *polished* hardcore.

Essentially, hardcore is the stuff of low- budget independent labels, thriving as punk did here from '76 onwards on a strictly street level. The past year has thrown up some hot items – Big Apple 'core (New York is crawling with bands)

from **Ludichrist** (*Immaculate Deception*), **Nuclear Assault** (*Game Over*, which includes the legendary 38-second blitzkreig, 'Hang The Pope') and Hare Krishna skinheads the **Cro-Mags** (*The Age Of Quarrel*). Plus there's the nomadic **D.R.I.** (Dirty Rotten Imbeciles)'s powerful *Crossover* album, and, funniest of all, New Jersey boys **Adrenalin O.D.** with *Humungousfungusamongus*, which is as crazed as it is unpronounceable.

Suicidal Tendencies: US skatecore fiends who've wriggled onto a major label.

As vital to thrash as they are to hardcore, independent labels were responsible for giving all of the aforementioned big guns a start in life, and it's these small, shoestring operations which continue to provide an outlet for the more difficult and innovative new bands. Labels like **Metal Blade** and **Megaforce** (US), **Roadrunner** (UK and Europe), **Music For Nations** (UK and Europe) and **Noise International** (based in Germany) have all been instrumental in promoting and nurturing new thrash, and it's the latter two who've really excelled over the past 12 months.

Music For Nations have ploughed some of the profits from over 60,000 British sales (a silver award) of

Bathory: Merciless Swedish death metal laced with the strangled vocals of Quorthon (above).

Metallica's *Master Of Puppets* into pushing a number of relatively unknown acts. Acts like **Possessed** (*Beyond The Gates*), **Agent Steel** (*Unstoppable Force*), **Death** (*Scream Bloody Gore*), **Dark Angel** (*Darkness Descends*), **Death Angel** (they may be young – drummer Andy Galeon is just 14! – but their *The Ultra-Violence* LP has a grip of iron) and **Bathory** (*Under The Sign Of The Black Mark* is more of that merciless Swedish death metal laced with the strangled vocals of the inimitable Quorthon).

Death metal (extra-heavy and oppressively morbid) has its place on the Noise label too – courtesy of **Celtic Frost**, whose *Into The Pandemonium* album is both baffling and brilliant; experimental, quirky and pretty much out on a limb.

It's certainly a brave and ambitious move from the Swiss trio. Their use of sampled sounds, female voices, strings, horns, scratchy rhythm tracks and a Wall Of Voodoo cover ('Mexican Radio') may alienate a big proportion of their "death or nothing" following, but that's obviously a risk which they're prepared to take.

Less adventurous yet far faster and tougher is **Voivod**'s *Killing Technology*, released early in '87. Easily their most listenable album to date (the other two are long hauls filled with incessant hammering) *Killing* is accomplished yet still as punky and acidic as ever. **Tankard** are quite punky too, and what they lack in cutting edge they *almost* make up for in pure fun. Their debut, *Zombie Attack*, is something of a German hardcore classic.

Helloween, grand, melodic and quick to boot, are currently Noise's big success story, having sold in excess of 100,000 copies of their second full album, *Keeper Of The Seven Keys – Part 1*, in their German homeland alone.

Keeper, the first test of their new singer, Michael Kiske, has it all – fine tunes, fine riffs and an appealing sense of humour – and with a headlining show at the Hammersmith Odeon already behind them, Helloween are tightly locked into an upward spiral.

And so, still, is thrash. The kids won't want to go back to crusty, pedestrian trad metal now that they've tasted the thrill of speed.

Everywhere, new speed combos are springing up like the reborn in a zombie flick; **Rage**, **Cyclone**, **Testament**, **Virus**, **Exhumer** (the last two are both signed to an all-new British indie specialist death/speed/hardcore label, Metalworks).

Alongside Helloween, Anthrax, Megadeth, Metallica, Slayer, and even Agent, Steel have all headlined at the Hammersmith's battered old Odeon over the past year. Simply, thrash is too tough to die. Too strong to fade. And too good to miss.

PAUL ELLIOTT

Agent Steel: Relatively unknown but a headliner at the Hammersmith Odeon.

HIP-HOP

In a year when sensation was in danger of becoming a mere rumour, the mighty **Def Jam** label (aided and abetted by the ghost of John Bonham) caused a brutal, bass-heavy convulsion in the body pop with a string of extraordinary hardcore rap releases. Not rap in the sense of corny images of break-dancing and graffiti, but rap re-invented as what label co-founder, **Rick Rubin,** called "Black Rock". "Def Jam make rock records for black people," he claimed, and consistently argued that hip-hop had more in common with heavy rock or hardcore punk than the disco or soul it was normally lumped with.

Rubin went further, insisting that Def Jam was the first rebellious black music of the '80s, the first black music that didn't have to dress itself up in Jerri curls and upwardly mobile show-biz values in order to be accepted into the main stream.

Def Jam's war against the gentrification of black music might have seemed like so much hot air if it wasn't for the fact that the grooves were so seismic. **LL Cool J** released his second album, *Bigger and Deffer,* and shed the minimalist homeboy persona of his debut *Radio,* in favour of a towering and monstrous tribute to his own ego. A self-proclaimed "Legend in Leather", with the taste of victory permanently in his mouth, LL crushed all opposition with a power-crazed and atheistic set of ego-raps that were further proof that rap had brutally replaced the essentially religious faith in an Other that lay at the heart of so much black music in the '60s, with a belief in Self above all else.

Run DMC released their best album yet with *Raising Hell,* and their collaboration with Aerosmith on 'Walk This Way', ensured that their grim-faced visages were as ubiquitous on MTV as Billy Idol's sneer. The band spent the rest of the year working on *Tougher Than Leather* (a sort of rap blaxploitation flick that's everything *Krush Groove* wasn't) and settling into their new role as The Ambassadors of Rap on Planet pop, doing the sort of good works that

celebrities are expected to perform in these post-Live Aid times performing at anti-crack benefits, taking part in high school literacy campaigns, that sort of thing.

Def Jam also unleashed a new act in **Public Enemy,** the so-called "Black Panthers of rap", who came up with the best rap album of the year in *Yo! Bum Rush The Show*. Combining avant-garde textures, boombox beats and an unrelenting sonic surface tension with an uncompromising line in Black Power politics, the album was a fierce attack on the "cold getting dumb" attitude of much contemporary rap. Public Enemy knew what time it was. And it wasn't "Time To Get Ill" as The Beastie Boys proclaimed, neither was it time to "Get Stupid Fresh" as Mantronix urged. "It's time to get educated and motivated" said Public Enemy.

Then there was the orgiastic agitation of **The Beastie Boys'** debut album, *Licensed to Ill* – the musical equivalent of an ape's anus pushed in the face of pop respectability. Noisy, nasty, loud, lewd and ideologically unsound, The Beasties

Mantronix: A brave attempt to bridge the gap between the street and the dancefloor.

eulogized hard drinking, hard beats, hard rock, hard dicks and the right not to be upwardly mobile, while all the time disrespecting women, gays, melodic decorum, grown-ups, socially aware soul-boys and the racial division between black and white music.

Much to everyone's surprise, *Licensed to Ill* stormed to the top of the American charts. Even more surprising were the tabloid headlines of the "Beastie Boys Bite Off Mongrels' Heads" variety that greeted their arrival in Britain. Behind the hysteria, what united both right and left, both *The Sun* and *City Limits,* was the accusation that the Beasties were somehow fake because they were really white kids from nice, middle-class homes. What seemed to annoy the British media the most was not so much the vileness of The Beasties' behaviour, but the fact that it wasn't rooted in under-privilege or deprivation.

Up until recently it was commonplace for cultural commentators to portray rap as the authentic voice of the inner-city, street music as opposed to fake, media-created music. But the rise of Def Jam, a label whose personnel and artists are largely drawn from the two New York suburbs, Queens and Long Island, has changed that. The fact that this most suburban of labels was producing the hardest, hardcore rap was one of the better ironies of the year.

The rise of the new generation of suburban rappers didn't go unnoticed in the original home of rap, the Boogie Down Bronx. After the demise of the first generation of Bronx rappers and DJ's like Bam and Grandmaster Flash, the Bronx looked to be a spent force. But this was the year that the Bronx bit back with a whole new generation of talent like **T. La Rock, Masters of Ceremony, Almighty El Cee, The Ultra-Magnetic MC's** and, the most hardcore of them all, the **Grand, Incredible Scott La Rock** and his rapping partner **"The Poet" aka Blastmaster KRS 1.**

The latter's debut album *Criminally Minded* was a deeply cynical, deeply syncopated slice of street regal, renegade rap with the emphasis on reggae-rap

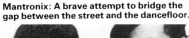
The Cookie Crew: Undermining the rule that Britishness and rap don't mix.

mutation. But this was reggae with all the herbally mellow elements ruthlessly excised to produce an unrelentingly harsh, sparse soundscape underpinned by the most primary of skankopated pulses over which KRS rapped lurid tales of sexual degradation, drug addiction and casual violence. "Fresh for '87, Suckers" he boasted and he wasn't wrong.

A way from New York, this year also saw the emergence of a burgeoning rap scene in Miami. Christened **Miami Bass,** this was rap with the emphasis on the bass-biology interface, the point where the bass end of the sonic spectrum rattles your rib-cage. The **2 Live Crew** and **MC Shy D** were the main artists while **Luke**

less fiercely minimal and more musical drawing on sources like Parliament, Hendrix, Steve Miller and Kraftwerk.

But it wasn't the music that Schoolly D became famous for, rather the Yo-Boy image of guns, gangs and the good life of which Schoolly was supposed to be the embodiment. When it was revealed that he, far from being a gun-toting, drug-snorting teenage psychopath, was a would-be young entrepreneur drawing on his experiences as a teenage gang member to make great rap records, you could hear the sighs of disappointment all over medialand. This year's exotic rap savage proved to be this year's smart cookie and the world's first yuppie Yo-Boy.

On a different planet altogether were **Mantronix** who released their second album, **Music Madness.** Too sophisticated for the hardcore rap crowd and too techno-raw for the club scene,

King Sun and D. Moet: Came up with the haunting rap ballad, 'Hey Love'.

To The Edit. The most futuristic music of the year but how many people were there to listen?

For those of you who regard hip-hop as Misogyny Central, then this year's stream of raps about "skeezers", "sluts" and "big-butted bitches" provided plenty of ammunition. But the fly girls weren't taking it all lying down. There was **Sweet Tee** and **Jazzy Joyce's** 'It's My Beat' as well as **Salt-N-Pepa's** debut album, *Hot, Cool And Vicious.* The latter boasted the sort of sound that sits in the pit of your stomach with Salt and Pepa, two female rappers from Queens, swapping rhymes and putting down the menfolk in a style that was sugar and spice and all things nasty.

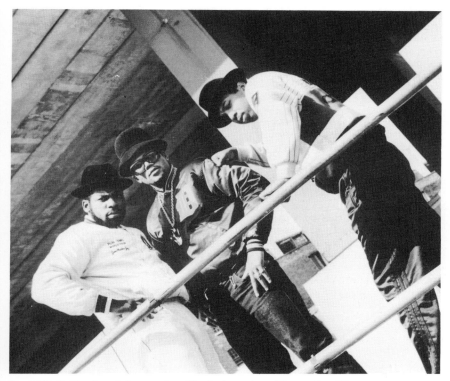
Run DMC: Settling into their new role as The Ambassadors of Rap on Planet Pop.

Skywalker was the main producer. The music was unrelentingly juvenile in content but showed a neat way of resolving its disparate influences into spectacular sequences of action-packed, rapidly-edited moments.

Over in Philadelphia, **Schoolly D** prompted the question "How hard can hardcore hip-hop get before turning into a pure pulse of sensation?" with a debut album of which the most musical element was the booming dub caverns that echoed throughout. His follow-up album, *Saturday Night – The Album,* was

Music Madness was a brave attempt to bridge the gap between the street and the dancefloor by re-establishing a relationship between electro and rap.

Commercially it failed but aesthetically it was a great triumph – a mish-mash of everything from Big Band-era jazz to the theme from *The Old Grey Whistle Test* fed through Mantronik's sampler. Everything, except MC Tee's rap, was stolen, dismantled and re-transmitted to create the sort of adventurous sonic playground that The Art Of Noise should have been assembling after *Close*

B ack in Britain things went from bad to not quite as bad as it used to be. Generally British rap is the pits, but with the emergence of **Faze One**, **The Three Wise Men** and **The Cookie Crew**, things started to change. The problem with British hip-hop is that Britishness and rap just don't mix – the former with its cramped, closed-in images of beer and pigeons, wet leaves and dogshit, is too feeble a vehicle to house the inflated desires and larger-than-life persons of the best rap. But this year the above-mentioned groups went some way towards undermining that rule.

And lest we forget, this was also the year of **Eric B's** 'Paid In Full', **The Skinny Boy's** monument to hip-hop wig-out 'Weightless', **Just Ice's** rudeboy rap in a reggae style as heard on the Mantronik-produced 'Back To The Old School', **King Sun's** haunting rap ballad 'Hey Love', **The Classical Two's** 'New Generation', **MC Shan's** 'Down By Law' and a host of other talents who burned brightly for an instant before disappearing under the weight of rap's everlasting search for the rhythm of the moment.

FRANK OWEN

REGGAE

"If them ask your name and number/Just tell them you a ragamuffin soldier/And if further, reggae ambassador/ Rule all over" ('Greetings' – Half Pint)

"Ragamuffin year this year/Ragamuffin year me say next year/Revolutioneer coming here/People you better beware/ Babylon better beware" ('Ragamuffin Year' – Junior Delgado)

The year of the ragamuffin was heralded by **Half Pint** with his 'Greetings' salutation. Released to a thunderous beat in the summer of 1986, it gave currency to an expression long in use in a general sort of way in reggae terminology. *"Greetings! I bring from Jah, ooh, eee,"* sang Half Pint, *"to all ragamuffins…"* and immediately identified an era.

Not that the ragamuffins themselves were anything new but the latest in a long

Half Pint: Heralded the Year of the Ragamuffin with his 'Greetings' salutation.

line of disaffected rude boys recognizable from rock steady days and even before. Nor had their quarrelsome inclinations changed much either, only now these were more openly expressed, as on **Super Black**'s ragamuffin 'Rambo' for Jammy's. *"Me is a youth don't deal with war,"* asserts Black, *"me is a youth don't check for war. Come to the test me will deal with war, hold a bwoy face me a go full it up a scar, broke a bwoy jawbone with a crowbar. Rambo me Rambo. Me ragamuffin and me jumbo."*

Quite apart from its ragamuffin connotations, the very rhythm of 'Greetings' provided a further lucrative spin-off for producer **George Phang** with an album devoted to the same and popular singles using the track such as Super Cat's 'Under Pressure' and Frankie Paul's heartfelt 'Alesha', a steady seller for months.

Reggae music has always been a law unto itself and a popular act will rarely be content in releasing just one new record at a time where two or even several might equally serve. **Frankie Paul** has been liberal with his voice ever since his appearance on the scene and in recent times would appear to have usurped Sugar Minott as reggae's most prolific recording artist.

Released at the same time as 'Alesha' in July 1986, his 'Shub In' for Sydney Crooks of The Pioneers went on to become one of the hits of the year, attaining the second spot on the reggae chart for six weeks, deprived of a Number One first by **Audrey Hall**'s 'Smile' and then by **Boris Gardiner**'s 'I Want To Wake Up With You', both national chart hits of great longevity.

In the meantime, a whole slew of Frankie Paul music became available. In August came 'Hungry Belly' for Vena, with whom the singer later recorded 'Tato' released the following February and 'Warning' in March. Also in August came 'Handcart Man' for Redman, who also released his 'We Are Di Best' in April of the following year. September brought 'You Are So Good To Me' and 'Bad Man Pick Me' and there were other

odd releases up to the end of the year.

He then had 'No Sizzling' for Skeng Don and 'Gun Shot' among his February releases, 'All People' for Spade and 'Kick Up A Rumpus' the following month and his own comment on the one Sharon's pre-natal condition on 'No Tek It Weh' for Black Scorpio up on pre in April. In May there was 'Rub A Dub With Feeling', 'Rubber Dub Market', 'Control The Area', 'I'm Missing You' for Prince Jazzbo and a couple for Prince Jammy, 'Cover Your Mouth' and 'Cool Now King Jammy's'. *"Clash of the century,"* he claimed on the latter, *"we run the country, every time"* and went on *"listen Frankie P round the microphone stand. Anywhere Jammy go them a shake off him hand, them say him are the ram dance man."*

Another May release by Frankie Paul, this time in company with barker **Joe Lick Shot** for 'Dance Caan Nice Wid-Out Wi' for the Ottey brothers, also gave him his first chart hit since 'Shub In', all those waxings and yet a mere nine months previous.

Lovindeer: Rejuvenated and helping to make the 'Boops' controversy a favourite topic.

Frankie Paul: Usurped Sugar Minott as reggae's most prolific recording artist.

There is a standing tradition of thematic bias in much reggae and never more so than at present. Recent years have seen such as the long-running 'One Dance' saga with all dissertation set to the classic 'Pressure And Slide' rhythm and this was followed by the "sugar daddy" controversy of 'Boops', with the majority of artists passing comment over a reworking of the rock steady 'Whip' rhythm.

Last year's 'What The Hell' from **Echo Minott** on the subject of marital strife was another which sparked much retort. It was originally released during midsummer but was not picked up on until September, by which time an answer record by UK based **Andrew Paul** from the wily Fashion outlet entitled 'What The Police Can Do' was in direct competition with Echo's own and they fought it out on the charts in the ensuing weeks.

Further retort from the rejuvenated **Lovindeer** on 'Babylon Boops' made it the favourite topic over the Christmas period and into the New Year. Concurrent with this Lovindeer was also scoring big with 'Man Shortage' which went on to top the local chart, while Echo Minott followed up for Jammy with the enchanting ring tune 'Emmanuel Road' for another hit the following year.

Another theme was Sharon's pregnancy already referred to, concerning a sister mythologized in reggae in much the same way as Hank Ballard's Annie according to R&B lore. The first of these was by **Screwdriver** on a tune entitled 'Don't Hide It' but it was **Little John**'s answer for the ubiquitous Jammy's 'Yes Mama' which was the big hit. There was further discussion, toaster **Peter Metro**'s 'Yes Daddy' for George Phang and another Screwdriver effort 'No Mama'. And there was Lovindeer popping up once again for another brisk-selling aside 'Me Do That', positively blue on 'Don't Bend Down'.

Another voice popularly heard was the piping tone of **Coco T**. He had a Top Ten hit in the autumn with 'Tune In' for Jammy, sang of the '86 Flood' for Harry J and 'Over Me' for Mello Sounds during the same period, as well as the popular 'Crying Time' towards the end of the year. 1987 saw 'Sweet Jamaica', the Greensleeves 'Medley' discomix and another hit for Jammy with 'Come Again' in March.

People had been predicting things for Nottingham duo **Natural Ites** ever since their stirring and melodic 'Picture On The Wall' in 1983 and four years later they were astride the chart with 'Lately', a superior brand of local produce sharing certain distinctions in common with **Undivided Roots**' 'Party Nite' of the previous year and **Matumbi**'s 'After Tonight' of yore. And the Natural Ites' own follow-up 'Cry For You' was in the same vein.

The sensation of the New Year was **Pinchers** who dislodged Natural Ites with his slack 'Agony' for Jammy, scoring again for the same producer with 'Sit Down Pon It'. Among a rash of freelance efforts from Pinchers released in their wake were included 'Grammy' for Vena, 'Me Love Me Like Me Enjoyment' for John Dread and a tune played on the sounds called 'Mass Out'.

Another off-colour Jammy protégé to find success was **Admiral Bailey**, whose new expression for the old Jamaican *pum pum* on 'Punany' was big in the clubs and a popular seller for months. He also achieved hit status and provoked further comment with his 'Two Year Old' about his own son.

A third, 'Big Belly Man', was another popular party piece. *"Now look at some of the impressive man,"* stated Bailey, *"like Papa Jammy's him a big belly man, Digital yes him a big belly man, Daddy Steelie him a big belly man, look pon Jack Scorpio a big belly man, look pon Josey Wales yes him a big belly man, look pon Shelley yes him a big belly man, look pon George Phang yes him a big belly man, I Admiral is a big belly man…"*

Also heard throughout the year in the dance-halls were the naggingly familiar tonsils of **King Kong** on tunes like 'Glamour Boy' towards the end of 1986, hits early the following year with 'Cake Of Success' and 'Digital We Digital', pre such as 'Ragamuffin A Pass', 'Agony And Pain', 'Babylon', 'Time Is The Master' and his own comment on Admiral Bailey's theme for 'Four Year Old'.

And there was a reawakening of interest in the **Wailing Souls** group and some good new music from them on 'Dance Hall Nice Again' in 1986 and 'Dog Bite', 'Full Moon', 'Informer' and 'Diamonds And Pearls' the following year. Dance-hall nice again indeed.

PENNY REEL

Reggae music has always been a law unto itself and a popular act will rarely be content in releasing just one new record at a time where two or even several might equally serve

JAZZ

J azz caught its breath over the last 12 months. In 1985-86, it bolted forward in Britain: you could see and hear people walking and talking jazz again, and quite a few were actually caught playing it. In the last year the players have got stronger, the "revival" has hardened into a solid base for further expansion and jazz, generally, has stayed around.

This was not a year for startling new surprises. Most of the faces remained the same. The fact that they were still there and kept the idea of a new jazz alive was enough to put it in magazines and on television, two areas that haven't exactly been saturated with this music in recent years. The BBC did another of their *Jazz Week* beanos, and it began to seem less like a crank's idea and more like good, inventive programming. After all, jazz has never been short on style.

It's this infiltration into the cultural mainstream which jazz has always struggled with. Given that it's a difficult music to start with – that is, you can't always whistle the tune after the first chorus – the "elitist" status which it's gathered has been its commercial downfall. With the record industry contracting to its own elite level – megastars who can sell millions, not paltry thousands – it seemed that a marketing problem area like jazz was at the bottom of the priority list. Instead, the scene has been set for an interesting change.

saxophone. Some suggest that his is a token success, a black crossover with a limited resonance for jazz itself. Yet the fact remains that Pine is playing turbulent post-Coltrane music which demands plenty of his audience.

A couple of points make for interesting conversation in this area. One is that the musicians themselves are no longer "purist". They weren't born to be jazz musicians. Today's young players grew up surrounded by many musics – rock, soul, jazz-rock, reggae, whatever – and their tastes are likely to be just as eclectic. Many are prepared to work in crossover bands, not just to make ends meet but because they actually enjoy it. They want to play different sorts of music. Attitudes towards stylistic boundaries have softened, just as the players themselves have got younger and younger (like policemen).

And a new audience, a *listening* audience, may be growing up alongside. A few developments have encouraged people to take listening a little more seriously. The wry suggestion has often been made that people turn to jazz only when there's nothing else worth listening to. What's really happened is a kind of progressive education for the ear. The

But Pine didn't only sound good, he *looked* like a youth icon, a handsome, well-dressed man with a saxophone

The huge success of **Courtney Pine's** debut album is the most striking instance of this direction. Pine, the young tenorman from Paddington, notched up a cool 50,000 sales for *Journey To The Urge Within* by the end of 1986, and he was picked as one of the cultural faces of the year in a *South Bank* round-up. But Pine didn't only sound good, he *looked* like a youth icon, a handsome, well-dressed man with a

fashionable acclaim for New Age music, contemporary composers like Michael Nyman and Philip Glass and the new music from Africa and Latin America have all helped to create a climate where a playing music like jazz can hold its own confident place. Few of the newer converts to jazz listen to jazz alone.

T he music's forward directions over the past year all seem based around these sorts of assimilation. The time of outrageous new innovation has long since cooled off, in Britain, Europe and America alike. Young British players like **Steve Williamson**, **Andy Sheppard**, **Iain Ballamy**, **Julian Arguelles** and **Phillip Bent** form a huge, floating collective of performers, building new bands or one-off projects almost at will: the music might be electric or acoustic, hard bop or hard funk, big band or duo.

Two leading American groups took their heritage apart with a similar enthusiasm. **The Leaders**, a supergroup with such spellbinding players as **Chico Freeman**, **Cecil McBee** and **Arthur Blythe**, played virtuoso sets where the influences glittered – as if it were some living jazz

The Courtney Pine Quartet: Playing turbulent post-Coltrane music which demands plenty.

Andy Sheppard: One of several young British players who formed a huge, floating collective.

hall of fame. **Brass Fantasy**, a band of trumpets and trombones and one drummer, is an outfit that roars exultantly through a similar breadth of material: their newest record includes versions of Michael Jackson's 'Thriller' and Lloyd Price's 'Personality'. Trumpeter **Lester Bowie** leads the band; he is also one of The Leaders.

At home, it's easier than ever to go out and hear jazz live, yet there are still too many players chasing too few (poorly paid) gigs. Fans and musicians alike love to complain about this situation – there are just as many starving rock players – but the "revival" hasn't set every part of the country on fire.

Local organizations, the backbone of British jazz, can struggle for an audience for any gig which has nothing to offer but the music itself. **London's National Jazz Centre** appeared to finally die an ignominious if mysterious death, with the premises remaining as a half-built hulk in Covent Garden. Nevertheless, the regional administrators remain full of enthusiasm. A club like Peter Ind's splendid **Bass Clef** thrived in its own cheerful way. This summer everybody was preparing busily for October 1987, which has been officially designated as National Jazz Month, climaxed by the British Jazz Awards.

Perhaps the most encouraging signs of

Wynton Marsalis: Continued to make many hackles rise with his outspoken comments.

all came from the record industry itself. In America, there has been renewed activity from majors like RCA, with plenty of reissues being prepared for the burgeoning CD market. In Britain, though, the trend at last began to move towards signing up new jazz, in the wake of Pine's extraordinary success. Island, who managed to win an industry award for the marketing of *Journey To The Urge Within*, took a further step by reactivating their **Antilles** subsidiary with a number of new signings: **The Jazz Warriors,** west country saxophonist Andy Sheppard and a slew of Americans. That, they said, was just the start.

A&R departments elsewhere weren't quite so quick, but at Editions EG (**Man Jumping**, **Bill Bruford's Earthworks**) and Virgin's new Venture subsidiary (**Lester Bowie**) a jazz direction looked solid enough. EMI continued to wheedle **Blue Note** into record chain stores and the club DJs who'd helped to give jazz the fresh push all seemed to have their own compilation album out. It felt like a team spirit was at work.

Pat Metheny and Ornette Coleman: A successful partnership record.

remarkable tours and records from the Norwegian saxophonist **Jan Garbarek** and the Dutchman **Willem Breuker** with his bizarre Kollektief.

We should also mention those two trumpeters, **Wynton** and **Miles**: **Mr Marsalis** continued to make many hackles rise with his outspoken comments on business, music and critics,

---

The fashionable acclaim for New Age music, contemporary composers like Michael Nyman and Philip Glass and the new music from Africa and Latin America have all helped to create a climate where playing music like jazz can hold its own confident place

---

A number of older spirits brought cause for celebration. There were at least two notable anniversaries: **Gil Evans** passed his 75th birthday with a towering London concert in May, his energy undiminished even if he felt a little too tired to make the party afterwards; and the equally noble **Dizzy Gillespie** chalked up 70 years at the Royal Festival Hall in July. **Ornette Coleman** reappeared with his first British concerts for seven years in April, and his **Prime Time Band** made a hurricane of harmolodic noise. Following his successful partnership record with guitarist **Pat Metheny**, Ornette has put together another three albums: this is a purple patch for the old rebel.

His great contemporary, **Cecil Taylor**, also visited to play solo. In exchange, perhaps, we sent plenty of our people over to the US in just one band, the mighty **Charlie Watts Orchestra**, which bemused American audiences with its sheer size. Meanwhile, other Europeans continued to create jazz in their own image: there were

Miles Davis: Scored his biggest hit with a rock audience since *Bitches Brew*.

but he put out one gorgeous record (*J Mood*) and left several more awaiting release, while **Mr Davis** scored his biggest hit with a rock audience since *Bitches Brew* with the elegant if rather chilly *Tutu*.

The mood is optimistic, not revolutionary. There's plenty to play and hear.

RICHARD COOK

BLUES

Just for the record, the heaviest impact ever made by a blues album on the US pop charts is still the No. 11 position achieved by Bobby Bland's *Here's The Man* in 1963. That doesn't mean, though, that **Robert Cray's** No. 13 peak position and gold album score *Strong Persuader* is anything other than the most important event to occur in the blues field so far this decade. Cray has sold over 700,000 copies of his major label debut, and before the album's chart life is over it is a dead cert for platinum. This is *serious business*.

Not even the magisterial BB King or the rockin' white boys like Johnny Winter, George Thorogood, Stevie Ray Vaughan or the Fabulous Thunderbirds have pulled off a coup like *Strong Persuader*, and the two most serendipitous aspects of the whole thing are (a) that it wasn't the result of anybody's marketing masterplan and (b) that it couldn't have happened to a more qualified guy. If Robert Cray hadn't happened, nobody would have had the imagination to invent him.

For a start, at a time when Buddy Guy – now past his 50th birthday – is *still* being referred to as one of "the younger bluesmen", Cray is a mere yearling of 34, clean-cut and exceptionally good-looking. His band are tight, funky, disciplined and unflashy. Cray's own mellifluous southern-soul voice and taut, spiky West Side guitar are straightforward and relatively unornamented, and his repertoire (composed by the band, the singer and manager/producers Dave Walker and Bruce Bromberg) is packed to bursting with memorable, melodic and lyrically sophisticated meditations on infidelity and despair.

His first album *Who's Been Talkin'* was cut for Giorgio Gomelski's Tomato label in 1978, remained unreleased until 1980 and managed to stay in the shops for all of six months before Tomato went under. It was several years before Cray recorded again, but *Bad Influence* – the result of this reunion between Cray and

the Bromberg/Walker team – was picked up for UK release by Demon. The album's lead song 'Phone Booth' was promptly covered by Albert King, and Cray began his formidable collection of WC Handy awards.

The follow-up album, *False Accusations*, strengthened Cray's status and Mercury Records began nosing after him; not because visions of platinum were dancing in their corporate head, but because signing Cray would demonstrate that they were a label who cared about

music and were concerned at least as much with quality as with sales. Result: Robert Cray is now only one hit single away from being the first blues singer to become a bona fide pop star. For thousands upon thousands of US record-buyers, *Strong Persuader* is the first blues album they've ever taken home.

Still, you may say, that's all very nice for Robert Cray and his band and for Mercury Records and for Bruce Bromberg and Dave Walker and their Hightone label, but is Cray's success simply a quirk of cultural history or is this finally the year that the blues hauls itself out of a rut and into the sunshine? Well, this may not be the millennium but there are a few favourable omens.

For a start, despite most of Chicago's musical headlines being made by the House crews, the blues is not only alive and well there, but it's actually thriving. There are blues bars and clubs all over the city now, and as many as 60 blues bands are in regular work. Recently, 43rd Street was officially renamed

Robert Cray is now only one hit single away from being the first blues singer to become a bona fide pop star

Muddy Waters Boulevarde, and Bruce Iglauer, boss of the town's premier blues label Alligator Records, reports that in the last couple of years Alligator's turnover has virtually doubled.

Much of this can be attributed to the success of the Grammy-winning *Showdown* team-up by Albert Collins, Johnny Copeland and someone called **Robert Cray**, to Collins' drastically heightened profile in the wake of his Live Aid stint with George Thorogood and his guest-shot on David Bowie's 'Underground' single, and to **Johnny Winter's** decision to sign to the label.

In Britain, the presence of a sizeable contingent of blues fans in the nation's ad agencies can be deduced from the spectacle of Renaults being driven down rain-splashed roads to the tune of **Otis Rush's** 'So Many Roads', of power-dressing career girls washing urban grime out of the hair accompanied by **Jimmy Reed's** 'Bright Lights Big City' and lovelorn young men grimly swilling Tennants Pilsner to the melancholy strains of someone sounding remarkably like **Champion Jack Dupree** crooning Little Walter's 'Mean Old World' ("it's a *mean pint*," growls a tough male voice apparently unconcerned with the niceties of the Trade Descriptions Act). As a logical companion piece to the unlikely alliance of clothing manufacturers and Campaigners For Real Soul, the blues is coming forward as a signifier of urban grit with a dash of glamour.

Meanwhile, video stores have been playing host to **Crossroads**, a peculiar blend of teen adventure and the legend of Robert Johnson in which Ralph (*Karate Kid*) Macchio attempts to sell his soul to learn how to play the blues. Apparently the methods used by earlier generations of white bluesers (excess boozing and doping, listening to lots of scratchy old albums, not washing) are inadequate for the Age of YUP.

The year also saw the usual flurry of activity in the customary fields of gigs and discs. **BB King** played his usual immaculate show, distinguished by some unselfconscious clowning and showboating as well as some of the rawest guitar he's played at a UK concert for years and marred only by a disgusting robin's-egg blue V-neck pullover under his inevitable Big Suit. **Buddy Guy** and **Junior Wells** showed up for a couple of gigs which generated a storm of indifference, but the cadaverous, Mephistophelian figure of **Clarence Gatemouth Brown** perched elegantly on a stool at Dingwalls clad in his customary cowboy finery and played a monster show comprising his usual blend of jump blues, big-band swing and fiddle-driven country music – the same stuff included on his *Real Life* album (Rounder Europa) along with the bonus of a flagwaving horn section.

Stevie Ray Vaughan showed up, braving the worst that Libyan terrorists could throw at him, and proved to be the Phil Cool of the overamped Stratocaster: five minutes of Jimi Hendrix, five minutes of Albert King, five minutes of BB, more Hendrix, a little Guitar Slim, yet more Hendrix. Who Stevie Ray himself is, we have yet to discover.

The Fabulous Thunderbirds rocked out the Town & Country in their usual amiable manner, Robert Somebody-or-other practically burned Hammersmith Palais to the ground, and then this same Robert was due to open on tour for Tina Turner following a guest appearance on her last TV special as a last-minute dep for a no-showing Wilson Pickett.

On the reissue front, **Charly**, **Ace** and the **Demon/Edsel** combine performed their usual sterling service, and **Atlantic** Records made the best of a fairly sporadic and patchy blues catalogue by marshalling everything they could find (including live performances by **BB King, Bobby Bland, Muddy Waters, Howlin' Wolf** and – with a smoking vesion of Bland's 'I Smell Trouble' – **Ike & Tina Turner**) into a luxurious eight-album boxed set entitled (not surprisingly) *Atlantic Blues*, a far from shabby companion to their larger and more expensive jazz and R&B collections.

Ace managed to unearth some previously unreleased **Guitar Slim** sides (which they teamed up with an equal number of **Earl King** out-takes), but unfortunately they weren't a patch on the classics. The follow ups to last year's miraculous Sonny Boy Williamson Chess boxed set – supposedly spotlighting Muddy Waters and Howlin' Wolf – are still only rumours. Charly's **Junior Wells** collection *Messin' With The Kid* is, happily, a fact.

Notable new albums included New

Walter "Wolfman" Washington: A magnificent voice halfway between Albert King and Isaac Hayes.

Orleans vet **Earl King's** *Glazed*, a team-up with **Roomful Of Blues**, a great band who've never had a decent vocalist, and from the same legendary burg, the featured debut of **Walter "Wolfman" Washington,** whose *Wolf Tracks* (Rounder Europa) showcases a magnificent voice halfway between Albert King and Isaac Hayes, not to mention some excellent songs, impressive guitar and swaggering brass arrangements.

Malaco Records – all the way from Jackson Mississippi, y'all – released **Bobby Bland's** *After All* and **Little Milton's** *Annie Mae's Cafe*, both of which are heartening moves in the direction of a return to form. And Alligator unleashed upon the world **Li'l Ed & The Blues Imperials**, a raucous, slide-powered quartet led by the late JB Hutto's little nephew and as hot a party band as could be desired.

Li'l Ed was first recorded as part of Alligator's *The New Bluebloods* project, a compilation of tracks by an even dozen of Chicago's current blues bands, but as soon as they got him in the studio they knew they were onto something. Ed and his tream cut something ridiculous like 40 tunes in three and a half hours, so his own album was inevitable. Alligator also have this year's best debut by a white blues band in **Little Charlie & The Nightcats'** *All The Way Crazy;* fast, loose and jivey almost to the point of caricature, but entertaining and soulful for all of that.

Once the consequences of Robert What's-his-name's success percolates through both to the major record companies and the younger musicians, things could get drastically interesting. If anything is likely for 1988, we could be seeing some highly radical funk-blues fusion on the way from some musicians who want to steer a course between the macho street-brag of rap and the upwardly mobile vacuity of too much of the current crop of crossover soul. It could just be that one day they'll be calling Robert Cray the Godfather Of The Blues.

CHARLES SHAAR MURRAY

As a logical companion piece to the unlikely alliance of clothing manufacturers and Campaigners For Real Soul, the blues is coming forward as a signifier of urban grit with a dash of glamour

COUNTRY

During the late 1970s and the first half of the 1980s, country music was almost deservedly regarded as a joke. The cloying sentimentality, coupled with increasingly smooth production techniques which removed every trace of emotion from lyrics whose writers had intended them to convey human feelings, reduced country music to the level of the Eurovision Song Contest at its worst.

One reason for the strong revival of

Dwight Yoakam: Toured to great acclaim and was reminiscent of a young Elvis Presley.

country music in the last two years apart from the fact that mainstream pop and rock has become so depressingly banal, is that country performers tend to be less egocentric and financially acquisitive than their counterparts in pop and rock.

This may be connected with the fact that they are almost always under the control of producers and A&R men, who realize that their jobs are on the line unless they come up with hits. Therefore they require to be convinced that their artist clients are able to write songs which are superior to those being conveyor-belted out by the army of lyricists and tunesmiths in and around Nashville.

Most of the time, even the most notable country artists do not insist on recording only their own compositions, and this selflessness has led to country music leading its competitors in terms of catchy tunes, artful lyrics and generally being memorable enough to stay in the mind for longer than a nanosecond.

A less subjective reason for the rebirth of country relates to the unlikely concept of five of the biggest record companies co-operating to launch a generic campaign through the Country Music Association, sharing the cost of each facet of the campaign equally.

Allegedly, the idea came from a marketing economist, who cleverly spotted that Europe as a whole is not too different in size from the US and has a population which is surely no less than the States. As the US is by far the biggest buyer of country music, raising interest in the genre in Europe should double profits. While not the most laudable of motives, the end result has been that sales of country records have significantly increased.

One element in the recipe which proved crucial was that many of the Nashville new breed had rejected the over-sophistication and clinical hygiene of their city's modern music, preferring instead the rougher and more heartfelt sounds of yesteryear which had at least partially led to the birth of rock 'n' roll.

Randy Travis: His second LP, *Always And Forever*, confirmed his earlier promise.

Superior songs, performances in '50s/'60s style with no synthesizers but fiddles, dobros, mandolins and even banjos occasionally, plus the idea of seeking fame but not necessarily money, united young performers.

Even so, the five companies – CBS, EMI, MCA, RCA and WEA – failed to get it right the first time. Of the ten artists nominated as stars of the campaign, one was an actor from *Dynasty*, four others were groups whose natural habitat was the cabaret circuit and another (**Hank Williams Jr.**) seemed to derive his appeal more from the fact that his father was arguably the biggest country star of all time than any great affinity for convincing country music (the most memorable portion of his autobiography related to the occasion when he fell off a mountain, cracked his head open and had to push his brain back into his head).

The other four nominees were better choices – mother and daughter team **The Judds** had the stripped down sound, looked like they were sisters and were called Naomi (mum) and Wynonna (although a recent rumour suggests far more mundane first names, like Christine and Shirley). They sounded good and sold a bit which encouraged

The Judds had the stripped down sound, looked like they were sisters and were called Naomi (mum) and Wynonna (although a recent rumour suggests far more mundane first names, like Christine and Shirley)

RCA to nominate them for the '87 campaign, during which they released their third LP in short order, made their British debut at the London Palladium and charmed Terry Wogan.

George Strait, a 1986 MCA nominee, might have become much more than a cult in Britain if he had followed a similar plan (although he is considerably better known now) while **Rosanne Cash** (daughter of Johnny) has been too busy having Rodney Crowell's children to think of touring to increase her already growing following.

The final '86 campaigner, old timer **Don Williams,** had signed with Capitol after many years elsewhere and was nominated on that basis. It was definitely not chic to admit to liking Don Williams (even though E. Clapton and P.D. Townshend said they did) during

Dan Seals: One of EMI's nominees for the majors' 1987 generic country campaign.

the fashion conscious years, although he actually adhered to the stereotype of using trad country instruments and didn't write all his own songs. The problem was that the oft used accusation of Don's apparent similarity to Jim Reeves was not easy to refute, even if anyone who saw him live became an instant lifelong fan. A glance at his audience revealed an age range of 50 years, from intrepid youngsters who could hardly believe that this avuncular figure was entertaining, through musos who wanted to watch Jim Horn on sax and Danny Flowers on guitar, to pensioners who've seen him every time since they heard 'I Recall A Gypsy Woman'.

The '87 campaign was obviously better understood by the labels promoting it. Two of the five labels only nominated a single act from their roster, these being **The Judds** (RCA) and **Randy Travis** (WEA), whose second LP, *Always And Forever,* confirmed the promise of the earlier *Storms Of Life*.

EMI still felt that **Dan Seals** was worth a bit of marketing effort, perhaps hoping that not too many would recall that he was previously half of England Dan & John Ford Coley whose early '70s outpourings were reminiscent of a pair of John Denvers. EMI's other choice, T. Graham Brown, seems to be a perfect example of the widening boundaries of country music. Brown is extremely good but should surely be classed as an R&B singer, although the British public's reluctance to buy his splendid *Tell It Like It Used To Be* is distressingly small-minded.

CBS nominated **Ricky Skaggs,** the artist widely regarded as the catalyst in driving country music back to its traditional roots, and a duo known as **The O'Kanes** whom some have likened (inaccurately) to the Everly Brothers. MCA went for **Reba McEntire,** a fine singer in the Tammy Wynette mould who is attracting attention but needs to appear in Britain to cement a following, and **Steve Earle,** a Springsteenish singer/songwriter whose *Guitar Town* LP became a favourite and who fitted a UK tour into a schedule which could make him a Hank Williams Senior-style legend unless he slows down a bit.

Others who attracted attention although they were not directly nominated for the '87 campaign included Texan singer/songwriter **Lyle Lovett,** a slew of new female country stars headed by **Nanci Griffith** who followed four small label LPs on Philo with the superb *Lone Star State Of Mind* on MCA, **Kathy Mattea** and **Patti Loveless**.

Steve Earle: A Springsteenish singer/songwriter whose *Guitar Town* LP became a favourite.

Then there was **Dwight Yoakam,** who toured to great acclaim and was reminiscent of a youngish Elvis Presley, the triumphant return of **Kris Kristofferson** with his finest album in years, *Repossessed,* and *Trio,* which united the prodigious talents of **Dolly Parton, Linda Ronstadt** and **Emmylou Harris.** Even **Johnny Cash** is experiencing a revival of popularity following a change of record label after 28 years with CBS.

All in all, country music is healthier and more marketable in Britain than it has been for many years. Even the unjustly ignored **Wes McGhee,** an Englishman who writes better Texan songs than many genuine Texans, has been signed by the influential publishers, Bug Music, in Nashville. Some credit must be due to the first Englishman to run the CMA's London office, Martin Satterthwaite, who has worked tirelessly to promote country music, and has become a focal point of a swiftly expanding industry which may finally start to be taken seriously in Britain.

JOHN TOBLER

FOLK

The supreme irony occurred in March 1987. Those old stormtroopers of folk music **The Dubliners** celebrated their silver jubilee with an Irish television special on Gay Byrne's infamous *Late Late Show*.

It was encouraging to see **U2** take the time and effort to perform a folk song, 'Springhill Mining Disaster' for the occasion (and it didn't really matter that they made a bit of a dog's dinner of it). It was touching to see one of the group's casualties, Cairon Bourke, in attendance to show moral support if no longer able to offer it physically. And it was oddly warming to see the most triumphant survivor of them all, Christy Moore, paying moving tribute in song to the Dubliners' main architect, Luke Kelly.

But it was **The Pogues** who, in one glorious unselfconscious foul swoop, took the whole crazy shooting match full circle and in their madness made perfect sense of the last 25 years. Kindred spirits to a T, they joined The Dubliners for a version of 'The Irish Rover' to awaken the dead. Match result: The Dubliners not only got to play with a drummer for the first time in their lives, they got their first hit single for 20 years; The Pogues got their first hit single EVER.

The sheer gut excitement of the exercise made monkeys out of those more

De Dannan: Came out with yet another faultless album in *Ballroom*.

purist commentators who had derided The Dubliners and their ilk for their non-progressiveness and their lack of vision in the wake of the Celtic music revolution in the seventies. The Dubliners and The Pogues made delightful bedfellows and both should be roundly applauded for publicly showing folk music the way to go home.

The other irony is that folk music has been determinedly reborn in the last year by . . . well, by not being folk music any more. After years of complaining about young people being put off folk music by its image of pewter tankards and 98-verse Scottish ballads, folk has undergone a radical change of image that borders on revolution. How? By simply not being called *folk music* any more. Easiest trick in the book – pop groups do it all the time – and it's worked . . . and *how*.

The magic word ROOTS has now insidiously replaced the word FOLK and, as if by magic, blinkers are being removed all over the UK and young hearts are flocking back to the music. Two years ago they wouldn't have thought twice about going to see the Scottish folk singer **Dick Gaughan**, but once they discovered he was really a ROOTS artist, Gaughan became the hottest gig in town.

Other events helped to facilitate this shift of course. It couldn't have happened without **Billy Bragg** blazing round the country spreading the word about Gaughan, **Leon Rosselson**, **The Watersons** and a lot more besides. It couldn't have happened without a former Bragg roadie **Andy Kershaw** getting a Radio 1 show in which he chose to defy the usual mind-numbing blandness of that particular station and promote ethnic music of all shapes and sizes. And it couldn't have happened without a shift in emphasis within the scene itself and the emergence of relatively fresh artists like **Rory McLeod** (who makes even Bragg look laid-back) and the brilliant teenage piper from Northumbria **Kathryn Tickell**.

The appearance of that magic word ROOTS has freed a lot of well-established artists, too, from the inhibitions forced on them by a certain concern for tradition and a slavish correctness that dates back to the early days of revival. Respect for the folk tradition is right and proper; to be handcuffed by it is plain dumb. So, in the last year we've had pillars of the folk club scene such as **Pete Coe** forming a strident and richly exciting new band **Red Shift**, and **John Kirkpatrick** going out on a limb with the sheer bravado of his songwriting on his *Blue Balloon* LP.

And with the onset of roots music, we have opened – at long last – the floodgates for ethnic musics from all over the world. With the exhilarating **Bhundu Boys** from Zimbabwe leading the way. An out and out pop group in their own country, here they fit snugly under a roots brolly. I hate to say it because of the decidedly iffy moral implications, but eight million copies of *Graceland* have had a crucial bearing on this too – **Paul Simon**'s mega-monster bringing African music and especially the wonderful **Ladysmith Black Mambazo** into worldwide consciousness.

The Bhundu Boys: An out and out pop group in Zimbabwe but fitting under the roots umbrella here.

The roots march was crystallized by three outstanding compilation albums released in the early summer – *Square Roots* from Ian Anderson's **Rogue Records**, *The Cutting Edge* from Pete Lawrence's enterprising new **Cooking Vinyl**, and *Globestyle Worldwide – Your Guide* from a label (**Globestyle**) specifically designed to bring to this country ethnic music from unlikely corners of the world.

In many ways Globestyle represent the most ambitious moves of the lot, in particular giving an airing to some stunning field recordings from Madagascar, while *Square Roots* introduced us to kora music from The Gambia with **Dembo Konte** and **Kausu Kuyateh** (who also had an LP

Shane McGowan of The Pogues with The Dubliners: Making delightful bedfellows!

entirely to themselves, followed by a highly successful UK tour). Including these two masters of such an exotic music on an album alongside the bizarre **3 Mustaphas 3** playing a Balkan arrangement of 'Speed The Plough' and **Billy Bragg** performing a traditional song 'Hold The Fort' or **Brendan Croker** from Leeds sounding like a vintage blues singer on 'That Naggin' Wife Of Mine' and the brilliant acapella group **Swan Arcade** blasting out Sting's song 'Children's Crusade', was itself a strong statement of intent.

The Cutting Edge concentrated more on homegrown talent but was, in its own way, even more ambitious, with the up-and-coming artists chosen to represent a brand-new face to the world. The likes of **Malcolm's Interview, We Free Kings, Pressgang, Black Spot Champions, The Deighton Family**, and **Mark T & The Brickbats** all display a rock eye's view with their verve and their single-mindedness. Promising new *rock* acts too – **The Proclaimers, The Band Of**

All for the cost of a pack of Duracels, the simple but charming record (she sings to a backdrop of chirping crickets) has been hugely successful and at the start of 1987 Michelle moved to Britain where her warmth and humour have also made her a great success on stage. Honest and unpredictable, she is the perfect antidote to the cutesy blandness of Suzanne Vega (with whom she's sometimes ludicrously compared, and her own pet hate).

The other British/transatlantic love affair was with an ex-con who'd spent the last few years busking in California, **Ted Hawkins**. Andy Kershaw was responsible for this one, stumbling on a Hawkins tape and playing it constantly on his radio show. When he came in for a tour, British audiences would barely let Hawkins go again, finding a beguiling beauty in the man's homespun honesty and a voice that was pure Sam Cooke. So what if he sang hackneyed songs like 'Country Roads'? Ted Hawkins was one of the stars of this folk year.

Not that the folkies were *entirely* at the mercy of the roots revolution. **Kathryn Tickell** – *everybody's* sweetheart – has been operating basically within the established folk club network, a network that also produced the superb **Will's Barn** live tape of a club night in Yorkshire with **The Watersons, The Copper Family, Bob Davenport** and **The Rakes** holding court. And that old campaigner **Ashley Hutchings** sang lead vocals for the first time on record with an ambitious concept

total disgust. The EFDSS, never truly in touch with the music it was supposed to be representing, is now surely an irrelevancy.

It has certainly been a remarkable milestone of a year, as suggested it would be by the immensely successful "Hottest Ceilidh In Town" anti-apartheid event at Kentish Town & Country Club. All in the cause of a giant bop, it brought together Billy Bragg, Richard Thompson, Rory McLeod and the rampant **Oyster Band**, now surely folk's fearless flagship, their frantic version of the old ritual song 'Hal-An-Tow' blowing any remaining cobwebs completely away and the *Step Outside* LP widely reckoned to be one of the best of the eighties.

Patrick Street: A new supergroup whose debut album was on a par with De Dannan's latest.

We even had a new supergroup born. While **Christy Moore**'s star shone and shone, **De Dannan** came out with yet another faultless album (*Ballroom*), **Moving Hearts** were reborn (again) and **Mary Coughlan** became a singing star and a vigorous divorce campaigner, Ireland's year was completed to perfection with the formation of **Patrick Street** (**Andy Irvine, Jackie Daly, Artie McGlynn** and **Kevin Burke**). Their debut album was on a par with De Dannan's latest and that's the highest praise of all.

Honorary mentions should also be made in despatches of **The Mekons**, the blinding **Whippersnapper, Fairport**'s 25th anniversary, **Capercaillie, Lick The Tins, Clive Gregson & Christine Collister**, the stunning all-girl gospel group **Sweet Honey In The Rock, Attacco Decente, Andy White, Pete Morton, Bill Caddick, Alistair Anderson, Le Rue** and the upsurge of British cajun groups.

This is one year that doesn't deserve to be forgotten in a hurry.

COLIN IRWIN

After years of complaining about young people being put off folk music by its image of pewter tankards and 98-verse Scottish ballads, folk has undergone a radical change of image that borders on a revolution

---

Holy Joy – are now being mentioned as having "roots" influences.

Cooking Vinyl's other great achievement was in the discovery of the young lady who's occupied the top of the British independent charts for much of the year, **Michelle Shocked.** The story of Pete Lawrence's discovery of La Shocked is a PR man's dream. On holiday in Texas, he heard her singing around a camp-fire after the main events were over and recorded her on a Sony Walkman. When he got back to England he set up Cooking Vinyl and turned the cassette into a record – *The Texas Camp Fire Tapes*.

album about, of all things, L-O-V-E.

But as if to emphasize what an epic year this has been, a soap opera to rival *Dallas* was being played out within the austere walls of Cecil Sharp House to decide whether that stout defender of the folk tradition, the **English Folk Dance & Song Society** should be introduced to the twentieth century or remain in the eighteenth. The membership voted to remain with the latter and the man proposing the sweeping changes (including the selling off of Cecil Sharp House in favour of a more economical headquarters out of London) quit in what one imagines was

DANCE

It last it happened. In 1987 all the possible permutations and combinations of musical notes to form that perfect melody had been used. What we are now witnessing more than ever is a craze of cover versions, re-hashes and re-releases, creating in itself a new art form.

The most dominant cult on the London underground club scene (what is heard there usually happens later across the country) was the **Rap/Hip-Hop** stylee, which has practically done away with the previously *de rigueur* soulful popular music of people like Cherelle and the SOS Band. All of a sudden everyone wanted to be underground. With Rap not only did you have hard street music but a movement complete with uniform, language and lifestyle: witness the explosion of kids in American flight jackets covered with badges, in Kangol hats *à la* LL Cool J, and wearing Volkswagen and Mercedes emblems fashioned as jewellery due to the Beastie Boys.

Previously hip-hop had failed to take off in non-specialist clubs, mainly because people didn't know how to dance to it. Most associated it with

breakdancing and invariably when hip-hop was played the whole dancefloor would be taken over by a few breakers and bodypoppers thus bringing the rest of the club to a standstill. Now hip-hop has a dance of its own that everyone can do: the Wop, a kind of flexing and jerking of the arms while bending the knees and generally making the whole body as flexible as possible – perfect for those slow beats.

endless plays to become dancefloor classics such as **LL Cool J**'s 'The Bells' but other notable floor-fillers of the year included 'My Adidas/Peter Piper' by **Run DMC**, 'The Word' by **The Junkyard Band**, 'Feelin' James' by **A Classic Production**, 'Saturday Night' by **Schoolly D** and 'I Know You Got Soul' by **Eric B & Rakim**.

A notable cousin of hip-hop was the **Rare Groove** scene, which centred around obscure seventies funk. Comparisons have been made with the Northern Soul scene (though without the religious devotion) but basically it's been hyped out of all proportion. Already record companies have been ransacking their back catalogues for such gems as **Maceo And The Macks**' 'Cross The Track', **The Jackson Sisters**' 'I Believe In Miracles' and whatever **James Brown** albums they can get their hands on – a questionable tactic since the whole fun of Rare Groove is that the tracks have to be searched out. To remain fun, the scene has to stay underground; only time will tell whether Rare Groove will die a death or, after

All of a sudden everyone wanted to be underground. With Rap not only did you have hard street music but a movement complete with uniform, language and lifestyle

Increasingly the rap underground came up with crossover hits – **The Real Rozanne**'s 'Bang Zoom', **Heavy D & The Boyz**' 'Mr Big Stuff', **Jazzy Jeff And Fresh Prince**'s 'Girls Ain't Nothing But Trouble' – as well as establishing **Run DMC**, **Mantronix** and the **Beastie Boys** as viable pop products. Nevertheless, in rap's fast-moving world the hits get played out very quickly on the dancefloor. Few survive

reaching a peak, return to its underground roots.

In London the absence of regular hip-hop clubs meant that your average b-boy had to make do with one-nighter trendy clubs which played a healthy proportion of rap. This "trendy" scene has evolved and itself fragmented into many different directions over the past few years. Having started off with the mixed/gay madness of Steve Strange's post-punk clubs, the New Romantic and electronic music gave way to funk with the arrival of "Le Beatroute" club. The birth of funkabilly club "The Dirtbox" saw an increase in numbers from a hard core of a mere hundred to almost a thousand; it also saw the divide between the straights and gays on the scene grow wider.

Originally straight clubbers frequented trendy gay discos because they were the only place to go where one wouldn't get bothered if wearing outrageous attire. Once the rockabilly style became popular and make-up and frilly shirts were out, many straight club-goers suddenly stopped pretending they were bisexual and reverted to a straight lifestyle. What was left of the avant-garde

The Junkyard Band: Their 'The Word' was one of the notable floor-fillers.

movement turned into the Gothic scene with clubs like "The Batcave".

After "The Dirtbox" and the many one-off warehouse parties came the legendary "Mud Club" which still continues. With these two clubs things got much funkier and rap started to take on greater importance. With other famous clubs like "The Language Lab" and "The Titanic" concentrating on rap – not to mention present-day house/hip-hop/rare groove-style clubs like "Delirium", "The Opera House" and "Raw" – the scene has come a long way since the New Romantics.

LL Cool J: Few rap hits survive endless plays to become classics like his 'The Bells'.

Nowadays the gay crowd tend to frequent strictly gay discos, though many still go to "straight" clubs such as the "Mud Club" or the "Wag Club" without being out of place. Likewise straight clubbers still visit mixed/gay venues such as "Taboo", "Sacrosanct" and "The Pyramid". Add to this the recent influx of black b-boys and funksters and you have a melting-pot club scene that is open-minded in attitude with little racism, sexism or violence.

Due to this confluence of different cults the scene has also grown vastly. The "Mud Club" started off with a loyal following of 300; clubs such as "The Opera House" and "Delirium" were attracting up to 2,000 each week before new venue management forced their closure. The scene grows even larger with the inclusion of rare groove clubs such as "Soul II Soul" and "Family Funktion" (both having a rootsier and more serious atmosphere than their trendy counterparts).

A new influx of stylish multi-racial teens, aged from 14-17, with a passion for hip-hop and house has also appeared in force – trying to sneak into trendy clubs with their elders (i.e. 18-24). At the straighter clubs like the "Mud Club" or "Delirium" they can find the wild, electric atmosphere of the street while at the more mixed/gay clubs like the "Cafe Du Paris", "Pyramid" or "Sacrosanct" they can take part in the avant-garde lunacy of the fashion world complete with its Hi-NRG/Eurobeat and trash disco soundtrack.

While in London the slower hip-hop and soul tempo reigns supreme, the North seems to be ruled by the faster Hi-NRG and House beats. Before House came along, the clubs in the North that had been influenced greatly by seventies disco would be serving Hi-NRG as their staple diet (though back in London much of this music would only be heard in gay discos).

While many of the **Hi-NRG/ Eurobeat** records are extremely poppy and commercial, most are hits only on the dancefloor. Few manage to cross over like **Taffy**'s 'I Love My Radio' or **Man 2 Man**'s 'Male Stripper'. Most notably, **Sinitta**'s 'So Macho' stayed for weeks in the lower reaches of the national chart on Northern sales alone before the South caught on. Among the most popular Eurobeat records this year were 'Again' by **Do Piano**, 'Music That You Can Dance To' by **Sparks**, 'Run To Me' by **Tracey Spencer**, 'Two Of Hearts' by **Stacey Q** and 'Fascinated' by **Company B**.

What Hi-NRG lacks, however, is the face of a movement, being mainly associated with gay culture and moustachioed clones sniffing poppers on the dancefloor – not the sort of image a female fan in her teens would be able to identify with. It also lacks a certain credibility, being seen as mass-produced plastic pop with few merits of its own. The number one Hi-NRG producer Ian Levine (DJ at the infamous Heaven) churns out many Levine/Trench compositions on his own Nightmare label, all of which are said to sound exactly the same by non-believers. Although all these records feature highly in the Eurobeat charts, none have gone on to match the success of Evelyn Thomas' worldwide hit 'High Energy'.

To dance fans addicted to that faster beat, **House** music came as a breath of fresh air and was also far more credible. Originating in Chicago and gaining underground status in various adventurous clubs a few years ago, these records were influenced not only by seventies disco and funky dance tracks by people like Isaac Hayes but also by Italian disco imports – hence the

Schooly D: His 'Saturday Night' was another of the year's notable floor-fillers.

Eurobeat connection.

Only a few House records, however, made the crossover from relative obscurity to popular success – 'Love Can't Turn Around' by **Farley "Jackmaster" Funk** and **Jesse Saunders** (featuring **Darryl Pandy** on vocals), 'Jack The Groove' by **Raze** (from New York) and, of course, 'Jack Your Body' by **J.M. Silk**. Further hits from Chicago's DJ International and Trax labels sadly failed to materialize but other popular House records were 'The House Music Anthem' by **Marshall Jefferson & On The House**, 'Move'

J.M. Silk: 'Jack Your Body' was one of the few House records to be a popular success.

by **Farm Boy**, 'Let The Music Move U' by **Raze,** 'This Brutal House' by **Nitro DeLuxe** and 'House Nation' by **The Housemaster Boyz & The Rude Boy Of House**.

A whole new wave of House-influenced hits – borrowing mainly the style and production sounds – also appeared, from **Mel & Kim**'s 'Showing Out' and 'Respectable' to even **Fleetwood Mac** and their 'Big Love' remix by **Arthur Baker**, not to mention the Stars On 45-sounding 'Jack Mix'es by **Mirage** which must surely be taking plagiarism to new limits. Leaders of the field, however, were producers **Stock, Aitken & Waterman** with their House/Hi-NRG pop fusion. It was the genius of this award-winning team that brought you the perfect pop of 'Respectable' along with many other mind-numbingly bland masterpieces from **Dead Or Alive**, **Bananarama**, **Samantha Fox** and **Princess** to eighties disco diva **Lana Pellay**.

Stock, Aitken & Waterman were one of the few British teams making successful club music mostly because other Brits hadn't got a clue or even been to a nightclub. Roll on the future when the new wave of British club-goers start turning out their own music. Having experienced for themselves what actually makes people dance in clubs and having been influenced by such a wide selection of sounds, how can this generation fail? The new music is coming sooner than you think.

MARK MOORE

AME

The Monkees: A late-sixties situation comedy but more entertaining than the usual rock video.

"Forward . . . into the past!" boomed a mock announcer during one of the Firesign Theatre's early seventies pot-comedy routines. Funny how a sentiment which elicited heady giggles in the days of *Future Now* and "free form" radio has become 15 years later, the unspoken *bon mot* of American rock. And even the sainted sixties are getting to be old hat! For the last 12 months or so, from the perma-frost corporate zone right down to the most heated underground streams, the music of the 1970s has been recycled, recreated and generally regarded as religion. Sometimes you can't tell the nostalgic merchants from the real-timers.

For anyone who came of age in the last decade, it's all rather bizarre. Or perhaps you predicted that Black Sabbath would not only become THE big influence on a new generation of bands but a sort of social force. If the Monkees really did "invent rock video" like MTV says they did, nobody noticed at the time. These days, even the critical favourites, from Run DMC to Randy Travis to REM to Robert Cray, are ransacking recent history for inspiration. Many find it, but at a cost which is more dear than anyone imagines.

"Look Out (Here Comes Tomorrow)"

The Monkees' 1986 comeback is still hard to fathom. By summer's end more than two million people had paid to see these three greying prefab sprouts. The second time around, though, nobody cared whether they could play their instruments or not. Mickey Dolenz, Peter Tork and Davy Jones mugged, sang and banged tambourines up front while a backing band sawed through

their catalogue of Brill Building Bubblegum hits. Film and video producer Mike Nesmith, the sole Monkee to actually do something since the group split in 1970, stayed on the sidelines 'til the tour's last date.

Much of the "credit" for this decade's dose of Monkeemania rests at **MTV**'s door. The rock video channel zealously hyped the made-for-TV group's return

Ozzy Osbourne: 'Paranoid' and 'Iron Man' – the 'Louis Louie' and 'Wild Thing' of headbanging.

with contests and promotions, and aired reruns of the simians' old show on what seemed like a round-the-clock basis. A late-sixties vintage situation comedy long on slapstick and shaggy dog stories, *The Monkees* was certainly more entertaining than the usual rock video grind.

All six of the Monkees' reissued albums as well as a new Greatest Hits compilation reached the *Billboard* Top 200 in 1986; the group even had a "new" Top 40 single called 'That Was Then, This Is Now'. The irony of The Monkees borrowing a backward-looking song from The Mosquitos – an obscure "psychedelic revival" group young enough to be their children – was completely lost on their new, barely teenaged fans.

Once a pre-pubescent phenomenon, always a pre-pubescent phenomenon: older kids' tastes run a bit more progressive. Lately, the cool date seems to be attending a concert by the seventies warhorse of your choice. Both the **Moody Blues** and **ELP** (Emerson Lake and the strategically-named Powell) were consistent draws on the concert trail last year. The Moody Blues' John Lodge told David Wild of *Rolling Stone* that "the audiences can be fifteen to sixteen years old. Quite honestly, that's a younger audience than we had in the first place." By all accounts, that was par for the course.

Rust Never Sleeps But Heavy Metal Endures

Like some perfectly preserved fossil, heavy metal has withstood the brutal passage of time. In spring 1987, albums by **Ozzy Osbourne** and a beast called **Whitesnake** sat comfortably in the Top Ten. Ozzy's is a double live album which prominently features both 'Paranoid' and 'Iron Man', the **Black Sabbath** "classics" which have

RICA

The Monkees: More than two million people paid to see these graying prefab sprouts.

Black Sabbath: Not only *the* big influence on a new generation but a sort of social force.

of the charts with their relatively innocuous 'Talk Dirty To Me'. Like the Gotham glitter originals, **Poison** could pass for girls on the cover of their debut album; pretty ones at that.

All of a sudden, the ornate, self-conscious trappings of mid-seventies decadence are everywhere. *Hammer Of The Gods*, Steven Davis's best-selling Led Zeppelin biography, has become a sort of bible for aspiring rockers. Punks who for years had sported politically correct buzz-cuts have let their locks flow and begun practising guitar solos. Actual shag haircuts have been spotted though flared trousers and platform shoes mercifully have not.

The sixties fixations of groups like REM and Hüsker Dü seem passé

Poison: Like The New York Dolls, they could pass for girls on their debut LP cover.

become, respectively, the 'Louie Louie' and 'Wild Thing' of headbanging. Whitesnake are an extensively derivative ensemble fronted by David Coverdale. His rather dubious claim to fame is succeeding Ian Gillan as **Deep Purple**'s lead singer; a rarefied pedigree by today's standards. Perseverance pays off, again and again.

Perhaps metal's built-in audience turnover (as predictable as puberty), ensures that the music itself remains morbidly consistent. With the notable exceptions of **Metallica** and the late **Black Flag**, the new generation of so-called thrash bands have only served to blur the distinction between punk and HM; they've effectively neutered both

styles. Yet as hard rock becomes more and more another predictable part of the mainstream, its seamy underside hasn't been forgotten. In fact, it's become immortalized.

A Made-For-TV Movie Starring Linda Blair With Soundtrack Music By The Sweet On Qualudes

A dozen years after the demise of the **New York Dolls**, a young quartet from Southern California stole the chords from 'Personality Crisis' and hit the top

compared to, say, **Sonic Youth**'s well-chewed cover of Sunset strip relic **Kim Fowley**'s 'Bubblegum'. Maverick producer **Rick Rubin** transformed the useless **Cult** into a Memorex Zeppelin, and littered the **Beastie Boys**' monumental novelty record with so many of Page and Bonzo's riffs that even Robert Plant's head must be spinning.

Starship: Grace Slick's negligible creative presence was the only real Jefferson connection.

Indeed, the only glimmer of hope in all this lies in the Def Jam stable's clever pastiches. **Run DMC**'s 'Walk This Way' was one of the few records released in the last year which took the raw material of the past to build something new, or at least unfamiliar. It was a resounding hit, but it's hard to believe that three black men from Queens would have been able

to break through on MTV if Steven Tyler and Joe Perry of Aerosmith hadn't "guest-starred" in their video. In 1986, you had to be shrewd to get over.

Bob "Rock And Roll Never Forgets" **Seger** played – and sold out – hundreds of arena one-nighters. **Boston** released their first LP in nine years (*Third Stage*) and went platinum in almost as many days. **Heart** rebounded from career-death's door with their first chart-topping album of the decade. The abbreviated **Starship** launched a pair of singles into the Top Ten, though Grace Slick's negligible creative presence was the only real Jefferson connection.

Perversely, the comeback campaigns of **Peter Frampton**, **Alice Cooper**, **Ted Nugent** and **Aerosmith** all stiffed, while **Bob Dylan's** media-celebrated tour with **Tom Petty & The Heartbreakers** was marred by inconsistency both on stage and at the box office. In Dylan's case, perhaps you just have to go away first. Jethro Tull would probably have cleaned up. When **Fleetwood Mac** resurfaced with the breathy, perfectly sculpted single in early 1987, its success seemed ordained. With disruptive influences like disco and underground rock relegated to their respective ghettos, from the rock monolith's point of view 1987 was even *better* than 1977.

"Kiss is the ultimate band" — Jon Bon Jovi, May 1987

Kiss: Obvious huckster compared to Jon Bon Jovi's blown-dry marketing savvy.

Well, compared to **Bon Jovi's** blown-dry marketing savvy, those four fire-breathing cartoon metallists were obvious hucksters. There's no denying the mind-snapping catchiness of 'Livin' On A Prayer' or 'Wanted Dead Or Alive' but expressions like "well-crafted hooks" and "wholesome appeal" just tell part of the story.

Jon Bongiovi served his teenage apprenticeship as a janitor in one of the top recording studios in New York City (where his cousin was a producer). He observed a variety of top artists at work and, his raw talent obvious, got to record some "demos" with top session players. Jon Bon Jovi was an astute student.

After two moderately successful albums, Bon Jovi and his namesake band tried something novel. They played potential tracks for *Slippery When Wet* to representative fans and polled them to decide what should ultimately be on the LP. The results are well-known to anyone recently within earshot of a radio. While I won't question the sincerity of Bon Jovi's populist notions, it should also be pointed out that this is a common practice in the advertising business, known as a focus group study. Bon Jovi were a music businessman's dream; a band that markets itself.

Musically, of course, Bon Jovi are an absolute seventies throwback, a glossed-over Bad Company. Considering the oldies-orientated "classic rock" format dominating radio stations at present, it's not surprising that the most popular new band sounds like they could have existed ten years before. The old chicken vs. the egg debate rages anew: do kids like old music because that's all they ever hear or do radio stations play old music because that's all kids want to hear?

The savvy calculation behind Bon Jovi's success may seem a bit creepy, but it's not surprising when you think about it. Pop music has always been a mirror, and today's young people seem to address issues of job security with an intensity their elders often find

Bon Jovi: A music businessman's dream – a band that markets itself.

unfathomable.

Reading interviews with popular but personality-less British groups like **The Outfield** and **Cutting Crew** can be quite revealing. You get the idea that they're very competent musicians who've actively chosen the soaked-in-the-seventies sound of American radio-rock not so much as a means of artistic expression but as a career path. Hard work, determination and a minute sensitivity to what's selling have replaced hard living, inspiration and an inflated awareness of what's happening as the modern rock and roller's credo.

A Little Old, A Little New, A Whole Lot Borrowed — But Is It The Blues?

As mainstream rock, heavy metal and rap and their offshoots came to be perceived solely as the soundtrack of adolescence, an older generation of fans, unsurprisingly, turned to the music they'd grown up with. Reissues became a growth industry in 1986-87, and the burgeoning CD format made repackaged music of the past that much more attractive to consumers turned off by Lionel Richie's teeth or Larry Blackmon's codpiece.

At roughly the same time, the Black Music and Country Charts in *Billboard* were swept by a wave of artists who seamlessly (shamelessly, some would say) drew on their roots to create records which weren't exactly new but certainly sounded fresher than the formulaic swill they displaced.

In a musical town whose very name had become synonymous with the sugary

Dwight Yoakam: Proving that an artist can draw from their musical heritage without merely repeating it.

string arrangements of producer Billy Sherril and the unctuous sentimentality of Kenny Rogers, the so-called New Traditionalists set Nashville on its ear. Smoothie **Randy Travis**, unapologetic rockers **Dwight Yoakam** and **Steve Earle**, Otis Redding-influenced belter **T. Graham Brown** and the dynamic mom and daughter duo **The Judds** have all proved that an artist can draw from their musical heritage without merely repeating it.

While many of the crooning proponents of **Retro Nuevo** soul are

Fleetwood Mac: From the rock monolith's point of view, 1987 was even better than 1977.

too polished and preening for comfort, **Anita Baker** and singer/guitarist **Robert Cray** embody the same type of wide-awake historical aesthetic as the new crop of country artists. Baker's giddy mix of gospel, R&B, funk and pop strikes many familiar nerves while retaining an effervescent flavour all its own, while Cray adds Stax-flavoured horns and totally modern lyrical concerns to his timeless blues guitar.

Unlike the white rockers, whose recaps of the past seem alternately cynical or naive, the Retro Nuevo and New Traditionalist movements at least seem tempered by some sense of current reality. Which is, admittedly, pretty bleak.

Nobody Deserves To Be Stuck With Huey Lewis

What happened? In 1984 pop music seemed to begin a period of diversity and innovation, the likes of which hadn't been heard since the mid-sixties. By 1987 the mainstream was standing still – if not flowing backward. **Prince** followed his eccentric muse down various sideroads, **Tina Turner** and **Cyndi Lauper** issued disappointingly cautious follow-ups to their ground-breaking block-busters. **Boy George** and **Duran Duran** aged painfully, and **Michael Jackson** seemed to grow more paranoid with each new business deal and missed album deadline. But the difference between 1984 and now can be summed up in two words: **Huey Lewis**.

Just compare the hits from Huey And The News' three-year-old album *Sports*

to last year's *Fore!*. 'I Want A New Drug' was funny and sly, underlying hedonism's diminished returns. 'Hip To Be Square', on the other hand, is mindless cheerleading: "*I'm working out most every day/ and watching what I eat.*" With their barbershop harmonies and bouncy bar-band riffs, Huey Lewis And The News are an agreeable group and if *Fore!* was merely another dumb, cheerful record they could easily be forgiven.

But after hearing 'Stuck On You' a few hundred times, I've come to resent Huey's sixties survivor as average-guy stance. He's not just accepting a mediocre, convictionless middle-age; he's *celebrating* it. After sharing the same friends, the same address, the same phone number with someone for "all these years," Huey decides that this must be it. "I'm so happy to be stuck with you." Has love really become just another compromise you learn to live with?

Rock and roll once offered an alternative to, or at least a release from, that brand of emotional fascism. But in the words of Lou Reed, "those were different times." Forward, into the past.

MARK COLEMAN

Boston: Released their first LP in nine years and went platinum in almost as many days.

I'm not kidding myself that I'm still an angry young rebel. I'm still angry, but I'm motivated by purely selfish reasons.
SIOUXSIE

My idea of the average person is someone in a crowd who's running towards me trying to tear my clothes off.
MICHAEL JACKSON

All of a sudden, we've got screaming teenagers at our concerts – throwing bras onstage!
RICHARD COLES, THE COMMUNARDS

I feel like Mr Magoo sometimes – like I'm just stumbling into success.
ROBBIE NEVIL

We still haven't quite crossed the border into where all the cool people totally hate you.
ADAM YAUCH, THE BEASTIE BOYS

I was having an affair with Jon Moss. In the beginning it was the most marvellous thing – but suddenly things changed. It's the Abba syndrome, isn't it? How do you love someone who bangs drums out of time deliberately to annoy you on stage?
BOY GEORGE

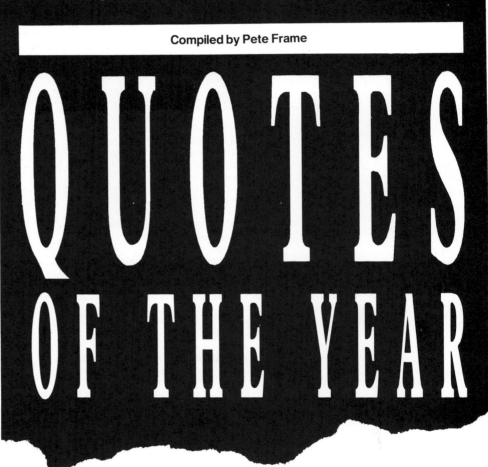

Compiled by Pete Frame

QUOTES OF THE YEAR

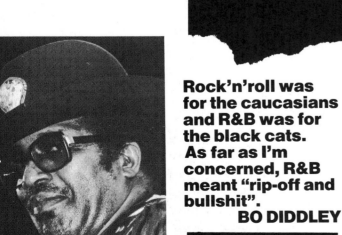

Rock'n'roll was for the caucasians and R&B was for the black cats. As far as I'm concerned, R&B meant "rip-off and bullshit".
BO DIDDLEY

These two girls in Scotland sent us down some plastic bags and asked us to jack off in them and send them back. I didn't though. You have to save some things for yourself.
PAUL RUTHERFORD, FRANKIE GOES TO HOLLYWOOD

We used to have all these girls taking pictures of themselves and sending them in. We had this thing called the Ugly Board in the office where we'd pin up all the ugly ones. It was a bit like Readers' Wives, only worse.
MARK, FRANKIE GOES TO HOLLYWOOD

We'll be a wart on the arse of the music business for some time to come.
NASHER, FRANKIE GOES TO HOLLYWOOD

Basically, America is a racist nation — it was founded on genocide. The blood of so many Red Indians is lying beneath the Empire State Building.
TERENCE TRENT D'ARBY

The ranks of the glamorous change constantly.
IGGY POP

I hardly read anything; I'm too lazy. I read all the classics, but only in comic form . . . so I just know the stories really.
MICK JONES, BIG AUDIO DYNAMITE

I think the number of countries that hate the English grows by the year – they're learning what the Irish, French, Welsh and Scottish have known for centuries.
SEAN, MICRODISNEY

We want to be the intellectual Wham!
PAT KANE, HUE AND CRY

I'd always been unsuccessful with girls, but then suddenly everything changed. People think you're quite sexy if you've written a few poems!
RICHARD JOBSON, THE ARMOURY SHOW

A lot of bands go around with shit on their teeth because they've kissed so many arses. Well, there's no shit on our teeth, okay?
PETE BURNS, DEAD OR ALIVE

There's one thing that annoys me when I come to London. I see all these fabulous looking males and they're all bent. Great shame. It seems to be the fashion.
TRACY TRACY, THE PRIMITIVES

Maybe the reason for all this disco shit is that people hate living in Thatcher's Britain so much that they need some mindless distraction.
AMANDA BROWN, THE GO BETWEENS

The music business is like having your head put in a dog turd.
SHANE MacGOWAN, THE POGUES

If Mozart were alive today, he would definitely play electronic.
RALF HUTTER, KRAFTWERK

It feels sort of like coming back from a war . . . alive . . . and surprised to be alive!
DAVID CROSBY

I like being the roughest, toughest woman in rock 'n' roll. I'm a specialist.
WENDY O WILLIAMS

Nicaragua was the sexiest revolution ever. There was a military presence, but everyone was so relaxed. Yet the moment I crossed the border into Salvador, I sensed this real malevolence in the soldiers.
BONO, U2

If I was reincarnated as a boy, maybe I'd like to be a cross between Paul Weller and Zodiac Mindwarp.
TRACEY, VOICE OF THE BEEHIVE

I'm not romantic; my wife would probably verify that.
MEATLOAF

We only get stroppy with interviewers whose first questions are "Are you gay? Are you bikers? Are you on acid?" We just smack them in the mouth and say "Fuck off!"
GAYE BYKERS ON ACID

Black music is just coming of age now in this country. We're doing the first native black English music.
D, THE THREE WISE MEN

Stirrups in gynaecology I don't use. They're unnecessary and dreadful. The rockin' gynae says "no" to stirrups!
HANK WANGFORD

Basically, we only behave like assholes when we're having to deal with assholes. We're nice to nice people.
PAUL WESTERBERG, THE REPLACEMENTS

I'm somebody who walks the line between taste and a complete lack of it.
MARTIN FRY, ABC

Since August, I've had three diseases. My eye exploded, my left testicle exploded and I got a rare skin disease my doctor put down to an exotic strain of flu and asked me who I'd been sleeping with.
RICHARD BEALS, HEAD

Big girls are supposed to look at all these skinny girls in magazines and feel like failures. Well, I don't.
ALISON MOYET

We want to pass a law saying that Dolly Parton has to show her tits in public at least twice a day.
AD ROCK, THE BEASTIE BOYS

Us cuntish human beings are fucking up this planet, and we've got to be aware of that and stop doing it.
MATTHEW ASHMAN, CHIEFS OF RELIEF

In a way, I'm a bit of an egotist. I'm not smarmy though.
PAUL KING

We seem to attract a better class of fan; they like to discuss various intellectual points with us. We'd rather go for a cup of tea with our fans than have sex with them.
BOB MOULD, HUSKER DU

I appear to be promiscuous, but I'm not. Just because many of my friends are female doesn't mean that I shag them all.
ZODIAC MINDWARP

We are, in fact, a tribute to Marvin Gaye.
KEVIN, GAYE BYKERS ON ACID

I never watched *Blue Peter*, which probably explains a great deal. All that making battleships out of old match boxes and bed sheets . . . I was never intrigued by that.
MORRISSEY, THE SMITHS

I like the pressure. It gives me eczema, but I enjoy it.
MICK HUCKNALL, SIMPLY RED

I want to live to be 100, in perfect health.
ROBERT SMITH, THE CURE

**You learn from reading stuff like Janis Joplin's biography that getting obliterated and going crazy all the time just equals one thing — sadness.
IAN ASTBURY, THE CULT**

When we did *Saturday Superstore*, I was really ill – I had to go off and throw up. I thought "I can't be sick over Mike Reid!" It might have been quite revolutionary, but a bit too distasteful all the same.
CORINNE DREWERY, SWING OUT SISTER

The most romantic thing I've ever done is fuck my girlfriend.
TOM, SLAYER

We know the records we put out are classics. People are sick of all the bullshit and see that the Godfathers can deliver something more.
PETER COYNE, THE GODFATHERS

I'm a great believer that of all the art forms, rock is the living art form. It's the living culture; it's the one thing that can actually move and change society.
DAVID BOWIE

Most of the hit records in America right now sound like an advert for passion fruit drink. The whole curse of TV is turning America into a homogenized mess.
JEFF TROTT, WIRE TRAIN

**If I became a female vocalist tomorrow, I don't think it would change things much. I'd still have to scrub the floor, balls or no balls.
PETE BURNS, DEAD OR ALIVE**

Because we were hip three years ago, people don't want to know now.
NICK MARSH, FLESH FOR LULU

AIDS has changed my life. I'm not as promiscuous as I used to be. I've adopted an intelligent approach to it. After all, I've already had a lot of lovers. I did have an AIDS test, and I'm alright.
FREDDIE MERCURY, QUEEN

I suggest we should burn the Queen Mother, and chop the Royal Family into small bits and sell them to Japanese tourists.
STAN CULLIMORE, THE HOUSEMARTINS

**Stupid pop stars flock to sing on Ferry Aid, which should have been called "Sun Aid", when the paper has decided to kill Elton John, one of our brothers as a musician. You have to despair.
STEVE SKAITH, LATIN QUARTER**

QUOTES OF THE YEAR

I seem to have become almost a subsidized artist as far as the record companies are concerned. They look around to see what's worth keeping from a certain aesthetic viewpoint.
TOM VERLAINE

I'd like to be able to write a song like 'Shaddap You Face'; to sit down in all seriousness and write lines like "itsa not sa bad, itsa nice-a place." Of course, we're not up to that standard yet.
JO, WE'VE GOT A FUZZBOX

We're stroppy, selfish people who know what we want – but whatever you do, don't tip us. God, there's nothing worse than being tipped . . . it's like the kiss of death!
SIMEON, CHAKK

On the way back from Holland we were strip-searched at the Customs. I had a man stick a spatula up my bum. The thing is, they're so nice about it – chatting while they're probing your orifices. He was asking what Beatles albums I had.
PETE, THE PRIMITIVES

The trouble is, American bands aren't cool. English bands are cool no matter how awful they are.
AIMEE MANN, TIL TUESDAY

We don't want to write songs about getting down or partying.
GARY CHRISTIAN, THE CHRISTIANS

I love reading about myself. I've still got the *NME* where I'm a clue in the crossword.
PETE WYLIE

**Take James Dean, a crappy American import who has been pushed down our throats for the past 20 years. He was a complete disaster, an absolute idiot in the way he lived his life, and yet he is always portrayed as some kind of hero and role model.
PAUL HEATON, THE HOUSEMARTINS**

**It's a bit strange taking your bra off for a photographer the first time, but you get used to it. Sometimes, they want you to do uncomfortable things, like posing with your bottom in the air, and you're wondering who's going to come through the door.
MEL, MEL AND KIM**

I get frustrated when George Michael gets voted "Songwriter Of The Decade", or whatever, when really people are just voting for his bank balance. That's the consideration these days – you're judged more on what you sell than on your actual talent or craftsmanship.
PAUL WELLER, THE STYLE COUNCIL

We love oral sex, don't we Paul?
HOLLY JOHNSON

I hate 18-year-old rookie cops coming up to me and asking what I'm doing, when I'm just innocently hanging around a public toilet.
DR ROBERT, THE BLOW MONKEYS

My biggest regret was never seeing the Osmonds.
JUNE MONTANA, BRILLIANT

By and large, Australian men are a horrible breed.
ROBERT FOSTER, THE GO BETWEENS

The wonderful thing about our audience is that they don't go around with their thumbs up their bums.
BRUCE DICKINSON, IRON MAIDEN

On my gravestone, it'll say "Ozzy Osbourne, born, died, bit the heads off things". . . what a fucking legacy!
OZZY OSBOURNE

I love it when my kitchen is all neat and in order. I'm obsessed with cleanliness.
NEIL TENNANT, THE PET SHOP BOYS

There's not a lot of misery in my face.
JIM KERR, SIMPLE MINDS

If we had enough money, we'd look like Earth Wind & Fire!
ARTHUR, THE BLUBBERY HELLBELLIES

A lot of bands are just like the boring hamburgers you buy in fast-food restaurants. You buy the Spandau burger and you just get indigestible stodge. We have balls and bite.
DAN BAIRD, THE GEORGIA SATELLITES

This may sound funny, but I'm not as eloquent as Billy Bragg.
DR ROBERT, THE BLOW MONKEYS

Oh, let's not talk about the yacht . . . I bought a new polaroid camera today.
NICK RHODES

Don't argue with me – because I go straight for the jugular.
MEATLOAF

I won't speak to the teen mags because all they want to talk about is hairspray and stuff, and it's all just a crock of shit. I don't want to sell the band on that.
JON BON JOVI, BON JOVI

I never did make anything that anyone wanted to hear while they were jogging. I'd rather make records that make people hit each other on the head with chairs.
PETE BURNS, DEAD OR ALIVE

I can't sing for toffee.
NICK BERRY

I like a good snog. Snogging's always been the first part of the chase and it's a shame, often, when it gets beyond that. Snogging's more exciting. Boys'll have to learn to hold their horses.
KEREN, BANANARAMA

I don't have much time to be domestic; I've got an iron, but I've never used it.
ROBERT SMITH, THE CURE

I'd like to make an album that was great enough for people to listen to in ten years' time and think "Cor, he was brilliant!"
RICHARD BUTLER, PSYCHEDELIC FURS

I should be exercising more. Creativity is far too sedentary. I just sit at a piano all day.
ROSIE VELA

I'm still carrying on as before – but now I use condoms.
LEMMY, MOTORHEAD

The music business is shit.
JIM REID, JESUS AND MARY CHAIN

There should be a code for pop stars laid down by the Musicians Union. They should adhere to guidelines the same as superheroes have to abide by a code in comics – and if they don't, they should be taken off display.
PAUL HEATON, HOUSEMARTINS

★ **QUOTES OF THE YEAR** ★

I'm tired of seeing Luther Vandross and all those guys come past me. They can't even carry my jockstrap. They know it. I know it.
BOBBY WOMACK

We all look useless. If I dress in a suit, I look like a bag of potatoes.
ALI CAMPBELL, UB40

I don't want to marry anyone who's lazy or anyone who thinks they can live off me. In fact, my husband has got to be extremely rich.
DORIS, 5 STAR

The low point of my year was when I had all my hair cut off. I cried for weeks afterwards. But then I started getting lots of fan mail saying how nice it was, so I cheered up after that.
LORRAINE, 5 STAR

My bedroom's all in black, and I've got a black suede headboard with a built-in CD player. What pop star hasn't?
BEN, CURIOSITY KILLED THE CAT

Basically, we're just four young guys off the street that are doing what we're doing. We're pretty bland people.
MIG, CURIOSITY KILLED THE CAT

EMI won't give me the budget to blow up a real helicopter. It's such a hassle.

TONY JAMES, SIGUE SIGUE SPUTNIK

I don't do acid now. I think that once you start getting messages from God on the telephone, six months after you've taken something, it's time to stop.

ZODIAC MINDWARP

Being spokesman for a generation is the worst job I've ever had.

BILLY BRAGG

I'm one of those people who think that masturbation should be taught in schools. It's especially important in today's climate of safe sex.

MARC ALMOND

Hardcore in general is portrayed as something unimportant, but we're probably eight times as intelligent as most of the people we've talked to in the music press.

EDDY SHRED, THE STUPIDS

I don't let AIDS stop me from going to bed with who I want. Rubbers are only good for erasing.

CHRIS VON ROHR, KROKUS

Jerry Hall called me "a fat ugly drag queen" and said I was both disgusting and corrupting the youth of Britain. Then, in the next video Mick Jagger does, he's wearing a dress!

BOY GEORGE

I love Run DMC. I'm a big hip-hop fan — if that's what it's called.

KIM WILDE

Being on a major label is like putting your car in for a service. They take it in and mess around with it, but you never know exactly what they've done or who is responsible. JOHN WHITEHEAD, IT'S IMMATERIAL

The best thing I've ever videoed by mistake was a news item showing Nancy Reagan falling off stage into a flower bed. We played it again and again. She's great for a laugh.

PETE BURNS, DEAD OR ALIVE

I once had a dream about Dusty Springfield. It was one of those erotic dreams, but it wasn't smutty. I dreamt she came out of a record cover and we had a love affair.

JIM REID, JESUS AND MARY CHAIN

It's a headache making records. It must be six headaches at Michael Jackson level.

RICHARD THOMPSON

If I could be doing anything, I'd be lying on the floor in my birthday suit, eating junk food and watching something dumb on TV.

ANITA BAKER

Let's face it, there's a bit of a stigma attached to me. Going off to buy a Nik Kershaw album isn't exactly cool.

NIK KERSHAW

There's something about standing on a stage with a microphone that compels you to be attractive. Even Sinatra became attractive – and he's an ugly little bastard with huge flapping ears.

ROBBIE COLTRANE

I'm talking about people meeting in Cleveland and swapping a small paper bag that decides whether your record gets played. You can't take these people on.

JIM KERR, SIMPLE MINDS

Everybody likes to loosen up now and then, but I don't wanna die doing it. I've never seen anything as addictive as crack; you can get hooked after one go. I'm not into it!

GENERAL KANE

Even if I come out in a dress like Marilyn Monroe, with my physique and the angles of my face, I still look like a male in drag.

GRACE JONES

As long as we keep drinking and making mistakes, everything will be alright.

ROB McKAHEY, STUMP

**I quite like being old; it's more fun than being young.
SHIRLIE (25), PEPSI AND SHIRLIE**

I polish my toenails, I shave my legs, I like perfume. I am a real conventional chick.
CHRISSIE HYNDE, THE PRETENDERS

It was chosen more for its collective meaning, that spurious authority it can carry: 'The Bible Of Pot Plants', 'The Bible Of Vitamins', it suggests a collective wisdom, which seemed appropriate because we nicked a lot of styles.
TONY SHEPHERD, THE BIBLE!

Somebody gave me a pair of crushed velvet boxer shorts for Christmas. It was a sweet gesture. I've worn them on my head once or twice, as a nightcap.
WAYNE HUSSEY, THE MISSION

Some people just have this unnatural glow around them. You know they are going to be dead in a few years, and it simply doesn't matter to them.
PETER CHRISTOPHERSON, COIL

The difference between Bananarama and us is that they're pretending and we're not. They pretend to be talented, they pretend to be able to sing, they pretend to be able to dance. We don't.
JO, BABY AMPHETAMINE

I'm glad I'm not David Bowie . . . he's such a third rate eclectic. I don't think I've ever been third rate.
MALCOLM McLAREN

At the turn of the eighties, I was doing £200 worth of cocaine a day. My nose is wrecked. If I had a piece of cotton wool, I could show you a trick.
FRANCIS ROSSI, STATUS QUO

Being rude onstage is brilliant; the fans love it. We're definitely going to have to become more obnoxious.
POP WILL EAT ITSELF

The Red Wedge once phoned to see if we'd play for them, but we basically told them to fuck off. In Northern Ireland, the Labour Party has a devastating record of atrocities.
DAMIAN O'NEILL, THAT PETROL EMOTION

I had a prison video of this man literally frying in the electric chair. His shoes are smoking, he's pissing himself and dribbling all over the place. First time I watched it, I was in a bit of a funny mood and actually thought it was quite funny.
NICK CAVE

Have you ever heard 40,000 people singing "Tommy is a wanker"? It was one of the greatest moments in my life – standing on that stage avoiding Coke bottles filled with piss.
TOMMY VANCE

When I go to see The Fall, I don't see many other 47-year-old men there . . . unless they're perverts!
JOHN PEEL

There is an incredible pressure on new bands in Glasgow. They're expected to be either a funky white soul band or some mutant offspring of the Velvet Underground.
RICKY ROSS, DEACON BLUE

It would be nice to say that we were part of a big scene and that modern music was really promising, but it's not. It's nearly all terrible.
MIKE GIBSON, THE GODFATHERS

One journalist asked me, isn't it exhausting to stay that deadpan throughout one song? I thought, one song? I've been that deadpan throughout my entire life!
SUZANNE VEGA

All the people with guts and brains are leaving Scotland. In 20 or 30 years, we'll have a pretty unintelligent population.
CRAIG REID, THE PROCLAIMERS

By the end of 1987, we'll have three hit singles and a hit album in this country, and we'll be starting to break into Europe.
MAGGIE DEMONDE, SCARLET FANTASTIC

The thing is that angst-ridden young white men have always made the best records, be it Lou Reed, Mark Smith, or . . . Julian Cope.
KEITH GREGORY, THE WEDDING PRESENT

When I dress up, I think "Oh my God, what will they think down in Watford?" Sometimes I feel like the prat of the century!
ELTON JOHN

Bono, Edge and Adam used to go to the back of the classroom and write songs. It wasn't surprising we all failed our exams.

LARRY MULLEN, U2

I give God the credit for being the co-writer. I'm just the guy who writes it down.
LIONEL RICHIE

The problem with drink is that it becomes a bit romanticized. When you're drunk all the time, you start thinking you're Dylan Thomas or Richard Burton.
MATT JOHNSON, THE THE

I've been here three times. The first time, I was an Ethiopian pirate around 6 BC. Then I was a painter in the 18th century, though I wasn't world class. Then I was a very talented country and western singer. A friend of mine is an exceptionally talented clairvoyant, and he told me.
TERENCE TRENT D'ARBY

I became a drug addict and an alcoholic. My nose was big enough to park a diesel truck inside!
LITTLE RICHARD

I used to say that history would bear me out. Now I realize that it'll be on a stretcher.
VAN DYKE PARKS

In the early seventies, all American music had an obligatory smile, neatly tied up in a bundle to be sold. My life was never like that.
SUZANNE VEGA

I remember seeing Carl Perkins, on my bus, on his knees, praying to die because the drink had worn off.
JOHNNY CASH

We've always been game for a laugh at other people's expense.
STEPHEN PASTEL, THE PASTELS

I hope people don't want to use my records as an excuse not to relate to their girlfriends or parents. I hope they stimulate thoughts like "God, I'll go downstairs and be nice to Mom."
ROBYN HITCHCOCK

I got involved in hardcore in 1983, when I was living in a squat in the Haight area of San Francisco. I really like the irony that the summer of love happened there, yet 16 years later it really was hate.
MICHELLE SHOCKED

Bob's a wet kisser. He leaves spit all round my mouth, but it's quite good because I can imagine that I'm kissing a lorry driver. I went to public school, you see, and every girl who went to public school wants to kiss a lorry driver.
PAULA YATES

You shouldn't be fucking all the time and not getting pregnant, because that's unnatural. If you have children, that keeps things in perspective.
CHRISSIE HYNDE, THE PRETENDERS

It's what's on the fucking record that counts. That's all that ever counts.
ELVIS COSTELLO

It's hard to find a reason to make another record, except for the fact that your record deal says you have to. But this year I hope to make a lot of money and fuck off for ever. That'd be nice.
TERRY HALL, THE COLOURFIELD

I never had any problems until I was about 28. Then I got successful and I got lazy and turned into a lard ass.
DOLLY PARTON

I think a lot of lyricists are self-centred, egotistical faggot dickheads who think they can screw any girl.
DAVE MUSTAINE, MEGADETH

I loved sex. The only thing I loved more than sex was a second helping.
LITTLE RICHARD

I think the music I've done has had some honesty and integrity, and I hope some class, in amongst today's quagmire of vinyl bullshit.

MARC ALMOND

I thought Michael Jackson would be a faggot, but he wasn't at all. He was cool, a cool person. He was like a godly figure; he had this sort of aura – as if when he's around, there's nothing wrong with the world.

JAY, RUN DMC

We're the ones who got everybody jobs. We made rapping work economically, so it couldn't be dismissed as a fad.

RUN, RUN DMC

I was never allowed to watch T Rex because my dad's got a thing about gays. I think it stems from something he went through in his youth.

DANIELLE DAX

Ann Summers' window is an absolute joke. How can you think of mingling your souls when you're wearing a nipple-less rubber catsuit?

JULIANNE, ALL ABOUT EVE

I hate the idea of morals in any form.

GENESIS P ORRIDGE

All my best numbers only ever took half an hour to write.

ROY ORBISON

The kids don't have to listen to Madonna. They've got a choice, an alternative – and that's us.

CC DeVILLE, POISON

★ QUOTES OF THE YEAR ★

Being in a band is a ludicrous occupation.

KEVIN LYCETT, THE MEKONS

People say to me "wouldn't you like to lead a normal life?" but to me this is a normal life.

JANET JACKSON

I'm sick of the right, I'm sick of the left, sick of Lenin, Marx, Reaganomics, Friedman and Keynes. Most of all, I'm sick of the middle. We need new dreams tonight. But where are the new dreamers?
BONO, U2

I would like to eventually turn into Germaine Greer.
MORRISSEY, THE SMITHS

I'm actually quite visceral, as you'd find out from people who know me. I mean, I fart a lot for one thing.

PETER ASTOR, THE WEATHER PROPHETS

I would strongly refute the suggestion that I'm trying to copy him (Phil Collins). That pisses me off. I feel that my influence on him hasn't been fairly acknowledged.

PETER GABRIEL

We were tripping, of course. It was acid, acid, acid. We were spaced constantly. We felt that acid was the great cure, a way to find everything.

NOEL REDDING, THE JIMI HENDRIX EXPERIENCE

We're just trying to have fun. There's that saying, you know . . . fuck art, let's dance.

KIM WILSON, THE FABULOUS THUNDERBIRDS

I do feel sexier now that I've lost weight. With a 34 waist, you do feel sexier than with a 54 waist.

LUTHER VANDROSS

It's not hip to be fucked-up any more, man. There's no fun to hard drugs. Your life gets to be trash.

DAVID CROSBY

I didn't recognize the importance of honour until I was 39. Before that, I was too serious to understand it.

HOLGER CZUKAY

Basically, America is a racist nation — it was founded on genocide. The blood of so many Red Indians is lying beneath the Empire State Building.
TERENCE TRENT D'ARBY

The ranks of the glamorous change constantly.
IGGY POP

I hardly read anything; I'm too lazy. I read all the classics, but only in comic form . . . so I just know the stories really.
MICK JONES, BIG AUDIO DYNAMITE

I think the number of countries that hate the English grows by the year – they're learning what the Irish, French, Welsh and Scottish have known for centuries.
SEAN, MICRODISNEY

We want to be the intellectual Wham!
PAT KANE, HUE AND CRY

I'd always been unsuccessful with girls, but then suddenly everything changed. People think you're quite sexy if you've written a few poems!
RICHARD JOBSON, THE ARMOURY SHOW

A lot of bands go around with shit on their teeth because they've kissed so many arses. Well, there's no shit on our teeth, okay?
PETE BURNS, DEAD OR ALIVE

There's one thing that annoys me when I come to London. I see all these fabulous looking males and they're all bent. Great shame. It seems to be the fashion.
TRACY TRACY, THE PRIMITIVES

Maybe the reason for all this disco shit is that people hate living in Thatcher's Britain so much that they need some mindless distraction.
AMANDA BROWN, THE GO BETWEENS

The music business is like having your head put in a dog turd.
SHANE MacGOWAN, THE POGUES

If Mozart were alive today, he would definitely play electronic.
RALF HUTTER, KRAFTWERK

It feels sort of like coming back from a war . . . alive . . . and surprised to be alive!
DAVID CROSBY

I like being the roughest, toughest woman in rock 'n' roll. I'm a specialist.
WENDY O WILLIAMS

Nicaragua was the sexiest revolution ever. There was a military presence, but everyone was so relaxed. Yet the moment I crossed the border into Salvador, I sensed this real malevolence in the soldiers.
BONO, U2

If I was reincarnated as a boy, maybe I'd like to be a cross between Paul Weller and Zodiac Mindwarp.
TRACEY, VOICE OF THE BEEHIVE

I'm not romantic; my wife would probably verify that.
MEATLOAF

We only get stroppy with interviewers whose first questions are "Are you gay? Are you bikers? Are you on acid?" We just smack them in the mouth and say "Fuck off!"
GAYE BYKERS ON ACID

Black music is just coming of age now in this country. We're doing the first native black English music.
D, THE THREE WISE MEN

Stirrups in gynaecology I don't use. They're unnecessary and dreadful. The rockin' gynae says "no" to stirrups!
HANK WANGFORD

Basically, we only behave like assholes when we're having to deal with assholes. We're nice to nice people.
PAUL WESTERBERG, THE REPLACEMENTS

I'm somebody who walks the line between taste and a complete lack of it.
MARTIN FRY, ABC

Since August, I've had three diseases. My eye exploded, my left testicle exploded and I got a rare skin disease my doctor put down to an exotic strain of flu and asked me who I'd been sleeping with.
RICHARD BEALS, HEAD

Big girls are supposed to look at all these skinny girls in magazines and feel like failures. Well, I don't.
ALISON MOYET

Would I go to South Africa? Only if the President sent me.

JAMES BROWN

I can see the art in everything from Les Dawson to the guy who shakes your cocktails.

ZODIAC MINDWARP

What could be more beautiful than the sound of 8,000 Germans whistling and shouting "Get off!"

COLIN NEWMAN, WIRE

After eight years of being Julian Cope, you tend to lose any real sense of the way you are. I worked out the other day that I've taken 150 acid trips – and now, when I tell stories about them, I'm not sure what happened when!

JULIAN COPE

If Jesus Christ came back now, he'd have to come back as a twat. To come back as he was would be too preposterous for this age.

JULIAN COPE

Do you know that chocolate gives off the same drug in your brain that you get when you're in love? We're very heavily into chocolate at the moment.

RUSSEL BURNS, WIN

It's never been an ambition of mine to be a mega pop star. All I ever really wanted was to headline at Dingwalls – and I never even got to do that!

ALISON MOYET

My hands are insured for a million pounds. Not by me, but by the company that organizes our tours.

MARK KING, LEVEL 42

For interviews, I used to carry a set of clockwork teeth with me. I used to let them clack away, look at the journalist, and say "you hippie cunt!"

MATTHEW ASHMAN, CHIEFS OF RELIEF

My tarantula's fine – she's just about to shed her skin. I've got two rats as well – Barry and Ian – and a black Asian scorpion called Bob.

MARC RILEY, THE CREEPERS

It's good these days, because you can get decaffeinated cappuccino – so you can be healthy and cool at the same time. time.

ROLAND GIFT, FINE YOUNG CANNIBALS

Our drummer is very energetic; he quite often gets a hard-on when he's playing. Drumming is his sex life. It's a bit of a shame for his girlfriend.

ANDERSON, CRAZYHEAD

Naked bodies can look very artistic; I have a sensual body and people say I have nice breasts.

MEL, MEL AND KIM

I like art that is generated without much consciousness of critics, other artists, fashion and commercial values. My current preoccupation, besides music, is the planning of an amusement park.

PETER GABRIEL.

People who go on about vegetarian stuff are really boring. Black pudding is an essential part of the British Sunday breakfast; probably just as essential as the Royal Family.

IAN McNABB, THE ICICLE WORKS

I once saw a photo of Pat Boone with his bollocks in a box. He had a cardboard box with a cut out hole and his balls hanging out of it!

ALI CAMPBELL, UB40

I've never voted in a general election. I don't think there's a party that represents anything of any worth.

KIRK BRANDON

Sweden is shit to play in. It's a hole.

FREDDIE WADLING, THE LEATHER NUN

I think the number of countries that hate the English grows by the year – they're learning what the Irish, French, Welsh and Scottish have known for centuries.
SEAN, MICRODISNEY

★ QUOTES OF THE YEAR ★

I was very good at embroidery at school.
STEVEN SEVERIN, THE BANSHEES

Our lyrics are about girls, drinking, getting drunk with girls, and hanging out with girls. Basically, we make fairly sexist drunk records.
MIKE D, THE BEASTIE BOYS

There's a fine line between being angry and being an idiot.
KIRK BRANDON

We get letters saying "this song changed my life," and you think "Oh, I wrote that on the bog in ten minutes!"
TONY LINEHAM, MIGHTY LEMON DROPS

If you're not screaming round the bar with your dick out, people think there's something wrong with you!
OZZY OSBOURNE

When I was about 23, I realized that I wasn't Jesus Christ – which I'm sure a lot of people secretly believe they are.
JULIAN COPE

I'm one of the world's vainest human beings, and I love it!
JOHN LYDON

I don't think that men's bodies look good in the nude at all.
SAMANTHA FOX

I'd be lying if I said I didn't think I was gorgeous.
DR ROBERT, BLOW MONKEYS

I don't want to be remembered. All right, that's a lie! It would be really good if people thought: "What a total prick he was!"
JOE STRUMMER

Not all my songs are about my dick, you know!
ZODIAC MINDWARP

There's a sort of healthy hatred within the group . . . but we hate everybody else more than we hate each other, so it's alright!
SHANE MacGOWAN, THE POGUES

I was just being silly one day and got fed up with my old name, Suzie. I decided to call myself Phranc because it reminded me of baked beans.
PHRANC

One of my regrets is not being discovered earlier. I was a 15 year old working in a South Wales glove factory when rock 'n' roll came out in 1955 . . . but I had to wait until I was 24, and by then, it was too late.

TOM JONES

I know this sounds really pretentious but, as a kid, I was given an IQ test and considered a genius.
TERENCE TRENT D'ARBY

Prince Charles came up to me and said "Your music vibrated my sternum." I didn't know whether to be pleased or broken up.

BRYAN ADAMS

When I first heard about AIDS, it seemed like another American plot to get rid of undesirables. DAVEY HENDERSON, WIN

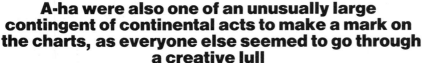

A-ha were also one of an unusually large contingent of continental acts to make a mark on the charts, as everyone else seemed to go through a creative lull

Once upon a time, there was just the disc, the record player, and the radio. You listened to the radio, bought the disc, played it on your record player, made it a hit. Even the TV hardly entered into it. Charting a single was once a simple, uncomplicated activity, but that's now about as obsolete a process as cranking up a gramophone. It's like a harmless pastime turned into a multi-media event, in which the fragile little piece of vinyl has all but been lost sight of.

This wretched loss of innocence has led to an incredible opening up of possibilities for the marketing men. Now you have pop on the film screen, in the national newspapers, on video, cable, telephone, TV soap operas, commercials, and still, thank God, good old-fashioned

radio. Radio is still largely responsible for breaking records but it has long since lost its monopoly on the consumer's ear.

Strangely enough, the more accessible pop music has become, the more it seems to have been reduced to a tool to sell things other than itself. Singles sales are down, and the turnover of chart acts has been swift and savage. The leading new members of this year's chart cast have reflected this instant-mash packaging of pop. A soap star, a boy in a jeans advert, a topless model – all found they could be pop stars without any tiresome dues paying, if they could come up with a good producer and/or a halfway decent tune.

The Top 75 as a breeding ground for new talent had almost been declared barren; few seemed able to develop any long-term prospects in that particular plot of land. Only a handful of major new British acts were broken via the singles

chart – the other chart occupants had to settle for being bizarre trailers for that mighty money-spinner known as "Various Artists" (now that's what I call a fast buck) and having considerably less than the statutory 15 minutes of celebrity status. Indeed, it was a year when the general consensus seemed to be that nostalgia was definitely just a thing of the past.

We busted into June '86 seemingly obsessed by the lure of the novelty record (ah – the summer silly season, repeated in '87 by **The Firm**'s remarkably daft number one, 'Star Trekkin'). **Spitting Image**, everyone's favourite TV puppet show, penned themselves an irritating pastiche of a continental pap record with 'The Chicken Song' and reached number one with it. This gave way to the only marginally less aggravating 'Spirit In The Sky', the psychedelically costumed **Doctor And The Medics** version of the old Norman Greenbaum hit.

This, unfortunately, was an omen of what was to come – a welter of cover versions of dusty old songs, as if collective inspiration had dried up. Originality, anyone? Not if it could be helped, it seemed. This retrogressive attitude kept the good Doctor at number one for three weeks, denying the top spot to the infinitely superior 'On My Own', a duetted ballad by **Patti LaBelle** and **Michael McDonald**. But whoever said this game was fair?

And the covers kept a-rolling: **Bananarama** hit with Shockin Blue's 'Venus', **Owen Paul** achieved one-hit wonder status with Marshall Crenshaw's 'My Favourite Waste Of Time', **Art Of Noise** resurrected ancient guitar hero Duane Eddy to revamp 'Peter Gunn', and taking the Belle Stars' crown as

GLES

The Pet Shop Boys: Wonderfully English and claiming a second number one hit.

Ben E. King: His 'Stand By Me' also featured in the American movie of the same name.

doyennes of the remake (a dubious honour if ever there was one), **Amazulu** commenced a string of cover hits with 'Too Good To Be Forgotten'.

In fact, an astonishing six number ones during this period were cover versions. **Boris Gardiner**'s smoochy lovers rock ballad 'I Want To Wake Up With You' was originally penned by Nashville veteran Ben Peters, and ended up ranking as 1986's third biggest seller after a three-week residency at number one. It led to premature speculation about reggae returning as a chart force, but all it really achieved was inclusion on no less than eight compilation albums as the song every Wayne wanted to dedicate to his Sharon.

But the one that really took the biscuit was **The Communards**' version of 'Don't Leave Me This Way', previously a hit for Harold Melvin and the Blue Notes (and indeed Thelma Houston), which surged into pole position in September '86 for four weeks and became the year's biggest seller. The curious combination of a familiar tune and Jimi Somerville's unique falsetto seemed to prove irresistible to the great British singles buyer.

The Housemartins, one of the few genuinely new, original acts to break big through the singles chart, very nearly got the Christmas number one with their acapella version of the Isley Brothers' 'Caravan Of Love' but didn't reckon on the public's hunger for nostalgia in the form of Jackie Wilson.

Then in March '87, after his crippling heroin addiction, **Boy George** came triumphantly back with 'Everything I Own', emulating Ken Boothe's performance by reaching number one. But it was, of course, a cover version – originally a non-reggae song written by David Gates of Bread. George later went to number one again as part of **Ferry Aid**, the Sun's "supergroup" effort to raise money for victims of the Zeebrugge Ferry disaster, which involved 120 "celebrities", some of distinctly dubious musical qualifications (hello Page Three girl Linda Lusardi and Anne Diamond) belting out a heartfelt version of 'Let It Be' alongside its author, Paul McCartney.

Nick Berry: The self-confessed meagerly talented "Wicksy" who stirred a million hearts.

Also featured singing along in the Ferry Aid chorus were Linda Davidson and Nedjet Salih, alias Mary and Ali from *EastEnders*, possibly the only pair on the cast of that show who hadn't yet released a single.

The Beeb's most popular programme spawned three hits, the first by Ange, aka **Anita Dobson**, who in August '86 released her beathy vocal version of the *EastEnders* theme entitled 'Anyone Can Fall In Love' which should've been subtitled 'Anyone Can Make A Bad Record', especially if they have a weekly TV audience of over 25 million.

At least she didn't get to sing it on the show, which the self-confessed, meagrely-talented **Nick Berry** cetainly did. As Wicksy, he stirred a million hearts with 'Every Loser Wins'; everyone wept over Lofty being jilted by Michelle and Nick saw his Simon May-penned tune rocket 62 places up the chart (a jump without precedent). A couple of impromptu performances by Wicksy at the piano in the bar of the Queen Vic caused the single to sell faster than anything since Band Aid and Wham! in 1984, and it subsequently stayed at number one for four weeks.

Simon May also wrote a lesser hit for **Letitia Dean** (Sharon) **and Paul Medford** (Kelvin), 'Somethin' Out Of Nothing', not to mention Marti Webb's 'Almost There', theme tune of the BBC's *Howard's Way* series.

The TV factor also worked for **Al Jarreau** and his *Moonlighting* theme tune, and indirectly for the star of that show, **Bruce Willis**, who launched himself as a pop singer with 'Respect Yourself' and 'Under The Boardwalk'. People seemed more at home with actors who sang than with singers who tried to act.

And how about models who tried to sing? No one believed **Samantha Fox** could but she did, raunching persistently in the charts with songs which invariably contained the words "do ya", "wanna" or "gonna", and thus becoming the ultimate rock chick. The ultimate instant heart-throb **Nick Kamen**, a smouldering pouty poseur with fifties appeal who took his jeans off in a *Levi's* 501 TV commercial. That action alone was enough to launch his career in pop with the flimsy 'Each Time You Break My Heart', along with a much-hyped connection with Madonna.

The slick *Levi's* TV campaign – all fifties teenage chic and pop video sensibility – became a chart phenonemon in itself. Using classic soul as its soundtrack, it spawned a series of hits for old soulsters.

This intense nostalgic activity peaked in February/March '87, when half of the Top 10 were originals or remakes of 15-year-old songs: **Ben E King**'s 'Stand By Me' (also featured on the score of the eponymous American film and a big hit there because of it); **Percy Sledge**'s 'When A Man Loves A Woman' (also used on the soundtrack of the mega-successful US war film *Platoon*); **Boy George**'s 'Everything I Own'; 'Great Pretender', **Freddie Mercury**'s version of the Platters hit, and 'I Get

Nick Kamen: A smouldering pouty poseur with fifties appeal who took his jeans off.

Starship: Surely the most unlikely bunch of ex-hippies ever to reach number one in the UK.

The Sweetest Feeling', the second posthumous hit for **Jackie Wilson**, following his big Christmas chart topper 'Reet Petite'.

Which brings us neatly to that other popular marketing ploy; have film theme, will travel, usually from the US to the UK charts. 'You Take My Breath Away' was a monster hit for American rockers **Berlin**, written by **Giorgio Moroder** for the soundtrack of the equally monstrous *Top Gun*. While resident at the top of the chart in November '86, it outsold its nearest rival by two to one. Likewise, **Starship**, surely the most unlikely bunch of ex-hippies ever to reach number one in the UK, had a four-week chart topper with 'Nothing's Gonna Stop Us Now', the theme from *Mannequin*.

The Psychedelic Furs did their career no harm whatsoever by flogging the rights to the title *Pretty In Pink* and subsequently remaking that 1981 hit for release as the film's title track. Brief celebrity status was also bestowed upon Australia's **Mental As Anything** for recording the theme to the outrageously successful Paul Hogan film *Crocodile Dundee*, and even **Rod Stewart** got in on the act with 'Love Touch', the theme from *Legal Eagles*.

Thee 12-inch format truly came of age in a year when 30 per cent of all singles sales could be attributed to extended mixes. This was largely accounted for by the formidable contribution of black music in all its forms – mainstream disco, soul, hip-hop, house, rap . . . the pigeonholes are as endless as the list of names. **Gwen Guthrie**, **Atlantic Starr**, **The Real Thing**, **Jaki Graham**, **Kool And The Gang**, **The Gap Band**, **Randy Crawford**, **Anita Baker**, **Luther Vandross**, **George Benson**, **Oran "Juice" Jones**, **Freddie Jackson** and the pop/soul crossover **Cameo**; all had sizeable hits or three as the beats per minute went on and on and on.

The biggest success story, however, was **Steve "Silk" Hurley**'s definitive dancefloor dominator 'Jack Your Body' –

the number one that never should have been, because it clocked in at over 25 minutes in total playing time thus contravening official chart regulations. But they got away with it, and it was the first house record to achieve the pinnacle, following the introductory ripples of **Farley Jackmaster Funk**'s 'Love Can't Turn Around' and **Raze**'s 'Jack The Groove'.

Club credibility with their first hit 'Showing Out' established the extremely photogenic **Mel & Kim** as marketable popsies with serious dancefloor appeal. With the help of the prolific **Stock/ Aitken/Waterman** production triumvirate (who really forged *the* distinctive dance sound of the year), they followed it up with the number one hit 'Respectable'.

Hip-hop and rap finally became commercially viable with **Lovebug Starski**, **Mantronix**, **Real Roxanne**, **DJ Jazzy Jeff** and **Fresh Prince**, and, of course, the mighty **Run DMC**, who rocked the house a

Madonna: Knocked everyone else into a cocked hat, breaking records by the dozen.

stage further with 'Walk This Way'. **The Beastie Boys** came along much later, but made a much bigger noise with 'Fight For Your Right' and 'No Sleep 'Til Brooklyn'.

Now closer to black music than would ever have been thought possible even a couple of years ago, heavy rock isn't often in the habit of taking up too many chart positions. This year, however, saw the emergence of a new hybrid – "pop metal" – building up a huge crossover audience. As part of its total global domination of singles charts, 'The Final Countdown' clocked up two weeks for Swedes **Europe** as the UK's number one. Rock also acquired some respectable hooklines with Americans **Bon Jovi**'s 'You Give Love A Bad Name' and **Van Halen**'s 'Why Can't This Be Love', with a respectable performance from the more traditionally heavy metal **Iron Maiden**.

T hese, then, were the prevailing trends which influenced the singles market with varying degrees of success. But all was not lost in this cut and thrust of multi-media marketing.

Plenty of acts were quietly clocking up hits and operating outside this invidious process. Many of the top acts of 1985 had vanished into oblivion more quickly than they had emerged, but the stalwarts really held their own. Both singles and albums charts, in fact, were totally dominated by the apparently infallible goddess of vinyl, **Madonna**. She knocked everyone else into a cocked hat, breaking records by the dozen, selling almost double the amount of singles as her nearest rival, registering four hits, three number ones and almost matching her success in 1985.

Madonna stood like a rock-solid Statue Of Liberty in a shifting tide of fortune. In July '86, 'Papa Don't Preach' nestled comfortably atop the charts for three weeks and took the sales of Madonna's first twelve British hits over the four million mark in two and a half years, matching the meteoric rise of Adam Ant. (Whatever happened to "Ant Music"?) Then came the title track of her album, 'True Blue' (one week at number one), 'Open Your Heart' (narrowly missed number one due to Christmas nostalgia),

Europe: The Swedes clocked up two weeks at number one with 'The Final Countdown'.

Talking of **Jacksons**, Michael's kid sister **Janet** paired up with scorchingly hot writers/producers **Jam And Lewis** (who also wrote and/or produced hits for **Robert Palmer**, **The Human League**, **Herb Alpert**, **The SOS Band** and **Alexander O'Neal**) to achieve six singles in the Top 50. They were all from her album *Control*; she was the only artist to accomplish this other than Five Star, who achieved the same with their album *Silk And Steel*. Ironically enough, the first act ever to do

Continentals didn't really pose a serious threat to the Anglo-American duopoly of the charts but Norwegian pop darlings **A-ha** certainly put a big dent in it. With the benefit of an innovative series of promotional videos, their sophisticated pop gained them four hit singles and nearly as many sales as Five Star. They were also one of an unusually large contingent of continental acts to make a mark on the charts, (almost always as a one-off) as everyone else seemed to go through something of a creative lull.

Of course, there had to be the song British tourists brought back from holiday with them, and this time it was the strangely subdued hi-NRG Europop of **Modern Talking** and 'Louie Louie'. Thank God the holidaymakers

Madonna knocked everyone else into a cocked hat, breaking records by the dozen, selling almost double the amount of singles as her nearest rival

then 'La Isla Bonita', a two-week number one which was almost as dead a cert as the Conservative election victory.

Meanwhile our very own gleamingly white-toothed **Five Star** became a regular hit machine with six smashes – five off the same album – from 'Can't Wait' to 'The Slightest Touch', they just couldn't go wrong. The commercial appeal of a surrogate Jackson Five seemed to mushroom; they were the only other act to sell a million singles.

Alison Moyet: A consistent British performer with a reliable track record.

this was Michael Jackson himself.

Prince continued to reign in a class of his own, releasing the classic 'Sign 'O' The Times' after three hits from his *Parade* album. The soft soul spectrum was well taken care of by the smooth talents of **Lionel Richie** and **Billy Ocean**.

C onsistent British performers weren't thick on the ground, but reliable track records were achieved by established acts like **Eurythmics**, **Queen**, **UB40**, **Level 42**, **Genesis**, **Alison Moyet**, **Simple Minds** and **The Smiths**, while promising foundations were laid by new bands **The Housemartins**, **Simply Red**, burgeoning goth rock band the **Mission** and the wonderfully English **Pet Shop Boys**. A round of applause too for ever-improving **Bangles** representing the visiting West Coast pop delegation.

Iggy Pop: Made an impressive comeback in a year of fickle fortune.

grew out of it as their tans faded and left the band to continue their staggering success throughout Europe. (Who says we'll ever be Europeans, eh?) The dubious Austrian charms of **Falco** also continued to please somebody, somewhere, but the real horror was provided by an unlikely duo by the names of **MC Miker G and DJ Sven**, who recorded a truly awful novelty version of Madonna's 'Holiday' entitled

'Holiday Rap', a Euro million-seller.

But onto more tasteful items, and the bands most likely to break through during '87 and '88. **Curiosity Killed The Cat** now seem guaranteed to have a reasonable chart career ahead of them after the success of 'Down To Earth', 'Ordinary Day' and the re-released debut single 'Misfit'; likewise the breezy **Swing Out Sister**, who pleased with 'Breakout', 'Surrender' and 'Twilight World'. And, not before time, Vince Clarke's **Erasure** established themselves as front runners.

These fledglings should take care not to get over-confident, however. Once upon a time, it seemed impossible to think that the Class of '84 – Duran Duran, Culture Club, Spandau Ballet, Thompson Twins – would ever have trouble getting hit singles. But that's exactly what's happened.

Duran Duran released their most credible single to date ('Skin Trade') and still failed to go to the top; **Culture Club** was abandoned in favour of George's solo career; **Spandau Ballet** did moderately well with 'Through The Barricades' but hardly matched their previous years' performance. While the British career of the **Thompson Twins** seems all but over. A pop audience has no mercy – ask **Paul Young**, and **Go West**, and **Nik Kershaw**, and **Frankie Goes To Hollywood** and **Howard Jones** and . . .

The most overblown chart event of the year was surely the fuss made over the **Wham!** split and "Final" gig. A brief hot spell which passed for the summer of '86 was ordered up especially for George and Andrew's last stand, with their swansong 'Edge Of Heaven', dominating the charts into July. Their arrogant presumption that it would debut at number one proved ill founded – the damn thing (released in lavish double-pack type formats) was just too expensive. **George Michael**'s solo career moved inexorably forward and upward when he clocked a second number one, aided by **Aretha Franklin** on 'Knew You Were (Waiting For Me)'. In '87 he

The The: Went gold with the brilliant album *Infected* but found no favour at Radio One.

attempted to soil his pristine image slightly by getting his first real solo single, 'I Want Your Sex', banned from the radio and TV. He still got into the top five.

In contrast to golden George, there were the usual crop of one-hit wonders. Say hello and wave goodbye to **Sly Fox**, **Real Roxanne**, **Jermaine Stewart**, **Hollywood Beyond**, **It Bites**, **Stan Ridgeway**, **Owen Paul**, **Taffy**, **Judy Boucher**, **Peter Cetera**, **Cutting Crew**, **Nu Shooz**, **Mr Mister**, **Su Pollard** and the remarkable **Sinitta**, whose 'So Macho' had a run of 17 weeks in the Top 75. But the one-hit wonder crown must surely (oh, please) go to **Chris De Burgh**, whose "heartfelt" ballad 'The Lady In Red' stayed at number one for three weeks and was allegedly Fergie's fave rave.

In fact it was a year of fickle fortune almost all round. **Paul Simon** and **Debbie Harry** made impressive comebacks, as did **Peter Gabriel**, **Status Quo**, **ABC**, **Iggy Pop** . . . and the pride of Pontypridd himself, **Tom Jones**. But the "Fifth Generation of Rock 'n' Roll" ended abruptly when **Sigue Sigue Sputnik**'s second single '21st Century Boy' failed to ignite the

Martin Stephenson of the Daintees: A sharp songwriter who deserves chart success.

Top 20. Even **Bob Geldof**, whose profile since Live Aid had been massive, failed to send record buyers to the shops in droves.

As always, there were the also rans and the near misses. **The The**, masterminded by Matt Johnson, went gold with the brilliant and controversial album *Infected* but never found favour at Radio 1. 'Sweet Bird Of Truth', an intense song about a fighter pilot over the Middle East, coincided with the American bombing of Libya and was immediately removed from the airwaves. Subsequently there was always an excuse not to include The The on the playlists; the same fate befell **Marc Almond**, who consistently put out charming and commercial singles but found that

Duran Duran: Released their most credible single but failed to go to the top.

someone, somewhere had their thumbs down.

Big Audio Dynamite received an enormous amount of critical approval but despite initial promise with 'E=MC^2', their newer cross-cultural rock noise didn't result in chart crossover. Similarly there was only a flicker on the chart front for promising new style rockers **Then Jericho**, set to follow in the footsteps of Simple Minds.

The celebrated end of the indie-pop market grazed the Top 100 and expectations were high for the likes of **That Petrol Emotion**, **The Bodines**, **Chakk** and **The Mighty Lemon Drops**, but despite signing to major labels, the results were disappointing. Then there were the songs dubbed "sadly ignored classics", like **The Bible**'s 'Graceland' and 'Mahalia', **Black**'s 'Everything's Coming Up Roses' and **The Lover Speaks** 'No More I Love You's'.

Justice will have been done if, during the coming year, the left-of-centre talents of the wonderful **Yello**, the sharp songwriting of **Martin Stephenson And The Daintees**, plus **Win**, **Hurrah!**, **Microdisney**, **The Big Dish** and **The Big Supreme** all find a place in the nation's hearts and charts.

ill many of this year's top sellers retain their placings in the year to come? Will anyone challenge the reign of the compilation album by putting together an LP's worth of hit singles? Will someone, somewhere be saying next year that **Westworld**, **Johnny Hates Jazz** and **Wet Wet Wet** were one-hit wonders? Predictions are dangerous but it seems likely that **Whitney Houston** is set to challenge Madonna's supremacy, and that **Living In A Box**, **Terence Trent D'Arby**, **Mel & Kim**, **Pepsi & Shirlie**, **The Blow Monkeys**, **Zodiac Mindwarp** and **The Beastie Boys** will rack up a few hits between them.

A fast, furious and merciless year. We'll never return to the days of the radio and the record player, days perhaps fondly remembered by one veteran, **David Bowie**. His single 'Day In, Day Out' was, quite astonishingly, his *forty-seventh* to date. Now, that's what I call a chart career . . .

BETTY PAGE

BEASTIE BOYS

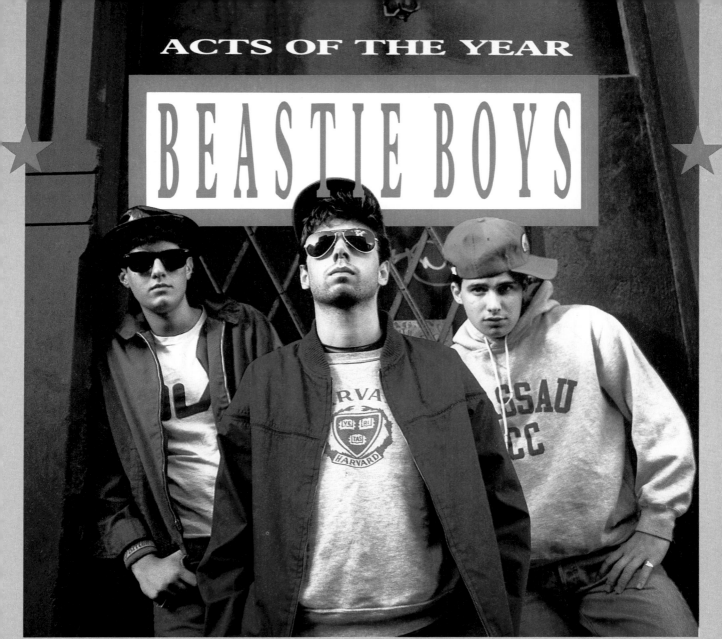

G oofy, oafish, nerdish, articulately insolent and most of all obnoxious – "we like that word" – the Beastie Boys' most obvious achievement in 1987 was to reinvent Moral Panic.

Not since Mods and Rockers nearly ended civilization as we know it by scuffling on Brighton beach, not since spaced-out hippies nearly ended civilization as we know it by waving flowers, not since Alice Cooper did something distasteful with snakes and babies, since the Sex Pistols caused level-headed laymen around the country to kick in their TVs in disgust etc. etc. have so many people been so shocked about something they neither knew or really cared about.

Even before they reached Britain in May, Adam Horovitz (Ad-Rock), Adam Yalch (MCA) and Michael Diamond

(Mike D) – three white rappers in their early 20s from New York – were already being referred to – by those who make their living out of outrage – as worse than Satan spawn. Right-wing Conservative MP and notorious self-publicist Peter Bruinvels spearheaded the campaign by demanding that the Home Secretary ban them. They were, he suggested, obscene, depraved, disgusting and perverting. More specifically their show incorporated semi-naked girls cavorting in a cage, much testicle-grabbing and spurting of beer from the groin and a 21ft imitation penis. Whatever, it didn't work. The Beastie Boys still came; Bruinvels lost his seat at the June general election.

The week before they arrived in Britain, while they were at the Montreux Festival (a massive mimed TV spectacular and media event in Switzerland), the Beastie Boys' real problem began. For weeks rumours had been flying that the Beastie Boys, hardly very famous in Britain or Europe, had

been invited precisely to cause as much fuss and generate as much free publicity as Frankie Goes To Hollywood had the year before. Frankie found that a little boozing – tame by Saturday night macho man standards – and some half-hearted equipment bashing was reported with dribbling enthusiasm by the press as a "£100,000 rampage".

Doubtless the Beastie Boys' actual antics while they were there – a few food fights, some general rowdiness, a couple of half upturned cars – would have fitted the bill adequately but for one British newspaper, the *Daily Mirror*, it wasn't enough. Instead they printed a front page story claiming that "the Beasties" (sic) had verbally and physically assaulted a group of dying handicapped children, using choice phrases like "go away, you fuckin' cripples".

Naturally this story was an "exclusive", almost certainly because it simply wasn't true. Naturally the denials and eye-witness refutations followed – they had in fact been signing autographs

BEASTIE BOYS

– but this couldn't prevent the story from being widely believed. The day before the three of them had been The Beastie Boys, a cult group who mixed abrasive rap rants with heavy metal guitar riffs. Now they were "the Beasties" and public enemy number one.

Over the next fortnight as their British tour got underway things got progressively out of control. The Beastie Boys, who had elsewhere in the world received little more than the expected reprimands and whose main aim was far more to get everyone in a Beastie Boys GET OFF MY DICK T-shirt than to cause uproar, were by turns shocked, upset and bewildered. Their record company received death threats. Hotels banned them. Taxi drivers swore at them. As their tour progressed the press bombarded them with a daily barrage of abuse.

On their final date in Liverpool the Beastie Boys were reported set upon by a mob hurling cans and bottles. After ten minutes they went offstage but not before several members of the audience

16th" birthday party – Mike D singing, MCA on bass and two other friends on guitar and drums. They released an EP 'Pollywog Stew' (released in Britain, incidentally, by the anarchist Crass organization) and then in 1983 a joke rap record called 'Cookie Puss' (around this time Ad-Rock joined and the others left).

A while later they met up with a young affluent rap and heavy metal fan called Rubin who was setting up his own label, Def Jam, with Run DMC's manager Russell Simmons. Their first few singles – 'Rock Hard', 'She's On It', 'It's The New Style' – did little and CBS, who'd licensed Def Jam presumably in the hope of chancing upon another Run DMC, by all accounts hated them. At one point after an incident involving a camera disappearing from the CBS offices ("we may be obnoxious but we're not thieves"; the band have always furiously denied the accusation) they were actually banned from coming in.

That only changed when their *Licensed To Ill* album was released. CBS hated it – their only apparent enthusiasm was for vetoing the band's working title, the typically tasteless *Don't Be A Faggot*. Perhaps understandably though they felt that an album whose sleeve showed an aeroplane violently squashed into the ground and which contained heavy-metal-meets-rap music and jokey bragging sexist doggerel was hardly going to pay for itself let alone knock the

And so on . . .

The Beastie Boys are proud of this tale and of many others of their uncompromising right to be obnoxious (or at least they were until things went wrong) because they clearly know that being obnoxious and doing what the hell they want brings large benefits. For one thing their fans love it. For another the media love it. And because the media love it so much there followed all the stories – great, dramatic, wild, wonderful, rock 'n' roll stories, the sort of stories that should have all been true even if some of them weren't.

Did they really seal and fill up a shower in a Los Angeles hotel, use it for mixed-sex party-time swimming and then kick open the door causing $10,000 damages? Did they really drill a hole between two rooms one above the other (they'd asked for *adjoining* rooms) at London's Holiday Inn and climb up and down on a rope between the two? Did they really see Madonna (who they supported on her 1985 American tour) brandishing her personal handgun, smashing a TV with the Beastie Boys' sledgehammer and tossing another TV at her minder for a prank? They weren't saying and to be fair the media weren't that bothered to find out.

As well as the stories there were the insults – great, dramatic, wonderful, rock 'n' roll insults – reported just as keenly. They slagged off journalists, they slagged off other bands and, verbally at least, they refused to respect anything. As they always answered when the recurrent charge of sexism was levelled against them, "We don't just put women down – we put *everyone* down."

Yes, *even* the handicapped were sometimes the butt of their humour if you knew where to look. Mike D told the American magazine *Contrast* about his rough childhood as a "kid with no legs." "Originally," he confided, "I was going to be the Handicapped Rapper." Plans only changed, he claimed, when the miracle of modern medicine grafted on two spanking new limbs "and, by golly, they work wonderful." More seriously, Ad-Rock told this writer of when he shaved his hair in tenth grade and lied to his French teacher that he'd had chemotherapy. It was, he said, "really funny for a while;" after a week and a half she found out and he "got in a *lot* of trouble."

The point being not that this proves that the Beastie Boys did swear at cripples – they didn't and it would have been most out of character if they had – but that the school of Respect-Nothing humour with which they toy can explode in their face at any time. They idolize *The Young Ones* (when they met Nigel Planer in London they were struck dumb with awe) and they'd probably heartily agree with the sentiments of *The Young Ones* scriptwriter Ben Elton who said "I can make jokes about *anything*." That's what they seemed to be trying but as they discovered it's all rather different when you try and live it 24 hours a day.

> **The day before the three of them had been The Beastie Boys, a cult group who mixed abrasive rap rants with heavy metal guitar riffs. Now they were "the Beasties" and public enemy number one**

were hurt. After interviewing witnesses, the police arrested Ad-Rock and he was bailed for £10,000 to appear for trial on a charge of Grievous Bodily Harm. Whether he was found guilty or innocent, this set the seal on an episode which had gone horribly horribly wrong.

So who were they, these Beastie Boys who caused all this fuss? Were they, as some suggested, just three wily youths making money and a name for themselves out of manufactured outrage? That was certainly a theory they enjoyed playing along with – "it's like Johnny Rotten, it sells records – you yell at a couple of people, piss in someone's mouth and the next thing you know you're number one in the pop chart" – but their history suggests something far less calculated.

The Beastie Boys began in the early '80s as an incompetent hardcore punk band formed to play MCA's "15th or

year's big success story, Bon Jovi, off the top of the album charts.

They couldn't have been more wrong. *Licensed To Ill* sold over two million copies in under two months, becoming the fastest selling first album in CBS' history. Predictably the office ban was embarrassingly cancelled – now the Beastie Boys could come in and do whatever they wanted and people would smile.

The hypocrisy wasn't lost on the Beastie Boys. With a mixture of amusement and disgust they told the story of a CBS representative whom they'd met on their American tour, someone who'd obviously been told that their gimmick was to be rude and obnoxious. Determined to "hang out" with them, he started jumping round the tour bus. They told him to "fuck off".

"Aw guys, you're *so* funny," he apparently guffawed back, priding himself on being in on the joke.

"Fuck off," they repeated.

"Ha ha ha. I get it," he unfortunately repeated.

"Fuck off!"

Not surprisingly in the midst of all this the Beastie Boys' actual music was ignored. The band complained – of course – but it was an inevitable consequence of their own hi-jinks. Nevertheless the music was actually good, often very good. Cynics who puffed "it's all hype" were wrong. You *can't* sell millions of albums just by dousing mediocre music in the spirit of teenage rebellion. Ask Sigue Sigue Sputnik.

Still, all that brattish rebelliousness was most definitely part of the appeal. Stuart Cosgrove from the *NME* speaking on Radio 4 (yes, they were taken *that* seriously) put his finger on it when he said they were about "The whole idea of wanting to party, staying up late, getting drunk, not getting your hair cut – actually quite trivial teenage fantasies of misbehaviour."

Of course he meant it as a condemnation as if the Beastie Boys should feel duty bound to be more serious. Cosgrove was just one of a whole wave of British writers who had been preaching a fanatical hip-hop gospel over the last couple of years for both musical and ideological reasons, and they all seemed rather slighted – betrayed even – when the music's most successful popularizers chose to chant not "Yo! Subvert the system! March on the capital!" but "Girls! To do the dishes! Girls! To clean up my room! Girls! To do the laundry! Girls! And in the bathroom!" Yes, it was sexist. Yes, it was pathetic. And yes, by and large it was harmless.

"By and large" because as much as the Beastie Boys trumpeted the irony in what they do (both by actually pointing it out and by the ludicrously mannered way they did everything) for some people they will always be what their worst critics say they are. For every ten people I saw in the audience when I joined their American tour who enjoyed the music and the fun and the idiocy of it all, there'd be one leering drunken character chanting along, joining in with what had become, I'd swear, the new uncaring chauvinistic anthems of their generation.

These are the people who will take the Beastie Boys' supposed manifesto (imagine it said by Rik from *The Young Ones* and you'll get the *intended* tone) at face value: "We're thinking towards a good time, we're thinking towards the consumption of beer, towards a person who's more interested in pussy than keeping a nine-to-five job, we're talking about a hedonistic attitude to life." And these people are something that all the irony in the world can't avoid.

In addition to the thousands of words used to describe the Beastie Boys' antics and the thousands more used to crucify them, it seemed at times as if there was hardly a magazine or newspaper without a piece *explaining* them – which in most cases meant trying to explain them *away*.

In America there was the ingenious Dastardly Short Hair Trick Theory which argued that the Beastie Boys were actually doing a sneaky Pied Piper act on American youth by tricking them into paying attention with their respectable short hair cuts (when of course they all really *wanted* to look like Jon Bon Jovi).

Then there was the They Must Be The New Monkees Theory – a huge logical jump based on the observation that Rick Rubin co-writes all their songs and that they play no instruments on stage. The Beastie Boys pointed out that they *did* play some of the little instrumentation on the album and that *they* also co-wrote the songs.

There was also the already mentioned Anyone Who Gets Onstage And Swears Can Make Millions As A Teen Anti-Hero Theory and finally the They're All Posh slur. This was based on the discovery that the Beastie Boys are all from reasonably well-to-do Jewish New York families. Ad-Rock's dad is hippie playwright Israel Horovitz, MCA's dad is a successful architect etc. But the Beastie Boys never pretended otherwise (they'll all talk quite happily about their parents) and secondly what difference does it make?

Bit by bit, however, the attacks, the slurs, the public vilification and finally the Liverpool prosecution have taken their toll. To the Beastie Boys' distress (if they really *were* as vile as they're often painted they shouldn't care but it seems they do care rather a lot) the whole escapade seems to have gone sour, a bit like an episode of *The Young Ones* when you blow up a house only to find out it was real explosive and there were real people inside.

Maybe the Beastie Boys were asking for it but the events of their European tour were never what they intended to happen. Perhaps the best Beastie Boys story – partly because it's true, partly because it sums up the witty nerdiness they treasure – is the one recounted by a *Rolling Stone* journalist as he toured Graceland with them.

There wasn't, he reported, much about Elvis's mansion that impressed them until they got to the dining room – a huge hall with a massive dinner table headed by a suitably ostentatious chair. Elvis didn't sit at *that* chair though, the guide faithfully explained. No, Elvis sat at the *side* of the table so that he could watch TV as he munched. On hearing this the Beastie Boys simply turned to each other and burst into a spontaneous round of applause.

Elvis, they'd clearly decided, was one of them. Millions of dollars in the bank and the best thing in life is still a TV dinner. Now that's how to be a Beastie Boy. At least that's how it's supposed to be – clowning about, being irresponsible, living out the longest, wildest teenage party ever. But sadly if that was the dream then it's a dream that has been wrested away from them, probably for ever.

CHRIS HEATH

If, gentle reader, you ever find yourself on the losing side of a pop-culture trivia quiz, rest assured that you can always help to even up the balance by asking your opponent to cite the connection between Spike Lee's brilliant low-budget urban comedy *She's Gotta Have It* and platinum funk combo Cameo. If you are offered the information that Cameo's leader is named Larry Blackmon and that the role played by Lee in his movie is that of a Brooklyn B-Boy named Mars Blackmon, you are then in a position to raise one eyebrow and generously concede a mere half-point.

The complete answer – you will volunteer – is that Tracy Camilla Johns, who starred in *She's Gotta Have It*, is the person who persuaded Larry Blackmon that it was time to have his Jerri-curls whacked off and replaced with a hard, angular Philadelphia flat-top. Following hot on the heels of the breakthrough hit 'She's Strange', the haircut was the final step in the transformation of Cameo from one Division II funk outfit among many to one of the best bands – regardless of style and category – in the world.

CAMEO

As far as most audiences in Britain were concerned, Cameo arrived fully-formed from nowhere with 'She's Strange'. In actual fact, they'd been around for almost a decade, and already had a history. Only the last two Cameo albums – *Single Life* and *Word Up!* – were even granted the honour of a UK release. *Single Life* was beefed up more than somewhat by the addition of 'She's Strange', the title track of a previous Cameo album but the covers of both albums spotlighted the trio who, for all intents and purposes, *are* Cameo: Nathan Leftenant (the one with the stumpy wee dreadlocks), Tomi Jenkins (the one with the high pure Smokey voice) and Big Larry himself, Cameo's writer/producer/arranger/conceptualiser/singer/frontman and all-purpose Big Cheese.

It was not always thus. As recently as 1980, Cameo resembled a coked-out football team dressed up funny. The cover of *Cameosis* depicts nine guys, fronted by a bearded Blackmon, emerging from a miasmic cloud of dry ice and draped in blue and white glitter outfits. The following year's *Knight Of The Sound Table* was scarcely a move in the right direction: by this time there were *ten* of them, though their dress-sense had improved slightly and Suburban Casual was the order of the day.

The music was tight and snappy: Cameo had drawn their inspiration from the street-funk bands of the '70s like Earth Wind & Fire, Brass Construction and Ohio Players (all 8- to 12-piece groups with hollering brass sections, Hendrixy guitarists and murderously precise choreography) as well as from George Clinton's Parliament/Funkadelic combine with their surreal, politicised trademark blend of stone cold funk, hard rock and barbed humour.

By 1982's *Alligator Woman*, Blackmon's concept of Cameo was beginning to refine itself in earnest. The travails of leading and organizing a band which sometimes swelled to as many as 12 people – all of whom wanted a say in everything – had wrecked his nerves to the point where it had literally made him ill and come within an ace of bankrupting the operation entirely. So he trimmed the group down to a five-piece, making up the difference with session players; by the time *She's Strange* was released in 1984, keyboard player Gregory Johnson had also vanished. All that remained to be purged were singer/guitarist Charlie Singleton . . . and the Jerri-curls.

Cameo were by no means an unsuccessful band even before 'She's Strange' fused ballad and rap with such offhand elegance. Blackmon had led his unwieldy crew through nearly ten years' worth of albums on Casablanca's Chocolate City subsidiary and later on his own Atlanta Artists label, averaging 500,000 copies of each album before the breakthrough with *She's Strange*. It's a respectable figure and a more than eloquent tribute to Blackmon's combination of musical and entrepreneurial acumen. He runs the band, runs the production company, produces the records, writes the songs, programmes the drum machines, sings the songs, directs the videos, does all the interviews . . . and still finds the time to run around in a red codpiece.

that rarest of all pop commodities: *personality*. In a crowded field with a strong tendency towards the generic, where audiences groove to and buy individual records rather than follow acts and where hot producers rule, Cameo literally cannot be mistaken for anybody else. That crunching beat and *nastay* vocal sound are totally unmistakable, and though they build their scaffolding with Yamaha DX7s – *four* of the bastards on stage at the '86 Hammersmith shows – and Blackmon's drum programmes, the computers are fleshed out with enough horns, voices, guitars and bass for it to feel like a party.

On stage, Cameo's show betrays the truth of all those stories about Blackmon watching every night from the wings when the band toured with George Clinton. Live, direct and in your face, Cameo serve up an incendiary cocktail of grooves, stunts and styles, all topped off with cartoony, absurdist macho most perfectly symbolized by Blackmon's most celebrated sartorial accessory.

With his iron-pumped superhero shoulders, clone-zone moustache and aircraft-carrier haircut, Blackmon appears as a caricature of masculinity (Freddie Mercury must be consumed with envy) and that codpiece is so far over the top that it renders the joke almost overt. The punchline is, of course, that it conceals far more than it reveals; while it draws attention to the wearer's pelvis, it also requires the observer to draw on his or her particular set of fantasies or expectations. Unlike traditional rock tight pants, it leaves *everything* to the imagination: a throwback to the R&B tradition of Big Suits. As virtuoso image-mongering and as a method of creating controversy out of nothing, it's nothing short of masterly.

It's possible to go quite a long way in pop by artful packaging of nothing in particular, but Cameo are as long on substance as style. The archetypal Cameo song 'She's Strange' boasts some startling

unfortunately not with me"). Funk is renowned for plenty of things, but once you get past George Clinton and Prince, wit is not amongst the field's more commonly recognized attributes.

Reputedly, Blackmon gets more than a wee bit irritable when Cameo are classified as a "funk" or "R&B" group – that's where they've *been*, not where or what they are – or compared overmuch to George Clinton. He is a phenomenally hard-working and disciplined man – no drinking, no drugging, lots of workouts and compulsory exercise classes for band and crew – and he's applying everything he's learned from the pop bizness to get Cameo as near to the top of the league as is humanly possible.

Most funk outfits who've become regulars in the pop charts have done so with ballads – later Kool & The Gang, for example, or Lionel Richie's epically horrendous clinch numbers for The Commodores – but Cameo are staying with their parodic variations on tuff-enuff grandstanding, and calling their music "black rock and roll".

Which, of course, it is. This is the aspect of their work most frowned-upon by white soul purists who seem to have accepted – quite uncritically – the notion that seminal black rockers from Chuck Berry, Bo Diddley and Little Richard right up to Jimi Hendrix and beyond are "honorary whites" and that black musicians who draw on their work in the same way that their white counterparts do are in some way "Tomming".

The similarities in presentation and machismo quotient between metal and rap combos are inescapable to anybody who's ever seen Run-DMC or LL Cool J work, let alone anybody who's listened to Funkadelic in their Hendrix mode, and Blackmon has simply grafted both these forms onto a basic funk framework, along with hefty doses of digital synthesis and a sizeable sense of humour.

With *Word Up*, Cameo thanked and acknowledged both God and Jean-Paul Gaultier, as well as clearing wall space for their platinum discs. While they're at it, they should make sure they've got room for the additional awards which they're bound to pick up over the next few years unless Blackmon cracks up under the strains imposed by the contradictions between his hedonistic public and lyrical stance, and his private life as a puritanical workaholic.

The most worrying Blackmon anecdote to emerge so far is the revelation that he's recently been seeing a shrink to help him deal with a little voice in his head which keeps suggesting that he ought to relax and let himself have a little fun occasionally. Maybe, when he's finally convinced himself that Cameo are successful enough, he might even allow himself a little holiday. Any way you check it, the man's earned it.

CHARLES SHAAR MURRAY

The reason that Cameo are rampaging across the pop charts is simply that Blackmon has learned exactly how to sell funk to a rock crowd in a big hall and to pop fans on the radio

---

The reason that Cameo are rampaging across the pop charts while, say, Con Funk Shun and lots of other people who're also capable of knocking out a fair dance tune aren't, is simply that Blackmon has learned exactly how to sell funk to a rock crowd in a big hall and to pop fans on the radio.

Since *She's Strange*, Cameo have had

lines ("*She's my twilight zone, my Al Capone/ she's my Rolling Stones and my Eva Peron*"), and Blackmon's lyrical acuity is apparent in virtually every Cameo tune, from the anti-Reaganite savagery of 'Talkin' Out The Side Of Your Neck' and the anti-war, anti-nuke reggae lilt of 'Little Boys With Dangerous Toys' to the détente-era rap anthem 'Urban Warrior' and the Big Bang yuppie satire of 'Fast Fierce And Funny' ("*I'm not a flaky kind of guy, you see/ I've got plenty of money, but

BON JOVI

I love my family dearly, of course, but I'd kill my mother for rock 'n' roll," the lead singer of 1987's most successful rock band confessed to *Smash Hits*. "I would sell my soul – that's a pretty sick thing to say, but I've said some pretty weird stuff to myself, you know. Like I'd give a day of my life for every day I can sing good. *That's* how much I dig it."

The multi-multi platinum *Slippery When Wet*, Bon Jovi's third smash LP, has set new records as the fastest selling album of all time in America, clocking up an average of one million copies sold every month. Further, unlike any other hard rock band in recent memory, they've scored two consecutive number one hits with 'You Give Love A Bad Name' and 'Living On A Prayer'. One New York radio station promoting a school spirit contest with a free Bon Jovi concert as the grand prize received 22 million entries; another station's listeners voted Jon Bon Jovi and Richard Gere the sexiest men in Manhattan.

Modest Jon, however, likes to downplay his role as a sex symbol, although it has certainly contributed to the success of Bon Jovi. In fact, he's rather turned the pigeon-holing pop industry on its collective ear by producing a hybrid of hard rock-pop that owes as much to the tunefulness of '70s glam rock as it does to the '80s heavy metal. The appeal is simple: fine musicianship, impassioned vocals, an accessible, if unremarkable image and monstrously anthemic songwriting.

Although it's only been in the last year that his music has become a pop phenomenon in Britain, Bon Jovi's been a runaway success in the States from his first single release, 'Runaway', appealing first to the headbanging crowd and – more crucially – their female peers. The group's eight month US tour was a sensation; sold-out stadiums and, in cities like Atlanta, Bon Jovi Days dedicated to them.

Born John Bongiovi, (the family name he inherited from his Sicilian father, a hair stylist who trims the band's locks to this day) on March 2, 1962, in Perth Amboy, New Jersey, Jon and his two younger brothers Tony and Matt were raised in nearby Sayreville, "a middle class kind of area with a lot of factories." By the time he was in junior high school, he was playing in garage bands in preparation for stardom. But his first public performance, with a band called Raze, was a true disaster. "We played a talent show and we had ideas of grandeur – a big tin foil sign that said Raze, this huge thing behind us," he recalls. "We came in *last*. My parents were there and they sort of crawled under their seats and said 'You should stay in school.' "

He did, wearing dark glasses to hide the fact that he'd been up playing rock and roll clubs all night, but he definitely decided that college wasn't for him. Neither, apparently, were the usual teenage professions – working in a junkyard, a fast food restaurant and a Kinney's shoe store – the last being a jacket-and-tie job, which Jon was relieved of with the words "Hey, rock star, you're fired!" when he dared to turn up the volume when Springsteen came on the radio.

His next job – acquired through Tony Bongiovi (producer for The Ramones and Talking Heads), and his dad's cousin – was more to his liking. "I had a job at the Power Station recording studio. I had a broom and a pot of coffee and I was the gofer. For 50 bucks a week for two years I slept on the floor in his place and learned about the music business. I met everyone, The Stones, Huey Lewis And The News, David Bowie, Meatloaf. It was weird 'cause I had a knock on my door one night at Wembley Arena and Meat was there and he says, 'Oh, you've come a long way from pouring coffee.'

The people that I met through the Power Station helped me in the business. It was a good experience."

Best of all, the owners of the Power Station let Jon use their studios when they were free, which allowed him the opportunity to record 'Runaway' with a group of musicians who were playing with John Waite and Rick Springfield. By 1982 Jon had joined forces with keyboard player David Bryan, with whom he had played several years before in a band called Atlantic City Expressway. Together they travelled to Los Angeles and approached record companies, staying in a cheap hotel and living on cheap plonk and junk food.

'Runaway', however, was beginning to get airplay around the country and Jon and David formed a band called Jon Bon Jovi and The Wild Ones, attracting drummer Tico Torres and bassist Alec John Such. Alec, who'd toured with Richie Sambora as part of Joe Cocker's band, encouraged the guitarist to check out the Wild Ones. Richie did and announced his intention to Jon: "I'm going to be your guitar player." In March of 1983 Bon Jovi was born, and the success of 'Runaway' secured them a recording contract with PolyGram Records.

These days the Bon Jovi mode of transportation is a private jet and Jon sometimes uses a lookalike Texan model named Jim Belling as a decoy. To protect his privacy he often registers into hotels as Harry Callahan,

> **"I had a job at the Power Station recording studio. I had a broom and a pot of coffee and I was the gofer. For 50 bucks a week for two years I slept on the floor and learned about the music business"**

particularly proud of their relationship with their audience. "I think we'll always be remembered for being fair and honest," Richie Sambora says. "For giving everything we've got and understanding that if you get a chance to make records and be this kind of band, it's a special thing. Never take it for granted." Bon Jovi don't. In fact, when they were working on *Slippery When Wet* in Vancouver, they let fans they met while recording vote on which songs should appear on the final product.

Jon credits at least part of the band's enormous success to their hard work, integrity (refusing to do anything but live performance videos) and personal friendship: "We're best friends, that's more important to me than being the best player or great looking. We always socialize. We even go on holidays together." Then there's Bon Jovi's sound, described by the main man as "not so poppy that heavy metal fans can't get into it and not so heavy that pop fans can't dig it. I think our music is so diversified, it pulls from so many roots that it kind of makes people listen to it despite whatever else they might think about hard rock.

"I am the primary songwriter," Jon admits, "but the band has got more and more involved. That's something I wanted done a long time ago because people just assumed that since we were called Bon Jovi that meant it was me, not a band."

Like it or not, Jon Bon Jovi is still the star. Still, he's one of the world's most reluctant sex symbols. "I hate it," Jon fumed to *Smash Hits*. "I won't speak to the teen mags because all they want to talk about is hair spray and stuff and I don't want to sell the band on that. We're just a rock and roll band. That's all we ever claimed to be. We never set out to change the world – rock and roll to me was always entertainment, it wasn't a place to be talking about politics or nuclear holocausts. As much as I love U2 and Little Steven's my idol, it's like '*You* write about that stuff.' I ain't concerned."

But, in fact, he is. Bon Jovi performed at the Farm Aid concerts in 1985 and 1986 and he's also actively involved with Operation Lift Off, a group that aids young cancer patients, ARMS (Action Research Into Muscular Sclerosis), and with his work on the anti-drug campaign. Though he got mixed up in the drug scene briefly because all his mates were doing it, he was saddened and sobered by those friends who died from it. "On behalf of our band," he has said, "I want to say, 'Yeah, we believe in this cause.' "

Luckily, being just a singer in a rock and roll band provides Jon Bon Jovi with a wonderful alternative. "That is better than any drugs or alcohol or money. I'd give up all my money for that sensation," he told *Smash Hits*. "When I fly out there over the audience and they're having fun, no matter how tired I might be, I am Superman!"

DAVID KEEPS

the detective played by his idol Clint Eastwood in the *Dirty Harry* films. Because the band's touring schedule is so exhausting, unless he's in a major city he sometimes has to have the name of the town taped to his microphone stand.

It's all for the sake of concentration, because the show's the thing. "We go out, smile and touch the kids in the first row because that's what I wanted the guy to do with me when I was in the first row," Jon says. But he does that one better, swinging out into the audience on ropes and singing an acoustic version of

'Silent Night' from a miniature stage in the centre of the auditorium. The fans love every minute of it, showering the band with screams and presents. Then, of course, there are more provocative gifts, but as Jon himself puts it, it's better to have underwear thrown at you than bottles. And that's certainly better than the – heavens to Morrissey! – pig's head that British heavy metal fans once threw onstage in Bon Jovi's early days. "That," Jon told a British magazine, "is a dumb kind of compliment."

For the most part, though, the band is

ACTS OF THE YEAR

As a future practitioner of American black music, Hucknall's roots aren't exactly orthodox. During his teenage years, he neither espoused the delights of Ford Escorts, cocktails and holidays in Ibiza, nor cranked out beer-soaked approximations of R&B favourites to equally sodden pub audiences. This man took the long way round: he studied Fine Art at Manchester Polytechnic, then played the guitar and sang in various Heavy Metal bands. Then – seeing as it was infinitely more suited to his wholehearted contempt for authority – he converted to punk, forming The Frantic Elevators.

After a couple of years spent making the sort of music the combo's devotees describe as "jangly", "gawky" and "not even fitting into the punk scene", Hucknall changed direction again. Months of sleeping on Liverpool DJ Roger Eagle's floor had exposed him to possibly the most awesome soul/R&B/blues/reggae record collection known to mankind. This crash course in the Sound Of The City showed him that passion could combine with proficiency in a way that actually *raised* credibility levels. Sure The Elevators split, but only after Hucknall had spent several months doing his damnedest to push them in his new found direction. Reasons cited for the break-up include the group not being able to meet Hucknall's exacting R&B requirements, and the abject commercial failure of their last single. Coming out on their own label, the record drained both the band's bank account and their creative reserves. They believed they could never better this single, no matter how far they progressed down their leader's adopted path. Indeed, with or

In May this year, the Singapore government declared Simply Red's *Men And Women* album an affront to public decency. Such was their sense of outrage, any record dealer found to be so much as stocking a copy became liable to prosecution. That anybody could find the LP's mildly erotic lyrics a corrupting influence is, in 1987, quite remarkable.

Before we go any further, it should be made clear that talking about Simply Red as an act without meaning Mick Hucknall, the group's singer and songwriter, as an individual is all but impossible. During their three years and two albums, Hucknall's presence is the only constant in the line-up, and it is solely his forceful personality and musical ambition that pushes them forward. The group name speaks volumes – "Red" was Hucknall's teenage nickname.

Since the group put many a purist's nose out of joint by audaciously covering an accepted dancefloor classic – The Valentine Bros' 'Money's Too Tight (To Mention)' – as a *first* single, back in 1985, Hucknall has courted adverse publicity. The unceremonious sacking of the original group members. His trumpeting his own worth in the Soul Man Stakes. The allegedly unfounded, but nonetheless widely reported, tales of the group's '86 US tour being a maelstrom of promiscuity. The loud declamations of pop star frippery – pronouncements that completely failed to take into account the most sartorially irritating aspects of Hucknall's own presentation: some sort of walking stick and a carefully angled hat. Etc. All in all, this was not the behaviour expected of a group whose lushly produced balladry and unintrusive funk swiftly found favour among the better heeled, better behaved record buyers on both sides of the Atlantic. But then Simply Red were never your run-of-the-mill blue-eyed soul boys.

SIMPL

without them, Hucknall himself has yet to top that tune. It was called 'Holding Back The Years'.

In 1984, after two years devoted to learning voice control and seeking out empathetic musicians, Hucknall emerged as A Soul Singer, fronting Simply Red. Demos were made, and a deal with Elektra Records was signed. Then, as if to demonstrate his unswerving commitment to the music, he sacked the group before they ever set foot in a recording studio. Whatever the motives, and here lies a debate between despotism and quality control, the new version of Simply Red – Tony Bowers (bass), Chris Joyce (drums), Sylvan Richardson (guitars), Tim Kellet (brass) and Fritz McIntyre (keyboards) – has yet to incur the singer's displeasure. They have played on each album and every tour.

Simply Red appeared at precisely the right time. After a couple of years of watching a nation of schoolkids actually enjoying spinning on their heads, and the memory of John Travolta's white flares blurring with the passage of time, grown ups wanted to dance again. Pre-George Clinton funk music was enjoying a resurgence, Lionel Richie was shifting vast amounts of albums and two-bit pop stars everywhere were keeping straight faces as they earnestly discussed their "gospel roots".

To the further annoyance of soul's self-appointed keepers, the public loved Hucknall's treatment of 'Money's Too Tight'. Aided by Culture Club producer Stewart Levine, Hucknall had smoothed off the burred edges, removing much of the original's desperation, and so made a moving song about being poor acceptable to well-fed BMW owners. No mean feat. 'Jericho' did much the same thing, but the song that consolidated Hucknall as A Voice To Be Reckoned With was that fateful Frantic Elevators composition 'Holding Back The Years'. Worldwide it sold several million – Neil Smith, the Elevators' guitarist and co-writer, was able to buy a house with his unexpected royalty cheques – yet ironically, as it had been only marginally reworked, it stood up as an example of the way Hucknall was rather than where he clearly fancied himself to be. As a pop ballad there's very few tunes that can touch it, but as a

RED

deep soul song there's not a lot that would want to.

Picture Book was the first Simply Red album. Produced by Levine, it was a bright, pleasant extension of the singles, tributes to hard times nuzzling up against tales of undying, often unreciprocated love. It was hugely successful (it is still selling at around the three million mark) as were the extensive UK and US tours that followed. Simply Red proved beyond doubt that they were a far better

than merely competent act, while Hucknall made it plain he could both write a good song and, in comparison with the other "voices" of the day, sing them.

But was it *soul*? Whether the people buying his records considered the semantics of this issue is open to question, but for both Hucknall and a large element of the music press it became a major talking point. He claimed it was; they were sure it wasn't. A bitter war of words began. Hucknall was cheerfully called (among other things) a parasite on the back of black music, arrogant, an opportunist and a hypocrite, and all manner of contradictions between his past and present personae were unearthed. He responded with the kind of surly, calculatedly undiplomatic statements that cemented his longstanding reputation as a stroppy sod – even at school he was apparently never one to shrink from confrontation. The rift has never really healed. His ability to get squarely up journalists' noses is probably the only remaining obstacle to Hucknall becoming that creature for which he reserves a special loathing – A Pop Star.

B ack in the studio for *Men And Women*, the second album, that enraged "sensitive" Singapore, Hucknall opted to let his records do the talking. He set about making what he hoped would be an unmistakably authentic-sounding black music album; Stewart Levine was dropped in favour of Alex Sadkin's (Grace Jones, Tom Tom Club, Thompson Twins) more abrasive results. Motown veteran Lamont Dozier was co-opted to co-write two songs, Bunny Wailer's 'Love Fire' and Sly's 'Let Me Have It All' were the chosen covers, and to the funk/ballads balance were added gospel, R&B and a touch of HM guitar. All bases covered, but was it *soul*?

Not really. What it was, was the sound of a young man with an extremely pleasing, but much too orderly voice, who had listened long and hard to the most inspired of certain music forms and was attempting to ape it, grunt for grunt and squeal for squeal. As one reviewer remarked, "His singing is in acute danger of descending into a mere collection of mannerisms." Even putting 'Holding Back The Years' aside, *Picture*

Book was a much better album simply because Hucknall wasn't labouring to prove a point. In fact, if he hadn't continually harped on about "soul" in interviews, he could have passed into media consciousness as a superior pop singer and thus avoided the pressure to find the funk on *Men And Women*. It seems there is quite a gulf between the way Hucknall sees what he does, and the way everyone else sees it.

Hopefully, the latest album's failure to live up to its predecessor's success will tell Hucknall something, while its still healthy sales will allow him the time to do something about it. If this headstrong young man can temper his aspirations to bring them in line with his limitations, there is no reason why Simply Red shouldn't be making excellent music for many years to come.

LLOYD BRADLEY

But was it *soul*? For both Hucknall and a large element of the music press it became a major talking point. He claimed it was; they were sure it wasn't

There she sat on a stool, smiling the sweetest smile of innocence, eyes bright and the key dangling from her ear, singing 'Let's Wait Awhile', a song of love for the AIDS generation. Janet Jackson, so very shy yet so seemingly assured, an imp, a true star. She was born for it. Her six brothers, Jermaine, Jackie, Marlon, Tito, Michael and Randy were already famous at it. One of her two sisters, Latoya, had tried it and was still trying. Only Maureen had demurred.

Janet Jackson, youngest of Joe and Katherine Jackson's nine children, had been born for it in Gary, Indiana in 1966 and now, sitting up there on her high stool 20 years later, hands folded neatly in her lap, she *was* it – the latest product of the Jackson hit factory, a tiny celebration of the modern pop, fragile and very, very rich. Papa Joe, self (?)-made American business man, was satisfied.

Joe and Katherine Jackson had ambitions. Joe had been a crane operator who played in a local R&B band called The Falcons. Katherine had been a blues and country singer. Many sons were visited upon them and their ambitions were turned on the offspring; they encouraged the boys to play instruments, they put them through daily rehearsals, groomed them for talent contests.

Thus The Jackson 5, gleaming and squealing and pulsating in terrible hippie-Afro trews, feted across two continents (America, Europe), weeny soul-pop hitmakers for the Motown corporation and the heroes of an ill-drawn Saturday morning kids cartoon TV show in which they would be attacked by giant killer basketballs from outer space etc., selling pop to the pre-pubescent generation in much the same way that She-Ra and Masters Of The Universe sell plastic toys today. The Jackson 5: an American growth industry. Joe looked at the girls and saw there was room for further development, further corporate growth.

All *she* really wanted to do was ride a horsie and be a jockey when she grew up, but at seven she was plumped into the entertainment business, appearing in *Jackson Summer Special* television shows and on stage with her brothers, playing the little Jimmy Osmond role of chirpingly precocious, prancing brat, a black Shirley Temple for the '70s. She did fair, juvenile impressions of Mae West and Donald Duck but, on the whole, she'd rather have been at home playing with her puppy and/or her crayons. She collected crayons. Whenever they went on tour to foreign parts, her brothers would return with

crayons. She even had crayons from Japan.

By the time she was nine, Janet had been broken in. Joe took her out of "normal" school and enrolled her at Valley High stage academy in California (the family had long ago moved from Gary to a secluded mansion in Encino) and here she was heavily coached for TV work in an atmosphere of push and privilege. Eventually, she would appear on the pseudo "black consciousness" and rather awful sit-com *Diff'rent Strokes* ("black consciousness" because it had black kids talking jive talk; pseudo because the central black kids were foster children of a white middle-class male who was frightfully rich and frightfully liberal, and besides you could understand the "jive" talk; awful – all of the above).

On *Diff'rent Strokes* she portrayed a squeaking tot, a buddy for the irritating dwarf-child "hero" Arnold. On *Good Times* (equally "black", equally awful) she played the battered child from next door – it was in the middle '70s that all American situation comedies began to tackle "real" "social" "issues": tears amongst the laughter, blubs before bedtime or the TV dinner, whichever came first (these things went out betwixt 6 and 7). Hence the chubby, appealing and entirely wholesome face of Janet Jackson got into *TV Guide*. Hence it was time, thought Papa Joe, for the newest bill-rolling commodity to make a record.

Janet Jackson, the LP, was released in 1982 when Janet was just 15. On the cover, Janet Jackson was seen beaming in a lily pond. The LP was what it was: a product issued off the back of a minor TV celebrity, a thing of little substance and scant imagination. The girl could sing a bit, that much was clear, but what she'd been given to sing was wretchedly

ineffectual.

And so back to TV, where now we find her plugging away in the chorus of the high energy, all-singing, all-dancing soap opera *Fame*. Such work was to eliminate some of the troublesome puppy fat – you can't hope to make it as a US entertainer if you tend to the pork (unless you play it for laughs). Janet shot down from 110 pounds to 94 and mother Katherine

JANET JACKS

declared herself "delighted".

Another LP, *Dream City*, showed Janet preening herself and beaming as before upon a motorcycle and revisiting the territories of stodgy MOR soul, despite productions courtesy of Jesse Johnson, Giorgio Moroder and brother Marlon Jackson. A duet with Cliff Richard on 'Two To The Power Of Love' was hardly destined to have a young public tottering on its heels in excitement and ecstasy, now, was it? Joe Jackson seemed to be guiding the fruit of his loins down a tunnelled career of glitzy mediocrity – a road to Vegas, Atlantic City or nowhere much at all like the brothers Michael had left behind. All this would change.

On 7 September 1984, The Jacksons were on the road (accompanied, yes, by Joe and Katherine) on their so-called *Victory* tour. Eighteen years old, Janet took this rare opportunity to make a personal "statement" by eloping with singer James DeBarge and becoming a married woman, an adult. It was time, she had decided, for her parents to let go. But her parents didn't. The horror and the guilt. I once asked Janet what happened then and she stared at her feet, *through* her

Her friends were dogs and giraffes and llamas and deers and she slept with pet snakes because "they're so cute". Her idea of rebellion was to throw a grape from a hotel window and hear it "pop" on the street below

feet, and silently squirmed . . . "Marriage was something I had to experience right then . . . We were young . . ." And? ". . . I do want to get married again . . . I hope . . . by the time I'm 30 . . . I hope . . ."

James DeBarge was very much persona non grata in the Encino household and the union ended after eight months. Janet, scurrying back to the family seat, was put to work once more. A&M, her record company, set her a diet to lose the puppy fat she'd won back since *Fame* and then despatched her to Minneapolis and into the hands of Jimmy Jam and Terry Lewis, producers and principal writers of *Control*, the album.

"*This is a story about control. My control. Control of what I say, control of what I do and this time I'm gonna do it my way . . . Because it's all about control. And I've got lots of it . . .*"

And – bang! – into a persuasive mixture of assurance and seduction on which the girl was telling us "*When I was 17 I did what people told me. Did what my father said and let my mother mould me . . .*" but all was different now because Miss Jackson had got wise and sassy and there's no one's gonna fool around with *her*, you hear? "*No my first name ain't Baby, it's Janet – Miss Jackson if you're nasty . . .*" What on earth had Jam and Lewis done to this naïve and protected teenager?

The strength and sheer sauce of the LP *Control* shone through, from the bossy to the sexual stuff, the guttural moans and the Frenchy whispers. A new team had reconstructed the junior Jackson, made her a character to be reckoned with and the image of brash confidence overlapped onto video: Janet in designer togs of the ghetto leaping amongst the lowlife, dancing like a knowing gamine within the sewer smoke, a cross between *The Warriors* and *West Side Story*.

Here was an eighties girl, like Madonna *above* the men, chewing gum and acting haughty, unavailable thank you very much. The wacko brother with the llama in the oxygen tent might have been green with envy, but no need. The image was an image. *Clever*, and it sold triple platinum – but an image nonetheless. The real Janet stayed at home in Encino, playing *Scrabble* and *Trivial Pursuit* with her mother . . .

"A special thanks to Mother for loving me, and for sticking by my side through this project no matter what it was I had decided to do. I Love You Very Much, Mother" gushed Janet on the LP credits. Father was dealt with in shorter fashion: "Special thanks to Joe Jackson Productions."

It was the parents who were still in control. Janet had never been out dancing in public until she was 19. Her friends were dogs and giraffes and llamas and deers and she slept with pet snakes because "they're so cute". Her idea of rebellion was to throw a grape from a hotel window and hear it "pop" on the street below. Interviewers would be bemused by her childlike airs as she giggled about bubblegum and the cute antics of the Jackson chimp, Bubbles, and the extravagant tricks he plays – roller skating, playing dead, juggling bananas and kissing to be clever.

Even Jimmy Jam and Terry Lewis had been taken aback by her lack of worldliness when first they met her and took her to a Minneapolis bar: "A couple of guys started talking to her and she came up to me," says Jimmy Jam, "and she said 'Why didn't you help me?' And I said 'I thought you took care of yourself.' She'd never had a chance to handle herself . . ."

And still she hasn't had that chance. She's big bucks and interested parties close in, drawing the reins tighter. But look at her on that stool, hear that young, unsullied and perfect voice, just imagine what this artiste could do if she ever *did* gain control. We love you dearly, Janet. Please write soon.

TOM HIBBERT

ACTS OF THE YEAR

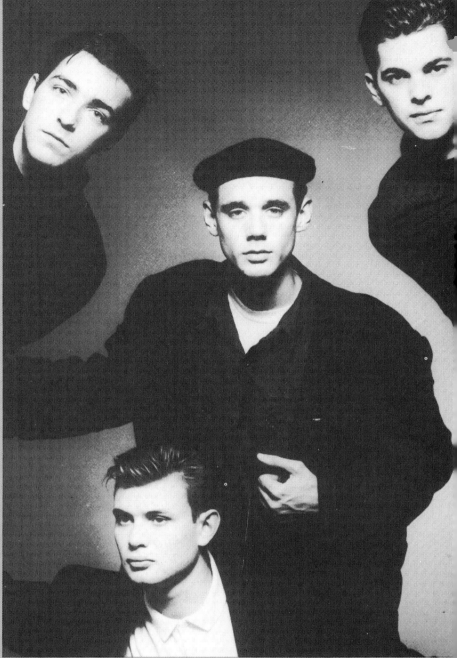

The opening bars of that first hit were hardly an auspicious start. After 'Misfit' had flopped on its first release, the group had put out a second single 'Down To Earth'. Shortly after the needle had settled into the groove the listener was assailed by the voice of Ben Volpierre-Pierrot delivering one of the most preposterous couplets in pop's history: "shooting stars in midnight pastures," he sang. "And hanging out in clouds beneath the moon."

Oh dear. Not only had this man espoused such unashamedly hippy-esque ruralist imagery but he used the phrase "hanging out" in the second line. And yet the performers of this ungainly lyric were destined to become the new British act of 1987, the group most likely to knock A-ha off their perch, the crew whose LP went straight to number one in the charts on pre-sale, the people most likely to have rumours made up about them in the press, and a band set to make *rather* a lot of money over the next few years.

But why *this* lot? Why of all the young hopefuls who were queueing up for stardom at the beginning of 1987 were Curiosity the ones to make it biggest?

Reason number one is that 1987 was always going to be the year of the good-looking pop star. All the contending groups had to have at least one member who was not even remotely ugly. Magazines like *Just Seventeen* had

CURIOSITY KILLED TE

bounded to prominence and were printing posters of pop "stars" who hadn't come within a million miles of a hit but were included simply on the strength of their looks. 1987 was, after all, the year when a fashion model called Nick Kamen could become a pop star despite the fact that he danced with the grace of a bank manager and had a voice reminiscent of chalk on glass.

There were plenty of groups who could boast a handsome member or two but the thing about Curiosity Killed The Cat was that *all four* of them fitted this bill, which is a real rarity. Even the bass player didn't look disgusting. Fans could argue endlessly about which one was their favourite member, which one they fancied – and they actually did.

Why, one of the group had even been a

bona fide model. Ben, the son of photographer Jean Claude Volpierre-Pierrot and his PR agent wife, had – much to his later embarrassment – posed for C&A and even "hung out" with Mike Read on the cover of his Pop Quiz game. He'd already proved his pin-up potential and, as audiences were later to discover, his casual pseudo-skanking would make Ben a singularly charismatic performer.

A nother rather rum thing that happened in 1987 which helped to pave the way for Curiosity's inexorable rise was that there was a real need for new *young* pop stars. Think about it. Freddie Mercury was 42. Phil Collins was 36. Mark Knopfler was 39. How can a teenager fantasize about a pop star if every star they see is having a hair transplant? Even the younger generation of stars were knocking on a bit now. Duran were definitely looking a bit long in the tooth and as for 1986's pop phenomenon A-ha – well, even old hands Duran could honestly boast that they were younger than the Norwegian trio.

By the start of 1987 there was a whole new younger audience who wanted new young pop stars of their own – not the ones their older brothers and sisters had consumed. Adults like Howard Jones, Nik Kershaw and Paul Young were now left hitless, Spandau Ballet were suddenly looking decidedly old hat and Duran Duran were having difficulty in making the Top 20 let alone the Top 10. The field was wide open to those still eligible for their under-26 railcards.

Plus there was another piece of image which made them gloriously marketable to their record company: rumour appeal. A-ha had turned out to be an unbearably prissy threesome and former pin-ups like Howard Jones and Nik Kershaw were now married and having babies. It was ages since there'd been a pop group who smacked of a certain youthful irresponsibility.

Within no time at all the tabloid press had caught on to the fact that Curiosity behaved like "normal" boys in their early twenties. All of a sudden there was a rumour that Ben was "hanging out" in the carnal sense with Paula Yates. The idea caught on with the John Blakes and Jill Pringles of Fleet Street and the next minute he was supposed to be sleeping with Eighth Wonder floozy Patsy Kensit! Then they dreamed up the idea that there

was some sort of liaison between the group and underage pop tart Mandy Smith – a notion only made more ludicrous by the fact that nobody could make up their mind whether it was Ben or Migi that she was supposed to be "dallying" with.

The crowning glory was a miraculous story invented by *The Sun* in which the group were supposed to have lured

Mandy and the disproportionate Maria Whittaker down to Ben's mansion (it's always a mansion). What actually went on was left to the innuendo of the newsprint but Ms Whittaker expressed her shock and disgust at the whole business.

All those tales had the resounding ring of untruth of course. There was one story that *The Sun* printed that was more plausible though: the one related by the group's jilted manager Antimo Rivetti which told quite simply of the sort of hanky panky that young men so often get up to. All it really proved was that, unlike so many pop stars in the Paul King mould, Curiosity actually *did* behave like 23-year-old boys. They were, after all, the sort of group who ended a live set with Nick, the bass player, cheerfully inviting girls in the audience to come back to meet the group at their hotel. Horrible, yes, but true.

the usual smattering of pop stars present. But Andy seemed to take a fancy to the group and agreed to direct the video for 'Misfit'. Within a few weeks they were "hanging out" in New York with the pop Svengali himself.

"He just liked us," the group explained afterwards. "We were the only young people at the exhibition." Let's hope Nick Rhodes, who was also present, hasn't read that. Of course, the video didn't turn out to be much cop but no matter, the right impression had been made.

But how, you may persist, could a group who tack the suffix "man" on to all of their sentences ever be truly trendy? Those who've never heard them speak or read an interview with them might have missed the fact that the group have very little to say for themselves but really do say "cool" a lot and actually employ phrases like "hanging out".

The LP, *Keep Your Distance*, turned out to be of relatively high quality, even if the late-eighties dance fizz actually bore a remarkable resemblance to mid-seventies jazz funk

W hat's more, unlike so many British groups since the Durans, Curiosity Killed The Cat are also blessed with that dubious quantity known as "trendiness". But how, you ask, can a group which calls one of their songs 'Tell (Wag)' after London's Wardour Street nighterie, really be trendy? Why, that's such an *uncool* thing to do.

But that's actually the point. To a teenage audience the very idea of the Wag Club is desperately trendy. The world of Crazy Larry's, of the Cafe De Paris, of warehouse parties – all favourites with the Curiosities – is one positively drenched in glamour for those who've not seen what they're actually like. And, after all, Curiosity must be trendy because magazines like *Elle*, *i-D* and *Ritz* loved them way before they'd had anything like a hit, and *Comme Des Garçons* invited them to travel to Paris to model menswear.

The point is that, unlike some groups, Curiosity Killed The Cat were never so trendy that they lost touch with their fans.

And just to show how trendy they really were, they won the patronage of Andy Warhol. The late photographer came to London to open an exhibition of his self-portraits and as ever there was

Ten years ago, when punk rock was at its height and when everyone's professed ambition was to destroy any remnants of the sixties, to be in possession of such a hippy vocabulary was a lynchable offence. But that's the big wheel of life: what was desperately untrendy ten years ago is suddenly hip now; the teenage audience – blissfully unaware of the awful connotations apparent to their elders – loves this new vocabulary.

And the music? The Press hailed it as "late-eighties dance fizz", which is a reasonable enough description. Aided by high-quality session musicians and the production of Stewart Levine who was finally chosen after a try out with Sly and Robbie, the LP, *Keep Your Distance*, turned out to be of relatively high quality, even if the late-eighties dance fizz actually bore a remarkable resemblance to mid-seventies jazz funk.

It's no surprise, therefore, that the group admits to admiring not only groups like the obligatory Chic, but also hoary old jazz funk people like Chic Corea and Weather Report alongside the more obscure reggae and soul musicians. But that's the big wheel turning again. To a teenager all this sounds sparklingly new.

So why *were* Curiosity Killed The Cat the act of the year? Because the glorious benefits of hindsight tell us that they were simply the perfect group for a year like 1987.

WILLIAM SHAW

ACTS OF THE YEAR

There's a story they tell about Paul Simon. There he is, enjoying the weekend at a friend's house out on Long Island. During a game of softball one of the guests slips and breaks a bone in his leg. Simon volunteers to take the victim – who is in some pain – to the hospital in the back of his car. As they go bumping down the backroads with the poor unfortunate doing his best to bite back the pain, Simon turns to his passenger and thoughtfully enquires if he wishes to hear the mixes of his new album.

The poor invalid is too distracted, gobstruck or awestruck to demur. After all, here he is being chauffeured by the man who wrote 'Bridge Over Troubled Water', 'Sound Of Silence', 'America' and 'Mrs Robinson' – among so many others – and wouldn't it be rather churlish to refuse? So off they rattle Casualty-wards to the accompaniment of the early mixes with Simon offering occasional comments and soliciting his passenger's opinions on the virtues of the material.

This anecdote almost explains why Paul Simon remains one of the least clubbable of internationally famous popular musicians. Even with multi-million selling albums like *Bridge Over Troubled Water*, *The Graduate*, and *There Goes Rhymin' Simon* under his belt he remains, if not a workaholic, then certainly a man whose all-encompassing enthusiasm for his work is inclined to blind him to the social niceties.

Very much the Manhattan bohemian made good, Simon sang his line on 'We Are The World' but didn't look that comfortable about it. He subsequently pulled out of Live Aid because he felt he was being messed around. One minute they wanted him on his own, then they wanted Artie, then he was going to duet with Dylan and finally they wouldn't guarantee him a soundcheck so he watched the whole thing on TV and then wished like hell he'd stayed in. He was still kicking himself over a year later when he came to London to promote the newly released *Graceland*.

The *Graceland* experience could hardly have been a more classic case of Simon's musical enthusiasm and ambition running away with his better judgement. It started with a pirate cassette of South African music. In townships like Soweto they call it "gumboots" in honour of the footwear used by the mineworkers. This music is steeped in its own pokey vernacular, closely based on the sound of the accordion and far removed from the pseudo-scientific calculations of Western pop music.

Simon, in his eyrie high above Central Park, played this tape and marvelled at its freshness and vigour. Although township jive is clearly a product of a variety of influences – ranging from Zulu chants through Victorian hymnals to Michael Jackson's *Thriller* – it is clearly a music at least as rich and complex as rockabilly or reggae. And – did Simon detect? – more commercial than all of them?

Once he'd been to South Africa, tracked down some of the musicians on that tape, recorded with them in Johannesburg, in some cases – specifically with 'The Boy In The Bubble' and 'I Know What I Know' – elaborating upon traditional material to produce new songs, then flown some of the musicians to New York and London for further recordings, mixed and re-mixed as is his custom, finally giving the whole thing an international patina by bringing in well-tried US session players before releasing it to a level of acclaim that he hadn't come near since *There Goes Rhymin' Simon* 13 long years earlier, *then*

some people said that of course the whole thing had been a carefully planned cultural hi-jack.

Tom Sabina, one of the many African National Congress spokesmen who was called upon to comment, summed up one widely held view when he described Simon as "opportunist. He knew very well that *Graceland* was going to be a success and he has made a lot of money out of it." Mr Sabina can be excused his touching faith in the predictability of the music business. The majority of the motives that were ascribed to Simon as the single 'You Can Call Me Al' began to take off and the brouhaha over *Graceland* whipped itself up into a regular media firestorm, ranged from the understandably naïve to the plain mischievous.

The politicians and leader writers decently confined themselves to arguing about the efficacy or otherwise of the United Nations boycott and Musicians Union regulations. Should he have gone to South Africa to record? Should he have brought the musicians out and made the album in New York? Should he have given them royalties rather than

triple the South African scale that he did pay?

It was when the music papers and the Fleet Street tabloids and the youth culture pundits weighed in that the debate turned seriously grotesque. Here the reality of one middle-aged New York pop star recording a handful of tunes with some South African musicians was lost in a vapour of *ishoos* and personal unpleasantness.

Groaning under the weight of their collective self-righteousness, the Forces of Progress and Enlightenment laid into Simon for his politics, his bank account, his stature, even his shirts. When his tour reached the Zimbabwean capital, a journalist asked how he could name his record after a place that so clearly reflected the slave-owning legacy of the American South. Many held that he could at least have included a song about the evil of apartheid, as if such a glib move would be sufficient to assure them that Simon was not an unrepentant fascist.

Questions of Right and Wrong were thus obscured by ludicrous efforts to pinpoint exactly who had the moral high ground. An open letter was handed in at London's Albert Hall stage door, signed by Billy Bragg, Paul Weller and Jerry Dammers amongst others, demanding that Simon give " a complete and heartfelt apology to the United Nations General Assembly" for his breach of the cultural boycott. Inevitably it was left to the *Sun* to climax this orgy of tosh by describing the audience at Simon's Albert Hall show as "Porsche-owning yuppies".

Unhappily Paul Simon is not well-equipped either to weather this kind of storm or to fight it off. Because the battle was essentially being staged between opposing sets of clichés and nobody's mind was likely to be changed, he would have been wisest to have adopted what you might call the Mick Jagger Defence – i.e. refuse to dignify the charges by offering any kind of defence. The people who bought and enjoyed *Graceland* weren't particularly bothered about the minutiae of the political case; those who were bothered about the politics hated the record.

And many of Simon's arguments were weak to say the least. Yes, the South African musicians had voted to work with him, but by that time he was already on his way to Johannesburg. In certain cases he had paid session fees because his collaborators wouldn't have trusted in the likelihood of subsequent royalty cheques. When you asked him if he honestly believed he'd done the right thing he'd say, of course he had. But there was enough of the old-fashioned liberal about him to suggest that he wasn't as sure as all that. The way the tour was organized – with co-headlining status for Miriam Makeba and Hugh Masekela and with Simon the only white face of 25 musicians on stage – added to the suspicion that he was trying to render himself bulletproof.

Ultimately it amounted to a battle between two opposing ways of looking at the world, each of them rooted in a different era. Simon's is an attitude formed in the '60s with a consequent emphasis on the virtues of synthesis, sincerity and moderation. Simon is not a political *naif* but his belief in the importance of motives puts him out of kilter in these categorical times. No matter whether the government's right or left, he said, it's the artist who gets screwed. "When they say that the UN has decided something they make you feel – or at least they try to make you feel – that God has spoken."

The opposition argument is an '80s argument. You're either part of the problem or part of the solution and musicians – particularly wealthy ones – cannot be exceptions. According to Jerry Dammers, "saying that you like Paul Simon's music is as irrelevant as saying we shouldn't boycott South African fruit because it tastes nice."

Thus Paul Simon became the first pop star to be boycotted, picketed, excoriated and pilloried because of a career miscalculation. Despite what Dammers says, Simon's final and only real defence is the manifest quality of *Graceland*, a record that sold millions of copies and won a Grammy by dint of its pure musical qualities. Only a cretin would argue that it has done anything but brought long-overdue recognition to South African musicians and at last thrown some positive light on the culture of the enslaved majority of that country's population. It does not make P.W. Botha look any better and will be played and enjoyed long after he is gone.

In one of his more convincing statements on the affair Simon offered his best defence: "The thing about culture is that it flows like water. It's not something that can just be cut off." If *Graceland* proves to have prised open a door through which African music can begin to find a wider audience then it's unlikely that history will judge him unkindly.

DAVID HEPWORTH

Groaning under the weight of their collective self-righteousness, the Forces Of Progress And Enlightenment laid into Simon for his politics, his bank account, his stature, even his shirts

Who'd have thought it would have turned out like this?

When we last left them, The Communards had just finished the first round-Britain Red Wedge tour. The lynchpin of the tour was Paul Weller's Style Council, with the odd guest spot by a solo Spandau or Smith, and the tour guide was the hugely charismatic Billy Bragg. Yet the surprise hit was The Communards, with the inspired pop of 'You Are My World', the deliberately tacky disco cover 'Don't Leave Me This Way', and Jimmy Somerville's gender-switch duet with Sarah-Jane Morris on the jazz standard 'Lover Man', she growling out a rude bluesy bass while he tipped the sound-meters into the red with his choiring falsetto.

Written off at the time as "self-indulgent crap",," by former colleague Steve Bronski, Somerville's new partnership with Richard Coles was a brave stab at artistic independence – a mix of campy flamenco, jazz covers, speedy electro and what Coles ruefully confessed was "that Petula Clark sound." It hardly seemed the likeliest contender for number one and the dubious attentions of Fleet Street, however, and if anything we wished them well while notching up another square peg failing to fit itself into a round hole.

It *was* a shaky start, with the first two singles, 'You Are My World' and 'Disenchanted', just denting the charts, but the intervening year proved their wellwishers' fears to be unfounded. It might be worth asking exactly which has changed shape – peg or hole, perhaps a little of both – but the nelly pinko Scots dwarf and his beanpole pal have broken it, and from the number of scraps they've had with both the press and fellow pop stars, they've come through with their politics and integrity dusty but intact.

The sales and chart positions – a platinum album, gold and silver singles around the world – and the sell-out

ACTS

CO

audiences speak for themselves, as do the interviews, statements, political appearances and benefits. Put them all together and you have that pop basilisk, the radical pop group who have won the hearts and minds of a nation that was meant to be too busy buying shares and voting Tory. Either they've sold us a pup or The Communards have succeeded where The Doors and Stones and The Clash and Poisongirls failed before them.

F THE YEAR

MUNARDS

Much of their success can be put down to their charm, on record and in person. Their style might be described as one of the sneakier examples of the "post-modern" smash-and-grab, mix 'n' match raid on the past. While elsewhere most of this is baldly obvious – retro soul from jeans ads, the latest wave of psychedelic affectation, the current alliance between scratch and HM, even the larcenous sampling of other people's records – The Communards' brief is so wide that there are few styles that they could not, beyond personal choice, address themselves to. (More: no matter how many orchestral musicians you gave them, they still wouldn't turn in a King Crimson album.)

It also goes some way beyond "eclecticism", a term that's something of a non-starter in this context. The Communards are not a disco sequencer setting, a flamenco swirl, a homage to Pet Clark or a touch song mood. Rather, the essence of The Communards is a larky sense of camp, a musical mischief, indulgence and enthusiasm.

They are also, of course, up-front personalities, and here some dubious forces come into play. As every journalist who has met them will attest, they give great copy; salt-of-the-earth politics, banter you could *eat*, sexy indiscretions and that perennial favourite – who is the intemperate Somerville dishing this week? They have also worked tirelessly on the AIDS front – Somerville even reuniting, tearfully, with the Bronskis to play an International AIDS Day benefit – and take every opportunity to bang the message home.

That the media should willingly publish their comments is not paradoxical; just as page three promotes the sexual attitudes condemned on page one, the media has found a way of having its cake and eating it on the subject of AIDS as well.

Somerville has been criticized for dragging other pop stars, notably the Pet Shop Boys, out of the closet, arguing that in times like these they have a moral duty to stand up publicly and be counted. It has been argued in return that this has to be a matter of personal choice and that no one has the right to come out of the closet on *anyone* else's behalf, but in this particular arena – the arena of money and fame hymned, however ironically, on the Pet Shop Boys' *Please* – gay club habitués Tennant and Lowe were pretty much fair game.

It could be said that Somerville did Tennant a favour by getting to him before *The Sun* did, and even if it didn't stop *The Sun* it did lessen the effect. It should also be noted that the pop closet is the carpentry of British attitudes and libel laws, and to condone such furniture is to side with the people who would like to board up all the closets and dump them over a cliff with their contents inside.

What is so special about The Communards is that, like the Bronskis before them, they do not lie or prevaricate about their sexuality, nor do they resort to fancy dress in what is often an attempt to appeal to a hostile public's sense of novelty. They are quite literally the gay next door – their album contained little explicit gay politics beyond the level of charged metaphor – and their very "ordinariness" itself is far more "subversive" than a space cadet in high heels with a goldfish bowl on his head. (Culturally, the British tend to site these creatures – the Davids and Marcs and Georges and Petes – at the end of the pier, where they are as much a harmless diversion as the other pier attractions. The only problem is they keep breaking down and we have to get new ones.) The Communards make no bizarre or exotic "excuse" for themselves, because they don't feel they have to.

Being the gay next door is not without its problems, though. Much is made of their queenly humour. Inside the gay sub-culture this is a dialect of sorts, but outside the ghetto it brings into play the notion of the Homosexual as Court Jester, the witty and sympathetic queen who is tolerated solely because of those two virtues. It also brings up the nasty Freudian notion of "conversion" by the right woman, if she could just get the chance. "We're a couple of closet straights and we've got two young wives locked away somewhere," Somerville cracked to one journalist last year. He might have been voicing a fantasy common among his fans.

That may seem unfair and extreme, and certainly irrelevant to a fair proportion of their audience, but it can't be dismissed when trying to explain their appeal. It's been argued that the appeal of such pop stars is non-sexual – a "safe" object of platonic desire for the 14-year-old schoolgirls who scream Jimmy's name at Communards concerts – but common misconceptions about homosexuals do not disappear when they become pop stars.

Ultimately, given the circumstances – not least those in the House of Commons – perhaps we should thank our lucky stars for what we've got. The Communards are not going to outsell Abba, nor will their pronouncements bring down a government. But they do acquit themselves impeccably on both, and it might be a key to their success that the two are in a sense separate. The *Communards* album is a collection of love songs and laments that, with the exception of 'Forbidden Fruit', are given political resonance by the simple fact that they are written and sung by men, and for other men at that. There is no 'Glad To Be Gay' on the album; if it's propaganda, it's by example, not slogan.

In the record shops and tour venues, these songs offer what homosexuals have been waiting for for decades – pop songs about *their* lives – while also offering a wider audience recognizably universal sentiments: love, longing, passion, loss. It could also be said that part of their appeal lies in the fact that their songs carry somewhat more emotional conviction than much "straight" pop.

And they continue to squawk on about gay rights, the Labour vote, CND, South Africa, the miners' strike. It could be argued that pop star politics are ultimately ineffectual, but I wouldn't underestimate the effect of their example, indeed their very existence. Even after the Tory victory, there's hope for civil liberties yet if these two tarts are still allowed to get up and play. JOHN GILL

It might be worth asking exactly which has changed shape — peg or hole, perhaps a little of both — but the nelly pinko Scots dwarf and his beanpole pal have broken it

They get up promptly in the morning in the large home (tennis court, recording studio, fish pond), they brush their teeth, they do their allotted household chores ("It's important to do that," they trill) sticking with discipline to the rota, and then they get on with the job . . . pop stars.

Sometimes Stedman, the oldest, will go to his room and scribble ideas for the latest set of costumes he's designing. Sometimes Doris will assemble the clan in the living room (the lawn if it's a fine day) and whip them through the choreography she's devised for the next single. Sometimes Lorraine will repair to the bathroom and pose before the mirror,

and dig the strength of mom dealing with such awesome problems as daughters' braces and Keith's dandruff. Wow!). God almighty, even the Brady Bunch made records. The family, in America, was big business.

But it took until the eighties with five black kids from Romford for the British pop industry to latch on to the winning ways of the scheme. And it's comparisons with The Jacksons, not just because of skin colour, that Five Star most draw (and readily encourage themselves).

Doris wants, as she has frequently noted, to marry Michael. Stedman used to model himself on Michael. They haven't featured in a kiddie TV cartoon but they've had a strip in *Look In* which

Jimmy Cliff and more. And then, like Joe, he began producing issue.

Ask the Five Star children how they formed their group in the first place and they will undoubtedly tell you, with their piping conviction, how the idea of a family group just came to them and how it was with trepidation that they approached their parents with that idea. Perhaps this is true. But the seeds of such a ruse had been planted, inarguably, by Buster himself: he has revealed that he'd been thinking about this very wheeze as far back as 1971 when he had stopped touring and when the youngest, Delroy, was still in nappies.

It was on Buster's own label, Tent Records, that the first Five Star product was released. He then negotiated a deal with RCA, got the kids their first appearance on the BBC's gruesome lunchtime jollity *Pebble Mill At One* (this is September 1983), and then we had a chart hit 'All Fall Down'.

Some near misses ('Let Me Be The One', 'Love Take Over', 'RSVP') followed before 'System Addict' made the top five and the rest, as they say, is history.

There was nothing that Five Star wouldn't do: they'd appear on television schlock things from *3,2,1* to *Paul Daniels* to those grotesque *Summer Specials* where everyone looks a jerk – apart from Five Star because, unlike Duncan Norvelle and the other panto losers, they were sincerely delighted to be there. They'd make the front cover of the good-natured pop magazines; the same week they'd be featured in the *Sunday Times* as a "phenomenon".

The joy was they didn't understand the difference. They were making good

They are so nice, polite and uncomplicated it's weird. This is a cynical biz and the Pearsons seem totally wacko

anticipating a future career in movies: "Serious doesn't look good on me." And sometimes Delroy, the youngest, will just pack up his tackle, bait and rod and retire for carp fishing.

It is all so homely, frighteningly innocent. They eat choc bars for breakfast. They have a cat called John who thinks he's a dog; they have a kitten called Puppy who thinks he's a puppy. They pour tomato ketchup over one another and shriek because it looks like BLOOD! Spooky!! They watch BBC schools broadcasts about changing car tyres because there's nothing else on. They make jokes about barbecuing the neighbours and then feel very, very guilty. They buy cars for £40,000 and then drive them up and down the garden path – nowhere else. None of them has ever had a "proper" boyfriend or girlfriend. Their only friends are each other and they all love their mother Dolores and father Buster *so* much.

All of the above they'll reveal with compelling honesty and naïvety; they are so nice, polite and uncomplicated it's weird. This is a cynical biz and the Pearsons seem totally wacko. But there's no sham at work here. These folk are simple, in the nicest possible sense . . .

The family, all-singing, all-prancing group has been seen before, most conspicuously in the late '60s/early '70s when there seemed to be a young teenage consuming public so willing to jump enthusiastically on the back of a cheerful set of brotherly/sisterly chums that apart from the genuine relatives – The Cowsills, The Carpenters, The Jacksons, The Osmonds – the formula was even stretched to fiction for the fantastically lovey-lovey Partridge Family (dig the "psychedelic" tour bus

is the next best thing. They love animals. They are loopy in their innocent approach to life. There are five of them. Black. The innocent pop of 'I Want You Back'/'ABC'/'All Fall Down'/'Find The Time'. And haven't we seen such dance routines somewhere before? Even in cartoon form, yes, we *have*!

The comparisons, almost chilling, go yet further. Buster Pearson admits that he has learned from the mistakes of Jackson père Joe. Buster would not have started his children as early as Joe and he's going to stay with them, never veering into recriminations with any

offspring (like Joe, on occasions has; Joe seems to treat his children as business clients who owe him loyalty: even now he is planning to launch his own *Cola* brand in direct opposition to Michael's multi-million dollar *Pepsi* campaign. Who will do *his* ads? Purrety weird). But like Joe, Buster still seems to be the driving force behind the family entertainment business, pushing forward, as far as he dare, the ambitions of the children.

And Buster, like Joe, was a sporadic musician. He escaped Jamaica at 17 and ended up a session guitarist, backing Wilson Pickett, Desmond Decker,

ACTS OF THE YEAR

FIVE ST

pop records, selling copies of their albums *Luxury of Life* and *Silk And Steel* (half a million each by current estimates) with refreshing lack of calculated promotion. We'll do anything. Daddy doesn't know when to say no.

"All the Jacksons knew about was how to perform," Buster has said. "I've made sure mine know every aspect of the music business. If something was to happen to me tomorrow, they could survive."

Of course, they *don't* know every aspect of the music business – but they're getting coaching. It's just like the old days. They're writing and producing on the B-side. For the moment though it has to be Buster who handles the business and he certainly sees no conflict between strict family morals and milking money wherever he can.

The man has business acumen – just look at the deal he struck with *Crunchie* (the chocolate bar with the honeycomb centre) – to sponsor the group's British tour of 1986. This was proper money – and not the usual arrangement of low profile emblems on tour tickets. *Crunchie* was everywhere. *Crunchie* banners on stage and environs, a free *Crunchie*/Five Star poster with every copy of *Silk And Steel*, even a free *Crunchie* bar with press copies of the LP. Yum!

And so free of sin and extravagance are the group that this industrial tie-up was the closest they'd ever come to the courtship of "controversy". It just wasn't on for a clean and pleasant pop troupe, suggested our national "news"papers, to be advocating a tooth-rotting product to our health-conscious nation's tinies. A rather pathetic little furore was whipped up and even the British Dental Association was dragged in on the "act". It came as no surprise to find that the 1987 tour was sponsored by *Ultrabrite* toothpaste. Five Star do not like to give offence.

Where do things go from here? The children – for children they are, however big they get – simply cannot believe that through hard work and premium dedication they will not become unbelievably, uncannily famous. Perhaps they will. Perhaps they will go mad and rebel like idols The Jacksons. But natural romance? According to Buster "before Five Star they were too young for such things; during Five Star they haven't the time." Which is possibly true, though he once told *Q* magazine that he'd always preserve the right of veto for any prospective suitor . . . "We've built up too much to let someone come in and take any of it away."

In the meantime they're content to ape The Jacksons: teeth, smiles, squeaks of innocence. A few fine records. The family that plays together, stays together. Until the playground closes down . . .

CHRIS HEATH/TOM HIBBERT

BRYAN ADAMS
Into The Fire (A&M)
... all Bry's songs fill the pre-requisite of American pop, sounding just like Coke or jeans adverts. Pristine and gormless pop metal that overwhelms and overplays its sub-Springsteen tinseltown teen anthems with posing pouch power chords and bullneck bravado. I can't quite make out what he's advertising though. Canadian lager perhaps?
Melody Maker

This is Springsteen country, but whereas one might *believe* Bruce is out there on the edge of the town, Bry, with his clean leather jacket, is always going to be someone you might pass in the high street on a Saturday morning carrying a Woolworths bag.
NME

. . . this is a studied, classy, straight down the line rock album – a bit old fashioned and just the sort of thing that you're not supposed to like!
Sounds

AFRIKA BAMBAATAA
Beware (The Funk Is Everywhere) (Tommy Boy)
How the mighty collapse when they can't see past mid-Manhattan.
NME

You know the sort of thing: harder than the rest, we've got this and we've got that etc. In no other form of music I can think of do lyrics amount to little more than shopping lists...
Sounds

... this is a meandering, overmanned excursion with more credits listed on the sleeve than at the end of *Spitting Image* and the only common purpose appears to be to celebrate Afrika Bambaataa. "Overseer Of Funk", titular head of state.
Melody Maker

A-HA
Scoundrel Days (WEA)
But as I write, the hotbed of talent that is A-ha continues to go unrecognized. The critics, the unbelievers, the philistines who see only the glossy posters and the fancy haircuts, will persist in sneering at these Scandinavian saucepots with all the insight and perception of a tree.
Sounds

It is *great*. Literally.
Melody Maker

The best teen pop at least made you jump about. A-ha make you sink into your chair.
NME

LEE AARON
Lee Aaron (10)
Lee Aaron is the sort of woman you'd expect to discover playing Foreigner on the stereo in her nifty white Mercedes convertible. With the lid off . . . If it's inoffensive, if it's shifted some serious units for someone else, and if you could confuse it with the soundtrack from the forthcoming Tom Cruise or Eddie Murphy box office blockbuster, then you can bet Lee Aaron will find room for it in her repertoire.
Sounds

GREGORY ABBOTT
Shake You Down (CBS)
Eight sensitive sparse, gentle, slow-paced, rhythmic, tender, harmoniously crooned "ballads" about L-O-V-E, all in the same vein as the hit single 'Shake You Down' and each one showing that Gregory is quite one of the most accomplished singers of "smoochie" songs in the spooniverse.
Smash Hits

... I reckon that a lot of you out there are going to love this man's voice to death. Forgive my self-indulgence, but I've waited years to write this sentence: A Star Is Born.
Melody Maker

My mum ... knows nothing about today's music ... but she says Gregory Abbott sounds like Leo Sayer with *even more feeling!!!* And you can't get any better than that, can you?
NME

As promised, it's much rougher and more ambitious than their first LP, but it's also crammed with even more ridiculously catchy tunes.
Smash Hits

THE GREG ALLMAN BAND
I'm No Angel (Epic)
There's no soul-baring in the lyrics, just the usual grind about women who done him wrong, but the emotion simply sounds right.
Q

MARC ALMOND
Mother Fist And Her Daughters (Virgin)
Almond's overripe tragedies are frequently exploded by tongues bursting through cheeks.
Q

Trust no one who claims to hate the voice of Marc Almond – if they're not lying outright, then they're drowning in a glassy sea of self-deception.
NME

Don't look for clever synth patches, searing sampled sounds or blistering solos. Look for heart, soul and sympathy – and find it. Marc Almond – a difficult artist, thank God.
Sounds

HERB ALPERT
Keep Your Eye On Me (A&M)
... his trumpet is so muted he often sounds like he's playing in the studio corridor.
Q

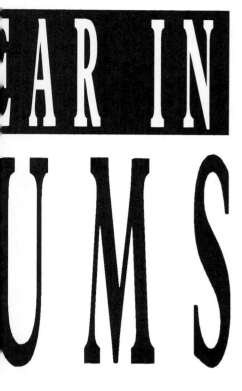

lyce Hibbert

EAR IN UMS

PHIL ALVIN
Unsung Stories (London)
An enjoyable, if ultimately unconvincing, project.
Sounds

If American myths and curios, deftly handled and skilfully embossed are your bag, then leave the hyped-up bluster of Talking Heads well alone and check out this collection. One of the most rewarding releases of the year.
NME

Unsung Stories is a gas, a genuinely vivacious collection of mostly obscure country blues, gospel and brawling big band jazz classics ... A rare and timeless delight.
Melody Maker

AMAZULU
Amazulu (Island)
Aren't Amazulu almost *unbearably* sweet and jolly? Even when they're singing about being broken-hearted, abandoned and thoroughly down in the dumps they sound like they're eating three Cadbury's cream eggs, while frolicking barefoot in a summery meadow.
Smash Hits

AND ALSO THE TREES
Virus Meadow (Reflex)
Like a wolf in sheep's clothing they disguise a malicious and grievous intent behind graceful, beautiful mottos and motifs. Spectacular lyrical fables are spun through a maze of inticing pleasantry that inevitably

explode without prior warning ... Sweetness incarnate but with grubby hands and black soul.
NME

... a scripted soundtrack for some long-forgotten Edgar Allen Poe tale.
Melody Maker

ADAM ANT
"Hits" (CBS)
Lapsed teenagers, now beer-bellied clerical officers with "Ant Music" tattooed across their craniums, will beg to differ, but the man's 15 minutes of inspiration were launched by the boisterous 'Dog Eat Dog' and lasted as long as it takes to peel an orange . . .

  Hits isn't comprehensively great, but buy the video and chuckle 'til your socks drop off.
Sounds

He probably WAS the first modern pop star, inasmuch as he understood the potential of video ... And his hits, all contained in this package, have endured amazingly well.
Melody Maker

ANTHRAX
Among The Living (Island)
There's nothing approaching raunch or boogie in this music; the last traces of R&B animalism have been scoured from heavy metal, and with them go sensuality and even narcissism.
Melody Maker

Anthrax are akin to social workers on speed.
Sounds

One of the very few successful bands to be named after a sheep disease...
Q

THE ART OF NOISE
Re-Works Of Art Of Noise
(Chrysalis)
Tesco's and Safeway's head offices will lap it up, because it takes supermarket muzak into a whole new realm.
Smash Hits

ASHFORD AND SIMPSON
Real Love (Capitol)
Nick and Val's thousandth *en famille* release is so eminently okay that I'm nearly lost for words.
Melody Maker

VIRGINIA ASTLEY
Hope In A Darkened Heart
(WEA)
Hope ... is a beautiful place, full of delights; but be warned, there's nothing nasty in Virginia's garden.
NME

By the middle of side one, you are longing for something jagged to rush out and slam into your rib-cage. More basically, you long for these dormant sighs to do *something*. Maybe Virginia should spend more time in rooms where people yell and scream some of the time, without ever stopping to dry their tears.
Sounds

... passive as the arrangements are, Astley's horribly affected, childlike vocal delivery renders the whole package a tad too irritating to ignore.
Melody Maker

ATLANTIC STARR
Secret Lovers — The Best Of Atlantic Starr (A&M)
Atlantic Starr are no dunderheads when it comes to emoting in best black music tradition. 'Send For Me' and the Chic-styled 'Am I Dreaming' are magic moments. Given low lights, a warm brandy and the right sort of company, I'd probably find additional praises for this Star-set mixture of rhythm 'n' romance.
NME

All In The Name Of Love
(WEA)
... they could release any three tracks off this LP as singles and suddenly become very famous indeed.
Smash Hits

ATTACCO DECENTE
United Kingdom Of America
(All Or Nothing Records)
These pop social workers have a wonderful musical perspective, fashioning a startlingly fresh barrage of sound out of a variety of acoustic implements.
Sounds

Attacco's insidious use of dulcimers and tongue drums ... does not compensate for

Geoff Smith's weak vocals, which sadly display neither the range nor the richness required to make this promising album compulsive listening.
Melody Maker

BAD COMPANY
Fame And Fortune (Atlantic)
For Bad Co '86 . . . still appear capable of handling their personal Big Bang of comeback with a fair modicum of righteous, if familiar, pure rock riffs.
NME

. . . an album that I approached with a mocking disbelief has won me over (to a point), not through sentiment but through quality.
Sounds

BALAAM AND THE ANGEL
The Greatest Story Ever Told
(Virgin)
An album that's about as threatening as Sir Geoffrey Howe and just as cuddly. If they get any more accessible, they will become Irish and sing about trees. An extremely *nice* record.
Sounds

It's snakes, angels, griffins, scrolls, and all kinds of everything totalling a harmonic rush of REM-ic sound, sights firmly established on American shores. Leeds meets West Coast.
NME

THE BALHAM ALLIGATORS
The Balham Alligators
(Special Delivery)
Swamp boogie at its stifling, steamy best.
Q

BEASTIE BOYS
Licensed To III (Def Jam)
They chant/rap about all the essential things in life, from the joys of being the school bully . . . to girlies' skirts, from preoccupations with trying to fill their "fat bellies" to, erm, girlies' skirts.
Smash Hits

The main sources of inspiration behind this record are . . . burgers, booze and chicks. I love them!
Sounds

You want smut? You want punk? You want heavy metal? Sick and tired of half-an-arse, half a brain-cell coy boy twee-twittery? You want music your parents will HATE? . . . This is aural pornography of the finest kind.
NME

Licensed To III is the cast of *Porkies* auditioning for the Pacino part in *Scarface* . . . It's brilliant. Best beat it and buy it.
Melody Maker

NICK BERRY
Nick Berry (BBC)
Nick Berry may be jolly good at pulling cheesy smirks in the boozer and saying "Leave it aht, Mum, alright?" and winking at Mary the so-called punk etc. etc. but a pop singer he is not – and he knows it. His apologetic warblings on this hastily assembled thing are embarrassing to say the very least. Dear oh dear oh dear oh dear. Why oh why oh why oh why? As N. Berry is the first to admit, this is simply *not* very good.
Smash Hits

THE B-52s
Bouncing Off The Satellites
(Island)
. . . all we have here is an album which is part Swing Out Sister and part Bananarama.
Sounds

That the B-52s aren't bigger than the Beach Boys or selling 1000 times more than the Curiosity complacency is a cause for national shame.
Melody Maker

THE BHUNDU BOYS
Tsvimbodzemoto (Disc Afrique)
. . . helpful subtitling on the sleeve assists the average Brit's enjoyment of the mood of the songs and thus we know that the happy-go-lucky melody 'Vakaparei' relates the value of "honesty and communication as a means to solving family problems."
Sounds

'Una Shuwa', for instance, warns *"guard your tongue to ensure you do not offend your friends."*
NME

Join the Bhundu celebration or have a grey day.
Melody Maker

BIG AUDIO DYNAMITE
No 10, Upping Street (CBS)
Upping St . . . is a decent literate, listenable slab of *le pop moderne* . . .
NME

So why does the record fall to pieces on side two?
Sounds

Side two leaves the beatbox at home and serves up brilliant, soulful, inventive pop.
Smash Hits

THE BIG DISH
Swimmer (Virgin)
. . . this album is the gangrenous underbelly of our decaying charts.
NME

. . . the literate, singer-songwriterly feel, plus Lindsay's aching vocals, combine with some of the best pop melodies around today to make this album something special.
Melody Maker

There's all the right curves and some of the right turns, but none of the real flesh.
Sounds

BLACK BRITAIN
Obvious (10)
. . . this is an unfortunately well-titled album.
Record Mirror

. . . just because they do their proselytizing in 4/4 time doesn't make me any more likely

to enjoy listening to them.
Melody Maker

File under Nice Guys Finish Last.
NME

A few more-than-half-decent tunes, an album with its heart in the right place . . . but is this enough?
Sounds

Powerful, true Brit city funk which burns where Five Star only twinkle.
Q

THE BLOW MONKEYS
She Was Only A Grocer's Daughter (RCA)

It will be said that Dr Robert has one musical idea and has written ten songs around it. This has some truth, but ignores the fact that he is skilful enough to turn it into a noisy, chattering LP, that is inspired, embarrassing, ambitious, determined, arrogant, stupid, delightful and, with looks like that, dreamy.
NME

Grocer's Daughter has taken some of pop's best moves and shuffled them with a deft touch to come up with a winning hand. It's rich, tender and soulful and leaves you with a saccharine smile. It's free from torment and challenging twists.
Sounds

PHILLIP BOA AND THE VOODOO CLUB
Aristocracie (Red Flame)

Pulling even more of his morbid fascinations of maternal mutilation, rejection and manipulation to the forefront, Boa has built on his suit of disquietening black humour, creating a record that combines the exotic perfection of a Black Forest summer with the desperate tones of Kurtz as he cries, "The horror, the horror."
Melody Maker

Philistrines (Red Flame)

An orchestra of violins and cellos fights for breathing space alongside a harsh male and a soft female vocal, an insistent dance drumbeat holds sway and vibrating guitars cut and slice tunes which latch on to the imagination and remain there.
NME

Whilst producing the most powerfully subversive pop I've heard for ages, his work is hampered by too many slipshod amateur hour Indie faults . . .
Melody Maker

BOGSHED
Step On It (Shellfish)

Step On It doesn't allow the way for wider popularity and instant success, but it does set up Bogshed for a long and worthwhile career as an underground institution.
Sounds

Tried And Tested Public Speaker (Shellfish)

Bogshed look destined to end up in the we-talked-about-them-last-year-but-let's-be-honest-they-weren't-very-good box.
Sounds

Bogshed aren't subtle, soothing and they aren't intellectual arbiters of taste, but they do make a loud noise well.
Melody Maker

BON JOVI
Slippery When Wet (Mercury)

They're American! They have long hair and appalling trousers! They haven't an original idea in their heads! They sing tiresome old "rock" clichés in hoarse voices to crunging guitar "riffs"! They wish they were Bruce Springsteen! That's all you need to know about Bon Jovi!
Smash Hits

With this album, Bon Jovi have hit third time lucky. They've become more mature, more confident, more accomplished, without simultaneously losing the spark of vitality and adventure that first urged them out of New Jersey and on to the bus.
Melody Maker

DAVID BOWIE
Never Let Me Down (EMI America)

One wonders, finally, if this album was really necessary.
Q

Wilfully lacking grandeur, all *too* immaculate, processed ageing rock for Americans called Phil and Steve and Don in record company offices.
Melody Maker

. . . a worried old hound trying to anticipate what the younger public wants to hear.
Sounds

If this is Bowie in his true, natural colours the suspicion that all along he had a warped art-school idea about pop music, an avant-garde superciliousness and the sort of talent more suited to real estate, advertising, or full-time loafing is now confirmed. Or maybe he should just start taking drugs again.
NME

BILLY BRAGG
Talking With The Taxman About Poetry (Go! Discs)

. . . there's lots more songs about politics and lots more songs about how being in love is a bit of a problem, all "sung" in that familiar tuneless gravelly voice . . . this is a spine-tinglingly good record.
Smash Hits

I'd say the attempt at creating a worthy and acceptable face for the Labour Party has taken its toll and is leaving Bragg flat.
Sounds

Qualifying Bragg for more than mere Good Blokedom, *Taxman* . . . is prosaic and compact, a chronicle not so much difficult as *direct*. And at £4.49 it's only 37.4p a song.
NME

BRIGANDAGE
Pretty Funny Thing (Gung Ho)

The production seems strangely tame, but the songs aren't. These are yesterday's positive punks, and they can occasionally be very, very touching, mostly where the voice shines.
NME

Ripped and torn, bruised and abused, Brigandage have returned with an album steeped in old traditions, burning with punky ebullience and dancing with a devil-may-care attitude.
Sounds

BRILLIANT
Kissing The Lips Of Life (WEA)

They produce some highly memorable soul with bubbling horns and piano, and some extremely dodgy electro-junk full of zappy sound effects. But the really brilliant (har har) thing about Brilliant is you never get bored.
Smash Hits

Brilliant are groovy but lazy, a time bomb on a *very* long fuse.
Sounds

THE BRILLIANT CORNERS
What's In A Word (SS 20)
The Brilliant Corners and their pinky and perky ethics are nothing less than adorable.
Melody Maker

This is 25 minutes of sad, silly, love songs and I for one haven't had enough of them. Buy these true-life stories ahead of the other fiction romances.
NME

JAMES BROWN
Gravity (Scotti Bros)
Lots of highly polished disco, soul during which JB can let loose his joyful, throaty squawks to his heart's content.
Smash Hits

It's polished, it's commercial – but it doesn't cut the mustard . . .
Melody Maker

So, once again, just when we thought the finale might be in sight, James Brown, bless his flares and five-inch turn-ups, has discarded his cloak of many years and returned, both dramatically and effectively, to centre stage.
NME

CHUCK BROWN AND THE SOUL SEARCHERS
Live Double Album
(Rhythm King Records)
We are talking heat-baked funk, injected with some sticky swing and sprinkled with the coolest of non-boring jazz brass and blues vocals. Chuck's voice stretches from the relaxed to the acute, his lyrics crack from his mouth like mineral and glass tumbling from an exploded Perrier bottle, all in slo-mo of course.
Sounds

BUCKS FIZZ
Writing On The Wall (Polydor)
How can you possibly hate the Fizz, eh gang? They are so determinedly uncool – more so now that they've dumped vixtress-in-chief Jay Aston – that you have to admire their brave ideological stance, don't you, eh gang? And as for their music – well, of course, it's awesomely brilliantly conceived pop music performed with relish and enough ticklish production tricks to distract attention from their vile clothes.
Smash Hits

The four members of Bucks Fizz defy critical analysis. There is little artistic merit and they seem expressionless people devoid of character or charisma.
Melody Maker

KATE BUSH
The Whole Story (EMI)
The Whole Story is big, black subversive pop, more useful and more enjoyable than the constipated jangling of a hundred and one little lads with big mouths and even bigger clothes allowances.
NME

Over the last nine years and five albums, Kate Bush, the most beautiful woman-child in Kent, has matured into quite the most sensual, expressive and creative artist this country can now boast. And this 12-track compilation of hits and near misses more than adequately documents her evolution . . .
Sounds

Far from being "The Whole Story", this collection reveals nothing . . . which is, of course, the crux of her appeal. And it's magnificent.
Melody Maker

DAVID BYRNE
Soundtrack From True Stories (EMI)
It's exactly the sort of music that people would play in lifts if the whole world had gone completely bonkers – in other words vaguely interesting, slightly disturbing and rather inconsequential.
Smash Hits

The whole album is a scrapbook of muzak in its various chameleon manifestations.
Sounds

CAMEO
Word Up (Club)
. . . while a lot of the second side slips into slightly routine dance music, side one contains two of the most indescribably brilliant songs ever – 'Word Up' itself (which sounds good even when you're not looking at Larry Blackmon's red cod-piece) and the more melodic next single, 'Candy'.
Smash Hits

But it couldn't outshine Cameo's music. For better or for worse, one of the lasting memories of 1986 must be that of Larry Blackmon's codpiece . . . Its title track remains the year's most distinctive slug of the dancefloor libido, while its successor, 'Candy', is smoother, sweeter, but no less effective.
Sounds

Word Up is here. It's as wordlessly effective as Larry Blackmon's shiny red genital crash-helmet. It causes laughter and movement with disarming ease. It is beyond words.
NME

Come off it, Larry, we all know what you'd really be most comfortable wearing! Spangly satin jump suits with sailcloth flares.
Melody Maker

STAN CAMPBELL
Stan Campbell (WEA)
He might not thank me for saying this, but the tone and phrasing are somewhat reminiscent of Michael McDonald . . .
Record Mirror

It's "interesting" rather than especially "good" . . .
Smash Hits

A grave disappointment.
Melody Maker

THE CARDIACS
Big Ship (Alphabet)
. . . If your taste is for the grotesque, then the Rocky Horror Cardiac Parody Request Spot could be just the tonic you need.
Sounds

Arrest these peasants before they get another chance.
Melody Maker

CARMEL
The Falling (London)
The Falling is a rare glimpse of bloodied realism. And by Harry, the girl carries it off by disguising half of them as swinging jazz railway tracks.
Sounds

Spotty though it may be, this is a brave and often fascinating album that manages the uncanny trick of sounding sophisticated yet rough-hewn, and always keeps one secret back for the next play.
Melody Maker

. . . throughout it all there's an undercurrent of bittersweet melancholia as poignant as weeping behind dark glasses.
NME

JEAN CARNE
Legendary Tracks
(Streetsounds)
Listen to absolutely anything on this album for subtle, mature, superior soul.
Melody Maker

Carne swoops and coos and growls, punch-drunk on her own vocal mobility, particularly when lacing G&H's Philly fizz.
NME

KIM CARNES
Light House (EMI America)
All the rough edges Kim Carnes' voice might suggest have been smoothed out and rounded down, the tense threat of danger which made 'Bette Davis Eyes' so appealing has been surgically removed and all that remains is that fundamentally country/MOR safety and security.
Sounds

. . . the material here – bar-room rockers and inconsequential, depressive ballads dressed up with studio trickery – offers little scope to the cracked beauty of the Carnes' voice.
NME

NICK CAVE AND THE BAD SEEDS
Your Funeral . . . My Trial
(Mute)
Theatrical, maybe; blameless, no.
Melody Maker

With *Your Funeral,* Nick Cave reaches a pinnacle of wilful tragedy and exhibits his blackest portrait yet of the thwarted outsider stalking the edge of town.
Sounds

He is probably the only man more openly religious than Cliff Richard . . .
Melody Maker

A CERTAIN RATIO
Force (Factory)
A Certain Radio, once a forced laugh, have contracted a smile and it suits them.
NME

Manchester's former mutant soulboys are at yet another turning point. Captured over eight tracks is the current flux, the left-field delights and MOR workouts . . .
Sounds

You *can* teach an old dog new tricks! After eternities painstakingly, sweatily marking out small spaces, jogging on the spot, A Certain Ratio have jerked from their sleeves a fine pop record, a forceful push. A real advance!
Melody Maker

EUGENE CHADBOURNE
Corpses Of Foreign Wars
(Fundamental)
A witty, silly, barbed album which realizes the historical supremacy of satire over the soapbox as a tool with which to bludgeon away at the Establishment.
Sounds

Vermin Of The Blues
(Fundamental)
By magnifying and exaggerating the redness of the neck, the lonesomeness of the heart, the meanness of the boogie, it is as if he wants to uncover the rabid, weird pulse that has determined rock 'n' roll since the beginning of time. Chuckle and worry.
Melody Maker

THE CHAMELEONS
Strange Times (Geffen)
The Chameleons make the most ordinary records in the world, that's about their only distinction.
Sounds

CHINA CRISIS
What Price Paradise (Virgin)
This is an album of rare pearls and no real passion. Its urbanity is overwhelming. It is almost impossible not to think of it as a James Last LP for those too young or too damned Habitat-hip to know better.
Melody Maker

China Crisis have abandoned their own distinctive, very English pop sensibility . . . What they've moved on to is an understated, largely bland, stylized and sophisticated rock music which has a spiritual home on the West Coast of America.
Sounds

China Crisis are a polite band. Worried about jagged edges, loose chords and jarring vocals, they airbrush their songs with a vapid wash which makes them slip down so easily you begin to wonder if you were listening to anything at all.
NME

ANNE CLARK
Hopeless Cases (10)
They should only let Johnny Gielgud and Johnny Betjeman read out loud on records.
NME

The music often struggles to make up the deficit in emotion lost by speaking rather than singing, but this is Anne's best album yet.
No 1

Angry but restrained, exasperated but in control, she reflects and redefines all our own frustrations and fears.
Sounds

THE COCTEAU TWINS
The Moon And The Melodies
(4AD)
The Moon And The Melodies? What melodies? . . . this is nothing more than "credible" wall-paper music for cry-baby toffs.
Smash Hits

This is the sort of record that it is difficult to describe without swearing. I rather like it although I can't imagine what I'm going to do with it.
NME

. . . you could shovel adjectives into its bottomless depths till the end of time, and you'd still be floundering, drowning in its beauty.
Melody Maker

COIL
Horse Rotorvator (K422)
Put preconceptions aside and enjoy.
Melody Maker

A qualified success, but often giddy.
Sounds

THE COLOURFIELD
Deception (Chrysalis)
There's no excuse for tarting up what is in reality a mildly pleasant pop record and trying to convince us that the fun has to come through such muso seriousness.
Melody Maker

Occasionally the result is too dreary for words but mostly it's quite a dense, fascinating and wonderfully miserable record.
Smash Hits

Even if it is Terry Hall's final attempt "to make as much money as possible and to piss-off for ever," *Deception* still puts The Colourfield right up there with The The and Dexys as purveyors of quality pop music.
Sounds

. . . either a joke that's fallen flat or a kitschy piece of heart-wrenching without the heart.
Q

THE COMSAT ANGELS
Chasing Shadows (Island)
The Comsat Angels' songwriting makes much of little, economically using ideas and sounds to create an overall impression that is fleeting yet subtle and soothing.
Sounds

CONCRETE BLONDE
Concrete Blonde (IRS)
It's all very '60s with its sharing of secrets and whispers of love. The music is gentle, easily consumed, yet it's not *too* comfortable.
Sounds

Happily, these bizarros trot out arrestingly picturesque portraits of urban squalor, their simple axis reverberating with a solid sense of sparse adventure; lean guitars stretching out to subvert the *overt* pop tones.
Melody Maker

ALICE COOPER
Constrictor (MCA)
Why do these middle-aged, paunch-belaboured, otherwise eminently

respectable businessmen feel a need to run around screaming at the top of their lungs about snakes, teenage frankensteins, terminators, gorillas and alley cats to the rhythm of a *boom chugga boom chugga chugga boom* drumbeat? . . . His performance is too tame and serene to appeal to all but the most sanitized of his genre.
NME

The hard rock equivalent of elevator music, laughably old fashioned, a hopeless stereotype of the genre.
Sounds

JULIAN COPE
Saint Julian (Island)
On his last LP, *Fried,* Julian Cope sounded so barking mad that one wasn't really expecting to hear from him again. But here he is again, sounding more accessible, poppy and *healthy* than he has done for ages.
Smash Hits

Can we cope with a leather clad pop pope? I'd like to think so.
Sounds

. . . for those of you waiting for this perfect fool to stop believing he's turned into a shopping arcade for a minute and start tapping into some less possessed pop sensibility, this could be your first, colourwashed Cope trip. Enjoy the ride.
Melody Maker

. . . has Christ come back as an acid casualty who collects Dinky toys and lives in Tamworth, Staffordshire? . . . the ability to behave like a big-headed prat has never done anyone in pop music any harm.
Q

ELVIS COSTELLO
AND THE ATTRACTIONS
Blood And Chocolate (Imp)
Like rock, Costello can find no new surprises in his head, so he re-visits the haunts of old records and themes with the made energy of a creative mind in thrall to its medium.
Sounds

. . . these new songs are much more punchy, direct and angry than he's been for years, rather like the stuff he used to do back in the late '70s.
Smash Hits

If *Blood And Chocolate* represents a return of sorts to the grit and bile that marked Costello's early albums, it is a welcome resurrection of a tough streak that has been underplayed since the turn of the decade.
NME

MARY COUGHLAN
Under The Influence (WEA)
Her voice is deep and rich and full of sex, and she comes over as both tough and touching.
Sounds

CRIME & THE CITY
SOLUTION
Room Of Lights (Mute)
This is where the blues have finally found asylum in the late '80s. It isn't a party.
Sounds

Through the wooden walls of a broken-down, trashed-up shack we hear a band play, a swampy blues band as dirty as the mess that surrounds us. They're playing a music of inordinate stilted and stuttering strength with tortured melody and an offbeat backroom crashing that jerks our feet through the mire . . . Maddened by the incongruity and weakened by our hurtling we storm from the hut and bury our heads in a steaming heap of alligator droppings. But the music *still* sounds brilliant.
Melody Maker

BRENDAN CROKER & THE
5 O'CLOCK SHADOWS
Boat Trips In The Bay
(Red Rhino)
Simply the best yet from the unshaven kings of West Yorkshire Creole pop . . . It's a stunningly spacious album; bold, brilliant and utterly mad! There's no passengers on this boat.
Record Mirror

THE CULT
Electric (Beggars Banquet)
This time they've scampered farther back along rock's lost highway to the late '60s and a time when fuzzy wah-wah guitars squeal akimbo, voices growl about "revolution", and everyone makes as much noise as they possibly can. This is an altogether more satisfactory state of affairs . . .
Smash Hits

Musically it sounds like a trip through the styles of the seventies from sub-T. Rex catchphrasing, through acid-scrambled

nonsense . . . to full blown Led Zeppelin bombast.
NME

Electric isn't pastiche – The Cult are too stupid and strutting and desperate for that. *Electric* is serious plagiarism and, if Jimmy Page has any wits left about him at all, writs should be arriving at Astbury's attorney any day now.
Melody Maker

. . . the neanderthal machismo evinced here in both the brutally efficient heavy rock swagger and the angel/whore lyricism deserves a spanking.
Q

CULTURE CLUB
This Time (Virgin)
. . . mostly it's a happy reminder of just how good, inventive and joyful a pop group Culture Club were at their best.
Smash Hits

. . . we should look back and admire this colourfulness – they always avoided the po-faced Bowie-isms of other grey-cheeked pop groups.
NME

Whether this mess of melting sugar lumps is valid isn't the thing – whether or not you can stomach it *is*.
Melody Maker

. . . the album has the complexion of a chicken plumped up by regular injections of water; not quite what it seems at first, but fairly tasty for all that.
Sounds

THE CURE
Kiss Me, Kiss Me, Kiss Me
(Fiction)
Now, in *Kiss Me, Kiss Me, Kiss Me,* they've made a rough, almost shoddy album full of fuzzy guitars and incompetent singing – slightly less fashionable in 1987 than admitting you're one of The Thompson Twins. They've also compounded their tactical mistake by making *Kiss Me . . .* a double album. Funny then, that despite all that this is a consistently good and frequently brilliant record.
Q

CURIOSITY KILLED THE CAT
Keep Your Distance . . .
(Phonogram)
. . . we're dealing with the shallow meaningfulness and subdued bounciness of semi-clever pop. No doubt these are experiences drawn from real life, delivered straight from the soul – the problem is that these are lives and souls that are fundamentally mediocre.
Melody Maker

. . . as the songs themselves are all extremely similar they do tend to blur into a soothing, jazzy, giant one-ness, pleasant and relaxing but not earth-shatteringly memorable. Basically it's designer background music.
Smash Hits

With their music a dripping tap of pallid monotone pop that has an affection if not a knack for funk, all eyes and ears are on Ben. (I've told you already, he's the one with the

beret who's always in Mandy Smith's photos).
Sounds

CUTTING CREW
Broadcast (Siren)
This collection of feeble melodies and embarrassingly twee lyrics is recommended only for those who like to puzzle over lines like "these four suspicious riders have been circling the borders of your bungalow."
Smash Hits

HOLGER CZUKAY
Rome Remains Rome (Virgin)
Holger's music suggests reverie and moods, it's full of exquisite pleasures. *Rome* is an unusual record, but it's hardly an inaccessible piece of noise.
Sounds

Rome Remains Rome is a perfectly tolerable record, and quite charming at times.
NME

ROGER DALTREY
Can't Wait To See The Movie
(10)
People don't buy records out of charity, Roger. Well, maybe they do, but not yours, old son.
Sounds

THE DAMNED
Anything (MCA)
All very nice if you like this sort of black comedy rock but not much fun otherwise.
Smash Hits

The bombast is fine but lacks any out-and-out vulgarity to launch it. Yearning and overdoing things musically until all is brittle with spit and polish, The Damned appear as gargoyles with expense accounts that know too much and care too little.
Sounds

TERENCE TRENT D'ARBY
Introducing The Hardline According to Terence Trent D'Arby (CBS)
It is a grasping of all great music regardless of style and category. Where D'Arby has the edge is that he has the talent to cross his tracks beautifully and turn this history into his own distinct and dynamic sound.
NME

He's pretty; he's charming, but arrogant; he's smooth; he's sexy; he's soulful (the real thing!); he's credible . . . but he also makes *great* pop records.
Record Mirror

Truly, there's nothing wrong enough with *The Hardline . . .* to lead anyone out of the wilderness and, truly, that's what's wrong with it.
Melody Maker

. . . It's a fine debut that leans into soul and R&B to emerge as fully realized pop for easy mass approval.
Sounds

MILES DAVIS
Tutu (WEA)
The music is often a blank canvas, a cosy foil for Miles to flash his metal against.
NME

Oddly enough, the overall feeling of the album is romantic, despite all the wallops and worms of squabbling sound in the foreground.
Melody Maker

DEACON BLUE
Raintown (CBS)
Raintown doesn't present a group, it merely suggests that you admire its production values.
Q

THE DEAD KENNEDYS
Bedtime For Democracy
(Alternative Tentacles)
"*Bedtime For Democracy*" the press release proudly boasts, "contains 21, yes twenty-one, new songs" and this is true. Unfortunately only three, yes *three*, are any good.
Melody Maker

So by releasing this the DK's are flicking the Vs at those who would like to shut them up. That this record is not entirely wonderful is perhaps but a small point.
Sounds

DEAD OR ALIVE
Mad, Bad And Dangerous To Know (Epic)
Splendid for going bonkers to down your local discotheque but not so splendid for playing just about anywhere else.
Smash Hits

It's outrageously funny and quite brilliant.
No 1

Mad, Bad And Dangerous To Know is a creamy example of modern pop music at its sickening best with overdubs, sexbeat remixes and coy, sniggering fetish songs like the curiously titled 'Come Inside'. And it's a good LP . . .
Sounds

DEEP PURPLE
House Of Blue Light (Polydor)
Deep Purple are lost, static, anachronistic, banking on nostalgia and still milking that same generation's fond loyalty. Consequently, this record is of scant interest to anybody under 25.
Sounds

If any of you can tolerate the idea of Deep Purple, we have been reliably informed this is their weakest album. If you can find it in your heart to *like* Deep Purple then you are as insensitive and self-seeking as they are. You deserve each other.
Melody Maker

THE DEL FUEGOS
Stand Up (London)
. . . The coolest in-car sound for this summer, and about as funky as white folk get these days.
Q

DIED PRETTY
Free Dirt (What Goes On)
. . . Died Pretty eschew the more common *trappings* of great songwriting and go straight to its cerebral and sensual core, returning to it a spirit, a self-respect and a pedigree paralleling that of the best '60s West Coast groups.
Sounds

DIF JUZ
Out Of The Trees (4AD)
Out Of The Trees may have several intriguing romantic atmospheres but ultimately it's like watching leaves fall – meditational but frustrating.
Sounds

Beneath that apparently dull exterior lies nothing. This is a record to kill time to for those who prefer it dead.
Melody Maker

THE DOLPHIN BROTHERS
Catch The Fall (Virgin)
. . . they're Simple Minds with an over-developed sense of ceremony and an under-developed grasp of essential cheap tricks like grandeur and personality.
Melody Maker

BILL DRUMMOND
The Man (Creation)
Thoroughly enchanting, ripe with Celtic sentimentality and telling personal revelations this is surely one of the oddest records of the year . . .
Melody Maker

The Man is a work of humble genius; the best kind.
Sounds

DRUM THEATRE
Everyman (Epic)
"The Drums" on this LP don't sound like anyone, they sound like . . . everyone except not as good.
Smash Hits

Well-meaning but disordered and over-eclectic, *Everyman* falls well short of qualifying for the benefit of the doubt.
Sounds

Everyman communicates less than the average government AIDS commercial.
Melody Maker

Even the drums are dull.
Q

DUKES OF STRATOSPHEAR
Psonic Psunspot (Virgin)
. . . *Psonic Psunspot* is all slithy toves, mimsy borogoves, gyres and gimbles and the mome raths outgrabe.
Melody Maker

DUMPTRUCK
Positively Dumptruck
(Bigtime)
. . . music for bookworms with the earnest sensitivity of poetry majors.
Sounds

DURAN DURAN
Notorious (EMI)
They've abandoned the ostentatious clothing of their high life, Sri Lankan tourist period, the new tone being set by 'Notorious', the least strident, least paranoid single since 'Rio'.
Sounds

It's a study in funk, sludge dredged up from an outmoded notion of what cuts in the clubs. It's a shock I know, but Duran are old-fashioned.
Melody Maker

It didn't hurt me at all to be locked in a room with *Notorious*, as I have a weakness for clever, contrived pop.
NME

BOB DYLAN
Knocked Out Loaded (CBS)
Knocked Out Loaded is shockingly bad. Barely coherent, it is probably his worst album to date, which is saying a lot considering how *Empire Burlesque, Shot Of Love* and *Self Portrait* were all really atrocious.
Melody Maker

SHEILA E
Pride And Passion (WEA)
. . . it is a messy affair that sees her shifting in style much more than is good for her.
Q

STEVE EARLE
AND THE DUKES
Exit O (MCA)
Steve Earle is one mean songwriter, a great singer and a fair player. The Dukes, his band, deliver with a vengeance, painting themselves onto his moods. *Exit O* is an album to keep on playing until it is lodged in your memory immovably.
Sounds

Earle can infect and rehabilitate traditional American mythology, matching its rounded formal instincts with a new spiritual dimension.
NME

For those Southern Baptist fundamentalists to whom even The Boss represents perfidious East Coast intellectualism, Steve Earle is a godsend.
Melody Maker

It is possible that Earle was bundled through the recording sessions at great speed and against his will?
Q

ECHO AND THE BUNNYMEN
Echo And The Bunnymen
(WEA)
Still, actual duff moments are few and far between and a half-decent Echo And The Bunnymen LP is still much better than most.
Smash Hits

. . . the first thing you notice about this album is how quiet it is; back with not so much a hop as a hare-lipped whisper, something which is entirely to their credit . . . The Bunnymen manage a naïve, bewildered innocence that contrasts with the self-deluding religious trance that U2 *still* opt for.
Sounds

. . . this LP is more a testament to the group's laziness and lack of interest in the business than their songwriting skills.
NME

THE EDGE
Captive (Virgin)
. . . it's a soundtrack of incidental music for a film and like most incidental music of any sort it's as dreary as stale yoghurt out of context.
Melody Maker

It is, after all, film music, consequently The Edge turns the volume down and twiddles his fingers gently to produce some beautiful (though rather insubstantial) pieces . . .
Smash Hits

. . . *Captive* stars Oliver Reed.
NME

EINSTÜRZENDE
NEUBAUTEN
Einstürzende Neubauten
(Some Bizzare)
Forget art, this is unadulterated drivel.
Record Mirror

. . . a fine record which will be talked about for months to come.
Sounds

This is music for something like "Aliens 6"
. . .
Melody Maker

ERASURE
The Circus (Mute)
Andy Bell has a voice which, apart from the understandable Moyet comparisons, is sturdy and reliable if a little inflexible.
NME

. . . Andy Bell sounds fatally similar not only to the hot-air balloon Moyet but also the dragon Annie Lennox.
Melody Maker

They're bouncy! They're fun! They start and stop in the right places! Perhaps they do all rely a bit too much on the same *plinka-plinka-plonka* noises, and perhaps Andy Bell does still sound uncannily like Alison Moyet, but they're not going to rub Erasure out very easily!(?)
Smash Hits

Vince Clarke remains one of the great unrecognized geniuses of modern pop.
Q

EU
Future Funk (Be Bop And Fresh)
. . . *Future Funk* captures mainmen Experience Unlimited on the DC Go Go circuit, trucking tracks that now come across somewhat flatly.
NME

EUROPE
The Final Countdown (Epic)
Europe can hardly be described as the most original band around . . . In fact the only surprises are that a) there's a song about the plight of the Cherokee Indian and b) they're Swedish (neither of which is very exciting, really is it?).
Smash Hits

EVERYTHING BUT THE GIRL
The Stars Shine Bright
(blanco y negro)
Caution lines this music like a woolly vest. God knows how they ever got associated with "jazz", or anything other than the mooniest pop music.
Sounds

I've been examining this record with a stethoscope, trying to find some pulse, some surge of life or honest intention, but I'm not sure I've succeeded.
NME

. . . simple, crystal clear melodies that might easily have been written two decades ago by masters of the pop form like Bacharach and David.
Melody Maker

F

FAITH BROTHERS
A Human Sound (Siren)
Like Billy Bragg without the jokes but with a full band plus a Labour Party social club full of strings. *A Human Sound* the Brothers second album, is a gauche combination of crystal clear, strumalong innocuousness and dot to dot rhetoric.
Sounds

I was hoping it was all a wind-up, hoping that the record would yield some interesting if scholarly fruitcakery. But, no, it seems the Brothers are *serious!*
Melody Maker

For some reason, the word that seems to sum up this cheerful, inoffensive, and not excessively striking record is "stocky".
NME

MARIANNE FAITHFULL
Strange Weather (Island)
. . . Jazz and blues semi-standards, each teased out through her distinctive jewelly gravelled voice . . .
Melody Maker

Faithfull really hasn't a voice to speak of, her interpretations rely on vocal method acting.
Sounds

FALCO
Emotional (WEA)
Falco is a dead unlikely pop-star, a shameless, screw-loose wonder without whom the charts would be an even poorer place.
NME

. . . it's difficult to tell *what* he's on about as he rants on in at least five languages (and all at the same time). None of this really matters, though, because this album is packed with outrageously catchy tunes . . .
Smash Hits

. . . the more I hear of the fellow's work, the further I nudge the pointer on the sliding scale away from complete dork in the direction of misunderstood genius.
Sounds

TAV FALCO'S PANTHER BURNS
Behind The Magnolia Curtain
(Fan Club)
. . . a kind of hyper-primitivism, a glorious shambles, rockabilly not so much souped-up as souped all-over-the-shop.
Melody Maker

THE FALL
Bend Sinister
(Beggars Banquet)
One of these days The Fall are going to surprise the world and release a record that *isn't* full of Mark E. Smith droning on twenty-to-the dozen about things that annoy him while scratch guitars, clanky drums and a cheap organ doodle repetitively in the background. But not, er, yet.
Smash Hits

The Fall are often, these days, erroneously put in the dock for the charge of remaining musicaly static. *Bend Sinister* with its soundtracks slithering through a garden of unearthly delights, throws the dock into the bay and drowns the judges in their own rhetoric.
Sounds

The Fall are un-pop too – anti-dance, anti-spectacle, unsensual – but they have carved out a *rival* territory of alien beauty that they can exploit indefinitely.
Melody Maker

And through the dog-eared pages of Roget's Thesaurus Mark Smith chases the English language; with an axe.
NME

FELA ANIKULAPO KUTI
Teacher Don't Teach Me Nonsense (London)
No fire, no venom, despite all he's been through, just vaguely chiding anti-government messages, conveyed with the anger of a postage stamp.
Melody Maker

FELT
Forever Breathes The Lonely Word (Creation)
. . . enchanting, timeless pop tunes – an utter masterpiece of quite *gorgeous*, magical lyrics, well wibbly organ "runs", chinkling guitars and a voice that can't sing in the same way as, say, Lloyd Cole can't sing, but is nevertheless completely mesmerizing.
Smash Hits

Felt haven't re-invented anything, won't change anything . . . But this is a great record.
NME

Forever . . . will never make converts to their weird and wired world, but it will delight the disciples.
Sounds

FIREHOSE
Ragin', Full-On (SST)
They deal in confusion, in the illusory layers which separate emptiness and saturation, jazz and rock, the unfinished and the whole. A subtle sense of quality surrounds each song.
Melody Maker

Great songs, amazing playing. . . the world's best trio.
NME

FIVE STAR
Silk And Steel (RCA)
Slick, quick and corny, this album has everything a couple of decades-worth of chart material is made of, each track calculated and honed to sound pretty much like the one preceding and the one following it.
NME

. . . all in all this 5 Star hot-under-the-collar, should-I-shouldn't-I-screw-you tease must be the highest of high camp because I can't help but collapse in a heap of giggles when these emotional retards (Deniece is over 18!) strut such filthy stuff.
Melody Maker

Silk And Steel comes streamlined and air-brushed, but its fever and cunning makes for poison soul.
Sounds

THE FLAMIN' GROOVIES
One Night Stand (ABC)
This first LP for eight years . . . proves that age has not diminished the Groovie's ability to kick out the jams.
Q

Dear oh dear! Not content with merely re-releasing old stuff, this lot of psychedelic popsters have felt the need to re-record it as well . . . Yuk!
Record Mirror

. . . its undignified inadequacies make it seem less a history, more a comedy, a tragedy even, a grim attestation best left in the private libraries of close friends and trusted relations.
Melody Maker

Completely silly, but then, that's all they ever were.
NME

FLEETWOOD MAC
Tango In The Night
(Warner Bros)
Fleetwood Mac aren't quite dinosaurs yet; more like humpbacked whales – lumbering, huge and a dying breed. While no record collection would be complete without *Rumours*, yours would certainly be more credible without *Tango In The Night*, a collection of 12 very boring, occasionally unlistenable rock songs of the very worst calibre.
Record Mirror

There's a dull, loping pace to just about everything; puerile lyrics and little twiddly keyboard hooks instead of actual tunes.
Sounds

They are the "History Men" of pop: out of date, dressed all wrong, and not funny.
Melody Maker

. . . hardly a comeback to rival that of Bobby Ewing's shower scene . . .
Q

FLESH FOR LULU
Long Live The New Flesh
(Beggars Banquet)
Flesh For Lulu have moved on from leather 'n' cheekbones sleaze to a cultivated and versatile form of rock conservatism.
Q

THE FLYING BURRITO BROTHERS
Dim Lights, Thick Smoke And Loud, Loud Music (Edsel)
Thank the Good Lord that there are people at Demon and Edsel who care enough to put these songs back in our record shops.
NME

JOHN FOGERTY
Eye Of The Zombie
(Warner Bros)
What he doesn't say with words, he says through his guitar and the pulse beat that squeezes your adrenalin up to tickle your spine.
Sounds

The abysmal LP title and the hideous cover are accurate indicators of the generally turgid r 'n' r that dominates this record.
NME

SAMANTHA FOX
Samantha Fox (Jive)
A small step for man, a huge step for lip gloss.
Melody Maker

Samantha Fox sings better than Anita Dobson – official!
Record Mirror

Not really naughty but nicely tawdry.
Sounds

FRANKIE GOES TO HOLLYWOOD
Liverpool(ZTT)
Even the "socially conscious" lyrics are laughable.
NME

The lyrics are the ripest gibberish dotted with words like "sun", "moon", "oceans","hell", "heaven", "sailboats of ice on desert sands" . . .
Melody Maker

Frankie Goes To Hollywood, their trainers, their handlers and everybody else connected with this slab of unexceptional plastic elevator muzak should be made to eat every copy pressed and every sleeve printed. *Liverpool* indeed!
Sounds

ARETHA FRANKLIN
Aretha (Arista)
Aretha is sufficient to nibble on for a few months, but let's hope the main course of a classic album isn't too far away.
Sounds

Recently I've been turning up the radio for *that* voice despite her material; this time round I'll be doing it because of it.
Melody Maker

It bears no roaring champions like *Freeway* or *Zoomin*. But for devotees of La Franklin, it will cause reams of affection to well up.
NME

DOUG E FRESH AND THE GET FRESH CREW
Oh My God (Cool Tempo)
. . . what really shines about this LP is the impressive range of ideas, moods and the sheer musicality of the finished whole . . .
Q

ROBERT FRIPP & THE LEAGUE OF CRAFTY GUITARISTS
Live! (Editions EG)
. . . a kind of pluck-in-cum-seminar in which players of varying levels of experience gather in secluded conditions to participate in various guitar events, or "challenge".
Melody Maker

. . . this is the sort of LP to provide the soundtrack to one of those speeded-up films on the miracles of botany.
NME

FRONT 242
Official Version (Red Rhino)
Front 242 are the worthless flipside of the traditional continental bent for experimentation. Uniformly unsurprising, alarmingly unambitious . . .
Sounds

It's a document that drips cynicism and mocks its listener by confusing the emotive with intellect. Each song is immensely

danceable and endlessly listenable while also being saturated in bloody thuggery.
Melody Maker

FRUITS OF PASSION
Fruits Of Passion (Siren)
Fruits Of Passion are in the grand tradition of British earnestness, soulful grit and shirtsleeves-rolled banality.
NME

THE FUGS
Starpeace (New Rose)
Starpeace sells itself (or not as the case may be) as a slice of social conscience/incontinence-drenched "Contemporary Opera", when it is in fact that old perishing nuisance The Rock Concept Album.
Melody Maker

FULL FORCE
Full Force Get Busy One Time (CBS)
Full Force don't really transcend categories, they just filch various bits – metal guitar, jazzy flourishes, the odd cosmetic touch of hip-hop scratch or echo – and squeeze them onto the same soundspace.
Melody Maker

The most important good things about Full Force are that a) two members are called Shy Shy and Bowlegged Lou, b) they shout out *"Don't even try it . . . word!"* a few times . . .
Sounds

FURNITURE
The Wrong People (Stiff)
It is a wonderful swirling, whirling potful of different sounds . . . And then to top it all there's the flugel horn – the flutesomely crooning flugel horn. From now on, no household LP should be without one.
Smash Hits

. . . a lush spiky fruity whirl of pop flying spontaneously from glib to grandiose to godlike.
Melody Maker

PETER GABRIEL
So (Charisma)
The constant struggle between Gabriel's intellect and his gut reactions is probably never going to produce a perfect album but it will give you some pretty fine highs along the way.
Sounds

DIAMANDA GALAS
Saint Of The Pit (Mute)
Saint Of The Pit contains an unparalleled purity, it is the gift of inspired spirituality working through the mastery of one of the most evocative and talented composers around.
NME

My problem with Diamanda Galas is never knowing when it's *appropriate* to listen. Not in company, for sure (murders conversation). But scarcely bearable on your own either. It's a rare day when my constitution is so hardy, my spirit so robust, that I'm eager to take the plunge.
Melody Maker

THE GAP BAND
Gap Band 8 (RCA)
For the most part these are just slow smoochy ballads all about the pursuit of love or – sniff, sniff – the loss of it . . .
Smash Hits

. . . a product of stunning anonymity.
Sounds

. . . this is far better than any album with the utterly useless title *Gap Band 8* could ever expect to be.
Q

BORIS GARDINER
Everything To Me (Revue)
Boris Gardiner as we all know and love him – warm, cuddly, soft, sensual, and full of sexist shit. Hang the bloody deejay.
Melody Maker

. . . Boris himself still looks like a member of the 1970 Brazilian World Cup squad.
Smash Hits

BOB GELDOF
Deep In The Heart Of Nowhere (Phonogram)
Sir Bob tells us that he very much wants to abandon being a professional saint and get back to being a pop star. Which is all very well, but the sad thing is that he doesn't write very good pop songs any more.
Smash Hits

I see that you've made a bit of effort with the old lyrics, but that doesn't help when the muzak is so obviously not happening. And you still can't sing, but you probably know that.
NME

Charity never really begins at home, so maybe Geldof won't be too taken aback if some of the critical fraternity divert themselves briefly from his great efforts to relieve the world of some of its suffering and square up to the uncomfortable task of declaring his first post-famine relief solo album an unqualified turkey.
Melody Maker

GENERAL PUBLIC
Hand To Mouth (Virgin)
. . . never have so many trip-wire rhythms, mountainous melodies and subtle words been wasted on such an anaemic, lethargic and turgid veneer of sound.
Sounds

. . . an LP that you might call "boring" if it wasn't so tedious that you wouldn't even dignify it with classification.
NME

. . . as an exercise in taking pop a few quick-steps further, *Hand To Mouth* stands head and shoulders above even the very

best of the rest.
Melody Maker

BOY GEORGE
Solid (Virgin)
For more than half of side two George sings
in a cheeky low gravelly voice over songs
which either sound like old Motown
stompers ('Just Ain't Enough') or '60s group
T. Rex . . .
Smash Hits

. . . some of his songs are ruined by a gritty
vocal treatment which sounds like a cross
between Tina Turner and Lou Rawls with
laryngitis.
Record Mirror

. . . a surprisingly strong record that draws
from influences as diverse as The Doors . . .
and classic soul . . .
Sounds

. . . he sounds more Ringo Starr than Tom
Jones . . .
Melody Maker

. . . he's beginning to lean more in the
direction of Billy Idol than Liberace.
Q

GEORGIA SATELLITES
Georgia Satellites (Elektra)
Fuelled on one part electricity and nine parts
Jack Daniels, the sound they are now
making is a God-almighty bar-room brawling
racket of the most *holy* kind. This record is
quite simply the best stomping, dirty,
carefree rock 'n' roll album I've ever heard.
Sounds

Imagine a musical *Gone With The Wind*
starring Status Quo, all Stratocasters and
southern accents, and that's the Georgia
Satellites.
NME

GIRLSCHOOL
Nightmare At Haple Cross
(GWR)
You can start where you like on this record
but you'll always end up with screeching
guitars and a drummer who's obviously only
playing two drums All Of The Time.
NME

PHILIP GLASS
Dancepieces (CBS)
Using his customary mix of electronic and
classical instruments Glass has
demonstrated again that building music,
lego-style, around repetitive phrases need
not be monotonous.
Q

THE GO-BETWEENS
Tallulah (Beggars Banquet)
. . . characteristically uneven, yielding wheat
and chaff in varying degrees. Once again, a
shambolic brilliance sits cheek-by-jowl with
an almost wilful sobriety.
Q

THE GODFATHERS
Hit By Hit (Corporate Image)
Their name, their well-dressed suits, their
Brylcreemed hair, their classic idea of cool
and their hard R&B pop all recall the misty
early sixties of *Room At The Top* and the
Edgar Wallace mysteries. Everything they
do captures a little English legend.
Melody Maker

THE GOLDEN PALOMINOS
Visions Of Excess (Celluloid)
This record is overwhelming; I had to play it
before it ate me.
NME

Visions Of Excess is a great, regressive step
into the land of the grey giants. It may be a
trick of the light, but for a moment, the
mountains appear to move . . .
Melody Maker

GO WEST
Dancing On The Couch
(Chrysalis)
Mechanically constructed with a spray-job
second to none, it's a thoroughly safe and
serviceable sound comfortably cruising the
B-roads between rock and pop.
NME

Evidently inspired by Lionel Richie's
Dancing On The Ceiling.
Record Mirror

. . . Go West appear to have moved on a
frontier or two, and their new home suits
them.
Q

JAKI GRAHAM
Breaking Away (EMI)
And I do like the way she dresses, so
modern and . . . well, *independent.*
Sounds

Yes, I know she wore that rubber dress and
everything and you COULDN'T see a panty
line, but I really think she should have left it
under her bed where it belongs.
Melody Maker

GRANDMASTER FLASH
Ba-Dop-Boom-Bang (Elektra)
. . . there are fully 14 tracks here . . . and all
of them sounding more like ideas for things
yet to be recorded than like well-finished
works.
Q

It's nice to see some humour and the
positive attitudes of 'I Am Somebody' and
'Get Yours'; as opposed to the sexism and
violence apparently so hip to many rappers
these days.
Record Mirror

What's left then is an extremely rich, slick
and sly album that borrows from all sorts of
sources, and employs a rich parade of
sorcery. Most notably, the Parliament/
Funkadelic squeeze and sleaze on the
preposterously silly 'I Smell Your
Underarms'.
Melody Maker

GRANGE HILL CAST
Grange Hill – The Album
(BBC)
If there has ever been anything more bizarre
in the history of popular music than *Grange
Hill*'s Imelda singing Cyndi Lauper's 'Girls
Just Wanna Have Fun', it is probably
Grange Hill's Banksie singing Dire Straits'
'The Walk Of Life' . . .
Smash Hits

EDDY GRANT
Born Tuff (Ice)
. . . *Born Tuff* is packed with listenable, toe-
tapping, bouncy tunes; even though Mr
Grant appears on the sleeve in a series of
defiant, straight-faced, hard-man poses
(with and without Raybans).
NME

Up at the recording studio Eddy is horrified
to find that he's lost the tapes that go
"brmmbubadumHEY!" on all his records,
and his A-Z of Brixton streets got lost in the
sea that morning . . . The only way out is
International Rock. Yes, that's it, MTV will
love it, all he needs is a few "raunchy" guitar
solos, lots of words about what nice weather
we're having, and a macho pun title like
Born Tuff.
Melody Maker

AL GREEN
Soul Survivor (A&M)
Old man Al's extraordinary vocal acrobatics
on the stock cabaret number 'He Ain't
Heavy' are more suited to Vegas than the
pulpit. In fact, it's an altogether
embarrassing experience.
Sounds

Green is surely the most laid-back, most
sensual preacher ever to warn against the
primrose path.
NME

GUNS 'N' ROSES
Appetite For Destruction
(Geffen)

It's a gruelling business wading through their creations, trying to think of some world where what they do could be seen as having even the slightest point . . .
Melody Maker

Peppered with a hundred expletives and held together by the *krunch!* of a million riffs, *Appetite For Destruction* is a screaming anti-pop celebration from beginning . . .
Sounds

GWEN GUTHRIE
Good To Go Lover (Polydor)

I've heard it all before, a bit fresher, somewhere else. But it's all so immaculately and personably sung that I play it more often than anything else around at the moment.
Melody Maker

Big girls don't cry as Gwen will testify. But, if you're hoping to find some real emotion, some tear stains and love pains, well, this just ain't the place.
NME

This record may pay a few bills but it also mortgages her soul.
Sounds

HALF MAN HALF BISCUIT
Back Again In The DHSS
(Probe Plus)

As this posthumous collection (basically it includes everything that wasn't on that first album) picks its way through the Indian summer of the best band from Liverpool since The Real Thing, you soon remember just why you called plain old *Back In The DHSS* the best debut release since *The Clash.*
Sounds

Every band should do what Half Man Half Biscuit did. Appear, be brilliant, leave. With one album at each end.
Melody Maker

. . . they show a healthy horror of a world . . . where adverts pretend that people have

peaches on cornflakes and where pop music is taken ever so seriously.
Q

DARYL HALL
Three Hearts In The Happy Ending Machine (RCA)

Overflowing with the type of deep soul which is more usually found in a bottle of after-shave, *Three Hearts In The Happy Ending Machine* will entrance those swinging young things who commute daily to computer and advertising companies.
NME

Soul should talk in emotional tongues. *Three Hearts* speaks like the Stock Exchange.
Sounds

DEBBIE HARRY
Rockbird (Chrysalis)

. . . plenty of the aggressive sprightly pop songs that Blondie used to do so well, the odd slightly swoonsome ballad and a couple of throwaway disco songs. How very nice it is to have her back.
Smash Hits

Her voice still reeks of sex as it flits from nymphomaniacal squeals of delight to chilling allure . . . Having suffered pale imitations for so long it's just sweet to welcome back the real thing.
Sounds

Debbie Harry coming out of retirement is rather like a middle-aged housewife getting a new hairdo and trying to go on a Club 18-30 holiday.
Record Mirror

Most of the album sounds indistinguishable from the latest Kim Wilde offering (sweet irony!) or a de-mystified Madonna . . .
NME

The question is, really, will a generation of 15 year olds reared on the output of Ciccone and Wilde – crudely-chiselled pretendresses to Debbie's glam throne – appreciate the real thing, now that she's back?
Melody Maker

HEAD
A Snog On The Rocks (Demon)

Combining swashbuckling pirate chic with the blackly be-leathered look, Head ruthlessly plunder several centuries of popular song idioms and swagger with the assorted arrogance of everyone from Vincent and Presley to Adam Ant and Billy Idol.
Sounds

Quite whether all those wayward jawbones and that stylized oikishness actually adds up to anything is unfortunately rather more of a mystery.
Melody Maker

HEAD OF DAVID
LP (Blast First)

See-sawing wildly between madness and self-immolation, their rapid-fire attack is a murderously *volcanic* melodic assassination attempt, featuring feedback as spinal curvative, plus "vocals" – more your average torture victim – veering towards the neanderthal.
Melody Maker

LP was the only vinyl to turn metal guitars mental again *and* say something worthwhile.
Sounds

This *LP* isn't exactly easy listening: crazed vocals screaming out despair over and over again, painting desolate landscapes of little hope and unrelenting submission; heavy metal guitars wrenching out riffs where you'd

imagine none would want to tread; grey surburban life EXPLODED into multi-coloured noise.
NME

HEART
Bad Animals (Capitol)
. . . yet another unpleasant dose of American stadium-rock, its large and expensively processed sound rolling around in all-too-familiar and always uninteresting circles.
Q

HEAVEN 17
Pleasure One (Virgin)
Heaven 17's decline since *Penthouse & Pavement* appears to be complete. They have really reached the bottom rung with this drab collection of neutered funk.
NME

Music, business and media alike have caught up with them. Heaven 17's misery is that they are intelligent young men who realize they've already nothing left to say.
Sounds

. . . they've opted to recoil into a semi-rocky "realism", of sorts, but it's boggy, well-trodden ground and they sink ignominiously.
Melody Maker

THE JIMI HENDRIX EXPERIENCE
Live At Winterland (Polydor)
Indie insects! Grebo gerbils! R&B runts! Listen to this, and you'll not only wonder why you ever bothered to make music, but you'll also wonder why you were ever *born*.
Melody Maker

NONA HENDRYX
Female Trouble (EMI America)
Female Trouble for all its gimmicky graphics and striking cover, is just too intense for total mainstream acceptance.
Record Mirror

Female Trouble attempts to frame an old-fashioned pelvic thrust of a voice in a high-tech market-crossover setting.
Sounds

HE SAID
Hail (Mute)
These arty pop record probings probably would've sounded very deep to most of us in 1978 but eight years later this dirge will only be listened to by lifelong post-punkers.
NME

With time and a conservation of ideas, He Said could create some engaging pop music that fulfils both the demands of the senses and the intellect. But until then, *Hail* will do just fine.
Sounds

NICK HEYWARD
Postcards From Home (Arista)
Nick seems to have finally kissed goodbye the chirpy pop songs and cheeky grins that Haircut 100 used to specialize in. Instead he has become An Adult – with distressing results.
Smash Hits

But neither he nor we can escape from the fact that Nick is happiest with rinky-dink ballads in which he can hang his sensitivity out to dry.
Melody Maker

. . . I sense COMPROMISE writ large across this release.
NME

HOLGER HILLER
Oben Im Eck (Mute)
Oben Im Eck is truly cathartic in the sense that those feelings aroused are beyond ones of that duality of pity and terror acted upon by his indie-peers.
NME

A cerebral rather than physical or emotional catharsis, *Oben Im Eck* is brilliant but not ultimately satisfying.
Sounds

ROBYN HITCHCOCK
Invisible Hitchcock
(Glass Fish)
Most people make the mistake of comparing Robyn Hitchcock to Syd Barratt, very few of them realize that he actually *is* Syd Barratt.
Melody Maker

Hitchcock revels in the ability to see both the beautiful face across the table *and* the cold baked beans on the plate in front of him. His near-as-dammit unique gift is the strength to use both these images when spontaneously getting up on that table and bursting into song.
Sounds

ROBYN HITCHCOCK AND THE EGYPTIANS
Elements Of Light (Glass Fish)
The world-weary delivery of wacko lyrics places Mr Hitchcock somewhere between Julian Lennon and a freak accident, which is more promising than it sounds.
NME

Musically speaking, it's-not-very-interesting psychedelic folk-pop, with an ethereal feel. Imagine the cast of *The Archers* doing *Sergeant Pepper*.
Record Mirror

Hitchcock's professional jerkiness *can* grow grinding, but this stays the right side of hysterical. Crack-brained convincing in fact.
Sounds

HOLLYWOOD BEYOND
If (WEA)
. . . more cluttered than cool.
Q

HOODOO GURUS
Blow Your Cool! (Chrysalis)
They've got a hole, it's a nice hole, and they can make a noise in it. A big happy racket with a crew of dancing maniacs hooting along, the sun postponing sleep for a few extra hours to stay and hear another one . . .
Melody Maker

Blow Your Cool! deserves every hackneyed cliché you can find: red hot, high energy, *bitchin'*.
Sounds

The Hoodoo Gurus' third album offers proof that a maniacal rock 'n' roll flourishes still, albeit in Australia.
Q

HOT CHOCOLATE
The Very Best Of Hot Chocolate (EMI)
ABC always wanted to be Hot Chocolate; Spandau Ballet *should* have wanted to be Hot Chocolate; any other chart hopeful should buy this album and *worship*.
Melody Maker

WHITNEY HOUSTON
Whitney (Arista)
At least five of the eleven tracks that make up *Whitney* are destined to become smash hit singles, and yet the album hangs together

in perfect diversity.
Record Mirror

You'll be glad to know her cats get a thank you in the six mile long credit list, however.
Smash Hits

. . . young Whitney is making a determined bid not simply to grow up, but to be *old*.
Q

THE HUMAN LEAGUE
Crash (Virgin)
. . . Phil and his chums making out like Minneapolis funksters, and nobody scoring exceptional marks for lyrics, the only consistent factor is a beat which marches relentlessly on through every number.
Sounds

. . . I've tried it all ways, morning, noon and night, drunk and sober, alone and in company, searching for that wink of wit, that cheeky chortle, that look that says they know what they're doing and everything's okay and on line but *still Crash* sounds crap.
Melody Maker

Big Philip is never further than a chorus away, laying down the law – *"Everyone is going to a party"* in the telling tones of a miserable get who gives the impression that he'd sooner be at home making fairy cakes.
NME

HURRAH!
Tell God I'm Here (Kitchenware)
When they're not battling between rock's loud chest-beating and pop's clever hooklines, Hurrah! are charging through the demands of daytime radio like phoney Vikings, pillaging and raping but never really ruling their domain.
Sounds

Hurrah! are big! bold! brassy! bursting with bloody brilliance and berfect bop! Or even perfect pop, a mysterious perfection blessed by the critics but eluded by God, better known as the Major Record Industry.
No 1

How they get away with this shuffling eclecticism and remain hip is something of a mystery.
Melody Maker

Excuse me, God, but there's this group you should know about.
Q

HÜSKER DÜ
Warehouse:
Songs And Stories (WEA)
Hüsker Dü are ecstatic, visionary, with all the lyricism and gilded pop splinters of the early '70s group Love. Indispensable.
No 1

. . . this music is psychedelia without drugs, a rock that has left behind loins, juice, even heat, and found a new, frosty kind of intensity. A celestial impulse.
Melody Maker

THE ICICLE WORKS
If You Want To Defeat Your
Enemy Sing His Song
(Beggars Banquet)
. . . a collection of, erm, massive rock anthems along the same lines as early Simple Minds or even (deep breath) U2.
Smash Hits

And whilst it's no disaster, there's little here that's *special*.
Sounds

BILLY IDOL
Whiplash Smile (Chrysalis)
This is an ode to peroxide.
NME

Thirty years of age, *still* one of the best-looking people on the planet, *still* creating quite sumptuous squealaway rock pop tunes and *still* with the only sneer in rock you can actually *hear*.
Smash Hits

Whiplash Smile is a perfect eighties response to the panicking realization that originality's no longer an option in pop – it could have been parody but it plumps for authenticity instead and there's *true* grit, *true*

glitter, true honest-to-goodness dumb faith to this record, a touching homage to a lost cause.
Melody Maker

IMMACULATE FOOLS
Dumb Poet (A&M)
Don't let this LP into your life.
Melody Maker

JAMES INGRAM
Never Felt So Good (Qwest)
Plush soul, a little over-polished for my taste, too full of its own sophistication, adept but not inspired. It could be *anybody*.
Sounds

IN TUA NUA
Vaudeville (Virgin)
In Tua Nua rope desire, love and evil into an indifferent lump to be stuck under the kitchen table. Big subjects and large landscaped melodies turn the epic into a stiff formulaic pose Bono might blush at.
Melody Maker

In Tua Nua have assimilated the more obvious purveyors of the decade's commercially viable rock music, from Simple Minds to The Pretenders . . . and added nothing of their own bar seamless technical proficiency and their folk tokenism.
Sounds

TIPPA IRIE
Is It Really Happening To Me
(UK Bubblers)
As a central figure in the renaissance of reggae MCing along with Smiley Culture, Tippa has a sure-tongued grasp of the need for lyrical variety *and* musical open-mindedness. Pop percolates through these grooves but not at the expense of the idiom's roots.
Sounds

Turn that noise up!
NME

IRON MAIDEN
Somewhere In Time (EMI)
Although we are informed that *Somewhere* takes HM forward into the '90s, in fact it leaves it where it always has been – floundering in 1974.
NME

To the fans *Somewhere In Time* . . . will be

as reassuring as a *Kerrang!* through the letterbox, as comforting as Tommy Vance on a Friday night, and homely as roast beef every Sunday lunchtime.
Sounds

IT BITES
The Big Lad In The Windmill
(Virgin)
I didn't expect so many words about honesty, men crying or being upset.
NME

. . . sometimes it's quite stirring. Then, however, one remembers how ultimately stultifying this kind of music was, is and will always be.
Melody Maker

Like being hit on the head by a flying dustcart while swimming in the Dead Sea, It Bites are unexpected and by me, at least, unwanted.
Sounds

IT'S IMMATERIAL
Life's Hard And Then You Die
(Siren)
This could well be the most miserable album title of the decade but never mind because the record itself shows that It's Immaterial write jolly good pop songs.
Smash Hits

Let's just say it's very good.
Sounds

JOE JACKSON
Will Power (A&M)
It's not that you resent Joe's insistence on trying to widen his musical outlook and escape the pop scramble with all its cheesy trimmings. It's just that, once in a while, you too would like to be able to derive some pleasure from his costly and daffy whims.
Sounds

At first we all thought he was Costello; then he became Cab Calloway, before turning into Cole Porter, and now this year's model. He's Leonard Bernstein.
NME

A soundtrack looking for a movie.
Melody Maker

As a musician working out from the field of popular music, Jackson has strayed dangerously far.
Q

JASON AND THE SCORCHERS
Still Standing (EMI)
The main point about The Scorchers, as with the Hoodoo Gurus, seems to be that varying genres – here, country, rock 'n' roll, R&B – can be clipped and slipped together without all potency being diluted, then slammed out.
Melody Maker

All things considered, though, this album is . . . alright.
Sounds

THE JAZZ BUTCHER
Big Questions (Glass)
. . . this fairly gigantic songwriting talent with his inimitable knack of grasping the essence *and* the idiocies of the deepest (and often darkest) emotions, literately and with guitars, has been consistently overlooked in a paranoid rush to write the man off as wacky burlesque.
Sounds

Distressed Gentlefolk (Glass)
. . . *Distressed Gentlefolk* is a *lot* of fun to listen to . . . but only if you remember to put it on, in the first place! What's happened?
Melody Maker

THE JETS
Crush On You (MCA)
A good effort but if you're wondering if they're the new Five Star the answer is: most definitely not.
Smash Hits

BILLY JOEL
The Bridge (CBS)
There is only one real justification for Billy Joel's existence. And that is that every time he has a hit, he makes a video and we all get to see Christie Brinkley on *Top Of The Pops*.
Sounds

DON JOHNSON
Heartbeat (CBS)
A jolly sight better than *Survivor*, anyway. It sounds as if it cost about a billion dollars to produce – which, of course, it probably did – and it's really not too bad in a Dan Hartman sort of way. Gosh.
Smash Hits

Our main man in Miami can actually sing more convincingly than he acts . . .
Record Mirror

PAUL JOHNSON
Paul Johnson (CBS)
This Harlesden boy has a creamy vocie that would melt a million hearts . . .
Sounds

. . . what he lacks is charisma, mystique, even fanciability. When it comes to his brand of dreamy, smoochy soul, the presence of at least one of these qualities is essential . . .
Melody Maker

GRACE JONES
Inside Story (Manhattan)
. . . it sounds rather as though it were written, played and sung by a computer. Maybe she's an android after all.
Smash Hits

That voice, like a messenger from some glamorous hell; that black-ice baritone, the sound responsible for the sweat on Russell Harty's top lip, remains the same.
NME

This is hardly Grace pushing it to the limits, just assured, measured, which seems just about right.
Sounds

HOWARD JONES
One To One (WEA)
And the songs? Well, they're still a-brim with wildly dippy why-can't-we-all-be-nice-to-each-other? political sentiments, but then that's Howard for you, isn't it?
Smash Hits

. . . he's still knocking out infuriatingly catchy synth motifs and he's still spouting the blindingly obvious.
Sounds

Howard the hack he may be. But Howard the schmuck he most definitely is not.
NME

JILL JONES
Jill Jones (Paisley Park)
If Prince was her girlfriend, he might have made something like this.
Record Mirror

Jones has the kind of soul-laden tonsils destined to give certain well established *black* artists a nasty shock . . .
Sounds

Basically, if you like Prince you're going to like this . . .
NME

SHIRLEY JONES
Always In The Mood
(Philadelphia International)
No fierce belter, Shirley is all poise and graceful soul queen majesty, the gossamer thread linking her to a gospel past at times seems barely visible.
NME

No dear, not the one who played David Cassidy's mom in *The Partridge Family*.
Melody Maker

THE JUDDS
Give A Little Love (RCA)
. . . this is the real stuff, accept no substitutes.
NME

After 15 tracks of The Judds and their Badoit-clear, butterfly-gentle vocals, though, it's almost imperative that one follows them up with a weighty dose of some godawful "alternative" band just to redress the balance a bit.
Melody Maker

Sex is here, too. Is there anything The Judds can't sing?
Sounds

These new fundamentalists will make sentimental fools of us all yet.
Q

THE JUSTIFIED ANCIENTS OF MU MU
1987 — What The F**k Is Going On (Sound Of Mu)
1987 . . . isn't a *bad* record, just disappointing, the sound of one good idea spread very thin, of novelty wearing off.
NME

1987 is the aural equivalent of a *Blue Peter* time capsule that's been compiled by the Val Singleton Youth Branch of Baader Meinhof.
Sounds

NICK KAMEN
Nick Kamen (WEA)
If anyone had ever before doubted the "genius" of Nick Kamen, well, here's the proof. That any man can be so famous and still be so utterly talent-free has indeed taken "genius" of some description . . . Unforgivably embarrassing.
Smash Hits

There are 501 reasons to dislike this album, but you know the one that counts; models are meant to date pop stars, not become them.
NME

Gentle tunes melt like honey in the warm summer sun. And Kamen's impotent voice weakly trails away.
Sounds

THE KANE GANG
Miracle (Kitchenware)
. . . truly class songs complemented by some great singing, arrangements and production.
Record Mirror

. . . efficient, clinical soul-pop that sounds as if it's been assembled from a kit.
NME

The Kane Gang ought, in fact to be filed next to Level 42 – Smart White Soul – rather than the grim, grey Style Council.
Melody Maker

There's a thin line between the sublime and the sickening, and often this album veers from cool Vandross to Volpeliere-Pierrot dross.
Sounds

MICK KARN
Dreams Of Reason Produce Monsters (Virgin)
. . . this little masterpiece of pure boredom will have you fast asleep in no time.
Smash Hits

Fortunately, few adolescents will be getting off their BMX bikes to plop this on to their turntable.
Sounds

. . . he combines his misunderstanding of mood and taste with his innate grasp of pseudo-religious waffle. It's a celestial moment of a magnitude unattained since *Omen III – The Final Conflict*.
Melody Maker

. . . one of those classic LPs where you can listen for ages at the wrong speed before noticing anything amiss.
Q

NICK KERSHAW
Radio Musicola (MCA)
The man is clearly a complete ninny if he thinks that any child over the age of eight is going to be impressed with his insights. This record is really boring and he sings like a pig.
NME

Radio Musicola is a fine, even mature, pop work . . .
Sounds

Sophisticated pop can be light and still have depth. *Radio Musicola* is sophisticated pop at its best.
Melody Maker

CHAKA KHAN
Destiny (Warner Bros)
It sounds like the popping of corks, it sounds like the LEB saying, Sorry, you were right, we over-charged you, it sounds like the kind of sunshine that renders hangovers irrelevant, it sounds like she's just phoned to say she's on her way even as I write, like waltzing on ice with a Persian tiger, like Auntie Chaka at her best. And that's something.
Sounds

KILLING JOKE
Brighter Than A Thousand Suns (EG)
These are pop's equivalents of fire and brimstone; sermons wrapped in big angry shapes, words of dark wisdom from the Nostradamus of Goth.
NME

Most of this album is *magnificent*, but being stupid bastards a while longer Killing Joke cleverly suffocate their own potential; lack of pruning rituals ensuring no hit singles fly here. STUPID . . .
Melody Maker

BEN E. KING
Stand By Me (Atlantic)
Although this isn't "the ultimate collection" that the sleeve proclaims (quite a few hits have been left out), it does prove that as a singer Ben E. King is a toff of the highest order.
Smash Hits

Jeans are boring. Jeans are what everybody wears. Jeans are what every Young Conservative yuppie guppy thinks are rebellious rock 'n' roll attire . . . Sometimes, even, your parents wear jeans. I had teachers who wore jeans . . . Ben E. King has nothing to do with jeans if you're over 12 years old, and is a great man.
Melody Maker

THE KINKS
Think Visual (London)
This old dog may not know any new tricks, but he can still perform his old ones to perfection.
Sounds

It's simple: the music on this album is very, very poor. And, what's more, it's very varied:

Ray Davies has done his homework and covered the ground pretty thoroughly. There aren't many ways of being substandard which he hasn't explored here.
NME

KOOL AND THE GANG
Forever (Phonogram)
This record is not excessively striking and soon I shall have forgotten it.
NME

Forever is *exactly* what Gang fans want from a record and, equally, exactly what *I don't* – corny Sunday afternoon jazz-funk baby food. Come on, *Journey* have got more soul than this.
Sounds

KRAFTWERK
Electric Cafe (EMI)
Their sound has changed little over the years and their sense of invention has all but evaporated along with their sense of melody, with only the occasional glimpse of their glorious past . . .
Sounds

They're cleaner and better than you'd imagine – but what really seduce are not the rhythm or the regularity but the glimmers, the blinks, the related background events, minor clockwork details, refractions of facial twitches. Ping!
Melody Maker

. . . this record has been soft-machine tested over and over and round and round the dance halls of Düsseldorf until its beats have been thoroughly perfected, forcing the listener to respond to its imperatives.
NME

ED KUEPPER
Rooms Of The Magnificent (Hot)
. . .an intuitively brilliant songwriter.
Sounds

I'll just say this and go. This is a record full of hunted thoughts. Ed Kuepper is my father. No, wait. Ed Kuepper is my honeypot. When he hits London later this month, I'll do anything he wants.
Melody Maker

LADYSMITH BLACK MAMBAZO
Shaka Zulu (WEA)
The fact that there is a large sticker displayed prominently on the front of this album with the words "Produced by Paul Simon" makes me a shade uneasy.
Record Mirror

And the faults with *Shaka Zulu* . . . unerring preciousness of it all and the irritating lack of variety . . . must surely be laid at Simon's door in his role of producer.
Melody Maker

It sounds more like a slowed down dub version of *Graceland*, without Simon's whining vocals.
NME

LATIN QUARTER
Mick And Caroline (Rockin' Horse)
The 'Loony Left' never sounded so sensible. Even N. Tebbit would be hard pressed to work up much of a froth about No-Nukes-Sanctions-Now politics the way Latin Quarter tell it.
NME

Spreading their lungs out a bit, blowing some of the fog away from their atmosphere, Latin Quarter have opted for a bit more of the humpty-bumpty sound with gleeful drumming spraying vigour up sensible hemlines.
Melody Maker

CYNDI LAUPER
True Colors (Portrait)
Stunningly lightweight, reassuringly middle-

of-the-road, mind numbingly dull, instantly forgettable. . .
Sounds

True Colors is a chart ballad, swathed in swarming synth sensitivity, that superficially attracts, coaxes and finally woos – transatlantic pop at its most persuasive . . .
NME

This human foghorn we can trust has integrity as, commercially speaking, she makes no crass concessions, preferring to play it hard: Russian roulette with all chambers full.
Melody Maker

THE LEATHER NUN
Lust Games (Wire)
Tie me to the mast if I wouldn't rather hear any 12 seconds of Barry Manilow's 'Could This Be Magic?' instead . . .
NME

A name like The Leather Nun you'd think these Swedes would have a sense of humour, but I don't see a shred of one here.
Melody Maker

Slow Death (Wire)
Money aside, there seems to be little point in this release . . .
NME

THE LEGENDARY PINK DOTS
Island Of Jewels
(Play It Again Sam)
Psychedelic coloured tunes with often monotonous, often thrilling Bowie/Bauhaus inflections, these haunting voices shouldn't be taken without an aspirin and the landing light left on.
Sounds

Island Of Jewels is baroque and outlandish, but rapturous too – the first whale among 1987's pop minnows.
Melody Maker

LEVEL 42
Running In The Family
(Polydor)
The bulk of their audience will surely have trouble relating to the group's new, existentialist bent. Luckily, though, the music itself is comfortingly familiar, percolating white funk sound and all.
Melody Maker

They've extracted the wit and replaced it with a sense of familial responsibility, added a discreet dusting of late 20th century angst, and processed the mixture into a clean, smokeless fuel that can heat up Wembley Arena's chilly wastes for weeks on end.
NME

Level 42 play sensible adult pop for sensible adult people.
Sounds

. . . like the last one (and the one before that and the one before that) it sounds slick and clever and enjoyable and somehow entirely lacking in that extra something special.
Q

HUEY LEWIS AND THE NEWS
Fore (Chrysalis)
Mind you, he'll make loads of money and when we are all older and wiser he'll be singing title themes for films like *Porkys 14*.
Smash Hits

Fore offers us another ten songs to skateboard to and neatly corners the market in urban surf music.
NME

But then *Fore* is pretty square, something the whole family can jive and sway to.
Sounds

LIGHT A BIG FIRE
Surveillance (Siren)
On the menu are lots of rich influences seasoned with some hot production, but trying to be all things to all people is something that's never easily digestible.
Record Mirror

All in all, worth checking out. Or chucking out.
Melody Maker

LIMAHL
Colour All My Days (EMI)
This LP is all that is dull, completely without imagination and sickeningly bland in the world of popular music: unbelievably boring, spring-along tweetie tunes, blipping and skipping and tooting and simpering on and on . . .
Smash Hits

Limahl, in anyone's language, is a big girl's blouse.
Melody Maker

Limahl is like one half of Dollar estranged from its very own Thereze.
Sounds

Limahl is the new David Essex, without the

looks, charm or flair, and this is a most uninspired collection of songs, full stop.
NME

LITTLE FEAT
As The Time Goes By – The Best Of Little Feat
(Warner Bros)
. . . it's a whole deal better than the shoddy double 'Hoy-Hoy' collection of a few years back, touching nearly all the necessary bases, and sounding as fresh and faultless as it did back then.
NME

LITTLE RICHARD
Lifetime Friend (WEA)
Little Richard still *oozes* energy, and although some songs are drippy "we're all God's children" gospel-type anthems, the best ones . . . have a "big band" sound with a sprinkling of manic piano bashing exuberance. Splendid.
Smash Hits

It is true that Dick runs out of puff now and then and that the backing band all have wooden legs but the spluttering bluster and one-take zappyness of the recordings makes this a far from worthless record.
NME

Lifetime Friend isn't much coming from the man who invented rock 'n' roll. In fact, this waste of rock's most transcendent bellows borders on sacrilegious.
Sounds

LITTLE STEVEN
Freedom No Compromise
(Manhattan)
. . . bludgeons rather than uplifts.
Q

LIVING IN A BOX
Living In A Box (Chrysalis)
. . . when Living In A Box's blood starts to boil, the shades of Otis Redding and James Brown sock it to us.
Q

LONE JUSTICE
Shelter (Geffen)
Lone Justice are, you see, the band that plays on every single US Yuppieflick about couples breaking up and getting together and buying sushi in parks. You know the bit when Mr Brat and The Sensitive Chick run along the pier waving balloons and holding onto their hats?
Melody Maker

Music for grown-ups, which is fine considering the bilge the kiddies are listening to these days.
Sounds

THE LONG RYDERS
Twin-Fisted Tales (Island)
It's always very tasteful, very acceptable, but it's a million galaxies away from being interesting.
NME

. . . this is a disappointing record that reveals its creators to be not Marlboro Man cowboys but LA dudes.
Melody Maker

. . . essentially this is little more than hash and beans. Real neighbourly, but characterless.
Q

LOVE AND ROCKETS
Express (Beggars Banquet)
No longer gentleman of the shade, the winter rains and ruins are over and a new light now shines through. There is interest without pretension, pop without mundanity.
Melody Maker

Frolicsome, flamboyant and not in the least bit flabby, Love And Rockets are actually quite . . . good?
Sounds

THE LOVER SPEAKS
The Lover Speaks (A&M)
Ringing with booms, croons and soaring falsettos, tripping dramatically over its own analytical word-play and inverted romantic clichés, it's something of a magnificent failure.
Sounds

LYDIA LUNCH
Hysterie (Widowspeak)
The myth that Lydia Lunch is merely a siren howling in the dark is gleefully and intelligently shot down in flames at last. Here's the ammo.
NME

Mood music for masochists.
Melody Maker

THE LYRES
Lyres Lyres (New Rose)
The Lyres have had their moments, but this latest import isn't one of them.
NME

Historically faithful, prime cult fertilizer, The Lyres exist in a timeless void and, for their fellow travellers, this music will be sweet indeed.
Sounds

PAUL McCARTNEY
Press To Play (EMI)
Thumbs aloft, I think.
NME

. . .whereas the legend-without-any-enigma would normally impress with craftsmanship, his sure touch as a brickie-of-vignettes seems to have stayed behind in the cocktail lounge, being easygoing with Noel Edmunds.
Sounds

Pointless but expensive.
Melody Maker

MICHAEL McDONALD
The Best Of Michael McDonald (WEA)
In the '70s Michael McDonald was making wonderfully syrupy, souly pop (for driving around California in a convertible car to) as of one The Doobie Brothers. And it's an old "Doobie's" song – 'What A Fool Believes' – that really stands out here; the rest is just middle-of-the-road slop.
Smash Hits

I hold no brief for mellow maturity, but there is something in the cracks at the edges of this grainy voice that contrasts poignantly with the ultra-hygienic music that surrounds it.
Melody Maker

FREDDIE McGREGOR
All In The Same Boat
(Real Authentic Sound)
McGregor speaks in the tongues of love and his music has the strength (and here we are not talking about macho volume) to turn your spine all soft and gooey.
Sounds

All In The Same Boat may not be the hippest platter of modern times, but it *is* a pleasure, a genuine pleasure.
Melody Maker

MADHOUSE
"8" (Paisley Park)
. . . if you're expecting Prince, forget it. We're talking *smooth* music here.
Sounds

The cover has a picture of a woman, a dog and a sandcastle. There is no mention of God anywhere.
Melody Maker

MADNESS
Utter Madness (Zarjazz)
With their best single for ages 'Waiting For The Ghost Train' (included here) in the charts and now this excellent compilation, full marks to Madness for bowing out on a high note.
Smash Hits

Utter Madness hasn't vacated my turntable since I brought it home, six hours ago now.
Melody Maker

. . . the diversity of their music and its humour will still scratch emotions for years to come.
Sounds

Utter Madness is a very necessary compilation. It shows us that there is much to celebrate and precious little to complain about. The maddest group in all the world will no longer compete. How could they do this to me?
NME

MANTRONIX
Music Madness (10)
Fleshless, soulless, faceless and fantastic.
Melody Maker

Fulfilling the most ghastly nightmares of what avant underground pop represents could be achievement, but the result is akin to aural epilepsy; not a holy war viral strain, more a genetic malfunction.
NME

As a listening experience this album is percolated with convulsions which will let you pass away a pleasant 40 minutes of back-flipping.
Sounds

MARILLION
Clutching At Straws (EMI)
. . . isn't it a bit self-indulgent to make a whole concept album out of the emotional fumblings of your rock 'n' roll lifestyle?
Record Mirror

My father tells me he recognizes some early Yes in there, too.
NME

The Marillion musicians, meanwhile, have, thankfully, learnt the art of brevity: there are

10 whole songs here and they are strangely unplagued by endless guitar solos . . .
Smash Hits

I can think of nothing more to say about Marillion than that they sound like Genesis . .
Melody Maker

Back in '77 such stuff was the Enemy, and the kindest thing for Fish and his pseudy band would have been to put them out of their misery with a bullet in the base of the skull. Nowadays, though, they're such a quaint throwback that I can't get too bothered.
Sounds

Were it not for the swirling curlicues of the arrangements against which he explores his relationship with the demon drink this could almost be Fish's country and western record, so conspicuously soaked is it in the self-pity that follows straight on the heels of self-indulgence.
Q

BRANFORD MARSALIS
Royal Garden Blues (CBS)
What you don't need to know, however, is the complete history of jazz in order to appreciate Branford's album as a work of great taste and sophistication.
Record Mirror

Wynton's brother is a very good saxophone player, and, whatever Wynton thinks, hanging out with Sting has not rotted his teeth.
Melody Maker

HUGH MASEKELA
Tomorrow (WEA)
Amiable, consoling, often tedious. For musicians only.
Melody Maker

Purists will almost certainly regard it as a sell-out, watering down Masekela's South African roots and adding enough studio sweeteners to make it palatable for the global market-place. But that's their problem.
Sounds

MEATLOAF
Blind Before I Stop (Arista)
Blind Before I Stop is a pop record made by a lot of people who don't seem to know what they're doing.
NME

Is this what two years on a mustard and tomato diet does to a man?
Sounds

MEAT PUPPETS
Mirage (SST)
. . . the easy picking guitar plangency of their heat-hazed songs now have a tension born of *latent* threat. In this barren, sweltering high noon, a feller might go stone loco any minute.
Sounds

THE MEKONS
Honky Tonkin' (Sin)
. . . the fiddles and accordians are excellent throughout but those awful approximations of yodels aren't quite so welcome . . .
Record Mirror

As strange, hapless and queasy as any pub near the Leeds Corn Exchange. Fiddles, melodeons, this is a lost, commercially unviable music for a lost, commercially unviable town. The Mekons are far out in the hills from pop, miles from anywhere.
Melody Maker

MEL & KIM
F.L.M. (Supreme)
If you like wonderfully tacky, totally unpretentious dance music where little catchy snippets of tunes and electronic drums a-clinking and a-clattering are more important than anything else in the world then you'll simply recognize *F.L.M.* as a "masterpiece" of sorts.
Smash Hits

They're bold, emancipated young hipsters and they're the best home-grown disco talent since Five Star disappeared up their own family tree.
Sounds

A veritable feast of unpretentious pop and a classic of its kind.
Q

THE MEMBRANES
Songs Of Love And Fury
(In Tape)
Like the Beatles not on drugs, like the Mary Chain on the Beatles, like Simon Hebdige on the function of pop, like crazy, daddio! No, I don't like this record.
NME

They're still the lumpiest, bumpiest ride in town, ugliness and beauty combined, like Charles Bronson in a pink satin wedding dress. A puddle of titles, noise, energy, heart and soul and whippersnapper ear-bending density. And why not?
Melody Maker

. . . this is Joy Division, The Fall and the punk rock pop tone all gathered together and thrown at one canvas in a fit of stunning genius.
Sounds

THE MEN THEY COULDN'T HANG
How Green Is The Valley
(MCA)
. . . although TMTCH play rather frisky music, their lyrics are often meaningful or serious, a good combination. They are also excellent musicians. I bet you've never heard a bouzouki played so well before.
Sounds

. . . infinitely more assured than its predecessor, a more fluent and timeless parade of crusading guitars, guts and guns.
Melody Maker

MICRODISNEY
Crooked Mile (Virgin)
Crooked Mile has obviously had about a squillion pounds spent on it and it shows in the big "production" here which does tend to smooth out the rather attractive rough edges in Cathal Coughlan and Sean O'Hagan's songs.
Smash Hits

Warm, wandering and intrinsically melodic, their music is a comfort and a sure pointer to quality in confused musical times.
Melody Maker

THE MIGHTY LEMON DROPS
Happy Head (Blue Guitar)
. . . both the Bunnymen and Julian Cope could probably sue for plagiarism, if so inclined. But, quite honestly, who cares?
Record Mirror

. . . yes, they're smaller than Echo, who were smaller than the Doors.
Melody Maker

There's a dignity in *Happy Head* that remains warm, emotive and superior to the undignified romp that The Mighty Lemon Drops have often been lumped in with . . . Place alongside the classics in the hall of fame.
Sounds

MIRACLE LEGION
Surprise Surprise Surprise
(Rough Trade)
. . . a superb guitar band in their own right, concocting lush, complex, folk-washed reveries . . .
Sounds

THE MISSION
The First Chapter (Phonogram)
Was there ever such a fine group of gloomerous swirlsters?
Smash Hits

By far the most entertaining aspect of this pompously titled collection is the sleeve notes . . .
NME

God's Own Medicine
(Phonogram)
For all their dodgy black "clothes", mouldly hats and make-up, The Mission's music is really rather . . . erm, *nice* – and quite swoonsomely enchanting.
Smash Hits

This year, a lot of people remembered how much they liked Led Zeppelin and The Mission remembered more loudly than most, carrying their fond reminiscences down to the very last detail of Simon Hinkler's twin-necked 'Jimmy Page' brand guitar. . . and if you *badly* wanted the first Mission album to be stupendous, as I did, you won't be cheated. Rich with spicy passion dripping from every note, this record (*that* title!) never once stumbles or falters, running on guitars of almost ridiculous clarity and relentless rhythm.
Sounds

This album is completely inane and I shall sell it tomorrow.
NME

The first time I was really impressed by The Mission was the night they became the only Top Thirty band in the universe to be turned away from the Limelight for not being famous enough. The second time I was really impressed by The Mission was last week when I finally started to listen to their music.
Melody Maker

MOMUS
The Poison Boyfriend
(Creation)
Momus writes witty, political, melancholy songs about people's frustrated desires, strained relationships, social awkwardness and blunted ambitions.
NME

. . . Momus is the person who brings back acute (as opposed to merely cute) insight, humour, sadness and sudden fumbling sex into the art of singer-songwriting . . .
Sounds

Never has melancholy sounded *quite* so articulate.
Melody Maker

THE MONKEES
Then And Now . . . The Best Of The Monkees (Arista)
. . . if this is The Monkees now I'd rather wait for The Archies revival.
Melody Maker

MOTLEY CRUE
Girls Girls Girls (Elektra)
A load of tripe it may be but worse has been done in the name of rock and roll than this harmless, pea-brained entertainment.
Q

ALISON MOYET
Raindancing (CBS)

There's less roaring singing and less emphasis on being intensely "soulful" but these are still ten fairly polite pop songs.
Smash Hits

Raindancing has its moments, but it's also got a bad case of rising damp.
NME

This great white anserine blob called Alison – surname designed to suggest champagne, a nuance of upward mobility (if you've got a crane handy) but never forgetting the common touch (she talks like an oik and her lyrics admit that men and women sometimes get into the same bed) – doesn't she just remind you of a belch?
Melody Maker

If music like this was all that she was capable of, however, *Raindancing* would not be a disappointment.
Q

ROBBIE NEVIL
C'est La Vie (Manhattan)

As a West Coast LP, it compares favourably with the like of Loggins and McDonald, but if you're expecting soul/dance, you've got Robbie wrong.
Record Mirror

COLIN NEWMAN
Commercial Suicide
(Crammed)

Colin Newman has assembled his own chamber orchestra, and hidden beneath the naturally deadpan title, the work is of maximum beauty.
NME

Commercial Suicide . . . suggests a washing-machine made entirely of wood – a useless model of usefulness.
Melody Maker

. . . a solemn, brooding atmosphere permeates, like the sound of a secular, 21st century church, built as a monument to the frail emotions of the human species.
Sounds

NEW MODEL ARMY
The Ghost Of Cain (EMI)

Some groups manage to mix *pop* music and politics – New Model Army don't. Even if you share their political views. a whole album full of what-a-mess-we're-making-of-the-world sentiments is just too depressing to take.
Smash Hits

It must take energy and vast resources of anti-talent to manufacture naffness quite so thorough and uncompromising as this.
NME

. . . there's no preaching, no tablets from on high, just people and places and steely, gritty hope. Rough diamonds.
Sounds

They may have hearts as big as this planet but their heads need realignment.
Melody Maker

NEW ORDER
Brotherhood (Factory)

I suspect, however, it'll only be fully appreciated in retrospect, as it does take so much effort on behalf of the listener.
Record Mirror

I can't decide.
Melody Maker

Brotherhood is flawed – of course! But to be human, idiosyncratic *and* popular right now is a rare distinction.
Sounds

This is a wonderful LP made by very silly people.
NME

NON
Blood And Flame (Mute)

. . . an album whose primary purpose is to act solely as background *ambience* – music for an industrial generation terrified of silence.
NME

RIC OCASEK
This Side Of Paradise (Geffen)

. . . it's jolly good – a clever mixture of superior American pop and electronic

gadgetry. Actually, it's a bit dreary at first but after a few plays really grows on you.
Smash Hits

He sounds, of course, like an utter dork.
NME

ALEXANDER O'NEAL
Hearsay (Tabu)

. . . he may well share the lurex sweaters of the truly great black crooners.
Sounds

ORCHESTRAL MANOEUVRES IN THE DARK
The Pacific Age (Virgin)

At the end of it, *just* another OMD LP. You feel kind of sorry for it, just wishing they had a mere hint of playfulness, the slightest touch of absurdity in their souls.
Sounds

. . . what grates here is the self-delusion; their sincere belief they're saying something important, even affecting us.
NME

This is a deeply sad record – as sad as wandering around the ruins of Citizen Kane's opera house.
Melody Maker

SHELLEYAN ORPHAN
Helleborine (Rough Trade)

Weird, pretty, and different from anything you've heard in ages.
NME

A cut in the quotient of preciousness could put Shelleyan Orphan on the right track, otherwise a lifetime of film soundtracks beckons.
Sounds

Helleborine is hippy nonsense.
Melody Maker

OZZY OSBOURNE
Tribute (Epic)

. . . will inspire many a lump in the throat.
Q

Of course, this is all for the most diehard Ozzy fans, of which I'm sure there are plenty. It's a case of open that closed mind (or, in some cases, the other way round) . . .
Sounds

MARIE OSMOND
I Only Wanted You (Capitol)
. . . it's the same wonderful candyfloss, each humalong number a dollop of heavily addictive gorgeous-tasting soap opera fluff.
Melody Maker

OVERKILL
Taking Over (Megaforce)
This is the kind of album that, if it walked in a pub and insisted that you drink with it, you'd be too scared to refuse.
Q

PARLIAMENT
Uncut Funk — The Bomb — The Best Of Parliament (Club)
. . . overloaded, cluttered with *too many* funky strands, draped with so many tangents, follies, flights of fancy, you fear the groove will collapse under the strain. But no, everything pushes forward, moves you.
Melody Maker

Besides, on the sleeve of this album you will find an indispensable "Teach Yourself P-Funk" glossary . . .
NME

DOLLY PARTON, LINDA RONSTADT & EMMYLOU HARRIS
Trio (Warner Bros)
The cover is an embarrassing Barbie Doll affair, and to emphasize the joke effect, there are even cut-out models of the gals (and accompanying outfits for us to play with). General glossiness, however, can't damage the harmonies, all countrified coyly, or the tears beneath the frilly-white dressings.
Melody Maker

THE PASTELS
Up For A Bit With The Pastels
(Glass)
Of course, serious fans — people who like Paul Young and Peter Gabriel — will point out that Stephen Pastel cannot sing. Well, my dear Yuppie chums, though wee Bastard Pastel's sickly vocals do flit from being enticing to plain dull, voices are not everything. Ask Phil Collins.
Sounds

From the swirling vortex of Stephen Pastel's ever-expanding head comes words of dippiness, meekness and sardonic humour. He delivers them all in that wonderful, plaintive, prosaic voice, which at times sounds like it's falling through a musical whirlpool.
NME

THE PENGUIN CAFE ORCHESTRA
Signs Of Life (EG)
. . . the PCO have put together a bunch of

pierced sweetness, and if it's never going to drive people out into the streets with torches and revolution on their minds, or inspire them to other valuable craziness, it's still there, tough and composed, to colour the days of a life.
NME

PET SHOP BOYS
Disco (Parlophone)
If you're the sort of person who hates 12" versions, then avoid *Disco* – if not then this daft mish-mash of crashing drums, stupid sound effects and insanely catchy tunes is quite highly recommended.
Smash Hits

. . . suspend your cynicism for three quarters of an hour and accept *Disco* on its own terms. Love it. Dance to it. Play it at your Xmas parties.
Sounds

The Pet Shop Boys are quite possibly the greatest pop group in the world. It is therefore entirely in order for them to release an album of remixes of their singles and B-sides.
NME

TOM PETTY & THE HEARTBREAKERS
Let Me Up, I've Had Enough
(MCA)
. . . supremely engineered rock and roll, music with the smoothest lines and glossiest finish, with every feature designed for maximum comfort and the handling perfect and predictable.
Q

Somebody built a by-pass round Tom Petty some years back and he's been blissfully unaware of the volume of traffic that's raced past him since. . . This is the sound of a man waving a white flag, you get the impression he's really had enough.
NME

The whole thing could have been concocted at any time over the last ten years, but with the lank hair, dishevelled voice and 12-string Rickenbacker still in place here, that's good enough.
Sounds

COURTNEY PINE
Journey To The Urge Within
(Island)
I'm pleased that this country has a musician who knows how to do more with his instrument than wave it at photographers.
Melody Maker

He is being ravished by his discovery of his belonging to history, to Tradition. I don't care what the pallid reptiles massed in Jazz Necropolis Central have to say on the matter; Courtney got it bad, and that is very, very good.
NME

What's excellent about Pine's stance is his absolute commitment to the hard jazz: no sappy bossa nova workouts or funky scraps of fusion.
Sounds

THE POLICE
Every Breath You Take — The Singles (A&M)
. . . although they could be embarrassingly pretentious at times, *Every Breath You Take* proves what an imaginative and clever group they really are. . . er, were.
Smash Hits

IGGY POP
Blah-Blah-Blah (A&M)
Blah-Blah-Blah is the real Iggy Pop, 1986 model and, like it or not, he sounds as sane and adult as anyone who boasts a past like his could hope to be . . . These are ominous, boundless rhythms thundering outside your

front door and, yup, Iggy Pop is back with a slam. *Still*, the last hero.
Sounds

How can such a tawdry and tired effort be reviewed in a lively and readable way? Well, frankly, it's impossible.
Melody Maker

The result is precisely what you would expect, Adult Orientated Decadence . . .
NME

THE PRETENDERS
Get Close (WEA)
Well dear lady, from title to terminal you are peddling us the inert poetry of the mundane . . .
Sounds

Pretenders LPs were always crap. *Get Close* is no exception.
NME

Still, *Get Close* is a little livelier than might have been expected from the old codgers credited here.
Melody Maker

MAXI PRIEST
Intentions (10)
Much of the problem lies with the production, handled predominantly by Aswad's Drummie Zeb with the rest of Aswad contributing instrumentally. Precise and crystal clear, *Intentions* simply lacks the energy, vitality and immediacy of both Priest's and Aswad's live performances . . .
NME

Stunningly produced, mainly by Aswad's Drummie Zeb, to sound as bright and shiny as possible, without freezing the warmth that characterizes the south Londoner's vocals . . .
Melody Maker

PRINCE
Sign 'O' The Times (WEA)
But if he *is* off his trolley, well, who cares? The best bits of this LP . . . are utterly *utterly* brilliant.
Smash Hits

. . . here he's often too absorbed with studio trickery, new found minimalism, a curious sense of humour or himself to give the material a resonance and life of its own.
NME

. . . this is a rambling, widescreen delight featuring a procession of brilliant cameos by each of its star's fascinating alter-egos.
Sounds

U should B ready 2 go 4 it.
Q

THE PROCLAIMERS
This Is The Story (Chrysalis)
. . . a glorious record, recorded in a week and performed with a thuggish, sensitive, personal missionary zeal. It's a holy hootnanny. Get yourself saved.
Melody Maker

Armed with just one guitar a harmonica and a set of bongos, 25-year-old twins Craig and Charlie Reid have come up with a witty and extremely listenable collection of folk-tinged pop.
NME

. . . some of the most evocative and thoroughly irresistible quality songwriting that you'll hear anywhere. Yes, they're *that* good, and any accolades thrown their way are no more than they deserve.
Sounds

. . . all these songs seem to split neatly between stories about losing your virginity or your job.
Q

PSYCHEDELIC FURS
Midnight To Midnight (CBS)
. . . while I can't find anything in *Midnight To Midnight* to tattoo permanently on to my experience, I'll happily work up a sweat to it for a while.
Melody Maker

They offer rock without raunch, dance music without sweat, and, wisely, they nick their sleeve designs off Prince.
NME

PUBLIC ENEMY
Yo! Bum Rush The Show
(Def Jam)
He's too smart and too committed to use rap as anything other than a means of black agitation, education, and liberation. His words are ammunition in the propaganda battle for power and against street siren. Learning breeds knowledge, knowledge breeds power, and power breeds reaction – hence the band's name.
Melody Maker

. . . these "black panthers of rap", when not illustrating just how good crack is, eat quiche. Their professed stand might be cobbled out of *Shaft*, '70s funk and Deep Purple in minute doses, but their worldview is pure semi-detached Long Island . . .
NME

QUEEN
Live Magic (EMI)
This album should be for all those who thought they *didn't* like Queen, like myself. Roll on the next live album.
Sounds

THE RAILWAY CHILDREN
Reunion Wilderness (Factory)
Reunion Wilderness is alas a fine pop postcard from the heart.
NME

In fact, it's a distinctly un-Scottish Postcard act . . .
Sounds

RED BOX
The Circle And The Square
(WEA)
Red Box are for the easily impressed amongst us. Don't buy this record, please.
Sounds

REM
Dead Letter Office (IRS)
. . . the best of it suggests that even what the group have discarded over the years is more intriguing than the official catalogues of most of their contemporaries.
Melody Maker

What you have here, *really,* is an invaluable set of chicken bones, clues (but *only* clues) to the mysery of REM's divinity.
NME

Life's Rich Pageant (IRS)
. . . alternates between '60s Byrdsian elektric folk and '80s garage rock, prickly with switchblades.
Sounds

Musically, it's a great leap forward from their earlier work, without dispensing with the essential REM-ness of things . . .
NME

. . .in terms of raw emotion it's up there with classic Motown.
Melody Maker

REO SPEEDWAGON
Life As We Know It (Epic)
The last track is called, without a trace of irony, 'Tired Of Gettin' Nowhere'.
Q

THE REPLACEMENTS
Pleased To Meet Me (Sire)
What can you say about a group who write a song about Alex Chilton?
Sounds

The welcome return of the world's most talented buncha winos.
NME

It's raucous, off its face, comic, brawling, lyrical, seeks out secret, forbidden places, gives voice to wonder and . . . is VERY LOUD INDEED!
Melody Maker

. . . another slap around the chops for those who reckon there's no pop life left in white American rock 'n' roll.
Q

THE RESIDENTS
Stars And Hank Forever
(Ralph Records)
. . . Side One is a more than palatable pop oddity. Just for God's sake don't turn it over.
Melody Maker

LIONEL RICHIE
Dancing On The Ceiling
(Motown)
This record is dull . . . Still, maybe there'll be some blind people in the videos.
NME

I'm paying him the highest compliment, I'm sending this album to my mum.
Sounds

STAN RIDGWAY
The Big Heat (IRS)
. . . a perfect combination of hummability and weirdness.
Sounds

TOM ROBINSON
Still Loving You (Castaway)
. . . Robinson is a great story-teller searching for a musical style.
Record Mirror

. . . a sad old business.
Melody Maker

I like it, but then like Tom I'm getting older.
Sounds

LINDA RONSTADT
For Sentimental Reasons
(Asylum)
. . . if you smuggle it home inside your anorak you might just get a very pleasant surprise.
Sounds

DIANA ROSS
Red Hot Rhythm And Blues
(EMI)
It's certainly the most listenable album Diana Ross has made since she left Motown.
Q

DAVID LEE ROTH
Eat 'Em And Smile
(Warner Bros)
There are tougher and nastier slugs of metal this year, but none which is so much fun.
Sounds

Eat 'Em And Smile is a tame commodity,

dressed in lamé tights and baseball boots; baring its teeth only to reveal a set of plastic lucky bag fangs.
NME

RUN DMC
Raising Hell (London)
. . . as the saliva spatters against your microphone, it brings Run DMC right into your living-room, and you can almost feel the specks of spit hitting your cheek.
Sounds

ST VITUS DANCE
Love Me Love My Dogma
(Probe Plus)
. . . will have you wondering what would have happened if Simon & Garfunkel had been to more Monkees gigs.
Record Mirror

. . . an album full of well marshalled contrivance and a feeling of a disenfranchised populace hissing under its breath.
Sounds

Quite what a shelf of Lucozade bottles is doing on the cover is anyone's guess . . .
NME

SALT 'N' PEPA
Hot Cool Viscious (Champion)
. . . dated female bragging.
Record Mirror

. . . the record manages to be très avant garde and the People's Choice all at the same time.
Melody Maker

It's irradiated freshness and not at all stupid.
NME

SAXON
Rock The Nations (EMI)
Saxon are cool, as far as their genre goes.
Melody Maker

The problem for Biff Byford is the same as it ever was: if she's hot she's too young and if she's old enough she's either a bitch or she doesn't notice you.
NME

But don't worry . . . Saxon aren't finished. The riffs may be losing their teeth but so what?
Sounds

SCHOOLLY D
Schoolly D (Schoolly D)
Schoolly D has reduced himself to nothing but armour, masks, the capacity for massive retaliation.
Melody Maker

Saturday Night (Rhythm King)
Unfortunately for him, there's more to making music than trying to become the *Dirty Harry* of rap.
Sounds

THE SHAMEN
Drop (Moshka)
They ain't afraid to be irrelevant by revisiting the Summer Of Love to set the record straight.
NME

SHRIEKBACK
Big Night Music (Island)
These moribund theoreticians have concocted an album of unfaltering dullness and no useful purpose.
Sounds

. . . warm as toast, a bubbling, velveteen, blue-eyed undertow of rhythms that even *smooches*.
No 1

To sum up: almost intriguing.
NME

SIGUE SIGUE SPUTNIK
Flaunt It (Parlophone)
It's all boys' music, desperately so . . . The little girls who make the rules for today's pop will surely find this trousery talk wearisome.
Sounds

. . . Sigue Sigue Sputnik aren't really in it for the music, so they won't mind me pointing out the fact that it's the biggest heap of garbage since the last heap of garbage.
NME

CARLY SIMON
Coming Around Again (Arista)
. . . high on gloss and low on just about everything else.
Sounds

The singing is flawless, the musicianship admirable, and even the production impeccable.
Q

PAUL SIMON
Graceland (Warner Bros)
Dance album of the year.
NME

. . . it would be churlish not to admit that on this LP there are three of the most marvellous melodies I have ever heard.
Sounds

SIMPLE MINDS
Live In The City Of Light
(Virgin)
As double live albums go, it's pretty good.
Q

SIMPLY RED
Men And Women (WEA)
What a supremely talented bunch of people Simply Red are.
Smash Hits

However, 'The Right Thing', the best song about bonking since Zodiac's 'Wild Child' *is* essential.
Sounds

His singing is in acute danger of descending to a mere collection of mannerisms: his grunts, melismas and "ooowww"s still sound borrowed. (The best white R&B singers don't borrow, they *steal*.)
Q

SIOUXSIE AND THE BANSHEES
Through The Looking Glass
(Polydor)
. . . the sort of thing they play on Soviet TV whenever the big chief pops his clogs.
Smash Hits

Should you be gifted with the ability to dance while you're splitting your sides then it's likely you'll enjoy this album.
Melody Maker

But when you consider that a compilation album of the original versions of the songs here would be far preferable to *Through The Looking Glass*, then it can't really be seen as a particularly worthwhile achievement.
Q

SLADE
You Boyz Make Big Noise
(RCA)
Slade may be virtually a national institution but this record has more genuine power and energy than a lorryload of contemporary metal product.
Q

SLAYER
Reign In Blood (London)
. . . for once it's possible to understand America's parents' worries about demonic utterings being hidden in the grooves of rock albums.
Sounds

SLY AND ROBBIE
Rhythm Killers
(Fourth & Broadway)
I'd rather a little less precision and a few more whoopee cushions.
Melody Maker

A pleasure and a privilege to hear.
Sounds

THE SMITHS
The World Won't Listen
(Rough Trade)
We're halfway to Paradise, here, now, with The Smiths.
NME

A career in outrage is a fine place to be but some jokes just aren't funny anymore.
Melody Maker

. . . *The World Won't Listen* converts Morrissey's private inadequacies into public triumphs.
Q

SOUL ASYLUM
Made To Be Broken
(Rough Trade)
. . . this is high-energy rock built around that unfashionable thing, the powerchord, and the idea that this is remotely embarrassing would never even *occur* to Soul Asylum.
Melody Maker

All asylum, no soul.
Sounds

Made To Be Broken is a brilliant record . . .
NME

SPANDAU BALLET
Through The Barricades
(CBS)
Gary Kemp writes *terrible* lyrics. On this LP he's discovered that love is like war . . .
Smash Hits

. . . songs for sports stars and pop stars in sports cars.
Record Mirror

How unarguably, unutterably, unrepentantly *vile*.
Melody Maker

These are the boys who joined the people's army because they liked the uniform.
NME

SPEAR OF DESTINY
Outland (10)
. . . almost entirely tune-free – wimfling on and *on* at a doomfully dull plodalong pace like some monstrously serious 40 minute "epic" song about being dead (or something).
Smash Hits

. . . Kirk loses whatever ability he had to write good songs, he sings more like early Chris De Burgh than ever before . . .
NME

. . . *Outland* is unlikely to threaten his status as the great unheeded mouthpiece of the great unwashed.
Sounds

RONNIE SPECTOR
Unfinished Business (CBS)
What's essential is that the sultriest, most brick-chewing New York twang in the business is finally back with a set of songs that summon up the yearning and innocence of her best sixties material, but place it in a contemporary context.
Melody Maker

BRUCE SPRINGSTEEN & THE E STREET BAND
Live 1975-85 (CBS)
One sturdy box with pleasing cover.
Smash Hits

I wouldn't particularly care to squander money on alternative versions of songs I've already got . . .
Melody Maker

Cheap at twice the price.
NME

STARSHIP
No Protection (RCA)
. . . it's all a bit like a particularly harrowing episode of *The Kids From Fame* when they let their hair down and really "rock out, man" and if *that* doesn't put you off, nothing will.
Smash Hits

STATUS QUO
In The Army Now (Vertigo)
. . . this is indeed an album worthy to be part-produced by that grand old doyen of pub rock, Dave Edmunds.
NME

After two years scouring the world for musicians as stupendously ugly as John Coughlan and Alan Lancaster, the Morecambe and Wise of rock are back, balder and more patently ridiculous than ever.
Melody Maker

JERMAINE STEWART
Frantic Romantic (10)
It's Hollywood and antiseptic sex is on the menu. It's an accurate caricature of today; the inward scream of mispronounced technology. Look at the wardrobe notes, Yamamoto, Gaultier, Claude Montana – no wonder he's in no hurry to take his clothes off, the little fop.
NME

Just one mulatto mannequin, peddling his wares without much werewithal.
Sounds

STRANGE CRUISE
Strange Cruise (EMI)
This is hedonism mixed with a life-denying urge to ponce around.
NME

In the great (well, mediocre) *Face* in the sky, he will appear in the adverts you flick through blankly at the back.
Sounds

The charmless young fashionhound who styles himself Steve Strange is an interesting character, inasmuch as he inspires such unanimous loathing from a normally divisive rock press.
Melody Maker

THE STRANGLERS
Dreamtime (Epic)
I do sometimes wonder why people feel the urge to buy records like this. Do they also buy Julian Lennon records?
NME

The Stranglers have a rather unspecial and increasingly frayed connection with the mundane.
Melody Maker

The Stranglers are always pushing back the boundary lines, which is good enough for me and you.
Sounds

Off The Beaten Track (Liberty)
If you're a barking mad Stranglers fan you've probably got all these B-sides and "oddities" already and if you're *not* a barking mad Stranglers fan you certainly won't want them.
Smash Hits

THE STYLE COUNCIL
The Cost Of Loving (Polydor)
. . . maybe The Style Council would be better going back to the more straight forward pop songs they used to be so brilliant at.
Smash Hits

I've got a lot of time for Weller but I get the impression he hasn't got much time for *us*.
Sounds

The problem is that Weller, ever earnest, has internalised too thoroughly the edict Rock Is Dead. For every past powerchord and epic gesture he now endeavours to atone, publically, by the slavish imitation of the most slick and redundant aspects of contemporary black music.
Melody Maker

Maybe the Cappuccino Kid's crossing over in an audience more to his liking, deliberately leaving 'Money-Go-Round'ers like me behind . . .
NME

. . . the group sounds little better than a pub band of balding musos who can play slickly enough but haven't got an interesting idea between them.
Q

SUDDEN SWAY
Spacemate (blanco y negro)
. . . good to have at the front of your collection if you want to persuade your parents that you're listening to "proper" music at last.
Melody Maker

They're all thumbs, they make great mistakes, their nonsense is *always* inspired.
Sounds

ANDY SUMMERS
XYZ (MCA)
. . . although he's won quite a few England caps for his playing, he wouldn't get into any team of mine with such a thin nasal rattle as this.
Sounds

. . . a sideman's solo album if ever there was one.
Q

SWANS
Holy Money (K422)
Gracefully brutal and aesthetically beautiful, Swans are forever . . . One of the albums of the year, at the very least.
Sounds

Public Castration Is A Good Idea (K422)
Listening to this album is like slowly being nailed to a placard that says "People Are Worthless".
NME

This sound is very much the constituency of pain, putrefaction and pleasure . . .
Sounds

. . . the moral equivalent of the Black Death . . .
Melody Maker

SWING OUT SISTER
It's Better To Travel (Phonogram)
Overall, it's an attractive mixture of infectious jazz and soul, though the instrumental tune 'Theme' goes all twinklingly oriental for some reason and there's even some Van Halenesque tinsy bursts of screechaway guitars on 'It's Not Enough'.
Smash Hits

You've got nine offence free tracks for the price of a couple of exotic cocktails.
Sounds

. . . the sort of pop songs your mind tells you are a little bit naff but which make you want to wave your arms about and sing along when no one's watching.
Q

DAVID SYLVIAN
Gone To Earth (Virgin)
Great for playing *Trivial Pursuit* to, but not a lot else.
Smash Hits

It aches to renege on emotion and hover, zenlike, as *art*. But the act of aching betrays

it with unwelcome frictions.
Melody Maker

Gone To Earth feels lovely; it doesn't run from danger but nestles in its lap and seduces it.
Sounds

TALKING HEADS
True Stories (EMI)
Musically it's not that different from the previous Talking Heads album *Little Creature*, but it's still excellent.
Smash Hits

. . . overall these nine songs jog gaily into the mind-slot marked Another Talking Heads LP.
NME

Does it matter if the unforgettable mingles with the mundane? Not here, not now.
Sounds

ANDY TAYLOR
Thunder (MCA)
. . . the kindest thing that can be said about this album is that one is glad he has got it out of the way.
Q

HELEN TERRY
Blue Notes (Virgin)
. . . one *might* expect *Blue Notes* would be interesting, perhaps full of curious touches and excursions into the odder byways of pop. Bloody *isn't* though, is it?
NME

Within a setting of invigorating modern dance soul classicism, Helen Terry reveals that she is now a performer of true stature . . . a singer of genuine quality.
Sounds

This has all the emotion of a postcard from Milton Keynes . . .
Melody Maker

THAT PETROL EMOTION
Babble (Polydor)
Babble then is a rare beast. Undeniably rock, undisputedly alive and as rigorously well-drilled, fired up and furiously stated as any angry music from any quarter.
NME

. . . an imaginative rock album of instinctive ferocity . . .
Q

THE THE
Infected (Some Bizarre)
Matt Johnson, alias The The, is an absolutely furious young man with a talent for writing brilliant menacing pop songs.
Smash Hits

The sound that comes out when Johnson throws back his head and screams is a formless, lupine howl. I love that sound. *Infected* was the most arousing pop record

in 1986, a scathing attack on numb normality.
Sounds

You can't fail to notice it, and you'll be impressed, sure. But you won't grow to love it.
NME

THEN JERICO
First (The Sound Of Music)
(London)
. . . just one more burst of wasted rhetoric.
Sounds

This LP rushes headlong into the squeaking purity of the compact disc, the state-of-the-art hi-fi, the up-to-scratch Walkperson.
NME

THIS MORTAL COIL
Filigree & Shadow (4AD)
. . . at heart, a dull, lifeless, profoundly uninteresting record . . .
Melody Maker

Filigree & Shadow translates, literally, as "ornamental and insubstantial": it may not sound exotic but, as a description of the contents go, it's a lot more honest.
NME

THRASHING DOVES
Bedrock Vice (A&M)
. . . it's guitar music of an indie-ish type, but the lure of the tunes is almost irresistible.
Melody Maker

. . . the most essential debut release of '87.
Sounds

THE THREE JOHNS
Crime Pays — Rock And Roll In The Demonocracy (Abstract)
It seems almost possible that the Johns three might be slipping into the pleasant pool of mediocrity they've been raging against this half decade.
Melody Maker

Messy, snappy, guttural, salivating, sordid, moving irregularly and close to the ground — have you ever noticed how dog-like the

music of The Three Johns is?
NME

TIMBUK 3
Greetings From Timbuk 3
(IRS)
Timbuk 3 are a humorous and powerful mixture of talent and perception.
Sounds

It's like Neil Young cooked spaghetti for David Byrne and the sauce, that took 14 hours to cook, is out of this world.
NME

THE TRIFFIDS
In The Pines (Hot)
. . . it's entirely remarkable.
NME

Rough and restful, offbeat and fun.
Melody Maker

. . . get to grips with these Triffids as soon as you dare.
Sounds

RUBY TURNER
Women Hold Up Half The Sky
(Jive)
Ruby Turner has a voice and a half; unfortunately most of this album disguises the fact.
Record Mirror

. . . God, this album is disappointing.
Melody Maker

TINA TURNER
Tina Turner (Capitol)
But Tina Turner does such a good job breathing life into some very dull and anonymous mainstream songs . . . that you actually want to hear them again.
Smash Hits

Another of the Living Goddesses of Las Vegas has made an LP with a significant amount of the songs produced by or featuring grisly white rockers . . .
NME

Maybe she *is* Rod Stewart for middle-class feminists . . . maybe the marketing boys

have wrapped her up in *cellophane*
. . . But she's *still* a cut above.
Melody Maker

TWISTED SISTER
Love Is For Suckers (Atlantic)
. . . they just can't get it into their (lovably)
thick skulls that the same old song and
dance simply won't do.
Sounds

ULTRAVOX
U-Vox (Chrysalis)
These days, there are two Ultravox songs –
the fast one and the slow one. There's little
deviation within either category . . .
Record Mirror

The idea of grandness seems to motivate
Ultravox, forever on the same spot, shouting
their glossy nothings.
Melody Maker

U2
The Joshua Tree (Island)
As always U2 remain in danger, at times, of
taking themselves just a *touch* too seriously
– but even *then* they still sound quite brilliant.
Smash Hits

U2 are out-of-touch, and, today at least, I
mean that as a compliment.
Melody Maker

U2 have taught themselves to play rock with
the virtuosity of experienced folk musicians.
It is that native lyricism which informs the
music of *The Joshua Tree* . . .
Sounds

. . . these vast, yearning soundscapes are
alive with the will to uplift. U2 have never lost
faith in rock's possibilities, the way that Paul
Weller did (to the point where he's now
wasting his time and talent lamentably).
Q

CAMPER VAN BEETHOVEN
Camper Van Beethoven
(Rough Trade)
The Frank Zappa of the Eighties? The Byrds
on acid? Don't ask me mate . . . I think it's
wonderful.
Melody Maker

LUTHER VANDROSS
**Forever, For Always,
For Love** (Epic)
The first truly dispensable Luther Vandross
album.
NME

For Luther fans only, but I guess that
includes quite a lot of you.
Record Mirror

Give Me The Reason (Epic)
Luther, like no other, can turn an unexciting
word like "*and*" into a party . . .
NME

SUZANNE VEGA
Solitude Standing (A&M)
. . . you can almost hear the rain pitter-
pattering down her grimy attic window as
she plinks her moody guitar and muses
glumly on "life".
Smash Hits

The more Suzanne Vegas in this world
the better.
Melody Maker

Nobody's expecting Mel & Kim but too much
of *Solitude Standing* is plain depressing.
Q

ROSIE VELA
Zazu (A&M)
I'm not fascinated, but I'm damnably allured.
NME

THE VELVET
UNDERGROUND
Another View (Polydor)
. . . little more than an LP's worth of
indulgent, arty farty prattlings . . .
Record Mirror

. . . mainly goes to prove that the gang can
be as self-indulgent as anyone else.
NME

TOM VERLAINE
Flash Light (Fontana)
Half the time he sounds barking mad,
cackling and grunting and going "uh-oh"
but he never goes *quite* over the top – and
sometimes you can almost dance to it.
In fact, it's wonderful.
Smash Hits

Verlaine really treads on no one else's toes,
writes songs that start where most finish and
still plays in that fidgety, angular way that
you can only dream about.
Sounds

Flash Light is an album of fascination,
intrigue, beauty and thrills . . .
NME

LOUDON WAINWRIGHT III
More Love Songs (Demon)
. . . will have hardened fans spluttering with
laughter at its sexual machinations.
Sounds

. . . what Loudon means when he talks about
LOVE is divorce, business, travel, politics
and sex. In other words, a slice of middle
American middle-aged *life*.
NME

WALL OF VOODOO
Happy Planet (IRS)
. . . as much of a puzzle as a
disappointment.
Q

JENNIFER WARNES
Famous Blue Raincoat (RCA)
These songs were never meant to be
addled, dazzled lumps. It's like – Elton John!
Elkie Brooks singing Tim Buckley!
Melody Maker

Jennifer Warnes revives Cohen's gnarled
poetry with a sensitivity you can easily warm
to and her style is perfectly poised to exploit
the spaces opened up by Suzanne Vega's
success.
Sounds

Famous Blue Raincoat is quite excellent,
quite beautiful.
Q

WASP
Inside the Electric Circus
(Capitol)
. . . they *can* be unbelievably crass . . . but I
really *don't* think a bloke wearing a flame-

spitting codpiece ought to be taken *that* seriously . . . They make too much money now to consider anything but safe metal albums. But the taming of WASP has polished them into a severe, rigorous metal-pop outfit.
Sounds

ROGER WATERS
Radio K.A.O.S. (EMI)
. . . Waters is stuck on the dark side of his own peculiar rock star timewarp.
Q

THE WEATHER PROPHETS
Mayflower (Elevation)
It's subtle and unimposing and takes a few listens to convince, but it's ultimately impressive.
Sounds

. . . less Ray Davies without the grain than Strawberry Switchblade's poetic big brother, the one who wears the black bin bag over his head.
Melody Maker

. . . strictly for Germans and the uninitiated.
NME

WE'VE GOT A FUZZBOX AND WE'RE GONNA USE IT
Bostin' Steve Austin' (WEA)
After nearly killing myself to enjoy this record I'm weepsome to report that it's nothing but *A BLOODY RACKET!!!*
Smash Hits

. . . Fuzzbox are much too sharp to turn into the next Bananarama.
Sounds

Dayglo Poly Styrene style, it is a sparkly gift-wrapped rip-off.
NME

WHITESNAKE
Whitesnake (EMI)
. . . enough good tunes to keep the snapping jaws of the pushy new metal speed kings at bay.
Sounds

. . . a compendium of wishy-washy heavy rock clichés . . . that had even the *Kerrang!* critic complaining about the "oh-so-corny lyrics".
Q

BARRENCE WHITFIELD & THE SAVAGES
Call Of The Wild (Demon)
. . . he's not the next James Brown but 'Call Of The Wild' is two-fingers-up to all those emotional amputees who pass their slob pub-rock off as rhythm 'n' blues.
Melody Maker

KIM WILDE
Another Step (MCA)
Say what you will about Kim Wilde, no one could ever accuse her of being Diana Ross.
Sounds

There's nothing more of interest to say except that she has very nice hair.
Smash Hits

Equipped with the bare necessities of sound, one could imagine your younger sister would produce a more sonorous noise than this.
NME

Her voice is remarkably similar, in its timbre and pitch, to Marie Osmond's . . .
Melody Maker

BRUCE WILLIS
The Return Of Bruno (Motown)
The best song here, 'Under The Boardwalk', is unhappily well beyond Willis's vocal capabilities, and not even deep-throat wah-oohs from The Temptations are enough to cover its embarrassment.
Q

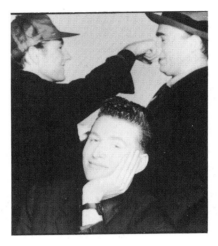

DANNY WILSON
Meet Danny Wilson (Virgin)
. . . falls between over-ambition and sheer, crafted pop inspiration.
NME

. . . big, bland and nigh on perfect.
Sounds

. . . not only rewarding depths of inventive panache but also a yearning emotionalism that lifts the music out of mere mannered accomplishment . . .
Q

JACKIE WILSON
15 Classic Tracks (Portrait)
. . . it's not hard to see why tired old superlatives like "classic" get trotted out once again – only this time they'd be right.
Smash Hits

. . . not even fit for the soul fanatic, merely for the soul historian.
Melody Maker

. . . poorly pressed, scrappy artefact, that demands your attention.
NME

THE WOODENTOPS
Live Hypno Beat Live (Rough Trade)
. . . The Woodentops are actually very brilliant at being thundering – with frantic but *tuneful* warblings, fwizzling thumpering rumblerdrums, demented wibbling organs and deliriously fine actual *songs*. And these aren't any crackly useless "live" noises either.
Smash Hits

. . . it's far from being an embarrassing backdoor "Best Of . . . " compilation.
NME

Not even for devotees and disciples. For dead people only . . .
Melody Maker

WORLD PARTY
Private Revolution (Chrysalis)
Nice songs, nice sentiments, but it's been tried before and it didn't work then . . .
Sounds

Some will call it greatness, some will call it a load of old baloney. I call it genius . . .
Melody Maker

X
See How We Are (Elektra)
A sharp contrast to the "Let's Pa-aaa-rty!!" attitude of the rest of the mainstream American market.
NME

. . . what it all boils down to is yet another bunch of growly yanks kicking ass and making vaguely the same sort of noise as about two million contemporaries.
Melody Maker

See How We Are. Indeed, I do and shudder.
Sounds

X-MAL DEUTSCHLAND
Viva (Phonogram)
. . . *Viva* is really rather rousing stuff and not half as dull as song titles like 'Eisengrau' or 'Feuerwerk' might suggest.
Smash Hits

Precisely panoramic pop for deep non-sheep who value stridency *as well* as sleep.
Melody Maker

XTC
Skylarking (Virgin)
. . . a record with more hooks than a docker's locker and yet as much chance of gracing *TOTP* as Robin Day.
NME

"This is Pop"? Maybe, but more in the fatherly sense than anything else.
Sounds

YELLO
One Second (Mercury)
. . . a sublime mix of electro-dance coupled with lush neo-classical melodies, plenty of adrenalin and lots of sparkle chucked in for good measure.
Record Mirror

There's hits and tunes and thoughts wriggling right across the year's most

exciting proposition.
Melody Maker

DWIGHT YOAKAM
Hillbilly Deluxe (Reprise)
Warners are obviously hoping to promote him as a country hunk, Nick Kamen gone a bit cowboy. He looks more like a Tijuana rent-boy.
Melody Maker

To these ears, this is about as pure country as you can get with that lonesome fiddle, guitars that sound like they enjoy being picked and harmonies that just linger.
Sounds

NEIL YOUNG
Landing On Water (Geffen)
He can't be well, and this record mustn't be encouraged. Shocking business, really.
Melody Maker

A work shaped with genuine skill and vision out of an imagination scarcely eroded by the passing of the years.
Sounds

NEIL YOUNG AND CRAZY HORSE
Life (Geffen)
. . . this album is worth a whole lot more than Suzanne Vega's entire repertoire of twee and vacuous introspection.
NME

. . . this rag-bag of ill-tempered patriotic posturing and menopausal raunch is final proof that the formerly great man has completely lost the plot.
Melody Maker

Though no doubt very decent and responsible for him to agonize about the outside world, I find Neil Young's hand-wringing patriotism hard to take. He just *sounds* tremendous.
Sounds

There's life in the old dinosaur yet.
Record Mirror

File under confused.
Q

PAUL YOUNG
Between Two Fires (CBS)
Paul Young's the sort who wins by default. Of course, you'd rather hear him than Rod Stewart or Tony Hadley.
Sounds

Nothing really awful then, just downright unexciting.
Smash Hits

. . . his songwriting fails him in the end and that is what ultimately condemns this record to the bargain basement pile.
Melody Maker

FRANK ZAPPA
Jazz From Hell (EMI)
Jazz From Hell is like airport muzak on a bad trip, an ugly collection of jagged bits and pieces that is, to be perfectly frank (ha!), very boring.
Sounds

When Utopia arrives, and most of our fun is outlawed with it, this is the music that will be ringing through the streets.
Melody Maker

ZERRA ONE
The Domino Effect (Mercury)
. . . not only a pile of over-blown pompous guff but boring, depressing and meaningless! I feel sick.
Smash Hits

A new rock for a spanking new year. Can't be bad.
Melody Maker

. . . monstrously uncool and a casual, assured success.
Sounds

WARREN ZEVON
Sentimental Hygiene (Virgin)
. . . Warren Zevon deserves your immediate reconsideration.
NME

Sentimental Hygiene sounds like a great way to go off the rails and claw back on.
Melody Maker

. . . streamlined *corporate* rock, a crisp but grey sound which cruises the late-night freeway but never hits either sunshine or the fast lane.
Sounds

ZODIAC MINDWARP AND THE LOVE REACTION
High Priest Of Love (Food)
High Priest Of Love is a ridiculously mannered, mildly funny and ultimately useless piece of rock product. Avoid.
NME

ALL OVER BAR T

Boy George flirted with Fleet Street and heroin and together they wiped him out. Tony Parsons comes to bury Boy George not to praise him.

Jolly George, the cartoon character who preferred Typhoo to fellatio, has the look of the concentration camp about him now. From daily tabloid to monthly glossy, hopeful sub-editors are calling the latest episode in the Boy George saga "The Boy Bounces Back" and the like but the cameras, once his happy ally, cannot conjure up a happy ending.

George Alan O'Dowd has emerged from the personal Belsen of heroin addiction looking as good as dead. Behind the make-up and fancy dress, there is a graveyard pallor to his skin, a grim set to his mouth and a shocked light in his eyes. Clearly he never dreamed that life could get this rough . . .

While his peers like Bendy Ben settle down to the first flush of spotty stardom or old Romantic classmates like Simon Le Bon and the Kemp brothers settle down to careers of lush mediocrity, Boy George is bled dry. He can be forgiven for his sins by Fleet Street (though of course his resurrection in that black and white cesspool is just as phoney as his crucifixion was) and he can even have the odd hit to follow up the embarrassingly abject 'Everything I Own' but it is all over bar the shouting for the former Boy.

Nothing is going to come out of that sad shell that is worth anything to anyone but the most mindless fan or the most money grabbing record company executive. It is there in his photographs and it is there in his work. The solo album *Sold* is in the bumwad league of the final Culture Club record, while the greatest hits

Boy George: You could make dolls out of a Beatle or the Boy, and they did.

package *The First Four Years – Twelve Worldwide Hits* was a study in shoddy melancholy. *The First* (there will be more?) *Four Years* (they couldn't even make it to a half-round number?) – *Twelve Worldwide Hits* ('Love Is Love' and 'The War Song' were hits in which world exactly?). You can't help thinking that the Boy deserved better than this.

The fantasy fate that Dave Rimmer invented for Boy George at the end of his excellent *Like Punk Never Happened* –

Boy George: When 'Do You Really . . .' appeared he couldn't have done more to put you at ease.

running Queenie's wine bar in the Old Kent Road, platinum records gathering dust on the walls and Marilyn playing the saloon bar bore – seemed derisive when the book came out in 1985. Now it seems like wishful thinking.

But in one way it seems inevitable that Boy George should end up the most spectacular wreck since the *Titanic*. He has, after all, always been a profoundly *reassuring* figure. That was the *point* of Boy George. He was always a comforting presence.

From 1981, when the heartbreakingly beautiful 'Do You Really Want To Hurt Me' appeared, he couldn't have done more to put you at ease. He was the screaming nelly who sang like a bird, the

androgynous figure who would reach for the digestive biscuits before he reached for the vaseline, an outrageous white rasta pantomime dame whose extremism, he implied, covered up nothing but an ordinary kid. Elvis went into the army to reassure the granny market and win their votes – George went into Fleet Street. Glib, pacy, thinking in headlines, the music taking second place – George and the Street of Shame were made for each other.

Even when the fall came – when George was getting over-exposed (the tabloids got bored with Boy George before he became tired of them), when Princess Margaret was calling him an "over-made-up-tart," instead of finding him cute. When his creative well had run dry and he was seeking ecstasy in other spheres – even when his fortunes dropped into the abyss from which there is no return, even *then* the Boy was a reassuring figure. He became fat and lazy, he buried himself alive in drugs – and it destroyed him. It took away everything but his life. The moral of this story was – you can't do that. How reassuring can you get?

George O'Dowd may be bright but he is not very intelligent. He flirted with Fleet Street and he did more than that with heroin and together they wiped him out. No pop star can keep the tabloids at a safe distance for ever simply because after a while they get bored and either the pop star comes up with a neat twist to his careers plotline or he gets dropped. George came up with the neat idea of killing himself. Now *that* kept Johnny Blake and the Bizarre boys interested!

After his fall from grace the next few episodes – the inevitable trail of dead bodies in his private life, the drug trials, the miracle cures and a messiah called methadone – were almost as tiresome and predictable as the music George started to make. But the lousy records didn't matter, which is some bitter irony for a man who essentially became famous by making a string of truly great singles. Like a Beatle, George had this shockingly high recognition factor – you could make dolls out of a Beatle or the Boy, and they did. Also like the Beatles, the thing you noticed first, and what in

HE POUTING

In one way it seems inevitable that Boy George should end up the most spectacular wreck since the *Titanic*. He has, after all, always been a profoundly *reassuring* figure

your heart of hearts you always liked best, was the music . . .

The difference between the Beatles and Boy George was two-fold. One difference was stamina ("The First Four Years" indeed) and the other was the difference between the sixties and the eighties and the reason for drug use in those times. Though there was always of course a degree of brainless hedonism about drug use in the Sixties, the Beatles and their contemporaries also experimented with chemicals for some kind of spiritual expansion and advancement, another shambling step towards the higher ground of consciousness.

In our time it is not like that. From the unemployed in the industrial wastelands to the pop stars who don't need a black card to get into the VIP lounge of the Limelight, drug use in the eighties is

never any more than – and never pretends to be anthing more than – a prayer for oblivion. Boy George was like anyone else who opted for that slow-motion suicide. It was all just too hard for him . . .

"*And next?*" as *Smash Hits* recently put it. "*Who knows?*" Who knows indeed . . . though there are only two possible punchlines to this sad joke. One is that the Boy will expire sometime over the next few years and Virgin will then be able to retrieve *Sold* from the remainder racks and re-release it as *The Immortal Boy George*. This premature death is not beyond the realms of possibility by any means, though old junkies do sometimes have a way of getting pickled in their poison and seem capable of shuffling on for ever (William Burroughs will certainly have a longer life than you and I).

The other possibility is that things will

go on as they are now, with the Boy singing "Red, gold and green, red, gold and green" to blue rinse matrons in Caesar's Palace in 15 years' time, sort of a Liberace with track marks.

His story *feels* as though it is over, but it is still possible to go to Hampstead tube station on a Saturday morning and follow the flock of Japanese schoolgirls to the door of his home. This sentimental pilgrimage, however, has less to do with George still being flesh and blood and breathing than it does with our culture's concept of celebrity. It hardly seems to matter that Mr O'Dowd is all washed up when he is still one of the most famous people on the planet.

Gilbert Adair says in his esssay "What Is Boy George For?" in his book *Myths And Memories*, "What Boy George truly represents is moderation, not excess. Underneath his glittering crust squats a homely little lad. For this, finally, is what Boy George is for: to personify, in an age of the media, and of "mediacrity", an age when fame is institutionalized, piped into the home like Muzak – to personify, as I say, a curious kind of Everyman."

Undoubtedly the life and squalid times of George urge you towards moderation rather than excess, but while it is possible that Adair is correct and the Boy is fame made Muzak – celebrity made into something you can pick off the supermarket shelf – what for the rest of us is merely a moral lesson is another man's life. It has always been hard to perceive George O'Dowd as another human being. He has always seemed larger – or smaller – than life.

The cartoon character is in a great deal of pain now, and where we once wished for him the inspiration to make music that would break our hearts, now the most we can hope for him is that he finds a course of non-addictive tablets that agree with his shattered body and mind, that will smother the unimaginable silent scream inside him and bring him the peace that he has earned.

Culture Club: George was the screaming nelly who sang like a bird.

KEEP TAKING

Tom Hibbert reports on the unholy alliance between telly and tabloid which has given birth to a whole new generation of useless pop stars. For them, marketing, not music, is the key.

Let's forget Ken Dodd for a minute. In the good old days (i.e. after yo-yos but before boil-in-the-bag noodles) it used to be understood that showbiz folk (i.e. something between a yo-yo and a noodle) did not make proper pop records. If they were overwhelmed by the urge to put themselves about on plastic, then the accepted medium was the comedy record. The chances were, anyway, that the showbiz person concerned was from what we shall laughingly call the world of comedy.

Thus Benny Hill, when the musical muse became too much to resist, found himself irresistibly drawn towards the tale of a randy milkman called Ernie. The musical framework of his epic served as a springboard from which he could bounce a dizzying set of *double entendres*. The point was that it was all a bit of a laugh, one of Benny's TV comedy routines transferred straight to plastic, without the intermediate efforts of a platoon of bearded men in baseball caps huffing away at winking, futuristic control boards and muttering darkly about EQ.

Nowadays, even the lowliest star of a coffee commercial boasts at least two of

person most famous for losing her clothes since Lady Godiva. And then she decides to make a record. The elderly might recall lasses of the sixties – girlie "personalities" who made similar career moves. Janice Nicholls for one. And another Samantha – Samantha Juste.

Janice was the "dolly bird" famous for squeaking "Oi'll give it foive" in a "funny" Birmingham accent on *Thank Your Lucky Stars*. And when she made her record, she merely exploited her cheekiness with a silly romp called . . . 'Oi'll Give It Five'. Samantha Juste was the dizzy dumb one who pretended to spin the discs behind Jimmy Savile on *Top Of The Pops*. She contrived a piece of pop nonsense called 'If Trees Could Talk' and was promptly never heard of again.

But this is the mid-eighties. No such novelty item for our Sam. Not for her trading on her bubbly Cockney "charm" or even her famed chest. No indeed. With a leather jacket and delicately torn jeans, Samantha Fox transforms herself into a sub-heavy metal streetwise gamine and yells out 'Touch Me (I Want Your Body)'. Soon Sam is a serious muso, a singing star throughout Europe and even in the States (where, apparently, she attracts a large gay following). Samantha has shown us the way. Get famous anyhow. Then you can

Nick Kamen: The pretty boy pop world had developed an inviting gap.

seems about to take his rightful place in the re-formed Beatles. How did this happen? Referring to the Madonna Episode, Nick quipped, "She loved my voice", thus conferring miraculous powers on wonder woman as the word which could have characterized Nick's career up to that point was "mute".

What had in fact happened was marketing. The pretty boy pop world had developed an inviting gap, owing to the fact that its leading practitioners had got serious, gone mad or spontaneously combusted. Into this gap popped Nick, who conveniently had always wanted to "do" music anyway. The years of modelling were promptly forgotten and quite right too. Who would want to dwell on an existence which involved having only one set of clothes and suffering burgeoning underwear trauma?

No sir, Nick was a quiffy troubador and always had been, since the days when he locked himself in a small room and learnt all the "licks" off his Su Pollard album. Now the past is a distant country, Nick has had a couple of what the marketing men call "hits" and released a whole LP, wherein he politely but expertly butchers a number of lesser known oldies. Nick knows the secret: keep safely tucked into the slipstream, avoid chubbiness and keep batting those crazy blue eyes. The material will eventually arrive because Nick Kamen is a marketable product.

Reeling under the blows of musical models, actors and soap queens, the staunch little empire of pop now found itself under siege from confident footballers

---

these becapped and bebearded gents as part of their entourage, ready at the drop of a hat to talk serious 48-track. The business of TV "characters" and "comedians" making music has become totally mega, an inescapable result of the unholy alliance between telly and tabloid which threatens to take over the world as we dimly perceive it.

Ah, tabloids. Curse of the eighties. Sire of the Page Three girl. "Saucy" Samantha Fox. "Our" Sam. A pair of bosoms and Samantha was up there pouting from filing cabinets on industrial estates around the nation, the

make the video . . .

Consider now the case of Nick Kamen. The first the world knew of Nick (apart that is from readers of *The Face* who had previously seen him modelling trousers on his head), was when he walked into a laundrette, wrestled briefly with his ideology and then drew some curious stares by the peculiar act of reading *The Spectator* in public. This intriguing moral fable was accompanied by the strains of a famous old pop song which young Nick had absolutely nothing to do with.

The next thing we know, the authorship of the famous old pop song has been reattributed in the minds of the hopelessly confused young, Nick has recorded a pop song written for him by Madonna and

THE TABLOIDS

Rupert Everett, on the other hand, has yet to find his niche. While Nick Kamen has stripped smirkingly to stardom, Rupert has opted for the "tortured artist with bells on" approach, which at the last sighting was listing dangerously. Mr Everett is a fully paid-up member of the Jon Bon Jovi "I would eat my poodle for rock 'n' roll" school of action, and barely a day goes by without this would-be popster warning us all of the dire consequences to his head should his bid for the top fail.

The initial problem concerned Rupert's first single: to walk into a record shop and ask for 'Generation Of Loneliness' by Rupert Everett would be an admission of total hipness failure. It just doesn't sound right and someone should have told him. Nevertheless, Rupert is a contender. He has a hand in his own material and will not be fobbed off with some pre-packed and greasy disco lash-up. To be sure, he knows Madonna (who doesn't?), but he wouldn't want her to write a song for him.

Instead, he has chosen as his musical guru none other than Bob Dylan, a musical guru of long standing. With ol' Bob, he has made a film and possibly "written" some music. Oozing this kind of credibility, Everett is in a position to snap pettishly at accusations that pop beckoned only after the concrete-clad failure of a couple of films. He's been writing songs since he was 16 and so anyone who sees him as a Johnny-come-lately can go and boil their head.

Taking the broader view, it could be said that anyone who looks like a cross between Sylvester Stallone and Tenpole Tudor is allowed to have a foot in both

Rupert Everett: Has opted for the "tortured artist with bells on" approach.

camps. Whatever, Everett is for the moment serious about his new career. Perhaps too serious.

Which is not an allegation one could make about the quasi-musical outpourings which have accompanied the rise of that hard-boiled (pop) opera *EastEnders*. Nick Berry, who plays something called Wicksy in the series, has freely admitted that he doesn't like his own voice, can't play the piano at all and did not start writing songs at 16, or any other time come to that. None of which prevented 'Every Loser Wins', a tune which richly fulfils the promise of its pea-brained title from leaping athletically to the top of the charts. This was a true spin-off, conceived in a moment, executed in a trice and forgotten in a jiffy.

The problem arises when we come to consider Anita Dobson, wild-eyed and toothy bar harridan in the series, but in real life the chanteuse extraordinaire responsible for the lilting strains of 'Anyone Can Fall In Love'. No problem as yet, file under Nick Berry. Enter Brian May, lofty guitarist from Queen, who claims to hear "anger and emotion" in Anita's speaking voice (possibly as a result of the character she plays being in a permanently angry and emotional state). Brian May has musical clout and he has decided to write songs for Anita to sing. The first one was called 'Talking Of Love' and was everything one could have hoped for. There may be more. Brian thinks that Anita is a "very rock 'n' roll person" and "has balls", so we can anticipate something quite special.

The point here is that an actress has had a measure of credibility conferred on her by direct intervention on the part of a platinum-suited "rocker" and members are allowed to introduce guests to their club. The twin-pronged attack of media saturation and pop glam by association will be hard to resist.

It is therefore a relief to leave the murky waters of the soaps for the clear air of the Corinthian peaks of football. There is no pretence here. Your average professional footballer thinks perfect pitch is an international stadium, doesn't mingle with the likes of Madonna and Bob Dylan and has always secretly yearned for the return of flared trousers.

When a football song staggers beerily and tunelessly over the horizon, the world knows to keep its head down. Fans buy them to mark some event in the team's season but they do *not* play them, nor are

Anita Dobson: Brian May from Queen hears "anger and emotion" in her speaking voice.

they sung on the terraces. The occasional participation of a musical celebrity in the proceedings lowers their value even further because the only fun to be had is seeing if the "singers" get the verse and chorus in the right order. The football song knows its place.

Or did, until Hoddle and Waddle and their expensively modulated hairstyles came on the scene. Their single resembled a traditional football song not one jot. It did not contain a variation on the sacred lyric: "We're going to hug and kiss each other and kick everyone else into a brain-damaged heap." It had the benefit of a "production job", which meant it did not actually frighten small children and pets. It had a tune.

Reeling under the blows of musical models, actors and soap queens, the staunch little empire of pop now found itself under siege from crisply confident footballers. A rumour that Ian "Beefy" Botham had a belter of a ballad up his sleeve could be the decisive factor.

So there we have it. There will, in future, be no respite from the pop burblings of those who were not born to bellow. No longer is it necessary to spend years perfecting techniques in a dark room and decades hawking demo tapes round record companies. As long as people keep taking the tabloids, new pop stars will appear from other areas of "the media", trailing clouds of producers and songwriters, safe in the knowledge that their PR is being well taken care of. The great-record buying public now appear to like what they know. Full stop.

GIRLS NEXT DOOR

They look like the extras not the stars, they dance round their Filofaxes and artistic considerations don't enter into it. Julie Burchill considers the appeal and pitfalls of being a pop starlet.

There had to be a non-boy Wham! sooner or later, a winning formula being what it is and the pop business being so flattering in its imitation. It SHOULD have been Joanne and Suzanne Humanne, the first girls to raise stage invasion to a high art, but they were too sated with platinum discs and disillusion. It COULD have been Pepsi and Shirlie, the two-tone Katharine Rosses of the Home Counties who finally got to strut their stuff when Butch and Sundance bit the bullet, but they didn't need it enough; they already had le petit mort(gages) and their place in the *Sun*.

These girls had no hunger, and no slogan; no three-minute manifesto, no GO FOR IT! Thus, at the last minute, coming from behind – CHEEKY! – on a prancing nag called FUN LOVE AND MONEY – a title worthy of Wham! at their bare-faced best – and making it through the tape not by a nose but by a rouged nipple, come Mel and Kim, the new Applebys of pop's eye for the main chance.

Mel and Kim give many collaterals to fame. One is cute and one is beautiful. They sing nicely and dance well. But their main strength is their airbrushed ordinariness. They look like extras from *Fame* or a Pepsi commercial, but not the stars. They look like 20 beige fruits of Anglo-Jamaican co-operation you pass in the street every day. They are the girls next door to the advertising agency; where they once danced around their handbags they now dance around their Filofaxes, but the everyday people shine through. From the East End to the West End, via catwalks and sweatshops, but they still say "Knowharramean?", not "Qu'est que c'est?"

Le pop: it's different for girls. Pop stars move from being dumb hunks to socially-concerned cocaine Communists in the space of one Red Wedge or Amnesty benefit. Pop stars do what they like, and they're still loved by their public; male homosexuality these days in pop is not the love that dare not speak its name but the love that shrieks its name in

Samantha Fox: The girl who rose without clothes, is obviously "nicer" than Diana Ross.

stereophonic sound. Unlike the Boy and the Bronskis, no pop star*let* could have had a number one hit with a single concerning the pleasures and pitfalls of being in love with another girl. It's DIFFERENT.

Pop is still Boystown, even if those

‘Treat Her Like A Lady' would be as hysterically funny as it is unthinkable. Pop stars DO; pop starlets ARE.

And what they are is so strictly regulated that their position makes your average straitjacket look like a wide open space. Ever since the Beatles, pretty boys have turned into sages of the ages and teen idols mutate into poets who don't blow it – five years from now we'll be huddled around our compact disc players trying blindly to unravel the riddle wrapped in an enigma that is the latest Nick Kamen triple concept album.

But girls stay put. They're Vamps (with its sub-divisions of Goddess – Sade, Diana – and Slag – Deborah Harry, Tina Turner), they're Chaps (Chrissie Hynde, Alison Moyet, incorporating the sub-division Wack – Slick, Sioux, Smith) or they're Wimps, known in mixed company as Girls Next Door. Then, of course, there is Genius – Dionne, Dusty – a bit thin on the ground since the demise of the silent songwriter. Occasionally there's a girl like Madonna,

---

Girls in pop do not sing self-glorifying gang anthems, or novelties, or protest songs; they don't even sing about social manners. Pop stars DO; pop starlets ARE

---

boys wear dresses. In private, pop starlets tend to be both serious and respectable, unlike their male counterparts. In public, whether it is Tina Turner at 50 singing about being a hooker (wasn't she meant to have regained her "dignity" when she shed her husband? Is it any more dignified to curry favour from five million men by proxy rather than one in actuality?) or Madonna singing about being a virgin, she is a female impersonator.

The pop starlet sells her talent in a way much more comparable with the stripper than the pop *star*. She does not narrate or pontificate; she teases, pleads and sells direct, without benefit of middle men such as self-respect or artistic considerations, to the ubiquitous and masculine "You". Girls in pop do not sing self-glorifying gang anthems, or novelties, or protest songs; they don't even sing about social manners. For instance, the female equivalent of

who with a hide of US Steel and a combination of beauty, brashness and brilliance manages to table-hop. But even Madonna could not find it within all her powers of enchantment to turn herself into a Girl Next Door.

Pepsi and Shirlie: The two-tone Katharine Rosses of the Home Counties.

Mel & Kim: Their main strength is their airbrushed ordinariness.

o one wants to be GND; least of all the girls themselves, after the first flush of fame and fortune has worn off. Why? It doesn't mean you're not considered beautiful (Kim Wilde, after being miscast as a Vamp at the start of her career, stands revealed after many tears, tantrums and transformations as a glorious GND), or sexy (Samantha Fox is a GND) or talented (Kate Bush is a GND). GNDs can be beautiful, sexy and talented; it is too easy and very cubist to point smirking at the Nolan Sisters when asked for a for-instance, and leave it at that.

But GNDs can't always be what they want. They can't be touched with genius, or autonomous, or solitary, or wild. As a rule, they don't write their own songs. A lot of them don't write their own cheques. They are pliable. Above all, they are NICE. Sex has nothing to do with it; Samantha Fox, the girl who rose without clothes, is obviously "nicer" than, say, Diana Ross, who never shed a stitch. GNDs do not *connive* or scheme; they think that being ruthless is what happens when the top blows off your house.

GNDs do exercise sexual prudence, though; they have steadies (Kim Wilde's was actually called GARY) and they live at home till unnaturally late. They tend to be rather family-orientated, and there is always a father or a brother lurking censoriously in the background in case some smutty hack wants to get smart and misinterpret perfectly innocent scenes from the videos, like Kim in the shower, swallowing and spitting out foamy water, or Kate bound hand and foot. Honestly, some people's dirty minds. . .

But sometimes their haloes slip down so far they could play hula hoop with

them. See the bad examples of Sandie Shaw and Marianne Faithfull, two Sixties GNDs from opposite ends of the social scale who came off the rails in a big way. Marianne Faithfull started out as an aristocratic teenager with a baby, a cleancut young husband, a face like a Rossetti angel and a habit of reading *Pride And Prejudice* on scuzzy tour buses. She ended up with a Mars Bar, Mick Jagger, a face like a Brueghel and a habit. Sort of the Lady Diana Spencer Story in reverse.

Sandie Shaw's was a less lurid, more

Bananarama: Making it on the backs of Jolley and Swain and cover versions.

stop-it-the-neighbours-are-talking lumpenprole tale. As GNDs go, poor Sandra was the Dreyfus of Dagenham; the essence of switched on yet clean-cut classless dollydom who was turned on good and proper when, after having it away with a married man, she was denounced in his subsequent divorce by a judge who called her "a spoilt and wilful girl who would stop at nothing to get her own way."

For a soldier, the equivalent would have been having your stripes torn off and your sword snapped in front of the

whole legion; all honour gone, all lace curtains twitching. Robbed of all working-class respectability, poor Sandra felt dispossessed enough to prance on down the Bohemian primrose path of multiple divorce, Eastern religion and making records with The Smiths. She probably had a great time – but she couldn't make those records any more, those great records she made when she was a little manipulated puppet on a string.

Even if they don't fall from grace accidentally, GNDs have a way of precipitating things when being the nation's sweetheart gets too much. Look at Sheena Easton and Olivia Newton-John; one minute saying please and thank you, the next prancing around brandishing riding crops and small purple pop stars from Minneapolis – kinky! – though not too successfully. They try being autonomous – *producing* themselves, if you please. Then they try *writing* – it's pathetic, really.

Think of Bananarama, making it on the backs of Jolley and Swain and cover versions, throwing fits of pique with the poor record company until they're allowed to record their own wretched efforts, limping in at number 93 with it and straight out with a bullet the next week then running back to Svengalis and bargain bins, looking for a new grave to rob when they found that Jolley and Swain had other starstruck fish to fry. It's not a *safe* life, being a GND; you're very dependent on the kindness of strangers. Where are Tracie Young and Dee C. Lee today?

Sticking pins in Mel and Kim dolls, probably. Because these really are ordinary girls; mixed marriage, divorce, violence, the battered wives refuge, truancy, demobbed at 15, pregnancy at 17 (Kim), waitressing, beaten up by boyfriend for taking clothes off in camera (Mel), cancer of the liver (Mel), a boyfriend called Wayne (Kim), a belief in horoscopes and reincarnation; an everyday story of working-class survival from an original set of sketches, by Hogarth, choreography by Debbie Allen.

Fame – will Mel and Kim live for ever? And will they live next door for ever? If Peter Waterman, their guiding limelight, has his way; "I'm not too keen on Mel and Kim going to the States – they don't pay you properly, and the record company would only give the girls dope, get them involved in cocaine."

But it is not cocaine that will spell the end of Mel and Kim as GNDs, and thus as flavour of the month. It is not the flats in Hampstead or the gambols in the Gambia. It's the fact that Kim has just written her first song, and plans to write many more. Like many GNDs, they are about to saunter down the cul-de-sac called creativity. We shall not see their like again (for six weeks, at least).

BLACK MUSIC - TRI

On one hand it was a year of unprecedented achievements — on the other there were thinly-veiled accusations of racism. Jim McFarlin reports on the problems that still face black musicians in America despite apparent prosperity.

The world of black music in America was anything but black and white over the past 12 months. 1986 marked the first time in history that three black female singers – Whitney Houston, Patti LaBelle and Janet Jackson – held the Nos. 1, 2 and 3 positions on *Billboard* magazine's US pop album charts simultaneously. But it was also a year in which two of black music's most celebrated male artists, P Funk godfather George Clinton and superstar producer-composer Quincy Jones, spoke

George Clinton: Widely quoted statements alleging exclusionary practices.

out with widely-quoted statements alleging exclusionary practices against rhythm and blues acts on pop record charts and radio playlists.

Miss Houston sold over eight million copies of her debut album for Arista Records, the best-selling first album ever for a black solo performer. Yet at the same time, three other solo women singers who scored No. 1 US black singles, Stephanie Mills ('I Have Learned To Respect The Power Of Love'), Jean Carne ('Closer Than Close') and Shirley Jones ('Do You Get Enough Love'), couldn't crack the Top 100 singles on the pop charts.

It was a year in which black-to-pop crossover success appeared to reach its all-time peak. Black artists commanded half the Top 10 positions on the US album charts at mid-year and historically unconventional acts enjoyed major

victories. Run DMC became the first rap group ever to earn a platinum LP and the blues-breaking Robert Cray Band went gold. In the midst of this musical nirvana, however, the need was felt to create a new action group called the Black Rock Coalition (BRC) to protest at the alienation of black musicians who play rock music from rock radio formats as well as the black music mainstream.

Why all these apparent discrepancies? Some have pointed, with irony and anger, to lingering effects of the discrimination which has long existed in the music industry.

It is generally conceded that black music was once systematically excluded from America's pop consciousness. Pat Boone's rise to fame in the 1950s by singing white cover versions of virtually every black hit of the day is given as the classic example. While the aura of black music prosperity surely seems to exist in the mid-1980s, the contention has been advanced that it is a partial and selective prosperity dictated solely by the record industry's bottom-line, a smokescreen to cover the remaining vestiges of racism in the music business. A few black performers at the very top are flourishing but far more must either conform or perish.

As examples, the fact is noted that it took Miss LaBelle 24 years and over a dozen record releases to achieve her first platinum album (the million-selling *Winner in You*) in 1986. Are we to believe that after nearly a quarter-century of thrilling vocals, Miss LaBelle suddenly stumbled upon the formula for commercial success with her last LP? More likely, she was finally smiled upon by the predominantly white moguls of MCA Records (who may have seen her as their answer to Capitol Records' blockbuster resurrection of Tina Turner) and given a substantial boost by her LP's signature single – a ground-breaking male-female inter-racial duet with Michael McDonald, 'On My Own'. As Miss LaBelle became fashionable to the lords of the music industry, she was, in turn, made accessible and palatable to the pop music-buying masses.

Sceptics also question whether Miss Houston, as exciting and magnetic a young talent as she is, could have burst

upon the pop scene as spectacularly as she did if Arista Records president (and noted star-maker) Clive Davis hadn't taken a personal interest in her career and spearheaded an immense promotional campaign. As Jerome Gasper, PolyGram Records vice-president of black music A&R, noted to *Billboard* magazine, "Clive Davis pulled out all the stops from the beginning on her. I wouldn't have been surprised if that record had sold only 400,000 units. But he believed and gave the record time to find its market."

One outgrowth of this "unequal opportunity" is the emergence of copycat black acts, as competing record labels scramble to share the fruits of a hot-selling sound and young hopefuls retool their styles in order to curry label interest. The dominance of star black female artists in 1986 helped set the stage for such 1987 would-be pop/soul queens as Lisa Lisa, Jody Watley, Donna Allen, Shirley Murdock, Mel'isa Morgan, Vesta Williams and, to a lesser degree, Anita Baker and Melba Moore.

Patti LaBelle: Finally smiled upon by the predominantly white moguls at MCA.

The platinum album consistency of Luther Vandross (another black superstar still waiting for a first Top 10 single) begat the ballad romanticism of Gregory Abbott, Freddie Jackson,

124

ND OR TRADITION?

Eugene Wilde and yet another comeback for the ageless Smokey Robinson. As the phenomenal accomplishments of Minneapolis-based producers Jimmy Jam and Terry Lewis have made self-contained production teams all the rage, here come David Frank and Mic Murphy of The System, the Deele's "L.A." Reid and Babyface and Michael Powell and Dean Gant.

Through numerous published comments from a variety of black musicians recently, the primary dilemma appears to be this: unlike their white counterparts, who are typically viewed as creative and innovative as their music becomes more divergent, black artists are directed towards being commercial rather than original. If their songs are too "black", there's a fear that they cannot cross over to the mass pop audience. If the songs are too "white", the fear is that they will not gain the strong foothold in black radio needed to act as a springboard to crossover potential.

Perhaps Clinton, "Dr Funkenstein", puts it best. "You have these black artists who get a pop smash and then keep copying that formula," he says. "Then they find out that white (radio) stations don't want them as regular guests because they're black, and black stations don't want them because they're too into

Members of The Black Rock Coalition with their President, Vernon Reid, centre.

A third outgrowth is that many white artists are becoming "blacker" in their musical approach – British performers, particularly Simply Red, Peter Gabriel, Steve Winwood and Robert Palmer, come instantly to mind – and are receiving more gracious acceptance on black playlists while many black artists are moving further away from classic R&B in search of that elusive crossover goal. As one US record executive lamented, "It's sad to see the brothers so

an 18-month study of the record industry which concluded that "a pattern of racial exclusion" makes the business "the sole preserve of white males".

The study, entitled "The Discordant Sound Of Music", alleged that blacks are "grossly under-represented" at professional and management levels of the industry despite being responsible for 25-30% of its annual revenues. Further, companies have no affirmative action programs or plans to increase their number of minority employees, and black artists who are not perceived to have crossover potential are handled differently than white acts and given smaller promotional budgets.

The NAACP report also noted a sad truth; there is tangible evidence of reverse discrimination among the black artists themselves. The vast majority of black entertainers have few if any blacks in supervisory or executive capacities. Though an artist is believed to have the ultimate say over whom he or she wants as a manager, record labels and agencies can apply subtle pressure to steer an act toward a person with whom they feel they can communicate more comfortably – i.e. a veteran manager, frequently white. As the report asked, "if black artists are not prepared to hire other black professionals, then who will?"

Songwriter-guitarist Vernon Reid, who formed the Black Rock Coalition in New York, sees little change. Reid contends black progressive artists are still told to "play it safe" at the outset of their recording careers, with the implied promise of expanding their musical horizons later – if they become a hit. Reid says even US college radio stations, supposedly the most receptive outlet for alternative music, doesn't seem to believe blacks are capable of creating adventurous new sounds like R.E.M. or The Replacements. The Bus Boys, those standard bearers of black/rock coalescence, have all but vanished.

Meanwhile, almost as if offering a placebo to the larger issues, the record industry has apparently overcome another long-standing pop taboo: the aforementioned success of the LaBelle-McDonald single has triggered a current deluge of inter-racial male/female pop duets, among them Carl Anderson and Gloria Loring ('Friends And Lovers'), Linda Ronstadt and James Ingram ('Somewhere Out There') and Aretha Franklin and George Michael ('I Knew You Were Waiting For Me'). Another step in breaking down the barriers? Another follow the leader response, more likely, another trend.

While the aura of black music prosperity surely seems to exist, it is a partial and selective prosperity dictated solely by the record industry's bottom-line, a smokescreen to cover the remaining racism in the music business

sounding white."

There are several ramifications to Clinton's suggestion. For one, the surging, omnipresent "Minneapolis sound" popularized by Prince in the early 1980s will likely continue to be copied to the point of distraction, or till it simply burns itself out. In the past year alone, Janet Jackson, Herb Alpert, Donna Allen, Sheila E., Jody Watley, Chico DeBarge and Jermaine Stewart, to name just a few, have borrowed and manipulated that basic groove.

Another is the possible trivialization of all the impressive contributions of black music to American culture in the past decade, if modern black music is viewed by the white recording establishment as a prevailing trend (like country and dance/disco in the 1970s) rather than a tradition.

concerned with crossing over, while white acts are increasingly working within R&B. We're selling out the only thing we've really got."

While many top representatives of major US record labels point proudly to broader pop acceptance for black acts and the growing popularity of rap, coupled with a promise of deeper commitment and marketing strategies for its highest-profile black acts, the root of the dilemma shows little sign of improving soon. Challenging the recording industry on racism, the National Association for the Advancement of Colored People (NAACP) recently released the results of

OUT OF AFRICA

To boycott or not to boycott? Can music separate itself from politics? These were the old questions that flared anew as Paul Simon's Graceland tour came to town. Simon Garfield examines the problems involved in dealing with music and apartheid.

In the end, we may find that the only songs that matter carry the words "Baby, I'm a love machine." For the present, some of the songs that matter most concern South Africa.

In 1987 the anti-apartheid debate fired the music world as never before. Not that it was a new issue: musicians have been inspired since the sixties by the horrors of Sharpeville and Soweto and touched by the brutalities and injustices unleashed on Biko, Mandela and a million silenced others. It's just that this time we had Paul Simon's *Graceland* album and tour, and it's fair to suggest that more insults were hurled, more temperatures raised and more beer spilt over Simon's plane trip to Johannesburg than any other single musical event.

Then again, most of the 1.3 million-plus who bought the LP in Britain – and millions more worldwide – didn't give a toss. The music was just dandy and sod anything else. The way Paul Simon saw it, at press conferences and in numerous interviews, there were no worries. He reaffirmed his loathing of apartheid at every opportunity and acknowledged the Botha regime as proto-fascist. He saw no reason to apologize for his actions, stressing that he would never perform in South Africa and that local musicians were paid triple the normal scale and received full songwriting credits (and presumably full royalties), although Los Lobos might have something to say on that subject.

Simon's explanation was that he "was approaching the subject from a cultural point of view . . . I am not an expert on South African politics." By his own admission, Simon unashamedly used South African music for his own ends. Speaking to *Musician* magazine, he explained how he was "just gonna go into the studio. The musicians would play until they found a groove that I liked. I wasn't trying to write South African songs, I was trying to write Paul Simon songs without emasculating the essence of that music."

He emerged with *Graceland*, one of the richest and most significant albums of the decade. With the huge inspiration and gifted assistance of Ladysmith Black Mambazo, General MD Shirinda & The Gaza Sisters, Stimela, The Boyoyo Boys and Ray Phiri, all revered and successful local musicians, Simon magicked a sound most Western record-buyers and radio producers could welcome as a courageous style of new pop. In one sense he'd done a Malcolm McLaren; pirated snappy and beautiful alien sounds from which he'd claim most of the royalties. And in one sense he'd served as an ambassador for the only important new music to reach five million pairs of ears last year.

The *Graceland* liner notes explain well enough the roots of Simon's South African odyssey but the notes are more interesting for what they omit. Nowhere is there any mention of any trepidation or apprehension of the political coals he was to rake, let alone direct political comment. Yet Simon couldn't escape the political controversy that grew, and grew

Johnny Clegg of Savuka ("We Have Risen"): a multi-racial Johannesburg-based pop-dance unit.

more complex, with each *Graceland* sale and live show.

The point was, of course, that you didn't *have* to be an expert on South African politics to recognize the evil of apartheid and its upholders, and thus Simon was blacklisted, boycotted and battered at press conferences. If the reason was clear-cut, the ensuing debate was less so. In strict terms, Simon had broken the 1980 United Nations cultural boycott by recording part of *Graceland* in South Africa and his actions, without consultation with or permission from any recognized anti-apartheid body, were seen as a deliberate and insensitive flaunting of internationally agreed conduct. As Stuart Cosgrove put it bluntly in the *NME*, "all they asked of us was to stop eating Del Monte sliced peaches, and Paul Simon's attitude told them to go fuck."

Others chose a quite diffrent tack. Sure Simon was naive, they said, but what was his crime? Was spreading the beat of resistance worldwide a corrupt thing? Should an artist opposed to the apartheid regime be punished for popularizing that country's joyous native music and thereby associating in the popular imagination South Africa with black rather than white faces?

The UN boycott was established in 1962, when a resolution called on all member states to avoid "all South African goods." The trade boycott was augmented in 1980 when the General Assembly asked countries "to sever diplomatic, military, nuclear, economic, cultural, academic and sports as well as other relations with the racist regime" in an attempt to persuade the Pretoria government to dismantle apartheid.

The problem for music and other cultural assets lies in the non-selective approach of a blanket ban. The *Graceland* affair highlighted a clear divide between the views of those within South Africa involved in the frontline of the struggle, and the anti-apartheid movements overseas. The UN argued against purchasing the album "because then you are putting money in the pockets of South Africans," but other anti-apartheid organizations, including the Pan-Africanist Congress and the Congress of Racial Equality (CORE), supported Simon. "He ought to get a goddamned medal, not blacklisted," said CORE's chairman Roy Innis. Further support for Simon came from two of apartheid's greatest musical opponents, the exiled singer Miriam Makeba and trumpeter Hugh Masekela (both of whom would later join him on tour).

The outlawed African National Congress maintained its opposition to the *Graceland* project, but it's known that the body is beginning to consider the possibilities of a strictly enforced boycott selectivity. There are obvious dangers in this, not least that any easing of the blanket ban may create a false impression that government-induced change is taking place, or that, however slightly, South Africa and apartheid are being

Labi Siffre: Some of the most level-headed comment on the Paul Simon affair.

brought in from the cold. Also, as UN's South Africa-related sub-committee chairman James Victor Gbeho told *Rolling Stone*, "if every performer would go to South Africa and claim that his visit is to benefit the black population, the boycott would be meaningless."

In Britain the campaign against Simon was spearheaded by Artists Against Apartheid, the body responsible for some excellent and influential fund and consciousness raising events. Its impassioned co-ordinator, ex-Special Jerry Dammers, believed that just buying the *Graceland* album was in itself a damaging defiance of the cultural boycott.

Addressing *Time Out*, he said, "I think the popularity of *Graceland* shows up the danger of a pop star breaking the boycott, because it may even make the boycott itself unpopular in the minds of the people who like the music and buy the LP. I don't know if that's what Simon wanted to do, but I think he has already done a lot of damage to the campaign . . . I hope the music of the South African people is not going to become just another valuable asset of that country to be exploited by the West in collaboration with the machinery of apartheid."

Some of the most level-headed comment on the affair came from Labi Siffre, the singer who composed the most successful anti-apartheid single of the year, 'Something Inside So Strong', inspired by a harrowing televised township shooting by the South African military. "With sanctions in general," he said, "I think you should ask the black people of South Africa. If they are happy with Paul Simon's record, and happy that he made the record, them I'm happy with it. Those people out of South Africa who are trying to do something for the country are supposedly doing it for the black people of South Africa. So I think if the black people of South Africa are for it, that's fine. It's not for an ego-trip for anybody else."

The controversy also threw up several wider issues. It was noted that Simon had turned down the opportunity of appearing on the (US) Artists Against Apartheid record attacking Sun City a year earlier, principally because the original demo tape had named all the artists who had performed there,

including friends such as Linda Ronstadt. The record, written by Little Steven and featuring Bono, Dylan, Springsteen and Miles Davis amongst many others, served to draw public attention to the $90 million white pleasure zone in the middle of the poverty of the black "homeland" of Bophuthatswana, "the Afrikaner's paradise in the black person's nightmare."

Some nine months later at a London press conference, Paul Simon was explaining his decision not to prohibit sales of *Graceland* in South Africa. Why, he asked, shouldn't people be able to buy the music of their own country? One reason was that the hefty tax on such sales would inevitably go to the government in Pretoria, and from there perhaps to the military. The SA sales veto had already been exercised by The

rousing shows in Britain this year, but not before sampling the sort of opposition Clegg hoped he'd left behind. There was further confusion over policing the boycott: were South African and South African-based musicians committed to the struggle and eager to spread the message abroad no better than those who'd played Sun City?

The Musicians' Union thought not. Clegg's SA residency was seen as incompatible with regular MU policy, and they opposed the granting of work permits and threatened to expel him from the union. The ANC, however, supported Clegg and his stance against apartheid, and a spokesman voiced the view that the best way forward with such issues was not through blind sloganeering but through consultation with the relevant progressive black elements within South Africa.

It was noted that Simon had turned down the opportunity of appearing on the (US) Artists United Against Apartheid record attacking Sun City a year earlier, principally because the original demo tape had named all the artists who had performed there, including friends such as Linda Ronstadt

Style Council, Spandau Ballet and Elvis Costello along with many less prominent musicians, and other artists like Blancmange chose instead to accept their SA royalties and send them directly to the ANC. Others still chose to sneer at what they perceived to be ineffectual tokenism.

Mixed reactons also greeted the arrival in Britain of "White Zulu" Johnny Clegg

Ladysmith Black Mambazo: The upshot of the *Graceland* controversy for them was a major contract.

& Savuka, a multi-racial Johannesburg-based freefall pop-dance unit. Rochdale-born Clegg, an ex-university lecturer, had moved to South Africa fascinated by Zulu culture, and in establishing his first band Juluka achieved a considerable victory in winning the right to perform as a multi-racial band before multi-racial audiences.

His new outfit Savuka ("We Have Risen") released an upbeat *Third World Child* album on EMI and played several

And the major upshot of last year's controversy and fine rhythm? Major contracts for Ladysmith Black Mambazo and Hugh Masekela (both WEA, the former produced by Paul Simon) and new deals for hot South African crossover musician Sipho Mabuse (Virgin) and Clegg & Savuka (EMI). Simon's personal stock inevitably increased tenfold and the boycott debate got its most widespread airing yet. Whether the mass record-buying public's own knowledge of the struggle of black South Africa increased proportionately with the prominence of these artists, or with the success of sympathetic records from the likes of UB40, Labi Siffre, Latin Quarter, Big Audio Dynamite and Boy George, will always be hard to tell.

But if anyone doubted the value of music-based protest-propaganda last year, they needed only to look at Botha's own efforts in this field. The "Bureau Of Information" released their "peace song", catchily titled 'Together We Can Build A Better Future', roping in (at great expense) some of the less sane elements of local musical talent (and resulting in arson attacks on several participants' homes). The song was not a big success.

According to local reports, the song heard most and played loudest in the township yards and record shacks was invariably something championed, diluted, moulded and Westernized by a runtish sixties folkie from New York.

A CONSPIRACY OF

In 1986 the British membership of Amnesty International rose by a third. In America it went up by 50,000 people. More than 60 per cent of these new members were under 25. Phil Sutcliffe investigates the beneficial effects of A.I.'s deliberate targetting of rock.

During Amnesty International's remarkable "Conspiracy Of Hope" tour of the USA in June, 1986, its stars – Sting, U2, Dire Straits, Phil Collins – met Veronica de Negri, one of the campaign activists who travelled with the rock star caravan. A middle-aged Chilean woman, she had survived imprisonment and torture under the Pinochet military regime but had been forced to live abroad for many years. She told them about her 19-year-old son Rodrigo who had grown up in exile and was about to return to his homeland for a visit at long last.

A couple of weeks later in Santiago, Rodrigo and a friend, Carmen Quintana, joined a street demonstration. They were unarmed and there is no suggestion that they were doing anything violent when,

apparently at random, troops snatched them from the crowd and dragged tham down an alley. They poured petrol over the two teenagers and set fire to them, beating them with rifle butts and mocking them while they burned. Then the soldiers bundled the bodies in blankets and dumped them on the outskirts of the city. All this is known because, despite appalling injuries, Carmen lived. Rodrigo died after three days in agony.

And so the "Conspiracy Of Hope" met horrifying reality. A direct line had connected their often rarefied world to the political victim savaged in the back alley – the very person Amnesty International has been standing up for since its foundation in 1961. Their reaction? What could it be? They did their shows. They gave their tracks to the *Conspiracy Of Hope* LP (titled *Rock For Amnesty* in the USA).

But what Amnesty has made many people realize is that such reactions to horror need not be essentially impotent cries of pain and anger. The atrocity was committed, the artist responds. The small piece of work sitting on a plastic disc acts as an amplifier and a magnifying glass. The tens of thousands who like the music come, look closer, make their own responses.

The dead cannot be reborn, but the prisoner of conscience can be freed, the torturer can be called off, the death sentence can be commuted. That's what AI's 600,000 "freedom writers" around the world demand with every letter they send to a president, a general, or a prison governor. And they get results – which is probably why, in the last year, Amnesty has become *the* pop cause and looks set to run and run, unlike some flavour-of-the-moment idealistic gestures.

The "Conspiracy Of Hope" tour targeted six named prisoners of conscience to highlight the general campaigning and awareness-raising. Two of them were subsequently released by regimes at opposite ends of the political spectrum: black trade union leader Thozamile Gqweta in South Africa and

human-rights activist Tatyana Osipova in the USSR.

Simple Minds dedicated their whole '86-87 world tour to Amnesty and in San Diego actually gave the audience postcards addressed to the Sri Lankan government in support of a Tamil activist called P Udoyarajan who had been in jail for three years. At least 400 cards were mailed and within six weeks he was released. Amnesty always stresses the difficulty of proving that such sequences of events are cause and effect, but there can be no serious doubt that the nagging weight of international, individual opinion plays its part.

These small victories for common decency are a few amongst hundreds that AI chalks up every year. The music connection undoubtedly helps – and it's no accident. "We targeted rock quite deliberately," says Pat Duffy, acting director of AI in Britain. "It appeals to a wide range and its roots are cross-cultural and classless. We want to become a mass movement so we must touch everyone."

In the past 18 months they've certainly reached out through the generations descending via veteran supporters Townshend and Clapton to Sting, Peter Gabriel and Mark Knopfler and finally a new array of '80s names like Simple Minds with their own ideas on how to point their fans' enthusiasm back out into the big world.

Simply Red began to carry the AI logo on their stationery. In his Christmas fan club mag Howard Jones asked readers to post cards they might have sent to him to a prisoner of conscience instead. UB40 invited AI to to insert membership forms in the sleeve of their last album. U2 let Amnesty leaflet some of their gigs (the association became so strong that it was reported that there were more Amnesty than U2 banners waved by the audiences on their '87 American tour).

Though Amnesty haven't attempted to stack all this support into a single monster event like Live Aid, the "Conspiracy" was hardly small potatoes with the six concert bills including U2, Sting, Gabriel, Bryan Adams, Jackson Browne, Lou Reed, Townshend, Carlos Santana and Ruben Blades and closing with a live MTV telecast from Giants Stadium, New Jersey.

The equivalent British effort, 1987's

Sting:
"It's the most civilized organization in the history of the world"

HOPE

"The Secret Policeman's Third Ball" – two nights of music and two of comedy at the London Palladium (co-ordinated by long-time Amnesty supporter, DJ Paul Gambaccini) – attracted names who had rarely or never previously allowed themselves to be associated with any political cause. Apart from Knopfler in a unique duet with Chet Atkins, there were Duran Duran, Kate Bush backed by old Pink Floyd friends Dave Gilmour and Nick Mason, Nik Kershaw, Bob Geldof (a recidivist from the original "Ball" in '79), Reed again and Joan Armatrading.

John Taylor (Duran Duran): "Because Amnesty International is apolitical it's a cause we shall always try to support"

"I think many people are worried that their careers will suffer if they become involved in something 'political'," Pat Duffy says, "but with Amnesty they don't feel that's a problem." It's also important to the stars offering themselves that what they do has proved itself in practice.

Of more profound and long-term significance is that in '86 British membership of Amnesty rose by a third to 37,000 while their American rolls went up by about 50,000 to 350,000. Duffy says that more than 60 per cent of new affiliates are "young" (under 25ish). AI are pretty scientific in assessing feedback from their rock-linked ventures: for example, membership forms are numbered so that they can tell whether the source of an application is, say, a U2 concert or a UB40 album.

To capitalize on the pop-star connection's basic capacity to attract attention, the charity has had to develop its skills in dealing with the business end of the music – record, video and TV companies. Unlike Live Aid which always intended to shut up shop within a year and leave it to the aid professionals, AI must think of the long haul (as in *for ever*, unless human nature takes a turn for the better). They need to keep on coming back to the people and companies who have helped them so they have to find ways of averting "compassion fatigue".

In essence, Amnesty have to, even *want* to, give helpful companies a piece of the action. "They are commercial organizations," says Duffy. "It's different to an artist doing a free show or donating a track. A company can't work for us for nothing or they won't be able to commit themselves to a full-scale promotion effort on Amnesty products."

A cautionary tale is the unexciting return on the "Conspiracy Of Hope" LP. PolyGram generously gave AI an advance of £170,000 and a McCartney-size 20 per cent royalty rate. But this created a situation where they couldn't allocate it promotional priority because profits wouldn't have covered additional costs. So it seemed that everywhere it was released the company was preoccupied with Bon Jovi's latest or, ironically enough, Bob Geldof's, and sales were slowish.

For the multi-media "Third Ball" Amnesty hope all the angles have been covered. "We're treading a precarious path between the charitable and the commercial," says Angus Margerison, general manager of Virgin Vision (Video) who ended up overseeing the whole project. "We have shareholders to think of now, you know. But the policy is we do one of these a year. So a deal was struck whereby Amnesty would have no financial risk, we'd cash-flow it all and keep a close watch on budgeting all the way through. We won't lose our shirts as long as we can cover that initial investment.

"That means we can offer them a high royalty, though I don't think I want to say exactly what it is, and come the autumn if we play it right we can market the thing as a total event and produce a synergy and . . ." He pauses from splashing about in biz-burble, draws breath, then delivers his considered punchline. "And get more people out of jail."

At press time the plan was to release the combined music and comedy film and two LPs (possibly packaged as a double), with separate videos and a book (published by Sidgwick & Jackson) also pitching at Christmas. Maybe a million

Robin Campbell (UB40): "It can't be wishy-washy to support basic human rights. In fact it's impossible not to support them. But it's important that Amnesty doesn't follow any *party* political lines"

quid for Amnesty, thinks Duffy. Half to two million depending, says Margerison. From Amnesty UK's perspective that means if it does well, it could bankroll them for a whole year – as well as recruiting more and more biro-bearing foot soldiers to the campaign.

To close, here are some thoughts on the wider implications: where a fondness for pop songs can sometimes lead us; why a rock concert can be a fundamentally different experience to a football match.

Yelena Bonner (Soviet dissident, former prisoner of conscience): "Amnesty can change the moral climate of the entire world, even in totalitarian countries and under repressive regimes."

Richard Reoch (AI): "If we don't raise *our* voices, there will only be the screams in the torture chambers and the endless silence of the secret graves."

To contact Amnesty International, send an SAE to:
UK: 5 Roberts Place, Bowling Green Lane, London EC1R 0BB. (*Phone: 01 251 8371*)
USA: PO Box 37137, Washington, DC 20013. (*Phone: 800 253 1100*)

ABROADCASTING

With the twin threats of Americanization and Europeanization looming large over British music broadcasting, Simon Frith wonders if 1987 will be the last year in which Radio One mattered so much.

Its anniversary wasn't celebrated with quite the same *fervour* as *Sgt Pepper's* (there weren't any CDs to sell) but in the 20 years since BBC Radio 1 started transmission in September 1967 it has done far more than the Beatles' sentimental masterwork to determine how British pop music is understood and organized.

To put it more precisely, if *Sgt Pepper* marked the moment when British rock became the central sound of international music marketing, Radio 1 ensured that this sound would remain something peculiarly British. This was the effect of its unique blend of US Top 40 and European public service principles: the daytime DJs domesticating the hits – all-purpose mood music for Simon Bates's bathetic romances and Steve Wright's little Englander routines, the evening DJs coming across as hiply enthusiastic youth workers – neither punk nor the very idea of an "indie" scene would have been possible without "Uncle" John Peel and his helpers.

Radio 1 "replaced" the 1960s pirate stations but it provides a pop service quite unlike their commercial model, and its supposed constraints have in fact been the source of its real strengths. To cater for everyone (and not just an advertiser's "demographic") means eclectic programming – British sales charts are the world's most confused and fast moving. Needletime agreements and the resulting airtime for cheap live sessions give off-peak shows the fervour of an alliance (musician, listener and DJ) *against* the mainstream industry.

The irony of this is that mainstream music policies are themselves a Radio 1 effect, something which the record companies continually resent. This kind of broadcasting is not at all in their best interests but has been, for 20 years now, the determining British means of promotion. It has no real radio competition (independent companies have a restricted, local impact), television time is short, and in the 1980s, at least, live tours and venues have had a declining sales influence while "club success" remains limited to club music.

Radio 1, in short, is still the way into the *Gallup* chart, and the *Gallup* chart is still the most important factor in the definition of British pop stardom. Record companies (majors and indies alike) have to organize their marketing around the single (which long ago ceased to be a money-maker in itself); they have to service the BBC youth audience (whether or not it is the real sales target).

Twenty years is a long time in the pop business and any institution that survives so long, whether a Beatles LP or a radio station, comes to seem a permanent part of the soundscape. 1987 may turn out, however, to be the last year in which Radio 1 mattered so much.

The return of a Tory government means that there will soon be at least two national radio services and though (for good advertising reasons) they'll be more like Radios 4 and 2 than Radio 1, even this will help companies break the youth-service selling system that is becoming less and less relevant to their needs. The Conservatives' victory will mean too the continued deregulation of television, increasing pressure on the BBC to

become a subscriber service, and the break-up of the ITV's regional monopolies. The idea (it's Rupert Murdoch's) is to increase Britain's TV opportunities, to give us all more programme "choice".

This is in political terms the "Americanization" of British broadcasting. The Thatcherites keep telling us about all those channels that the Californians have, but in commercial practice it will mean "Europeanization". (The new subscriber and advertiser markets will be organized across EEC boundaries.) In terms of pop outlets we've been here before – somewhere deep in my subconscious the meaning of rock and roll is tangled up with the experience of Radio Luxembourg.

Luxembourg's commercial station began its evening English language service in 1933, even then offering a flow of ads and records in deliberate contrast to the BBC's measured uplift. By the time I started listening in the 1950s it was a straightforward teen outlet – not so

If *Sgt Pepper* marked the moment when British rock became the central sound of international music marketing, Radio One ensured that this sound would remain something peculiarly British

much competition for the BBC's Light Programme as a way into a completely different world. On Lux we listened to American records (rather than British studio sessions) played by cool DJs (not plummy presenters) in between advertisements that treated us as already-consuming adults rather than soon-to-grow-out-of-it children.

Lux lost its ideological importance sometime in the early 1960s, even before Radio 1 (and in its early days Radio 1 still had no evening service), partly because the pirates were slicker and more up-to-the-minute, but partly too because the Beatles fitted better into the BBC format. We were happy to hear *them* live in the studio, cheeky youth club stars, and subsequent pop movements, from progressive rock through punk to white noise bands and shamblers, have consistently sounded more convincing in John Peel's sceptically affectionate terms than in Lux's pushier sales formats.

Radio Luxembourg does still broadcast, though, and catching it in 1987 (twiddling the dial in a Helsinki hotel room) was like getting an electric shock. My mind was emptied of history (who in 1959 believed that Britain would ever have *any* rock and roll importance?) and the music seemed mysterious again.

The important thing about rock and roll in those days wasn't that it was American (it wasn't the sound of the imported films and television shows) but that it was somehow Out There, a noise in suspense over Europe, brought to us for some unknown reason by football-pool tipsters and acne-cream companies as a youth secret. What mattered as we tuned our transistors wasn't that parents disapproved but that they didn't even know the music existed.

In 1987 Europe the mystery is soon dissolved by the British familiarity of the records (Curiosity Killed The Cat, Cutting Crew, Cocteau Twins), but my nagging sense of displacement returned when I switched from radio to television.

All over Northern Europe now (everywhere except most parts of Britain) peopls have access to *Music Box, Sky Trax* (which puts out a magazine, *Sky, just* like Lux's old *Fab 208*) and *MTV-Europe*, English language pop video services for non-English viewers, shop window displays of the latest musical goods held together by coy English VJs and "review" panels of minor English stars.

For the first time I understood properly that there really is a world of British pop fame that has nothing to do with British critics or British fans or British consumers at all – we still think that pan-European television music means the Eurovision Song Contest.

The rise of Euro-video promotion doesn't mean there'll be any dent made in Anglo-American pop hegemony (Radio Luxembourg never did anything much for Luxembourg's music-makers). There may be new sorts of Euro-star (A-ha, Europe) but the satellite and cable services themselves are dominated by British and American capital (Richard Branson's and W.H. Smith's in *Music Box*, Rupert Murdoch's in *Skytrax*, Robert Maxwell's and British Telecom's in *MTV*), by British and American performers. What these services do signal, though, is the increasing importance of the Euro-audience.

This is a matter of straight consumer economics. The UK has long been a less significant source of both record and concert income than West Germany, and the video channels have now put together a single North European youth market with much greater purchasing power than our own beleaguered teens. What is striking about this market is its *casual* appropriation of the consumer dream – British label pop is simply as bright and disposable as Italian label sportswear and American label fast-food.

Twenty-five years ago the Beatles provided cheap labour just for the German leisure business. Today British musicians are providing cheap labour (and videos) all across Europe. In this period British pop stars haven't so much taken over continental culture as become ever more dependent on it.

This is a matter of straight consumer economics. The video channels have now put together a single North European youth market with much greater purchasing power than our own beleaguered teens

This fact of financial life for Britain's embattled labels and musicians has remained oddly hidden from the rest of us – music writers still treat European (as against American) pop tastes with derision – but the point is that while we remain the most important source of pop talent, we are fast becoming the least important pop consumers.

Our *theories* of pop – all those arguments about who matters and what it means, Radio 1 talk and the music weeklies' diatribes – are irrelevant now to the new sales process. Most European countries have better rock magazines than ours anyway, better music coverage in their daily press, more sophisticated cultural arguments, more civilized rock clubs and festivals.

In this setting – the video programmes giving it dramatic clout – UK musical taste, our distinctive combination of cosiness and cultishness, has lost its influence on even our own performers' careers. Radio 1's ingratiating and earnest approach to "youth music" is beginning to sound really quite quaint – like the Light Programme in the 1950s. How long can it survive?

TRANSCENDENTAL

It had to happen — the generation weaned on Led Zeppelin demand their revenge. Mat Snow traces the revival of the rock group from Gothic gloom to a new Age Of Hilarious.

"If you read the lyrics of your Tears For Fears and people, they've all got *big* opinions on *big* subjects. I've got no opinions on these things and I think people just wanted someone to come along and say, Listen, I don't give a shit either. I don't care about all this stuff. Let's just party!" (*Zodiac Mindwarp, 1987*)

"We just ain't funky dudes. I'm just totally proud of the music I listen to – of not going through life embarrassed and really wishing I'd listened to James Brown records when I was 14. I'm very happy I used to listen to Led Zeppelin." (*Billy Duffy, The Cult, 1987*)

T o anyone for whom punk was a watershed in taste and attitude, such statements sound like the last word in reaction, a bizarre return to the dinosaur early '70s when the last flickers of the '60s rock community were extinguished by big money, big technology, and stardom's bunker mentality. Just as these ageing punks wring their hands at the likes of The Cult, Mission, Mindwarp et al, so they fail to grasp the connection with their megaselling brat-pack Noo Yawk cousins, The Beastie Boys. The tie-in is a four-letter word: AC/DC.

AC/DC: A loud, catchy, self-mockingly juvenile guilt-free trip.

Even though this Anglo-Australian Heavy Metal act has acquired a huge global following over the last ten years with their loud, catchy, self-mockingly juvenile guilt-free trip, only now has their influence filtered into the post-punk circles who would once have dismissed AC/DC's anti-style as irretrievably crass and non-U.

Such precious self-importance couldn't last forever, especially in today's climate where the time-hallowed teen pleasures of sex 'n' drugs 'n' pocket money are once more increasingly forbidden. Caught between the knowing, taunting self-promotion of Madonna, Paul Weller's uptight strictures and the swottish foppery of The Smiths, what can a poor boy do 'cept to sing for a rock 'n' roll band?

What people who knock the new rock dinosaurs also misunderstand (such is the ideological tunnel vision to which former punks are prey) is that the whole megadecibel hog stampede possesses (and proceeds from) a fully functioning sense of absurdity. Which is a relief, for the roots of the new rock revivalism lie in the most po-faced scene of all.

B y the time the Goth movement was in full swing in 1981-2, its main initiators Siouxsie And The Banshees were moving into the less monochrome territory. Though camp and androgyny dominated the Goth look, its sound was inclined to be a mirthless, dank thundering about in the void where life-forms trod uneasily if at all. With its strongholds in the north of England, it wouldn't overstate matters to say that Goth both reflected and theatricalized adolescent gloom about lack of prospects and also consciously rejected moneyed metropolitan glamour.

With hindsight you can identify the prototype of the new dinosaur rock in the best and most successful of the original Goth bands. From Leeds, The Sisters Of Mercy boasted in singer Andrew Eldritch a splendid pastiche of the right-on rocker's worst nightmare. Clad in black leather, long greasy locks half-obscuring a gaunt, impassive face already mystified by biker's reflector shades, he would drawl funereally through the Sisters' Mandrax-paced set whilst a single malarial spotlight hazed him in a shroud of cigarette smoke. And in the sick but interesting footsteps of his lizard-king guru Jim Morrison, he once even grew a beard.

The Sisters Of Mercy: With hindsight the prototype of the new dinosaur rock.

With his studied flair, Andrew Eldritch has now disappeared in a cloud of rumour and counter-rumour, not only bequeathing two former Sisters, Wayne Hussey and Craig Adams, to form The Mission, but also declaring the no-go zone of heavy rock open to scrutiny, approval and even pillage. This was typified in the Sisters' embracing of former untouchables The Rolling Stones in a claustrophobic and monotonous version of 'Gimme Shelter', a song which hindsight reveals as the anthem to Altamont when the hippie dream gave way to heavy rock's apolitical apocalyptic power-trip.

Amongst the major record companies, Arista saw which way the wind might blow, but too early. They signed an inferior Goth outfit called The Danse Society whose soporific version of the Stones' '2000 Light Years From Home' flopped in '84. When the big push started the following year, it would be a pincer movement spearheaded by two independently-moving prongs – The Cult and Zodiac Mindwarp.

What people who knock the new rock dinosaurs also misunderstand is that the whole megadecibel hog stampede possesses (and proceeds from) a fully functioning sense of absurdity

NEBRIATION

The Cult: Unearthed a blitzkrieg macho glamour long buried beneath the punk decade.

By 1985 The Cult looked seriously in danger of terminal contraction. Formed in Goth's *annus mirabilis* of 1982 by a born-again Red Indian resident of Bradford called Ian Astbury, with each year The Southern Death Cult shortened their name as substitute for finding a new musical idea. As Death Cult, they looked stuck in a limbo of pandering to an increasingly rigid Goth scene. As just The Cult they seemed in imminent danger of disappearing up their own definite article.

Then, flying in the face of confident predictions of demise, The Cult released a string of hit singles in 1985-6 plus an appalling but big-selling album called *Love*. Though the music was epic, swirling, pompously atmospheric and quite sexless, the promo videos made a grand spectacle of barbarian locks, guitar heroism, light shows and cock-rock gyrations. By looking back at Led Zeppelin's *The Song Remains The Same*, The Cult had unearthed a blitzkrieg macho glamour long buried beneath the punk decade of ideological soundness, minimalism and ironic distancing. By the end of '86 all The Cult needed to make the great leap to full-blown Zep-hood was for the music to catch up with the image.

Also from Bradford, Zodiac Mindwarp zoomed straight to the heart of the best without any boring intermediate Gothic stages. A cartoonist by trade and loon by nature, the former

Mark Manning identified the unwashed, spaced-out biker image as being both closest to his normal lifestyle and one that every other pop sub-cult bar Heavy Metal could unite in loathing. In a world crowded with fashion options, he stumbled upon one of the few ready-made images in which, because it requires no self discipline (au contraire), today's misfit can find a carefree drunken home.

Oddly enough, it was urbane style magazine *The Face* that first profiled Zodiac Mindwarp And The Love Reaction. It thoroughly enjoyed this provincial dirty joke at hip London's expense, and so made the band very trendy indeed – the latest freakshow for the jaded. Zodiac lived up to the caricature and more, in which his conspicuously inebriated spending of a large slice of Phonogram's £80,000 recording advance figured prominently. He played the over-loaded, over-endowed and over-the-top rock star to the hilt, though at one time he looked as if he might be his own publicity's first casualty – broke, brain-damaged and without even having got it together to make a mega-selling, malodorous mutha of a record.

By spring '87 he'd got his head round the problem and had a Top 20 hit with 'Prime Mover', launched on the back of one of rock's all-time preposterous videos, directed by Ade Edmonson (note that The Beastie Boys also credit the deceptively sophisticated male juvenile mayhem of The Young Ones as an influence). Zodiac may yet capitalize on the short-lived flush of the groovy but anaemic Doctor And The Medics, whose smash-hit version of Norman Greenbaum's 'Spirit In The Sky' in the summer of '86 heralded the public dawning of the Age of Hilarious.

Affiliated to the parodic, grebo end of the Spinal Tap spectrum are Leicester's Gaye Bykers On Acid (a Virgin signing so totally committed to all that is kinky, vile and weird that the fact that one of their members' father is a Conservative councillor has been turned into a perversely hip credential) and the Black Country's Pop Will Eat Itself.

Though the latter are close in mood to the surrealist classroom humour of Liverpool's late lamented Half Man Half Biscuit, their squalid appearance and chainsaw guitars qualify an appearance in this pantheon of plonkerdom. Note also that their superior version of Sigue Sigue Sputnik's 'Love Missile F1-11' implicitly acknowledges the marketing genius of

Tony James, whose noble mission to reintroduce vulgarity into the charts only failed because he ran out of cards up his sleeve.

More faithful to the Gothic metal-sheen and Vincent Price delivery are The Mission, fronted by Wayne Hussey. In their visual presentation The Mission evoke both the devil worshipping dandyism of early Black Sabbath and the beery, acid-fried brotherhood of Hawkwind. In his hilariously spoof rock star interviews,

The Mission: More faithful to the Gothic sheen and Vincent Price delivery.

Wayne claims that the Mormonism of his upbringing has now given way to transcendental inebriation, and the truth of this is demonstrably true. Wayne is a splendid parody rock star; what The Mission lack – despite handsome sales of their Phonogram album *God's Own Medicine* and accompanying singles – is a musical style that kicks ass *and* pokes fun.

Significantly, it took the production of Def Jam's Rick Rubin – the producer-cum-entrepreneur behind Run DMC and the Beastie Boys (and, of course, an AC/DC fan) – to strip away the last veils of Gothic gloom from The Cult and expose them as shameless cock-rockers.

Including their matchless Stones/Zeppelin pastiche 'Love Removal Machine', The Cult's album *Electric* is state of the art retro-rock, one of the best records of 1972. Their live show is cock-rock cabaret in excelsis: all the naffer aspects of the original period – the clothes, the drum solos, the guitar wankery, etc – are still recognizable but now streamlined for today's short attention span. Steppenwolf's hoary 'Born To Be Wild' and The Troggs' even more venerable 'Wild Thing' are amusing live highlights, and that the latter tune has now re-entered the repertoire of London Underground's buskers denotes a frightening degree of cultural penetration already.

No sleep till Hammersmith, folks.

NOTHING BUT A HO

Disco, they say, never died in the Windy City but Ian Cranna discovers there's more to the Chicago House than dance music and torrid tales

Chicago, you'd think from reading much of the wilfully romanticized "street" nonsense spouted in the British music press, has changed very little since the days of Al Capone except that synthesizers have replaced machine guns.

Wheeler-dealer black kids, one would read, would sign for one company and then cross the street to sign with another under a different name. The mutual bitching made Joan Rivers look like the milk of human kindness while backstabbing was an everyday part of going about your business. Everything was stolen from something else and nobody would ever give anybody else credit.

In fact, Chicago is a remarkably civilized city, if perhaps somewhat less than wildly exciting. In reality, the much celebrated pseudonyms have far more to do with (a) avoiding the jeers of your peers, (b) the fantasy creations (for fun) of local label pioneers Jesse Saunders and Vince Lawrence or (c) the pressing need for local musicians to make some quick money to pay off credit card bills than any Robin Hood notions of pulling a fast one to rip off the Boss Man.

Chicago musicians are also remarkably reluctant to badmouth each other publicly (business – where the real tangling takes place – is another matter entirely) and also quick to praise. Stealing other people's ideas is, after all, a time-honoured and universal practice. It's what you do with them that counts and House artists are thrilled that their local music has been greeted with approval in New York, let alone on the other side of the world. In short, Chicago House musicians are among the most pleasant and least arrogant you could wish to meet.

But whence all the fuss in the first place? And what exactly *is* House? Disco, they say, never died in the Windy City. The more aggressive rap culture hasn't taken off in Chicago and local tastes are naturally more conservative (this is the Mid West, after all) and this applies to music as

much as anything.

At the end of the day, House is a distinctive localized dance form, its threads pulled together from a variety of other styles but looked down upon by the more traditionally minded local musicians – until it took off. It's basically urban black dance music which adheres to the basics of good time dance music –

Farley Jackmaster Funk: Insists he started and christened House music.

a thumping beat with a particular emphasis on kick beats and hi-hats, and distinctive because it's made mostly electronically – dark, eerily empty washes of synthesizer, drum machines and sampling with a minimum of vocal distractions in contrast with the energy of the music.

Being independent releases, the records are necessarily low budget affairs but, as so often happens, lack of means to indulge oneself keeps things direct and the main idea to the forefront. Beneath the superficial simplicity and similarity, the true creativity starts which is what makes House such a fascinating phenomenon.

Curiously for a city so oriented towards dance music, Chicago has remarkably few clubs. It had none at all in 1977 when an astute local businessman, noting the weekend commuting to New York clubs, invited New York DJ Frankie Knuckles out to Chicago and so, slowly at first, was established the now legendary Warehouse Club. In the wake of its success came others, notably The Playground set up by Jesse Saunders and Vince Lawrence, and The Music Box where Ron Hardy held sway.

It's Frankie Knuckles who is generally

acknowledged as the real Godfather Of House, although Farley Jackmaster Funk (one of the DJs who grew up in Knuckles' wake) has staked his claim and he's sticking to it. The music Knuckles was playing – a blend of imports both from Britain (arty but succinct electronic music like the Art Of Noise) and from Europe (especially Italian disco) with '70s soul (especially the lush but forceful records of Philadelphia International) was generally known as "underground" if anything. Initially House was so difficult to define because it was so joyously open and free of rigid boundaries – such is the spirit of true House.

But Knuckles, according to Jesse Saunders (himself another early DJ), is more a programmer than a DJ; this is perhaps a bit hard on the big man (Knuckles is actually his real name) but the distinction is that DJs used more tricks of the trade like sampling to create a harder sound, and Farley was already one of these. Farley insists *he* started and christened House, though he is quick to give credit to the kid from whom he picked up the name.

As for the assertion that House was created by black gays for black gays, Knuckles (whose Warehouse crowd was principally gay) shrugs that he merely attracted a party crowd that was already on the go to advertised ad hoc parties. Others like Farley, more touchy about their masculinity, will insist that their crowd was straight and that different clubs had different crowds. These days visible gays and straight couples mix easily at House gigs, though some black gays – who set the pace with their stylish dressing and chic shaped haircuts now adopted throughout Chicago – can be scathing about the newcomers.

It was from the DJ tricks of the trade that the House record scene first started with a 12" of rhythm tracks intended by Farley for other DJs, although Jamie Principle's 'Waiting On My Angel' is generally accepted as the first House record. A legend in Chicago but virtually unknown outside it, this introverted, deeply spiritual youth with a sound like a black electropop Bowie has all the makings of a future superstar, especially now that he has a major deal with EMI.

As other DJs tried to stay ahead of the competition by adding their own musical trimmings and so found they could write their own songs, other releases followed: Saunders again with his own Jes Say (geddit?) label and (later) Steve "Silk" Hurley, and then the more daring of the local musicians: Marshall Jefferson hiding under the name of Virgo, and so on. And so too developed a local slang based around the themes of "jacking" – music, dancing and sex.

As with punk in Britain, the major local talents were the first to latch on to House as a vehicle for their own ideas

establishing DJ International and Trax Records respectively. Alas, short-sighted greed seems to have prevailed. It's a tragedy both for the development of House music and for Chicago itself (now devoid of major labels) that these two should have forfeited the trust of the local stars. In their wake have sprung up a host of lesser labels with lesser resources (and generally lesser talents) while the genuinely creative flounder in search of proper guidance.

House music was thus several years old by the time it was "officially" introduced to Britain by the music press in August 1986. To the bemused British, Darryl Pandy became the public face of House

entrepreneurs having left Chicago for the business meccas of Los Angeles or New York. The future of House lies in the stranded musical talents in Chicago being lucky or determined enough to secure proper managerial guidance and major label deals. Sadly there can be little future for House in Chicago alone.

But is there that much to get worked up about? Yes, for there are genuine talents to develop, but sadly the average British punter may never know the full power and glory that is House, for it is in a Chicago House club that the pieces finally fit and all is revealed. Here, from midnight till ten or eleven the next morning, the DJ really comes into his own. In a long, dark – very dark – room the music pounds and pounds. In the centre of the dancefloor a strobelight will be flickering, exaggerating the movements of Chicago's finest as they twist and turn with a mixture of stylishness and abandon, screaming and throwing their hands in the air with approval as a recognized favourite hits the speakers.

And the music – always the music – it's seamless stuff, relentlessly exciting and irresistibly powerful as the different songs fade in and out of each other – sometimes just a snatch, sometimes nearly a whole track – with various electronic tricks, trademarks and extra rhythm tracks adding their own reinforcements. To a newcomer it's a thrilling and awe-inspiring experience.

Initially House was so difficult to define because it was so joyously open and free of rigid boundaries — such is the spirit of true House

that actually transcended it: Adonis (locking himself away in his West Side home in search of perfection with thousands of songs on tape, and whose early records like 'No Way Back' helped define the typical House sound), Fingers Inc (the truly creative keyboard player and former jazz drummer Larry Heard and gifted but as yet undisciplined gospel singer Robert Owens), the aforementioned Marshall Jefferson (a highly likeable and ceaselessly energetic keyboard player whose chess scalps include the Illinois state champion). These are three of the more obvious names who stand to be around for years to come.

And then came the bad news. Local business talent was quick to spot the earning potential of House with first Rocky Jones and then Larry Sherman

Darryl Pandy: Became the public face of House when he sang on 'Love Can't Turn Around'.

as he sang 'Love Can't Turn Around' while Farley (who'd stolen the song from Isaac Hayes and the idea for doing it from Steve "Silk" Hurley) mimed to singer Kevin Irving's backing vocals on *Top Of The Pops* and Jesse Saunders' name mysteriously disappeared from the label credits. (Of such dealings are public legends, however misleading, born.)

And then was launched through the clubs Steve "Silk" Hurley's crossover monster 'Jack Your Body'. But why no appearances? Having parted company with DJ International (a small matter of the accounting discrepancy between reported sales of 17,000 and anticipated sales of over 100,000), JM Silk sat in Chicago blissfully unaware of the frantic demand while DJ International told callers the musicians were "out of town". (Of such dealings are public legends, however misleading, reinforced. Oh dear.)

So where does House go from here? Everyone agrees that it has to become more professional and more song-oriented to gain exposure. Part of the problem is that House records are so long that they're only just getting going when most pop records are winding down – a dancefloor DJ's delight but a radio DJ's nightmare. Strange to relate, the future of House depends upon business as much as musical talent, most experienced

Frankie Knuckles: The New York DJ who became The Godfather Of Chicago House.

There is no bar, no drunkenness and no trouble as people literally dance the night away. Although House is now accepted in other clubs, at a hardcore House club the crowd will be almost entirely black. Yours truly was one of only three white people all night at a Frankie Knuckles gig at the shortlived Gallery club yet there was no hint of heaviness, merely the occasional glance from the curious and solicitous hospitality from a beaming organizer. That's Chicago for you but it doesn't make for such a good story, does it?

TAINTED LOVE

Sex may be very rock 'n' roll indeed but pop stars have been very reluctant about facing up to AIDS. John Gill examines the music industry's awkward response to the killer disease.

On April Fool's Day 1987, George Michael, Bob Geldof, Womack & Womack, Herbie Hancock, Aswad, The Communards, Bananarama, Holly Johnson and a swathe of guests took over Wembley Arena for "The Party", the main event among dozens organized around International AIDS Day. During the weeks around the Day itself, there were other concerts, dance, film, theatre, fashion and cabaret events, all aimed at raising money for AIDS research, education and support, both in Europe and abroad. The event raised hundreds of thousands of pounds and gained respectable publicity, but it was all rather *bonsai* compared to Live Aid.

This is no criticism of the organizers, committed individuals of myriad sexual persuasions from the arts who gave freely of their time and expertise to attempt something different to an expensive and pointlessly alarmist government ad campaign, as well as topping up inadequate government health funding which had left major research hospitals competing with each other for charity hand-outs and the proceeds of benefits held by gay pubs and nightclubs.

There was no satellite link-up, no telethon with Geldof swearing at people to give money, and certainly no TV collage of People With AIDS accompanied by The Cars' 'Who's Gonna Take You Home?'. The Party – the night where the conscience-pop suffix found a ghastly reason to throw its own party – was a litmus test for the late 1980s concern with, well, *concern*.

AIDS is a fatally simply disease, carried by certain body fluids and transmitted in exclusive circumstances. Yet for so rock 'n' roll a disease – rock 'n' roll, like "jazz", meaning "fuck" in its original context – the black-and-white threat of AIDS has become surrounded by so many rumours, lies, myths, scares, moral attitudes and notions of cause and blame that such a massive subject, and one so close to home, may literally bankrupt Pop's conscience.

English avant-gardists Coil threw down a gauntlet of sorts a few years back, with a cover of Soft Cell's 'Tainted Love' where all proceeds from sales went to the AIDS charity, the Terrence Higgins Trust, and there has been a smattering of AIDS-related soul tearjerkers and agitrock tunes since, but Pop's reaction to the disease might best be described as having gone red in the face. Unless you're a punk or a member of ELP, love is an abiding and central subject of pop, yet pop has signally failed to address itself to this new need for change in all our lives. As the disease spreads, more and more people will become aware of its reality. Meanwhile, Pop twitters on as ever, not exactly ignorant of AIDS but acknowledging it reluctantly, like some awful family secret.

The trouble is, the moral and political complications around AIDS are silencing almost as many as are speaking out. A Le Bon or Geldof can appear on television pushing safer sex, but many more are backpeddling fiercely away from the subject, probably because of the gay connection (even though it's naïve young straights who are now most at risk from ignorance). In the real world, exposure means you might lose your job or home. In the wacky world of pop, you get – as has already happened – a call from *The Sun* asking if you deny that you have AIDS. The next day's headline runs "Pop Star X Denies S/He Has AIDS".

George Michael: From "Choose Life" T-shirts to Safe Sex videos

On a recent trip to San Francisco, I was stunned at the level of fundraising activities to help various AIDS organizations and charities. The full weight of American enterprise has been brought to bear on the disease. Yet another out gay rock critic lamented that America had yet to do anything on the scale of either International AIDS Day or even the government's "Ignorance" ad campaign.

It struck me then that there is a crucial difference between AIDS and all the other social issues with which pop has concerned itself. At the end of the day, whatever it achieves, cause-pop is still largely a matter of posturing, and there is something faintly obscene about posturing on the subject of a terminal disease.

There is also the fact that, locally and excluding the minority infected through shared needles, AIDS is a disease of the young, healthy and employable. When we raise funds, we do not do so to help the disenfranchised of the Third World, an endangered species or some threatened aspect of the environment. We raise funds to subsidize the health service, to plaster over cracks in the welfare state that have appeared because our taxes are diverted elsewhere, cracks that will continue to widen.

Days before finishing this piece, I was called by Simon Booth of Working Week. He, the Communards and a number of other bands werre drumming up PR for a youth festival due to be held in Portugal, where AIDS is rife and yet officially does not exist – sufferers die of "pneumonia" or "cancer". Their appearance at the festival would, he said, finally make AIDS an issue in Portugal, no small feat. It seems, then, that cause-pop can still find a role in the era of AIDS.

But if AIDS has already given us a fair indication of pop's care, commitment and capability, I do not look forward to the next few years. While figures rise steadily in Europe and America, the disease is exploding in Africa and threatens to bankrupt half the continent. What AIDS is doing to the continent makes the 'Who's Gonna Take You Home?' scenes from the Live Aid broadcast look like a party. I wonder if Wembley and Philadelphia will be as crowded the next time round.

THE BEST AND WORST
ALBUM COVERS
OF THE YEAR

It hasn't been a particularly innovative year for sleeve design – probably because the harsh commercial climate necessitates a hard sell approach. Still, it's easy to produce exciting design if you're given complete freedom to be arty-farty and obscure (e.g. 23 Envelope's work for 4AD). It's when the marketing department insists that the artist's mugshot and name are the only decoration allowed (as often

happens) that a designer's imagination is truly put to the test, and there are a few good and bad examples here.

The best covers are on the left; each is paired with an example of how *not* to do it. The choice here was depressingly wide but I've tried to avoid easy targets (e.g. heavy metal, poverty-stricken indie groups and almost anything American). Most of the horrors are by people who should know better . . .

● **FELT / Forever Breathed The Lonely Word** *(Creation)* Design: Shanghai Packaging (i.e. Lawrence of Felt)
● **SUZANNE VEGA / Solitude Standing** *(A&M)* Art Direction: Jeffrey Gold; Design: Melanie Nissen

● Here we start with two blurred, murky and not initially inspiring photographs of sensitive and wimpy songwriters. In Felt's case, inspired use of what resembles a failed home snapshot (the other half of the face is on the rear, along with minimal type) results in a masterpiece of understatement, reflecting the nebulous melancholia of the music within. The

Suzanne Vega cover, whilst starting with a similar image, is just weedy; a limp, vacuous photo languishing damply amidst badly placed and utterly unsympathetic '50s typography, and in a foul colour to boot. The result is sickeningly twee, and evocative of nothing more than the flowery wallpaper and brown crimplene of suburban coffee mornings.

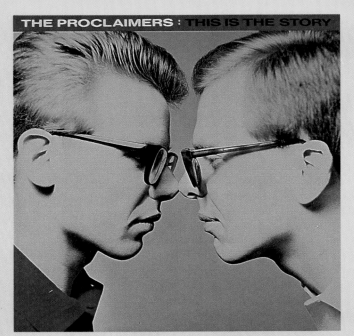

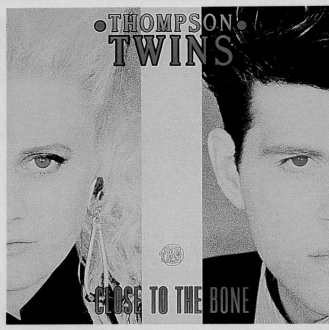

● **THE PROCLAIMERS / This Is The Story** *(Chrysalis)* Design: John Pasche (Chrysalis Records)
● **THOMPSON TWINS / Close To The Bone** *(Arista)* Design: Andie Airfix/Satori

● How to present twins – and how not to. The Proclaimers' elegant sleeve is a classic – a brilliantly memorable photo by Nick Knight which, without even seeming to try, gives the Reid twins an immediately identifiable "image" guaranteed never to date or become embarrassing. The designer, admirably, has avoided the temptation to be a typographic show-off and just let the photo speak for itself. It's a refreshingly unpretentious sleeve, unlike The Thompson Twins' tragic cover: a wanton smash-up of half-baked pretention, boring photography and extremely bad design. If there's a single worst element in this graphic mish-mash, it's the type – revolting, ill-matched faces filled with graduated orange '70s-style airbrushing – yuk!

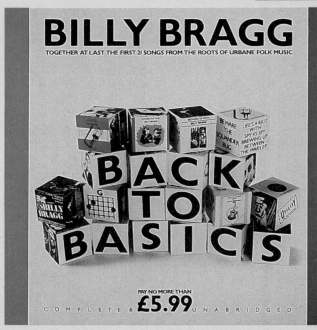

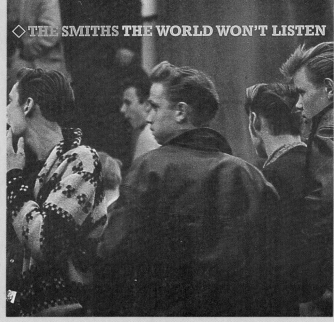

● **BILLY BRAGG/Back To Basics** *(Go! Discs)* Design: Caramel Crunch
● **THE SMITHS / The World Won't Listen** *(Rough Trade)* Design: Morrissey; Layout: Karen Gaugh

● These two compilation LPs continue a style already set by the artists' previous records. Billy Bragg's is fresh and clean, with excellent typography and not an element out of place. The way his sleeves suggest the look of old Penguin book covers without actually copying them is very clever, and this one neatly sums up all the others. The Smiths' famous "cover star" formula, however, is wearing a bit thin. The image is all-important, but they seem to be running out of interesting ideas for photos. In this case, not only is the photo mundane, but the type's awful too – pea-green, heavy and work-a-day. There's nothing here to stimulate the imagination at all – in fact it's even worse than *The Queen Is Dead*, and that was unspeakable . . .

● **PET SHOP BOYS / Disco** *(EMI)* Design: Mark Farrow
● **SIOUXSIE & THE BANSHEES / Tinderbox** *(Polydor)* Design: The Quay Brothers

● These two sleeves don't have anything in common except that they're both purplish and peculiar. The PSB's cover is slightly mystifying – a seemingly random video still of Chris Lowe's head and some daringly minuscule type. It's charmingly eccentric though, and so calming you could probably meditate over it. The Banshees' cover, meanwhile, is an assault on the eye – certainly the worst of the selection here. The question is – why? Why has it got a photo of a tornado on the front? Why is it surrounded by a badly cut-out engraving of a frame? Why use such dreadful type? And, above all, why print it in such a foul, cheapo-looking colour? The Banshees usually have fairly plush sleeves, but even the most hopeless indie group would be insulted by this one.

● **PRINCE / Sign 'O' The Times** *(WEA)* Design: No credit given
● **DAVID BOWIE / Never Let Me Down** *(EMI)* Design: Mick Haggerty

● For pop "legends", both Bowie and Prince have had variable sleeves. Prince's *Parade* is a classic, whereas *Around The World In A Day* makes the Fuzzbox's effort look tasteful. This one's a goodie, although there's not much to it: but it's so blurred and unspecific that you can interpret it how you will. David Bowie's sleeves are usually a good idea badly done, and this is no exception. Basically, it tries too hard. You're obviously meant to read loads into it but it's far too literal – all the so-called "meaningful" props have been too carefully assembled, and what *is* he wearing? The type is hideously overdone as well, and has nothing to do with the photo. A load of overblown guff masquerading as "art", in other words.

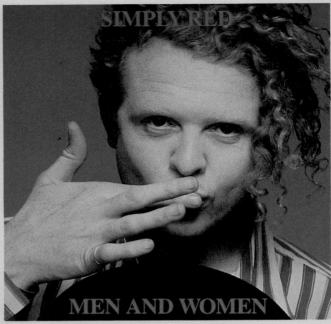

● **BLOW MONKEYS / She Was Only The Grocer's Daughter** *(RCA)* Design: Mainartery
● **SIMPLY RED / Men And Women** *(WEA)* Design: WEA Records

● The camera really does lie: here are two not-actually-very-handsome people looking devastatingly (well, *quite*) attractive courtesy of a bright flashlight and rather a lot of white make-up. They're both good photos, but it's what the designer's done with them that makes the difference. Doctor Robert has been left alone – just two subtle bars of blue and no logo, which is fine on

such a memorable image. But poor old Mick Hucknall is a victim of insensitive type – he's hemmed in by hulking red letters which don't match the picture and ruin its composition. Tiny white type carefully placed in the top left hand corner would have been a far better solution. Not only that, but the sleeve's printed on thin, naff card; it feels more like a 12″ single than an LP.

● **FUZZBOX / Bostin' Steve Austin** *(WEA)* Design: Andie Airfax/Satori
● **THE LEATHER NUN / Lustgames** *(Wire)* Design: Bengt Aronsson

● Both these sleeves, presumably, are supposed to be disgustingly tacky (if they're not, then the designers should be shot). The difference is that the Fuzzbox's sleeve is so horrible that it's brilliant, whereas the Leather Nun's is just plain revolting. It takes genius to produce something as pathetically home-made looking as *Bostin' Steve Austin* – a perfect pastiche of

felt-pen epics with which bored schoolgirls "decorate" their exercise books. (It must have taken an iron will not to include *any* redeeming features.) The whole thing's quite clearly meant as a joke, whereas with *Lustgames* you're not so sure – maybe the designer thinks it's a masterpiece. Either way, its true horror is so blatantly obvious it needs no further explanation . . .

● **ZODIAC MINDWARP** / *High Priest Of Love* *(Phonogram)* Design: Zodiac Mindwarp
● **THE CULT** / *Electric* *(Beggar's Banquet)* Design: Keith Breedon/Ai; Art Direction: Storm Thorgeson

● Heavy rock is noted for its disgusting artwork – airbrushed monsters and scantily clad females, as a rule. There are exceptions though – Zodiac Mindwarp, as befits someone who was art editor of the brilliantly designed *Flexipop* magazine, has a brilliantly designed LP sleeve. No airbrushing for him; a futuristic computer image is married with dainty classical type and a couple of pagan snakes. It works beautifully, right down to the bit of "apocalyptic" prose at the bottom. The Cult, meanwhile, have resurrected a '70s cliche – one better forgotten unfortunately, i.e. Roger Dean-style lettering. It's done so badly, too – an amateurishly cross-hatched logo which you can't read, a dull photo, and murky colours. Terminally depressing.

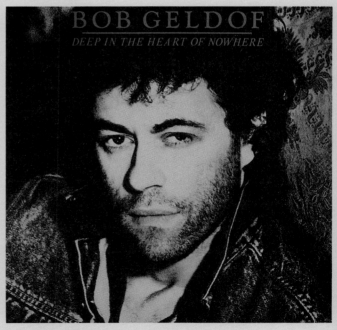

● **HOLGER HILLER** / *Oben Im Eck* *(Mute)* Design: Town And Country Planning
● **BOB GELDOF** / *Deep In The Heart Of Nowhere* *(Phonogram)* Design: Mike Storey (Phonogram Records)

● Just as black and white films can be more atmospheric than colour ones, so too black and white sleeves can have a lot more impact. Holger Hiller's for instance; a dreamy collage of impressionistic photos with only a spot of red and minimal type. The other side has a different photo and the same wording; both work as the "front", and you can gaze at either for hours without getting bored. (The only grumble is that it's annoying having no track listing to consult.) Bob Geldof's monochrome effort is probably meant to look "serious" and "worthy", like a grainy cinema verité documentary. Unfortunately it merely succeeds in looking pompous, thanks to a particularly stilted photo. Not only that, but it makes him look suspiciously like George Michael . . .

● **THE CURE / Kiss Kiss** *(Polydor)* Design: Andy Vela & Porl Thompson/Parched Art

● **YELLO / One Second** *(Phonogram)* Design: Ernst Gamper

● The oldest cliché in the book: a pair of pouting red lips. Perfectly justified in the Cure's case, given the album's title, and anyway it's a totally original approach. As with all Cure sleeves, there's tremendous attention to detail; the back of the LP is a huge giant eye, the two inner bags feature more giant polaroids of Robert Smith's features, and every bit of hand-crafted calligraphy is millimetre precise. Compared to the Cure's luscious lips, Yello's are a pair of ugly old rubber tyres – the disembodied mouth hangs grotesquely in space without a face to relate to. And what has it got to do with the record? Obviously the designer just fancied displaying one of his paintings to the world, but does the world want to see it? I think not.

● **VARIOUS 4AD ARTISTS / Lonely Is An Eyesore** *(4AD)* Design: 23 Envelope

● **NEW ORDER / The Peel Sessions** *(Strange Fruit)* Design: Wyke Studios

● 23 Envelope's work is usually self-indulgent and *Lonely Is An Eyesore* is no exception; you need an electron microscope to decipher the type. Still, it's a beautiful piece of decorative art and 4AD fans are used to obscurity. The Peel Sessions covers also use type and texture as the sole decoration, but they're a complete eyesore. They must have cost quite literally 1p to produce – knocked up in some local studio to the worst standards of DIY "design" (I use the term loosely) and printed in one colour (black) on disgustingly textured card. How dare the BBC inflict such a disgraceful design on the public? For a few pence more they could have had a perfectly decent sleeve. My cat could do a better job than this, and I haven't even *got* a cat.

● **THE UNDERNEATH / Lunatic Dawn Of The Dismantlers** *(El)* Design: Karl Blake (i.e. The Underneath)

● **THE DAMNED / Anything** *(MCA)* Design: The Leisure Process

● Well! Who'd have thought a load of old spanners, some painted plasticene (or maybe it's alphabetti spaghetti) and what appears to be the most repulsive Christmas jumper in the universe could end up looking as brilliant as The Underneath's sleeve? Its only fault is the wonky spacing – it reads as "Dism Antlers", not "Dismantlers" – but let's not be pedantic. This

meisterwerk is probably a complete accident, seeing as the back is appallingly designed, but who cares? It's a work of consummate genius anyway. The Damned's sleeve is a painted 3D model too – but what a horrid one! It looks like all the creepy cod-Victorian whimsy that was popular in the early '70s – and that stuff was abysmal even back in those tasteless days.

● **23 SKIDOO / Just Like Everybody** *(Bleeding Chin)* Design: Neville Brody

● **VARIOUS / Hitmix 86** *(Stylus)* Design: Mainartery

● These days you have to look closely at Neville Brody's work to check it isn't by one of his countless imitators. 23 Skidoo's retrospective compilation is the genuine article, and though it's Nev doing what comes easiest to him – almost self parody, in fact – there's no denying that he really is a talented and innovative typographer (an extremely rare breed these days). It's simple,

modern, delicately coloured and perfectly structured – a delight. *Hitmix 86* is one of the squillions of imitators – an advertising agency's idea of "trendy" design. It fulfils the function of leering garishly off a shelf at you but so does a Pot Noodle and that's no recommendation. Over-the-top is an understatement – every copy should come with a free sickbag.

This was the year that the music video finally fell asleep in front of the television. After ten-odd years of increasingly hollow aesthetic gestures, distorted copycatism from the film and advertising industries, a global role in the business of boosting consumer avarice, and the conquering of space (satellites) and time (they've rewritten the fifties and are currently at work on the sixties), the whole video body politic is just very, very overweight and very, very tired. And we're tired too, and, well, a bit sad.

Five years ago, when the handsome newcomer started to squall and throw things at the wall it all looked very exciting, like a film student's summer of '76. But, like punk, video turned out to be a brief lesson in appropriation – another spectacle rearranged and inflated for eye-drugged Top Shoppers. Video taught us that the Next Big Thing should not be slotted between Shake 'n' Vac commercials and wounded children in Beirut.

Video also taught us that photographs in general are fast becoming sneaky, complex organisms full of weird motivations and visual class distinctions – do you get the references, does Super-8 make you feel nostalgic, why are those people scowling at you?

For now video is asleep in a pin-striped suit, entirely critic-proof and quite lacking in zesty ideas or startling developments. The money continues to roll in. Like America, the business of video is business . . .

★

TOP FIVE

1

GEORGECLINTON-PARLIAMENTFUN-KADELIC THE MOTHERSHIP CONNECTION Live From Houston
(**Virgin Vision,** 30 mins.)
In which 26 episodes of *Lifestyles Of The Rich And Famous* were melted down for George Clinton's shoulderpads.
This is a celestial performance from the Sun King of funk (filmed in 1977) and when the master tells the flock, "Free your mind and your ass will follow" you can almost spot young Prince Rogers Nelson taking notes in row 92.

2

THE DEAD KENNEDYS Live In San Francisco
(**Hendring,** 60 mins.)
Tasteless, incisive and guaranteed free of yuppie lifestyle-mongering, this live set sees California's finest greeting flying fans in a snakepit and lurching smartly through American politics (from 'Moral Majority': *"I'm a hope dope pusher/be addicted to the Lord"*). This is alert stuff (from the *Bedtime For Democracy* LP) and proof positive that Jello Biafra is the hardest working man in showbusiness.

3

SEVERED HEADS Severed Heads
(**IKON Video,** 30 mins.)
Sardonic electronics from the Aussie cut-up duo, plus seriously ravishing images from the band's own video synthesizer. With five segments, including the neurotic 'Dead Eyes Opened'. Overall, *Severed Heads* is a combination of hollow laughter and an explosion in a paint factory – is this what they mean by 'video art'?

4

MAHALIA JACKSON Mahalia
(**Hendring,** 72 mins.)
Inspiration to Dr. King and elder example to Aretha, Mahalia Jackson was the last, greatest classic gospel singer. These concerts were filmed shortly before her death in 1972 and in an unobtrusive way show us her physical frailness and spiritual invincibility. *Mahalia* is a haven from the advert-think and grim flesh contests of pop.

5

PET SHOP BOYS Television
(**Picture Music International,** 30 mins.)
Because 'West End Girls' still looks like a post-mod's Swinging London. These six promos are not blazingly original, or even heart-stoppingly stylish, but directors Morahan and Watson have a knack for alluring graphics and playful irony. Besides, Chris Lowe is one of the great deadpan camera starers of our time.

THE ALARM. Spirit of '76

(*Hendring,* 90 mins.)

This is an MTV-sponsored look at a recent Alarm concert in Los Angeles, and the sleeve notes make one thing clear about the proceedings: "It was a long day indeed." And so it was. No doubt about it. The minutes positively flub past us, wearily wending their way across four Welshmen in full cry and an audience full of Yanks who scream "Awright!" a lot. The *longueurs* increase with mawkish, laddish hymns like 'Howling Wind', 'Knife Edge', 'Blaze Of Glory', 'Spirit Of '76', and 'Where Were You When The Storm Broke?'.

All in all, it was a day of good faith, moral sincerity, and all the songwriting ability of four spatulas pretending to be U2. A day you'll leave to the Awrights of your parish.

CHET BAKER. Live At Ronnie Scott's

(*Hendring,* 58 mins.)

Only in the jazz world – which respects wrinkles, women and low-lifes, and cares little for the cut of your picture disc – could a middle-aged trumpet player sit at a drab little table and say to Elvis Costello: "They told me nobody could work with false teeth, but I didn't buy that." And Baker isn't smiling, which is part of his appeal.

He's an honest-to-goodness American Plain Man – his ex-con's face tells us that he's seen it all, done it all, and doesn't really want to talk about it. This tape does him justice – long after you've settled into Baker's feline, languid playing you notice how understated the camera work is, how whisper-subtle the lighting, and how finely textured the accompaniment (Michael Grailler on piano, Riccardo Del Fra on bass).

No wonder Costello and Van Morrison felt compelled to pop for a ticket – that night, the glow of jazz beat out the glare of the charts. Recommended.

BAUHAUS. Archive

(*Beggars Banquet,* 40 mins.)

Archive features an unusually gaseous example of what promo directors call a "linking device". Linking devices are something record companies need to unify and update old concert footage someone's discovered in the stockroom. Here, director Christopher Robin Collins, who should know better, has produced a plot about an old magician stumbling upon a dusty film projector. The machine starts up and darned if we aren't whisked back to a Bauhaus concert, circa 1980.

But even as you're seduced by the band's pointy boots and the beautifully inept lighting – not to mention Pete Murphy doing his anorexic-Christ act in 'Stigmata Martyr', or barking on all fours during 'Hair Of The Dog' – Collins keeps cutting back to his bored Actors Equity magician, blinking at the film projector. By rights, of course, this man should have torn off a mask to reveal himself as Pete Murphy, but video laws prevail and the projector blows up.

Murphy's pitch, as it happens, is a whole catalogue of art school gestures but I love him anyway. Practise your spidery dancing to 'Lagartija Nick', 'Kick In The Eye', 'Dark Entries', 'A God In An Alcove' and 'Passion Of Lovers'.

▶

VIDEO

BIG COUNTRY. Live: Seer
(*Virgin Vision,* 55 mins.)
This is a filmed record of the New York date in Big Country's 1986 tour, and as such inspires both pity and terror; few bands work so hard at squashing their virtues and promoting their vices. On the plus side, Big Country are unquestionably hard-working and sincere – they always look like doughty Scots saplings – and they don't do cover versions.

But throttling any enjoyment you might take from 'Fields Of Fire' or 'Look Away' is the band's lyrical shagginess, musical conservatism and extreme low marks in style (what *is* that Spinal Tap-like thingy on stage?). Their right-on gestures are annoying – what does archive footage of factories have to do with hotel rooms and catering trucks? And as for all that drop-jawed wailing – is it a clarion call to arms, or is it the kind of thing guitar players like to do in stadiums?

THE BLOW MONKEYS. Digging Your Video
(*RCA Video* 20 mins.)
It's hard to know what to say about these promos – 'Forbidden Fruit', 'Digging Your Scene', 'Wicked Ways', 'Don't Be Scared Of Me' – except that Dr. Robert is suffering from one of the more common camera neuroses – he loves the lens, but he's not sure that the lens loves him. He's singing, he's dancing, the lamé suit gleams under the lights but doubt hangs off every curl of the lip – does he look good? Does he look bad? Will Paula ever have him on *The Tube* again? One day there will exist a spa for distressed glamour boys, where Dr. Robert and Martin Fry can sit out in deck chairs, practising tossing the hair out of their eyes. Meanwhile, against all odds, Blow Monkeys singles continue to improve.

BON JOVI. Breakout: The Video Singles
(*Channel 5,* 27 mins.)
Considerable banality here, and why not? If they weren't tight-jeaned and streak-haired they wouldn't be able to appear in promos like 'She Don't Know Me', which brandishes a girl with a gun, or 'Runaway', which is about nuclear waste and teenage absenteeism. There are six promos in total, including Jon Bon Jovi's anguished bit of dialogue: "If I stopped playing, what have I got?"

DAVID BOWIE. Day-In-Day-Out
(*Picture Music International,* 18 mins.)
Julien Temple needs to avoid David and Mick's phone calls: they keep demanding the same old designer-danger scenarios, and they want them to be meaningful. As usual with Temple's work *Day-In* aims at being devilishly glam but also wants to "say something"; in this case, the message seems to be that society forces photogenic mothers to become hookers. But we've seen it all before – the ghetto trash looks straight out of 'Undercover', as do the tense glances and views from speeding cars.

Day-In is a menagerie of Templeisms: the unconvincing lovers-against-the-world plot, the paranoia, the pursuit, the crack editing and the high fashion flesh peddling (in Temple's films, prostitution is the best way to meet a pop star). Still Bowie looks better than he has in years, so Temple will probably be doing the next one. And neither version of *Day-In* is nearly as bad as 'Loving The Alien', a harrowingly fey promo rather sheepishly tacked on at the end.

CAMEO. The Videosingles
(*PolyGram,* 30 mins)
Few people have more insinuating vowel sounds than Larry Blackmon – he sounds like W.C. Fields in ecstasy, phoning in the hits from under a pile of silk sheets. These five promos are surprisingly up to scratch – they're sleek-dirty and mock-sophisticated, with polished production values (check the lighting in 'Word Up') and some taut pussyfooting in the dance sequences. In a nutshell, we have here an exquisite, flashing gem that wishes it could put its hand on your knee. Most Views Of Codpiece: 'Candy'.

CULTURE CLUB. The First Four Years
(*Virgin Vision,* 50 mins.)
In retrospect, you can see how hard George had to work not to look threatening. With or without That Voice he was a pop problem, being a tall, husky bloke in make-up and strange clothes, busting out all over in semiotic come-ons. The O'Dowd genius lay in deciding which signals would get him on *Saturday Superstore*, and which wouldn't.

In, then, went the mischievous smiles, the tippy-toe dancing and the baggy, international clobber. Out went chin stubble, complaining and any buried longings for tight rubberwear. Quite necessarily, the early Culture Club promos were giddy, kiddy things, full of Tinkertoy sexuality and a genuine generosity of spirit (no one was ever embarrassed or made to look nasty in a Culture Club video).

Later, of course, the usual parabola of success distorted the band's good sense, causing George to look frayed ('Karma Chameleon'), pissed off ('It's A Miracle') and over-indulged ('Victims'). The much-publicised 'War' video was a mistake, rendered invalid by The Toilet Tissue Syndrome – pretty pictures tarting up an ugly process for TV.

But 'Black Money' is wonderful, and 'Do You Really Want To Hurt Me' titillatingly old-fashioned. And to watch these videos is to singalonga Culture Club; the Voice is still delectable.

THE DURUTTI COLUMN. Domo Arigato: Live In Japan
(*IKON Video,* 60 mins.)

There's an inviting hush about this performance – the audience is composed and attentive, and the camera treats Vini Reilly like a renowned cellist, or a senior surgeon. This is exactly the right approach, since Durutti music has always had an airy, cerebral flavour – it's music suitable for nature documentaries, or enormous empty rooms. With 'Sketch For Summer', 'Mercy Dance', 'E.E.', 'Belgian Friends', and 'Missing Boy'. Reilly's eccentricities show themselves in the song titles – eg. 'Blind Elevator Girl' – and in his face, which is the mug of an Elizabethan dogcatcher. On the other hand, drummer Bruce Mitchell looks like Sir John Betjeman. Recommended.

BOB DYLAN With Tom Petty And The Heartbreakers. Hard To Handle
(*Virgin Vision,* 56 mins.)

. . . which sees the veteran sociologist live on stage in Australia, looking like a broke-down Keith Richards and singing like a combination of Tony Curtis and hanging judge. 'Ballad Of A Thin Man' is merciless and 'It's Alright, Ma' is windy and magisterial. I even liked 'In The Garden' (though Tom Petty didn't). But Dylan scholars will be hard pressed to defend some of the lyrics; here's a couplet from 'Lenny Bruce', honkingly delivered: "*Maybe he had some problems/ but he sure was funny . . .*"

SHEILA E. Live Romance 1600
(*Picture Music International,* 58 mins.)

There's a strong undercurrent of self-surveillance here; Janet Jackson may be famous for it, but Sheila E is plainly no amateur in the discipline department. Though she exudes a sort of compact gusto and dresses in a *haute* bordello style (her audience are musos, potheads, lovers, and *Dynasty* fans, not yuppies), Escovedo is as alert and precisely choreographed as any Jackson.

Unfortunately, her professionalism fails to boost the show beyond mere good cheer. There's something missing: memorable hooks, maybe, or vocals with personality plus. Whatever the problem, you're glad to see Prince arrive for 'A Love Bizarre'; suddenly the people at the back start pushing, and the music sounds sensational. The stage comes alive, which almost makes up for having to sit through 'Toybox'.

EUROPE. The Final Countdown
(*CBS Fox Video,* 14 mins.)

If Europe were a brand of ale, they'd be called Metal Lite. Here are three promos from the fearless but gormless Scandinavian screamers: 'The Final Countdown' (with bits of "video art" in it), 'Carrie' (the customary "sensitive" video) and 'Rock The Night' (the mandatory global-party video). Shockingly, Europe are quite svelte, being a lot more persuasive and engrossing than, say, the Banshees.

JIMI HENDRIX. Johnny B. Goode
(*Virgin Vision,* 26 mins.)

A brief Hendrix sampler, with the collaged 'Are You Experienced?' short, and live versions of the title track (from the Berkeley Community Center concert) and 'All Along The Watchtower' (from the Atlanta Pop Festival). There's also an unappealing little film-student piece called 'Art Attack', which is filler, and a troupe of lumpen dancers interfering with 'Voodoo Chile'. Throughout, Hendrix seems briefly glimpsed; enthusiasts would be better off with the Warners bio-video released last year.

BUDDY HOLLY. The Real Buddy Holly Story
(*Picture Music International,* 90 mins.)

At the insistence of their leader, The Crickets gave out business cards with each demo tape. This documentary makes it clear that there was no dawdling around Buddy Holly, who "hadda have creases in his Levi's, real neat, alla time". Elsewhere in this rather too-earnest tribute we discover that Holly was no Clark Kent – those who knew him found him quite steely.

The Real Buddy Holly Story is high on personal reminiscences (back-porch interviews with publishers, managers, etc. etc.) and low on archive footage (unsurprising, given Holly's early death). Its love of detail is sometimes distracting – who could relish accounts of how the boys tiled Norman Petty's studio? But some excellent points are made about the originality of Holly's playing, and their famous *Ed Sullivan* TV appearance is delightful.

Elvis cultists will be interested to discover the heavy-lidded one in his earliest photos ever, backstage with Holly and Johnny Cash. And there's a useful idea in video packaging from PMI: the price includes two audio cassettes of The Crickets' greatest hits.

VIDEO

WHITNEY HOUSTON. The Number One Video Hits
(*RCA Video,* 18 mins.)
A four-song EP with the best-known hits 'How Will I Know' and 'Saving All My Love For You'. But the winsome 'You Give Good Love' contains the greatest number of semiotic morsels: when Houston's hip, painstakingly casual boyfriend visits an emporium marked 'Design House' you know that noir yuppiedom (and New Manism) is here to stay. In video, males traditionally spend their time smashing things. But the postpunk New Man *shops*, and still pulls beautiful birds like Whitney Houston. Conclusion: advertising changes everything.

INXS. The Swing And Other Stories
(*PolyGram,* 58 mins.)
The invisible Aussie behind this eleven-song starting kit is director Richard Lowenstein. He's excellent – in fact he's far too good for the band, being alert and inventive while the musos are laid-back and charmless (Interviewer: "Your producer gave a new dimension to the band, didn't he?" *Inx*: "He did, yeah.")

Rather than string together antique promos back to back, Lowenstein has spun out the new material ('Dancing On The Jetty', 'All The Voices') and then chopped in bits of the old ham and baloney (including the sublimely awful 'Don't Change', 'Original Sin' and 'The Spy Of Love', none directed by Lowenstein). 'I Send A Message' is a first in the history of vulgarity – it is proud of putting TV sets in a Buddhist temple – but 'Burn For You' is fine and 'Melting In The Sun' is hot. But will Britain ever buy their records?

MICK JAGGER. Running Out Of Luck
(*CBS Fox,* 86 mins.)
. . . in which you notice that Jagger's body is *too* whippet-thin, *too* fanatically maintained; he has the trad-rocker's fear of a fat middle age. Of course, the unlovely joke is that all that flab has shifted to his mind . . .

Directed by Julien Temple and with a script by both Temple and Jagger, these 90 minutes of pure ego hokum concern "the fantasies and fears of the world's most celebrated and envied rock star". What really happens is that Mick and Jerry have a fight, and Mick subsequently wanders around Rio until Rae Dawn Chong sleeps with him. The songs are worthless and the supposedly self-mocking humour is clammy and unfunny, but Temple has lost none of his gift for staging musical sequences.

Cineastes take note: Dennis Hopper has a bit part here, which casts a new light on his role in *Blue Velvet*; it seems the man shouts and acts wiggy in all his films.

BILLY JOEL. The Video Album Vols. I&II
(*CBS Fox,* 90 mins.)
Probably unintentionally, this two-volume set looks very much like a tribute to Baby Boomer success – it's a travelogue for older yuppies. We start with the schoolboy poetry and acrylic flares of the seventies ('Piano Man') and then move to the first stirrings of fame ('Honesty') to penthouse paranoia ('Pressure') to marrying the model ('Uptown Girl') and settling down.

Like Bowie, Jagger et al before him the 40-ish Joel begins to issue nostalgic po'-boy singles that remind him of his youth; the accompanying promos are tricked up in Real Rock Values (no-frills interiors, the band looking studiedly casual, lots of joshing with the technicians). At the very end, Joel crowns himself with the last, biggest bit of cred available to a white middle-class tycoon; he records a duet with Ray Charles. And it's absolutely horrible to watch.

KATRINA AND THE WAVES. Walking On Sunshine EP
(*Picture Music International,* 30 mins.)
This is like being lunged at by a dental health pamphlet, or being mugged by a macramé kit. Katrina Lescanich and her largely Brit back-up are just terrifyingly plucky, always smiling and looking on the bright side of things. Their one chart success – 'Walking On Sunshine' is entirely muck resistant, even when performed in a grotty club. There are four other tunes on display here, each of which seems to say "Have a nice day".

LATIN QUARTER. In Concert
(*RCA Video,* 60 mins.)
This is a live date recording for the ITV *Meltdown* series. Here are comfy, jazzy tunes with noodling bass lines and badly organized lyrics about Nicaragua; Latin Quarter seem to have sprung from the corner of a Biff cartoon. 'Radio Africa' though, manages to gain a toe-hold in the memory.

LEVEL 42. Live At Wembley
(*Channel 5,* *73 mins.*)

The shock is that while Mark King and his supper-club ordinaires are amiably working through 'The Chinese Way' or 'Lessons In Love', the camera pulls back to reveal thousands of ecstatic Top Shoppers, all dipping and swaying to dance tunes only they can hear. Level 42 are the canine whistles of the chart scene – everyone can hear their call but the critics.

Somehow, Level 42 have become Very Big. They've acquired a global band's accessories: camera cranes, eye-boggling lighting and a papal stage. *Live At Wembley* is two encores, eleven songs (including a sinuous version of 'Living It Up') and the recent promo for 'Running In The Family'.

LOOSE ENDS. Loose Ends
(*Virgin Vision,* *18 mins.*)

Who are these people? Why are they so ordinary, so well-meaning? Whoever they are, their version of Bowie's 'Golden Years' is honeyed and flirtatious, and is therefore a success. The video, though, is quite rancid. Also includes the advert-like promos 'Emergency (Dial 999)', 'Magic Touch', 'Hangin' On A String' and 'Stay A Little While, Child'.

MADNESS. Utter Madness
(*Virgin Vision,* *46 mins.*)

Madness promos were and are among the best videos ever made; their malarkey-riddled essays on the British character belong right up there with the Pythons. And like the Pythons they're people you miss – the space they leave in your affections can't be filled by anyone else. Fall in love again with 'The Sun And The Moon', 'Our House', 'Michael Caine', 'Yesterday's Men', 'Uncle Sam', 'Wings Of A Dove' and '(Waiting For) The Ghost Train'. Videos that float like a butterfly and sting like a bee.

MARILLION. The Videos 1982-6
(*Picture Music International,* *28 mins.*)

Featuring surprisingly self-mocking commentary from compère Fish, this eight-song retrospective is crammed with cod-romantic junk. But it's likeable cod-romantic junk; Marillion don't take themselves too seriously. Proof of this lies with Fish, who not only wears mascara under his Ray-Bans but who is subject to slitty-eyed visions of destruction, like Nostradamus or Joan Collins. But don't splash out on my account – if you're not in the mood for hoarsely-sung juvenilia, stay away. With 'Market Square Heroes', 'Heart Of Lothian', 'Garden Party', 'Kayleigh', 'Lavender' and the totally silly 'Assassing'.

FREDDIE MERCURY. Video EP
(*Picture Music International,* *20 mins.*)

With the promos 'I Was Born To Love You', 'Living On My Own', 'Time' and 'Made In Heaven'. None of these were made by Russell Mulcahy or Brian Grant, the two directors who most often manufacture loaves-and-fishes scenarios for Queen. Not to worry though – fans will find the usual clone armies, Freddie's unique overbite, and lost continents of diamanté. Bombastic, of course, but surprisingly effective.

THE MISSION. Crusade
(*Channel 5,* *60 mins.*)

So what if the Mish add up to a lot of Gothic margarine? They're not as tasty as their predecessors The Sisters Of Mercy but unfortunately the electro-crazy charts of '82 weren't ready for the return of purple scarves. Now, however, batty mysticism is here to stay – there will always be people who go for styrofoam cathedrals on stage and lyrics like, "*Take my hand I'll lead you/ to the garden of delight.*"

The Mission are straightforward about themselves – they're The Incredible String Band with Ray-Bans and nasty baritones. Here director Tony Van Den Ende has shot them live in soupy darkness, with the occasional druggy special effect (opening flowers) and lots of fans stupefied over the smoke machines. The set features material from *God's Own Medicine.*

MR. MISTER. Videos From The Real World
(*RCA Video,* *14 mins.*)

Showbusiness! Mr. Mister give their all to sentiments like "the broken record goes round and round" and "I'll never learn to fly again", songs which are accompanied by views of eagles and deranged fashion models. Verdict: sprightly but stupid.

VIDEO

QUEEN. Live In Budapest
(*Picture Music International,* 90 mins.)
Here are 22 Queen hits performed with nipple-bursting intensity in the Nepstadium, Budapest, which is quite possibly the largest venue in the universe. From the air, Queen look like a flashlight lying in a dark tennis court. Fact: it took 17 cameramen to film this concert, but only one critic to yawn at it.

LIONEL RICHIE. The Making Of Dancing On The Ceiling: Come On Up
(*Hendring,* 29 mins.)
This video of the-making-of-another-video cops the 1986 Serious Moonlight Award for unnecessarily bothering consumers. This is thin territory indeed – the hit in question isn't that interesting, and neither are the "major choreographed numbers". Absurdly, the interviewees treat a common or garden variety film set as if it were a NASA project (blueprints and all). Naturally, Fred Astaire's name is dragged through the mud and, naturally, they all hug each other at the end.

SIGUE SIGUE SPUTNIK. Sex Bomb Boogie EP
(*Picture Music International,* 10 mins.)
In which we discover how Tony James, bless his misguided wardrobe, made the mistake only a capital R-Rock Fan would make – he assumed the kids wanted sweat 'n' spurts 'n' danger. What the kids actually wanted, of course, were cool cookies like Ben Curiosity and Corinne Drewery, who'd probably wrinkle their pretty noses at all that slavering display. Poor old Sigue Sigue Sputnik flung pills and matches at their audience; uninterested, the kids drifted off for a cup of cappuccino.

And so the visual product has arrived, though *SBB* isn't quite the million-dollar techno-snort you might expect. There're some large screens behind the band, and snips from *The Terminator*, and some meant-to-be spine-tingling computer text, but not much else. Truth be told, wrinklies and Tories already watch these things in their own videos – there's nothing particularly incendiary about pictures of jet planes. The Sputs' problem is this: they want to be monolithic, atrocious and amoral, but advertising has pipped them at the post. Hideous to relate, your average Kit-E-Kat advert is more disturbing than *Sex Bomb Boogie*.

SPEAR OF DESTINY. The Epic Videos
(*CBS Fox,* 11 mins.)
In 1987, it's gratifying to see a good-looking lad lose control of himself on stage. Even as today's career pin-ups are being sober and responsible, Kirk Brandon is behaving as if punk actually happened; the ghost of '76 is flailing away in his schizo smiles and crack-hipped dancing. Brandon is plainly an original, but in 'All My Love' he comes perilously close to imitating a cack funk band, what with those wailing horns and shrill back-up singers. If he keeps on like this, a fate worse than the Eurythmics awaits him. Three promos, including 'The Wheel', and 'Prisoner Of Love'.

STATUS QUO. Rockin' Through The Years
(*Channel 5,* 103 mins.)
I'm quite fond of the Quo; they're like New Order without the genius, or four Billy Braggs from hell. And they're consistent – Francis Rossi looks the same now as he did in 1973. This 26 song retrospective was one of the big sellers of the year, and it ranges from the engagingly duff ('Paper Plane') to the totally senile ('Dear John', the worst video ever made).

But they're above criticism, somehow, because Rossi looks genuinely sly in a tux ('Marguerita Time') and because everything they do fuels a thousand happy hours in a thousand bars in all corners of the earth, which is not bad for a bunch of brickies who never look at the camera. Curiously, the band's best singles were released during The Turbulent Years: 'Rockin' All Over The World' ('77), 'Again And Again' ('78) and 'Whatever You Want' ('79). The sleeve lists release dates and highest chart positions.

THE STYLE COUNCIL. Jerusalem
(*Palace,* 60 mins.)
At one point in this flaky filmette the script really lets us have it – it suddenly abandons the spoiled-brat hi-jinx and coy Edwardian beach scenes for something much plainer, much more decisive. This is the point where the band is hauled before a judge, who condemns them for being "intelligent" and "well-dressed" and for using "melodies". Which is a relief, actually; I don't know about you but I hate floundering around not knowing who's brilliant and who's not; I like a band that *tells* me how superior they are, preferably in E-Z Yoof terms.

Jerusalem commits cinematic hara-kari with its smug, scattered attitude: the songs are pompous and tinny, the script goes nowhere fast and James Brown need not top himself in envy of the Weller wardrobe. But worse than the band's arch game-playing is their sniping at easy targets, e.g., the stereotyped thick copper, the stereotyped neurotic TV host, the stereotyped dumb American etc. etc. And as for the band's much-vaunted political concern – there's nothing in *Jerusalem* but the politics of self-regard.

THE THE. Infected
(*CBS Fox Video*, 46 mins.)

It's easy to see why critics love Matt Johnson – he's literate, pissed off, right-on, and well-dressed. But tasteful scorn alone cannot build a brilliant video; the truly great vids have imaginative bite, and a certain humility. *Infected*, for all its ga-ga publicity, is just not that extraordinary. It looks as ego-ridden as any other project – featuring Johnson as apocalyptic glamourpuss – and its "message" (that Americans are dangerously stupid) is hardly provocative; nobody is telling us to give all our possessions away, or to stop buying records, or to ban television. *Infected* is just another stars-in-sunglasses video, heavy on the artistic garlic.

To be fair, some bits of this South American venture are better than others (the outcome was bound to be spotty, since several directors handled the eight tracks). 'Angels Of Deception' isn't bad, and 'Heartland' slips only once. Otherwise, however, it's Matt the angst-wrestling hero all the way, whether sweating, scowling, posing in industrial wasteland, confronting writhing hookers or watching a blonde slop Coca-Cola on her breasts (cultural imperialism metaphor).

Final Score: Showbiz Values 20 – Matt Johnson's Criticism Of Same 0.

TRAFFIC. Live At Santa Monica '72
(*Channel 5*, 64 mins.)

Traffic songs meandered their way towards genius; most of them are a combination of savage waffling and one or two unforgettable keyboard hooks. Here, the whole band wander around a sticky stage shaking their hair, wearing swirling hippie shirts and possibly digesting swirling hippie drugs (Jim Capaldi appears to be watching the eye of God opening on the floor). Curiously, Winwood is one of the few performers whose faces are absolutely unreadable – he could be singing the phone book.

The music is just staggeringly good: 'Freedom Rider', 'Low Spark Of High Heeled Boys', 'Light Up Or Leave Me Alone', and 'Glad', which is accompanied by priceless psychedelic effects from underground film-maker Chick Strand. The best archive video of the year.

TINA TURNER. Break Every Rule
(*Picture Music International*, 60 mins.)

This is possibly the most over-directed video of the year; absolutely nothing here is spontaneous. Turner's audience is stuffed with improbable fashion plates who know the words to every song, and director David Mallet is careful not to deviate from a menu of yuppie entertainments: there's a little techno-wit (from Max Headroom), a little black-and-white nostalgia ('Overnight Sensation'), a little advertising (the *Pepsi* commercial, which gets on your nerves) and a little new talent (Robert Cray, guesting in the excellent, un-screamed 'A Change Is Gonna Come').

The lady herself is a combination of force of nature and Vegas headliner, which is a fairly interesting place to be. Watch old rules broken and new ones reinforced in Steve Cropper and Eddie Floyd's '634-5789', Robert Palmer's 'Addicted To Love' and the Bowie-penned 'Girls', not so much songs as Yup campaigns.

UB40. CCCP
(*Virgin Vision*, 60 mins.)

The problem with the un-Western tour videos – Bowie in Singapore, Wham! in China – is that they often degenerate into six or seven tea-towel scenes, e.g., Jamming With The Locals, Posing By The Monuments, Joking About The Food, etc. etc. *CCCP* is not entirely free of this – instead of wacky encounters with fur hats we might have had more dialogue from the Soviets, or even one or two thoughts from the band. The film suffers from too much subway riding and not enough chat, but since the band perform with such supernatural magnificence on stage I'm forgetting to complain.

The jaunty, racially jumbled Brummies are perfect for beginning pop fans who resolutely occupy every seat in The House Of Sports, Leningrad, looking either confused, suspicious, or completely agog. 'Keep On Moving' chips away at their glaze, and 'Please Don't Make Me Cry' and 'Rat In Mi Kitchen' has them up on their feet. At the end, the Campbell brothers' generosity and husky sweetness captivates the audience – strangers turn into music lovers, and 'Don't Break My Heart' takes everyone's breath away. All the hits, directed by the band's sax player Brian Travers. Acquire!

VARIOUS. Hits 5
(*CBS Fox Video*, 57 mins.)

With Everything But The Girl looking out of sync, Five Star looking to get on, Howard Jones looking like the career that time forgot, Little Richard looking 20 years younger, The Stranglers looking 20 years older, Hollywood Beyond looking up, Nick Kamen looking good, Red Box looking for love and Owen Paul looking for trouble (with the deathless assertion to his lady love: "I don't care/ if being with you/ is meaningless or ridiculous").

VIDEO

VARIOUS. Kerrang! Video Kompilation – 20 Rock Monsters
(*Virgin Vision/Picture Music International*, 90 mins.)

Unfortunately no *nouvelle vague* here – no speed-metal from, say, Metallica or Megadeth – just the usual icons (dry ice, scary monsters, Big Hair) duly saluted. Still, everyone has something to contribute: Motorhead, for example, cop the best song title, which is 'Killed By Death'. Iron Maiden have the most tattoos. Marillion opt for the most popular video theme in history – the ever-persuasive Asylum/Straitjacket storyline. And Wendy O. Williams gets her knickers in a twist during 'It's My Life', biting other women in the arm and trying to run people down in her car. Clearly, Williams is Barbara Cartland with spikes on; an ageless heroine in pursuit of her own kind of glamour.

VARIOUS. Move Closer: The Alternative Video Selection
(*CBS Fox*, 50 mins.)

We never discover the reason behind the "alternative" billing. Because the compilers selected some artistes from the Thinking Label, Mute Records? Because the other CBS Hits videos are rubbish? But all things considered this is a decent enough collection. Pick Hits: Oran "Juice" Jones' domestic arrangements ('The Rain'), Erasure's laundry ('Sometimes'), Alison Moyet's exuberance ('Is This Love?') and Paul Young's legs ('Why Does A Man Have To Be Strong?').

VARIOUS. Now That's What I Call Music 8
(*Picture Music International*, 80 mins.)

This one contains the customary clutch of hits and one aspiring technical trend. It seems that slow-motion Super-8 was last year's favourite film technique; both Duran Duran's 'Notorious' and Orchestral Manoeuvres' 'Forever Live And Die' are full of grainy, floating microphones and drifting profiles (not to mention the blurry waistlines – Super-8 is the over-thirties' godsend). Other than this, you might well be reminded that both the single and the video in the number one slot last year ('Don't Leave Me This Way') are, well, ordinary. Standouts in this collection include The Pet Shop Boys' 'Suburbia', Erasure's 'Sometimes' and Swing Out Sister's giddy 'Breakout'.

VARIOUS. Now That's What I Call Music 9
(*Virgin Vision*, 60 mins.)

Probably the most comprehensive hits package of the year – only a middling prospect, I admit – with Boy George, 'Everything I Own'; Pepsi And Shirlie, 'Heartache'; Hot Chocolate, 'You Sexy Thing', Curiosity Killed The Cat, 'Down To Earth'; UB40, 'Rat In Mi Kitchen'; The Blow Monkeys, 'It Doesn't Have To Be That Way'; Freddie Mercury, Simply Red, the extremely dire Housemartins and the paralysingly unpleasant clip made for Jackie Wilson's 'Reet Petite'. That little clay monster was too eager to please; there was a sort of shuffling sho-nuffism in every step. Would they have made the same "little man" for, say, Buddy Holly or Eddie Cochran?

VARIOUS. Soul Cellar
(*CBS Fox*, 57 mins.)

Featuring clips from the SOS Band, Cherelle, Alexander O' Neal, Miami Sound Machine, Philip Bailey, The Manhattans, and Lisa Lisa And Cult Jam with Full Force. With the exception of Dee C. Lee's restrained 'Hold On' the collection looks insistent but tacky: here are the vaselined close-ups, EastEnderish lighting and ceaseless flaunting of naff leather goods endemic to new soul video.

There are reasons for this outbreak of tat, among them a lack of British directors in Minneapolis and a certain Yankee laissez-faire. The Stateside soul/funk bunch were never as visually aspirant – as delightfully pretentious – as, say, the English Blitz kids (from whom video sprang). Americans just aren't art-school moody; somehow you can't imagine the Flyte Tyme crew ripping off Jean Cocteau.

Meanwhile, in the Sharon-like environs of the local disco, critics are given the bum's rush and everything about *Soul Cellar* proves to be a massive hit.

WHAM! The Final
(*CBS Fox*, 14 mins.)

And so ends the duo that made spun sugar look easy, the credits rolling up over a flurry of fringed jackets, backlighting, critical raves and mumsy daydreaming. George Michael will move astutely and deservedly from international talent to global star, but will he find better video directors? In retrospect the promos here – 'The Edge Of Heaven', 'A Different Corner', 'Where Did Your Heart Go?' – look unexceptional and soft-focused, like a marriage of Dulux advert and Next market research. Their last bow deserved better.

REVIEWED BY DESSA FOX

BOOKS

A selection of the year's publications reviewed by our panel of experts.

● BIOGRAPHIES

THE BEATLES BOOK
(Omnibus)

While hardly living up to the lines on the cover proclaiming "the most thorough companion to The Beatles' music available" and "the one book that every Beatles fan should own", this collection of hitherto scattered writings by such heavyweight scribes as Lester Bangs, Dave Marsh, Lenny Kaye, David Fricke and many more is a valuable addition to any serious fan's Beatle library. It includes Lennon's *Playboy* interview, a McCartney interview by Vic Garbarini (the interviewer on the McCartney interview LP which was deleted on the same day as it was released), a George Martin chat, lots of factual compilations (discographies, *Sgt Pepper* sleeve) and so on. Probably few new insights for dedicated Beatlemaniacs but a useful collection which will be of interest to a broader market. *(JT)*

THE BEATLES
Geoffrey Giuliano *(Sidgwick & Jackson)*

Coffee table city! A beautifully produced, luxurious (it weighs over 3lbs, with only 224 pages!) attempt to find something new to say about the moptops. It doesn't really succeed verbally but has a fairly well chosen pictorial content, although at £14.95 it should have. Less a history of the Beatles than a collection of reminiscences from people who the author, an actor/Beatle fan, ran across – the Indian gent who taught George sitar, someone who lived a few doors down the road from Ringo when he was a kid, one of the Dakotas (Billy J. Kramer's group), Father McKenzie (as in 'Eleanor Rigby'), Ronnie Hawkins, etc., etc.

Hardly any of them have any virtue other than that they have rarely, if ever, been interviewed before about the Beatles and this is a book for Beatle completists rather than for those who want to learn something about the group. The desire to say something new on this subject is now resulting in the bottom of the barrel being scraped, although the pictures are in many cases rare. This makes this incomplete non-statistical tome worth having, but probably not worth buying unless you already have a rhinestone-encrusted toothbrush or need another Beatles book. *(JT)*

STARVING FOR ATTENTION
Cherry Boone O'Neill *(Dell)*

From the 1950s, when he made millions from his sanitized cover versions of black rock & rollers' tunes, Pat Boone has been Mr Clean incarnate. A Born Again Christian evangelist, his showbiz career would probably be dead by now were it not for his four blushing daughters whom he thrust on stage at an early age. With him, as the Boone Family, they have captured the hearts – we will not say minds – of Right Wing Middle America. But behind the outer image of happiness and stability lies a less comfortable truth, and this book – the harrowing story of renegade elder daughter Cherry's struggle with anorexia nervosa (the slimming disease that ultimately killed Karen Carpenter) – proves anew that behind the American Dream lies the American Nightmare.

A disappointment from the beginning to her strict disciplinarian father – Pat always wanted sons and was still spanking his daughters when they reached 18 – Cherry's hair-raising story follows her from chubby teen with unrealistically high expectations of herself to emaciated clothes-horse trapped in a never-ending circle of bouts of endless gorging followed by forced vomiting. These in turn eventually led her into the final indignities of shoplifting laxatives and eating out of the dog's dish. A sobering book, despite its kitsch cover and purple prose. *(Kris Kirk)*

ALIAS DAVID BOWIE
Peter & Leni Gillman *(Hodder & Stoughton)*
STARDUST: THE LIFE AND TIMES OF DAVID BOWIE
Tony Zanetta & Henry Edwards *(Michael Joseph)*

Always long on implications and subtexts, David Bowie's career has always been far more fascinating to critics and biographers than those of many people who've consistently outsold him. (Who would *you* rather read about, Bowie or Foreigner?)

Ex-*Sunday Times* Insight Team person Peter Gillman teams up with his wife Leni to produce an earnestly Freudian work which links virtually everything in Bowie's life to his family background and his institutionalized brother and teenage hero Terry. In doing so they devote pages of painstaking drivel to analyses of those songs which they consider relevant to their theme and ditch everything which doesn't fit. Their journalistic competence is infinitely superior to that of anybody else who's ever attempted to tackle the job, but sadly they are woefully (blissfully?) unaware of why Bowie was an important artist in the first place and what qualities went into earning him sufficient magnitude to be worthy of their attention.

By contrast, Zanetta and Edwards have some first-hand knowledge of their subject. Zanetta was part of the Mainman management team who were in charge of Bowie's career in the Ziggy era and *Stardust* is full of the venom, spite and bile of the jilted lover. For gossip freaks only. *(CSM)*

IN OTHER WORDS . . . DAVID BOWIE
Ed. Kerry Juby *(Omnibus)*

Spun off from a radio series narrated by Angie Bowie in which various friends, enemies, lovers and associates of David Bowie

reminisced about their time in the great man's orbit, this book has the naughty, indulgent, guilty attraction of a bunch of people having a good old gossip over a box of chocolates. Tony Visconti, for example, still hasn't forgiven Bowie for spending more time canoodling with Angie than playing music during the *Man Who Sold The World* sessions; former MainMan honcho Tony Zanetta and ex-manager Ken Pitt are still trotting out many of the same anecdotes from their own tell-all Bowie books; Nile Rodgers (whose name is misspelled throughout) is as thoroughly diplomatic as you might expect and Mick Ronson still sounds faintly confused by the whole business. Nicolas Roeg and Brian Eno are, as you might expect, the most insightful into the creative process of Bowie The Artist, and the picture researcher deserves a large drink for unearthing some mind-boggling period trivia. Bowie fans (not as numerous a breed as they were a few years ago) will gobble it up, e'en unto the last caramel. *(CSM)*

JAMES BROWN
James Brown with Bruce Tucker *(Sidgwick & Jackson)*
This James-Brown-tells-Bruce-Tucker-his-life-story book is a fascinating read for more reasons than the exhaustively complete James Brown discography at the back. It opens with a first hand account of what it was like to be dirt-poor and black in America's Deep South 50 years ago: running from the Klan, nickel and dime hustles, being sent home from school for having no proper clothes, prison . . . Brown's childhood was far from comfortable. His late teens and early twenties on the "chittlin circuit" – scuzzy R&B nightclubs – were not much different from any band's beginnings: broken down vans, not getting paid, falling asleep at work the next day and so on. But what makes this book such compulsive reading is the last and longest part (after Brown has made it) which provides as frank and open a picture as possible of a pop star whose sense of self-importance is seriously out of control. The man wrote to President Johnson about his income tax problem – he hadn't paid any for years and was being taken to court – and was genuinely surprised not to get a reply. From reading this, you're led to believe that Brown never made a mistake in his life, was responsible for *every* development in popular music since the minuet, was irresistible to all women and was the best dressed man in the world. Gripping stuff!

Although Brown's musical, social and political sway over black America from 1964 to 1974 was vast, it was not nearly so great as he imagines. Perhaps one day Cliff White of Charly Records will write *the* James Brown biog; he's close enough to know, yet removed enough to be objective. *(LB)*

I USED TO BE AN ANIMAL BUT I'M ALL RIGHT NOW
Eric Burdon *(Faber & Faber)*
No doubt Faber consultant Pete Townshend felt that a book on one of the genuinely great groups of the mid-sixties was long overdue and he was right. This, unfortunately, isn't it – Burdon's book is rather too full of fanciful and barely remembered anecdotes which have not withstood the test of time as well as his music. Is there a conspiracy this year among publishers to omit discographies? Burdon, the various Animals and the numerous solo projects need to be documented, as they are a significant chapter in rock history. However, this undisciplined and disconnected skip through a quarter of a century of sometimes successful battles with the rock hierarchy leaves the reader (and some of its characters, I hear) frustrated by its shoddiness, although a few of its anecdotal passages pose interesting mysteries. Tell us, Eric, what was your *real* relationship with Jimi Hendrix, and what really happened to Mike Jeffrey? *(JT)*

ALL ACROSS THE TELEGRAPH: A BOB DYLAN HANDBOOK
Edited by John Bauldie & Michael Gray *(Sidgwick & Jackson)*
This engrossing, occasionally hilarious and deeply learned book is a collection of pieces from the pages of *The Telegraph*, a British magazine devoted to documenting the life and examining the works of pop music's most enduringly interesting figure. These range from fascinating footnotes (Did he really play with Bobby Vee? Who was Mr Jones?) through Legends Unravelled (the real story of the bike accident and The Basement Tapes) and portraits of supporting players (like A.J. Weberman and Jacques Levy) to reviews and essays which combine enormous knowledge with reasoned criticism. Deserves to take up permanent residence at the bedside of any Dylan fan with a sense of humour and should be followed by a second volume at the earliest opportunity. *(DH)*

THE BASKETBALL DIARIES AND THE BOOK OF NODS
Jim Carroll *(Faber & Faber)*
"At 13 years of age, Jim Carroll writes better prose than 89% of the

novelists working today," claimed Jack Kerouac when these tales of sex, dope, petty crime, basketball and Catholic guilt were first published in the '60s. He certainly seems to have led a full life between the ages of 12 and 15, and the terse, slangy side-of-the-mouth prose in which he recounts it is even more alarmingly precocious than the events he describes. The "mature" work in *The Book Of Nods*, which is tacked onto the end of *The Basketball Diaries*, is considerably less impressive: turgid prose poems of the extremely deep and meaningful variety. Carroll turned rock poet in the '70s and, encouraged by Patti Smith, recorded a few albums for CBS but has notably failed to produce anything as savagely inspired and off-handedly evocative as that astonishing debut. *(CSM)*

NO DIRECTION HOME: THE LIFE & MUSIC OF BOB DYLAN
Robert Shelton *(New English Library)*
Shelton was the journalist whose *New York Times* review first singled Dylan out from the mass of Greenwich Village folkies and over the subsequent 25 years he's enjoyed a certain amount of the artist's trust. As a biography this is the equal of Anthony Scaduto's 1971 effort while ironically suffering from the same inclination to interpret everything in the light of his mid-'60s work. Shelton is sincere in his love for Dylan and his wish to see him installed beside other Great American Poets but when it comes to the lupine appeal of the man's rock and roll and the crucial importance of his humour, Shelton is still caught flat-footed. During Dylan's lifetime that could be the fate of all his biographers. *(DH)*

KINDS OF LOVING
Lee Everett Alkin *(Columbus)*
Now a happily-married trance medium and faith healer, Lee Everett has had an up-and-down life both privately and professionally. These cheery reflections, however, prove that the one-time common law wife of British rock & roller the late Billy Fury and later spouse of gay DJ Kenny Everett is still the hard-working, wise-cracking, down-to-earth Yorkshire lass she was back in the fifties. Then, as Audrey Valentine Middleton, she escaped her job in Sheffield's Co-op Funeral Department by running away to London with a musician on a rock & roll package tour.

It's these early years of singing in the Two Is coffee bar (where Tommy Steele was discovered), stripping at the Panama Club and pleasuring maharajahs at the Embassy Club which are the saltiest and most entertaining part of the book, reminding us of how little the tackier end of showbiz/pop has changed over the years. Though Lee's detailed account of her troubled later years of being married to a closeted homosexual is painfully sad, it's also ultimately quite inspiring. *(Kris Kirk)*

FIVE STAR: THE STORY SO FAR
Daryl Grant *(Zomba)*
An archetypal scissors-and-paste quick cash-in job: 48 pages with lots of pictures (half in colour) and workmanlike text full of slavish hyperbole ("that they're currently Britain's top pop act is beyond any doubt") and quotes cobbled together from uncredited press interviews, notably *Smash Hits*, with lots of condescending fake ENTHUSIASM in capital letters and inept jokes (in brackets with exclamation marks!). Just under half this scintillating prose is the band's "story" (so far being their first tour in October 1986), notable for being completely devoid of any tiresome intrusions like comment or insight from a writer who doesn't even appear to know that Tent Records is Buster (Dad) Pearson's own label, let alone actually *met* Five Star. (Grant must be the only writer in existence not to find the Pearson children even *slightly* weird.) Other contents include a few personal details on each member, the skimpiest of tour accounts, some utterly uninteresting Five Star facts (e.g. what was number one when each member was born) and four apparently random song lyrics. A "slim" volume that will satisfy neither fan nor critic, its sole redeeming feature is Dolores (Mum) Pearson's recipe for bread pudding. *(IC)*

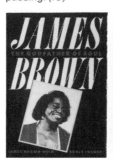

GENESIS: I KNOW WHAT I LIKE
Armando Gallo *(Omnibus)*
This is tagged as a "special limited reprint" to meet fans' demands – a marginally updated edition of the 1980 original (which is where the main narrative still stops). What you've really got here is a classic book written, photographed and designed by a lifelong fan of the band. The important point, however, is that photo-journalist Gallo has been driven by his devotion to the group to ensure that he's produced a book that's worthy of them. In fact, it's a yardstick by which other "fan" books should be judged. The detail is impressive, the original material copious and the historical references accurate. As a non-devotee of Genesis, I also found it engrossing reading – God knows how enjoyable real followers will find it. Well done to all involved (which basically means Gallo, Omnibus, Gallo, Gallo and Gallo). *(Brian Harrigan)*

REMEMBERING BUDDY
John Goldrosen & John Beecher *(GRR/Pavilion)*
This expanded, updated version of Goldrosen's 1965 *Buddy Holly: His Life And Music* is as loving and comprehensive as could be desired, now taking in the explosion of interest in the bespectacled one which followed Paul McCartney's acquisition of the Holly catalogue and the making of the *Buddy Holly Story* biopic which featured Gary Busey in the title role; it paints a persuasive and authentic picture of the Lubbock protégé. Far from the Shy Guy presented through the music, Holly emerges as an energetic, confident-to-the-point-of-arrogance young musician whose interests ranged from country to Ray Charles, and who was one of the few fifties figures whose creative career could well have stretched through the sixties and beyond if he hadn't taken that ill-fated airplane ride.

Among Goldrosen and Beecher's revelations is a far less cosy relationship with his producer Norman Petty than previous accounts would suggest and the demonstration that, while the movie did casual violence to many of the facts of Holly's career, the celluloid incarnation was at least psychologically true.

This updated edition is in a handsomely designed and profusely illustrated large format, and nobody with any significant degree of interest in Buddy Holly could do better than check it out. *(CSM)*

ALBERTA HUNTER: A CELEBRATION IN BLUES
Frank C. Taylor with Gerald Cook *(McGraw-Hill)*
One of the classic blues singers of the twenties, Alberta Hunter not only survived until 1984 but enjoyed a remarkable renaissance in her career, writing and performing the score for the Robert Altman production *Remember My Name* and playing for Carter at the White House while well into her eighties. In between times she enjoyed a sizeable reputation in Europe, entertained US troops virtually all the way through World War II and adopted a second career as a nurse, eventually getting her marching papers because the authorities felt that at 70 she should retire. In fact she was 82 at the time.

Warm, witty, feisty, generous and stingy, Hunter was simultaneously a staunch Christian and a performer of some of the raunchiest blues of the time. This dichotomous, charismatic personality emerges in well-rounded glory from this exceptionally loving biography, and characters as disparate as Louis Armstrong, Noel Coward, Ethel Waters and Somerset Maugham flit though her history. For all lovers of the blues in all its myriad forms, this is a small treasure. *(CSM)*

ELTON JOHN
Chris Charlesworth *(Bobcat)*
Where the majority of Bobcat Books appear to be rather thin volumes hastily assembled to take advantage of the latest new sensation (and why not, if there's a market?), this still thin volume provides a very readable skeleton account of the life and times of possibly Britain's best loved rock star. Charlesworth would not put his name to anything less than acceptable and while this is universes away from being the ultimate Elton book (Paul

Gambaccini is rumoured to be writing the official biog), the pictorial content of this enlarged pamphlet (plus a quite accurate text which, like every other Elton book, is thin on the post 1974/5 era) makes it a worthwhile purchase. *(JT)*

HELLFIRE: THE JERRY LEE LEWIS STORY
Nick Tosches *(Dell)*
This hallucinatory, poetic meditation on the life and times of The Killer – and incidentally those of his evangelist cousin Jimmy Lee Swaggart (now, thanks to Pearlygate, almost as famous as Jerry Lee himself) – brings the years between the Depression and the rock and roll years to steamy, menacing life. In Tosches' prose, redolent of moonshine whisky, honky-tonks and revivalist tent-shows, the story of this piano-pounding Louisiana wildman – forever trapped between the beckoning allure of rock and roll damnation and the forbidding and forbidden promised land of holiness and salvation – takes on archetypal and iconic stature.

Naturally, it hits all the predictable highs and lows of Lewis's career (the first recordings at Sun, the marriage to his 13-year-old cousin Myra, the fall from stardom, the road back, the divorces, the booze and drug bouts, his son's fatal motorcycle accident, the endless cycle of fall and repentance) but finds unpredictable insights and revelations to accompany each one. As sly and epic, wild and crazy, sleazy and sanctified as its subject, *Hellfire* is one of the few great rock biographies, towering over the cynical, slapdash cut-and-paste merchants as Grahame Greene or Eric Ambler do over Jeffrey Archer or Frederick Forsyth. *(CSM)*

McCARTNEY
Chris Salewicz *(Queen Anne Press)*
Unofficial biographies such as this usually have their inherent advantages and disadvantages. Lack of access to the subject can lead to gaping holes, though lack of accountability often makes for increased candour and readability. Here the pros outweigh the cons.

From *McCartney* we learn that once Paul got to the stage where people would want to write about him, his stage-managing of every public aspect of his life was meticulous. So much so that an entirely accurate account of things from his own lips would be rather too much to hope for. Thus forced to rely on research for his account of the young Paul, Salewicz has left no stone unturned – family, scout leaders, teachers and publicans all present a fascinating picture of the professional nice guy who once hung frogs on a barbed wire fence for fun. Where the book falls down is after The Beatles became successful and, understandably, the flow of willing supergrasses and unwitting dirt-dishers suddenly dries up. (This isn't a crucial complaint, however, as most of this can be found elsewhere.)

What *McCartney* is, then, is an account of growing up in Liverpool just after the war which is so engaging that the Beatles era becomes a bit of an intrusion and whose second half, without any fresh insight on such important factors as the rows with Lennon or the lunacy surrounding Apple and *Sgt Pepper*, is a bit of a bore. A book for McCartney completists or, paradoxically, those with not much interest in the Fab Four. *(LB)*

MARILLION: THE SCRIPT
Clive Gifford *(Omnibus)*
Yet another "biography" of a band which ends up as a hagiography as the author takes the part of devoted and unshakeably correct fan, with anyone who offers so much as a hint of criticism being presented as an ignorant loony and the music press set up as some curious Great Satan. Scissors, paste, scrapbooks and back issues of music papers have a lot to answer for when they end up as something like this. Okay, Marillion fans will eat this with a fork and spoon but it really doesn't add very much to the fund of human knowledge. Incidentally, Fish comes across as a really good bloke, which is just as well because that's exactly what he is. He also deserves a more imaginative and perceptive biographer than Clive Gifford. Oh, and Carol Clerk of *Melody Maker* comes across as a really perceptive critic which, again, is just as well because that's exactly what she is. She, not Gifford, should have been given this book to write. *(Brian Harrigan)*

WILLIE NELSON
Michael Bane *(Dell)*
That Willie Nelson has made an immense contribution to popular music in general, and country/"outlaw" music in particular, is not a subject for debate. The sub-title of this large print mass market paperback is "An unauthorized biography" and while Bane obviously almost worships Willie, it's equally obvious that he wasn't able to get very close to him and therein lies the major fault of his book. It's a skimpy overview which glosses over too much of Nelson's long and glorious career for those who might expect at least some documentation, and this contains none at all. No discography, no list

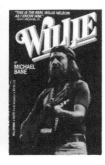

of compositions and cover versions, in fact not much at all really. His somewhat unconvincing explanation of how Nelson bucked the Nashville system was much better dealt with in the 15-year-old *Rise And Rise Of Redneck Rock*, and this half-hearted effort still leaves the field totally clear for a better researched biography. For new (or undemanding) fans only. *(JT)*

PAPA JOHN
John Phillips with Jim Jerome *(Dolphin/Doubleday US; Virgin UK)*
As songwriter-in-chief with The Mamas And The Papas and composer of Scott MacKenzie's archetypal '67 smash 'San Francisco (Wear Some Flowers In Your Hair)', John Phillips was one of the chief propagandists of Hippie. With this book, he may not succeed in trashing the few extant remnants of the ethos of the movement, but he certainly presents a memorable portrait of himself as one of the most arrogant, callous, weak-willed and self-indulgent assholes ever to crucify himself in print for money.

A self-pitying tale of massive drug abuse and indiscriminate screwing, *Papa John* leaves a trail of pubic scalps, dirty syringes and squandered fortunes through the sixties and seventies, with the likes of Otis Redding, Jimi Hendrix, Mick Jagger and Keith Richards putting in guest appearances along the way. For connoisseurs of rock and roll squalor and Tory MPs everywhere, this will prove a rare treat. No doubt it is intended to demonstrate Phillips' contrition at his (literally) wasted years and his loathing of his dissolute past, but that doesn't account for the book's all-pervasive air of smugness. As good a piece of evidence as any that Hippie was a direct ancestor of Yuppism and the New Right. *(CSM)*

ELVIS AND GLADYS
Elaine Dundy *(Dell US/Futura UK)*
ELVIS IN PRIVATE
Ed. Peter Haining *(Robert Hale)*
If the finest critical analysis of Elvis Presley's musical achievement still remains Greil Marcus' *Presliad* (included in his definitive *Mystery Train*), then Elaine Dundy's *Elvis And Gladys* stands unchallenged as the most painstaking, intuitive and insightful account of the Icon's formative years and early stardom. Free from all bias and attitude except a compassionate and inquisitive interest in the human reality behind the all-pervasive myth, Dundy's book carries a genuine emotional impact that cuts straight through all the familiar Presleyan platitudes.

Its most important achievement – apart from its exemplary evocation of the Southern experience of the Depression – is its rehabilitation of Gladys Presley (who is normally depicted as a classic Freudian stereotype of a grasping, possessive mother) and its ruthless debunking of the myth of Colonel Tom Parker. Indeed, it is difficult for anybody other than the most thoroughly bedazzled Presley orthodoxist to emerge from a perusal of *Elvis And Gladys* not wishing that the most famous artist/manager team in all of rock and roll had never met.

Haining, on the other hand, supplies the most conventional hagiography imaginable, aided by contributions from everybody from Chet Atkins and John Lennon to Jimmy Savile and Priscilla Presley. Its sole saving grace is a fine selection of photographs. *(CSM)*

QUEEN: A MAGIC TOUR
Text: Peter Hillmore. Photography: Denis O'Regan *(Sidgwick & Jackson)*
A 96 page A4-sized glossy paperback, this is a primarily visual record of Queen's "A Kind Of Magic" tour of Europe in the summer of 1986. Almost all of the book is taken up with O'Regan's straightforward concert photography (mostly in colour): the band playing, a brief backstage glimpse, the band playing, a couple of concert tickets, the band playing, a stadium shot or two, the band playing, a spot of larking about for the cameras, the band playing etc etc. The text is kept right down to a 3½ page introduction by way of Hillmore's distinctly journeyman descriptions – just about tolerable until it comes to the music ("Freddie began to run closer still, drawn inexorably to the deafening roar until he was at the very edge of the stage . . ."), plus the inevitable tour credits at the back. It's competent, solid, even colourful stuff but entirely unimaginative in concept and execution. Perfect for Queen fans, in other words. *(IC)*

QUEEN: A VISUAL DOCUMENTARY
Ken Dean *(Omnibus)*
The very embodiment of what the Trades Descriptions Act is all about. This is called a "visual documentary" and, by golly, that's exactly what it is. No more, no less. The words that break up the rather impressive pictures are brisk and informative without really telling you anything more than a Queen fan would already know. But really this is a time for congratulating the photographers, not least

the underrated Barry Plummer who has come up with a stack of good stuff. Nice production and good design also make for good value for Mercury's mob. And by the way, isn't Brian May photogenic? (Unlike poor Freddie who's never come across as attractive.) *(Brian Harrigan)*

HOW CAN I KEEP FROM SINGING: PETE SEEGER
David King Dunaway *(Harrap)*
Folksinger Pete Seeger's biography is as much a history of the American Left as of any section of the music business as such: modern readers may have some difficulty understanding why the political and media establishments were so terrified of a tall, thin man who played the banjo. Nevertheless, this middle-class New England radical – whose ancestors came over to the US on the *Mayflower,* no less – faced the full fury of the House Un-American Activities Committee, and as recently as 1968 got the popular Smothers Brothers kicked off TV for giving him a platform to sing a song opposing the Vietnam war.

Though his work, and his compositions like 'Little Boxes', 'If I Had A Hammer' and 'Where Have All The Flowers Gone?' were important precursors of the commercial folk boom of the late fifties and early sixties, his steadfast adherence to leftist politics prevented him from receiving the benefit of the dues he paid for so many years. Powerfully and plainly written, Dunaway's book is a portrait of a decent and stubborn man who was sufficiently un-American to care passionately about other people even as he clung to an anachronistic and idealized vision of the Common Folk. *(CSM)*

SEX PISTOLS: THE INSIDE STORY
Fred and Judy Vermorel *(Omnibus)*
Even nine years after its first publication this is still the most wonderful book ever written about the brief phenomenon that was punk rock.

The other notable tome from that era – Tony Parsons' and Julie Burchill's *The Boy Looked At Johnny* – froths with venomous punkish ravings that seem quaintly dated now but Fred and Judy Vermorel were ex-students of mass media at the Polytechnic of Central London (Fred was an old Situationist chum of Pistols manager Malcolm McLaren) and opted for a calmer, fly-on-the-wall documentary approach. They collect press cuttings, telexes, transcripts, school reports and letters and then juxtapose them so they narrate the odd and frantic tale. Producers, managers, parents, promoters, the group: all are here. Rotten is allowed to show himself from time to time as a boastful, cocky, precocious prat while McLaren is permitted to reveal that he's hardly above being a bit of a wally, and it's this verisimilitude which lifts the book far above the usual old claptrap of pop biographies.

The real backbone of the book, however, is the gorgeously down to earth diary of Sophie, Glitterbest's put-upon secretary. While McLaren is issuing statements all over the shop and making grandiose gestures, she's the one who has to get back receipts for petty cash, arrange a dentist for Johnny Rotten and see that Nancy Spungen makes it to the court on time. These gloriously mundane details haul the book miles away from the usual punk rock mythologising. Imagine the scene: while the TV-watching nation was supposedly reeling with shock at the lads' four letter word behaviour with Bill Grundy, Paul Cook's mum was at home saying "Oh! That's the shirt I washed for Paul last week." Lovely.

In the meantime this new edition has been spruced up with lots of new photos, a new discography and some background notes on McLaren and Situationism. *(WS)*

GLORY DAYS
Dave Marsh *(Sidgwick & Jackson)*
Buried somewhere in this massive (478 pages) sequel to Marsh's earlier Springsteen epic *Born To Run* is about half of an excellent book about America's most popular rock entertainer and the significance of his triumph during the Reagan era. Unfortunately, since Marsh considers that *everything* about Bruce Springsteen is important, the interesting stuff is virtually choked senseless by a

remorseless flood of trivial data. Even more unfortunately, since Springsteen is managed by Marsh's best friend with the assistance of Mrs Marsh, the book is about as objective as the party political broadcast which it so often resembles. When writing about almost any other subject, Marsh is one of the most acute rock commentators you could ever hope to read. On Springsteen, his range narrows until it encompasses little more than the space between hectoring advocacy and fannish drivel.

This is a shame, since Springsteen's career is an extraordinary one and the nature of his achievement – mounting what amounts to an alternative vision of America during the most demented orgy of nationalistic chest-beating in modern history – is more than worthy of some serious analysis. *Glory Days* comes frustratingly close to providing just that, but Marsh's need to subordinate everything to his canonization of Bruce as The Greatest Living American wins out every time. *(CSM)*

STATUS QUO: THE AUTHORISED BIOGRAPHY (25TH ANNIVERSARY EDITION)
John Shearlaw *(Sidgwick & Jackson)*
There can be few Quo fans who are not by now familiar with this sturdy, informative volume, which, like the band itself, seems to get spruced up and trotted out again every year or so. This new edition brings the band's history up to date, from the "End Of The Road" tour through their re-formation for Live Aid to Rossi and Parfitt's continuing without Alan Lancaster, despite his court action to try and stop them using the name.

Shearlaw is one of the very few who can write intelligently and entertainingly about Status Quo at any length but, while his love of the band is never in doubt, it has to be said that the recent additions to this venerable volume are well below standard. The narrative is very bitty and lacks the balanced historical overview of the earlier chapters, while the writing has degenerated almost beyond recognition into scrappy, lazy hack journalism which relies on exclamation marks rather than thoughtful use of language to make its point. In addition, the usual veil is drawn over some of the more interesting personal politics of the band (just *why* Rossi couldn't continue to work with Lancaster is never satisfactorily explained), the fudged handling of the resultant court case is a great missed opportunity for a bit of human drama, and Shearlaw has taken to thrusting himself far too far forward into the story. It really does read like he genuinely couldn't be bothered to write a proper history.

There is some new source material here for Quo fans but if I were them I'd hang on in the hope that Shearlaw will be shamed into rewriting this new portion for the next edition. *(IC)*

BARBRA STREISAND – THE WOMAN, THE MYTH, THE MUSIC
Shaun Considine *(Dell)*
An eye-popping biography of the Brooklyn-born multi-millionairess (latest estimate of earnings: $100m-plus) who still recycles her Christmas cards. From her first gig at a 1960s Greenwich Village gay bar talent contest through to her recent expensive filmic flop (a drag musical bastardization of Isaac Bashevis Singer's *Yentl*) and beyond, Babs has – according to this well-researched and wildly entertaining unauthorized muckrake – spent her life trampling over anyone who stood in her path to all-round Genghis Khandom.

From her own Yiddish Momma (whom she banned from her shows) to ex-hubbie/slave Elliot Gould (whom she made wear a chauffeur's cap when he drove her), from the co-writers whose production and arranging credits she nicked to the fellow-duettists whose thunder she stole (Neil Diamond, Donna Summer), from the leading men she bedded (Ryan O'Neal, Warren Beatty et al) to those who escaped her three-inch fangs (Robert Redford), there are few who describe La Streisand in other than zoological terms.

With the memory of an elephant (boy, does she enjoy revenge), the appetite of a horse, the killer instinct of a barracuda and, according to *Hello Dolly* co-star Walter Matthau, "less talent than a butterfly's fart," the most monstrous ego in showbiz now spends half

her life building huge barns on her LA estate just to house her spreading collection of antiques, and the other half plotting increasingly jaw-dropping projects such as her planned film treatment of *Macbeth* with Marlon Brando playing hubbie.

If you're a sucker for dirt-digging showbiz bios, this is *the one*; it kept me up till 5am. *(Kris Kirk)*

TALKING HEADS: A BIOGRAPHY
Jerome Davis *(Omnibus)*
This smaller American paperback (a *Billboard* publication) turns out to be the proverbial parson's egg. It starts off with the formidable disadvantage that the author has evidently not been able to talk to the band themselves and is thus unable to check that all he has gleaned from interviews elsewhere is in fact true. He is also unable to dig out the real whys and wherefores – we are told only that adolescent Byrne liked black music but not why – and similarly the book lacks the artists' own insights on their work except when already reported by someone else. The same goes too for the band's own interpersonal relationships (crucial in Talking Heads); it would have been fascinating, for example, to know what the rest of the group (and Byrne, come to that) made of Byrne's apparent crack-up in London on their second British tour.

Inevitably too there are glaring gaps – the story that Byrne made the rest of the group re-audition for Talking Heads after they got their record deal with Sire isn't even mentioned – and hasty glossings over – Chris Frantz barely features and the promised examination of Tina Weymouth's strength as a person (given almost equal billing with Byrne's artistry in the introduction) never really materializes except in the most cursory fashion.

For all that, however, Davis has made a pretty thorough job of digging up past acquaintances and people on the fringe of the group, and there is a lot of illuminating to be found here. Particularly interesting (if rather bitty) is the chapter on the young Byrne and his development in personality and as a conceptual artist. It's this source material, plus a competent history of the group and a couple of reproductions of the student Byrne's curious questionnaires (a pity about the photographs) that ultimately make this a book worth having. *(IC)*

I TINA
Tina Turner with Kurt Loder *(Penguin)*
Pop star autobiographies – especially ghosted ones like this – tend to be rather dodgy affairs, probably because most pop stars are too career-minded to sanction the publishing of anything that might taint their public image. *I Tina* avoids the worst of that bland sanitization – not, one suspects, because Tina Turner is any less calculating than most pop stars, but because the most interesting part of her life – when she was with Ike Turner in the '60s and early '70s – is distant enough for her to treat as history.

Whether or not she tells the absolute truth about that period, she spins a chillingly unattractive tale of a husband obsessed with money, power, drugs and sex as means of disguising his own inadequacies. Sensibly Kurt Loder – who has conformed to the common modern biographical convention of just presenting the story as chunks of speech, mostly from Tina but also from friends and family – doesn't waste too long on the subsequent years when the shutters come down and the tale is reduced to a list of concert tours and record contracts.

Some might find the soap opera qualities of the whole thing a bit nauseating – the poor girl-who-had-nothing who finds fame but only at the expense of happiness and who walks out with nothing again only to return truly triumphant after her years in the wilderness – but then that might be just how it happened. *(CH)*

DREAMGIRL: MY LIFE AS A SUPREME
Mary Wilson with Patricia Romanowski and Ahrgus Juillard *(Sidgwick & Jackson)*
If life is unfair, then the music business is just like life only more so. Mary Wilson's reminiscences of her years with The Supremes (or, to be more accurate, her years with Diana Ross; The Supremes continued with a variety of lead singers for six years after Ross went nova) is a fairly scarifying account of what happens to people when they become commodities. A cautionary modern fairy-tale, it casts Diana Ross as the Bad Princess, Motown bossman and founder Berry Gordy as the Wicked Uncle and the late Florence Ballard – the best singer of the three but perpetually relegated to the back line – as the Tragic Heroine.

Motown, as the company's publicists have never tired of telling us, was a family but like many families it was prone to jealousies, conflicts and the occasional outbreak of sheer brutality. *Dreamgirl* is a vivid and unashamedly partisan account of Wilson's journey from the Mississippi Delta to the Detroit housing projects, stardom and

finally showbiz limbo and the nostalgia circuit. Her anger is rarely tainted with bitterness, but when planning your next dinner party it would still be inadvisable to seat her next to Diana Ross. *(CSM)*

ZAPPA
Julian Colbeck *(Virgin)*
Obviously an admirer, Colbeck's failure to come to grips with the prolific, highly intelligent but generally commercially unviable erstwhile chief Mother of Invention is at least honourable. It would probably take a book the size of the one you're reading, with quite small print, to even start an investigation into the Zappa phenomenon, and while such a mythical volume might be bought by the ardent fans, there aren't enough of them to make such a volume profitable. Occasionally as obscure as its subject (who *did* win the court case over Zappa being banned by the Albert Hall? I read that passage several times, yet I still don't know), this isn't a bad read, although a discography and formal track and line up listings would have immeasurably improved it. Nice read, shame about the documentation. *(JT)*

● MISCELLANEOUS

BLACK HEART MAN: A JOURNEY INTO RASTA
Derek Bishton *(Chatto & Windus)*
Of the scores of books, pamphlets, magazine articles and theses on the subject of Ras Tafari, this slim study by a "drop-out journalist trying to put [his] old hippy politics into practice" is particularly singular.

Bishton's "journey" is an attempt to reconcile what he sees as "the two pillars of the Rasta credo which non-Rastas find most difficulty in taking seriously – the divinity of Haile Selassie and repatriation to Africa as an inevitability for black people in the West." It took him from Handsworth in Birmingham to the Pinnacle hill in Jamaica via Shashamene in Ethiopia, the land granted by Selassie to the black peoples of the West (in particular the Jamaican Ras Tafari) in appreciation of their fighting support when Mussolini invaded the country during the thirties.

The conclusion of Bishton's pilgrimage is his contention that whatever the reservations of Europeans on the validity of Ras Tafari, they are in any case not in a position to pass judgement, having systematically suppressed the voice of the black race throughout history. "I began to realize," he writes, "that it was the rigours of the European intellectual tradition which had been responsible for turning black people into slaves and was even now defining the terms in which Rastas should be viewed."

He cites as an example the case of Edward Wilmot Blyden. How many people, white or black, have ever heard of Edward Wilmot Blyden, let alone anything he said or wrote, asks Bishton. "It's not surprising, because virtually none of his work is in print. The outstanding black intellectual of the nineteenth century – and about the only place you can be sure of finding a book with his name on it is in the British Library."

And in his small way, a self-loathing *backra* (white man) ridden with liberal guilt, Derek Bishton goes some distance towards redressing the balance. *(PR)*

TRUE STORIES
David Byrne *(Faber & Faber)*
David Byrne always looks like the sort of person who spends half the morning picking bits of fluff off his clothes and it's that sort of painstaking attention to detail that makes *True Stories* one of the very few book-of-the-films to be worthwhile.

The text is in two main parts. First there's a lucid account from Byrne of how the film came about – from the collection he started in 1983 of bizarre newspaper stories about everyday folk to his individual method of scriptwriting i.e. covering a wall with sketches of different scenes then constantly rearranging and editing them until they had "some sort of flow". Secondly there's the film's script which runs down a quarter of each double page for 160 pages, spelling out not just the words spoken but the long filming instructions and scene settings that make explicit most of what is left implicit in the film itself.

The rest of the book is mostly taken up with beautifully printed photographs, some relating directly to the film, some simply tangentially related to a theme being touched on in the script. There are also some of the sketches Byrne made, reprinted articles that interest him (e.g. *The Wall Street Journal*'s "Why Do Hot Dogs Come In Packs Of 10 And Buns in 8s and 12s?") and short commentaries by Byrne on things like Parades ("parades are horrible . . .") and See-Through Houses ("houses look best when they're not finished . . .").

Whether Byrne's strange playful obsession with the trivial and the odd deserves this sort of attention or should just be dismissed as post-art school dilettantism is debatable but certainly there couldn't be a much more witty, intelligent and beautifully compiled presentation of it than this. *(CH)*

THE KNEBWORTH ROCK FESTIVALS
Chryssie Lytton Cobbold *(Omnibus)*
Our Chryssie (don't you just love the "y" instead of the "i"?) is the lady who, along with husband David, apparently owns Knebworth House. At the beginning of 1974, promotor Freddie Bannister approached the two of them with the idea that their gaff was the perfect spot for a rock festival. Unfortunately they agreed and thus was born a series of possibly the most boring outdoor festivals ever staged in the UK. Chryssie does her best to make them seem even more tedious. She's in the ideal position to give us the ynsyde ynformatyon but instead reveals that she has all the news sense of . . . well, the average stately home owner. The great Freddie Bannister vs manager Peter Grant ticket controversy is glossed over, the shambolic Capital Jazz Festival is left uninvestigated and the whole concept of outdoor fest isn't even tackled. Actually, one begins to wonder if Chryssie isn't just a teensy bit dim, especially when she talks about husband David going off with Ree Styles (singer with The Tubes) who was their most "way out" (Chryssie's quotes) visitor to date. "The combination of Ree and vodka obviously affected David," she gushes. "In the end he got into the Rolls with her and set off across the park. I never thought I would see him again but she turned him out at the lodge gates!" Oh Chryssie – get serious! *(Brian Harrigan)*

LYRICS 1962–1985
By Bob Dylan *(Jonathan Cape)*
For a man who claims not to read a fraction of the things written about him and to pay his own past little mind Dylan has been busy in the archives of late. First there was *Biograph* and now we have a fat volume which takes the whole of his 1973 collection *Writings & Drawings* and adds the massive amount of words he's bashed out between *Planet Waves* and *Empire Burlesque*. The change of title and the division of all the songs into album sections suggests that these are presented as *libretti* rather than stand-alone poems. At the very least it affords the chance to make out every last word he's singing on the records (or, interestingly, what he *meant* to sing); at best it's the written testament of an extraordinary imagination and evidence of his unrelenting energy. As Tony Hancock threatened to tell Saint Peter: "'ere you are, mate. Add *that* lot up!" *(DH)*

THE INCOMPLETE WORKS OF JAMIE REID: UP THEY RISE
Text: Jamie Reid and Jon Savage. Design: Malcolm Garrett and Jamie Reid *(Faber & Faber)*
Jamie Reid is most famous as the man responsible for the ransom note lettering and the safety pin through the Queen's nose during the Sex Pistols' heyday. This Sex Pistols period (their section is called 'Sex' – the other two are 'Death' and 'Birth') takes up the second part of this book, which is both an (auto)biography and an anthology of his work.

The Sex Pistols are undoubtedly the book's main selling point – Reid gives only the second compelling account of those times after Fred and Judy Vermorel's *The Inside Story* and some of the unused artwork (like the Richard Branson 'No One Is Innocent' sleeve) is engrossing. The rest of the book is fascinating too, however, as Reid explains how he journeyed from student sit-ins and Situationism in the '60s, through a printing and magazine co-operative, two years in the Hebrides and the Sex Pistols in the '70s, to his current multi-media project called "Leaving The Twentieth Century" (as in "please wash your hands before leaving . . .") with actress Margi Clarke.

It's a path which only makes sense when you look at the different impulses battling within Reid: what he calls a "spiritual socialism", a slightly hippy idealism and a simple love of art. Sometimes you get

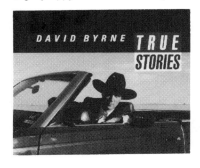

the impression that he really wishes the last of those could get out more. Hidden away, almost sadly, in tiny type beneath an abstract painting (reproduced, like the rest of the book, in disappointing black and white) he says, ''I have been and always will be a painter. The Sex Pistols were just a diversion.'' *(CH)*

VISUAL AID
Various *(Pantheon Books, New York)*
Inspired by Band Aid, USA For Africa and the continuing need to keep funds flowing to the drought-stricken Africans, here's *Visual Aid* – a handsome 160 page hardcover collection of previously unpublished portraiture from some of the top photographic names in the fields of entertainment, style and fashion: Annie Liebowitz, Robert Mapplethorpe, David Bailey (his work shot in a makeshift studio at Live Aid in London), Matthew Rolston, Sheila Metzner, Herb Ritts, Snowdon, Greg Gorman and Andy Warhol (whose contributions are some of the Polaroids he took as a basis for later paintings). The subjects include Bruce Springsteen, Mick Jagger, Norman Mailer, Elvis Costello, Jane Fonda, Cyndi Lauper, Michael Jackson, a faceless Madonna, Nancy Reagan, Grace Jones, Tom Waits, Joan Collins, the Metropolitan Insurance Building of New York and, of course, Bob Geldof.

The standard of photography is, needless to say, extremely high, as are the standards of printing and production. It's an invidious task to pick highlights from such a collection but some beautiful Pre-Raphaelite influenced fashion pictures from Sheila Metzner, some startling flora, fauna and fashion shots from Snowdon and Greg Gorman's casual but enthralling all-girl group portrait of Jessica Lange, Goldie Hawn, Jane Fonda, Sally Field and Barbra Streisand together all provided something special, while Annie Liebowitz shows she's still not short of effective surprises. At $30.00 you'll have to dig deep for *Visual Aid* but it will be money well spent in every sense. *(IC)*

ASK: THE CHATTER OF POP
Paul Morley *(Faber & Faber)*
Basically, *Ask* is an anthology of the best interviews recorded by Paul Morley, all but one for the *NME* between 1976 and his departure in the early '80s for ZTT Records. As such it's rather good. Simply by following through trains of thought and by pressing his subjects with slightly obscure questions, he digs out answers that at least give the illusion of being unusually illuminating. Cynics could be excused thinking in places that he's intent on showing just two things – that Paul Morley is cleverer than most pop stars and that he's dared taunt them with the proof – but even when he's quite clearly taking an obscene pleasure in watching pop stars unwittingly hang themselves with their own ridiculous utterances, he's always still revealing more about them than about himself. The most refreshing thing about the whole book is that – whether he is being insolent to Alice Cooper or sycophantic to Sting – he's clearly brimming with a genuine fascination both with people and their motivations, and with pop music itself. *(CH)*

THE TOP 100 ALBUMS
Presented by Paul Gambaccini *(GRR 2/Pavilion)*
The idea of there being a definitive chart of albums compiled on a meritorious basis is an attractive one but ultimately such a list would have to be drawn up by one person with sufficient informed taste and breadth and depth of knowledge. Such a person does not exist. In their absence we lesser mortals keep getting saddled with pointless abstractions such as this coffee table paperback which seize on any flimsy excuse – here the 30th anniversary of the first rock album (*Elvis Presley*, actually) to top the American LP charts – to try to pass themselves off as some kind of collective critical guide for collectors. (For ''collectors'' read ''beginners''. Or ''morons''.)

What you actually get here is a hopelessly ill-judged panel of . . . *broadcasters*. (Since when has MTV been synonymous with sound critical taste in music? Or DJs, for that matter?) Presumably the intention is to make for a more populist, accessible approach but the result is simply a compromise compilation which is no use to anyone

and certainly has no claim to being the ''top'' list of albums. You might as well do your own with your friends; it'd be a lot more interesting.

The resulting chart contains all the dopey, half-baked and downright ludicrous results you might expect from such a witless selection. Predictably *Sergeant Pepper* is number one (debatable in itself) but lower down Carole King's *Tapestry* (30), Graham Parker & The Rumour's *Squeezing Out Sparks* (43) and Huey Lewis & The News' *Sports* (72) rate higher than *Beatles For Sale* (71), Prince's *Purple Rain* (90) and Eurythmics' *Sweet Dreams* (97).

Things can only get better with the following section which depicts the ''top'' 100 album sleeves with their US and UK catalogue numbers and track listings, followed by a commentary from fact fetishist Gambaccini. This annotation is all the more irritating because he has the makings of a perceptive guide if only he could stir himself from his fawning approach and numbing use of clichés.

This part of the book is followed in turn by the most interesting section – the individual listings of the so-called ''professionals'' themselves. It is actually fascinating to know what public figures list as their favourite records (Can Mark Ellen's favourite LP *really* be Dillinger's *CB200*??!) but so dismal and unknown are most of the participants that ultimately the only response possible is who *cares* what these people think, especially if they're responsible for that ridiculous chart at the front?

When the first volume of this kind, *Critics' Choice*, appeared in the '70s, *Cashbox* sneered ''Here's a real non-book for ya!'' How right they were, and that goes for this useless sequel as well. A curse on coffee tables everywhere. *(IC)*

● GENERAL

DESIGNER BOYS & MATERIAL GIRLS: MANUFACTURING THE '80S POP DREAM
Dave Hill *(Blandford Press)*
The main problem with this book is that the author adheres far too rigidly to his underlying thesis – that in the '80s pop music can be seen as a product of a number of different strategies. That's the reason why the 16 profiles comprising this book – The Police, Madness, Spandau Ballet, Madonna and so on – are so unconvincing; the brief career summaries and the manipulative theories he's added on simply don't glue together. It's very noticeable that his favourites, rather predictably the Elvis Costello's and the Madness's, are precisely those who are most out at sea in mid '80s pop music and who he therefore tends to cast sympathetically as victims.

Elsewhere his lack of affection (no sin in itself) is compounded by a worrying lack of command over his material – without trying I noted over 30 factual mistakes as I read through. Most of all, Dave Hill writes as if things very rarely happen by accident, as if everyone in pop music is fairly bright and as if you can explain why people manically fling their arms about while listening to the latest Bananarama single in their bedroom by a careful examination of Bananarama's career. Pop music isn't that simple, nor is it that boring. *(CH)*

THE HIP
Brian Case, Roy Carr and Fred Dellar *(Faber & Faber)*
A brilliant piece of marketing ensured that this slight but highly entertaining book copped hold of the interest in jazz style at precisely the right moment. After *Absolute Beginners*, this set something of the record straight on who the real masters of cool were: from the classic study of Chet Baker on the cover inwards, the photographic content was superb (though sometimes peculiarly designed) and the text offered a neat, racy little history on the jazz argot and appearance as it grew up in the '50s and '60s. A jazz book for audiences who weren't necessarily interested in jazz, the energy and ingenuity of its approach managed to mirror some parts of the music itself. One day, perhaps, a collector's item. *(RC)*

EXPENSIVE HABITS: THE DARK SIDE OF THE MUSIC INDUSTRY
Simon Garfield *(Faber & Faber)*
Simon Garfield is possibly the first music journalist to bother to understand the business side of pop music – not just the general principles but the smallprint as well – and it's that wealth and depth of knowledge that makes *Expensive Habits* so compelling.

Most of the basic stories here are fairly common knowledge – that Wham! earned little more than a pittance from their first wave of success, that the Beatles' financial affairs were a constant catastrophe, that people like Hazel O'Connor can be strangled into silence by legal wranglings – and it's Garfield's painstaking step-by-step explanation of what went on that is so interesting. Much of it is

like a nightmarish piece of fiction except that it's hard to believe characters could be this naïve, this stupid, this incompetent or this Machiavellian.

Occasionally the tales are funny too. In the last chapter – a collection of quotes and anecdotes – Dave Robinson, former head of Stiff Records, recounts how Richard Branson only remembered an ancient unresolved business disagreement when the two of them were together on the golf course and Branson was fuming at having taken nine shots on the fourteenth hole. The writ arrived the following week . . . *(CH)*

● REFERENCE

COUNTRY MUSIC USA
Bill C. Malone *(Equation)*
This weighty tome with 562 pages, of which the last 47 are the index (!), is a scholarly and brilliantly researched book. An object lesson in being on top of one's subject, it makes fascinating reading for those who wish to learn more about a musical genre which is experiencing a strong rise in popularity. Malone is a professor of history at a New Orleans university, and while this is an undeniably useful book for a critic, it is also rather hard going at times. The straightforward biographical chapters, such as that on Jimmie Rodgers, are factually impeccable but lack a sense of humour and, more importantly, a sense of enjoyment. As source material or the basis for research this could hardly be bettered, but don't expect to read this in under 50 sittings. *(JT)*

HOW TO MAKE IT BIG IN THE MUSIC BUSINESS
Bob Monaco and James Riordan *(Omnibus)*
First of all it has to be stated that nobody – but nobody – can give you a copper-bottomed guarantee that you will be able to make it in the music business. If such a formula existed, everybody would be using it. The best you can hope for is a manual that will set out the various situations you are likely to encounter and, with the benefit of experience, advise you in accurate, encouraging, layman's language what to do and what not to do. This is such a book.

Monaco and Riordan are two American record producers, while Riordan has also had pretty wide all round music business experience. What they do is to take the various myths, misconceptions and attitude problems that are common among inexperienced (and not so inexperienced) music business aspirants and then tell you how it *really* is in an honest, succinct and highly readable style. For example: "A band should have a leader. As much as people try it, four guys can't lead a band because it doesn't work." Voila! Hundreds of hours of other people's sufferings in one easy-to-swallow capsule.

Having dealt with the personal angles, the authors then move on to the kind of situations and characters in the music business that the aspirant is likely to have to deal with – songs, demos, studios, professional people (managers, agents, lawyers) and record labels – and dish out the same kind of informed, no nonsense approach and sound advice. "Firing your best friend can be a real hassle but if you have a mutual understanding before you begin to work together, the problem is lessened considerably." Voila! Hindsight beforehand.

One note of caution, however. This book is American and both the scale of operations and certain situations may be different in each country. For example, though it may not be worthwhile in America, it is a very good idea to form your own music publishing company in Britain. That reservation aside, this book should be compulsory reading for anyone considering getting involved with the music business. It will save you – and those dealing with you – a lot of unnecessary trouble and grief. In the music business there can be few greater assets. *(IC)*

HM LPS
Produced by Masateru Makino.
Designed by Takashi Yamada *(Omnibus)*
An extraordinary book, presumably first published in Japan and then snapped up by Omnibus for publication in the UK. It is nothing more and nothing less than reproductions of 434 heavy metal album covers, with the title, band and catalogue number printed underneath. There are no credits for the designers or artists, nor is there any kind of narrative, explanation or critique. Just 434 album sleeves. The book, however, is littered with typesetting errors: Dio's *Holy Diver* becomes *Holly Diver* putting an entirely different complexion on young Ronnie's entire persona. *Storm* becomes *Storme*, The Scorpions' *Virgin Killer* becomes *Virin Killer* etc etc. Motorhead, incidentally, become Moterhead. So what does all this prove? Firstly, that the Japanese can't spell. Secondly, that Omnibus' proof-readers can't be bothered. And thirdly, that HM bands go for the same old crappy visuals (Vikings, women, horror, death etc) because those sleeves which actually portray the band do nothing so much as underline the fact that HM bands inevitably look like a bunch of wallies. *(Brian Harrigan)*

THE NEW ILLUSTRATED ROCK HANDBOOK
Consultant: Mike Clifford *(Salamander)*
It's difficult not to groan these days when one sees yet another increasingly meaningless "rock encyclopedia" bearing down on you, especially when it claims to be "the ultimate rock reference work – no fan or aspiring performer should be without it!" On the other hand no book that boasts the combined knowledge of knowledgeable historians and trivia experts like Peter Frame and John Tobler deserves to be dismissed out of hand. Inevitably there are quibbles over omissions (surely Nick Drake merits inclusion?) or who gets relegated to the thumbnail sketch appendix but mostly this book covers its chosen ground pretty well, given the virtually impossible nature of the task so great is the diversity and sheer volume of mainstream music these days. In fact it also breaks some new ground by including a new section including Management/Promotion Personalities, Record Companies and Musical Instruments, though this part is as yet distinctly sketchy.

Inevitably too there are mistakes, mostly on a nit-picking level though there are errors of fact: The Fairport Convention's first LP was on Polydor not Island, Scritti Politti is *not* Italian for political writings, Squeeze did not write the play *Labelled With Love* nor did they appear in it and it's disappointing to see the oft-repeated myth about The Jackson 5 being discovered by Diana Ross included here (it was in fact Gladys Knight). In fact black music receives something of a short shrift here (perhaps to be expected from a rock listing) though it's surprisingly good on pop.

If informed taste and sheer volume of comprehensive information are the book's main strengths then its extremely elastic definition of "original line-up" and its "selective" LP listings by artist are its main weaknesses. In fact the latter often appears downright misleading: Simple Minds first three LPs on Arista are listed with their Virgin re-release dates of years later; the original Mamas And Papas only recorded four studio LPs yet this book lists seven titles, of which no fewer than six are subsequent rehashed compilations.

So, not the "ultimate reference work" it proclaims to be but with 272 pages, over 650 pictures and sleeves and more than 300,000 words, this still represents an extremely useful (if hardly definitive) guide to mainstream rock music for the interested reader. *(IC)*

JAZZ: THE ESSENTIAL COMPANION
Ian Carr, Digby Fairweather & Brian Priestley *(Grafton)*
A splendidly authoritative biographical dictionary of most of the major performers in jazz. Though there are flaws – a sometimes foolish bias towards British jazz, which is and always has been a minor league phenomenon, and some too writerly accounts of figures who are no more than footnotes – this must be the best shot yet at clearing away the smoke around the huge number of jazz musicians and their many schools. The longer entries on Parker, Armstrong and the like seldom resort to the hackneyed summary, and there are fascinating revelations on players that might otherwise be mere names on record sleeves. It is that rarity, a well-written and very readable jazz book, and the sort of thing to be frequently pulled off the shelf. One might have asked, though, for more and better photographs. *(RC)*

THE BPI CERTIFIED AWARDS

© **The British Phonographic Industry Ltd, reprinted with permission. The qualifying sales levels for BPI Gold and Platinum awards are, respectively, 500,000 units and 1,000,000 units (singles), and 100,000 units and 300,000 units (LPs). Sales of cassettes and compact discs are included.**

To qualify for Double or Triple Platinum, a single or album must have been released since January 1985 or have appeared in the *Gallup* **charts since then if it was released earlier. Multi-Platinum is a new category introduced in February 1987 to acknowledge sales over Triple Platinum.**

MULTI PLATINUM
(Over 900,000 units)

Phil Collins: No Jacket Required (Virgin) *Apr 87* (1.2m)
Dire Straits: Brothers In Arms (Vertigo) *Feb 87* (2.4m)
Five Star: Silk And Steel (RCA) *Apr 87* (1.2m)
Fleetwood Mac: Rumours (WEA) *Mar 87* (1.8m)
Michael Jackson: Thriller (Epic) *Mar 87* (2.4m)
Madonna: True Blue (Sire) *Mar 87* (1.2m)
Meatloaf: Bat Out Of Hell (Epic) *Mar 87* (1.2m)
Alison Moyet: Alf (CBS) *Mar 87* (1.2m)
Mike Oldfield: Tubular Bells (Virgin) *Apr 87* (1.5m)
Queen: Greatest Hits (EMI) *Apr 87* (1.8m)
Sade: Diamond Life (Epic) *Mar 87* (1.2m)
Paul Simon: Graceland (Warner Bros) *Apr 87* (1.2m)
Various: Now That's What I Call Music 6 (EMI) *Apr 87* (1.2m)
Various: Now That's What I Call Music 8 (EMI) *Feb 87* (1.2m)
Wham!: Make It Big (Epic) *Mar 87* (1.2m)

TRIPLE PLATINUM
(900,000 units)

Phil Collins: Face Value (Virgin) *Mar 87*
Eurythmics: Revenge (RCA) *Jan 87*

Five Star: Silk And Steel (RCA) *Jan 87*
Genesis: Invisible Touch (Virgin) *Jul 87*
Whitney Houston: Whitney Houston (Arista) *Oct 86*
Madonna: True Blue (Sire) *Nov 86*
Queen: Greatest Hits (EMI) *Apr 86*
Paul Simon: Graceland (Warner Bros) *Jan 87*
U2: The Joshua Tree (Island) *Jul 87*
U2: Live (Under a Blood Red Sky) (Island) *Apr 87*
Various: Now That's What I Call Music 1 (EMI) *Dec 86*
Various: Now That's What I Call Music 8 (EMI) *Dec 86*
Various: Hits 5 (RCA) *Dec 86*
Wham!: Fantastic (Epic) *Mar 87*

DOUBLE PLATINUM
(600,000 units)

A-ha: Hunting High And Low (Warner Bros) *Sep 86*
Kate Bush: Hounds Of Love (EMI) *Dec 86*
Kate Bush: The Whole Story (EMI) *Dec 86*
Eurythmics: Revenge (RCA) *Nov 86*
Five Star: Silk And Steel (RCA) *Dec 86*
Peter Gabriel: So (Virgin) *Mar 87*
Genesis: Invisible Touch (Virgin) *Mar 87*
Whitney Houston Whitney (Arista) *Jul 87*

Level 42: World Machine (Polydor) *Oct 86*
Madonna: True Blue (Sire) *Sep 86*
The Police: Every Breath You Take – The Singles (A&M) *Dec 86*
Queen: It's A Kind Of Magic (EMI) *Oct 86*
Paul Simon: Graceland (Warner Bros) *Dec 86*
Simple Minds: Once Upon A Time (Virgin) *Oct 86*
Simply Red: Picture Book (Elektra) *Mar 87*
U2: The Unforgettable Fire (Island) *Apr 87*
U2: The Joshua Tree (Island) *Apr 87*
Various: Now That's What I Call Music 2 (EMI) *Dec 86*
Various: Now That's What I Call Music 3 (EMI) *Dec 86*
Various: Now That's What I Call Music 7 (EMI) *Oct 86*
Various: Now That's What I Call Music 8 (EMI) *Dec 86*
Various: Now That's What I Call Music 9 (EMI) *Apr 87*
Various: Hits 5 (RCA) *Dec 86*

PLATINUM
(300,000 units)

A-ha: Scoundrel Days (Warner Bros) *Dec 86*
The Bangles: Different Light (CBS) *Jan 87*

George Benson: Love Songs (Warner Bros) *Dec 86*
Bon Jovi: Slippery When Wet (Phonogram) *Jan 87*
Chris De Burgh: Into The Light (A&M) *Aug 86*
Kate Bush: The Whole Story (EMI) *Nov 86*
The Communards: Communards (London) *Jan 87*
Curiosity Killed The Cat: Keep Your Distance (Phonogram) *Jul 87*
Eric Clapton: August (Duck) *Apr 87*
Everly Brothers: Walk Right Back (WEA) *Feb 87*
Eurythmics: Revenge (RCA) *Sep 86*
Five Star: Luxury Of Life (RCA) *Oct 86*
Five Star: Silk And Steel (RCA) *Oct 86*
Foster & Allen: Reminiscing (Stylus) *Jan 87*
Hot Chocolate: The Very Best Of (EMI) *Apr 87*
Housemartins: London 0 Hull 4(Go! Discs) *Dec 86*
Whitney Houston: Whitney (Arista) *Jun 87*
Janet Jackson: Control (A&M) *May 87*
League Unlimited Orchestra: Love And Dancing (Virgin) *Nov 86*
Level 42: Running In The Family (Polydor) *Apr 87*
Huey Lewis & The News: Fore (Chrysalis) *Dec 86*
Michael McDonald: Sweet Freedom (Warner Bros) *Mar 87*
The Mamas & The Papas: 20 Greatest Hits (EMI) *Nov 86*
The Monkees: Best Of (EMI) *Dec 86*
Alison Moyet: Raindancing (CBS) *Apr 87*
Original Cast: Phantom Of The Opera (Polydor) *Feb 87*
Pet Shop Boys: Please (EMI) *Jan 87*
The Police: Every Breath You Take – The Singles (A&M) *Nov 86*
Queen: A Kind Of Magic (EMI) *Aug 86*
Queen: Live Magic (EMI) *Jan 87*
Lionel Richie: Dancing On The Ceiling (Motown) *Sep 86*
Paul Simon: Graceland (Warner Bros) *Oct 86*
Simple Minds: New Gold Dream (Virgin) *Jan 87*
Simple Minds: Live: In The City Of Light (Virgin) *Jun 87*
Simply Red: Picture Book (Elektra) *Jul 86*
Simply Red: Men And Women (Elektra) *Mar 87*
Spandau Ballet: Through The Barricades (CBS) *May 87*
Tina Turner: Break Every Rule (Capitol) *Mar 87*
U2: The Joshua Tree (Island) *Mar 87*
Various: Now That's What I Call Music 7 (EMI) *Aug 86*
Various: Now That's What I Call Music 9 (EMI) *Apr 87*
Various: South Pacific (CBS) *Dec 86*
Various: Top Gun – Original Soundtrack (WEA) *Dec 86*
Suzanne Vega: Solitude Standing (A&M) *Jun 87*
Wham!: The Final (Epic) *Dec 86*
Whitesnake: Live In The Heart Of The City (EMI) *Apr 87*
Paul Young: Between Two Fires (CBS) *Jan 87*

GOLD (100,000 units)

Bryan Adams: Into The Fire (A&M) *Apr 87*
A-ha: Scoundrel Days (Warner Bros) *Oct 86*
The Bangles: Different Light (CBS) *Nov 86*
Anita Baker: Rapture (Elektra) *Dec 86*
Beastie Boys: Licensed To Ill (Def Jam) *Jun 87*
George Benson: While The City Sleeps (WEA) *Sep 86*
Big Audio Dynamite: This Is B.A.D. (CBS) *Oct 86*
Big Country: The Seer (Phonogram) *Oct 86*
Bon Jovi: Slippery When Wet (Phonogram) *Nov 86*
David Bowie: Never Let Me Down (EMI) *May 87*
Elkie Brooks: No More The Fool (Legend) *Jan 87*
Jackson Browne: Running On Empty (Asylum) *Sep 86*
Kate Bush: The Whole Story (EMI) *May 87*
Cameo: Word Up! (Phonogram) *Jan 87*
The Cars: Greatest Hits (Elektra) *Oct 86*
Eric Clapton: August (Duck) *Dec 86*
The Communards: Communards (London) *Sep 86*
The Cult: Electric (Beggars Banquet) *Jun 87*
Culture Club: This Time (Virgin) *May 87*
Curiosity Killed The Cat: Keep Your Distance (Phonogram) *May 87*

Terence Trent D'Arby: The Hardline According To (CBS) *Jun 87*
Barbara Dickson: The Right Moment (K-Tel) *Nov 86*
Placido Domingo: Collection (Stylus) *Mar 87*
The Drifters: Very Best Of (Telstar) *Dec 86*
Duran Duran: Notorious (EMI) *Dec 86*
Deanna Durbin: Can't Help Singing (EMI) *Nov 86*
Erasure: The Circus (Mute) *Apr 87*
Europe: The Final Countdown (Epic) *Dec 86*
Everything But The Girl: Eden (Blanco Y Negro) *Dec 86*
Five Star: Silk And Steel (RCA) *Aug 86*
Fleetwood Mac: Tango In The Night (Warner Bros) *Apr 87*
Foster & Allen: Reminiscing (Stylus) *Nov 86*
Frankie Goes To Hollywood: Liverpool (ZTT) *Jan 87*
Bob Geldof: Deep In The Heart Of Nowhere (Phonogram) *Dec 86*
Debbie Harry: Rockbird (Chrysalis) *Jan 87*
Buddy Holly: 20 Love Songs (EMI) *Nov 86*
Hot Chocolate: The Very Best Of (EMI) *Feb 87*
Whitney Houston: Whitney (Arista) *Jun 87*
Huddersfield Choral Society: The Carols Album (EMI) *Dec 86*
Human League: Crash (Virgin) *Oct 86*
Billy Idol: Whiplash Smile (Chrysalis) *Nov 86*
The Ink Spots: The Best Of (EMI) *Nov 86*
Iron Maiden: Somewhere In Time (EMI) *Oct 86*
Janet Jackson: Control (A&M) *Sep 86*
Japan: Gentlemen Take Polaroids (Virgin) *Nov 86*
Jean Michel Jarre: Rendezvous (Polydor) *Aug 86*
Elton John: Leather Jackets (Rocket) *Nov 86*
Aled Jones: An Album Of Hymns (Telstar) *Dec 86*
Howard Jones: One To One (Warner Bros) *Oct 86*
Kiri Te Kanawa: Christmas With Kiri (Polydor) *Dec 86*
James Last: Maestro Of Melody (Readers Digest) *Mar 87*
Level 42: Running In The Family (Polydor) *Mar 87*
Huey Lewis & The News: Fore (Chrysalis) *Sep 86*
Marillion: Clutching At Straws (EMI) *Jun 87*
Paul McCartney: Press To Play (EMI) *Sep 86*
Michael McDonald: Sweet Freedom (Warner Bros) *Dec 86*
Mel & Kim: FLM (Supreme) *Apr 87*
Matt Monro: The Very Best Of (EMI) *Dec 86*
Alison Moyet: Raindancing (CBS) *Apr 87*
Stevie Nicks: Rock A Little (EMI) *Jan 87*
Alexander O'Neal: Alexander O'Neal (Tabu) *Dec 86*
Original Cast: Phantom Of The Opera (Polydor) *Feb 87*
Elaine Paige: Christmas (WEA) *Dec 86*
Robert Palmer: Riptide (Island) *Aug 86*
Luciano Pavarotti: The Pavarotti Collection (Stylus) *Sep 86*
Pet Shop Boys: Please (EMI) *Jan 87*
The Police: Every Breath You Take – The Singles (A&M) *Nov 86*
The Pretenders: Get Close (WEA) *Dec 86*
The Pretenders: Learning To Crawl (WEA) *Feb 87*
Prince: Parade (Paisley Park) *Jul 86*
Prince: Sign Of The Times (Paisley Park) *Apr 87*
Cliff Richard & The Shadows: Very Best Of (Readers Digest) *Jun 87*
Lionel Richie: Dancing On The Ceiling (Motown) *Aug 86*
Santana: Viva Santana (K-Tel) *Dec 86*
Paul Simon: Graceland (Warner Bros) *Sep 86*
Simple Minds: Live: In The City Of Light (Virgin) *Jun 87*
Simple Minds: Sons And Fascination (Virgin) *Nov 87*
Simply Red: Men And Women (Elektra) *Mar 87*
Frank Sinatra: New York New York (WEA) *Jul 87*
The Smiths: The World Won't Listen (Rough Trade) *Mar 87*
Spandau Ballet: Through The Barricades (CBS) *Nov 87*
Bruce Springsteen & The E Street Band: Live 1975-85 (CBS) *Nov 86*
Status Quo: In The Army Now (Phonogram) *Oct 86*
The Style Council: The Cost Of Loving (Polydor) *Mar 87*
Supertramp: The Autobiography Of (A&M) *Oct 86*
Swing Out Sister: It's Better To Travel (Phongram) *Apr 87*
Talking Heads: True Stories (EMI) *Nov 86*
The The: Infected (CBS) *Jan 87*
U2: The Joshua Tree (CBS) *Mar 87*
UB40: Rat In The Kitchen (DEP International) *Jan 87*

Ultravox: Ultravox (Chrysalis) *Oct 86*
Luther Vandross: Give Me The Reason (Epic) *Feb 87*
Van Halen: 1984 (Warner Bros) *Jul 87*
Various: Atlantic Soul Classics (WEA) *Jul 87*
Various: Black Magic (Stylus) *Jan 87*
Various: Formula 32 (Polydor) *Nov 86*
Various: Friends And Lovers (K-Tel) *Jul 87*
Various: Greatest Hits Of 1986 (Telstar) *Dec 86*
Various: Holiday Album (CBS) *Jul 87*
Various: Hot Mix 86 (Stylus) *Nov 86*
Various: The Island Story (Island) *Jul 87*
Various: Lovers (Telstar) *Dec 86*
Various: Motown Chartbusters (Telstar) *Dec 86*
Various: Move Closer (CBS) *Mar 87*
Various: Now Dance 86 (EMI) *Nov 86*
Various: Now That's What I Call Music 7 (EMI) *Aug 86*
Various: Now That's What I Call Music 9 (EMI) *Apr 87*
Various: Now – The Summer Album (EMI) *Jul 86*
Various: Simon Bates – Our Tune (Polydor) *Nov 86*
Various: Sixties Mania (Telstar) *Dec 86*
Various: South Pacific (CBS) *Oct 86*
Various: The Chart (Telstar) *Dec 86*
Various: Together (K-Tel) *Dec 86*
Various: Top Gun – Original Soundtrack (CBS) *Nov 86*
Suzanne Vega: Solitude Standing (A&M) *May 87*
Whitesnake: Whitesnake (EMI) *Jul 87*
Roger Whittaker: His Finest Collection (Polygram) *Jul 87*
Bruce Willis: The Return Of Bruno (Motown) *Jul 87*
Steve Winwood: Back In The Highlife (Island) *Aug 86*
Paul Young: Between Two Fires (CBS) *Nov 86*

SINGLES

GOLD (500,000 units)

Berlin: Take My Breath Away (Epic) *Nov 86*
The Communards: Don't Leave Me This Way (London) *Sep 86*
Chris De Burgh: Lady In Red (A&M) *Aug 86*
Europe: The Final Countdown (Epic) *Nov 86*
Freeez: I.O.U. (Beggars Banquet) *Feb 87*
Boris Gardiner: I Want To Wake Up With You (PRT) *Sep 86*
The Housemartins: Caravan Of Love (Go! Discs) *Nov 86*
Ben E. King: Stand By Me (CBS) *Mar 87*
Madonna: Papa Don't Preach (Sire) *Aug 86*
Mel & Kim: Respectable (Supreme) *Apr 87*
George Michael & Aretha Franklin: I Knew You Were Waiting (Epic) *Jan 87*
Sinitta: So Macho (Fanfare) *Sep 86*
Starship: Nothing's Gonna Stop Us Now (RCA) *Jun 87*
Various (Ferry Aid): Let It Be (CBS) *Mar 87*
Jackie Wilson: Reet Petite (PRT) *Jan 87*

DOUBLE PLATINUM (2,000,000 units)

Wings: Mull Of Kintyre (EMI) *Nov 86*

PLATINUM (1,000,000 units)

nil

THE RIAA CERTIFIED AWARDS

Recording Industry Awards Of America Inc, reprinted with permission.

The qualifying levels for RIAA Gold and Platinum awards are, respectively, 1,000,000 units and 2,000,000 units (singles), and 500,000 units and 1,000,000 units (LPs). Sales of cassettes and compact discs are included.

Totals for this period show a substantial increase in the Platinum and Multi-Platinum LP categories due to the new eligibility of recordings released prior to 1976. Such recordings are indicated by an asterisk (*). The figures at the end of the Multi-Platinum entries indicate the million level reached.

MULTI-PLATINUM
(2,000,000 units and above)

Aerosmith: Greatest Hits (Columbia) *Nov 86* (2m)
*Aerosmith: Toys In The Attic (Columbia) *Nov 86* (4m)
*Aerosmith: Get Your Wings (Columbia) *Nov 86* (2m)
*Aerosmith: Aerosmith (Columbia) *Nov 86* (2m)
Alabama: My Home's In Alabama (RCA) *Aug 86* (2m)
*America: History (Greatest Hits) (Warner Bros) *Oct 86* (4m)
Anita Baker: Rapture (Elektra) *Mar 87* (2m)
The Bangles: Different Light (Columbia) *Feb 87* (2m)
The Beastie Boys: Licensed To Ill (Def Jam) *Apr 87* (3m)
*Black Sabbath: Paranoid (Warner Bros) *Oct 86* (3m)
*Blood Sweat & Tears: Blood Sweat & Tears (Columbia) *Nov 86* (3m)
Bon Jovi: Slippery When Wet (Mercury) *Apr 87* (7m)
Boston: Boston (Epic) *Oct 86* (9m)
Boston: Don't Look Back (Epic) *Oct 86* (4m)
Boston: Third Stage (MCA) *Feb 87* (4m)
*Johnny Cash: Greatest Hits (Columbia) *Nov 86* (2m)
*Johnny Cash: At San Quentin (Columbia) *Nov 86* (2m)
*Johnny Cash: At Folsom Prison (Columbia) *Nov 86* (2m)
Cheap Trick: At Budokan (Epic) *Nov 86* (3m)
*Chicago: Chicago Transit Authority (Columbia) *Nov 86* (2m)
*Chicago: Chicago V (Columbia)
*Chicago: Chicago VI (Columbia) *Nov 86* (2m)
*Chicago: Chicago IX (Greatest Hits) (Columbia)

Nov 86 (2m)
*Chicago: Chicago X (Columbia) *Nov 86* (2m)
Cinderella: Night Songs (Mercury) *Feb 87* (2m)
Culture Club: Colour By Numbers (Virgin) *Nov 86* (4m)
Charlie Daniels Band: Million Mile Reflections (Epic) *Nov 86* (2m)
Deep Purple: Machine Head (Warner Bros) *Oct 86* (2m)
Dire Straits: Dire Straits (Warner Bros) *Oct 86* (2m)
*Doobie Brothers: The Captain And Me (Warner Bros) *Oct 86* (2m)
*The Doors: The Doors (Elektra) *Jun 87* (2m)
*The Doors: L.A. Woman (Elektra) *Jun 87* (2m)
The Doors: Greatest Hits (Elektra) *Jun 87* (2m)
*Bob Dylan: Greatest Hits (Columbia) *Nov 86* (2m)
*Earth Wind & Fire: That's The Way Of The World (Columbia) *Nov 86* (2m)
*Earth Wind & Fire: Gratitude (Columbia) *Nov 86* (2m)
*Fleetwood Mac: Fleetwood Mac (Reprise) *Oct 86* (5m)
*Dan Fogelberg: Souvenirs (Epic) *Nov 86* (2m)
John Fogerty: Centerfield (Warner Bros) *Sep 86* (2m)
Genesis: Invisible Touch (Atlantic) *Oct 86* (2m)
Heart: Heart (Capitol) *Aug 86* (4m)
Heart: Little Queen (Portrait) *Nov 86* (2m)
*Jimi Hendrix: Are You Experienced? (reprise) *Oct 86* (2m)
*Jimi Hendrix: Smash Hits (Reprise) *Oct 86* (2m)
Bruce Hornsby And The range: The Way It Is (RCA) *Apr 87* (2m)
Whitney Houston: Whitney Houston (Arista) *Feb 87* (8m)
Julio Iglesias: 1100 Bel Air Place (Columbia) *Feb 87* (3m)
Janet Jackson: Control (A&M) *Apr 87* (4m)
*Billy Joel: Piano Man (Columbia) *Nov 86* (2m)
Billy Joel: The Bridge (Columbia) *Apr 87* (2m)
*Janis Joplin: Pearl (Columbia) *Nov 86* (3m)
Kansas: Leftoverture (Kirshner) *Nov 86* (3m)

Kansas: Point Of Know Return (Kirshner) *Nov 86* (3m)
Huey Lewis & The News: Sports (Chrysalis) *Jul 87* (7m)
Huey Lewis & The News: Fore! (Chrysalis) *Dec 86* (2m)
Madonna: Like A Virgin (Sire) *Jul 87* 7m)
Madonna: True Blue (Sire) *Feb 87* (4m)
Meatloaf: Bat Out Of Hell (Epic) *Nov 86* (4m)
Molly Hatchet: Flirtin' With Disaster (Epic) *Nov 86* (2m)
*Willie Nelson: Red Headed Stranger (Columbia) *Nov 86* (2m)
Willie Nelson: Greatest Hits (And Some That Will be) (Columbia) *Nov 86* (3m)
Ted Nugent: Ted Nugent (Epic) *Nov 86* (2m)
Billy Ocean: Love Zone (Jive) *Dec 86* (2m)
*Original Cast: My Fair Lady (Columbia) *Nov 86* (3m)
*Peter, Paul & Mary: Peter, Paul And Mary (Warner Bros) *Oct 86* (2m)
*Pink Floyd: Wish You Were Here (Columbia) *Nov 86* (3m)
Quiet Riot: Metal Health (PSH) *Nov 86* (4m)
REO Speedwagon: Hi Infidelity (Epic) *Nov 86* (7m)
Lionel Richie: Dancing On The Ceiling (Motown) *May 87* (2m)
Run DMC: Raising Hell (PRF) *Apr 87* (3m)
*Santana: Santana (Columbia) *Nov 86* (2m)
*Santana: Abraxas (Columbia) *Nov 86* (4m)
*Santana: Third Album (Columbia) *Nov 86* (2m)
*Seals & Crofts: Greatest Hits (Warner Bros) *Oct 86* (2m)
*Simon & Garfunkel: Parsley, Sage, Rosemary & Thyme (Columbia) *Nov 86* (3m)
*Simon & Garfunkel: Bookends (Columbia) *Nov 86* (2m)
*Simon & Garfunkel: Bridge Over Troubled Water (Columbia) *Nov 86* (5m)
*Simon & Garfunkel: Greatest Hits (Columbia) *Nov 86* (5m)
Paul Simon: Graceland (Warner Bros) *May 87* (2m)
*Sly & The Family Stone: Greatest Hits (Epic) *Nov 86* (3m)

Soundtrack – Original Movie: Top Gun (Columbia) *Apr 87* (4m)
Soundtrack – Original Movie: Eddie & The Cruisers (STB) *Dec 86* (2m)
***Soundtrack:** Jonathan Livingston Seagull (Columbia) *Nov 86* (2m)
***Soundtrack:** West Side Story (Columbia) *Nov 86* (3m)
***Bruce Springsteen:** Born To Run (Columbia) *Nov 86* (3m)
Bruce Springsteen: Bruce Springsteen & The E Street Band Live 1975-85 (Columbia) *Feb 87* (3m)
***Barbra Streisand:** Christmas Album (Columbia) *Nov 86* (2m)
***Barbra Streisand:** Greatest Hits (Columbia) *Nov 86* (2m)
***James Taylor:** Sweet Baby James (Warner Bros) *Oct 86* (3m)
U2: The Joshua Tree (Island) *May 87* (2m)
Van Halen: 1984 (Warner Bros) *Jul 87* (6m)
Van Halen: 5150 (Warner Bros) *Oct 86* (3m)
Steve Winwood: Back In The Highlife (Island) *Apr 87* (2m)
***Edgar Winter Group:** They Only Come Out At Night (Epic) *Nov 86* (2m)
***Neil Young:** After The Goldrush (Reprise) *Oct 86* (2m)
***Neil Young:** Harvest (Reprise) *Oct 86* (3m)
ZZ Top: Eliminator (Warner Bros) *Jul 87* (6m)

PLATINUM
(2,000,000 units)

AC/DC: Who Made Who (Atlantic) *Mar 87*
Bryan Adams: Into The Fire (A&M) *Jun 87*
***Aerosmith:** Toys In The Attic (Columbia) *Nov 86*
***Aerosmith:** Get Your Wings (Columbia) *Nov 86*
***Aerosmith:** Aerosmith (Columbia) *Nov 86*
Alabama: The Touch (RCA) *Jan 87*
***America:** America (Warner Bros) *Oct 86*
***America:** History Greatest Hits (Warner Bros) *Oct 86*
***Lynn Anderson:** Rose Garden (Columbia) *Oct 86*
Association: Greatest Hits (Warner Bros) *Oct 86*
Anita Baker: Rapture (Elektra) *Oct 86*
Bangles: Different Light (Columbia) *Dec 86*
Beastie Boys: Licensed To Ill (Columbia) *Feb 87*
Jeff Beck: Wired (Epic) *Nov 86*
***Jeff Beck:** Blow By Blow (Epic) *Nov 86*
***Black Sabbath:** Black Sabbath (Warner Bros) *Oct 86*
***Black Sabbath:** Sabbath, Bloody Sabbath (Warner Bros) *Oct 86*
***Black Sabbath:** Master Of Reality (Warner Bros) *Oct 86*
***Black Sabbath:** Black Sabbath – Vol 4 (Warner Bros) *Oct 86*
***Black Sabbath:** Paranoid (Warner Bros) *Oct 76*
***Blood, Sweat & Tears:** Greatest Hits (Columbia) *Nov 86*
***Blood, Sweat & Tears:** Blood, Sweat & Tears (Columbia) *Nov 86*
Bon Jovi: 7800 Degree Farenheit (Mercury) *Feb 87*
Bon Jovi: Bon Jovi (Mercury) *Apr 87*
Bon Jovi: Slippery When Wet (Mercury) *Oct 86*
Boston: Third Stage (MCA) *Nov 86*
***The Byrds:** Greatest Hits (Columbia) *Nov 86*
Cameo: Word Up (Atlanta Artists) *Dec 86*
***Wendy Carlos:** Switched On Bach (CBS) *Nov 86*
***Johnny Cash:** Greatest Hits (Columbia) *Nov 86*
***Johnny Cash:** At San Quentin (Columbia) *Nov 86*
***Johnny Cash:** At Folsom Prison (Columbia) *Nov 86*
***Chicago:** Chicago Transit Authority (Columbia) *Nov 86*
***Chicago:** Chicago III (Columbia) *Nov 86*
***Chicago:** IV (At Carnegie Hall) (Columbia) *Nov 86*
***Chicago:** Chicago V (Columbia) *Nov 86*
***Chicago:** Chicago VI (Columbia) *Nov 86*
***Chicago:** Chicago VII (Columbia) *Nov 86*
***Chicago:** Chicago VIII (Columbia) *Nov 86*

***Chicago:** Chicago IX – Greatest Hits (Columbia) *Nov 86*
Cinderella: Night Songs (Mercury) *Nov 86*
Club Nouveau: Lean On Me (Tommy Boy) Warner Bros) *May 87*
Club Nouveau: Life, Love & Pain (Warner Bros) *Apr 87*
***Ray Conniff:** Somewhere My Love (Columbia) *Nov 86*
***Alice Cooper:** Billion Dollar Babies (Warner Bros) *Nov 86*
***Alice Cooper:** Greatest Hits (Warner Bros) *Nov 86*
***Alice Cooper:** Killer (Warner Bros) *Nov 86*
***Bill Cosby:** The Best Of (Warner Bros) *Oct 86*
***Bill Cosby:** Bill Cosby Is A Very Funny Fellow Right! (Warner Bros) *Oct 86*
***Bill Cosby:** Wonderfulness (Warner Bros) *Oct 86*
***Bill Cosby:** I Started Out As A Child (Warner Bros) *Oct 86*
***Mac Davis:** Baby Don't Get Hooked On Me (Columbia) *Nov 86*
***Deep Purple:** Made In Japan (Warner Bros) *Oct 86*
***Deep Purple:** Machine Head (Warner Bros) *Oct 86*
Neil Diamond: Serenade (Columbia) *Nov 86*
Dio: The Last In Line (Warner Bros) *Feb 87*
Dokken: Under Lock And Key (Elektra) *Apr 87*
***Doobie Brothers:** What Were Once Vices Now Are Habits (Warner Bros) *Oct 86*
***Doobie Brothers:** Toulouse Street (Warner Bros) *Oct 86*
***Doobie Brothers:** The Captain & Me (Warner Bros) *Oct 86*
***The Doors:** The Doors (Elektra) *Jun 87*
***The Doors:** Waiting For The Sun (Elektra) *Jun 87*
***The Doors:** The Soft Parade (Elektra) *Jun 87*
***The Doors:** The Doors – 13 (Elektra) *Jun 87*
***The Doors:** L.A. Woman (Elektra) *Jun 87*
***The Doors:** Best of (Electra) *Jun 87*
Duran Duran: Notorious (Capitol) *Jan 87*
***Bob Dylan:** Greatest Hits Volume II (Columbia) *Nov 86*
***Bob Dylan:** Nashville Skyline (Columbia) *Nov 86*
***Bob Dylan:** Greatest Hits (Columbia) *Nov 86*
***Earth, Wind & Fire:** Open Our Eyes (Columbia) *Nov 86*
Earth, Wind & Fire: That's The Way Of The World (Columbia) *Nov 86*
***Earth, Wind & Fire:** Gratitude (Columbia) *Nov 86*
***Fleetwood Mac:** Fleetwood Mac (Reprise) *Nov 86*
Fleetwood Mac: Tango In The Night (Warner Bros) *Jul 87*
***Dan Fogelberg:** Souvenirs (Epic) *Nov 86*
***Foghat:** Fool For The City (Bearsville) *Oct 86*
Kenny G: Duotones (Arista) *Jun 87*
***Peter Gabriel:** So (Geffen) *Aug 86*
***Art Garfunkel:** Breakaway (Columbia) *Nov 86*
***Genesis:** Invisible Touch (Atlantic) *Aug 86*
***Grateful Dead:** American Beauty (Warner Bros) *Oct 86*
***Grateful Dead:** Workingman's Dead (Warner Bros) *Oct 86*
***Grateful Dead:** Skeletons From The Closet (Best Of) (Warner Bros) *Dec 86*
***Arlo Guthrie:** Alice's Restaurant (Reprise) *Oct 86*
***Herbie Hancock:** Head Hunters (Columbia) *Nov 86*
Heart: Bad Animals (Capitol) *Jul 87*
***Jimi Hendrix:** Electric Ladyland (Reprise) *Oct 86*
***Jimi Hendrix:** Axis: Bold As Love (Reprise) *Oct 86*
***Jimi Hendrix:** Smash Hits (Reprise) *Oct 86*
***Jimi Hendrix:** Are You Experienced? (Reprise) *Oct 86*
***Bruce Hornsby And The Range:** The Way It Is (RCA) *Dec 86*
***Johnny Horton:** Greatest Hits (Columbia) *Nov 86*
Billy Idol: Whiplash Smile (Chrysalis) *Jan 87*
***Janis Ian:** Between The Lines (Columbia) *Nov 86*
Iron Maiden: The Number Of The Beast (Capitol) *Oct 86*
Iron Maiden: Piece Of Mind (Capitol) *Nov 86*
Freddie Jackson: Just Like The First Time (Capitol) *Jan 87*
Billy Joel: The Bridge (Columbia) *Oct 86*

***Billy Joel:** Piano Man (Columbia) *Nov 86*
***Janis Joplin:** Cheap Thrills (Columbia) *Nov 86*
***Janis Joplin:** Greatest Hits (Columbia) *Nov 86*
***Janis Joplin:** Pearl (Columbia) *Nov 86*
The Judds: Rockin' With The Rhythm (RCA) *Oct 86*
Cyndi Lauper: True Colors (Portrait) *Nov 86*
Huey Lewis & The News: Fore! (Chrysalis) *Dec 86*
***Gordon Lightfoot:** Sundown (Reprise) *Oct 86*
***Gordon Lightfoot:** Gord's Gold (Reprise) *Oct 86*
***Loggins & Messina:** Full Sail (Columbia) *Nov 86*
***Loggins & Messina:** Loggins & Messina (Columbia) *Nov 86*
Madonna: True Blue (Sire) *Sep 86*
***Johnny Mathis:** All-Time Greatest Hits (Columbia) *Nov 86*
***Johnny Mathis:** Johnny's Greatest Hits (Columbia) *Nov 86*
***Johnny Mathis:** Heavenly (Columbia) *Nov 86*
***Johnny Mathis:** Merry Christmas (Columbia) *Nov 86*
Miami Sound Machine: Primitive Love (Epic) *Oct 86*
***Steve Miller Band:** The Joker (Capitol) *Jul 87*
***Joni Mitchell:** Blue (Reprise) *Oct 86*
***Joni Mitchell:** Ladies Of The Canyon (Reprise) *Oct 86*
The Monkees: Then & Now . . . The Best Of The Monkees (Arista) *Jan 87*
Montrose: Montrose (Warner Bros) *Oct 86*
***Van Morrison:** Moondance (Warner Bros) *Oct 86*
Motley Crue: Girls Girls Girls (Elektra) *Jul 87*
Willie Nelson: Red Headed Stranger (Columbia) *Nov 86*
Ted Nugent: Ted Nugent (Epic) *Nov 86*
***O'Jays:** Family Reunion (Philadelphia International) *Nov 86*
Original Broadway Cast: Evita – Premiere American Recording (MCA) *Oct 86*
***Original Cast:** Sesame Street Original T.V. Cast Album (Columbia) *Nov 86*
***Original Cast:** My Fair Lady (Columbia) *Nov 86*
Robert Palmer: Riptide (Island) *Sep 86*
Dolly Parton: Greatest Hits (RCA) *Oct 86*
Dolly Parton, Linda Ronstadt & Emmylou Harris: Trio (Warner Bros) *Jul 87*
Pet Shop Boys: Please (Capitol) *Sep 86*
***Peter, Paul & Mary:** The Best Of (Ten Years Together) (Warner Bros) *Oct 86*
***Peter, Paul & Mary:** Peter, Paul & Mary (Warner Bros) *Oct 86*
***Pink Floyd:** Wish You Were Here (Columbia) *Nov 86*
Poison: Look What The Cat Dragged In (Capitol) *Apr 87*
The Police: Every Breath You Take The Singles (A&M) *Jan 87*
Prince: Sign Of The Times (Paisley Park) *Jul 87*
***Richard Pryor:** Is It Something I Said? (Reprise) *Oct 86*
***Gary Puckett & The Union Gap:** Greatest Hits (Columbia) *Nov 86*
Ratt: Dancing Under Cover (Atlantic) *Feb 87*
***Charlie Rich:** Behind Closed Doors (Epic) *Nov 86*
Lionel Richie: Dancing On The Ceiling (Motown) *Oct 86*
***Marty Robbins:** Gunfighter Ballads & Trail Songs (Columbia) *Nov 86*
David Lee Roth: Eat 'Em And Smile (Warner Bros) *Sep 86*
Run-D.M.C.: King Of Rock (PRF) *Feb 87*
***Santana:** Santana (Columbia) *Nov 86*
***Santana:** Abraxas (Columbia) *Nov 86*
***Santana:** Third Album (Columbia) *Nov 86*
***Santana:** Caravanserai (Columbia) *Nov 86*
***Santana:** Santana's Greatest Hits (Columbia) *Nov 86*
***Carlos Santana & Buddy Miles:** Carlos Santana & Buddy Miles 'Live' (Columbia) *Nov 86*
Scorpions: World Wide Live (Mercury) *Sep 86*
***Seals & Crofts:** Greatest Hits (Warner Bros) *Oct 86*
***Simon & Garfunkel:** Parsley, Sage, Rosemary & Thyme (Columbia) *Nov 86*
***Simon & Garfunkel:** Bookends (Columbia) *Nov 86*
***Simon & Garfunkel:** Bridge Over Troubled Water (Columbia) *Nov 86*

*Simon & Garfunkel: Greatest Hits (Columbia) *Nov 86*

*Paul Simon: There Goes Rhymin' Simon (Columbia) *Nov 86*

*Paul Simon: Paul Simon (Columbia) *Nov 86*

Paul Simon: Graceland (Warner Bros) *Dec 86*

*Frank Sinatra: Greatest Hits (Reprise) *Oct 86*

*Sly & The Family Stone: Stand! (Epic) *Nov 86*

*Sly & The Family Stone: Sly & The Family Stone's Greatest Hits (Epic) *Nov 86*

*Soundtrack: Camelot (Warner Bros) *Oct 86*

*Soundtrack: Funny Girl (Columbia) *Nov 86*

*Soundtrack: Jonathan Livingston Seagull (Columbia) *Nov 86*

*Soundtrack: West Side Story (Columbia) *Nov 86*

*Bruce Springsteen: Born To Run (Columbia) *Nov 86*

Spyrogyra: Morning Dance (MCA) *Jun 87*

George Strait: George Strait's Greatest Hits (MCA) *Feb 87*

*Barbra Streisand: My Name Is Barbra, Two (Columbia) *Nov 86*

*Barbra Streisand: Greatest Hits (Columbia) *Nov 86*

*Barbra Streisand: Christmas Album (Columbia) *Nov 86*

*Barbra Streisand: Stoney End (Columbia) *Nov 86*

*Barbra Streisand: Live In Concert At The Forum (Columbia) *Nov 86*

*Barbra Streisand: The Way We Were (Columbia) *Nov 86*

Talking Heads: Speaking In Tongues (Sire) *Dec 86*

*James Taylor: Mud Slide Slim & The Blue Horizon (Warner Bros) *Oct 86*

*James Taylor: Sweet Baby James (Warner Bros) *Oct 86*

*Ten Years After: A Space In Time (Columbia) *Nov 86*

Randy Travis: Always And Forever (Warner Bros) *Jul 87*

Randy Travis: Storms Of Life (Warner Bros) *Feb 87*

Tina Turner: Break Every Rule (Capitol) *Nov 86*

U2: The Joshua Tree (Island) *May 27*

Luther Vandross: Never Too Much (Epic) *Dec 86*

Luther Vandross: Give Me The Reason (Epic) *Dec 86*

Various: Disney's Children's Favourites Volume II (Disney) *Oct 86*

Wham!: Music From The Edge Of Heaven (Columbia *Oct 86*

Whitesnake: Whitesnake (Geffen) *Jun 87*

Whodini: Escape (Jive) *May 87*

*Andy Williams: The Andy Williams Christmas Album (Columbia) *Nov 86*

*Andy Williams: Love Story (Columbia) *Nov 86*

*Edgar Winter Group: They Only Come Out At Night (Epic) *Nov 86*

Steve Winwood: Back In The High Life (Warner Bros) *Oct 86*

*Gary Wright: The Dream Weaver (Warner Bros) *Oct 86*

*Neil Young: After The Gold Rush (Reprise) *Oct 86*

*Neil Young: Harvest (Reprise) *Oct 86*

*Neil Young: Everybody Knows This Is Nowhere (Reprise) *Oct 86*

Neil Young: Decade (Reprise) *Dec 86*

GOLD (1,000,000 units)

Gregory Abbott: Shake You Down (Colombia) *Feb 87*

AC/DC: Who Made Who (Atlantic) *Aug 86*

Bryan Adams: Into The Fire (A&M) *Jun 87*

Alabama: The Touch (RCA) *Jan 87*

Herb Alpert: Keep Your Eye On Me (A&M) *Jun 87*

Atlantic Starr: All In The Name Of Love (Warner Bros) *Jun 87*

Anita Baker: Rapture (Elektra) *Aug 86*

Bananarama: True Confessions (London) *Oct 86*

The Beastie Boys: Licensed To Ill (Def Jam) *Feb 87*

The Bellamy Brothers: Greatest Hits (MCA) *Oct 86*

Bon Jovi: Slippery When Wet *Oct 86*

Boston: Third Stage (MCA) *Oct 86*

David Bowie: Never Let Me Down (EMI) *Jul 87*

Cameo: Word Up (Atlanta Artists) *Oct 86*

Belinda Carlisle : Belinda (IRS) *Nov 86*

Peter Cetera: Solitude/Solitaire (Warner Bros) *Nov 86*

Chicago: Chicago 18 (FMN) *Dec 86*

Cinderella: Night Songs (Mercury) *Oct 86*

Eric Clapton: Behind The Sun (Duck) *Feb 87*

Eric Clapton: August (Duck) *Apr 87*

Patsy Cline: Sweet Dreams (Soundtrack) (MCA) *Apr 87*

Club Nouveau: Life, Love And Pain (Warner Bros) *Mar 87*

John Conlee: Greatest Hits (MCA) *Nov 86*

Bill Cosby: Best Of (Warner Bros) *Oct 86*

Bill Cosby: Those Of You With Or Without Children, You'll Understand (Geffen) *Aug 86*

Robert Cray: Strong Persuader (Mercury) *Mar 87*

Crowded House: Crowded House (Capitol) *May 87*

The Cure: Standing On A Beach – The Singles (Elektra) *Feb 87*

Cutting Crew: Broadcast (Virgin) *Jun 87*

El DeBarge: El DeBarge (Gordy) *Sep 86*

Chris De Burgh: Into The Light (A&M) *Jul 87*

Depeche Mode: Some Great Reward (Sire) *Oct 86*

Dio: The Last In Line (Warner Bros) *Feb 87*

*The Doors: Best Of (Elektra) *Jun 87*

The Doors: Alive, She Cried (Elektra) *Jun 87*

Duran Duran: Notorious (Capitol) *Jan 87*

Europe: The Final Countdown (Epic) *Apr 87*

Eurythmics: Revenge (RCA) *Sep 86*

Evie: Come On, Ring Those Bells (Word) *Jun 87*

Expose: Exposure (Arista) *Jun 87*

Fleetwood Mac: Tango In The Night (Warner Bros) *Jul 87*

John Fogerty: Eye Of The Zombie (Warner Bros) *Nov 86*

Samantha Fox: Touch Me (Jive) *Apr 87*

Aretha Franklin: Aretha (Arista) *Dec 86*

Kenny G: Duotones (Arista) *May 87*

Peter Gabriel: Security ('82 LP) (Geffen) *May 87*

Genesis: Invisible Touch (Atlantic) *Aug 86*

Georgia Satellites: Georgia Satellites (Elektra) *Feb 87*

Glass Tiger: The Thin Red Line (Manhattan) *Mar 87*

Amy Grant: My Father's Eyes (Myrrh) *Apr 87*

Amy Grant: The Collection (Myrrh) *Feb 87*

Lee Greenwood: Inside Out (MCA) *Nov 86*

Emmylou Harris: Pieces Of The Sky (Reprise) *Oct 86*

Corey Hart: First Offense (Capitol) *Jan 87*

Heart: Bad Animals (Capitol) *Jul 87*

Bruce Hornsby And The Range: The Way It Is (RCA) *Nov 86*

Billy Idol: Whiplash Smile (Chrysalis) *Jan 87*

Inxs: The Swing (Atlantic) *Apr 87*

Iron Maiden: Somewhere In Time (Capitol) *Nov 86*

Iron Maiden: Killers (Capitol) *Jan 87*

Freddie Jackson: Just Like The First Time (Capitol) *Dec 86*

Bob James & David Sanborn: Double Vision (Warner Bros) *Jan 87*

The Jets: The Jets (MCA) *Sep 86*

Billy Joel: The Bridge (Columbia) *Oct 86*

Don Johnson: Heartbeat (Epic) *Nov 86*

The Judds: The Heartland (RCA) *Apr 87*

Kool & The Gang: Forever (Mercury) *Jan 87*

Cyndi Lauper: True Colors (Portrait) *Nov 86*

Huey Lewis & The News: Fore! (Chrysalis) *Dec 86*

Lisa Lisa & Cult Jam With Full Force: Lisa Lisa And Cult Jam With Full Force (Columbia) *Oct 86*

Reba McEntire: Whoever's In New England (MCA) *Jan 87*

Reba McEntire: What Am I Gonna Do About You (MCA) *Apr 87*

Madonna: True Blue (Sire) *Sep 86*

Metallica: Master Of Puppets (Asylum) *Nov 86*

Midnight Star: Headlines (Solar) *Aug 86*

Eddie Money: Can't Hold Back (Columbia) *Dec 86*

The Monkees: Then And Now (Best Of) (Arista) *Aug 86*

The Monkees: Greatest Hits (Arista) *Aug 86*

Motley Crue: Girls Girls Girls (Elektra) *Jul 87*

Shirley Murdock: Shirley Murdock! (Elektra) *May 87*

Anne Murray: Country (Capitol) *Mar 87*

Willie Nelson: The Troublemaker (Columbia) *Dec 86*

Willie Nelson: Half Nelson (Columbia) *Apr 87*

New Edition: Under The Blue Moon (MCA) *Jan 87*

Nu Shooz: Poolside (Atlantic) *Oct 86*

Jeffrey Osborne: Emotional (A&M) *Aug 86*

Dolly Parton, Linda Ronstadt & Emmylou Harris: Trio (Warner Bros) *Jul 87*

Sandi Patti: Hymns Just For You (IPT) *Dec 86*

Sandi Patti: Morning Like This (Myrrh) *Feb 87*

Sandi Patti: Songs From The Heart (BSN) *Mar 87*

Poison: Look What The Cat Dragged In (Capitol) *Mar 87*

The Police: Every Breath You Take – The Singles (A&M) *Jan 87*

The Pretenders: Get Close (Sire) *Dec 86*

Prince: Sign Of The Times (Paisley Park) *Jul 87*

Richard Pryor: That Nigger's Crazy (Reprise) *Oct 86*

Ratt: Dancing Undercover (Atlantic) *Nov 86*

R.E.M.: Life's Rich Pageant (IRS) *Jan 87*

Ready For The World: Long Time Coming (MCA) *Jan 87*

Lionel Richie: Dancing On The Ceiling (Motown) *Oct 86*

Linda Ronstadt: For Sentimental Reasons (Elektra) *Dec 86*

David Lee Roth: Eat 'Em And Smile (Warner Bros) *Sep 86*

Roxy Music: Avalon (Warner Bros) *Dec 86*

Dan Seals: Won't Be Blue Any More (EMI) *Feb 87*

Paul Simon: Graceland (Warner Bros) *Oct 86*

S.O.S. Band: Sands Of Time (Tabu) *Apr 87*

Soundtrack – Original Movie: Ruthless People (Epic) *Aug 86*

Soundtrack – Original Movie: Stand By Me (Atlantic) *Dec 86*

Bruce Springsteen: Bruce Springsteen & The E Street Band Live 1975-85 (Columbia) *Feb 87*

Spyrogyra: Carnival (MCA) *Jun 87*

Steppenwolf: 16 Greatest Hits (MCA) *Dec 86*

Ray Stevens: He Thinks He's Ray Stevens (MCA) *Feb 87*

George Strait: Strait From The Heart (MCA) *Feb 87*

George Strait: 7 (MCA) *Sep 86*

George Strait: Ocean Front Property (MCA) *Mar 87*

Stryper: To Hell With The Devil (ENG) *Mar 87*

Talking Heads: True Stories (Sire) *Nov 86*

George Thorogood & The Destroyers: Live (EIA) *Dec 86*

Randy Travis: Storms Of Life (Warner Bros) *Oct 86*

Randy Travis: Always And Forever (Warner Bros) *Jul 87*

Tina Turner: Break Every Rule (Capitol) *Nov 86*

U2: The Joshua Tree (Island) *May 87*

Luther Vandross: Give Me The Reason (Epic) *Dec 86*

Suzanne Vega: Solitude Standing (A&M) *Jul 87*

Billy Vera & The Beaters: By Request (Best Of) (Capitol) *Mar 87*

Andreas Vollenweider: White Winds (CBS) *Aug 86*

Andreas Vollenweider: Down To The Moon (CBS) *Feb 87*

Jody Watley: Jody Watley (MCA) *Apr 87*

Wham!: Music From The Edge Of Heaven (Columbia) *Aug 86*

The Whispers: Just Gets Better With Time (Solar) *Jul 87*

Whitesnake: Whitesnake (Geffen) *Jun 87*

Hank Williams Jnr: Montana Cafe (Warner Bros) *Dec 86*

Bruce Willis: The Return Of Bruno (Manhattan) *Mar 87*

Steve Winwood: Back In The High Life (Island) *Sep 86*

Yaz: Upstairs At Eric's (Sire) *Oct 86*

Dwight Yoakam: Guitars, Cadillacs Etc Etc (Reprise) *Jan 87*

VICTOR FELDMAN
Died 12 May, 1987, aged 53.

Apparently dying of a heart attack, this British born pianist, drummer and vibraphone player was one of the best known jazz musicians on the West Coast of America. Among his credits in the 1950s and 1960s was work with such major names as Benny Goodman, Miles Davis, Woody Herman and Cannonball Adderley. He recorded a number of albums of his own and a list of those for whom he played sessions reads like a *Who's Who* of the rock era. Among the names were Greg Allman, The Beach Boys, Bobby Bland, Kim Carnes, Johnny Cash, Christopher Cross, Dion, Phil Everly, The Four Tops, Marvin Gaye, Elton John, B.B.King, Lulu, Melanie, Joni Mitchell, Randy Newman, Leo Sayer, Boz Scaggs, Carly Simon, Steely Dan, James Taylor, Allen Toussaint, Tom Waits and Frank Zappa. This only partly complete list covers the fields of pop, rock, country, folk, R&B, jazz, etc. Feldman was probably unknown to millions who heard his contributions to numerous albums but was obviously held in high esteem by musicians among his contemporaries.

ANDRES SEGOVIA
Died 3 June, 1987, aged 94.

Segovia, the master of the Spanish guitar, died of heart failure in Madrid, having returned to his native land during an American tour during which he was hospitalized in New York. Segovia's achievement was to convince the classical music establishment that the guitar was a serious instrument on which to play classical music. One of his 30-odd albums for MCA won a Grammy Award in 1958 and he also recorded for CBS and RCA.

YOGI HORTON
Died 8 June, 1987, aged 33.

A noted studio drummer in New York and a longtime member of Luther Vandross's backing band, Horton committed suicide, apparently depressed about lack of recognition.

TURK MURPHY
Died 30 May, 1987, aged 71.

Strongly featuring in the traditional jazz revival of the 1950s, trombonist Murphy first attracted attention as a member of Lu Watters' Yerba Buena Jazz band during the 1940s and later led his own group which revived the music of early trad stars like Louis Armstrong and Jelly Roll Morton. His was the arrangement used on the hit versions of 'Mack The Knife' by Armstrong and Bobby Darin.

DANNY KAYE
Died 3 March, 1987, aged 74.

Hardly a pop star but well known in times past for his acting roles in such musical films as *White Christmas*, *Hans Christian Andersen* and *The Five Pennies*, Danny Kaye died of heart failure. Although his only British hit single was 'Wonderful Copenhagen' (a Top Five hit in 1953!), Kaye was probably best known for another song from the Hans Andersen film, 'The Ugly Duckling', and he is also remembered as a major comedian for such classic performances as his title role in *The Secret Life Of Walter Mitty*.

BOLA SETE
Died 14 February, 1987, aged 63.

Another notable ethnic guitarist, Sete's style was forged in his native South America where he was virtually a superstar. He recorded several solo jazz albums which were released in North America and Europe, also recording with Dizzy Gillespie among others. He died of pneumonia and respiratory failure.

TONY STRATTON-SMITH
Died 19 March, 1987, aged 53.

Ex-journalist, erstwhile record company boss and bon viveur extraordinaire, "Strat" (as he was known around Soho) died of cancer. Most notable in the music world for turning Genesis from struggling public school boys who had been dropped by Decca after one LP into international superstars, his Charisma label also released albums by Lindisfarne, the Monty Python team, Van der Graaf Generator and many others during the seventies. Stratton had recently sold the label to Virgin Records after becoming more interested in horse racing later in his life.

NORMAN HARRIS
Died 20 March, 1987, aged 39.

One of the major figures of the "Philly sound" of the seventies, Harris was guitarist and/or arranger on hits by the O'Jays, Teddy Pendergrass, Harold Melvin & The Bluenotes and MFSB, the hit-making session group of which he was a member. He also worked with non-Philadelphia International acts like The Stylistics and also produced The Trammps among others. He died of heart failure.

ROBERT PRESTON
Died 21 March, 1987, aged 68.

A theatrical (Broadway) and movie (Hollywood) star of long standing, Preston died of lung cancer. His most memorable role was as the leading actor in *The Music Man*, a show which gave the world such contrasting hits as '76 Trombones' (which Preston performed on the million selling original cast LP), and 'Till There Was You' (which he didn't sing but which became well known due to the cover version on *With The Beatles* sung by Paul McCartney).

DAVID SAVOY Jr.
Died 7 February, 1987, aged 24.

Savoy, who committed suicide, was the manager of Minneapolis-based Hüsker Dü. The band postponed its national tour in his memory.

KATE WOLF
Died 10 December, 1986, aged 44.

Folk singer/songwriter Wolf made six albums for Kaleidoscope Records before dying of complications which occurred during a bone marrow transplant operation in an attempt to cure leukaemia.

BUDDY RICH
Died 2 April, 1987, aged 69.

Never really recovering from the effects of an operation to remove a brain tumour, Rich was arguably the best known drummer in modern jazz. He worked during his twenties with major names like Tommy Dorsey and Artie Shaw, later joining Harry James's Orchestra, which he left during the mid-sixties to form his own big band. Rich was the antithesis of the quiet percussionist who rarely

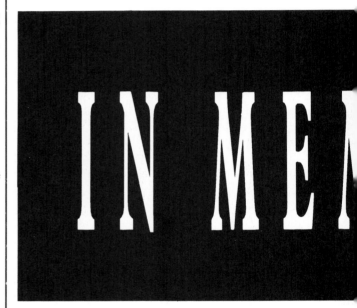

speaks, being more like the jazz world's Keith Moon, both instrumentally and also in his often outspoken comments. He recorded for numerous labels in a lengthy career, and was also a talented singer and occasional comedian.

LIBERACE
Died 4 February, 1987, aged 67.

Wladziu Liberace, the pianist whose approach to classical music (presenting it with almost vaudevillian undertones) made him immensely popular, particularly with his vast female fan following, died either of emphysema or AIDS. His *Liberace At The Piano* LP topped the US LP chart in 1952 and four of his other albums reached the Top 20 of that chart before the advent of rock 'n' roll. His popularity was such that he sold out concerts at both Carnegie Hall and Madison Square Garden in 1953 and his latterday TV series fuelled his largely middle-aged following during the 1960s.

LEE DORSEY
Died 2 December, 1986, aged 59.
One of the major names of New Orleans R&B music with five well known US Top 40 hits to his name, ex-professional boxer turned singer Dorsey grew up with the likes of Fats Domino. He was discovered at the age of 30 working in a car repair business where independent producer Renauld Richard heard

him singing while working underneath a motor. His hottest period came between 1961 and 1966, when 'Ya Ya', 'Do-Re-Mi', 'Ride Your Pony', 'Working In The Coalmine' and 'Holy Cow' were all hits in America, while two others, 'Get Out Of My Life Woman' and 'Confusion', were also British hits. His later work was often produced by Allen Toussaint and he was most recently in the news when he toured as opening act for The Clash, although his last original album was released during the late seventies. He died of emphysema.

SIPPIE WALLACE
Died 1 November, 1986, aged 88.
Starting her record career as a blues singer in the 1920s, she became a gospel singer in the 1930s, then fell into obscurity until the 1960s when Bonnie Raitt can take the credit for reviving her career by recording her songs, touring with her and helping her to acquire a new record deal with Atlantic. Sippie Wallace is presumed to have died of old age.

EDDIE "LOCKJAW" DAVIS
Died 3 November, 1986, aged 65.
Jazz saxophonist Davis worked spasmodically with the Count Basie band for over 20 years but more recently cut a number of albums under his own steam. He died of kidney failure.

THAD JONES
Died 20 August, 1986, aged 63.
Modern jazz trumpeter Jones, who died of cancer, achieved fame with the Count Basie band before forming the celebrated Thad Jones-Mel Lewis Jazz Orchestra which achieved sufficient popularity to tour the world and record several albums. His brother is drummer Elvin Jones, and he spent much of his later life living in Denmark.

CARMOL TAYLOR
Died 5 December, 1986, aged 53.
A country music songwriter and performer – he wrote hits like 'The Grand Tour' for George Jones plus items for Tammy Wynette and Barbara Mandrell – Taylor died of cancer.

DESI ARNAZ
Died 2 December, 1986, aged 69.
Another lung cancer victim, Arnaz was a singer and bandleader whose greatest fame came with his long participation in the TV series, *I Love Lucy*, which starred his real-life wife, Lucille Ball.

RON KASS
Died 17 October, 1986, Aged 51.
Well known in the record industry (he was President of the MGM label in America and Chairman of Warner Bros in Britain at various times, as well as founding President of Apple Records), Kass has received more recent publicity as ex-husband of Joan Collins. He died of cancer.

CLIFF BURTON
Died 27 September, 1986, aged 24.
Burton, bass player for noted metallurgists Metallica, died when the group's tour bus overturned in Sweden.

RUTH POLSKY
Died 7 September, 1986, aged 30.
An American promoter/agent, Polsky died after being run over by a taxi. Her pioneering work in presenting new British acts in America led to her working with the likes of Adam & The Ants, Echo & The Bunnymen, New Order and Sade.

JOHN HURLEY
Died 16 August, 1986, aged 45.
Hurley, who wrote 'Son Of A Preacher Man' and 'Love Of The Common People' and was also a country singer, died of liver failure and brain haemorrhage.

PAUL BUTTERFIELD
Died 4 May, 1987, aged 44.
Singer/harmonica player Butterfield was arguably the US equivalent of Alexis Korner or John Mayall in bringing R&B music to a predominantly white rock audience. His cohorts in the Butterfield Blues Band included guitarists Mike Bloomfield and Elvin Bishop, and his first two LPs, *The Paul Butterfield Blues Band* and *East West*, were essential items in the mid-sixties and both have recently been reissued on Edsel Records. His band provided the backing for Bob Dylan at the Newport Folk Festival in 1965,

causing much controversy among folk purists since they were Dylan's first electric backing band. He also appeared at the celebrated "Last Waltz" concert with The Band in 1976, although his profile had dropped considerably since the sixties. It is presumed that Butterfield, like Bloomfield (who died in 1981 aged 36), died as a result of drug abuse.

MOSES ASCH
Died 19 October, 1986, aged 81.
Folkways Records founder Asch died of a heart attack. Folkways is believed to be the oldest independent label still active and its catalogue includes material by Leadbelly, Woody Guthrie, Pete Seeger, Big Bill Broonzy and Coleman Hawkins. A Polish immigrant, Asch launched Folkways in 1947 and operated with a policy of pressing his own discs and manufacturing his own sleeves; this allowed him to keep every title on the label in catalogue, amounting to over 2,000 LPs.

ALFRED LION
Died 2 February, 1987, aged 78.
A German born immigrant who moved to New York in his late twenties and soon afterwards founded Blue Note records as a hobby, Lion died of congestive heart failure. With his partner Francis Wolff, Lion built the small jazz label into a major force, pioneering the recording of modern jazz and bebop in the 1940s and 1950s, and working in the early part of their careers with Thelonious Monk, Miles Davis, John Coltrane, Herbie Hancock, Ornette Coleman and Jimmy Smith, among many others. Lion sold the label to Liberty Records in 1967 and a continuing series of reissues of the label's catalogue via EMI in Britain has kept Blue Note's name alive to date.

FRED ASTAIRE
Died 22 June, 1987, aged 88.
While he was hardly a rock star, there can be little doubt of the influence singer and dancer Fred Astaire exerted over the rock generation. The timeless musical films in which he starred, most notably with his longtime dancing partner Ginger Rogers, remain classics and have been eagerly bought on home video by several generations of fans who enjoy the romantic escapism of movies like *Top Hat, Easter Parade, Flying Down To Rio* and many others, as well as the quicksilver brilliance of

his superlative footwork. Born Frederick Austerlitz on a farm in Omaha, Nebraska, in 1899 to an Austrian immigrant family, Astaire's movie career began in 1933, despite the report which was made on his first screen test: "Can't act. Can't sing. Slightly bald. Dances a little." He subsequently starred in around 40 feature films, mostly musicals, although he was also an accomplished dramatic actor as demonstrated in the 1959 cinematic version of the Neville Shute novel *On The Beach*. He won an Academy Award in 1949, not for anything specific but for his overall contribution to motion picture techniques. Astaire died of pneumonia in a Hollywood hospital in the arms of his second wife – if it could be said that any form of dying could be romantic, Fred Astaire even managed to achieve that with the dignity and all round decency which typified his career.

TEDDY WILSON
Died 31 July, 1986, aged 73.

Jazz pianist Wilson was the sensitive accompanist on Billie Holiday records but perhaps his most significant era was as the black pianist in the otherwise white Benny Goodman Trio in the fifties, when racially mixed acts were virtually unknown. He also played with Louis Armstrong and recorded under his own name. He died after a long illness.

GORDON MILLS
Died July/August 1986, aged 51.

The proprietor of MAM Records and Music Publishers, Mills discovered Tom Jones, Engelbert Humperdinck and Gilbert O'Sullivan and also had the foresight to release Dave Edmunds' chart-topping 'I Hear You Knocking' single when others could not see its potential. In later life, Mills was involved in many lawsuits, especially with O'Sullivan.

ANDY WARHOL
Died 22 February, 1987, aged 58.

The contribution to the rock era made by Andy Warhol, the son of a Czechoslovakian immigrant family, is not easy to quantify. One of his last endeavours in the pop music world was to make a video with Curiosity Killed The Cat, while his *Interview* magazine was a long running, if often rather obscure, publication which dealt with the glamorous side of rock stars. His most quoted utterance was "In the future everyone will be famous for

fifteen minutes," which may have been said either in jest or for effect or both, but is one of the great truisms of popular music. He had achieved his original fame/notoriety through his innovative screen prints and a painting he had done of a Campbell's soup can was auctioned for several thousand dollars in 1970. However, perhaps his biggest contribution to rock music was his patronage of the Velvet Underground who were the house band at New York's Cafe Bizarre until Warhol made them the resident musical part of his multi-media stage show known as The Exploding Plastic Inevitable. The front of the group's first LP bore the words "Andy Warhol" and a picture of a banana (which could be peeled off), only mentioning the album's actual title, *The Velvet*

Underground & Nico Produced By Andy Warhol, on the rear and the spine! Warhol was a respected pioneer of the Pop Art movement, although the precise detail of what he actually did is difficult to pin down – perhaps his contribution to both art and music was more philosophical than tangible. He died of a heart attack in his sleep in New York after gall bladder surgery shortly before.

BOUDLEAUX BRYANT
Died 25 June, 1987, aged 67.

Chiefly notable as co-writer with his wife Felice of numerous hits for the Everly Brothers at the start of their career, including 'Bye Bye Love', 'Wake Up Little Susie', 'Bird Dog' and 'All I Have To Do Is Dream', Boudleaux Bryant died of cancer in a Nashville hospital. He and his wife have been called Nashville's earliest full time songwriters and their timeless songs have been recorded by such

notables as Ricky Nelson, Roy Orbison, Trini Lopez, Henry Mancini, Count Basie, Chet Atkins and Mitch Miller. Their first hit as a songwriting team came in 1948 and one estimate of the number of records sold featuring one or more of the Bryants' reputed 1,500 plus songs is 300 million. Others who recorded their excellent songs include Bob Dylan, Simon & Garfunkel, Elvis Presley, The Beach Boys, The Grateful Dead, Ray Charles, James Taylor and Carly Simon.

JOHN HAMMOND SNR.
Died 10 July, 1987, aged 76.

John Hammond Snr., who died after a long illness, was the ultimate talent scout of not only the rock era, but also the preceding latter part of the jazz age. While he will mostly be remembered by the current generation for his championing of both Bob Dylan and Bruce Springsteen, Hammond's career began in the 1930s after he moved away from writing (he was a reviewer for *Melody Maker*, as well as contributing to many American publications). Among the notable acts whom he championed and in many cases produced were Fletcher Henderson, Coleman Hawkins, Benny Carter, Bessie Smith, Billie Holiday and many others. He organized the historic "Spirituals To Swing" concerts held at New York's Carnegie Hall and also showcased two further jazz age luminaries in Count Basie (whom he persuaded to move to New York) and Teddy Wilson, the black pianist who played with Benny Goodman (Hammond's brother-in-law) after the latter had strongly recommended the

move, remarkable at the time as racially integrated groups were unknown.

Hammond was not initially very impressed with rock music, but was the first person to recognize the potential of Dylan, Aretha Franklin (although the records he made with her were inferior to her hits) and Springsteen, none of whom broke through into superstardom until some years after they had been championed by Hammond. He was also an early supporter of George Benson and was the main motivation behind the re-issue of the material by Robert Johnson which ought to be in every serious blues fan's collection.

Most of his working life was spent with Columbia (CBS), but he also worked for Brunswick, Mercury and Vanguard, among other labels. His fascinating autobiography (available in Penguin) is obligatory reading for anyone who wants to know about the history of popular music, while his son, John Paul Hammond, still performs as a singer/guitarist of the R&B/folk persuasion. The death of John Hammond Snr. leaves a gap which is unlikely ever to be filled.

THE YEAR'S CHARTS

August 1986 — July 1987

FEATURING THE MUSIC WEEK AND RADIO & RECORDS NEWS CHARTS

WEEK ENDING AUGUST 2 1986
S I N G L E S UK A L B U M S

#	Singles	Albums
1	THE LADY IN RED — CHRIS DE BURGH (A&M)	TRUE BLUE — MADONNA (SIRE)
2	PAPA DON'T PREACH — MADONNA (SIRE)	THE FINAL — WHAM! (EPIC)
3	LET'S GO ALL THE WAY — SLY FOX (CAPITOL)	INTO THE LIGHT — CHRIS DE BURGH (A&M)
4	EVERY BEAT OF MY HEART — ROD STEWART (WARNER BROS)	A KIND OF MAGIC — QUEEN (EMI)
5	SO MACHO — SINITTA (FANFARE)	REVENGE — EURYTHMICS (RCA)
6	CAMOUFLAGE — STAN RIDGWAY (IRS/MCA)	RIPTIDE — ROBERT PALMER (ISLAND)
7	WHAT'S THE COLOUR OF MONEY? — HOLLYWOOD BEYOND (WEA)	BROTHERS IN ARMS — DIRE STRAITS (VERTIGO/PHONOGRAM)
8	SING OUR OWN SONG — UB40 (DEP INTERNATIONAL/VIRGIN)	EVERY BEAT OF MY HEART — ROD STEWART (WARNER BROS)
9	I DIDN'T MEAN TO TURN YOU ON — ROBERT PALMER (ISLAND)	PICTURE BOOK — SIMPLY RED (ELEKTRA)
10	FIND THE TIME — FIVE STAR (TENT/RCA)	BACK IN THE HIGH LIFE — STEVE WINWOOD (ISLAND)
11	ROSES — HAYWOODE (CBS)	NOW – THE SUMMER ALBUM — VARIOUS (EMI/VIRGIN)
12	MY FAVOURITE WASTE OF TIME — OWEN PAUL (EPIC)	HUNTING HIGH AND LOW — A-HA (WARNER BROS)
13	SOME CANDY TALKING — THE JESUS AND MARY CHAIN (BLANCO Y NEGRO)	INVISIBLE TOUCH — GENESIS (CHARISMA/VIRGIN)
14	SMILE — AUDREY HALL (GERMAIN)	THE SEER — (MERCURY/PHONOGRAM)
15	FIGHT FOR OURSELVES — SPANDAU BALLET (REFORMATION)	LONDON 0 HULL 4 — THE HOUSEMARTINS (GO! DISCS)
16	VENUS — BANANARAMA (LONDON)	SO — PETER GABRIEL (VIRGIN)
17	AIN'T NOTHIN' GOIN' ON BUT THE RENT — GWEN GUTHRIE (BOILING POINT/POLYDOR)	TOUCH ME — SAMANTHA FOX (JIVE)
18	PANIC — THE SMITHS (ROUGH TRADE)	STREET LIFE – 20 GREAT HITS — BRYAN FERRY/ROXY MUSIC (EG/POLYDOR)
19	HIGHER LOVE — STEVE WINWOOD (ISLAND)	WHITNEY HOUSTON — WHITNEY HOUSTON (ARISTA)
20	HAPPY HOUR — THE HOUSEMARTINS (GO! DISCS)	DRIVE TIME USA — VARIOUS (K-TEL)

S I N G L E S US A L B U M S

#	Singles	Albums
1	GLORY OF LOVE — PETER CETERA (FULL MOON/WARNER BROS)	BACK IN THE HIGH LIFE — STEVE WINWOOD (ISLAND)
2	PAPA DON'T PREACH — MADONNA (SIRE/WARNER BROS)	INVISIBLE TOUCH — GENESIS (ATLANTIC)
3	SLEDGEHAMMER — PETER GABRIEL (GEFFEN)	SO — PETER GABRIEL (GEFFEN)
4	MAD ABOUT YOU — BELINDA CARLISLE (IRS/MCA)	5150 — VAN HALEN (WARNER BROS)
5	LOVE TOUCH — ROD STEWART (WARNER BROS)	EAT 'EM AND SMILE — DAVID LEE ROTH (WARNER BROS)
6	HIGHER LOVE — STEVE WINWOOD (ISLAND)	REVENGE — EURYTHMICS (RCA)
7	WE DON'T HAVE TO TAKE OUR CLOTHES OFF — JERMAINE STEWART (TEN/ARISTA)	WALKABOUT — FIXX (MCA)
8	VENUS — BANANARAMA (LONDON/PG)	THE SEER — BIG COUNTRY (MERCURY/PG)
9	THE EDGE OF HEAVEN — WHAM! (COLUMBIA)	STRENGTH IN NUMBERS — 38 SPECIAL (A&M)
10	DANCING ON THE CEILING — LIONEL RICHIE (MOTOWN)	SCARECROW — JOHN C. MELLENCAMP (RIVA/PG)
11	INVISIBLE TOUCH — GENESIS (ATLANTIC)	LANDING ON WATER — NEIL YOUNG (GEFFEN)
12	TAKE MY BREATH AWAY — BERLIN (COLUMBIA)	LIKE A ROCK — BOB SEGER & THE SILVER . . . (CAPITOL)
13	RUMORS — TIMEX SOCIAL CLUB (JAY)	GTR — GTR (ARISTA)
14	SUZANNE — JOURNEY (COLUMBIA)	TOM COCHRANE & RED RIDER — TOM COCHRANE & RED RIDER (CAPITOL)
15	SWEET FREEDOM — MICHAEL McDONALD (MCA)	SOUNDTRACK — RUTHLESS PEOPLE (EPIC)
16	ALL THE LOVE IN THE WORLD — OUTFIELD (COLUMBIA)	THE OTHER SIDE OF LIFE — MOODY BLUES (POLYDOR/PG)
17	YOU SHOULD BE MINE — JEFFREY OSBORNE (A&M)	AFTERBURNER — ZZ TOP (WARNER BROS)
18	DANGER ZONE — KENNY LOGGINS (COLUMBIA)	KNOCKED OUT LOADED — BOB DYLAN (COLUMBIA)
19	OPPORTUNITIES — PET SHOP BOYS (EMI AMERICA)	LIFES RICH PAGEANT — REM (IRS/MCA)
20	WORDS GET IN THE WAY — MIAMI SOUND MACHINE (EPIC)	EMERSON, LAKE & POWELL — EMERSON, LAKE & POWELL (POLYDOR/PG)

WEEK ENDING AUGUST 9 1986
S I N G L E S UK A L B U M S

#	Singles	Albums
1	THE LADY IN RED — CHRIS DE BURGH (A&M)	TRUE BLUE — MADONNA (SIRE)
2	SO MACHO — SINITTA (FANFARE)	INTO THE LIGHT — CHRIS DE BURGH (A&M)
3	PAPA DON'T PREACH — MADONNA (SIRE)	THE FINAL — WHAM! (EPIC)
4	CAMOUFLAGE — STAN RIDGWAY (IRS/MCA)	A KIND OF MAGIC — QUEEN (EMI)
5	I WANT TO WAKE UP WITH YOU — BORIS GARDINER (REVUE/CREOLE)	REVENGE — EURYTHMICS (RCA)
6	LET'S GO ALL THE WAY — SLY FOX (CAPITOL)	RIPTIDE — ROBERT PALMER (ISLAND)
7	FIND THE TIME — FIVE STAR (TENT/RCA)	BROTHERS IN ARMS — DIRE STRAITS (VERTIGO/PHONOGRAM)
8	WHAT'S THE COLOUR OF MONEY? — HOLLYWOOD BEYOND (WEA)	RAT IN THE KITCHEN — UB40 (DEP INTERNATIONAL/VIRGIN)
9	EVERY BEAT OF MY HEART — ROD STEWART (WARNER BROS)	PICTURE BOOK — SIMPLY RED (ELEKTRA)
10	I DIDN'T MEAN TO TURN YOU ON — ROBERT PALMER (ISLAND)	FLAUNT IT — SIGUE SIGUE SPUTNIK (PARLOPHONE)
11	PANIC — THE SMITHS (ROUGH TRADE)	EVERY BEAT OF MY HEART — ROD STEWART (WARNER BROS)
12	AIN'T NOTHIN' GOIN' ON BUT THE RENT — GWEN GUTHRIE (BOILING POINT/POLYDOR)	HUNTING HIGH AND LOW — A-HA (WARNER BROS)
13	SING OUR OWN SONG — UB40 (DEP INTERNATIONAL/VIRGIN)	BACK IN THE HIGH LIFE — STEVE WINWOOD (ISLAND)
14	ROSES — HAYWOODE (CBS)	INVISIBLE TOUCH — GENESIS (CHARISMA/VIRGIN)
15	FIGHT FOR OURSELVES — SPANDAU BALLET (REFORMATION/CBS)	SO — PETER GABRIEL (VIRGIN)
16	SHOUT — LULU (DECCA/LONDON)	THE SEER — BIG COUNTRY (MERCURY/PHONOGRAM)
17	CALLING ALL THE HEROES — IT BITES (VIRGIN)	NOW – THE SUMMER ALBUM — VARIOUS (EMI/VIRGIN)
18	SMILE — AUDREY HALL (GERMAIN)	LONDON 0 HULL 4 — THE HOUSEMARTINS (GO! DISCS)
19	RED SKY — STATUS QUO (VERTIGO/PHONOGRAM)	QUEEN GREATEST HITS — QUEEN (EMI)
20	SOME CANDY TALKING — THE JESUS AND MARY CHAIN (BLANCO Y NEGRO)	STREET LIFE – 20 GREAT HITS — BRYAN FERRY/ROXY MUSIC (EG/POLYDOR)

S I N G L E S US A L B U M S

#	Singles	Albums
1	PAPA DON'T PREACH — MADONNA (SIRE/WARNER BROS)	BACK IN THE HIGH LIFE — STEVE WINWOOD (ISLAND)
2	GLORY OF LOVE — PETER CETERA (FULL MOON/WARNER BROS)	INVISIBLE TOUCH — GENESIS (ATLANTIC)
3	HIGHER LOVE — STEVE WINWOOD (ISLAND)	SO — PETER GABRIEL (GEFFEN)
4	MAD ABOUT YOU — BELINDA CARLISLE (IRS/MCA)	REVENGE — EURYTHMICS (RCA)
5	VENUS — BANANARAMA (LONDON/PG)	EAT 'EM AND SMILE — DAVID LEE ROTH (WARNER BROS)
6	DANCING ON THE CEILING — LIONEL RICHIE (MOTOWN)	5150 — VAN HALEN (WARNER BROS)
7	TAKE MY BREATH AWAY — BERLIN (COLUMBIA)	LANDING ON WATER — NEIL YOUNG (GEFFEN)
8	WE DON'T HAVE TO TAKE OUR CLOTHES OFF — JERMAINE STEWART (TEN/ARISTA)	WALKABOUT — FIXX (MCA)
9	THE EDGE OF HEAVEN — WHAM! (COLUMBIA)	STRENGTH IN NUMBERS — 38 SPECIAL (A&M)
10	RUMORS — TIMEX SOCIAL CLUB (JAY)	SCARECROW — JOHN C. MELLENCAMP (RIVA/PG)
11	SLEDGEHAMMER — PETER GABRIEL (GEFFEN)	LIFES RICH PAGEANT — REM (IRS/MCA)
12	SWEET FREEDOM — MICHAEL McDONALD (MCA)	GTR — GTR (ARISTA)
13	LOVE TOUCH — ROD STEWART (WARNER BROS)	THE SEER — BIG COUNTRY (MERCURY/PG)
14	STUCK WITH YOU — HUEY LEWIS AND THE NEWS (CHRYSALIS)	AFTERBURNER — ZZ TOP (WARNER BROS)
15	YOU SHOULD BE MINE — JEFFREY OSBORNE (A&M)	LIKE A ROCK — BOB SEGER & THE SILVER . . .
16	ALL THE LOVE IN THE WORLD — OUTFIELD (COLUMBIA)	TOM COCHRANE & RED RIDER — TOM COCHRANE & RED RIDER (CAPITOL)
17	WORDS GET IN THE WAY — MIAMI SOUND MACHINE (EPIC)	THE BRIDGE — BILLY JOEL (COLUMBIA)
18	FRIENDS AND LOVERS — C. ANDERSON/G. LORING (CARRERE/CBS)	KNOCKED OUT LOADED — BOB DYLAN (COLUMBIA)
19	INVISIBLE TOUCH — GENESIS (ATLANTIC)	NO GURU, NO METHOD, NO TEACHER — VAN MORRISON (MERCURY/PG)
20	BABY LOVE — REGINA (ATLANTIC)	THE OTHER SIDE OF LIFE — MOODY BLUES (POLYDOR/PG)

WEEK ENDING AUGUST 16 1986

S I N G L E S   UK   A L B U M S

#	SINGLES		ALBUMS
1	THE LADY IN RED — CHRIS DE BURGH (A&M)		TRUE BLUE — MADONNA (SIRE)
2	I WANT TO WAKE UP WITH YOU — BORIS GARDINER (REVUE/CREOLE)		INTO THE LIGHT — CHRIS DE BURGH (A&M)
3	SO MACHO — SINITTA (FANFARE)		A KIND OF MAGIC — QUEEN (EMI)
4	ANYONE CAN FALL IN LOVE — ANITA DOBSON/SIMON MAY ORCH (BBC)		THE FINAL — WHAM! (EPIC)
5	AIN'T NOTHIN' GOIN' ON BUT THE RENT — GWEN GUTHRIE (BOILING POINT/POLYDOR)		RIPTIDE — ROBERT PALMER (ISLAND)
6	CAMOUFLAGE — STAN RIDGWAY (IRS/MCA)		BROTHERS IN ARMS — DIRE STRAITS (VERTIGO/PHONOGRAM)
7	PAPA DON'T PREACH — MADONNA (SIRE)		REVENGE — EURYTHMICS (RCA)
8	SHOUT — LULU (DECCA/LONDON)		PICTURE BOOK — SIMPLY RED (ELEKTRA)
9	FIND THE TIME — FIVE STAR (TENT/RCA)		RAT IN THE KITCHEN — UB40 (DEP INTERNATIONAL/VIRGIN)
10	CALLING ALL THE HEROES — IT BITES (VIRGIN)		HUNTING HIGH AND LOW — A-HA (WARNER BROS)
11	PANIC — THE SMITHS (ROUGH TRADE)		BACK IN THE HIGH LIFE — STEVE WINWOOD (ISLAND)
12	LET'S GO ALL THE WAY — SLY FOX (CAPITOL)		THE PAVAROTTI COLLECTION — LUCIANO PAVAROTTI (STYLUS)
13	WHAT'S THE COLOUR OF MONEY? — HOLLYWOOD BEYOND (WEA)		EVERY BEAT OF MY HEART — ROD STEWART (WARNER BROS)
14	EVERY BEAT OF MY HEART — ROD STEWART (WARNER BROS)		FLAUNT IT — SIGUE SIGUE SPUTNIK (PARLOPHONE)
15	I DIDN'T MEAN TO TURN YOU ON — ROBERT PALMER (ISLAND)		THE ORIGINALS — VARIOUS (TOWERBELL)
16	FIGHT FOR OURSELVES — SPANDAU BALLET (REFORMATION/CBS)		INVISIBLE TOUCH — GENESIS (CHARISMA/VIRGIN)
17	I CAN PROVE IT — PHIL FEARON (ENSIGN/CHRYSALIS)		SO — PETER GABRIEL (VIRGIN)
18	DANCING ON THE CEILING — LIONEL RICHIE (MOTOWN)		QUEEN GREATEST HITS — QUEEN (EMI)
19	RED SKY — STATUS QUO (VERTIGO/PHONOGRAM)		NOW – THE SUMMER ALBUM — VARIOUS (EMI/VIRGIN)
20	ROSES — HAYWOODE (CBS)		STREET LIFE – 20 GREAT HITS — BRYAN FERRY/ROXY MUSIC (EG/POLYDOR)

S I N G L E S   US   A L B U M S

#	SINGLES		ALBUMS
1	PAPA DON'T PREACH — MADONNA (SIRE/WARNER BROS)		INVISIBLE TOUCH — GENESIS (ATLANTIC)
2	HIGHER LOVE — STEVE WINWOOD (ISLAND)		BACK IN THE HIGH LIFE — STEVE WINWOOD (ISLAND)
3	VENUS — BANANARAMA (LONDON/PG)		SO — PETER GABRIEL (GEFFEN)
4	TAKE MY BREATH AWAY — BERLIN (COLUMBIA)		REVENGE — EURYTHMICS (RCA)
5	DANCING ON THE CEILING — LIONEL RICHIE (MOTOWN)		EAT 'EM AND SMILE — DAVID LEE ROTH (WARNER BROS)
6	GLORY OF LOVE — PETER CETERA (FULL MOON/WARNER BROS)		5150 — VAN HALEN (WARNER BROS)
7	MAD ABOUT YOU — BELINDA CARLISLE (IRS/MCA)		LANDING ON WATER — NEIL YOUNG (GEFFEN)
8	RUMORS — TIMEX SOCIAL CLUB (JAY)		CAN'T HOLD BACK — EDDIE MONEY (COLUMBIA)
9	STUCK WITH YOU — HUEY LEWIS & THE NEWS (CHRYSALIS)		LIFES RICH PAGEANT — REM (IRS/MCA)
10	SWEET FREEDOM — MICHAEL McDONALD (MCA)		THREE HEARTS IN THE HAPPY ... — DARYL HALL (RCA)
11	THE EDGE OF HEAVEN — WHAM! (COLUMBIA)		WALKABOUT — FIXX (MCA)
12	WE DON'T HAVE TO TAKE OUR CLOTHES OFF — JERMAINE STEWART (TEN/ARISTA)		THE BRIDGE — BILLY JOEL (COLUMBIA)
13	FRIENDS AND LOVERS — C. ANDERSON/G. LORING (CARRERE/CBS)		GTR — GTR (ARISTA)
14	WORDS GET IN THE WAY — MIAMI SOUND MACHINE (EPIC)		LIKE A ROCK — BOB SEGER & THE SILVER ... (CAPITOL)
15	BABY LOVE — REGINA (ATLANTIC)		AFTERBURNER — ZZ TOP (WARNER BROS)
16	YOU SHOULD BE MINE — JEFFREY OSBORNE (A&M)		THE THIN RED LINE — GLASS TIGER (MANHATTAN)
17	DREAMTIME — DARYL HALL (RCA)		STRENGTH IN NUMBERS — 38 SPECIAL (A&M)
18	WALK THIS WAY — RUN DMC (PROFILE)		KNOCKED OUT LOADED — BOB DYLAN (COLUMBIA)
19	SLEDGEHAMMER — PETER GABRIEL (GEFFEN)		SCARECROW — JOHN C. MELLENCAMP (RIVA/PG)
20	DON'T FORGET ME (WHEN I'M GONE) — GLASS TIGER (MANHATTAN)		NO GURU, NO METHOD, NO TEACHER — VAN MORRISON (MERCURY/PG)

WEEK ENDING AUGUST 23 1986

S I N G L E S   UK   A L B U M S

#	SINGLES		ALBUMS
1	I WANT TO WAKE UP WITH YOU — BORIS GARDINER (REVUE/CREOLE)		NOW, THAT'S WHAT I CALL MUSIC 7 — VARIOUS (VIRGIN/EMI)
2	THE LADY IN RED — CHRIS DE BURGH (A&M)		TRUE BLUE — MADONNA (SIRE)
3	SO MACHO — SINITTA (FANFARE)		DANCING ON THE CEILING — LIONEL RICHIE (MOTOWN)
4	ANYONE CAN FALL IN LOVE — ANITA DOBSON/SIMON MAY ORCH (BBC)		A KIND OF MAGIC — QUEEN (EMI)
5	AIN'T NOTHIN' GOIN' ON BUT THE RENT — GWEN GUTHRIE (BOILING POINT/POLYDOR)		INTO THE LIGHT — CHRIS DE BURGH (A&M)
6	CALLING ALL THE HEROES — IT BITES (VIRGIN)		THE FINAL — WHAM! (EPIC)
7	DANCING ON THE CEILING — LIONEL RICHIE (MOTOWN)		BROTHERS IN ARMS — DIRE STRAITS (VERTIGO/PHONOGRAM)
8	I CAN PROVE IT — PHIL FEARON (ENSIGN/CHRYSALIS)		RIPTIDE — ROBERT PALMER (ISLAND)
9	CAMOUFLAGE — STAN RIDGWAY (IRS/MCA)		RENDEZ-VOUS — JEAN-MICHEL JARRE (DREYFUS/POLYDOR)
10	SHOUT — LULU (DECCA/LONDON)		PICTURE BOOK — SIMPLY RED (ELEKTRA)
11	GIRLS AND BOYS — PRINCE AND THE REVOLUTION (PAISLEY PARK)		THE HEAT IS ON — VARIOUS (PORTRAIT)
12	BROTHER LOUIE — MODERN TALKING (RCA)		REVENGE — EURYTHMICS (RCA)
13	PAPA DON'T PREACH — MADONNA (SIRE)		EVERY BEAT OF MY HEART — ROD STEWART (WARNER BROS)
14	PANIC — THE SMITHS (ROUGH TRADE)		RAT IN THE KITCHEN — UB40 (DEP INTERNATIONAL/VIRGIN)
15	WE DON'T HAVE TO TAKE OUR CLOTHES OFF — JERMAINE STEWART (10/VIRGIN)		HUNTING HIGH AND LOW — A-HA (WARNER BROS)
16	FIND THE TIME — FIVE STAR (TENT/RCA)		THE ORIGINALS — VARIOUS (TOWERBELL)
17	BREAKING AWAY — JAKI GRAHAM (EMI)		QUEEN GREATEST HITS — QUEEN (EMI)
18	GLORY OF LOVE — PETER CETERA (FULL MOON/WARNER BROS)		BACK IN THE HIGH LIFE — STEVE WINWOOD (ISLAND)
19	HUMAN — HUMAN LEAGUE (VIRGIN)		INVISIBLE TOUCH — GENESIS (CHARISMA/VIRGIN)
20	WHAT'S THE COLOUR OF MONEY? — HOLLYWOOD BEYOND (WEA)		THE QUEEN IS DEAD — THE SMITHS (ROUGH TRADE)

S I N G L E S   US   A L B U M S

#	SINGLES		ALBUMS
1	HIGHER LOVE — STEVE WINWOOD (ISLAND)		INVISIBLE TOUCH — GENESIS (ATLANTIC)
2	TAKE MY BREATH AWAY — BERLIN (COLUMBIA)		BACK IN THE HIGH LIFE — STEVE WINWOOD (ISLAND)
3	VENUS — BANANARAMA (LONDON/PG)		SO — PETER GABRIEL (GEFFEN)
4	DANCING ON THE CEILING — LIONEL RICHIE (MOTOWN)		EAT 'EM AND SMILE — DAVID LEE ROTH (WARNER BROS)
5	PAPA DON'T PREACH — MADONNA (SIRE/WARNER BROS)		CAN'T HOLD BACK — EDDIE MONEY (COLUMBIA)
6	STUCK WITH YOU — HUEY LEWIS AND THE NEWS (CHRYSALIS)		REVENGE — EURYTHMICS (RCA)
7	RUMORS — TIMEX SOCIAL CLUB (JAY)		5150 — VAN HALEN (WARNER BROS)
8	SWEET FREEDOM — MICHAEL McDONALD (MCA)		LIFES RICH PAGEANT — REM (IRS/MCA)
9	FRIENDS AND LOVERS — C. ANDERSON/G. LORING (CARRERE/CBS)		LANDING ON WATER — NEIL YOUNG (GEFFEN)
10	GLORY OF LOVE — PETER CETERA (FULL MOON/WARNER BROS)		THREE HEARTS IN THE HAPPY ... — DARYL HALL (RCA)
11	WORDS GET IN THE WAY — MIAMI SOUND MACHINE (EPIC)		THE BRIDGE — BILLY JOEL (COLUMBIA)
12	BABY LOVE — REGINA (ATLANTIC)		WALKABOUT — FIXX (MCA)
13	MAD ABOUT YOU — BELINDA CARLISLE (IRS/MCA)		LIKE A ROCK — BOB SEGER & THE SILVER ... (CAPITOL)
14	DREAMTIME — DARYL HALL (RCA)		THE THIN RED LINE — GLASS TIGER (MANHATTAN)
15	WALK THIS WAY — RUN DMC (PROFILE)		NINE LIVES — BONNIE RAITT (WARNER BROS)
16	DON'T FORGET ME (WHEN I'M GONE) — GLASS TIGER (MANHATTAN)		THE SPORT OF KINGS — TRIUMPH (MCA)
17	WE DON'T HAVE TO TAKE OUR CLOTHES OFF — JERMAINE STEWART (TEN/ARISTA)		STRENGTH IN NUMBERS — 38 SPECIAL (A&M)
18	MAN SIZE LOVE — KLYMAXX (MCA)		LIVE — G. THOROGOOD & DESTROYERS (EMI AMERICA)
19	LOVE ZONE — BILLY OCEAN (JIVE/ARISTA)		BOOMTOWN — DAVID & DAVID (A&M)
20	THE EDGE OF HEAVEN — WHAM! (COLUMBIA)		GTR — GTR (ARISTA)

WEEK ENDING AUGUST 30 1986

SINGLES — UK — ALBUMS

#	Singles	Albums
1	I WANT TO WAKE UP WITH YOU — BORIS GARDINER (REVUE/CREOLE)	NOW, THAT'S WHAT I CALL MUSIC 7 — VARIOUS (VIRGIN/EMI)
2	SO MACHO — SINITTA (FANFARE)	DANCING ON THE CEILING — LIONEL RICHIE (MOTOWN)
3	THE LADY IN RED — CHRIS DE BURGH (A&M)	TRUE BLUE — MADONNA (SIRE)
4	BROTHER LOUIE — MODERN TALKING (RCA)	A KIND OF MAGIC — QUEEN (EMI)
5	DON'T LEAVE ME THIS WAY — COMMUNARDS (LONDON)	INTO THE LIGHT — CHRIS DE BURGH (A&M)
6	WE DON'T HAVE TO TAKE OUR CLOTHES OFF — JERMAINE STEWART (10/VIRGIN)	SILK AND STEEL — FIVE STAR (TENT/RCA)
7	ANYONE CAN FALL IN LOVE — ANITA DOBSON/SIMON MAY ORCH (BBC)	REVENGE — EURYTHMICS (RCA)
8	AIN'T NOTHIN' GOIN' ON BUT THE RENT — GWEN GUTHRIE (BOILING POINT/POLYDOR)	THE FINAL — WHAM! (EPIC)
9	GLORY OF LOVE — PETER CETERA (FULL MOON/WARNER BROS)	THE HEAT IS ON — VARIOUS (PORTRAIT)
10	HUMAN — HUMAN LEAGUE (VIRGIN)	PICTURE BOOK — SIMPLY RED (ELEKTRA)
11	DANCING ON THE CEILING — LIONEL RICHIE (MOTOWN)	BROTHERS IN ARMS — DIRE STRAITS (VERTIGO/PHONOGRAM)
12	GIRLS AND BOYS — PRINCE AND THE REVOLUTION (PAISLEY PARK)	RIPTIDE — ROBERT PALMER (ISLAND)
13	CALLING ALL THE HEROES — IT BITES (VIRGIN)	RENDEZ-VOUS — JEAN-MICHEL JARRE (DREYFUS/POLYDOR)
14	I CAN PROVE IT — PHIL FEARON (ENSIGN/CHRYSALIS)	PARADE — PRINCE AND THE REVOLUTION (PAISLEY PARK)
15	WHEN I THINK OF YOU — JANET JACKSON (A&M)	INVISIBLE TOUCH — GENESIS (CHARISMA/VIRGIN)
16	BREAKING AWAY — JAKI GRAHAM (EMI)	THE PAVAROTTI COLLECTION — LUCIANO PAVAROTTI (STYLUS)
17	A QUESTION OF TIME (REMIX) — DEPECHE MODE (MUTE)	HUNTING HIGH AND LOW — A-HA (WARNER BROS)
18	THE WAY IT IS — BRUCE HORNSBY AND THE RANGE (RCA)	COMMUNARDS — COMMUNARDS (LONDON)
19	SHOUT — LULU (DECCA/LONDON)	QUEEN GREATEST HITS — QUEEN (EMI)
20	LOVE CAN'T TURN AROUND — F. 'JACKMASTER' FUNK (CHICAGO/LONDON)	THE ORIGINALS — VARIOUS (TOWERBELL)

SINGLES — US — ALBUMS

#	Singles	Albums
1	HIGHER LOVE — STEVE WINWOOD (ISLAND)	BACK IN THE HIGH LIFE — STEVE WINWOOD (ISLAND)
2	TAKE MY BREATH AWAY — BERLIN (COLUMBIA)	INVISIBLE TOUCH — GENESIS (ATLANTIC)
3	DANCING ON THE CEILING — LIONEL RICHIE (MOTOWN)	SO — PETER GABRIEL (GEFFEN)
4	VENUS — BANANARAMA (LONDON/PG)	FORE! — HUEY LEWIS AND THE NEWS (CHRYSALIS)
5	STUCK WITH YOU — HUEY LEWIS AND THE NEWS (CHRYSALIS)	CAN'T HOLD BACK — EDDIE MONEY (COLUMBIA)
6	FRIENDS AND LOVERS — C. ANDERSON/G. LORING (CARRERE/CBS)	EAT 'EM AND SMILE — DAVID LEE ROTH (WARNER BROS)
7	SWEET FREEDOM — MICHAEL McDONALD (MCA)	LIFES RICH PAGEANT — REM (IRS/MCA)
8	PAPA DON'T PREACH — MADONNA (SIRE/WARNER BROS)	REVENGE — EURYTHMICS (RCA)
9	WORDS GET IN THE WAY — MIAMI SOUND MACHINE (EPIC)	THREE HEARTS IN THE HAPPY . . . — DARYL HALL (RCA)
10	DREAMTIME — DARYL HALL (RCA)	5150 — VAN HALEN (WARNER BROS)
11	BABY LOVE — REGINA (ATLANTIC)	THE BRIDGE — BILLY JOEL (COLUMBIA)
12	WALK THIS WAY — RUN DMC (PROFILE)	LIKE A ROCK — BOB SEGER & THE SILVER . . . (CAPITOL)
13	DON'T FORGET ME (WHEN I'M GONE) — GLASS TIGER (MANHATTAN)	LANDING ON WATER — NEIL YOUNG (GEFFEN)
14	RUMORS — TIMEX SOCIAL CLUB (JAY)	BOOMTOWN — DAVID & DAVID (A&M)
15	THROWING IT ALL AWAY — GENESIS (ATLANTIC)	NINE LIVES — BONNIE RAITT (WARNER BROS)
16	LOVE ZONE — BILLY OCEAN (JIVE/ARISTA)	THE SPORT OF KINGS — TRIUMPH (MCA)
17	MAN SIZE LOVE — KLYMAXX (MCA)	WALKABOUT — FIXX (MCA)
18	WHEN I THINK OF YOU — JANET JACKSON (A&M)	LIVE — G. THOROGOOD & DESTROYERS (EMI AMERICA)
19	THE CAPTAIN OF HER HEART — DOUBLE (A&M)	THE THIN RED LINE — GLASS TIGER (MANHATTAN)
20	GLORY OF LOVE — PETER CETERA (FULL MOON/WARNER BROS)	SLIPPERY WHEN WET — BON JOVI (MERCURY/PG)

WEEK ENDING SEPTEMBER 6 1986

SINGLES — UK — ALBUMS

#	Singles	Albums
1	I WANT TO WAKE UP WITH YOU — BORIS GARDINER (REVUE/CREOLE)	NOW, THAT'S WHAT I CALL MUSIC 7 — VARIOUS (VIRGIN/EMI)
2	DON'T LEAVE ME THIS WAY — COMMUNARDS (LONDON)	DANCING ON THE CEILING — LIONEL RICHIE (MOTOWN)
3	WE DON'T HAVE TO TAKE OUR CLOTHES OFF — JERMAINE STEWART (10/VIRGIN)	TRUE BLUE — MADONNA (SIRE)
4	BROTHER LOUIE — MODERN TALKING (RCA)	A KIND OF MAGIC — QUEEN (EMI)
5	GLORY OF LOVE — PETER CETERA (FULL MOON/WARNER BROS)	INTO THE LIGHT — CHRIS DE BURGH (A&M)
6	RAGE HARD — FRANKIE GOES TO HOLLYWOOD (ZTT/ISLAND)	SILK AND STEEL — FIVE STAR (TENT/RCA)
7	SO MACHO — SINITTA (FANFARE)	IN THE ARMY NOW — STATUS QUO (VERTIGO/PHONOGRAM)
8	HUMAN — HUMAN LEAGUE (VIRGIN)	PICTURE BOOK — SIMPLY RED (ELEKTRA)
9	THE LADY IN RED — CHRIS DE BURGH (A&M)	REVENGE — EURYTHMICS (RCA)
10	WHEN I THINK OF YOU — JANET JACKSON (A&M)	THE HEAT IS ON — VARIOUS (PORTRAIT)
11	AIN'T NOTHIN' GOIN' ON BUT THE RENT — GWEN GUTHRIE (BOILING POINT/POLYDOR)	THE FINAL — WHAM! (EPIC)
12	DANCING ON THE CEILING — LIONEL RICHIE (MOTOWN)	INVISIBLE TOUCH — GENESIS (CHARISMA/VIRGIN)
13	GIRLS AND BOYS — PRINCE AND THE REVOLUTION (PAISLEY PARK)	WHILE THE CITY SLEEPS . . . — GEORGE BENSON (WARNER BROS)
14	(I JUST) DIED IN YOUR ARMS — CUTTING CREW (SIREN/VIRGIN)	BROTHERS IN ARMS — DIRE STRAITS (VERTIGO/PHONOGRAM)
15	THE WAY IT IS — BRUCE HORNSBY AND THE RANGE (RCA)	RENDEZ-VOUS — JEAN-MICHEL JARRE (DREYFUS/POLYDOR)
16	LOVE CAN'T TURN AROUND — F. 'JACKMASTER' FUNK (CHICAGO/LONDON)	COMMUNARDS — COMMUNARDS (LONDON)
17	ANYONE CAN FALL IN LOVE — ANITA DOBSON/SIMON MAY ORCH (BBC)	CONTROL — JANET JACKSON (A&M)
18	CALLING ALL THE HEROES — IT BITES (VIRGIN)	RIPTIDE — ROBERT PALMER (ISLAND)
19	I CAN PROVE IT — PHIL FEARON (ENSIGN/CHRYSALIS)	PARADE — PRINCE AND THE REVOLUTION (PAISLEY PARK)
20	A QUESTION OF TIME (REMIX) — DEPECHE MODE (MUTE)	HUNTING HIGH AND LOW — A-HA (WARNER BROS)

SINGLES — US — ALBUMS

#	Singles	Albums
1	DANCING ON THE CEILING — LIONEL RICHIE (MOTOWN)	BACK IN THE HIGH LIFE — STEVE WINWOOD (ISLAND)
2	STUCK WITH YOU — HUEY LEWIS AND THE NEWS (CHRYSALIS)	FORE! — HUEY LEWIS AND THE NEWS (CHRYSALIS)
3	TAKE MY BREATH AWAY — BERLIN (COLUMBIA)	INVISIBLE TOUCH — GENESIS (ATLANTIC)
4	HIGHER LOVE — STEVE WINWOOD (ISLAND)	SO — PETER GABRIEL (GEFFEN)
5	FRIENDS AND LOVERS — C. ANDERSON/G. LORING (CARRERE/CBS)	CAN'T HOLD BACK — EDDIE MONEY (COLUMBIA)
6	VENUS — BANANARAMA (LONDON/PG)	LIFES RICH PAGEANT — REM (IRS/MCA)
7	DREAMTIME — DARYL HALL (RCA)	EAT 'EM AND SMILE — DAVID LEE ROTH (WARNER BROS)
8	SWEET FREEDOM — MICHAEL McDONALD (MCA)	REVENGE — EURYTHMICS (RCA)
9	WORDS GET IN THE WAY — MIAMI SOUND MACHINE (EPIC)	LIKE A ROCK — BOB SEGER & THE SILVER . . . (CAPITOL)
10	BABY LOVE — REGINA (ATLANTIC)	THE BRIDGE — BILLY JOEL (COLUMBIA)
11	WALK THIS WAY — RUN DMC (PROFILE)	THE SPORT OF KINGS — TRIUMPH (MCA)
12	DON'T FORGET ME (WHEN I'M GONE) — GLASS TIGER (MANHATTAN)	THREE HEARTS IN THE HAPPY . . . — DARYL HALL (RCA)
13	THROWING IT ALL AWAY — GENESIS (ATLANTIC)	BOOMTOWN — DAVID & DAVID (A&M)
14	LOVE ZONE — BILLY OCEAN (JIVE/ARISTA)	NINE LIVES — BONNIE RAITT (WARNER BROS)
15	WHEN I THINK OF YOU — JANET JACKSON (A&M)	5150 — VAN HALEN (WARNER BROS)
16	HEAVEN IN YOUR EYES — LOVERBOY (COLUMBIA)	LIVE — G. THOROGOOD & DESTROYERS (EMI AMERICA)
17	RUMORS — TIMEX SOCIAL CLUB (JAY)	LANDING ON WATER — NEIL YOUNG (GEFFEN)
18	THE CAPTAIN OF HER HEART — DOUBLE (A&M)	SLIPPERY WHEN WET — BON JOVI (MERCURY/PG)
19	PAPA DON'T PREACH — MADONNA (SIRE/WARNER BROS)	TUFF ENUFF — FABULOUS THUNDERBIRDS (CBS ASSOCIATED)
20	TWO OF HEARTS — STACEY Q (ATLANTIC)	MEASURE FOR MEASURE — ICEHOUSE (CHRYSALIS)

WEEK ENDING SEPTEMBER 13 1986
S I N G L E S UK A L B U M S

#	SINGLES	ALBUMS
1	DON'T LEAVE ME THIS WAY — COMMUNARDS (LONDON)	NOW, THAT'S WHAT I CALL MUSIC 7 — VARIOUS (VIRGIN/EMI)
2	I WANT TO WAKE UP WITH YOU — BORIS GARDINER (REVUE/CREOLE)	DANCING ON THE CEILING — LIONEL RICHIE (MOTOWN)
3	WE DON'T HAVE TO TAKE OUR CLOTHES OFF — JERMAINE STEWART (10/VIRGIN)	SILK AND STEEL — FIVE STAR (TENT/RCA)
4	RAGE HARD — FRANKIE GOES TO HOLLYWOOD (ZTT/ISLAND)	GRACELAND — PAUL SIMON (WARNER BROS)
5	GLORY OF LOVE — PETER CETERA (FULL MOON/WARNER BROS)	TRUE BLUE — MADONNA (SIRE)
6	HOLIDAY RAP — M.C. MIKER 'G' & DEEJAY SVEN (DEBUT)	A KIND OF MAGIC — QUEEN (EMI)
7	BROTHER LOUIE — MODERN TALKING (RCA)	REVENGE — EURYTHMICS (RCA)
8	(I JUST) DIED IN YOUR ARMS — CUTTING CREW (SIREN/VIRGIN)	PRESS TO PLAY — PAUL McCARTNEY (MPL/PARLOPHONE)
9	SO MACHO — SINITTA (FANFARE)	INTO THE LIGHT — CHRIS DE BURGH (A&M)
10	HUMAN — HUMAN LEAGUE (VIRGIN)	THE HEAT IS ON — VARIOUS (PORTRAIT)
11	LOVE CAN'T TURN AROUND — F. 'JACKMASTER' FUNK (CHICAGO/LONDON)	IN THE ARMY NOW — STATUS QUO (VERTIGO/PHONOGRAM)
12	WHEN I THINK OF YOU — JANET JACKSON (A&M)	PICTURE BOOK — SIMPLY RED (ELEKTRA)
13	WORD UP — CAMEO (CLUB/PHONOGRAM)	WHILE THE CITY SLEEPS … — GEORGE BENSON (WARNER BROS)
14	YOU GIVE LOVE A BAD NAME — BON JOVI (VERTIGO/PHONOGRAM)	COMMUNARDS — COMMUNARDS (LONDON)
15	WALK THIS WAY — RUN DMC (LONDON)	CONTROL — JANET JACKSON (A&M)
16	THORN IN MY SIDE — EURYTHMICS (RCA)	INVISIBLE TOUCH — GENESIS (CHARISMA/VIRGIN)
17	THE WAY IT IS — BRUCE HORNSBY AND THE RANGE (RCA)	THE WAY IT IS — BRUCE HORNSBY AND THE RANGE (RCA)
18	WASTED YEARS — IRON MAIDEN (EMI)	BROTHERS IN ARMS — DIRE STRAITS (VERTIGO/PHONOGRAM)
19	THE LADY IN RED — CHRIS DE BURGH (A&M)	THE FINAL — WHAM! (EPIC)
20	AIN'T NOTHIN' GOIN' ON BUT THE RENT — GWEN GUTHRIE (BOILING POINT/POLYDOR)	RENDEZ-VOUS — JEAN-MICHEL JARRE (DREYFUS/POLYDOR)

S I N G L E S US A L B U M S

#	SINGLES	ALBUMS
1	STUCK WITH YOU — HUEY LEWIS AND THE NEWS (CHRYSALIS)	FORE! — HUEY LEWIS AND THE NEWS (CHRYSALIS)
2	DANCING ON THE CEILING — LIONEL RICHIE (MOTOWN)	BACK IN THE HIGH LIFE — STEVE WINWOOD (ISLAND)
3	FRIENDS AND LOVERS — C. ANDERSON/G. LORING (CARRERE/CBS)	INVISIBLE TOUCH — GENESIS (ATLANTIC)
4	TAKE MY BREATH AWAY — BERLIN (COLUMBIA)	SO — PETER GABRIEL (GEFFEN)
5	DREAMTIME — DARYL HALL (RCA)	CAN'T HOLD BACK — EDDIE MONEY (COLUMBIA)
6	THROWING IT ALL AWAY — GENESIS (ATLANTIC)	LIFES RICH PAGEANT — REM (IRS/MCA)
7	DON'T FORGET ME (WHEN I'M GONE) — GLASS TIGER (MANHATTAN)	EAT 'EM AND SMILE — DAVID LEE ROTH (WARNER BROS)
8	WHEN I THINK OF YOU — JANET JACKSON (A&M)	BOOMTOWN — DAVID & DAVID (A&M)
9	HIGHER LOVE — STEVE WINWOOD (ISLAND)	LIKE A ROCK — BOB SEGER & THE SILVER … (CAPITOL)
10	WALK THIS WAY — RUN DMC (PROFILE)	THE SPORT OF KINGS — TRIUMPH (MCA)
11	LOVE ZONE — BILLY OCEAN (JIVE/ARISTA)	THE BRIDGE — BILLY JOEL (COLUMBIA)
12	BABY LOVE — REGINA (ATLANTIC)	NINE LIVES — BONNIE RAITT (WARNER BROS)
13	HEAVEN IN YOUR EYES — LOVERBOY (COLUMBIA)	REVENGE — EURYTHMICS (RCA)
14	WORDS GET IN THE WAY — MIAMI SOUND MACHINE (EPIC)	SLIPPERY WHEN WET — BON JOVI (MERCURY/PG)
15	TWO OF HEARTS — STACEY Q (ATLANTIC)	MEASURE FOR MEASURE — ICEHOUSE (CHRYSALIS)
16	HEARTBEAT — DON JOHNSON (EPIC)	TUFF ENUFF — FABULOUS THUNDERBIRDS (CBS ASSOCIATED)
17	TYPICAL MALE — TINA TURNER (CAPITOL)	ESPECIALLY FOR YOU — SMITHEREENS (ENIGMA)
18	LOVE WALKS IN — VAN HALEN (WARNER BROS)	THREE HEARTS IN THE HAPPY … — DARYL HALL (RCA)
19	VENUS — BANANARAMA (LONDON/PG)	THE WAY IT IS — BRUCE HORNSBY & THE RANGE (RCA)
20	SWEET FREEDOM — MICHAEL McDONALD (MCA)	LIVE — G. THOROGOOD & DESTROYERS (EMI AMERICA)

WEEK ENDING SEPTEMBER 20 1986
S I N G L E S UK A L B U M S

#	SINGLES	ALBUMS
1	DON'T LEAVE ME THIS WAY — COMMUNARDS (LONDON)	NOW, THAT'S WHAT I CALL MUSIC 7 — VARIOUS (VIRGIN/EMI)
2	WE DON'T HAVE TO TAKE OUR CLOTHES OFF — JERMAINE STEWART (10/VIRGIN)	BREAK EVERY RULE — TINA TURNER (CAPITOL)
3	GLORY OF LOVE — PETER CETERA (FULL MOON/WARNER BROS)	REVENGE — EURYTHMICS (RCA)
4	(I JUST) DIED IN YOUR ARMS — CUTTING CREW (SIREN/VIRGIN)	GRACELAND — PAUL SIMON (WARNER BROS)
5	I WANT TO WAKE UP WITH YOU — BORIS GARDINER (REVUE/CREOLE)	SILK AND STEEL — FIVE STAR (TENT/RCA)
6	WORD UP — CAMEO (CLUB/PHONOGRAM)	TRUE BLUE — MADONNA (SIRE)
7	RAGE HARD — FRANKIE GOES TO HOLLYWOOD (ZTT/ISLAND)	CRASH — HUMAN LEAGUE (VIRGIN)
8	HOLIDAY RAP — M.C. MIKER 'G' & DEEJAY SVEN (DEBUT)	SLIPPERY WHEN WET — BON JOVI (VERTIGO/PHONOGRAM)
9	WALK THIS WAY — RUN DMC (LONDON)	A KIND OF MAGIC — QUEEN (EMI)
10	THORN IN MY SIDE — EURYTHMICS (RCA)	DANCING ON THE CEILING — LIONEL RICHIE (MOTOWN)
11	LOVE CAN'T TURN AROUND — F. 'JACKMASTER' FUNK (CHICAGO/LONDON)	FORE! — HUEY LEWIS AND THE NEWS (CHRYSALIS)
12	BROTHER LOUIE — MODERN TALKING (RCA)	COMMUNARDS — COMMUNARDS (LONDON)
13	RAIN OR SHINE — FIVE STAR (TENT/RCA)	THE HEAT IS ON — VARIOUS (PORTRAIT)
14	SO MACHO — SINITTA (FANFARE)	INTO THE LIGHT — CHRIS DE BURGH (A&M)
15	YOU GIVE LOVE A BAD NAME — BON JOVI (VERTIGO/PHONOGRAM)	PICTURE BOOK — SIMPLY RED (ELEKTRA)
16	HUMAN — HUMAN LEAGUE (VIRGIN)	THE WAY IT IS — BRUCE HORNSBY AND THE RANGE (RCA)
17	SWEET FREEDOM — MICHAEL McDONALD (MCA)	BROTHERS IN ARMS — DIRE STRAITS (VERTIGO/PHONOGRAM)
18	PRETTY IN PINK — PSYCHEDELIC FURS (CBS)	INVISIBLE TOUCH — GENESIS (CHARISMA/VIRGIN)
19	WHEN I THINK OF YOU — JANET JACKSON (A&M)	WHILE THE CITY SLEEPS … — GEORGE BENSON (WARNER BROS)
20	RUMORS — TIMEX SOCIAL CLUB (COOLTEMPO/CHRYSALIS)	PRESS TO PLAY — PAUL McCARTNEY (MPL/PARLOPHONE)

S I N G L E S US A L B U M S

#	SINGLES	ALBUMS
1	STUCK WITH YOU — HUEY LEWIS AND THE NEWS (CHRYSALIS)	FORE! — HUEY LEWIS AND THE NEWS (CHRYSALIS)
2	THROWING IT ALL AWAY — GENESIS (ATLANTIC)	BACK IN THE HIGH LIFE — STEVE WINWOOD (ISLAND)
3	DREAMTIME — DARYL HAL (RCA)	EYE OF THE ZOMBIE — JOHN FOGERTY (WARNER BROS)
4	FRIENDS AND LOVERS — C. ANDERSON/G. LORING (CARRERE/CBS)	THIS SIDE OF PARADISE — RIC OCASEK (GEFFEN)
5	WHEN I THINK OF YOU — JANET JACKSON (A&M)	CAN'T HOLD BACK — EDDIE MONEY (COLUMBIA)
6	DON'T FORGET ME (WHEN I'M GONE) — GLASS TIGER (MANHATTAN)	TRUE STORIES — TALKING HEADS (SIRE/WARNER BROS)
7	DANCING ON THE CEILING — LIONEL RICHIE (MOTOWN)	SO — PETER GABRIEL (GEFFEN)
8	HEAVEN IN YOUR EYES — LOVERBOY (COLUMBIA)	INVISIBLE TOUCH — GENESIS (ATLANTIC)
9	LOVE ZONE — BILLY OCEAN (JIVE/ARISTA)	LIFES RICH PAGEANT — REM (IRS/MCA)
10	TWO OF HEARTS — STACEY Q (ATLANTIC)	BOOMTOWN — DAVID & DAVID (A&M)
11	HEARTBEAT — DON JOHNSON (EPIC)	THE SPORT OF KINGS — TRIUMPH (MCA)
12	TYPICAL MALE — TINA TURNER (CAPITOL)	EAT 'EM AND SMILE — DAVID LEE ROTH (WARNER BROS)
13	WALK THIS WAY — RUN DMC (PROFILE)	THE BRIDGE — BILLY JOEL (COLUMBIA)
14	TRUE COLORS — CYNDI LAUPER (PORTRAIT/CBS)	SLIPPERY WHEN WET — BON JOVI (MERCURY/PG)
15	LOVE WALKS IN — VAN HALEN (WARNER BROS)	NINE LIVES — BONNIE RAITT (WARNER BROS)
16	TAKE MY BREATH AWAY — BERLIN (COLUMBIA)	LIKE A ROCK — BOB SEGER & THE SILVER … (CAPITOL)
17	I DIDN'T MEAN TO TURN YOU ON — ROBERT PALMER (ISLAND)	ESPECIALLY FOR YOU — SMITHEREENS (ENIGMA)
18	HIGHER LOVE — STEVE WINWOOD (ISLAND)	THE WAY IT IS — BRUCE HORNSBY & THE RANGE (RCA)
19	MISSIONARY MAN — EURYTHMICS (RCA)	MEASURE FOR MEASURE — ICEHOUSE (CHRYSALIS)
20	BABY LOVE — REGINA (ATLANTIC)	TUFF ENUFF — FABULOUS THUNDERBIRDS (CBS ASSOCIATED)

WEEK ENDING SEPTEMBER 27 1986

S I N G L E S   UK   A L B U M S

#	Singles	Albums
1	DON'T LEAVE ME THIS WAY — COMMUNARDS (LONDON)	SILK AND STEEL — FIVE STAR (TENT/RCA)
2	WE DON'T HAVE TO TAKE OUR CLOTHES OFF — JERMAINE STEWART (10/VIRGIN)	NOW, THAT'S WHAT I CALL MUSIC 7 — VARIOUS (VIRGIN/EMI)
3	WORD UP — CAMEO (CLUB/PHONOGRAM)	GRACELAND — PAUL SIMON (WARNER BROS)
4	RAIN OR SHINE — FIVE STAR (TENT/RCA)	REVENGE — EURYTHMICS (RCA)
5	(I JUST) DIED IN YOUR ARMS — CUTTING CREW (SIREN/VIRGIN)	BREAK EVERY RULE — TINA TURNER (CAPITOL)
6	GLORY OF LOVE — PETER CETERA (FULL MOON/WARNER BROS)	TRUE BLUE — MADONNA (SIRE)
7	THORN IN MY SIDE — EURYTHMICS (RCA)	TRUE STORIES — TALKING HEADS (EMI)
8	WALK THIS WAY — RUN DMC (LONDON)	FORE! — HUEY LEWIS AND THE NEWS (CHRYSALIS)
9	I WANT TO WAKE UP WITH YOU — BORIS GARDINER (REVUE/CREOLE)	COMMUNARDS — COMMUNARDS (LONDON)
10	LOVE CAN'T TURN AROUND — F. 'JACKMASTER' FUNK (CHICAGO/LONDON)	A KIND OF MAGIC — QUEEN (EMI)
11	HOLIDAY RAP — M.C. MIKER 'G' & DEEJAY SVEN (DEBUT)	DANCING ON THE CEILING — LIONEL RICHIE (MOTOWN)
12	SWEET FREEDOM — MICHAEL McDONALD (MCA)	INTO THE LIGHT — CHRIS DE BURGH (A&M)
13	RUMORS — TIMEX SOCIAL CLUB (COOLTEMPO/CHRYSALIS)	SLIPPERY WHEN WET — BON JOVI (VERTIGO/PHONOGRAM)
14	(FOREVER) LIVE AND DIE — ORCH. MANOEUVRES IN THE DARK (VIRGIN)	CRASH — HUMAN LEAGUE (VIRGIN)
15	STUCK WITH YOU — HUEY LEWIS AND THE NEWS (CHRYSALIS)	THE HEAT IS ON — VARIOUS (PORTRAIT)
16	RAGE HARD — FRANKIE GOES TO HOLLYWOOD (ZTT/ISLAND)	BLOOD & CHOCOLATES — E. COSTELLO & THE ATTRACTIONS (IMP DEMON)
17	BROTHER LOUIE — MODERN TALKING (RCA)	INVISIBLE TOUCH — GENESIS (CHARISMA/VIRGIN)
18	PRETTY IN PINK — PSYCHEDELIC FURS (CBS)	THE WAY IT IS — BRUCE HORNSBY AND THE RANGE (RCA)
19	ONE GREAT THING — BIG COUNTRY (MERCURY/PHONOGRAM)	BROTHERS IN ARMS — DIRE STRAITS (VERTIGO/PHONOGRAM)
20	YOU GIVE LOVE A BAD NAME — BON JOVI (VERTIGO/PHONOGRAM)	PICTURE BOOK — SIMPLY RED (ELEKTRA)

S I N G L E S   US   A L B U M S

#	Singles	Albums
1	STUCK WITH YOU — HUEY LEWIS AND THE NEWS (CHRYSALIS)	FORE! — HUEY LEWIS AND THE NEWS (CHRYSALIS)
2	THROWING IT ALL AWAY — GENESIS (ATLANTIC)	BACK IN THE HIGH LIFE — STEVE WINWOOD (ISLAND)
3	WHEN I THINK OF YOU — JANET JACKSON (A&M)	EYE OF THE ZOMBIE — JOHN FOGERTY (WARNER BROS)
4	DREAMTIME — DARYL HALL (RCA)	THIS SIDE OF PARADISE — RIC OCASEK (GEFFEN)
5	DON'T FORGET ME (WHEN I'M GONE) — GLASS TIGER (MANHATTAN)	CAN'T HOLD BACK — EDDIE MONEY (COLUMBIA)
6	TYPICAL MALE — TINA TURNER (CAPITOL)	TRUE STORIES — TALKING HEADS (SIRE/WARNER BROS)
7	HEARTBEAT — DON JOHNSON (EPIC)	BOOMTOWN — DAVID & DAVID (A&M)
8	HEAVEN IN YOUR EYES — LOVERBOY (COLUMBIA)	LIFES RICH PAGEANT — REM (IRS/MCA)
9	TRUE COLORS — CYNDI LAUPER (PORTRAIT/CBS)	SO — PETER GABRIEL (GEFFEN)
10	TWO OF HEARTS — STACEY Q (ATLANTIC)	INVISIBLE TOUCH — GENESIS (ATLANTIC)
11	FRIENDS AND LOVERS — C. ANDERSON/G. LORING (CARRERE/CBS)	THE SPORT OF KINGS — TRIUMPH (MCA)
12	I DIDN'T MEAN TO TURN YOU ON — ROBERT PALMER (ISLAND)	EAT 'EM AND SMILE — DAVID LEE ROTH (WARNER BROS)
13	LOVE ZONE — BILLY OCEAN (JIVE/ARISTA)	SLIPPERY WHEN WET — BON JOVI (MERCURY/PG)
14	LOVE WALKS IN — VAN HALEN (WARNER BROS)	THE WAY IT IS — BRUCE HORNSBY & THE RANGE (RCA)
15	DANCING ON THE CEILING — LIONEL RICHIE (MOTOWN)	ESPECIALLY FOR YOU — SMITHEREENS (ENIGMA)
16	MISSIONARY MAN — EURYTHMICS (RCA)	THE BRIDGE — BILLY JOEL (COLUMBIA)
17	SWEET LOVE — ANITA BAKER (ELEKTRA)	BREAK EVERY RULE — TINA TURNER (CAPITOL)
18	A MATTER OF TRUST — BILLY JOEL (COLUMBIA)	GREETINGS FROM TIMBUK3 — TIMBUK3 (IRS/MCA)
19	WALK THIS WAY — RUN DMC (PROFILE)	LANDING ON WATER — NEIL YOUNG (GEFFEN)
20	ALL CRIED OUT — LISA LISA & CULT JAM & FULL FORCE (COLUMBIA)	DEEP END — PETE TOWNSHEND (ATCO)

WEEK ENDING OCTOBER 4 1986

S I N G L E S   UK   A L B U M S

#	Singles	Albums
1	DON'T LEAVE ME THIS WAY — COMMUNARDS (LONDON)	GRACELAND — PAUL SIMON (WARNER BROS)
2	RAIN OR SHINE — FIVE STAR (TENT/RCA)	SILK AND STEEL — FIVE STAR (TENT/RCA)
3	TRUE BLUE — MADONNA (SIRE)	REVENGE — EURYTHMICS (RCA)
4	WORD UP — CAMEO (CLUB/PHONOGRAM)	NOW, THAT'S WHAT I CALL MUSIC 7 — VARIOUS (VIRGIN/EMI)
5	THORN IN MY SIDE — EURYTHMICS (RCA)	TRUE BLUE — MADONNA (SIRE)
6	WE DON'T HAVE TO TAKE OUR CLOTHES OFF — JERMAINE STEWART (10/VIRGIN)	BREAK EVERY RULE — TINA TURNER (CAPITOL)
7	(I JUST) DIED IN YOUR ARMS — CUTTING CREW (SIREN/VIRGIN)	COMMUNARDS — COMMUNARDS (LONDON)
8	WALK THIS WAY — RUN DMC (LONDON)	TALKING WITH THE TAXMAN ABOUT POETRY — BILLY BRAGG (GO! DISCS)
9	YOU CAN CALL ME AL — PAUL SIMON (WARNER BROS)	TRUE STORIES — TALKING HEADS (EMI)
10	GLORY OF LOVE — PETER CETERA (FULL MOON/WARNER BROS)	FORE! — HUEY LEWIS AND THE NEWS (CHRYSALIS)
11	(FOREVER) LIVE AND DIE — ORCH. MANOEUVRES IN THE DARK (VIRGIN)	A KIND OF MAGIC — QUEEN (EMI)
12	STUCK WITH YOU — HUEY LEWIS AND THE NEWS (CHRYSALIS)	INTO THE LIGHT — CHRIS DE BURGH (A&M)
13	LOVE CAN'T TURN AROUND — F. 'JACKMASTER' FUNK (CHICAGO/LONDON)	INVISIBLE TOUCH — GENESIS (CHARISMA/VIRGIN)
14	I'VE BEEN LOSING YOU — A-HA (WARNER BROS)	DANCING ON THE CEILING — LIONEL RICHIE (MOTOWN)
15	ALWAYS THERE — MARTI WEBB/SIMON MAY ORCH (BBC)	BROTHERS IN ARMS — DIRE STRAITS (VERTIGO/PHONOGRAM)
16	RUMORS — TIMEX SOCIAL CLUB (COOLTEMPO/CHRYSALIS)	THE HEAT IS ON — VARIOUS (PORTRAIT)
17	SWEET FREEDOM — MICHAEL McDONALD (MCA)	PICTURE BOOK — SIMPLY RED (ELEKTRA)
18	MONTEGO BAY — AMAZULU (ISLAND)	SLIPPERY WHEN WET — BON JOVI (VERTIGO/PHONOGRAM)
19	IN TOO DEEP — GENESIS (VIRGIN)	HUNTING HIGH AND LOW — A-HA (WARNER BROS)
20	I WANT TO WAKE UP WITH YOU — BORIS GARDINER (REVUE/CREOLE)	IN THE ARMY NOW — STATUS QUO (VERTIGO/PHONOGRAM)

S I N G L E S   US   A L B U M S

#	Singles	Albums
1	THROWING IT ALL AWAY — GENESIS (ATLANTIC)	THIRD STAGE — BOSTON (MCA)
2	WHEN I THINK OF YOU — JANET JACKSON (A&M)	FORE! — HUEY LEWIS AND THE NEWS (CHRYSALIS)
3	STUCK WITH YOU — HUEY LEWIS AND THE NEWS (CHRYSALIS)	BACK IN THE HIGH LIFE — STEVE WINWOOD (ISLAND)
4	TYPICAL MALE — TINA TURNER (CAPITOL)	THIS SIDE OF PARADISE — RIC OCASEK (GEFFEN)
5	TRUE COLORS — CYNDI LAUPER (PORTRAIT/CBS)	EYE OF THE ZOMBIE — JOHN FOGERTY (WARNER BROS)
6	HEARTBEAT — DON JOHNSON (EPIC)	TRUE STORIES — TALKING HEADS (SIRE/WARNER BROS)
7	I DIDN'T MEAN TO TURN YOU ON — ROBERT PALMER (ISLAND)	CAN'T HOLD BACK — EDDIE MONEY (COLUMBIA)
8	DON'T FORGET ME (WHEN I'M GONE) — GLASS TIGER (MANHATTAN)	BOOMTOWN — DAVID & DAVID (A&M)
9	HEAVEN IN YOUR EYES — LOVERBOY (COLUMBIA)	SO — PETER GABRIEL (GEFFEN)
10	TWO OF HEARTS — STACEY Q (ATLANTIC)	SLIPPERY WHEN WET — BON JOVI (MERCURY/PG)
11	DREAMTIME — DARYL HALL (RCA)	THE WAY IT IS — BRUCE HORNSBY & THE RANGE (RCA)
12	SWEET LOVE — ANITA BAKER (ELEKTRA)	LIFES RICH PAGEANT — REM (IRS/MCA)
13	ALL CRIED OUT — LISA LISA & CULT JAM & FULL FORCE (COLUMBIA)	THE SPORT OF KINGS — TRIUMPH (MCA)
14	LOVE WALKS IN — VAN HALEN (WARNER BROS)	EAT 'EM AND SMILE — DAVID LEE ROTH (WARNER BROS)
15	HUMAN — HUMAN LEAGUE (VIRGIN/A&M)	INVISIBLE TOUCH — GENESIS (ATLANTIC)
16	A MATTER OF TRUST — BILLY JOEL (COLUMBIA)	WELCOME HOME — 'TIL TUESDAY (EPIC)
17	TAKE ME HOME TONIGHT — EDDIE MONEY (COLUMBIA)	BREAK EVERY RULE — TINA TURNER (CAPITOL)
18	GIRL CAN'T HELP IT — JOURNEY (COLUMBIA)	GREETINGS FROM TIMBUK3 — TIMBUK3 (IRS/MCA)
19	MISSIONARY MAN — EURYTHMICS (RCA)	ESPECIALLY FOR YOU — SMITHEREENS (ENIGMA)
20	AMANDA — BOSTON (MCA)	FAME AND FORTUNE — BAD COMPANY (ATLANTIC)

WEEK ENDING OCTOBER 11 1986

S I N G L E S UK A L B U M S

TRUE BLUE MADONNA (SIRE)	**1**	GRACELAND PAUL SIMON (WARNER BROS)
RAIN OR SHINE FIVE STAR (TENT/RCA)	**2**	SILK AND STEEL FIVE STAR (TENT/RCA)
DON'T LEAVE ME THIS WAY COMMUNARDS (LONDON)	**3**	SOMEWHERE IN TIME IRON MAIDEN (EMI)
EVERY LOSER WINS NICK BERRY (BBC)	**4**	TRUE BLUE MADONNA (SIRE)
YOU CAN CALL ME AL PAUL SIMON (WARNER BROS)	**5**	REVENGE EURYTHMICS (RCA)
WORD UP CAMEO (CLUB/PHONOGRAM)	**6**	SOUTH PACIFIC K. TE KANAWA, J. CARRERAS, S. VAUGHAN (CBS)
THORN IN MY SIDE EURYTHMICS (RCA)	**7**	NOW, THAT'S WHAT I CALL MUSIC 7 VARIOUS (VIRGIN/EMI)
I'VE BEEN LOSING YOU A-HA (WARNER BROS)	**8**	COMMUNARDS COMMUNARDS (LONDON)
IN THE ARMY NOW STATUS QUO (VERTIGO/PHONOGRAM)	**9**	BROTHERHOOD NEW ORDER (FACTORY)
SUBURBIA PET SHOP BOYS (PARLOPHONE)	**10**	BREAK EVERY RULE TINA TURNER (CAPITOL)
WE DON'T HAVE TO TAKE OUR CLOTHES OFF JERMAINE STEWART (10/VIRGIN)	**11**	A KIND OF MAGIC QUEEN (EMI)
(FOREVER) LIVE AND DIE ORCH. MANOEUVRES IN THE DARK (VIRGIN)	**12**	INTO THE LIGHT CHRIS DE BURGH (A&M)
WALK THIS WAY RUN DMC (LONDON)	**13**	FORE! HUEY LEWIS AND THE NEWS (CHRYSALIS)
(I JUST) DIED IN YOUR ARMS CUTTING CREW (SIREN/VIRGIN)	**14**	TALKING WITH THE TAXMAN ABOUT POETRY BILLY BRAGG (GO! DISCS)
STUCK WITH YOU HUEY LEWIS AND THE NEWS (CHRYSALIS)	**15**	THE PACIFIC AGE ORCH. MANOEUVRES IN THE DARK (VIRGIN)
MONTEGO BAY AMAZULU (ISLAND)	**16**	TRUE STORIES TALKING HEADS (EMI)
ALWAYS THERE MARTI WEBB/SIMON MAY ORCH (BBC)	**17**	BROTHERS IN ARMS DIRE STRAITS (VERTIGO/PHONOGRAM)
TRUE COLORS CYNDI LAUPER (PORTRAIT)	**18**	INVISIBLE TOUCH GENESIS (CHARISMA/VIRGIN)
ALL I ASK OF YOU CLIFF RICHARD & SARAH BRIGHTMAN (POLYDOR)	**19**	DANCING ON THE CEILING LIONEL RICHIE (MOTOWN)
WALK LIKE AN EGYPTIAN BANGLES (CBS)	**20**	STREET SOUND EDITION 18 VARIOUS (STREET SOUNDS)

S I N G L E S US A L B U M S

WHEN I THINK OF YOU JANET JACKSON (A&M)	**1**	THIRD STAGE BOSTON (MCA)
THROWING IT ALL AWAY GENESIS (ATLANTIC)	**2**	FORE! HUEY LEWIS AND THE NEWS (CHRYSALIS)
TYPICAL MALE TINA TURNER (CAPITOL)	**3**	THIS SIDE OF PARADISE RIC OCASEK (GEFFEN)
TRUE COLORS CYNDI LAUPER (PORTRAIT/CBS)	**4**	BACK IN THE HIGH LIFE STEVE WINWOOD (ISLAND)
I DIDN'T MEAN TO TURN YOU ON ROBERT PALMER (ISLAND)	**5**	EYE OF THE ZOMBIE JOHN FOGERTY (WARNER BROS)
HEARTBEAT DON JOHNSON (EPIC)	**6**	TRUE STORIES TALKING HEADS (SIRE/WARNER BROS)
HUMAN HUMAN LEAGUE (VIRGIN/A&M)	**7**	BOOMTOWN DAVID & DAVID (A&M)
AMANDA BOSTON (MCA)	**8**	THE WAY IT IS BRUCE HORNSBY & THE RANGE (RCA)
SWEET LOVE ANITA BAKER (ELEKTRA)	**9**	SLIPPERY WHEN WET BON JOVI (MERCURY/PG)
ALL CRIED OUT LISA LISA & CULT JAM & FULL FORCE (COLUMBIA)	**10**	CAN'T HOLD BACK EDDIE MONEY (COLUMBIA)
STUCK WITH YOU HUEY LEWIS AND THE NEWS (CHRYSALIS)	**11**	SO PETER GABRIEL (GEFFEN)
TAKE ME HOME TONIGHT EDDIE MONEY (COLUMBIA)	**12**	WELCOME HOME 'TIL TUESDAY (EPIC)
DON'T FORGET ME (WHEN I'M GONE) GLASS TIGER (MANHATTAN)	**13**	EAT 'EM AND SMILE DAVID LEE ROTH (WARNER BROS)
TRUE BLUE MADONNA (SIRE/WARNER BROS)	**14**	BREAK EVERY RULE TINA TURNER (CAPITOL)
GIRL CAN'T HELP IT JOURNEY (COLUMBIA)	**15**	FAME AND FORTUNE BAD COMPANY (ATLANTIC)
A MATTER OF TRUST BILLY JOEL (COLUMBIA)	**16**	THE SPORT OF KINGS TRIUMPH (MCA)
TWO OF HEARTS STACEY Q (ATLANTIC)	**17**	GREETINGS FROM TIMBUK3 TIMBUK3 (IRS/MCA)
HEAVEN IN YOUR EYES LOVERBOY (COLUMBIA)	**18**	ENOUGH IS ENOUGH BILLY SQUIER (CAPITOL)
I'LL BE OVER YOU TOTO (COLUMBIA)	**19**	INVISIBLE TOUCH GENESIS (ATLANTIC)
NEXT TIME I FALL PETER CETERA AND AMY GRANT (FULL MOON)	**20**	PLAY DEEP OUTFIELD (COLUMBIA)

WEEK ENDING OCTOBER 18 1986

S I N G L E S UK A L B U M S

EVERY LOSER WINS NICK BERRY (BBC)	**1**	GRACELAND PAUL SIMON (WARNER BROS)
TRUE BLUE MADONNA (SIRE)	**2**	SCOUNDREL DAYS A-HA (WARNER BROS)
RAIN OR SHINE FIVE STAR (TENT/RCA)	**3**	SILK AND STEEL FIVE STAR (TENT/RCA)
YOU CAN CALL ME AL PAUL SIMON (WARNER BROS)	**4**	TRUE BLUE MADONNA (SIRE)
IN THE ARMY NOW STATUS QUO (VERTIGO/PHONOGRAM)	**5**	SOUTH PACIFIC K. TE KANAWA, J. CARRERAS, S. VAUGHAN (CBS)
DON'T LEAVE ME THIS WAY COMMUNARDS (LONDON)	**6**	REVENGE EURYTHMICS (RCA)
ALL I ASK OF YOU CLIFF RICHARD & SARAH BRIGHTMAN (POLYDOR)	**7**	WORD UP CAMEO (CLUB/PHONOGRAM)
SUBURBIA PET SHOP BOYS (PARLOPHONE)	**8**	SOMEWHERE IN TIME IRON MAIDEN (EMI)
WALK LIKE AN EGYPTIAN BANGLES (CBS)	**9**	NOW, THAT'S WHAT I CALL MUSIC 7 VARIOUS (VIRGIN/EMI)
I'VE BEEN LOSING YOU A-HA (WARNER BROS)	**10**	COMMUNARDS COMMUNARDS (LONDON)
THORN IN MY SIDE EURYTHMICS (RCA)	**11**	A KIND OF MAGIC QUEEN (EMI)
WORD UP CAMEO (CLUB/PHONOGRAM)	**12**	THE CHART VARIOUS (TELSTAR)
TRUE COLORS CYNDI LAUPER (PORTRAIT)	**13**	FORE! HUEY LEWIS AND THE NEWS (CHRYSALIS)
ALWAYS THERE MARTI WEBB/SIMON MAY ORCH (BBC)	**14**	INTO THE LIGHT CHRIS DE BURGH (A&M)
(FOREVER) LIVE AND DIE ORCH. MANOEUVRES IN THE DARK (VIRGIN)	**15**	ZAGORA LOOSE ENDS (VIRGIN)
MONTEGO BAY AMAZULU (ISLAND)	**16**	BREAK EVERY RULE TINA TURNER (CAPITOL)
STUCK WITH YOU HUEY LEWIS AND THE NEWS (CHRYSALIS)	**17**	BROTHERS IN ARMS DIRE STRAITS (VERTIGO/PHONOGRAM)
WE DON'T HAVE TO TAKE OUR CLOTHES OFF JERMAINE STEWART (10/VIRGIN)	**18**	LONDON 0 HULL 4 THE HOUSEMARTINS (GO! DISCS)
WALK THIS WAY RUN DMC (LONDON)	**19**	BROTHERHOOD NEW ORDER (FACTORY)
WORLD SHUT YOUR MOUTH JULIAN COPE (ISLAND)	**20**	INVISIBLE TOUCH GENESIS (CHARISMA/VIRGIN)

S I N G L E S US A L B U M S

TYPICAL MALE TINA TURNER (CAPITOL)	**1**	THIRD STAGE BOSTON (MCA)
TRUE COLORS CYNDI LAUPER (PORTRAIT/CBS)	**2**	FORE! HUEY LEWIS AND THE NEWS (CHRYSALIS)
I DIDN'T MEAN TO TURN YOU ON ROBERT PALMER (ISLAND)	**3**	THIS SIDE OF PARADISE RIC OCASEK (GEFFEN)
WHEN I THINK OF YOU JANET JACKSON (A&M)	**4**	BACK IN THE HIGH LIFE STEVE WINWOOD (ISLAND)
AMANDA BOSTON (MCA)	**5**	EYE OF THE ZOMBIE JOHN FOGERTY (WARNER BROS)
HUMAN HUMAN LEAGUE (VIRGIN/A&M)	**6**	TRUE STORIES TALKING HEADS (SIRE/WARNER BROS)
TRUE BLUE MADONNA (SIRE/WARNER BROS)	**7**	THE WAY IT IS BRUCE HORNSBY & THE RANGE (RCA)
SWEET LOVE ANITA BAKER (ELEKTRA)	**8**	SLIPPERY WHEN WET BON JOVI (MERCURY/PG)
ALL CRIED OUT LISA LISA & CULT JAM & FULL FORCE (COLUMBIA)	**9**	BOOMTOWN DAVID & DAVID (A&M)
TAKE ME HOME TONIGHT EDDIE MONEY (COLUMBIA)	**10**	WELCOME HOME 'TIL TUESDAY (EPIC)
THROWING IT ALL AWAY GENESIS (ATLANTIC)	**11**	SO PETER GABRIEL (GEFFEN)
HEARTBEAT DON JOHNSON (EPIC)	**12**	CAN'T HOLD BACK EDDIE MONEY (COLUMBIA)
I'LL BE OVER YOU TOTO (COLUMBIA)	**13**	FAME AND FORTUNE BAD COMPANY (ATLANTIC)
GIRL CAN'T HELP IT JOURNEY (COLUMBIA)	**14**	BREAK EVERY RULE TINA TURNER (CAPITOL)
NEXT TIME I FALL PETER CETERA AND AMY GRANT (FULL MOON)	**15**	KBC BAND KBC BAND (ARISTA)
YOU GIVE LOVE A BAD NAME BON JOVI (MERCURY/PG)	**16**	GREETINGS FROM TIMBUK3 TIMBUCK3 (IRS/MCA)
A MATTER OF TRUST BILLY JOEL (COLUMBIA)	**17**	ENOUGH IS ENOUGH BILLY SQUIER (CAPITOL)
THE RAIN ORAN 'JUICE' JONES (DEF JAM/COLUMBIA)	**18**	INVISIBLE TOUCH GENESIS (ATLANTIC)
IN YOUR EYES PETER GABRIEL (GEFFEN)	**19**	THE SPORT OF KINGS TRIUMPH (MCA)
WORD UP CAMEO (ATLANTA ARTISTS/PG)	**20**	GEORGIA SATELLITES GEORGIA SATELLITES (ELEKTRA)

WEEK ENDING OCTOBER 25 1986

S I N G L E S UK A L B U M S

#	SINGLES	ALBUMS
1	EVERY LOSER WINS — NICK BERRY (BBC)	GRACELAND — PAUL SIMON (WARNER BROS)
2	TRUE BLUE — MADONNA (SIRE)	SCOUNDREL DAYS — A-HA (WARNER BROS)
3	ALL I ASK OF YOU — CLIFF RICHARD & SARAH BRIGHTMAN (POLYDOR)	SILK AND STEEL — FIVE STAR (TENT/RCA)
4	IN THE ARMY NOW — STATUS QUO (VERTIGO/PHONOGRAM)	TRUE BLUE — MADONNA (SIRE)
5	YOU CAN CALL ME AL — PAUL SIMON (WARNER BROS)	REVENGE — EURYTHMICS (RCA)
6	WALK LIKE AN EGYPTIAN — BANGLES (CBS)	THE CHART — VARIOUS (TELSTAR)
7	RAIN OR SHINE — FIVE STAR (TENT/RCA)	WORD UP — CAMEO (CLUB/PHONOGRAM)
8	SUBURBIA — PET SHOP BOYS (PARLOPHONE)	SOUTH PACIFIC — K. TE KANAWA, J. CARRERAS, S. VAUGHAN (CBS)
9	DON'T LEAVE ME THIS WAY — COMMUNARDS (LONDON)	U-VOX — ULTRAVOX (CHRYSALIS)
10	MIDAS TOUCH — MIDNIGHT STAR (SOLAR/MCA)	ONE TO ONE — HOWARD JONES (WEA)
11	YOU'RE EVERYTHING TO ME — BORIS GARDINER (REVUE/CREOLE)	NOW, THAT'S WHAT I CALL MUSIC 7 — VARIOUS (VIRGIN/EMI)
12	TRUE COLORS — CYNDI LAUPER (PORTRAIT)	COMMUNARDS — COMMUNARDS (LONDON)
13	ALWAYS THERE — MARTI WEBB/SIMON MAY ORCH (BBC)	ORIGINAL SOUNDTRACK 'TOP GUN' — VARIOUS (CBS)
14	DON'T GET ME WRONG — THE PRETENDERS (REAL/WEA)	LONDON 0 HULL 4 — THE HOUSEMARTINS (GO! DISCS)
15	THE WIZARD — PAUL HARDCASTLE (CHRYSALIS)	SOMEWHERE IN TIME — IRON MAIDEN (EMI)
16	I'VE BEEN LOSING YOU — A-HA (WARNER BROS)	BROTHERS IN ARMS — DIRE STRAITS (VERTIGO/PHONOGRAM)
17	THORN IN MY SIDE — EURYTHMICS (RCA)	A KIND OF MAGIC — QUEEN (EMI)
18	WORD UP — CAMEO (CLUB/PHONOGRAM)	FORE! — HUEY LEWIS AND THE NEWS (CHRYSALIS)
19	WORLD SHUT YOUR MOUTH — JULIAN COPE (ISLAND)	INTO THE LIGHT — CHRIS DE BURGH (A&M)
20	(FOREVER) LIVE AND DIE — ORCH. MANOEUVRES IN THE DARK (VIRGIN)	IN THE ARMY NOW — STATUS QUO (VERTIGO/PHONOGRAM)

S I N G L E S US A L B U M S

#	SINGLES	ALBUMS
1	TRUE COLORS — CYNDI LAUPER (PORTRAIT/CBS)	THIRD STAGE — BOSTON (MCA)
2	AMANDA — BOSTON (MCA)	FORE! — HUEY LEWIS AND THE NEWS (CHRYSALIS)
3	I DIDN'T MEAN TO TURN YOU ON — ROBERT PALMER (ISLAND)	GET CLOSE — PRETENDERS (SIRE/WARNER BROS)
4	TYPICAL MALE — TINA TURNER (CAPITOL)	THIS SIDE OF PARADISE — RIC OCASEK (GEFFEN)
5	HUMAN — HUMAN LEAGUE (VIRGIN/A&M)	EYE OF THE ZOMBIE — JOHN FOGERTY (WARNER BROS)
6	TRUE BLUE — MADONNA (SIRE/WARNER BROS)	WHIPLASH SMILE — BILLY IDOL (CHRYSALIS)
7	TAKE ME HOME TONIGHT — EDDIE MONEY (COLUMBIA)	BACK IN THE HIGH LIFE — STEVE WINWOOD (ISLAND)
8	SWEET LOVE — ANITA BAKER (ELEKTRA)	THE WAY IT IS — BRUCE HORNSBY & THE RANGE (RCA)
9	NEXT TIME I FALL — PETER CETERA AND AMY GRANT (FULL MOON)	SLIPPERY WHEN WET — BON JOVI (MERCURY/PG)
10	I'LL BE OVER YOU — TOTO (COLUMBIA)	TRUE STORIES — TALKING HEADS (SIRE/WARNER BROS)
11	WHEN I THINK OF YOU — JANET JACKSON (A&M)	WELCOME HOME — 'TIL TUESDAY (EPIC)
12	YOU GIVE LOVE A BAD NAME — BON JOVI (MERCURY/PG)	BOOMTOWN — DAVID & DAVID (A&M)
13	THE RAIN — ORAN 'JUICE' JONES (DEF JAM/COLUMBIA)	KBC BAND — KBC BAND (ARISTA)
14	WORD UP — CAMEO (ATLANTA ARTISTS/PG)	SO — PETER GABRIEL (GEFFEN)
15	HIP TO BE SQUARE — HUEY LEWIS AND THE NEWS (CHRYSALIS)	BREAK EVERY RULE — TINA TURNER (CAPITOL)
16	LOVE WILL CONQUER ALL — LIONEL RICHIE (MOTOWN)	CAN'T HOLD BACK — EDDIE MONEY (COLUMBIA)
17	ALL CRIED OUT — LISA LISA & CULT JAM & FULL FORCE (COLUMBIA)	ENOUGH IS ENOUGH — BILLY SQUIER (CAPITOL)
18	THROWING IT ALL AWAY — GENESIS (ATLANTIC)	FAME AND FORTUNE — BAD COMPANY (ATLANTIC)
19	EMOTION IN MOTION — RIC OCASEK (GEFFEN)	GREETINGS FROM TIMBUK3 — TIMBUK3 (IRS/MCA)
20	THE WAY IT IS — BRUCE HORNSBY & THE RANGE (RCA)	GEORGIA SATELLITES — GEORGIA SATELLITES (ELEKTRA)

WEEK ENDING NOVEMBER 1 1986

S I N G L E S UK A L B U M S

#	SINGLES	ALBUMS
1	EVERY LOSER WINS — NICK BERRY (BBC)	GRACELAND — PAUL SIMON (WARNER BROS)
2	IN THE ARMY NOW — STATUS QUO (VERTIGO/PHONOGRAM)	TRUE BLUE — MADONNA (SIRE)
3	ALL I ASK OF YOU — CLIFF RICHARD & SARAH BRIGHTMAN (POLYDOR)	SILK AND STEEL — FIVE STAR (TENT/RCA)
4	WALK LIKE AN EGYPTIAN — BANGLES (CBS)	BETWEEN TWO FIRES — PAUL YOUNG (CBS)
5	TRUE BLUE — MADONNA (SIRE)	LIVERPOOL — FRANKIE GOES TO HOLLYWOOD (ZTT/ISLAND)
6	YOU CAN CALL ME AL — PAUL SIMON (WARNER BROS)	SCOUNDREL DAYS — A-HA (WARNER BROS)
7	TAKE MY BREATH AWAY — BERLIN (CBS)	THE CHART — VARIOUS (TELSTAR)
8	MIDAS TOUCH — MIDNIGHT STAR (SOLAR/MCA)	ORIGINAL SOUNDTRACK 'TOP GUN' — VARIOUS (CBS)
9	SUBURBIA — PET SHOP BOYS (PARLOPHONE)	WHIPLASH SMILE — BILLY IDOL (CHRYSALIS)
10	DON'T GET ME WRONG — THE PRETENDERS (REAL/WEA)	REVENGE — EURYTHMICS (RCA)
11	YOU'RE EVERYTHING TO ME — BORIS GARDINER (REVUE/CREOLE)	GET CLOSE — THE PRETENDERS (WEA)
12	TRUE COLORS — CYNDI LAUPER (PORTRAIT)	LONDON 0 HULL 4 — THE HOUSEMARTINS (GO! DISCS)
13	RAIN OR SHINE — FIVE STAR (TENT/RCA)	GIVE ME THE REASON — LUTHER VANDROSS (EPIC)
14	NOTORIOUS — DURAN DURAN (EMI)	DANCING ON THE CEILING — LIONEL RICHIE (MOTOWN)
15	YOU KEEP ME HANGIN' ON — KIM WILDE (MCA)	SOUTH PACIFIC — K. TE KANAWA, J. CARRERAS, S. VAUGHAN (CBS)
16	ASK — THE SMITHS (ROUGH TRADE)	FORE! — HUEY LEWIS AND THE NEWS (CHRYSALIS)
17	TO HAVE AND TO HOLD — CATHERINE STOCK (SIERRA)	BROTHERS IN ARMS — DIRE STRAITS (VERTIGO/PHONOGRAM)
18	THINK FOR A MINUTE — THE HOUSEMARTINS (GO! DISCS)	THE AUTOBIOGRAPHY OF SUPERTRAMP — SUPERTRAMP (A&M)
19	THE WIZARD — PAUL HARDCASTLE (CHRYSALIS)	PLEASE — PET SHOP BOYS (PARLOPHONE)
20	ALWAYS THERE — MARTI WEBB/SIMON MAY ORCH (BBC)	WORD UP — CAMEO (CLUB/PHONOGRAM)

S I N G L E S US A L B U M S

#	SINGLES	ALBUMS
1	AMANDA — BOSTON (MCA)	THIRD STAGE — BOSTON (MCA)
2	HUMAN — HUMAN LEAGUE (VIRGIN/A&M)	GET CLOSE — PRETENDERS (SIRE/WARNER BROS)
3	TRUE BLUE — MADONNA (SIRE/WARNER BROS)	FORE! — HUEY LEWIS AND THE NEWS (CHRYSALIS)
4	I DIDN'T MEAN TO TURN YOU ON — ROBERT PALMER (ISLAND)	WHIPLASH SMILE — BILLY IDOL (CHRYSALIS)
5	TRUE COLORS — CYNDI LAUPER (PORTRAIT/CBS)	EYE OF THE ZOMBIE — JOHN FOGERTY (WARNER BROS)
6	TAKE ME HOME TONIGHT — EDDIE MONEY (COLUMBIA)	THIS SIDE OF PARADISE — RIC OCASEK (GEFFEN)
7	NEXT TIME I FALL — PETER CETERA AND AMY GRANT (FULL MOON)	THE WAY IT IS — BRUCE HORNSBY & THE RANGE (RCA)
8	I'LL BE OVER YOU — TOTO (COLUMBIA)	BACK IN THE HIGH LIFE — STEVE WINWOOD (ISLAND)
9	YOU GIVE LOVE A BAD NAME — BON JOVI (MERCURY/PG)	SOUNDTRACK — COLOR OF MONEY (MCA)
10	HIP TO BE SQUARE — HUEY LEWIS AND THE NEWS (CHRYSALIS)	TRUE STORIES — TALKING HEADS (SIRE/WARNER BROS)
11	THE RAIN — ORAN 'JUICE' JONES (DEF JAM/COLUMBIA)	WELCOME HOME — 'TIL TUESDAY (EPIC)
12	WORD UP — CAMEO (ATLANTA ARTISTS/PG)	KBC BAND — KBC BAND (ARISTA)
13	LOVE WILL CONQUER ALL — LIONEL RICHIE (MOTOWN)	SLIPPERY WHEN WET — BON JOVI (MERCURY/PG)
14	THE WAY IT IS — BRUCE HORNSBY & THE RANGE (RCA)	BOOMTOWN — DAVID & DAVID (A&M)
15	TYPICAL MALE — TINA TURNER (CAPITOL)	SO — PETER GABRIEL (GEFFEN)
16	EVERYBODY HAVE FUN TONIGHT — WANG CHUNG (GEFFEN)	GEORGIA SATELLITES — GEORGIA SATELLITES (ELEKTRA)
17	EMOTION IN MOTION — RIC OCASEK (GEFFEN)	CAN'T HOLD BACK — EDDIE MONEY (COLUMBIA)
18	SWEET LOVE — ANITA BAKER (ELEKTRA)	THE LACE — BENJAMIN ORR (ELEKTRA)
19	ALL CRIED OUT — LISA LISA & CULT JAM & FULL FORCE (COLUMBIA)	INVISIBLE TOUCH — GENESIS (ATLANTIC)
20	I AM BY YOUR SIDE — COREY HART (EMI AMERICA)	BREAK EVERY RULE — TINA TURNER (CAPITOL)

WEEK ENDING NOVEMBER 8 1986

S I N G L E S UK A L B U M S

#	Singles	Albums
1	TAKE MY BREATH AWAY BERLIN (CBS)	EVERY BREATH YOU TAKE – THE SINGLES THE POLICE (A&M)
2	EVERY LOSER WINS NICK BERRY (BBC)	GRACELAND PAUL SIMON (WARNER BROS)
3	IN THE ARMY NOW STATUS QUO (VERTIGO/PHONOGRAM)	NOW DANCE 86 VARIOUS (EMI/VIRGIN)
4	WALK LIKE AN EGYPTIAN BANGLES (CBS)	TRUE BLUE MADONNA (SIRE)
5	ALL I ASK OF YOU CLIFF RICHARD & SARAH BRIGHTMAN (POLYDOR)	SILK AND STEEL FIVE STAR (TENT/RCA)
6	YOU KEEP ME HANGIN' ON KIM WILDE (MCA)	ORIGINAL SOUNDTRACK 'TOP GUN' VARIOUS (CBS)
7	NOTORIOUS DURAN DURAN (EMI)	SCOUNDREL DAYS A-HA (WARNER BROS)
8	SHOWING OUT MEL & KIM (SUPREME)	WHIPLASH SMILE BILLY IDOL (CHRYSALIS)
9	MIDAS TOUCH MIDNIGHT STAR (SOLAR/MCA)	REVENGE EURYTHMICS (RCA)
10	DON'T GET ME WRONG THE PRETENDERS (REAL/WEA)	GET CLOSE THE PRETENDERS (WEA)
11	TRUE BLUE MADONNA (SIRE)	NO. 10 UPPING ST. BIG AUDIO DYNAMITE (CBS)
12	SOMETHING OUTA NOTHING LETITIA DEAN & PAUL MEDFORD (BBC)	LIVERPOOL FRANKIE GOES TO HOLLYWOOD (ZTT/ISLAND)
13	YOU CAN CALL ME AL PAUL SIMON (WARNER BROS)	BETWEEN TWO FIRES PAUL YOUNG (CBS)
14	ASK THE SMITHS (ROUGH TRADE)	THE CHART VARIOUS (TELSTAR)
15	LIVIN' ON A PRAYER BON JOVI (VERTIGO/PHONOGRAM)	FORE! HUEY LEWIS AND THE NEWS (CHRYSALIS)
16	DON'T GIVE UP PETER GABRIEL & KATE BUSH (VIRGIN)	DREAMTIME THE STRANGLERS (EPIC)
17	BREAKOUT SWING OUT SISTER (MERCURY/PHONOGRAM)	A KIND OF MAGIC QUEEN (EMI)
18	SUBURBIA PET SHOP BOYS (PARLOPHONE)	LONDON 0 HULL 4 THE HOUSEMARTINS (GO! DISCS)
19	TRUE COLORS CYNDI LAUPER (PORTRAIT)	REMINISCING FOSTER & ALLEN (STYLUS)
20	THROUGH THE BARRICADES SPANDAU BALLET (REFORMATION/CBS)	SLIPPERY WHEN WET BON JOVI (VERTIGO/PHONOGRAM)

S I N G L E S US A L B U M S

#	Singles	Albums
1	AMANDA BOSTON (MCA)	THIRD STAGE BOSTON (MCA)
2	HUMAN HUMAN LEAGUE (VIRGIN/A&M)	GET CLOSE PRETENDERS (SIRE/WARNER BROS)
3	TRUE BLUE MADONNA (SIRE/WARNER BROS)	WHIPLASH SMILE BILLY IDOL (CHRYSALIS)
4	NEXT TIME I FALL PETER CETERA AND AMY GRANT (FULL MOON)	FORE! HUEY LEWIS AND THE NEWS (CHRYSALIS)
5	TAKE ME HOME TONIGHT EDDIE MONEY (COLUMBIA)	SOUNDTRACK COLOR OF MONEY (MCA)
6	HIP TO BE SQUARE HUEY LEWIS AND THE NEWS (CHRYSALIS)	EYE OF THE ZOMBIE JOHN FOGERTY (WARNER BROS)
7	YOU GIVE LOVE A BAD NAME BON JOVI (MERCURY/PG)	LIVING IN THE 20TH CENTURY STEVE MILLER BAND (CAPITOL)
8	THE WAY IT IS BRUCE HORNSBY & THE RANGE (RCA)	THE WAY IT IS BRUCE HORNSBY & THE RANGE (RCA)
9	I'LL BE OVER YOU TOTO (COLUMBIA)	THIS SIDE OF PARADISE RIC OCASEK (GEFFEN)
10	WORD UP CAMEO (ATLANTA ARTISTS/PG)	KBC BAND KBC BAND (ARISTA)
11	LOVE WILL CONQUER ALL LIONEL RICHIE (MOTOWN)	BACK IN THE HIGH LIFE STEVE WINWOOD (ISLAND)
12	I DIDN'T MEAN TO TURN YOU ON ROBERT PALMER (ISLAND)	SLIPPERY WHEN WET BON JOVI (MERCURY/PG)
13	EVERYBODY HAVE FUN TONIGHT WANG CHUNG (GEFFEN)	TRUE STORIES TALKING HEADS (SIRE/WARNER BROS)
14	THE RAIN ORAN 'JUICE' JONES (DEF JAM/COLUMBIA)	WELCOME HOME 'TIL TUESDAY (EPIC)
15	TRUE COLORS CYNDI LAUPER (PORTRAIT/CBS)	GEORGIA SATELLITES GEORGIA SATELLITES (ELEKTRA)
16	EMOTION IN MOTION RIC OCASEK (GEFFEN)	BOOMTOWN DAVID & DAVID (A&M)
17	WALK LIKE AN EGYPTIAN BANGLES (COLUMBIA)	THE LACE BENJAMIN ORR (ELEKTRA)
18	TO BE A LOVER BILLY IDOL (CHRYSALIS)	CAN'T HOLD BACK EDDIE MONEY (COLUMBIA)
19	FREEDOM OVERSPILL STEVE WINWOOD (ISLAND/WARNER BROS)	INVISIBLE TOUCH GENESIS (ATLANTIC)
20	I AM BY YOUR SIDE COREY HART (EMI AMERICA)	SO PETER GABRIEL (GEFFEN)

WEEK ENDING NOVEMBER 15 1986

S I N G L E S UK A L B U M S

#	Singles	Albums
1	TAKE MY BREATH AWAY BERLIN (CBS)	EVERY BREATH YOU TAKE – THE SINGLES THE POLICE (A&M)
2	YOU KEEP ME HANGIN' ON KIM WILDE (MCA)	NOW DANCE 86 VARIOUS (EMI/VIRGIN)
3	WALK LIKE AN EGYPTIAN BANGLES (CBS)	GRACELAND PAUL SIMON (WARNER BROS)
4	SHOWING OUT MEL & KIM (SUPREME)	ORIGINAL SOUNDTRACK 'TOP GUN' VARIOUS (CBS)
5	BREAKOUT SWING OUT SISTER (MERCURY/PHONOGRAM)	TRUE BLUE MADONNA (SIRE)
6	IN THE ARMY NOW STATUS QUO (VERTIGO/PHONOGRAM)	SILK AND STEEL FIVE STAR (TENT/RCA)
7	EVERY LOSER WINS NICK BERRY (BBC)	SLIPPERY WHEN WET BON JOVI (VERTIGO/PHONOGRAM)
8	THROUGH THE BARRICADES SPANDAU BALLET (REFORMATION/CBS)	THE GREATEST HITS OF 1986 VARIOUS (TELSTAR)
9	DON'T GIVE UP PETER GABRIEL & KATE BUSH (VIRGIN)	THE AUTOBIOGRAPHY OF SUPERTRAMP SUPERTRAMP (A&M)
10	ALL I ASK OF YOU CLIFF RICHARD & SARAH BRIGHTMAN (POLYDOR)	HIT MIX '86 VARIOUS (STYLUS)
11	LIVIN' ON A PRAYER BON JOVI (VERTIGO/PHONOGRAM)	GET CLOSE THE PRETENDERS (WEA)
12	NOTORIOUS DURAN DURAN (EMI)	REMINISCING FOSTER & ALLEN (STYLUS)
13	FOR AMERICA RED BOX (SIRE/WEA)	REVENGE EURYTHMICS (RCA)
14	THE FINAL COUNTDOWN EUROPE (EPIC)	A KIND OF MAGIC QUEEN (EMI)
15	DON'T GET ME WRONG THE PRETENDERS (REAL/WEA)	LIVERPOOL FRANKIE GOES TO HOLLYWOOD (ZTT/ISLAND)
16	SOMETHING OUTA NOTHING LETITIA DEAN & PAUL MEDFORD (BBC)	BETWEEN TWO FIRES PAUL YOUNG (CBS)
17	MIDAS TOUCH MIDNIGHT STAR (SOLAR/MCA)	SO PETER GABRIEL (VIRGIN)
18	BECAUSE I LOVE YOU SHAKIN' STEVENS (EPIC)	LONDON 0 HULL 4 THE HOUSEMARTINS (GO! DISCS)
19	TRUE BLUE MADONNA (SIRE)	SCOUNDREL DAYS A-HA (WARNER BROS)
20	(WAITING FOR) THE GHOST TRAIN MADNESS (ZARJAZZ/VIRGIN)	TOGETHER VARIOUS (K-TEL)

S I N G L E S US A L B U M S

#	Singles	Albums
1	AMANDA BOSTON (MCA)	LIVE/1975–85 BRUCE SPRINGSTEEN & E STREET (COLUMBIA)
2	HUMAN HUMAN LEAGUE (VIRGIN/A&M)	THIRD STAGE BOSTON (MCA)
3	TRUE BLUE MADONNA (SIRE/WARNER BROS)	GET CLOSE PRETENDERS (SIRE/WARNER BROS)
4	NEXT TIME I FALL PETER CETERA AND AMY GRANT (FULL MOON)	WHIPLASH SMILE BILLY IDOL (CHRYSALIS)
5	HIP TO BE SQUARE HUEY LEWIS AND THE NEWS (CHRYSALIS)	SOUNDTRACK COLOR OF MONEY (MCA)
6	THE WAY IT IS BRUCE HORNSBY & THE RANGE (RCA)	LIVING IN THE 20TH CENTURY STEVE MILLER BAND (CAPITOL)
7	YOU GIVE LOVE A BAD NAME BON JOVI (MERCURY/PG)	EYE OF THE ZOMBIE JOHN FOGERTY (WARNER BROS)
8	EVERYBODY HAVE FUN TONIGHT WANG CHUNG (GEFFEN)	KBC BAND KBC BAND (ARISTA)
9	LOVE WILL CONQUER ALL LIONEL RICHIE (MOTOWN)	THIS SIDE OF PARADISE RIC OCASEK (GEFFEN)
10	WORD UP CAMEO (ATLANTA ARTISTS/PG)	THE WAY IT IS BRUCE HORNSBY & THE RANGE (RCA)
11	TAKE ME HOME TONIGHT EDDIE MONEY (COLUMBIA)	FORE! HUEY LEWIS AND THE NEWS (CHRYSALIS)
12	WALK LIKE AN EGYPTIAN BANGLES (COLUMBIA)	BACK IN THE HIGH LIFE STEVE WINWOOD (ISLAND)
13	TO BE A LOVER BILLY IDOL (CHRYSALIS)	GEORGIA SATELLITES GEORGIA SATELLITES (ELEKTRA)
14	I'LL BE OVER YOU TOTO (COLUMBIA)	SLIPPERY WHEN WET BON JOVI (MERCURY/PG)
15	THE RAIN ORAN 'JUICE' JONES (DEF JAM/COLUMBIA)	THE LACE BENJAMIN ORR (ELEKTRA)
16	FREEDOM OVERSPILL STEVE WINWOOD (ISLAND/WARNER BROS)	BOOMTOWN DAVID & DAVID (A&M)
17	EMOTION IN MOTION RIC OCASEK (GEFFEN)	TRUE STORIES TALKING HEADS (SIRE/WARNER BROS)
18	YOU KNOW I LOVE YOU . . . DON'T YOU? HOWARD JONES (ELEKTRA)	CAN'T HOLD BACK EDDIE MONEY (COLUMBIA)
19	NOTORIOUS DURAN DURAN (CAPITOL)	INVISIBLE TOUCH GENESIS (ATLANTIC)
20	DON'T GET ME WRONG PRETENDERS (SIRE/WARNER BROS)	POWER KANSAS (MCA)

WEEK ENDING NOVEMBER 22 1986

S I N G L E S UK A L B U M S

#	Singles	Albums
1	TAKE MY BREATH AWAY — BERLIN (CBS)	HITS 5 — VARIOUS (CBS/RCA ARIOLA/WEA)
2	YOU KEEP ME HANGIN' ON — KIM WILDE (MCA)	EVERY BREATH YOU TAKE – THE SINGLES — THE POLICE (A&M)
3	SHOWING OUT — MEL & KIM (SUPREME)	THE WHOLE STORY — KATE BUSH (EMI)
4	BREAKOUT — SWING OUT SISTER (MERCURY/PHONOGRAM)	LIVE/1975–1985 — BRUCE SPRINGSTEEN & E STREET BAND (CBS)
5	THE FINAL COUNTDOWN — EUROPE (EPIC)	NOW DANCE 86 — VARIOUS (EMI/VIRGIN)
6	THROUGH THE BARRICADES — SPANDAU BALLET (REFORMATION/CBS)	GRACELAND — PAUL SIMON (WARNER BROS)
7	LIVIN' ON A PRAYER — BON JOVI (VERTIGO/PHONOGRAM)	TRUE BLUE — MADONNA (SIRE)
8	WALK LIKE AN EGYPTIAN — BANGLES (CBS)	ORIGINAL SOUNDTRACK 'TOP GUN' — VARIOUS (CBS)
9	DON'T GIVE UP — PETER GABRIEL & KATE BUSH (VIRGIN)	SILK AND STEEL — FIVE STAR (TENT/RCA)
10	FOR AMERICA — RED BOX (SIRE/WEA)	SLIPPERY WHEN WET — BON JOVI (VERTIGO/PHONOGRAM)
11	FRENCH KISSIN' IN THE USA — DEBBIE HARRY (CHRYSALIS)	THE GREATEST HITS OF 1986 — VARIOUS (TELSTAR)
12	EACH TIME YOU BREAK MY HEART — NICK KAMEN (WEA)	THE AUTOBIOGRAPHY OF SUPERTRAMP — SUPERTRAMP (A&M)
13	GHOSTDANCING — SIMPLE MINDS (VIRGIN)	HIT MIX '86 — VARIOUS (STYLUS)
14	BECAUSE I LOVE YOU — SHAKIN' STEVENS (EPIC)	GOD'S OWN MEDICINE — THE MISSION (MERCURY/PHONOGRAM)
15	ALL I ASK OF YOU — CLIFF RICHARD & SARAH BRIGHTMAN (POLYDOR)	REMINISCING — FOSTER & ALLEN (STYLUS)
16	SOMETIMES — ERASURE (MUTE)	SO — PETER GABRIEL (VIRGIN)
17	IN THE ARMY NOW — STATUS QUO (VERTIGO/PHONOGRAM)	BROTHERS IN ARMS — DIRE STRAITS (VERTIGO/PHONOGRAM)
18	(WAITING FOR) THE GHOST TRAIN — MADNESS (ZARJAZZ/VIRGIN)	REVENGE — EURYTHMICS (RCA)
19	SWEET LOVE — ANITA BAKER (ELEKTRA)	A KIND OF MAGIC — QUEEN (EMI)
20	NOTORIOUS — DURAN DURAN (EMI)	WHITNEY HOUSTON — WHITNEY HOUSTON (ARISTA)

S I N G L E S US A L B U M S

#	Singles	Albums
1	HIP TO BE SQUARE — HUEY LEWIS AND THE NEWS (CHRYSALIS)	LIVE/1975–85 — BRUCE SPRINGSTEEN & E STREET (COLUMBIA)
2	NEXT TIME I FALL — PETER CETERA AND AMY GRANT (FULL MOON)	THIRD STAGE — BOSTON (MCA)
3	THE WAY IT IS — BRUCE HORNSBY & THE RANGE (RCA)	GET CLOSE — PRETENDERS (SIRE/WARNER BROS)
4	HUMAN — HUMAN LEAGUE (VIRGIN/A&M)	SOUNDTRACK — COLOR OF MONEY (MCA)
5	AMANDA — BOSTON (MCA)	LIVING IN THE 20TH CENTURY — STEVE MILLER BAND (CAPITOL)
6	TRUE BLUE — MADONNA (SIRE/WARNER BROS)	WHIPLASH SMILE — BILLY IDOL (CHRYSALIS)
7	EVERYBODY HAVE FUN TONIGHT — WANG CHUNG (GEFFEN)	THE WAY IT IS — BRUCE HORNSBY & THE RANGE (RCA)
8	YOU GIVE LOVE A BAD NAME — BON JOVI (MERCURY/PG)	GEORGIA SATELLITES — GEORGIA SATELLITES (ELEKTRA)
9	LOVE WILL CONQUER ALL — LIONEL RICHIE (MOTOWN)	KBC BAND — KBC BAND (ARISTA)
10	WALK LIKE AN EGYPTIAN — BANGLES (COLUMBIA)	THE LACE — BENJAMIN ORR (ELEKTRA)
11	TO BE A LOVER — BILLY IDOL (CHRYSALIS)	THIS SIDE OF PARADISE — RIC OCASEK (GEFFEN)
12	WORD UP — CAMEO (ATLANTA ARTISTS/PG)	BACK IN THE HIGH LIFE — STEVE WINWOOD (ISLAND)
13	NOTORIOUS — DURAN DURAN (CAPITOL)	SLIPPERY WHEN WET — BON JOVI (MERCURY/PG)
14	YOU KNOW I LOVE YOU . . . DON'T YOU? — HOWARD JONES (ELEKTRA)	BOOMTOWN — DAVID & DAVID (A&M)
15	DON'T GET ME WRONG — PRETENDERS (SIRE/WARNER BROS)	EYE OF THE ZOMBIE — JOHN FOGERTY (WARNER BROS)
16	TAKE ME HOME TONIGHT — EDDIE MONEY (COLUMBIA)	FORE! — HUEY LEWIS AND THE NEWS (CHRYSALIS)
17	FREEDOM OVERSPILL — STEVE WINWOOD (ISLAND/WARNER BROS)	POWER — KANSAS (MCA)
18	IS THIS LOVE — SURVIVOR (SCOTTI BROS/CBS)	CAN'T HOLD BACK — EDDIE MONEY (COLUMBIA)
19	(FOREVER) LIVE AND DIE — ORCH. MANOEUVRES IN THE DARK (VIRGIN)	TRUE STORIES — TALKING HEADS (SIRE/WARNER BROS)
20	C'EST LA VIE — ROBBIE NEVIL (MANHATTAN)	SO — PETER GABRIEL (GEFFEN)

WEEK ENDING NOVEMBER 29 1986

S I N G L E S UK A L B U M S

#	Singles	Albums
1	TAKE MY BREATH AWAY — BERLIN (CBS)	HITS 5 — VARIOUS (CBS/RCA ARIOLA/WEA)
2	THE FINAL COUNTDOWN — EUROPE (EPIC)	THE WHOLE STORY — KATE BUSH (EMI)
3	YOU KEEP ME HANGIN' ON — KIM WILDE (MCA)	EVERY BREATH YOU TAKE – THE SINGLES — THE POLICE (A&M)
4	SHOWING OUT — MEL & KIM (SUPREME)	ORIGINAL SOUNDTRACK 'TOP GUN' — VARIOUS (CBS)
5	BREAKOUT — SWING OUT SISTER (MERCURY/PHONOGRAM)	TRUE BLUE — MADONNA (SIRE)
6	LIVIN' ON A PRAYER — BON JOVI (VERTIGO/PHONOGRAM)	SLIPPERY WHEN WET — BON JOVI (VERTIGO/PHONOGRAM)
7	SOMETIMES — ERASURE (MUTE)	THROUGH THE BARRICADES — SPANDAU BALLET (REFORMATION/CBS)
8	EACH TIME YOU BREAK MY HEART — NICK KAMEN (WEA)	NOW DANCE 86 — VARIOUS (EMI/VIRGIN)
9	FRENCH KISSIN' IN THE USA — DEBBIE HARRY (CHRYSALIS)	THE GREATEST HITS OF 1986 — VARIOUS (TELSTAR)
10	FOR AMERICA — RED BOX (SIRE/WEA)	SILK AND STEEL — FIVE STAR (TENT/RCA)
11	THROUGH THE BARRICADES — SPANDAU BALLET (REFORMATION/CBS)	LIVE/1975–1985 — BRUCE SPRINGSTEEN & E STREET BAND (CBS)
12	DON'T GIVE UP — PETER GABRIEL & KATE BUSH (VIRGIN)	HIT MIX '86 — VARIOUS (STYLUS)
13	SWEET LOVE — ANITA BAKER (ELEKTRA)	GRACELAND — PAUL SIMON (WARNER BROS)
14	WALK LIKE AN EGYPTIAN — BANGLES (CBS)	INFECTED — THE THE (SOME BIZZARE/EPIC)
15	IF I SAY YES — FIVE STAR (TENT/RCA)	DISCO — PET SHOP BOYS (EMI)
16	GHOSTDANCING — SIMPLE MINDS (VIRGIN)	BROTHERS IN ARMS — DIRE STRAITS (VERTIGO/PHONOGRAM)
17	THE SKYE BOAT SONG — ROGER WHITTAKER & DES O'CONNOR (TEMBO)	LOVERS — VARIOUS (TELSTAR)
18	BECAUSE I LOVE YOU — SHAKIN' STEVENS (EPIC)	REVENGE — EURYTHMICS (RCA)
19	WARRIORS (OF THE WASTELAND) — FRANKIE GOES TO HOLLYWOOD (ZTT/ISLAND)	THE AUTOBIOGRAPHY OF SUPERTRAMP — SUPERTRAMP (A&M)
20	ALL I ASK OF YOU — CLIFF RICHARD & SARAH BRIGHTMAN (POLYDOR)	SO — PETER GABRIEL (VIRGIN)

S I N G L E S US A L B U M S

#	Singles	Albums
1	THE WAY IT IS — BRUCE HORNSBY & THE RANGE (RCA)	LIVE/1975–85 — BRUCE SPRINGSTEEN & E STREET (COLUMBIA)
2	HIP TO BE SQUARE — HUEY LEWIS AND THE NEWS (CHRYSALIS)	THIRD STAGE — BOSTON (MCA)
3	EVERYBODY HAVE FUN TONIGHT — WANG CHUNG (GEFFEN)	GET CLOSE — PRETENDERS (SIRE/WARNER BROS)
4	WALK LIKE AN EGYPTIAN — BANGLES (COLUMBIA)	LIVING IN THE 20TH CENTURY — STEVE MILLER BAND (CAPITOL)
5	TO BE A LOVER — BILLY IDOL (CHRYSALIS)	AUGUST — ERIC CLAPTON (DUCK/WARNER BROS)
6	AMANDA — BOSTON (MCA)	WHIPLASH SMILE — BILLY IDOL (CHRYSALIS)
7	NOTORIOUS — DURAN DURAN (CAPITOL)	THE WAY IT IS — BRUCE HORNSBY & THE RANGE (RCA)
8	NEXT TIME I FALL — PETER CETERA AND AMY GRANT (FULL MOON)	GEORGIA SATELLITES — GEORGIA SATELLITES (ELEKTRA)
9	YOU GIVE LOVE A BAD NAME — BON JOVI (MERCURY/PG)	THE LACE — BENJAMIN ORR (ELEKTRA)
10	YOU KNOW I LOVE YOU . . . DON'T YOU? — HOWARD JONES (ELEKTRA)	SOUNDTRACK — COLOR OF MONEY (MCA)
11	DON'T GET ME WRONG — PRETENDERS (SIRE/WARNER BROS)	SLIPPERY WHEN WET — BON JOVI (MERCURY/PG)
12	LOVE WILL CONQUER ALL — LIONEL RICHIE (MOTOWN)	BACK IN THE HIGH LIFE — STEVE WINWOOD (ISLAND)
13	IS THIS LOVE — SURVIVOR (SCOTTI BROS/CBS)	POWER — KANSAS (MCA)
14	HUMAN — HUMAN LEAGUE (VIRGIN/A&M)	BOOMTOWN — DAVID & DAVID (A&M)
15	TRUE BLUE — MADONNA (SIRE/WARNER BROS)	KBC BAND — KBC BAND (ARISTA)
16	C'EST LA VIE — ROBBIE NEVIL (MANHATTAN)	THIS SIDE OF PARADISE — RIC OCASEK (GEFFEN)
17	SHAKE YOU DOWN — GREGORY ABBOTT (COLUMBIA)	SO — PETER GABRIEL (GEFFEN)
18	LAND OF CONFUSION — GENESIS (ATLANTIC)	LIVE ALIVE — STEVIE RAY VAUGHAN & DOUBLE TROUBLE (EPIC)
19	STAND BY ME — BEN E. KING (ATLANTIC)	CAN'T HOLD BACK — EDDIE MONEY (COLUMBIA)
20	WORD UP — CAMEO (ATLANTA ARTISTS/PG)	FORE! — HUEY LEWIS AND THE NEWS (CHRYSALIS)

S I N G L E S — UK — A L B U M S

#	Singles	Albums
1	THE FINAL COUNTDOWN — EUROPE (EPIC)	NOW, THAT'S WHAT I CALL MUSIC 8 — VARIOUS (EMI/VIRGIN/POLYGRAM)
2	TAKE MY BREATH AWAY — BERLIN (CBS)	HITS 5 — VARIOUS (CBS/RCA ARIOLA/WEA)
3	SOMETIMES — ERASURE (MUTE)	THE WHOLE STORY — KATE BUSH (EMI)
4	LIVIN' ON A PRAYER — BON JOVI (VERTIGO/PHONOGRAM)	EVERY BREATH YOU TAKE – THE SINGLES — THE POLICE (A&M)
5	EACH TIME YOU BREAK MY HEART — NICK KAMEN (WEA)	ORIGINAL SOUNDTRACK 'TOP GUN' — VARIOUS (CBS)
6	BREAKOUT — SWING OUT SISTER (MERCURY/PHONOGRAM)	TRUE BLUE — MADONNA (SIRE)
7	YOU KEEP ME HANGIN' ON — KIM WILDE (MCA)	SILK AND STEEL — FIVE STAR (TENT/RCA)
8	FRENCH KISSIN' IN THE USA — DEBBIE HARRY (CHRYSALIS)	SLIPPERY WHEN WET — BON JOVI (VERTIGO/PHONOGRAM)
9	SHOWING OUT — MEL & KIM (SUPREME)	GRACELAND — PAUL SIMON (WARNER BROS)
10	THE SKYE BOAT SONG — ROGER WHITTAKER & DES O'CONNOR (TEMBO)	THROUGH THE BARRICADES — SPANDAU BALLET (REFORMATION/CBS)
11	FOR AMERICA — RED BOX (SIRE/WEA)	REMINISCING — FOSTER & ALLEN (STYLUS)
12	THE RAIN — ORAN 'JUICE' JONES (DEF JAM)	NOW DANCE 86 — VARIOUS (EMI/VIRGIN)
13	SWEET LOVE — ANITA BAKER (ELEKTRA)	THE GREATEST HITS OF 1986 — VARIOUS (TELSTAR)
14	SO COLD THE NIGHT — COMMUNARDS (LONDON)	LOVERS — VARIOUS (TELSTAR)
15	SHAKE YOU DOWN — GREGORY ABBOTT (LONDON)	DIFFERENT LIGHT — BANGLES (CBS)
16	IF I SAY YES — FIVE STAR (TENT/RCA)	NOTORIOUS — DURAN DURAN (EMI)
17	THROUGH THE BARRICADES — SPANDAU BALLET (REFORMATION/CBS)	BROTHERS IN ARMS — DIRE STRAITS (VERTIGO/PHONOGRAM)
18	WAR — BRUCE SPRINGSTEEN & E STREET BAND (CBS)	REVENGE — EURYTHMICS (RCA)
19	WARRIORS (OF THE WASTELAND) — FRANKIE GOES TO HOLLYWOOD (ZTT/ISLAND)	LIVE/1975–1985 — BRUCE SPRINGSTEEN & E STREET BAND (CBS)
20	LAND OF CONFUSION — GENESIS (VIRGIN)	DISCO — PET SHOP BOYS (EMI)

S I N G L E S — US — A L B U M S

#	Singles	Albums
1	THE WAY IT IS — BRUCE HORNSBY & THE RANGE (RCA)	LIVE/1975–85 — BRUCE SPRINGSTEEN & E STREET (COLUMBIA)
2	EVERYBODY HAVE FUN TONIGHT — WANG CHUNG (GEFFEN)	THIRD STAGE — BOSTON (MCA)
3	WALK LIKE AN EGYPTIAN — BANGLES (COLUMBIA)	AUGUST — ERIC CLAPTON (DUCK/WARNER BROS)
4	HIP TO BE SQUARE — HUEY LEWIS AND THE NEWS (CHRYSALIS)	LIVING IN THE 20TH CENTURY — STEVE MILLER BAND (CAPITOL)
5	NOTORIOUS — DURAN DURAN (CAPITOL)	GET CLOSE — PRETENDERS (SIRE/WARNER BROS)
6	DON'T GET ME WRONG — PRETENDERS (SIRE/WARNER BROS)	GEORGIA SATELLITES — GEORGIA SATELLITES (ELEKTRA)
7	TO BE A LOVER — BILLY IDOL (CHRYSALIS)	THE WAY IT IS — BRUCE HORNSBY & THE RANGE (RCA)
8	YOU KNOW I LOVE YOU . . . DON'T YOU? — HOWARD JONES (ELEKTRA)	WHIPLASH SMILE — BILLY IDOL (CHRYSALIS)
9	IS THIS LOVE — SURVIVOR (SCOTTI BROS/CBS)	THE LACE — BENJAMIN ORR (ELEKTRA)
10	NEXT TIME I FALL — PETER CETERA AND AMY GRANT (FULL MOON)	SOUNDTRACK COLOR OF MONEY (MCA)
11	SHAKE YOU DOWN — GREGORY ABBOTT (COLUMBIA)	SLIPPERY WHEN WET — BON JOVI (MERCURY/PG)
12	C'EST LA VIE — ROBBIE NEVIL (MANHATTAN)	POWER — KANSAS (MCA)
13	YOU GIVE LOVE A BAD NAME — BON JOVI (MERCURY/PG)	THIS SIDE OF PARADISE — RIC OCASEK (GEFFEN)
14	LAND OF CONFUSION — GENESIS (ATLANTIC)	BACK IN THE HIGH LIFE — STEVE WINWOOD (ISLAND)
15	CONTROL — JANET JACKSON (A&M)	SO — PETER GABRIEL (GEFFEN)
16	WAR — BRUCE SPRINGSTEEN & E STREET BAND (COLUMBIA)	BOOMTOWN — DAVID & DAVID (A&M)
17	STAND BY ME — BEN E. KING (ATLANTIC)	LIVE ALIVE — STEVIE RAY VAUGHAN & DOUBLE TROUBLE (EPIC)
18	HUMAN — HUMAN LEAGUE (VIRGIN/A&M)	KBC BAND — KBC BAND (ARISTA)
19	LOVE WILL CONQUER ALL — LIONEL RICHIE (MOTOWN)	THINK VISUAL — KINKS (MCA)
20	AMANDA — BOSTON (MCA)	FORE! — HUEY LEWIS AND THE NEWS (CHRYSALIS)

S I N G L E S — UK — A L B U M S

#	Singles	Albums
1	THE FINAL COUNTDOWN — EUROPE (EPIC)	NOW, THAT'S WHAT I CALL MUSIC 8 — VARIOUS (EMI/VIRGIN/POLYGRAM)
2	SOMETIMES — ERASURE (MUTE)	HITS 5 — VARIOUS (CBS/RCA ARIOLA/WEA)
3	CARAVAN OF LOVE — THE HOUSEMARTINS (GO! DISCS)	THE WHOLE STORY — KATE BUSH (EMI)
4	THE RAIN — ORAN 'JUICE' JONES (DEF JAM)	EVERY BREATH YOU TAKE – THE SINGLES — THE POLICE (A&M)
5	TAKE MY BREATH AWAY — BERLIN (CBS)	LIVE MAGIC — QUEEN (EMI)
6	SHAKE YOU DOWN — GREGORY ABBOTT	GRACELAND — PAUL SIMON (WARNER BROS)
7	LIVIN' ON A PRAYER — BON JOVI (VERTIGO/PHONOGRAM)	TRUE BLUE — MADONNA (SIRE)
8	OPEN YOUR HEART — MADONNA (SIRE)	ORIGINAL SOUNDTRACK 'TOP GUN' — VARIOUS (CBS)
9	EACH TIME YOU BREAK MY HEART — NICK KAMEN (WEA)	SILK AND STEEL — FIVE STAR (TENT/RCA)
10	SO COLD THE NIGHT — COMMUNARDS (LONDON)	SLIPPERY WHEN WET — BON JOVI (VERTIGO/PHONOGRAM)
11	FRENCH KISSIN' IN THE USA — DEBBIE HARRY (CHRYSALIS)	REMINISCING — FOSTER & ALLEN (STYLUS)
12	BREAKOUT — SWING OUT SISTER (MERCURY/PHONOGRAM)	DIFFERENT LIGHT — BANGLES (CBS)
13	THE SKYE BOAT SONG — ROGER WHITTAKER & DES O'CONNOR (TEMBO)	SOUTH PACIFIC — K. TE KANAWA, J. CARRERAS, S. VAUGHAN (CBS)
14	REET PETITE — JACKIE WILSON (SMP)	LOVERS — VARIOUS (TELSTAR)
15	YOU KEEP ME HANGIN' ON — KIM WILDE (MCA)	THE GREATEST HITS OF 1986 — VARIOUS (TELSTAR)
16	CRY WOLF — A-HA (WARNER BROS)	REVENGE — EURYTHMICS (RCA)
17	LAND OF CONFUSION — GENESIS (VIRGIN)	FORE! — HUEY LEWIS AND THE NEWS (CHRYSALIS)
18	SHOWING OUT — MEL & KIM (SUPREME)	THROUGH THE BARRICADES — SPANDAU BALLET (REFORMATION/CBS)
19	SHIVER — GEORGE BENSON (WARNER BROS)	SIXTIES MANIA — VARIOUS (TELSTAR)
20	FOR AMERICA — RED BOX (SIRE/WEA)	NOW – THE CHRISTMAS ALBUM — VARIOUS (EMI/VIRGIN)

S I N G L E S — US — A L B U M S

#	Singles	Albums
1	EVERYBODY HAVE FUN TONIGHT — WANG CHUNG (GEFFEN)	LIVE/1975–85 — BRUCE SPRINGSTEEN & E STREET (COLUMBIA)
2	WALK LIKE AN EGYPTIAN — BANGLES (COLUMBIA)	THIRD STAGE — BOSTON (MCA)
3	THE WAY IT IS — BRUCE HORNSBY & THE RANGE (RCA)	AUGUST — ERIC CLAPTON (DUCK/WARNER BROS)
4	NOTORIOUS — DURAN DURAN (CAPITOL)	GET CLOSE — PRETENDERS (SIRE/WARNER BROS)
5	DON'T GET ME WRONG — PRETENDERS (SIRE/WARNER BROS)	LIVING IN THE 20TH CENTURY — STEVE MILLER BAND (CAPITOL)
6	SHAKE YOU DOWN — GREGORY ABBOTT (COLUMBIA)	GEORGIA SATELLITES — GEORGIA SATELLITES (ELEKTRA)
7	IS THIS LOVE — SURVIVOR (SCOTTI BROS/CBS)	THE WAY IT IS — BRUCE HORNSBY & THE RANGE (RCA)
8	YOU KNOW I LOVE YOU . . . DON'T YOU? — HOWARD JONES (ELEKTRA)	SLIPPERY WHEN WET — BON JOVI (MERCURY/PG)
9	C'EST LA VIE — ROBBIE NEVIL (MANHATTAN)	THE LACE — BENJAMIN ORR (ELEKTRA)
10	CONTROL — JANET JACKSON (A&M)	SOUNDTRACK COLOR OF MONEY (MCA)
11	LAND OF CONFUSION — GENESIS (ATLANTIC)	WHIPLASH SMILE — BILLY IDOL (CHRYSALIS)
12	HIP TO BE SQUARE — HUEY LEWIS AND THE NEWS (CHRYSALIS)	POWER — KANSAS (MCA)
13	WAR — BRUCE SPRINGSTEEN & E STREET BAND (COLUMBIA)	THIS SIDE OF PARADISE — RIC OCASEK (GEFFEN)
14	NEXT TIME I FALL — PETER CETERA AND AMY GRANT (FULL MOON)	SO — PETER GABRIEL (GEFFEN)
15	TO BE A LOVER — BILLY IDOL (CHRYSALIS)	THINK VISUAL — KINKS (MCA)
16	STAND BY ME — BEN E. KING (ATLANTIC)	BACK IN THE HIGH LIFE — STEVE WINWOOD (ISLAND)
17	SOMEDAY — GLASS TIGER (MANHATTEN)	FORE! — HUEY LEWIS AND THE NEWS (CHRYSALIS)
18	AT THIS MOMENT — BILLY VERA & THE BEATERS (RHINO)	STRONG PERSUADER — ROBERT CRAY BAND (MERCURY/PG)
19	LOVE IS FOREVER — BILLY OCEAN (JIVE/ARISTA)	LIVE ALIVE — STEVIE RAY VAUGHAN & DOUBLE TROUBLE (EPIC)
20	VICTORY — KOOL & THE GANG (MERCURY/PG)	CAN'T HOLD BACK — EDDIE MONEY (COLUMBIA)

WEEK ENDING DECEMBER 20 1986
S I N G L E S UK A L B U M S

CARAVAN OF LOVE THE HOUSEMARTINS (GO! DISCS)	**1**	**NOW, THAT'S WHAT I CALL MUSIC 8** VARIOUS (EMI/VIRGIN/POLYGRAM)
REET PETITE JACKIE WILSON (SMP)	**2**	**HITS 5** VARIOUS (CBS/RCA ARIOLA/WEA)
THE FINAL COUNTDOWN EUROPE (EPIC)	**3**	**THE WHOLE STORY** KATE BUSH (EMI)
OPEN YOUR HEART MADONNA (SIRE)	**4**	**GRACELAND** PAUL SIMON (WARNER BROS)
SOMETIMES ERASURE (MUTE)	**5**	**EVERY BREATH YOU TAKE – THE SINGLES** THE POLICE (A&M)
THE RAIN ORAN 'JUICE' JONES (DEF JAM)	**6**	**TRUE BLUE** MADONNA (SIRE)
SHAKE YOU DOWN GREGORY ABBOTT (CBS)	**7**	**LIVE MAGIC** QUEEN (EMI)
SO COLD THE NIGHT COMMUNARDS (LONDON)	**8**	**SILK AND STEEL** FIVE STAR (TENT/RCA)
LIVIN' ON A PRAYER BON JOVI (VERTIGO/PHONOGRAM)	**9**	**NOW – THE CHRISTMAS ALBUM** VARIOUS (EMI/VIRGIN)
CRY WOLF A-HA (WARNER BROS)	**10**	**FORE!** HUEY LEWIS AND THE NEWS (CHRYSALIS)
TAKE MY BREATH AWAY BERLIN (CBS)	**11**	**ORIGINAL SOUNDTRACK 'TOP GUN'** VARIOUS (CBS)
IS THIS LOVE? ALISON MOYET (CBS)	**12**	**SLIPPERY WHEN WET** BON JOVI (VERTIGO/PHONOGRAM)
EACH TIME YOU BREAK MY HEART NICK KAMEN (WEA)	**13**	**REVENGE** EURYTHMICS (RCA)
FRENCH KISSIN' IN THE USA DEBBIE HARRY (CHRYSALIS)	**14**	**SWEET FREEDOM** MICHAEL McDONALD (WARNER BROS)
BIG FUN THE GAP BAND (TOTAL EXPERIENCE/RCA)	**15**	**DIFFERENT LIGHT** BANGLES (CBS)
LAND OF CONFUSION GENESIS (VIRGIN)	**16**	**REMINISCING** FOSTER & ALLEN (STYLUS)
STEP RIGHT UP JAKI GRAHAM (EMI)	**17**	**SCOUNDREL DAYS** A-HA (WARNER BROS)
THE SKYE BOAT SONG ROGER WHITTAKER & DES O'CONNOR (TEMBO)	**18**	**SOUTH PACIFIC** K. TE KANAWA, J. CARRERAS, S. VAUGHAN (CBS)
BREAKOUT SWING OUT SISTER (MERCURY/PHONOGRAM)	**19**	**LONDON 0 HULL 4** THE HOUSEMARTINS (GO! DISCS)
BECAUSE OF YOU DEXYS MIDNIGHT RUNNERS (MERCURY)	**20**	**LOVERS** VARIOUS (TELSTAR)

S I N G L E S US A L B U M S

WALK LIKE AN EGYPTIAN BANGLES (COLUMBIA)	**1**	**LIVE/1975–85** BRUCE SPRINGSTEEN & E STREET (COLUMBIA)
EVERYBODY HAVE FUN TONIGHT WANG CHUNG (GEFFEN)	**2**	**AUGUST** ERIC CLAPTON (DUCK/WARNER BROS)
NOTORIOUS DURAN DURAN (CAPITOL)	**3**	**THIRD STAGE** BOSTON (MCA)
SHAKE YOU DOWN GREGORY ABBOTT (COLUMBIA)	**4**	**GET CLOSE** PRETENDERS (SIRE/WARNER BROS)
IS THIS LOVE SURVIVOR (SCOTTI BROS/CBS)	**5**	**LIVING IN THE 20TH CENTURY** STEVE MILLER BAND (CAPITOL)
C'EST LA VIE ROBBIE NEVIL (MANHATTAN)	**6**	**GEORGIA SATELLITES** GEORGIA SATELLITES (ELEKTRA)
THE WAY IT IS BRUCE HORNSBY & THE RANGE (RCA)	**7**	**THE WAY IT IS** BRUCE HORNSBY & THE RANGE (RCA)
CONTROL JANET JACKSON (A&M)	**8**	**SLIPPERY WHEN WET** BON JOVI (MERCURY/PG)
LAND OF CONFUSION GENESIS (ATLANTIC)	**9**	**WHIPLASH SMILE** BILLY IDOL (CHRYSALIS)
DON'T GET ME WRONG PRETENDERS (SIRE/WARNER BROS)	**10**	**THE LACE** BENJAMIN ORR (ELEKTRA)
AT THIS MOMENT BILLY VERA & THE BEATERS (RHINO)	**11**	**SO** PETER GABRIEL (GEFFEN)
WAR BRUCE SPRINGSTEEN & E STREET (COLUMBIA)	**12**	**FORE!** HUEY LEWIS AND THE NEWS (CHRYSALIS)
OPEN YOUR HEART MADONNA (SIRE/WARNER BROS)	**13**	**STRONG PERSUADER** ROBERT CRAY BAND (MERCURY/PG)
SOMEDAY GLASS TIGER (MANHATTEN)	**14**	**THINK VISUAL** KINKS (MCA)
YOU KNOW I LOVE YOU . . . DON'T YOU? HOWARD JONES (ELEKTRA)	**15**	**POWER** KANSAS (MCA)
VICTORY KOOL & THE GANG (MERCURY/PG)	**16**	**CAN'T HOLD BACK** EDDIE MONEY (COLUMBIA)
LOVE IS FOREVER BILLY OCEAN (JIVE/ARISTA)	**17**	**SOUNDTRACK** COLOR OF MONEY (MCA)
STAND BY ME BEN E. KING (ATLANTIC)	**18**	**KBC BAND** KBC BAND (ARISTA)
CHANGE OF HEART CYNDI LAUPER (PORTRAIT/CBS)	**19**	**THIS SIDE OF PARADISE** RIC OCASEK (GEFFEN)
THE FUTURE'S SO BRIGHT . . . TIMBUK3 (IRS/MCA)	**20**	**STILL STANDING** JASON & THE SCORCHERS (EMI AMERICA)

WEEK ENDING DECEMBER 27 1986
S I N G L E S UK A L B U M S

REET PETITE JACKIE WILSON (SMP)	**1**	**NOW, THAT'S WHAT I CALL MUSIC 8** VARIOUS (EMI/VIRGIN/POLYGRAM)
CARAVAN OF LOVE THE HOUSEMARTINS (GO! DISCS)	**2**	**THE WHOLE STORY** KATE BUSH (EMI)
THE FINAL COUNTDOWN EUROPE (EPIC)	**3**	**GRACELAND** PAUL SIMON (WARNER BROS)
OPEN YOUR HEART MADONNA (SIRE)	**4**	**HITS 5** VARIOUS (CBS/RCA ARIOLA/WEA)
SOMETIMES ERASURE (MUTE)	**5**	**TRUE BLUE** MADONNA (SIRE)
THE RAIN ORAN 'JUICE' JONES (DEF JAM)	**6**	**EVERY BREATH YOU TAKE – THE SINGLES** THE POLICE (A&M)
CRY WOLF A-HA (WARNER BROS)	**7**	**SILK AND STEEL** FIVE STAR (TENT/RCA)
IS THIS LOVE? ALISON MOYET (CBS)	**8**	**LIVE MAGIC** QUEEN (EMI)
SHAKE YOU DOWN GREGORY ABBOTT (CBS)	**9**	**REVENGE** EURYTHMICS (RCA)
LIVIN' ON A PRAYER BON JOVI (VERTIGO/PHONOGRAM)	**10**	**NOW – THE CHRISTMAS ALBUM** VARIOUS (EMI/VIRGIN)
SO COLD THE NIGHT COMMUNARDS (LONDON)	**11**	**SLIPPERY WHEN WET** BON JOVI (VERTIGO/PHONOGRAM)
BIG FUN THE GAP BAND (TOTAL EXPERIENCE/RCA)	**12**	**FORE!** HUEY LEWIS AND THE NEWS (CHRYSALIS)
BECAUSE OF YOU DEXYS MIDNIGHT RUNNERS (MERCURY)	**13**	**SWEET FREEDOM** MICHAEL McDONALD (WARNER BROS)
TAKE MY BREATH AWAY BERLIN (CBS)	**14**	**DIFFERENT LIGHT** BANGLES (CBS)
STEP RIGHT UP JAKI GRAHAM (EMI)	**15**	**THE FINAL** WHAM! (EPIC)
LAND OF CONFUSION GENESIS (VIRGIN)	**16**	**MUSIC FROM 'THE SINGING DETECTIVE'** VARIOUS (BBC)
DREAMIN' STATUS QUO (VERTIGO/PHONOGRAM)	**17**	**LONDON 0 HULL 4** THE HOUSEMARTINS (GO! DISCS)
NO MORE THE FOOL ELKIE BROOKS (LEGEND)	**18**	**AN ALBUM OF HYMNS** ALED JONES (TELSTAR)
FRENCH KISSIN' IN THE USA DEBBIE HARRY (CHRYSALIS)	**19**	**SCOUNDREL DAYS** A-HA (WARNER BROS)
THE SKYE BOAT SONG ROGER WHITTAKER & DES O'CONNOR (TEMBO)	**20**	**ORIGINAL SOUNDTRACK 'TOP GUN'** VARIOUS (CBS)

S I N G L E S US A L B U M S

NO US CHARTS PUBLISHED

WEEK ENDING JANUARY 3 1987
S I N G L E S   UK   A L B U M S

REET PETITE JACKIE WILSON (SMP)	**1**	NOW, THAT'S WHAT I CALL MUSIC 8 VARIOUS (EMI/VIRGIN/POLYGRAM)
CARAVAN OF LOVE THE HOUSEMARTINS (GO! DISCS)	**2**	TRUE BLUE MADONNA (SIRE)
THE FINAL COUNTDOWN EUROPE (EPIC)	**3**	GRACELAND PAUL SIMON (WARNER BROS)
OPEN YOUR HEART MADONNA (SIRE)	**4**	THE WHOLE STORY KATE BUSH (EMI)
CRY WOLF A-HA (WARNER BROS)	**5**	HITS 5 VARIOUS (CBS/RCA ARIOLA/WEA)
THE RAIN ORAN 'JUICE' JONES (DEF JAM)	**6**	SILK AND STEEL FIVE STAR (TENT/RCA)
SOMETIMES ERASURE (MUTE)	**7**	EVERY BREATH YOU TAKE – THE SINGLES THE POLICE (A&M)
IS THIS LOVE? ALISON MOYET (CBS)	**8**	REVENGE EURYTHMICS (RCA)
SHAKE YOU DOWN GREGORY ABBOTT (CBS)	**9**	LIVE MAGIC QUEEN (EMI)
LIVIN' ON A PRAYER BON JOVI (VERTIGO/PHONOGRAM)	**10**	MUSIC FROM 'THE SINGING DETECTIVE' VARIOUS (BBC)
SO COLD THE NIGHT COMMUNARDS (LONDON)	**11**	FORE! HUEY LEWIS AND THE NEWS (CHRYSALIS)
BIG FUN THE GAP BAND (TOTAL EXPERIENCE/RCA)	**12**	SLIPPERY WHEN WET BON JOVI (VERTIGO/PHONOGRAM)
TAKE MY BREATH AWAY BERLIN (CBS)	**13**	DIFFERENT LIGHT BANGLES (CBS)
LAND OF CONFUSION GENESIS (VIRGIN)	**14**	SWEET FREEDOM MICHAEL McDONALD (WARNER BROS)
DREAMIN' STATUS QUO (VERTIGO/PHONOGRAM)	**15**	THE FINAL WHAM! (EPIC)
BECAUSE OF YOU DEXYS MIDNIGHT RUNNERS (MERCURY)	**16**	ORIGINAL SOUNDTRACK 'TOP GUN' VARIOUS (CBS)
STEP RIGHT UP JAKI GRAHAM (EMI)	**17**	LONDON 0 HULL 4 THE HOUSEMARTINS (GO! DISCS)
NO MORE THE FOOL ELKIE BROOKS (LEGEND)	**18**	NOW – THE CHRISTMAS ALBUM VARIOUS (EMI/VIRGIN)
FRENCH KISSIN' IN THE USA DEBBIE HARRY (CHRYSALIS)	**19**	SCOUNDREL DAYS A-HA (WARNER BROS)
EACH TIME YOU BREAK MY HEART NICK KAMEN (WEA)	**20**	AN ALBUM OF HYMNS ALED JONES (TELSTAR)

S I N G L E S   US   A L B U M S

WALK LIKE AN EGYPTIAN BANGLES (COLUMBIA)	**1**	AUGUST ERIC CLAPTON (DUCK/WARNER BROS)
NOTORIOUS DURAN DURAN (CAPITOL)	**2**	LIVE/1975–85 BRUCE SPRINGSTEEN & E STREET (COLUMBIA)
SHAKE YOU DOWN GREGORY ABBOTT (COLUMBIA)	**3**	THIRD STAGE BOSTON (MCA)
C'EST LA VIE ROBBIE NEVIL (MANHATTAN)	**4**	GET CLOSE PRETENDERS (SIRE/WARNER BROS)
IS THIS LOVE SURVIVOR (SCOTTI BROS/CBS)	**5**	LIVING IN THE 20TH CENTURY STEVE MILLER BAND (CAPITOL)
CONTROL JANET JACKSON (A&M)	**6**	GEORGIA SATELLITES GEORGIA SATELLITES (ELEKTRA)
LAND OF CONFUSION GENESIS (ATLANTIC)	**7**	SLIPPERY WHEN WET BON JOVI (MERCURY/PG)
EVERYBODY HAVE FUN TONIGHT WANG CHUNG (GEFFEN)	**8**	THE WAY IT IS BRUCE HORNSBY & THE RANGE (RCA)
AT THIS MOMENT BILLY VERA & THE BEATERS (RHINO)	**9**	FORE! HUEY LEWIS AND THE NEWS (CHRYSALIS)
OPEN YOUR HEART MADONNA (SIRE/WARNER BROS)	**10**	STRONG PERSUADER ROBERT CRAY BAND (MERCURY/PG)
SOMEDAY GLASS TIGER (MANHATTAN)	**11**	SO PETER GABRIEL (GEFFEN)
DON'T GET ME WRONG PRETENDERS (SIRE/WARNER BROS)	**12**	WHIPLASH SMILE BILLY IDOL (CHRYSALIS)
THE WAY IT IS BRUCE HORNSBY & THE RANGE (RCA)	**13**	THINK VISUAL KINKS (MCA)
VICTORY KOOL & THE GANG (MERCURY/PG)	**14**	CAN'T HOLD BACK EDDIE MONEY (COLUMBIA)
CHANGE OF HEART CYNDI LAUPER (PORTRAIT/CBS)	**15**	THE LACE BENJAMIN ORR (ELEKTRA)
LOVE IS FOREVER BILLY OCEAN (JIVE/ARISTA)	**16**	KBC BAND KBC BAND (ARISTA)
WAR BRUCE SPRINGSTEEN & E STREET (COLUMBIA)	**17**	STILL STANDING JASON & THE SCORCHERS (EMI AMERICA)
WE'RE READY BOSTON (MCA)	**18**	POWER KANSAS (MCA)
ALL I WANTED KANSAS (MCA)	**19**	PRIVATE REVOLUTION WORLD PARTY (CHRYSALIS)
THE FUTURE'S SO BRIGHT . . . TIMBUK3 (IRS/MCA)	**20**	THIS SIDE OF PARADISE RIC OCASEK (GEFFEN)

WEEK ENDING JANUARY 10 1987
S I N G L E S   UK   A L B U M S

REET PETITE JACKIE WILSON (SMP)	**1**	NOW, THAT'S WHAT I CALL MUSIC 8 VARIOUS (EMI/VIRGIN/POLYGRAM)
CARAVAN OF LOVE THE HOUSEMARTINS (GO! DISCS)	**2**	THE WHOLE STORY KATE BUSH (EMI)
IS THIS LOVE? ALISON MOYET (CBS)	**3**	TRUE BLUE MADONNA (SIRE)
THE FINAL COUNTDOWN EUROPE (EPIC)	**4**	GRACELAND PAUL SIMON (WARNER BROS)
CRY WOLF A-HA (WARNER BROS)	**5**	SILK AND STEEL FIVE STAR (TENT/RCA)
OPEN YOUR HEART MADONNA (SIRE)	**6**	HITS 5 VARIOUS (CBS/RCA)
SOMETIMES ERASURE (MUTE)	**7**	EVERY BREATH YOU TAKE – THE SINGLES THE POLICE (A&M)
THE RAIN ORAN 'JUICE' JONES (DEF JAM)	**8**	SLIPPERY WHEN WET BON JOVI (VERTIGO/PHONOGRAM)
BIG FUN THE GAP BAND (TOTAL EXPERIENCE/RCA)	**9**	LIVE MAGIC QUEEN (EMI)
SHAKE YOU DOWN GREGORY ABBOTT (CBS)	**10**	REVENGE EURYTHMICS (RCA)
NO MORE THE FOOL ELKIE BROOKS (LEGEND)	**11**	SCOUNDREL DAYS A-HA (WARNER BROS)
SO COLD THE NIGHT COMMUNARDS (LONDON)	**12**	DIFFERENT LIGHT BANGLES (CBS)
LIVIN' ON A PRAYER BON JOVI (VERTIGO/PHONOGRAM)	**13**	FORE! HUEY LEWIS AND THE NEWS (CHRYSALIS)
LAND OF CONFUSION GENESIS (VIRGIN)	**14**	ORIGINAL SOUNDTRACK 'TOP GUN' VARIOUS (CBS)
STEP RIGHT UP JAKI GRAHAM (EMI)	**15**	LONDON 0 HULL 4 THE HOUSEMARTINS (GO! DISCS)
TAKE MY BREATH AWAY BERLIN (CBS)	**16**	BROTHERS IN ARMS DIRE STRAITS (VERTIGO/PHONOGRAM)
DREAMIN' STATUS QUO (VERTIGO/PHONOGRAM)	**17**	SWEET FREEDOM MICHAEL McDONALD (WARNER BROS)
JACK YOUR BODY STEVE 'SILK' HURLEY (LONDON)	**18**	THE FINAL WHAM! (EPIC)
HYMN TO HER THE PRETENDERS (REAL)	**19**	COMMUNARDS COMMUNARDS (LONDON)
OVER THE HILLS AND FAR AWAY GARY MOORE (10/VIRGIN)	**20**	DISCO PET SHOP BOYS (EMI)

S I N G L E S   US   A L B U M S

SHAKE YOU DOWN GREGORY ABBOTT (COLUMBIA)	**1**	AUGUST ERIC CLAPTON (DUCK/WARNER BROS)
AT THIS MOMENT BILLY VERA & THE BEATERS (RHINO)	**2**	THIRD STAGE BOSTON (MCA)
C'EST LA VIE ROBBIE NEVIL (MANHATTAN)	**3**	GET CLOSE PRETENDERS (SIRE/WARNER BROS)
OPEN YOUR HEART MADONNA (SIRE/WARNER BROS)	**4**	SLIPPERY WHEN WET BON JOVI (MERCURY/PG)
CONTROL JANET JACKSON (A&M)	**5**	THE WAY IT IS BRUCE HORNSBY & THE RANGE (RCA)
LAND OF CONFUSION GENESIS (ATLANTIC)	**6**	LIVE/1975–85 BRUCE SPRINGSTEEN & E STREET (COLUMBIA)
NOTORIOUS DURAN DURAN (CAPITOL)	**7**	LIVING IN THE 20TH CENTURY STEVE MILLER BAND (CAPITOL)
SOMEDAY GLASS TIGER (MANHATTAN)	**8**	GEORGIA SATELLITES GEORGIA SATELLITES (ELEKTRA)
IS THIS LOVE SURVIVOR (SCOTTI BROS/CBS)	**9**	FORE! HUEY LEWIS AND THE NEWS (CHRYSALIS)
CHANGE OF HEART CYNDI LAUPER (PORTRAIT/CBS)	**10**	STRONG PERSUADER ROBERT CRAY BAND (MERCURY/PG)
WALK LIKE AN EGYPTIAN BANGLES (COLUMBIA)	**11**	SO PETER GABRIEL (GEFFEN)
WILL YOU STILL LOVE ME? CHICAGO (WARNER BROS)	**12**	CAN'T HOLD BACK EDDIE MONEY (COLUMBIA)
VICTORY KOOL & THE GANG (MERCURY/PG)	**13**	WHIPLASH SMILE BILLY IDOL (CHRYSALIS)
WE'RE READY BOSTON (MCA)	**14**	THINK VISUAL KINKS (MCA)
EVERYBODY HAVE FUN TONIGHT WANG CHUNG (GEFFEN)	**15**	KBC BAND KBC BAND (ARISTA)
LIVIN' ON A PRAYER BON JOVI (MERCURY/PG)	**16**	PRIVATE REVOLUTION WORLD PARTY (CHRYSALIS)
TOUCH ME SAMANTHA FOX (JIVE/RCA)	**17**	STILL STANDING JASON & THE SCORCHERS (EMI AMERICA)
KEEP YOUR HANDS TO YOURSELF GEORGIA SATELLITES (ELEKTRA)	**18**	THE LACE BENJAMIN ORR (ELEKTRA)
ALL I WANTED KANSAS (MCA)	**19**	BOOMTOWN DAVID & DAVID (A&M)
THIS IS THE TIME BILLY JOEL (COLUMBIA)	**20**	POWER KANSAS (MCA)

WEEK ENDING JANUARY 17 1987

SINGLES UK ALBUMS

#	SINGLES	ALBUMS
1	REET PETITE — JACKIE WILSON (SMP)	THE WHOLE STORY — KATE BUSH (EMI)
2	JACK YOUR BODY — STEVE 'SILK' HURLEY (LONDON)	GRACELAND — PAUL SIMON (WARNER BROS)
3	IS THIS LOVE? — ALISON MOYET (CBS)	TRUE BLUE — MADONNA (SIRE)
4	BIG FUN — THE GAP BAND (TOTAL EXPERIENCE/RCA)	NOW, THAT'S WHAT I CALL MUSIC 8 — VARIOUS (EMI/VIRGIN/POLYGRAM)
5	NO MORE THE FOOL — ELKIE BROOKS (LEGEND)	LIVE MAGIC — QUEEN (EMI)
6	C'EST LA VIE — ROBBIE NEVIL (MANHATTAN/EMI)	SLIPPERY WHEN WET — BON JOVI (VERTIGO/PHONOGRAM)
7	CARAVAN OF LOVE — THE HOUSEMARTINS (GO! DISCS)	EVERY BREATH YOU TAKE – THE SINGLES — THE POLICE (A&M)
8	HYMN TO HER — THE PRETENDERS (REAL)	DIFFERENT LIGHT — BANGLES (CBS)
9	SOMETIMES — ERASURE (MUTE)	REVENGE — EURYTHMICS (RCA)
10	SURRENDER — SWING OUT SISTER (MERCURY/PHONOGRAM)	SILK AND STEEL — FIVE STAR (TENT/RCA)
11	THE RAIN — ORAN 'JUICE' JONES (DEF JAM)	SWEET FREEDOM — MICHAEL McDONALD (WARNER BROS)
12	OPEN YOUR HEART — MADONNA (SIRE)	HITS 5 — VARIOUS (CBS/RCA)
13	CRY WOLF — A-HA (WARNER BROS)	GET CLOSE — THE PRETENDERS (REAL/WEA)
14	THE FINAL COUNTDOWN — EUROPE (EPIC)	FORE! — HUEY LEWIS AND THE NEWS (CHRYSALIS)
15	IT DIDN'T MATTER — THE STYLE COUNCIL (POLYDOR)	BROTHERS IN ARMS — DIRE STRAITS (VERTIGO/PHONOGRAM)
16	LAND OF CONFUSION — GENESIS (VIRGIN)	MUSIC FROM 'THE SINGING DETECTIVE' — VARIOUS (BBC)
17	BALLERINA GIRL — LIONEL RICHIE (MOTOWN)	SCOUNDREL DAYS — A-HA (WARNER BROS)
18	REAL WILD CHILD — IGGY POP (A&M)	LONDON 0 HULL 4 — THE HOUSEMARTINS (GO! DISCS)
19	SHAKE YOU DOWN — GREGORY ABBOTT (CBS)	COMMUNARDS — COMMUNARDS (LONDON)
20	OVER THE HILLS AND FAR AWAY — GARY MOORE (10/VIRGIN)	ORIGINAL SOUNDTRACK 'TOP GUN' — VARIOUS (CBS)

SINGLES US ALBUMS

#	SINGLES	ALBUMS
1	AT THIS MOMENT — BILLY VERA & THE BEATERS (RHINO)	AUGUST — ERIC CLAPTON (DUCK/WARNER BROS)
2	OPEN YOUR HEART — MADONNA (SIRE/WARNER BROS)	GET CLOSE — PRETENDERS (SIRE/WARNER BROS)
3	SHAKE YOU DOWN — GREGORY ABBOTT (COLUMBIA)	THIRD STAGE — BOSTON (MCA)
4	C'EST LA VIE — ROBBIE NEVIL (MANHATTAN)	SLIPPERY WHEN WET — BON JOVI (MERCURY/PG)
5	LAND OF CONFUSION — GENESIS (ATLANTIC)	THE WAY IT IS — BRUCE HORNSBY & THE RANGE (RCA)
6	CONTROL — JANET JACKSON (A&M)	LIVING IN THE 20TH CENTURY — STEVE MILLER BAND (CAPITOL)
7	SOMEDAY — GLASS TIGER (MANHATTEN)	GEORGIA SATELLITES — GEORGIA SATELLITES (ELEKTRA)
8	CHANGE OF HEART — CYNDI LAUPER (PORTRAIT/CBS)	STRONG PERSUADER — ROBERT CRAY BAND (MERCURY/PG)
9	WILL YOU STILL LOVE ME? — CHICAGO (WARNER BROS)	FORE! — HUEY LEWIS AND THE NEWS (CHRYSALIS)
10	LIVIN' ON A PRAYER — BON JOVI (MERCURY/PG)	SO — PETER GABRIEL (GEFFEN)
11	WE'RE READY — BOSTON (MCA)	LIVE/1975–85 — BRUCE SPRINGSTEEN & E STREET (COLUMBIA)
12	IS THIS LOVE — SURVIVOR (SCOTTI BROS/CBS)	CAN'T HOLD BACK — EDDIE MONEY (COLUMBIA)
13	TOUCH ME — SAMANTHA FOX (JIVE/RCA)	SOUNDTRACK — GOLDEN CHILD (CAPITOL)
14	KEEP YOUR HANDS TO YOURSELF — GEORGIA SATELLITES (ELEKTRA)	WHIPLASH SMILE — BILLY IDOL (CHRYSALIS)
15	VICTORY — KOOL & THE GANG (MERCURY/PG)	THINK VISUAL — KINKS (MCA)
16	JACOB'S LADDER — HUEY LEWIS AND THE NEWS (CHRYSALIS)	KBC BAND — KBC BAND (ARISTA)
17	NOTORIOUS — DURAN DURAN (CAPITOL)	PRIVATE REVOLUTION — WORLD PARTY (CHRYSALIS)
18	THIS IS THE TIME — BILLY JOEL (COLUMBIA)	BOOMTOWN — DAVID & DAVID (A&M)
19	YOU GOT IT ALL — JETS (MCA)	POWER — KANSAS (MCA)
20	STAY THE NIGHT — BENJAMIN ORR (ELEKTRA)	RAISED ON RADIO — JOURNEY (COLUMBIA)

WEEK ENDING JANUARY 24 1987

SINGLES UK ALBUMS

#	SINGLES	ALBUMS
1	JACK YOUR BODY — STEVE 'SILK' HURLEY (LONDON)	THE WHOLE STORY — KATE BUSH (EMI)
2	REET PETITE — JACKIE WILSON (SMP)	GRACELAND — PAUL SIMON (WARNER BROS)
3	IS THIS LOVE? — ALISON MOYET (CBS)	LIVE MAGIC — QUEEN (EMI)
4	C'EST LA VIE — ROBBIE NEVIL (MANHATTAN/EMI)	DIFFERENT LIGHT — BANGLES (CBS)
5	NO MORE THE FOOL — ELKIE BROOKS (LEGEND)	TRUE BLUE — MADONNA (SIRE)
6	BIG FUN — THE GAP BAND (TOTAL EXPERIENCE/RCA)	NOW, THAT'S WHAT I CALL MUSIC 8 — VARIOUS (EMI/VIRGIN/POLYGRAM)
7	SURRENDER — SWING OUT SISTER (MERCURY/PHONOGRAM)	SLIPPERY WHEN WET — BON JOVI (VERTIGO/PHONOGRAM)
8	HYMN TO HER — THE PRETENDERS (REAL)	GET CLOSE — THE PRETENDERS (REAL/WEA)
9	IT DIDN'T MATTER — THE STYLE COUNCIL (POLYDOR)	SWEET FREEDOM — MICHAEL McDONALD (WARNER BROS)
10	REAL WILD CHILD — IGGY POP (A&M)	THE HOUSE OF BLUE LIGHT — DEEP PURPLE (POLYDOR)
11	WASTELAND — THE MISSION (MERCURY/PHONOGRAM)	EVERY BREATH YOU TAKE – THE SINGLES — THE POLICE (A&M)
12	SOMETHING IN MY HOUSE — DEAD OR ALIVE (EPIC)	THE VERY BEST OF ELKIE BROOKS — ELKIE BROOKS (TELSTAR)
13	RAT IN MI KITCHEN — UB40 (DEP INTERNATIONAL/VIRGIN)	NO MORE THE FOOL — ELKIE BROOKS (LEGEND)
14	THIS WHEEL'S ON FIRE — SIOUXSIE & THE BANSHEES (WONDERLAND)	REVENGE — EURYTHMICS (RCA)
15	DOWN TO EARTH — CURIOSITY KILLED THE CAT (MERCURY)	DISCO — PET SHOP BOYS (EMI)
16	WALKING DOWN YOUR STREET — BANGLES (CBS)	BROTHERS IN ARMS — DIRE STRAITS (VERTIGO/PHONOGRAM)
17	SOMETIMES — ERASURE (MUTE)	AUGUST — ERIC CLAPTON (DUCK/WARNER BROS)
18	THE RAIN — ORAN 'JUICE' JONES (DEF JAM)	FORE! — HUEY LEWIS AND THE NEWS (CHRYSALIS)
19	BALLERINA GIRL — LIONEL RICHIE (MOTOWN)	SILK AND STEEL — FIVE STAR (TENT/RCA)
20	ALMAZ — RANDY CRAWFORD (WARNER BROS)	INVISIBLE TOUCH — GENESIS (VIRGIN)

SINGLES US ALBUMS

#	SINGLES	ALBUMS
1	OPEN YOUR HEART — MADONNA (SIRE/WARNER BROS)	AUGUST — ERIC CLAPTON (DUCK/WARNER BROS)
2	AT THIS MOMENT — BILLY VERA & THE BEATERS (RHINO)	SLIPPERY WHEN WET — BON JOVI (MERCURY/PG)
3	WILL YOU STILL LOVE ME? — CHICAGO (WARNER BROS)	THIRD STAGE — BOSTON (MCA)
4	LIVIN' ON A PRAYER — BON JOVI (MERCURY/PG)	GET CLOSE — PRETENDERS (SIRE/WARNER BROS)
5	CHANGE OF HEART — CYNDI LAUPER (PORTRAIT/CBS)	THE WAY IT IS — BRUCE HORNSBY & THE RANGE (RCA)
6	LAND OF CONFUSION — GENESIS (ATLANTIC)	LIVING IN THE 20TH CENTURY — STEVE MILLER BAND (CAPITOL)
7	SOMEDAY — GLASS TIGER (MANHATTEN)	STRONG PERSUADER — ROBERT CRAY BAND (MERCURY/PG)
8	WE'RE READY — BOSTON (MCA)	GEORGIA SATELLITES — GEORGIA SATELLITES (ELEKTRA)
9	TOUCH ME — SAMANTHA FOX (JIVE/RCA)	CAN'T HOLD BACK — EDDIE MONEY (COLUMBIA)
10	JACOB'S LADDER — HUEY LEWIS AND THE NEWS (CHRYSALIS)	SO — PETER GABRIEL (GEFFEN)
11	KEEP YOUR HANDS TO YOURSELF — GEORGIA SATELLITES (ELEKTRA)	PRIVATE REVOLUTION — WORLD PARTY (CHRYSALIS)
12	SHAKE YOU DOWN — GREGORY ABBOTT (COLUMBIA)	FORE! — HUEY LEWIS AND THE NEWS (CHRYSALIS)
13	C'EST LA VIE — ROBBIE NEVIL (MANHATTAN)	WHIPLASH SMILE — BILLY IDOL (CHRYSALIS)
14	CONTROL — JANET JACKSON (A&M)	GAUDI — ALAN PARSONS PROJECT (ARISTA)
15	YOU GOT IT ALL — JETS (MCA)	KBC BAND — KBC BAND (ARISTA)
16	STAY THE NIGHT — BENJAMIN ORR (ELEKTRA)	THINK VISUAL — KINKS (MCA)
17	STOP TO LOVE — LUTHER VANDROSS (EPIC)	SOUNDTRACK — GOLDEN CHILD (CAPITOL)
18	BALLERINA GIRL — LIONEL RICHIE (MOTOWN)	BOOMTOWN — DAVID & DAVID (A&M)
19	LOVE YOU DOWN — READY FOR THE WORLD (MCA)	THE HOUSE OF BLUE LIGHT — DEEP PURPLE (MERCURY/PG)
20	TALK TO ME — CHICO DeBARGE (MOTOWN)	RAISED ON RADIO — JOURNEY (COLUMBIA)

WEEK ENDING JANUARY 31 1987
S I N G L E S UK A L B U M S

#	Singles	Albums
1	JACK YOUR BODY — STEVE 'SILK' HURLEY (LONDON)	GRACELAND — PAUL SIMON (WARNER BROS)
2	I KNEW YOU WERE WAITING — ARETHA FRANKLIN AND GEORGE MICHAEL (EPIC)	THE WHOLE STORY — KATE BUSH (EMI)
3	C'EST LA VIE — ROBBIE NEVIL (MANHATTAN/EMI)	DIFFERENT LIGHT — BANGLES (CBS)
4	IS THIS LOVE? — ALISON MOYET (CBS)	LIVE MAGIC — QUEEN (EMI)
5	NO MORE THE FOOL — ELKIE BROOKS (LEGEND)	TRUE BLUE — MADONNA (SIRE)
6	REET PETITE — JACKIE WILSON (SMP)	GET CLOSE — THE PRETENDERS (REAL/WEA)
7	HEARTACHE — PEPSI & SHIRLIE (POLYDOR)	NO MORE THE FOOL — ELKIE BROOKS (LEGEND)
8	DOWN TO EARTH — CURIOSITY KILLED THE CAT (MERCURY)	SWEET FREEDOM — MICHAEL McDONALD (WARNER BROS)
9	SURRENDER — SWING OUT SISTER (MERCURY/PHONOGRAM)	SLIPPERY WHEN WET — BON JOVI (VERTIGO/PHONOGRAM)
10	ALMAZ — RANDY CRAWFORD (WARNER BROS)	NOW, THAT'S WHAT I CALL MUSIC 8 — VARIOUS (EMI/VIRGIN/POLYGRAM)
11	BIG FUN — THE GAP BAND (TOTAL EXPERIENCE/RCA)	EVERY BREATH YOU TAKE – THE SINGLES — THE POLICE (A&M)
12	RAT IN MI KITCHEN — UB40 (DEP INTERNATIONAL/VIRGIN)	THE VERY BEST OF ELKIE BROOKS — ELKIE BROOKS (TELSTAR)
13	WASTELAND — THE MISSION (MERCURY/PHONOGRAM)	AUGUST — ERIC CLAPTON (DUCK/WARNER BROS)
14	SOMETHING IN MY HOUSE — DEAD OR ALIVE (EPIC)	DANCING ON THE CEILING — LIONEL RICHIE (MOTOWN)
15	I LOVE MY RADIO — TAFFY (TRANSGLOBAL/RHYTHM KING/MUTE)	REVENGE — EURYTHMICS (RCA)
16	HYMN TO HER — THE PRETENDERS (REAL)	THE HOUSE OF BLUE LIGHT — DEEP PURPLE (POLYDOR)
17	REAL WILD CHILD — IGGY POP (A&M)	SILK AND STEEL — FIVE STAR (TENT/RCA)
18	THIS WHEEL'S ON FIRE — SIOUXSIE & THE BANSHEES (WONDERLAND)	BROTHERS IN ARMS — DIRE STRAITS (VERTIGO/PHONOGRAM)
19	IT DIDN'T MATTER — THE STYLE COUNCIL (POLYDOR)	DISCO — PET SHOP BOYS (EMI)
20	JACK THE GROOVE — RAZE (CHAMPION)	MUSIC FROM 'THE SINGING DETECTIVE' — VARIOUS (BBC)

S I N G L E S US A L B U M S

#	Singles	Albums
1	OPEN YOUR HEART — MADONNA (SIRE/WARNER BROS)	AUGUST — ERIC CLAPTON (DUCK/WARNER BROS)
2	LIVIN' ON A PRAYER — BON JOVI (MERCURY/PG)	SLIPPERY WHEN WET — BON JOVI (MERCURY/PG)
3	WILL YOU STILL LOVE ME? — CHICAGO (WARNER BROS)	THIRD STAGE — BOSTON (MCA)
4	CHANGE OF HEART — CYNDI LAUPER (PORTRAIT/CBS)	THE WAY IT IS — BRUCE HORNSBY & THE RANGE (RCA)
5	AT THIS MOMENT — BILLY VERA & THE BEATERS (RHINO)	STRONG PERSUADER — ROBERT CRAY BAND (MERCURY/PG)
6	JACOB'S LADDER — HUEY LEWIS AND THE NEWS (CHRYSALIS)	LIVING IN THE 20TH CENTURY — STEVE MILLER BAND (CAPITOL)
7	WE'RE READY — BOSTON (MCA)	CAN'T HOLD BACK — EDDIE MONEY (COLUMBIA)
8	TOUCH ME — SAMANTHA FOX (JIVE/RCA)	GET CLOSE — PRETENDERS (SIRE/WARNER BROS)
9	KEEP YOUR HANDS TO YOURSELF — GEORGIA SATELLITES (ELEKTRA)	PRIVATE REVOLUTION — WORLD PARTY (CHRYSALIS)
10	YOU GOT IT ALL — JETS (MCA)	GEORGIA SATELLITES — GEORGIA SATELLITES (ELEKTRA)
11	BALLERINA GIRL — LIONEL RICHIE (MOTOWN)	GAUDI — ALAN PARSONS PROJECT (ARISTA)
12	LOVE YOU DOWN — READY FOR THE WORLD (MCA)	KBC BAND — KBC BAND (ARISTA)
13	STOP TO LOVE — LUTHER VANDROSS (EPIC)	WHIPLASH SMILE — BILLY IDOL (CHRYSALIS)
14	STAY THE NIGHT — BENJAMIN ORR (ELEKTRA)	INVISIBLE TOUCH — GENESIS (ATLANTIC)
15	BIG TIME — PETER GABRIEL (GEFFEN)	THE HOUSE OF BLUE LIGHT — DEEP PURPLE (MERCURY/PG)
16	TALK TO ME — CHICO DeBARGE (MOTOWN)	BY THE LIGHT OF THE MOON — LOS LOBOS (SLASH/WARNER BROS)
17	I'LL BE ALRIGHT WITHOUT YOU — JOURNEY (COLUMBIA)	SO — PETER GABRIEL (GEFFEN)
18	LAND OF CONFUSION — GENESIS (ATLANTIC)	BOOMTOWN — DAVID & DAVID (A&M)
19	SOMEDAY — GLASS TIGER (MANHATTEN)	THE FINAL COUNTDOWN — EUROPE (EPIC)
20	C'EST LA VIE — ROBBIE NEVIL (MANHATTAN)	FORE! — HUEY LEWIS AND THE NEWS (CHRYSALIS)

WEEK ENDING FEBRUARY 7 1987
S I N G L E S UK A L B U M S

#	Singles	Albums
1	I KNEW YOU WERE WAITING — ARETHA FRANKLIN AND GEORGE MICHAEL (EPIC)	GRACELAND — PAUL SIMON (WARNER BROS)
2	HEARTACHE — PEPSI & SHIRLIE (POLYDOR)	THE WHOLE STORY — KATE BUSH (EMI)
3	JACK YOUR BODY — STEVE 'SILK' HURLEY (LONDON)	DIFFERENT LIGHT — BANGLES (CBS)
4	ALMAZ — RANDY CRAWFORD (WARNER BROS)	LIVE MAGIC — QUEEN (EMI)
5	DOWN TO EARTH — CURIOSITY KILLED THE CAT (MERCURY)	NO MORE THE FOOL — ELKIE BROOKS (LEGEND)
6	C'EST LA VIE — ROBBIE NEVIL (MANHATTAN/EMI)	SWEET FREEDOM — MICHAEL McDONALD (WARNER BROS)
7	I LOVE MY RADIO — TAFFY (TRANSGLOBAL/RHYTHM KING/MUTE)	AUGUST — ERIC CLAPTON (DUCK/WARNER BROS)
8	NO MORE THE FOOL — ELKIE BROOKS (LEGEND)	GET CLOSE — THE PRETENDERS (REAL/WEA)
9	SURRENDER — SWING OUT SISTER (MERCURY/PHONOGRAM)	TRUE BLUE — MADONNA (SIRE)
10	IS THIS LOVE? — ALISON MOYET (CBS)	THE VERY BEST OF ELKIE BROOKS — ELKIE BROOKS (TELSTAR)
11	IT DOESN'T HAVE TO BE THIS WAY — THE BLOW MONKEYS (RCA)	NOW, THAT'S WHAT I CALL MUSIC 8 — VARIOUS (EMI/VIRGIN/POLYGRAM)
12	SHOPLIFTERS OF THE WORLD UNITE — THE SMITHS (ROUGH TRADE)	SLIPPERY WHEN WET — BON JOVI (VERTIGO/PHONOGRAM)
13	REET PETITE — JACKIE WILSON (SMP)	SILK AND STEEL — FIVE STAR (TENT/RCA)
14	YOU SEXY THING — HOT CHOCOLATE (EMI)	RAPTURE — ANITA BAKER (ELEKTRA)
15	RAT IN MI KITCHEN — UB40 (DEP INTERNATIONAL/VIRGIN)	DANCING ON THE CEILING — LIONEL RICHIE (MOTOWN)
16	ONCE BITTEN TWICE SHY — VESTA WILLIAMS (A&M)	EVERY BREATH YOU TAKE – THE SINGLES — THE POLICE (A&M)
17	BIG FUN — THE GAP BAND (TOTAL EXPERIENCE/RCA)	BROTHERS IN ARMS — DIRE STRAITS (VERTIGO/PHONOGRAM)
18	HYMN TO HER — THE PRETENDERS (REAL)	REVENGE — EURYTHMICS (RCA)
19	THE MUSIC OF THE NIGHT — MICHAEL CRAWFORD (POLYDOR)	THE FINAL COUNTDOWN — EUROPE (EPIC)
20	JACK THE GROOVE — RAZE (CHAMPION)	ZAZU — ROSIE VELA (A&M)

S I N G L E S US A L B U M S

#	Singles	Albums
1	LIVIN' ON A PRAYER — BON JOVI (MERCURY/PG)	AUGUST — ERIC CLAPTON (DUCK/WARNER BROS)
2	WILL YOU STILL LOVE ME? — CHICAGO (WARNER BROS)	SLIPPERY WHEN WET — BON JOVI (MERCURY/PG)
3	OPEN YOUR HEART — MADONNA (SIRE/WARNER BROS)	READY OR NOT — LOU GRAMM (ATLANTIC)
4	JACOB'S LADDER — HUEY LEWIS AND THE NEWS (CHRYSALIS)	THE WAY IT IS — BRUCE HORNSBY & THE RANGE (RCA)
5	CHANGE OF HEART — CYNDI LAUPER (PORTRAIT/CBS)	THIRD STAGE — BOSTON (MCA)
6	YOU GOT IT ALL — JETS (MCA)	STRONG PERSUADER — ROBERT CRAY BAND (MERCURY/PG)
7	KEEP YOUR HANDS TO YOURSELF — GEORGIA SATELLITES (ELEKTRA)	PRIVATE REVOLUTION — WORLD PARTY (CHRYSALIS)
8	TOUCH ME — SAMANTHA FOX (JIVE/RCA)	GAUDI — ALAN PARSONS PROJECT (ARISTA)
9	BALLERINA GIRL — LIONEL RICHIE (MOTOWN)	LIVING IN THE 20TH CENTURY — STEVE MILLER BAND (CAPITOL)
10	BIG TIME — PETER GABRIEL (GEFFEN)	GEORGIA SATELLITES — GEORGIA SATELLITES (ELEKTRA)
11	LOVE YOU DOWN — READY FOR THE WORLD (MCA)	CAN'T HOLD BACK — EDDIE MONEY (COLUMBIA)
12	STOP TO LOVE — LUTHER VANDROSS (EPIC)	BY THE LIGHT OF THE MOON — LOS LOBOS (SLASH/WARNER BROS)
13	WE'RE READY — BOSTON (MCA)	INVISIBLE TOUCH — GENESIS (ATLANTIC)
14	I'LL BE ALRIGHT WITHOUT YOU — JOURNEY (COLUMBIA)	KBC BAND — KBC BAND (ARISTA)
15	TALK TO ME — CHICO DeBARGE (MOTOWN)	GET CLOSE — PRETENDERS (SIRE/WARNER BROS)
16	RESPECT YOURSELF — BRUCE WILLIS (MOTOWN)	THE HOUSE OF BLUE LIGHT — DEEP PURPLE (MERCURY/PG)
17	I WANNA GO BACK — EDDIE MONEY (COLUMBIA)	THE FINAL COUNTDOWN — EUROPE (EPIC)
18	AT THIS MOMENT — BILLY VERA & THE BEATERS (RHINO)	BOOMTOWN — DAVID & DAVID (A&M)
19	MANDOLIN RAIN — BRUCE HORNSBY & THE RANGE (RCA)	BACK IN THE HIGH LIFE — STEVE WINWOOD (ISLAND/WARNER BROS)
20	FIGHT FOR YOUR RIGHT (TO PARTY) — BEASTIE BOYS (DEF JAM/COLUMBIA)	THE LACE — BENJAMIN ORR (ELEKTRA)

WEEK ENDING FEBRUARY 14 1987

S I N G L E S UK A L B U M S

#	SINGLES	ALBUMS
1	I KNEW YOU WERE WAITING — ARETHA FRANKLIN AND GEORGE MICHAEL (EPIC)	GRACELAND — PAUL SIMON (WARNER BROS)
2	HEARTACHE — PEPSI & SHIRLIE (POLYDOR)	THE COST OF LOVING — THE STYLE COUNCIL (POLYDOR)
3	DOWN TO EARTH — CURIOSITY KILLED THE CAT (MERCURY)	AUGUST — ERIC CLAPTON (DUCK/WARNER BROS)
4	ALMAZ — RANDY CRAWFORD (WARNER BROS)	DIFFERENT LIGHT — BANGLES (CBS)
5	IT DOESN'T HAVE TO BE THIS WAY — THE BLOW MONKEYS (RCA)	THE WHOLE STORY — KATE BUSH (EMI)
6	I LOVE MY RADIO — TAFFY (TRANSGLOBAL/RHYTHM KING/MUTE)	NO MORE THE FOOL — ELKIE BROOKS (LEGEND)
7	THE MUSIC OF THE NIGHT — MICHAEL CRAWFORD (POLYDOR)	SILK AND STEEL — FIVE STAR (TENT/RCA)
8	JACK YOUR BODY — STEVE 'SILK' HURLEY (LONDON)	TRUE BLUE — MADONNA (SIRE)
9	MALE STRIPPER — MAN 2 MAN MEETS MAN PARRISH (BOLTS)	SWEET FREEDOM — MICHAEL McDONALD (WARNER BROS)
10	YOU SEXY THING — HOT CHOCOLATE (EMI)	LIVE MAGIC — QUEEN (EMI)
11	STAY OUT OF MY LIFE — FIVE STAR (TENT/RCA)	NOW, THAT'S WHAT I CALL MUSIC 8 — VARIOUS (EMI/VIRGIN/POLYGRAM)
12	SHOPLIFTERS OF THE WORLD UNITE — THE SMITHS (ROUGH TRADE)	MIDNIGHT TO MIDNIGHT — THE PSYCHEDELIC FURS (CBS)
13	NO MORE THE FOOL — ELKIE BROOKS (LEGEND)	GET CLOSE — THE PRETENDERS (REAL/WEA)
14	ONCE BITTEN TWICE SHY — VESTA WILLIAMS (A&M)	DANCING ON THE CEILING — LIONEL RICHIE (MOTOWN)
15	IS THIS LOVE? — ALISON MOYET (CBS)	SLIPPERY WHEN WET — BON JOVI (VERTIGO/PHONOGRAM)
16	C'EST LA VIE — ROBBIE NEVIL (MANHATTAN/EMI)	GIVE ME THE REASON — LUTHER VANDROSS (EPIC)
17	BEHIND THE MASK — ERIC CLAPTON (DUCK/WARNER BROS)	BROTHERS IN ARMS — DIRE STRAITS (VERTIGO/PHONOGRAM)
18	RUNNING IN THE FAMILY — LEVEL 42 (POLYDOR)	RAPTURE — ANITA BAKER (ELEKTRA)
19	STAND BY ME — BEN E. KING (ATLANTIC)	ABSTRACT EMOTIONS — RANDY CRAWFORD (WARNER BROS)
20	ROCK THE NIGHT — EUROPE (EPIC)	REVENGE — EURYTHMICS (RCA)

S I N G L E S US A L B U M S

#	SINGLES	ALBUMS
1	LIVIN' ON A PRAYER — BON JOVI (MERCURY/PG)	READY OR NOT — LOU GRAMM (ATLANTIC)
2	WILL YOU STILL LOVE ME? — CHICAGO (WARNER BROS)	AUGUST — ERIC CLAPTON (DUCK/WARNER BROS)
3	JACOB'S LADDER — HUEY LEWIS AND THE NEWS (CHRYSALIS)	SLIPPERY WHEN WET — BON JOVI (MERCURY/PG)
4	YOU GOT IT ALL — JETS (MCA)	THE WAY IT IS — BRUCE HORNSBY & THE RANGE (RCA)
5	KEEP YOUR HANDS TO YOURSELF — GEORGIA SATELLITES (ELEKTRA)	THIRD STAGE — BOSTON (MCA)
6	BIG TIME — PETER GABRIEL (GEFFEN)	GAUDI — ALAN PARSONS PROJECT (ARISTA)
7	OPEN YOUR HEART — MADONNA (SIRE/WARNER BROS)	PRIVATE REVOLUTION — WORLD PARTY (CHRYSALIS)
8	RESPECT YOURSELF — BRUCE WILLIS (MOTOWN)	GEORGIA SATELLITES — GEORGIA SATELLITES (ELEKTRA)
9	BALLERINA GIRL — LIONEL RICHIE (MOTOWN)	STRONG PERSUADER — ROBERT CRAY BAND (MERCURY/PG)
10	LOVE YOU DOWN — READY FOR THE WORLD (MCA)	BY THE LIGHT OF THE MOON — LOS LOBOS (SLASH/WARNER BROS)
11	MANDOLIN RAIN — BRUCE HORNSBY & THE RANGE (RCA)	LIFE AS WE KNOW IT — REO SPEEDWAGON (EPIC)
12	I'LL BE ALRIGHT WITHOUT YOU — JOURNEY (COLUMBIA)	INVISIBLE TOUCH — GENESIS (ATLANTIC)
13	I WANNA GO BACK — EDDIE MONEY (COLUMBIA)	I'M NO ANGEL — GREGG ALLMAN BAND (EPIC)
14	TOUCH ME — SAMANTHA FOX (JIVE/RCA)	CAN'T HOLD BACK — EDDIE MONEY (COLUMBIA)
15	FIGHT FOR YOUR RIGHT (TO PARTY) — BEASTIE BOYS (DEF JAM/COLUMBIA)	SOUNDTRACK — OVER THE TOP (COLUMBIA)
16	LET'S WAIT AWHILE — JANET JACKSON (A&M)	BACK IN THE HIGH LIFE — STEVE WINWOOD (ISLAND/WARNER BROS)
17	STOP TO LOVE — LUTHER VANDROSS (EPIC)	THE FINAL COUNTDOWN — EUROPE (EPIC)
18	SOMEWHERE OUT THERE — LINDA RONSTADT & JAMES INGRAM (MCA)	THE HOUSE OF BLUE LIGHT — DEEP PURPLE (MERCURY/PG)
19	CHANGE OF HEART — CYNDI LAUPER (PORTRAIT/CBS)	LIVING IN THE 20TH CENTURY — STEVE MILLER BAND (CAPITOL)
20	BRAND NEW LOVER — DEAD OR ALIVE (EPIC)	THE LACE — BENJAMIN ORR (ELEKTRA)

WEEK ENDING FEBRUARY 21 1987

S I N G L E S UK A L B U M S

#	SINGLES	ALBUMS
1	STAND BY ME — BEN E. KING (ATLANTIC)	'THE PHANTOM OF THE OPERA' — VARIOUS (POLYDOR)
2	I KNEW YOU WERE WAITING — ARETHA FRANKLIN AND GEORGE MICHAEL (EPIC)	GRACELAND — PAUL SIMON (WARNER BROS)
3	DOWN TO EARTH — CURIOSITY KILLED THE CAT (MERCURY)	THE VERY BEST OF HOT CHOCOLATE — HOT CHOCOLATE (RAK)
4	HEARTACHE — PEPSI & SHIRLIE (POLYDOR)	AUGUST — ERIC CLAPTON (DUCK/WARNER BROS)
5	WHEN A MAN LOVES A WOMAN — PERCY SLEDGE (ATLANTIC)	SILK AND STEEL — FIVE STAR (TENT/RCA)
6	MALE STRIPPER — MAN 2 MAN MEETS MAN PARRISH (BOLTS)	PICTURE BOOK — SIMPLY RED (ELEKTRA)
7	ALMAZ — RANDY CRAWFORD (WARNER BROS)	DIFFERENT LIGHT — BANGLES (CBS)
8	IT DOESN'T HAVE TO BE THIS WAY — THE BLOW MONKEYS (RCA)	THE WHOLE STORY — KATE BUSH (EMI)
9	STAY OUT OF MY LIFE — FIVE STAR (TENT/RCA)	SO — PETER GABRIEL (VIRGIN)
10	RUNNING IN THE FAMILY — LEVEL 42 (POLYDOR)	LIVE MAGIC — QUEEN (EMI)
11	THE MUSIC OF THE NIGHT — MICHAEL CRAWFORD (POLYDOR)	BROTHERS IN ARMS — DIRE STRAITS (VERTIGO/PHONOGRAM)
12	I LOVE MY RADIO — TAFFY (TRANSGLOBAL/RHYTHM KING/MUTE)	GIVE ME THE REASON — LUTHER VANDROSS (EPIC)
13	YOU SEXY THING — HOT CHOCOLATE (EMI)	RAPTURE — ANITA BAKER (ELEKTRA)
14	COMING AROUND AGAIN — CARLY SIMON (ARISTA)	ABSTRACT EMOTIONS — RANDY CRAWFORD (WARNER BROS)
15	BEHIND THE MASK — ERIC CLAPTON (DUCK/WARNER BROS)	THE COST OF LOVING — THE STYLE COUNCIL (POLYDOR)
16	ONCE BITTEN TWICE SHY — VESTA WILLIAMS (A&M)	REVENGE — EURYTHMICS (RCA)
17	ROCK THE NIGHT — EUROPE (EPIC)	NO MORE THE FOOL — ELKIE BROOKS (LEGEND)
18	CRUSH ON YOU — THE JETS (MCA)	SWEET FREEDOM — MICHAEL McDONALD (WARNER BROS)
19	LIVE IT UP — MENTAL AS ANYTHING (EPIC)	SLIPPERY WHEN WET — BON JOVI (VERTIGO/PHONOGRAM)
20	JACK YOUR BODY — STEVE 'SILK' HURLEY (LONDON)	NOW, THAT'S WHAT I CALL MUSIC 8 — VARIOUS (EMI/VIRGIN/POLYGRAM)

S I N G L E S US A L B U M S

#	SINGLES	ALBUMS
1	LIVIN' ON A PRAYER — BON JOVI (MERCURY/PG)	READY OR NOT — LOU GRAMM (ATLANTIC)
2	JACOB'S LADDER — HUEY LEWIS AND THE NEWS (CHRYSALIS)	AUGUST — ERIC CLAPTON (DUCK/WARNER BROS)
3	YOU GOT IT ALL — JETS (MCA)	GAUDI — ALAN PARSONS PROJECT (ARISTA)
4	WILL YOU STILL LOVE ME? — CHICAGO (WARNER BROS)	SLIPPERY WHEN WET — BON JOVI (MERCURY/PG)
5	BIG TIME — PETER GABRIEL (GEFFEN)	I'M NO ANGEL — GREGG ALLMAN BAND (EPIC)
6	RESPECT YOURSELF — BRUCE WILLIS (MOTOWN)	THE WAY IT IS — BRUCE HORNSBY & THE RANGE (RCA)
7	MANDOLIN RAIN — BRUCE HORNSBY & THE RANGE (RCA)	LIFE AS WE KNOW IT — REO SPEEDWAGON (EPIC)
8	KEEP YOUR HANDS TO YOURSELF — GEORGIA SATELLITES (ELEKTRA)	GEORGIA SATELLITES — GEORGIA SATELLITES (ELEKTRA)
9	LET'S WAIT AWHILE — JANET JACKSON (A&M)	BY THE LIGHT OF THE MOON — LOS LOBOS (SLASH/WARNER BROS)
10	I WANNA GO BACK — EDDIE MONEY (COLUMBIA)	THIRD STAGE — BOSTON (MCA)
11	I'LL BE ALRIGHT WITHOUT YOU — JOURNEY (COLUMBIA)	SOUNDTRACK — OVER THE TOP (COLUMBIA)
12	FIGHT FOR YOUR RIGHT (TO PARTY) — BEASTIE BOYS (DEF JAM/COLUMBIA)	PRIVATE REVOLUTION — WORLD PARTY (CHRYSALIS)
13	SOMEWHERE OUT THERE — LINDA RONSTADT & JAMES INGRAM (MCA)	BACK IN THE HIGH LIFE — STEVE WINWOOD (ISLAND/WARNER BROS)
14	NOTHING'S GONNA STOP US NOW — STARSHIP (GRUNT/RCA)	INVISIBLE TOUCH — GENESIS (ATLANTIC)
15	LOVE YOU DOWN — READY FOR THE WORLD (MCA)	STRONG PERSUADER — ROBERT CRAY BAND (MERCURY/PG)
16	BRAND NEW LOVER — DEAD OR ALIVE (EPIC)	THE HOUSE OF BLUE LIGHT — DEEP PURPLE (MERCURY/PG)
17	TONIGHT, TONIGHT, TONIGHT — GENESIS (ATLANTIC)	CAN'T HOLD BACK — EDDIE MONEY (COLUMBIA)
18	LEAN ON ME — CLUB NOUVEAU (WARNER BROS)	FREEDOM — SANTANA (COLUMBIA)
19	BALLERINA GIRL — LIONEL RICHIE (MOTOWN)	CROWDED HOUSE — CROWDED HOUSE (CAPITOL)
20	OPEN YOUR HEART — MADONNA (SIRE/WARNER BROS)	PASSION — ROBIN TROWER (GNP/CRESCENDO)

WEEK ENDING FEBRUARY 28 1987

SINGLES UK ALBUMS

#	SINGLES (UK)	ALBUMS (UK)
1	STAND BY ME — BEN E. KING (ATLANTIC)	'THE PHANTOM OF THE OPERA' — VARIOUS (POLYDOR)
2	WHEN A MAN LOVES A WOMAN — PERCY SLEDGE (ATLANTIC)	THE VERY BEST OF HOT CHOCOLATE — HOT CHOCOLATE (RAK)
3	DOWN TO EARTH — CURIOSITY KILLED THE CAT (MERCURY)	GRACELAND — PAUL SIMON (WARNER BROS)
4	MALE STRIPPER — MAN 2 MAN MEETS MAN PARRISH (BOLTS)	AUGUST — ERIC CLAPTON (DUCK/WARNER BROS)
5	I KNEW YOU WERE WAITING — ARETHA FRANKLIN AND GEORGE MICHAEL (EPIC)	SILK AND STEEL — FIVE STAR (TENT/RCA)
6	HEARTACHE — PEPSI & SHIRLIE (POLYDOR)	PICTURE BOOK — SIMPLY RED (ELEKTRA)
7	RUNNING IN THE FAMILY — LEVEL 42 (POLYDOR)	LIVE MAGIC — QUEEN (EMI)
8	LIVE IT UP — MENTAL AS ANYTHING (EPIC)	DIFFERENT LIGHT — BANGLES (CBS)
9	CRUSH ON YOU — THE JETS (MCA)	GIVE ME THE REASON — LUTHER VANDROSS (EPIC)
10	COMING AROUND AGAIN — CARLY SIMON (ARISTA)	THE FINAL COUNTDOWN — EUROPE (EPIC)
11	SONIC BOOM BOY — WESTWORLD (RCA)	SO — PETER GABRIEL (VIRGIN)
12	ROCK THE NIGHT — EUROPE (EPIC)	THE WHOLE STORY — KATE BUSH (EMI)
13	STAY OUT OF MY LIFE — FIVE STAR (TENT/RCA)	BROTHERS IN ARMS — DIRE STRAITS (VERTIGO/PHONOGRAM)
14	IT DOESN'T HAVE TO BE THIS WAY — THE BLOW MONKEYS (RCA)	REVENGE — EURYTHMICS (RCA)
15	THE RIGHT THING — SIMPLY RED (WEA)	NOW, THAT'S WHAT I CALL MUSIC 8 — VARIOUS (EMI/VIRGIN/POLYGRAM)
16	BEHIND THE MASK — ERIC CLAPTON (DUCK/WARNER BROS)	RAPTURE — ANITA BAKER (ELEKTRA)
17	MANHATTAN SKYLINE — A-HA (WARNER BROS)	TRUE BLUE — MADONNA (SIRE)
18	LOVE REMOVAL MACHINE — THE CULT (BEGGARS BANQUET)	SLIPPERY WHEN WET — BON JOVI (VERTIGO/PHONOGRAM)
19	THE MUSIC OF THE NIGHT — MICHAEL CRAWFORD (POLYDOR)	NO MORE THE FOOL — ELKIE BROOKS (LEGEND)
20	YOU SEXY THING — HOT CHOCOLATE (EMI)	DISCO — PET SHOP BOYS (EMI)

SINGLES US ALBUMS

#	SINGLES (US)	ALBUMS (US)
1	JACOB'S LADDER — HUEY LEWIS AND THE NEWS (CHRYSALIS)	READY OR NOT — LOU GRAMM (ATLANTIC)
2	LIVIN' ON A PRAYER — BON JOVI (MERCURY/PG)	I'M NO ANGEL — GREGG ALLMAN BAND (EPIC)
3	BIG TIME — PETER GABRIEL (GEFFEN)	AUGUST — ERIC CLAPTON (DUCK/WARNER BROS)
4	LET'S WAIT AWHILE — JANET JACKSON (A&M)	SOUNDTRACK — OVER THE TOP (COLUMBIA)
5	MANDOLIN RAIN — BRUCE HORNSBY & THE RANGE (RCA)	LIFE AS WE KNOW IT — REO SPEEDWAGON (EPIC)
6	RESPECT YOURSELF — BRUCE WILLIS (MOTOWN)	GAUDI — ALAN PARSONS PROJECT (ARISTA)
7	YOU GOT IT ALL — JETS (MCA)	BY THE LIGHT OF THE MOON — LOS LOBOS (SLASH/WARNER BROS)
8	LEAN ON ME — CLUB NOUVEAU (WARNER BROS)	SLIPPERY WHEN WET — BON JOVI (MERCURY/PG)
9	NOTHING'S GONNA STOP US NOW — STARSHIP (GRUNT/RCA)	GEORGIA SATELLITES — GEORGIA SATELLITES (ELEKTRA)
10	I WANNA GO BACK — EDDIE MONEY (COLUMBIA)	BACK IN THE HIGH LIFE — STEVE WINWOOD (ISLAND/WARNER BROS)
11	SOMEWHERE OUT THERE — LINDA RONSTADT & JAMES INGRAM (MCA)	THE WAY IT IS — BRUCE HORNSBY & THE RANGE (RCA)
12	FIGHT FOR YOUR RIGHT (TO PARTY) — BEASTIE BOYS (DEF JAM/COLUMBIA)	THIRD STAGE — BOSTON (MCA)
13	TONIGHT, TONIGHT, TONIGHT — GENESIS (ATLANTIC)	PRIVATE REVOLUTION — WORLD PARTY (CHRYSALIS)
14	BRAND NEW LOVER — DEAD OR ALIVE (EPIC)	STRONG PERSUADER — ROBERT CRAY BAND (MERCURY/PG)
15	WILL YOU STILL LOVE ME? — CHICAGO (WARNER BROS)	THE HOUSE OF BLUE LIGHT — DEEP PURPLE (MERCURY/PG)
16	LET'S GO — WANG CHUNG (GEFFEN)	CROWDED HOUSE — CROWDED HOUSE (CAPITOL)
17	I'LL BE ALRIGHT WITHOUT YOU — JOURNEY (COLUMBIA)	FREEDOM — SANTANA (COLUMBIA)
18	THE FINAL COUNTDOWN — EUROPE (EPIC)	INVISIBLE TOUCH — GENESIS (ATLANTIC)
19	KEEP YOUR HANDS TO YOURSELF — GEORGIA SATELLITES (ELEKTRA)	NEVER ENOUGH — PATTY SMYTH (COLUMBIA)
20	COME GO WITH ME — EXPOSE (ARISTA)	CAN'T HOLD BACK — EDDIE MONEY (COLUMBIA)

WEEK ENDING MARCH 7 1987

SINGLES UK ALBUMS

#	SINGLES (UK)	ALBUMS (UK)
1	STAND BY ME — BEN E. KING (ATLANTIC)	'THE PHANTOM OF THE OPERA' — VARIOUS (POLYDOR)
2	WHEN A MAN LOVES A WOMAN — PERCY SLEDGE (ATLANTIC)	THE WORLD WON'T LISTEN — THE SMITHS (ROUGH TRADE)
3	LIVE IT UP — MENTAL AS ANYTHING (EPIC)	THE VERY BEST OF HOT CHOCOLATE — HOT CHOCOLATE (RAK)
4	MALE STRIPPER — MAN 2 MAN MEETS MAN PARRISH (BOLTS)	GRACELAND — PAUL SIMON (WARNER BROS)
5	CRUSH ON YOU — THE JETS (MCA)	PICTURE BOOK — SIMPLY RED (ELEKTRA)
6	RUNNING IN THE FAMILY — LEVEL 42 (POLYDOR)	SILK AND STEEL — FIVE STAR (TENT/RCA)
7	EVERYTHING I OWN — BOY GEORGE (VIRGIN)	AUGUST — ERIC CLAPTON (DUCK/WARNER BROS)
8	DOWN TO EARTH — CURIOSITY KILLED THE CAT (MERCURY)	LIVE MAGIC — QUEEN (EMI)
9	THE GREAT PRETENDER — FREDDIE MERCURY (PARLOPHONE)	THE FINAL COUNTDOWN — EUROPE (EPIC)
10	I GET THE SWEETEST FEELING — JACKIE WILSON (SMP)	GIVE ME THE REASON — LUTHER VANDROSS (EPIC)
11	THE RIGHT THING — SIMPLY RED (WEA)	DIFFERENT LIGHT — BANGLES (CBS)
12	COMING AROUND AGAIN — CARLY SIMON (ARISTA)	REVENGE — EURYTHMICS (RCA)
13	MANHATTAN SKYLINE — A-HA (WARNER BROS)	BROTHERS IN ARMS — DIRE STRAITS (VERTIGO/PHONOGRAM)
14	SONIC BOOM BOY — WESTWORLD (RCA)	THE WHOLE STORY — KATE BUSH (EMI)
15	HEARTACHE — PEPSI & SHIRLIE (POLYDOR)	SO — PETER GABRIEL (VIRGIN)
16	ROCK THE NIGHT — EUROPE (EPIC)	TRUE BLUE — MADONNA (SIRE)
17	I KNEW YOU WERE WAITING — ARETHA FRANKLIN AND GEORGE MICHAEL (EPIC)	COMMUNARDS — COMMUNARDS (LONDON)
18	LOVE REMOVAL MACHINE — THE CULT (BEGGARS BANQUET)	NOW, THAT'S WHAT I CALL MUSIC 8 — VARIOUS (EMI/VIRGIN/POLYGRAM)
19	STAY OUT OF MY LIFE — FIVE STAR (TENT/RCA)	RAPTURE — ANITA BAKER (ELEKTRA)
20	IT DOESN'T HAVE TO BE — ERASURE (MUTE)	SLIPPERY WHEN WET — BON JOVI (VERTIGO/PHONOGRAM)

SINGLES US ALBUMS

#	SINGLES (US)	ALBUMS (US)
1	JACOB'S LADDER — HUEY LEWIS AND THE NEWS (CHRYSALIS)	READY OR NOT — LOU GRAMM (ATLANTIC)
2	LEAN ON ME — CLUB NOUVEAU (WARNER BROS)	I'M NO ANGEL — GREGG ALLMAN BAND (EPIC)
3	LET'S WAIT AWHILE — JANET JACKSON (A&M)	AUGUST — ERIC CLAPTON (DUCK/WARNER BROS)
4	MANDOLIN RAIN — BRUCE HORNSBY & THE RANGE (RCA)	SOUNDTRACK — OVER THE TOP (COLUMBIA)
5	NOTHING'S GONNA STOP US NOW — STARSHIP (GRUNT/RCA)	LIFE AS WE KNOW IT — REO SPEEDWAGON (EPIC)
6	TONIGHT, TONIGHT, TONIGHT — GENESIS (ATLANTIC)	BACK IN THE HIGH LIFE — STEVE WINWOOD (ISLAND/WARNER BROS)
7	LIVIN' ON A PRAYER — BON JOVI (MERCURY/PG)	SLIPPERY WHEN WET — BON JOVI (MERCURY/PG)
8	BIG TIME — PETER GABRIEL (GEFFEN)	BY THE LIGHT OF THE MOON — LOS LOBOS (SLASH/WARNER BROS)
9	RESPECT YOURSELF — BRUCE WILLIS (MOTOWN)	GEORGIA SATELLITES — GEORGIA SATELLITES (ELEKTRA)
10	SOMEWHERE OUT THERE — LINDA RONSTADT & JAMES INGRAM (MCA)	NEVER ENOUGH — PATTY SMYTH (COLUMBIA)
11	YOU GOT IT ALL — JETS (MCA)	GAUDI — ALAN PARSONS PROJECT (ARISTA)
12	LET'S GO — WANG CHUNG (GEFFEN)	BROADCAST — CUTTING CREW (VIRGIN)
13	THE FINAL COUNTDOWN — EUROPE (EPIC)	CROWDED HOUSE — CROWDED HOUSE (CAPITOL)
14	BRAND NEW LOVER — DEAD OR ALIVE (EPIC)	STRONG PERSUADER — ROBERT CRAY BAND (MERCURY/PG)
15	I WANNA GO BACK — EDDIE MONEY (COLUMBIA)	THE HOUSE OF BLUE LIGHT — DEEP PURPLE (MERCURY/PG)
16	COME GO WITH ME — EXPOSE (ARISTA)	FREEDOM — SANTANA (COLUMBIA)
17	I KNEW YOU WERE WAITING — ARETHA FRANKLIN & GEORGE MICHAEL (ARISTA)	PRIVATE REVOLUTION — WORLD PARTY (CHRYSALIS)
18	DON'T DREAM IT'S OVER — CROWDED HOUSE (CAPITOL)	THIRD STAGE — BOSTON (MCA)
19	MIDNIGHT BLUE — LOU GRAMM (ATLANTIC)	THE WAY IT IS — BRUCE HORNSBY & THE RANGE (RCA)
20	FIGHT FOR YOUR RIGHT (TO PARTY) — BEASTIE BOYS (DEF JAM/COLUMBIA)	GRACELAND — PAUL SIMON (WARNER BROS)

WEEK ENDING MARCH 14 1987

SINGLES UK ALBUMS

#	Singles	Albums
1	EVERYTHING I OWN — BOY GEORGE (VIRGIN)	THE VERY BEST OF HOT CHOCOLATE — HOT CHOCOLATE (RAK)
2	STAND BY ME — BEN E. KING (ATLANTIC)	'THE PHANTOM OF THE OPERA' — VARIOUS (POLYDOR)
3	I GET THE SWEETEST FEELING — JACKIE WILSON (SMP)	THE WORLD WON'T LISTEN — THE SMITHS (ROUGH TRADE)
4	THE GREAT PRETENDER — FREDDIE MERCURY (PARLOPHONE)	GRACELAND — PAUL SIMON (WARNER BROS)
5	LIVE IT UP — MENTAL AS ANYTHING (EPIC)	PICTURE BOOK — SIMPLY RED (ELEKTRA)
6	WHEN A MAN LOVES A WOMAN — PERCY SLEDGE (ATLANTIC)	SILK AND STEEL — FIVE STAR (TENT/RCA)
7	RESPECTABLE — MEL & KIM (SUPREME)	AUGUST — ERIC CLAPTON (DUCK/WARNER BROS)
8	CRUSH ON YOU — THE JETS (MCA)	WILD FRONTIER — GARY MOORE (10/VIRGIN)
9	MALE STRIPPER — MAN 2 MAN MEETS MAN PARRISH (BOLTS)	LIVE MAGIC — QUEEN (EMI)
10	RUNNING IN THE FAMILY — LEVEL 42 (POLYDOR)	GIVE ME THE REASON — LUTHER VANDROSS (EPIC)
11	MOONLIGHTING 'THEME' — AL JARREAU (WEA INTERNATIONAL)	SAINT JULIAN — JULIAN COPE (ISLAND)
12	THE RIGHT THING — SIMPLY RED (WEA)	THE FINAL COUNTDOWN — EUROPE (EPIC)
13	COMING AROUND AGAIN — CARLY SIMON (ARISTA)	BROTHERS IN ARMS — DIRE STRAITS (VERTIGO/PHONOGRAM)
14	MANHATTAN SKYLINE — A-HA (WARNER BROS)	COMMUNARDS — COMMUNARDS (LONDON)
15	DOWN TO EARTH — CURIOSITY KILLED THE CAT (MERCURY)	THROUGH THE LOOKING GLASS — SIOUXSIE & THE BANSHEES (WONDERLAND)
16	WEAK IN THE PRESENCE OF BEAUTY — ALISON MOYET (CBS)	REVENGE — EURYTHMICS (RCA)
17	IT DOESN'T HAVE TO BE — ERASURE (MUTE)	STAND BY ME (THE ULTIMATE COLLECTION) — BEN E. KING (ATLANTIC)
18	SONIC BOOM BOY — WESTWORLD (RCA)	IMPRESSIONS — VARIOUS (K-TEL)
19	LOVE REMOVAL MACHINE — THE CULT (BEGGARS BANQUET)	DIFFERENT LIGHT — BANGLES (CBS)
20	SIGN 'O' THE TIMES — PRINCE (PAISLEY PARK/WARNER BROS)	THE WHOLE STORY — KATE BUSH (EMI)

SINGLES US ALBUMS

#	Singles	Albums
1	LEAN ON ME — CLUB NOUVEAU (WARNER BROS)	READY OR NOT — LOU GRAMM (ATLANTIC)
2	NOTHING'S GONNA STOP US NOW — STARSHIP (GRUNT/RCA)	I'M NO ANGEL — GREGG ALLMAN BAND (EPIC)
3	LET'S WAIT AWHILE — JANET JACKSON (A&M)	SOUNDTRACK — OVER THE TOP (COLUMBIA)
4	MANDOLIN RAIN — BRUCE HORNSBY & THE RANGE (RCA)	BACK IN THE HIGH LIFE — STEVE WINWOOD (ISLAND/WARNER BROS)
5	TONIGHT, TONIGHT, TONIGHT — GENESIS (ATLANTIC)	NEVER ENOUGH — PATTY SMYTH (COLUMBIA)
6	JACOB'S LADDER — HUEY LEWIS AND THE NEWS (CHRYSALIS)	BROADCAST — CUTTING CREW (VIRGIN)
7	LET'S GO — WANG CHUNG (GEFFEN)	AUGUST — ERIC CLAPTON (DUCK/WARNER BROS)
8	THE FINAL COUNTDOWN — EUROPE (EPIC)	LIFE AS WE KNOW IT — REO SPEEDWAGON (EPIC)
9	SOMEWHERE OUT THERE — LINDA RONSTADT & JAMES INGRAM (MCA)	SLIPPERY WHEN WET — BON JOVI (MERCURY/PG)
10	COME GO WITH ME — EXPOSE (ARISTA)	CROWDED HOUSE — CROWDED HOUSE (CAPITOL)
11	I KNEW YOU WERE WAITING — ARETHA FRANKLIN & GEORGE MICHAEL (ARISTA)	BY THE LIGHT OF THE MOON — LOS LOBOS (SLASH/WARNER BROS)
12	BIG TIME — PETER GABRIEL (GEFFEN)	GEORGIA SATELLITES — GEORGIA SATELLITES (ELEKTRA)
13	LIVIN' ON A PRAYER — BON JOVI (MERCURY/PG)	STRONG PERSUADER — ROBERT CRAY BAND (MERCURY/PG)
14	DON'T DREAM IT'S OVER — CROWDED HOUSE (CAPITOL)	WISHES — JON BUTCHER (CAPITOL)
15	MIDNIGHT BLUE — LOU GRAMM (ATLANTIC)	THE HOUSE OF BLUE LIGHT — DEEP PURPLE (MERCURY/PG)
16	RESPECT YOURSELF — BRUCE WILLIS (MOTOWN)	GRACELAND — PAUL SIMON (WARNER BROS)
17	BRAND NEW LOVER — DEAD OR ALIVE (EPIC)	FREEDOM — SANTANA (COLUMBIA)
18	THAT AIN'T LOVE — REO SPEEDWAGON (EPIC)	MIDNIGHT TO MIDNIGHT — PSYCHEDELIC FURS (COLUMBIA)
19	WHAT YOU GET IS WHAT YOU SEE — TINA TURNER (CAPITOL)	SOUNDTRACK — LIGHT OF DAY (BLACKHEART/CBS)
20	YOU GOT IT ALL — JETS (MCA)	GAUDI — ALAN PARSONS PROJECT (ARISTA)

WEEK ENDING MARCH 21 1987

SINGLES UK ALBUMS

#	Singles	Albums
1	EVERYTHING I OWN — BOY GEORGE (VIRGIN)	THE JOSHUA TREE — U2 (ISLAND)
2	RESPECTABLE — MEL & KIM (SUPREME)	MEN AND WOMEN — SIMPLY RED (WEA)
3	I GET THE SWEETEST FEELING — JACKIE WILSON (SMP)	THE VERY BEST OF HOT CHOCOLATE — HOT CHOCOLATE (RAK)
4	THE GREAT PRETENDER — FREDDIE MERCURY (PARLOPHONE)	'THE PHANTOM OF THE OPERA' — VARIOUS (POLYDOR)
5	LIVE IT UP — MENTAL AS ANYTHING (EPIC)	MOVE CLOSER — VARIOUS (CBS)
6	STAND BY ME — BEN E. KING (ATLANTIC)	GRACELAND — PAUL SIMON (WARNER BROS)
7	WEAK IN THE PRESENCE OF BEAUTY — ALISON MOYET (CBS)	THE WORLD WON'T LISTEN — THE SMITHS (ROUGH TRADE)
8	MOONLIGHTING 'THEME' — AL JARREAU (WEA INTERNATIONAL)	PICTURE BOOK — SIMPLY RED (ELEKTRA)
9	WHEN A MAN LOVES A WOMAN — PERCY SLEDGE (ATLANTIC)	SILK AND STEEL — FIVE STAR (TENT/RCA)
10	CRUSH ON YOU — THE JETS (MCA)	AUGUST — ERIC CLAPTON (DUCK/WARNER BROS)
11	RESPECT YOURSELF — BRUCE WILLIS (MOTOWN)	LIVE MAGIC — QUEEN (EMI)
12	RUNNING IN THE FAMILY — LEVEL 42 (POLYDOR)	THE FINAL COUNTDOWN — EUROPE (EPIC)
13	MALE STRIPPER — MAN 2 MAN MEETS MAN PARRISH (BOLTS)	COMMUNARDS — COMMUNARDS (LONDON)
14	FIGHT FOR YOUR RIGHT (TO PARTY) — BEASTIE BOYS (DEF JAM)	STAND BY ME (THE ULTIMATE COLLECTION) — BEN E. KING (ATLANTIC)
15	IT DOESN'T HAVE TO BE — ERASURE (MUTE)	BROTHERS IN ARMS — DIRE STRAITS (VERTIGO/PHONOGRAM)
16	SIGN 'O' THE TIMES — PRINCE (PAISLEY PARK/WARNER BROS)	WILD FRONTIER — GARY MOORE (10/VIRGIN)
17	LOVING YOU IS SWEETER THAN EVER — NICK KAMEN (WEA)	GIVE ME THE REASON — LUTHER VANDROSS (EPIC)
18	THE RIGHT THING — SIMPLY RED (WEA)	IMPRESSIONS — VARIOUS (K-TEL)
19	TONIGHT, TONIGHT, TONIGHT — GENESIS (VIRGIN)	SO — PETER GABRIEL (VIRGIN)
20	COMING AROUND AGAIN — CARLY SIMON (ARISTA)	REVENGE — EURYTHMICS (RCA)

SINGLES US ALBUMS

#	Singles	Albums
1	LEAN ON ME — CLUB NOUVEAU (WARNER BROS)	THE JOSHUA TREE — U2 (ISLAND)
2	NOTHING'S GONNA STOP US NOW — STARSHIP (GRUNT/RCA)	READY OR NOT — LOU GRAMM (ATLANTIC)
3	TONIGHT, TONIGHT, TONIGHT — GENESIS (ATLANTIC)	I'M NO ANGEL — GREGG ALLMAN BAND (EPIC)
4	LET'S WAIT AWHILE — JANET JACKSON (A&M)	BROADCAST — CUTTING CREW (VIRGIN)
5	MANDOLIN RAIN — BRUCE HORNSBY & THE RANGE (RCA)	NEVER ENOUGH — PATTY SMYTH (COLUMBIA)
6	LET'S GO — WANG CHUNG (GEFFEN)	BACK IN THE HIGH LIFE — STEVE WINWOOD (ISLAND/WARNER BROS)
7	THE FINAL COUNTDOWN — EUROPE (EPIC)	SLIPPERY WHEN WET — BON JOVI (MERCURY/PG)
8	I KNEW YOU WERE WAITING — ARETHA FRANKLIN & GEORGE MICHAEL (ARISTA)	SOUNDTRACK — OVER THE TOP (COLUMBIA)
9	COME GO WITH ME — EXPOSE (ARISTA)	CROWDED HOUSE — CROWDED HOUSE (CAPITOL)
10	DON'T DREAM IT'S OVER — CROWDED HOUSE (CAPITOL)	WISHES — JON BUTCHER (CAPITOL)
11	MIDNIGHT BLUE — LOU GRAMM (ATLANTIC)	AUGUST — ERIC CLAPTON (DUCK/WARNER BROS)
12	SOMEWHERE OUT THERE — LINDA RONSTADT & JAMES INGRAM (MCA)	MIDNIGHT TO MIDNIGHT — PSYCHEDELIC FURS (COLUMBIA)
13	THE FINER THINGS — STEVE WINWOOD (ISLAND/WARNER BROS)	STRONG PERSUADER — ROBERT CRAY BAND (MERCURY/PG)
14	WALKING DOWN YOUR STREET — BANGLES (COLUMBIA)	LIFE AS WE KNOW IT — REO SPEEDWAGON (EPIC)
15	THAT AIN'T LOVE — REO SPEEDWAGON (EPIC)	GRACELAND — PAUL SIMON (WARNER BROS)
16	WHAT YOU GET IS WHAT YOU SEE — TINA TURNER (CAPITOL)	THE HOUSE OF BLUE LIGHT — DEEP PURPLE (MERCURY/PG)
17	SIGN 'O' THE TIMES — PRINCE (PAISLEY PARK/WARNER BROS)	BY THE LIGHT OF THE MOON — LOS LOBOS (SLASH/WARNER BROS)
18	JACOB'S LADDER — HUEY LEWIS AND THE NEWS (CHRYSALIS)	FROZEN GHOST — FROZEN GHOST (ATLANTIC)
19	THE HONEYTHIEF — HIPSWAY (COLUMBIA)	GEORGIA SATELLITES — GEORGIA SATELLITES (ELEKTRA)
20	BIG TIME — PETER GABRIEL (GEFFEN)	FREEDOM — SANTANA (COLUMBIA)

S I N G L E S UK A L B U M S

#	Singles	Albums
1	RESPECTABLE — MEL & KIM (SUPREME)	THE JOSHUA TREE — U2 (ISLAND)
2	EVERYTHING I OWN — BOY GEORGE (VIRGIN)	RUNNING IN THE FAMILY — LEVEL 42 (POLYDOR)
3	I GET THE SWEETEST FEELING — JACKIE WILSON (SMP)	MEN AND WOMEN — SIMPLY RED (WEA)
4	WITH OR WITHOUT YOU — U2 (ISLAND)	MOVE CLOSER — VARIOUS (CBS)
5	THE GREAT PRETENDER — FREDDIE MERCURY (PARLOPHONE)	THE VERY BEST OF HOT CHOCOLATE — HOT CHOCOLATE (RAK)
6	WEAK IN THE PRESENCE OF BEAUTY — ALISON MOYET (CBS)	'THE PHANTOM OF THE OPERA' — VARIOUS (POLYDOR)
7	RESPECT YOURSELF — BRUCE WILLIS (MOTOWN)	GRACELAND — PAUL SIMON (WARNER BROS)
8	LIVE IT UP — MENTAL AS ANYTHING (EPIC)	SILK AND STEEL — FIVE STAR (TENT/RCA)
9	LET'S WAIT AWHILE — JANET JACKSON (BREAKOUT/A&M USA)	PICTURE BOOK — SIMPLY RED (ELEKTRA)
10	SIGN 'O' THE TIMES — PRINCE (PAISLEY PARK/WARNER BROS)	LIVE MAGIC — QUEEN (EMI)
11	FIGHT FOR YOUR RIGHT (TO PARTY) — BEASTIE BOYS (DEF JAM)	AUGUST — ERIC CLAPTON (DUCK/WARNER BROS)
12	IT DOESN'T HAVE TO BE — ERASURE (MUTE)	THE WORLD WON'T LISTEN — THE SMITHS (ROUGH TRADE)
13	MOONLIGHTING 'THEME' — AL JARREAU (WEA INTERNATIONAL)	SO — PETER GABRIEL (VIRGIN)
14	STAND BY ME — BEN E. KING (ATLANTIC)	INVISIBLE TOUCH — GENESIS (VIRGIN)
15	BIG TIME — PETER GABRIEL (VIRGIN)	IMPRESSIONS — VARIOUS (K-TEL)
16	LOVING YOU IS SWEETER THAN EVER — NICK KAMEN (WEA)	GIVE ME THE REASON — LUTHER VANDROSS (EPIC)
17	CRUSH ON YOU — THE JETS (MCA)	TRUE BLUE — MADONNA (SIRE)
18	TONIGHT, TONIGHT, TONIGHT — GENESIS (VIRGIN)	THE FINAL COUNTDOWN — EUROPE (EPIC)
19	WHEN A MAN LOVES A WOMAN — PERCY SLEDGE (ATLANTIC)	STAND BY ME (THE ULTIMATE COLLECTION) — BEN E. KING (ATLANTIC)
20	MALE STRIPPER — MAN 2 MAN MEETS MAN PARRISH (BOLTS)	WILD FRONTIER — GARY MOORE (10/VIRGIN)

S I N G L E S US A L B U M S

#	Singles	Albums
1	NOTHING'S GONNA STOP US NOW — STARSHIP (GRUNT/RCA)	THE JOSHUA TREE — U2 (ISLAND)
2	LEAN ON ME — CLUB NOUVEAU (WARNER BROS)	READY OR NOT — LOU GRAMM (ATLANTIC)
3	TONIGHT, TONIGHT, TONIGHT — GENESIS (ATLANTIC)	I'M NO ANGEL — GREGG ALLMAN BAND (EPIC)
4	I KNEW YOU WERE WAITING — ARETHA FRANKLIN & GEORGE MICHAEL (ARISTA)	BROADCAST — CUTTING CREW (VIRGIN)
5	LET'S GO — WANG CHUNG (GEFFEN)	NEVER ENOUGH — PATTY SMYTH (COLUMBIA)
6	DON'T DREAM IT'S OVER — CROWDED HOUSE (CAPITOL)	SLIPPERY WHEN WET — BON JOVI (MERCURY/PG)
7	COME GO WITH ME — EXPOSE (ARISTA)	WISHES — JON BUTCHER (CAPITOL)
8	MIDNIGHT BLUE — LOU GRAMM (ATLANTIC)	MIDNIGHT TO MIDNIGHT — PSYCHEDELIC FURS (COLUMBIA)
9	THE FINER THINGS — STEVE WINWOOD (ISLAND/WARNER BROS)	BACK IN THE HIGH LIFE — STEVE WINWOOD (ISLAND/WARNER BROS)
10	WALKING DOWN YOUR STREET — BANGLES (COLUMBIA)	FROZEN GHOST — FROZEN GHOST (ATLANTIC)
11	LET'S WAIT AWHILE — JANET JACKSON (A&M)	AUGUST — ERIC CLAPTON (DUCK/WARNER BROS)
12	MANDOLIN RAIN — BRUCE HORNSBY & THE RANGE (RCA)	STRONG PERSUADER — ROBERT CRAY BAND (MERCURY/PG)
13	SIGN 'O' THE TIMES — PRINCE (PAISLEY PARK/WARNER BROS)	BIG LIFE — NIGHT RANGER (CAMEL/MCA)
14	THE FINAL COUNTDOWN — EUROPE (EPIC)	CROWDED HOUSE — CROWDED HOUSE (CAPITOL)
15	WHAT YOU GET IS WHAT YOU SEE — TINA TURNER (CAPITOL)	SOUNDTRACK — OVER THE TOP (COLUMBIA)
16	(I JUST) DIED IN YOUR ARMS — CUTTING CREW (VIRGIN)	CAN'T HOLD BACK — EDDIE MONEY (COLUMBIA)
17	THE HONEYTHIEF — HIPSWAY (COLUMBIA)	BY THE LIGHT OF THE MOON — LOS LOBOS (SLASH/WARNER BROS)
18	DOMINOES — ROBBIE NEVIL (MANHATTAN)	THUNDER — ANDY TAYLOR (MCA)
19	LA ISLA BONITA — MADONNA (SIRE/WARNER BROS)	GEORGIA SATELLITES — GEORGIA SATELLITES (ELEKTRA)
20	STONE LOVE — KOOL & THE GANG (MERCURY/PG)	THE HOUSE OF BLUE LIGHT — DEEP PURPLE (MERCURY/PG)

S I N G L E S UK A L B U M S

#	Singles	Albums
1	LET IT BE — FERRY AID (SUN/ZEEBRUGGE DISASTER FUND)	NOW, THAT'S WHAT I CALL MUSIC 9 — VARIOUS (VIRGIN/EMI/POLYGRAM)
2	RESPECTABLE — MEL & KIM (SUPREME)	THE JOSHUA TREE — U2 (ISLAND)
3	LET'S WAIT AWHILE — JANET JACKSON (BREAKOUT/A&M USA)	RUNNING IN THE FAMILY — LEVEL 42 (POLYDOR)
4	WITH OR WITHOUT YOU — U2 (ISLAND)	MOVE CLOSER — VARIOUS (CBS)
5	LA ISLA BONITA — MADONNA (SIRE)	MEN AND WOMEN — SIMPLY RED (WEA)
6	EVERYTHING I OWN — BOY GEORGE (VIRGIN)	'THE PHANTOM OF THE OPERA' — VARIOUS (POLYDOR)
7	LEAN ON ME — CLUB NOUVEAU (KING JAY/WARNER BROS)	THE VERY BEST OF HOT CHOCOLATE — HOT CHOCOLATE (RAK)
8	WEAK IN THE PRESENCE OF BEAUTY — ALISON MOYET (CBS)	GRACELAND — PAUL SIMON (WARNER BROS)
9	I GET THE SWEETEST FEELING — JACKIE WILSON (SMP)	LIVE MAGIC — QUEEN (EMI)
10	THE GREAT PRETENDER — FREDDIE MERCURY (PARLOPHONE)	SO — PETER GABRIEL (VIRGIN)
11	RESPECT YOURSELF — BRUCE WILLIS (MOTOWN)	PICTURE BOOK — SIMPLY RED (ELEKTRA)
12	SIGN 'O' THE TIMES — PRINCE (PAISLEY PARK/WARNER BROS)	AUGUST — ERIC CLAPTON (DUCK/WARNER BROS)
13	BIG TIME — PETER GABRIEL (VIRGIN)	SILK AND STEEL — FIVE STAR (TENT/RCA)
14	LIVE IT UP — MENTAL AS ANYTHING (EPIC)	CONTROL — JANET JACKSON (A&M)
15	IF YOU LET ME STAY — TERENCE TRENT D'ARBY (CBS)	INVISIBLE TOUCH — GENESIS (VIRGIN)
16	FIGHT FOR YOUR RIGHT (TO PARTY) — BEASTIE BOYS (DEF JAM)	TRUE BLUE — MADONNA (SIRE)
17	EVER FALLEN IN LOVE — FINE YOUNG CANNIBALS (LONDON)	BROTHERS IN ARMS — DIRE STRAITS (VERTIGO/PHONOGRAM)
18	LOVING YOU IS SWEETER THAN EVER — NICK KAMEN (WEA)	IMPRESSIONS — VARIOUS (K-TEL)
19	IT DOESN'T HAVE TO BE — ERASURE (MUTE)	GIVE ME THE REASON — LUTHER VANDROSS (EPIC)
20	MOONLIGHTING 'THEME' — AL JARREAU (WEA INTERNATIONAL)	THE WORLD WON'T LISTEN — THE SMITHS (ROUGH TRADE)

S I N G L E S US A L B U M S

#	Singles	Albums
1	NOTHING'S GONNA STOP US NOW — STARSHIP (GRUNT/RCA)	THE JOSHUA TREE — U2 (ISLAND)
2	I KNEW YOU WERE WAITING — ARETHA FRANKLIN & GEORGE MICHAEL (ARISTA)	INTO THE FIRE — BRYAN ADAMS (A&M)
3	LEAN ON ME — CLUB NOUVEAU (WARNER BROS)	COME AS YOU ARE — PETER WOLF (EMI AMERICA)
4	DON'T DREAM IT'S OVER — CROWDED HOUSE (CAPITOL)	BROADCAST — CUTTING CREW (VIRGIN)
5	TONIGHT, TONIGHT, TONIGHT — GENESIS (ATLANTIC)	READY OR NOT — LOU GRAMM (ATLANTIC)
6	THE FINER THINGS — STEVE WINWOOD (ISLAND/WARNER BROS)	I'M NO ANGEL — GREGG ALLMAN BAND (EPIC)
7	MIDNIGHT BLUE — LOU GRAMM (ATLANTIC)	WISHES — JON BUTCHER (CAPITOL)
8	COME GO WITH ME — EXPOSE (ARISTA)	SLIPPERY WHEN WET — BON JOVI (MERCURY/PG)
9	WALKING DOWN YOUR STREET — BANGLES (COLUMBIA)	FROZEN GHOST — FROZEN GHOST (ATLANTIC)
10	SIGN 'O' THE TIMES — PRINCE (PAISLEY PARK/WARNER BROS)	NEVER ENOUGH — PATTY SMYTH (COLUMBIA)
11	LET'S GO — WANG CHUNG (GEFFEN)	MIDNIGHT TO MIDNIGHT — PSYCHEDELIC FURS (COLUMBIA)
12	(I JUST) DIED IN YOUR ARMS — CUTTING CREW (VIRGIN)	BIG LIFE — NIGHT RANGER (CAMEL/MCA)
13	LA ISLA BONITA — MADONNA (SIRE/WARNER BROS)	STRONG PERSUADER — ROBERT CRAY BAND (MERCURY/PG)
14	WITH OR WITHOUT YOU — U2 (ISLAND)	CAN'T HOLD BACK — EDDIE MONEY (COLUMBIA)
15	DOMINOES — ROBBIE NEVIL (MANHATTAN)	AUGUST — ERIC CLAPTON (DUCK/WARNER BROS)
16	LOOKING FOR A NEW LOVE — JODY WATLEY (MCA)	BY THE LIGHT OF THE MOON — LOS LOBOS (SLASH/WARNER BROS)
17	STONE LOVE — KOOL & THE GANG (MERCURY/PG)	BACK IN THE HIGH LIFE — STEVE WINWOOD (ISLAND/WARNER BROS)
18	COME AS YOU ARE — PETER WOLF (EMI AMERICA)	THUNDER — ANDY TAYLOR (MCA)
19	WHAT'S GOING ON — CYNDI LAUPER (PORTRAIT/CBS)	CROWDED HOUSE — CROWDED HOUSE (CAPITOL)
20	LET'S WAIT AWHILE — JANET JACKSON (A&M)	WHITESNAKE — WHITESNAKE (GEFFEN)

WEEK ENDING APRIL 11 1987
S I N G L E S UK A L B U M S

#	Singles (UK)	Albums (UK)
1	LET IT BE — FERRY AID (SUN/ZEEBRUGGE DISASTER FUND)	NOW, THAT'S WHAT I CALL MUSIC 9 — VARIOUS (VIRGIN/EMI/POLYGRAM)
2	RESPECTABLE — MEL & KIM (SUPREME)	THE JOSHUA TREE — U2 (ISLAND)
3	LA ISLA BONITA — MADONNA (SIRE)	RUNNING IN THE FAMILY — LEVEL 42 (POLYDOR)
4	LET'S WAIT AWHILE — JANET JACKSON (BREAKOUT/A&M USA)	SIGN 'O' THE TIMES — PRINCE (PAISLEY PARK/WARNER BROS)
5	WITH OR WITHOUT YOU — U2 (ISLAND)	MEN AND WOMEN — SIMPLY RED (WEA)
6	LEAN ON ME — CLUB NOUVEAU (KING JAY/WARNER BROS)	THE CIRCUS — ERASURE (MUTE)
7	IF YOU LET ME STAY — TERENCE TRENT D'ARBY (CBS)	MOVE CLOSER — VARIOUS (CBS)
8	THE IRISH ROVER — THE POGUES AND THE DUBLINERS (STIFF)	WHITESNAKE 1987 — WHITESNAKE (EMI)
9	WEAK IN THE PRESENCE OF BEAUTY — ALISON MOYET (CBS)	GRACELAND — PAUL SIMON (WARNER BROS)
10	EVER FALLEN IN LOVE — FINE YOUNG CANNIBALS (LONDON)	INTO THE FIRE — BRYAN ADAMS (A&M)
11	ORDINARY DAY — CURIOSITY KILLED THE CAT (MERCURY)	'THE PHANTOM OF THE OPERA' — VARIOUS (POLYDOR)
12	I GET THE SWEETEST FEELING — JACKIE WILSON (SMP)	THE VERY BEST OF HOT CHOCOLATE — HOT CHOCOLATE (RAK)
13	EVERYTHING I OWN — BOY GEORGE (VIRGIN)	TRUE BLUE — MADONNA (SIRE)
14	CAN'T BE WITH YOU TONIGHT — JUDY BOUCHER (ORBITONE)	CONTROL — JANET JACKSON (A&M)
15	SIGN 'O' THE TIMES — PRINCE (PAISLEY PARK/WARNER BROS)	SO — PETER GABRIEL (VIRGIN)
16	BIG TIME — PETER GABRIEL (VIRGIN)	AUGUST — ERIC CLAPTON (DUCK/WARNER BROS)
17	WANTED DEAD OR ALIVE — BON JOVI (VERTIGO/PHONOGRAM)	LIVE MAGIC — QUEEN (EMI)
18	RESPECT YOURSELF — BRUCE WILLIS (MOTOWN)	GIVE ME THE REASON — LUTHER VANDROSS (EPIC)
19	DAY-IN DAY-OUT — DAVID BOWIE (EMI AMERICA)	BROTHERS IN ARMS — DIRE STRAITS (VERTIGO/PHONOGRAM)
20	THE GREAT PRETENDER — FREDDIE MERCURY (PARLOPHONE)	PICTURE BOOK — SIMPLY RED (ELEKTRA)

S I N G L E S US A L B U M S

#	Singles (US)	Albums (US)
1	I KNEW YOU WERE WAITING — ARETHA FRANKLIN & GEORGE MICHAEL (ARISTA)	THE JOSHUA TREE — U2 (ISLAND)
2	NOTHING'S GONNA STOP US NOW — STARSHIP (GRUNT/RCA)	INTO THE FIRE — BRYAN ADAMS (A&M)
3	DON'T DREAM IT'S OVER — CROWDED HOUSE (CAPITOL)	READY OR NOT — LOU GRAMM (ATLANTIC)
4	THE FINER THINGS — STEVE WINWOOD (ISLAND/WARNER BROS)	COME AS YOU ARE — PETER WOLF (EMI AMERICA)
5	(I JUST) DIED IN YOUR ARMS — CUTTING CREW (VIRGIN)	BROADCAST — CUTTING CREW (VIRGIN)
6	SIGN 'O' THE TIMES — PRINCE (PAISLEY PARK/WARNER BROS)	I'M NO ANGEL — GREGG ALLMAN BAND (EPIC)
7	MIDNIGHT BLUE — LOU GRAMM (ATLANTIC)	WISHES — JON BUTCHER (CAPITOL)
8	WALKING DOWN YOUR STREET — BANGLES (COLUMBIA)	FROZEN GHOST — FROZEN GHOST (ATLANTIC)
9	LA ISLA BONITA — MADONNA (SIRE/WARNER BROS)	SLIPPERY WHEN WET — BON JOVI (MERCURY/PG)
10	WITH OR WITHOUT YOU — U2 (ISLAND)	MIDNIGHT TO MIDNIGHT — PSYCHEDELIC FURS (COLUMBIA)
11	LOOKING FOR A NEW LOVE — JODY WATLEY (MCA)	BIG LIFE — NIGHT RANGER (CAMEL/MCA)
12	DOMINOES — ROBBIE NEVIL (MANHATTAN)	CAN'T HOLD BACK — EDDIE MONEY (COLUMBIA)
13	LEAN ON ME — CLUB NOUVEAU (KING JAY/WARNER BROS)	STRONG PERSUADER — ROBERT CRAY BAND (MERCURY/PG)
14	STONE LOVE — KOOL & THE GANG (MERCURY/PG)	AUGUST — ERIC CLAPTON (DUCK/WARNER BROS)
15	COME AS YOU ARE — PETER WOLF (EMI AMERICA)	BY THE LIGHT OF THE MOON — LOS LOBOS (SLASH/WARNER BROS)
16	WHAT'S GOING ON — CYNDI LAUPER (PORTRAIT/CBS)	WHITESNAKE — WHITESNAKE (GEFFEN)
17	COME GO WITH ME — EXPOSE (ARISTA)	UNDER THE VOLCANO — ROCK & HYDE (CAPITOL)
18	TONIGHT, TONIGHT, TONIGHT — GENESIS (ATLANTIC)	THUNDER — ANDY TAYLOR (MCA)
19	LET'S GO — WANG CHUNG (GEFFEN)	ELECTRICITY — CULT (SIRE/WARNER BROS)
20	BIG LOVE — FLEETWOOD MAC (WARNER BROS)	CROWDED HOUSE — CROWDED HOUSE (CAPITOL)

WEEK ENDING APRIL 18 1987
S I N G L E S UK A L B U M S

#	Singles (UK)	Albums (UK)
1	LET IT BE — FERRY AID (SUN/ZEEBRUGGE DISASTER FUND)	NOW, THAT'S WHAT I CALL MUSIC 9 — VARIOUS (VIRGIN/EMI/POLYGRAM)
2	LA ISLA BONITA — MADONNA (SIRE)	RAINDANCING — ALISON MOYET (CBS)
3	LEAN ON ME — CLUB NOUVEAU (KING JAY/WARNER BROS)	THE JOSHUA TREE — U2 (ISLAND)
4	CAN'T BE WITH YOU TONIGHT — JUDY BOUCHER (ORBITONE)	ELECTRIC — THE CULT (BEGGARS BANQUET)
5	LET'S WAIT AWHILE — JANET JACKSON (BREAKOUT/A&M USA)	MOVE CLOSER — VARIOUS (CBS)
6	RESPECTABLE — MEL & KIM (SUPREME)	RUNNING IN THE FAMILY — LEVEL 42 (POLYDOR)
7	IF YOU LET ME STAY — TERENCE TRENT D'ARBY (CBS)	GRACELAND — PAUL SIMON (WARNER BROS)
8	WITH OR WITHOUT YOU — U2 (ISLAND)	MEN AND WOMEN — SIMPLY RED (WEA)
9	EVER FALLEN IN LOVE — FINE YOUNG CANNIBALS (LONDON)	SIGN 'O' THE TIMES — PRINCE (PAISLEY PARK/WARNER BROS)
10	LIVING IN A BOX — LIVING IN A BOX (CHRYSALIS)	THE CIRCUS — ERASURE (MUTE)
11	THE IRISH ROVER — THE POGUES AND THE DUBLINERS (STIFF)	INTO THE FIRE — BRYAN ADAMS (A&M)
12	ORDINARY DAY — CURIOSITY KILLED THE CAT (MERCURY)	THIS TIME — CULTURE CLUB (VIRGIN)
13	WANTED DEAD OR ALIVE — BON JOVI (VERTIGO/PHONOGRAM)	WHITESNAKE 1987 — WHITESNAKE (EMI)
14	THE SLIGHTEST TOUCH — FIVE STAR (TENT/RCA)	THE VERY BEST OF HOT CHOCOLATE — HOT CHOCOLATE (RAK)
15	WEAK IN THE PRESENCE OF BEAUTY — ALISON MOYET (CBS)	TRUE BLUE — MADONNA (SIRE)
16	STILL OF THE NIGHT — WHITESNAKE (EMI)	CONTROL — JANET JACKSON (A&M)
17	DAY-IN DAY-OUT — DAVID BOWIE (EMI AMERICA)	'THE PHANTOM OF THE OPERA' — VARIOUS (POLYDOR)
18	LET MY PEOPLE GO-GO — THE RAINMAKERS (MERCURY/PHONOGRAM)	AMONG THE LIVING — ANTHRAX (ISLAND)
19	KEEP YOUR EYE ON ME (SPECIAL MIX) — HERB ALPERT (BREAKOUT/A&M)	SO — PETER GABRIEL (VIRGIN)
20	ANOTHER STEP — KIM WILDE & JUNIOR (MCA)	SILK AND STEEL — FIVE STAR (TENT/RCA)

S I N G L E S US A L B U M S

#	Singles (US)	Albums (US)
1	I KNEW YOU WERE WAITING — ARETHA FRANKLIN & GEORGE MICHAEL (ARISTA)	THE JOSHUA TREE — U2 (ISLAND)
2	(I JUST) DIED IN YOUR ARMS — CUTTING CREW (VIRGIN)	INTO THE FIRE — BRYAN ADAMS (A&M)
3	DON'T DREAM IT'S OVER — CROWDED HOUSE (CAPITOL)	TANGO IN THE NIGHT — FLEETWOOD MAC (WARNER BROS)
4	THE FINER THINGS — STEVE WINWOOD (ISLAND/WARNER BROS)	READY OR NOT — LOU GRAMM (ATLANTIC)
5	LA ISLA BONITA — MADONNA (SIRE/WARNER BROS)	COME AS YOU ARE — PETER WOLF (EMI AMERICA)
6	SIGN 'O' THE TIMES — PRINCE (PAISLEY PARK/WARNER BROS)	I'M NO ANGEL — GREGG ALLMAN BAND (EPIC)
7	WITH OR WITHOUT YOU — U2 (ISLAND)	BROADCAST — CUTTING CREW (VIRGIN)
8	LOOKING FOR A NEW LOVE — JODY WATLEY (MCA)	FROZEN GHOST — FROZEN GHOST (ATLANTIC)
9	NOTHING'S GONNA STOP US NOW — STARSHIP (GRUNT/RCA)	WISHES — JON BUTCHER (CAPITOL)
10	WALKING DOWN YOUR STREET — BANGLES (COLUMBIA)	SLIPPERY WHEN WET — BON JOVI (MERCURY/PG)
11	DOMINOES — ROBBIE NEVIL (MANHATTAN)	BIG LIFE — NIGHT RANGER (CAMEL/MCA)
12	WHAT'S GOING ON — CYNDI LAUPER (PORTRAIT/CBS)	MIDNIGHT TO MIDNIGHT — PSYCHEDELIC FURS (COLUMBIA)
13	STONE LOVE — KOOL & THE GANG (MERCURY/PG)	CAN'T HOLD BACK — EDDIE MONEY (COLUMBIA)
14	COME AS YOU ARE — PETER WOLF (EMI AMERICA)	AUGUST — ERIC CLAPTON (DUCK/WARNER BROS)
15	BIG LOVE — FLEETWOOD MAC (WARNER BROS)	UNDER THE VOLCANO — ROCK & HYDE (CAPITOL)
16	MIDNIGHT BLUE — LOU GRAMM (ATLANTIC)	BY THE LIGHT OF THE MOON — LOS LOBOS (SLASH/WARNER BROS)
17	HEAT OF THE NIGHT — BRYAN ADAMS (A&M)	WHITESNAKE — WHITESNAKE (GEFFEN)
18	THE LADY IN RED — CHRIS DE BURGH (A&M)	ELECTRICITY — CULT (SIRE/WARNER BROS)
19	SERIOUS — DONNA ALLEN (21/ATCO)	STRONG PERSUADER — ROBERT CRAY BAND (MERCURY/PG)
20	TALK DIRTY TO ME — POISON (ENIGMA/CAPITOL)	LITTLE AMERICA — LITTLE AMERICA (GEFFEN)

WEEK ENDING APRIL 25 1987
S I N G L E S UK A L B U M S

#	SINGLES	ALBUMS
1	LA ISLA BONITA — MADONNA (SIRE)	NOW, THAT'S WHAT I CALL MUSIC 9 — VARIOUS (VIRGIN/EMI/POLYGRAM)
2	CAN'T BE WITH YOU TONIGHT — JUDY BOUCHER (ORBITONE)	RAINDANCING — ALISON MOYET (CBS)
3	LEAN ON ME — CLUB NOUVEAU (KING JAY/WARNER BROS)	F.L.M. — MEL & KIM (SUPREME)
4	LET IT BE — FERRY AID (SUN/ZEEBRUGGE DISASTER FUND)	THE JOSHUA TREE — U2 (ISLAND)
5	RESPECTABLE — MEL & KIM (SUPREME)	MOVE CLOSER — VARIOUS (CBS)
6	LIVING IN A BOX — LIVING IN A BOX (CHRYSALIS)	RUNNING IN THE FAMILY — LEVEL 42 (POLYDOR)
7	IF YOU LET ME STAY — TERENCE TRENT D'ARBY (CBS)	TANGO IN THE NIGHT — FLEETWOOD MAC (WARNER BROS)
8	THE SLIGHTEST TOUCH — FIVE STAR (TENT/RCA)	GRACELAND — PAUL SIMON (WARNER BROS)
9	LET'S WAIT AWHILE — JANET JACKSON (BREAKOUT/A&M USA)	THIS TIME — CULTURE CLUB (VIRGIN)
10	EVER FALLEN IN LOVE — FINE YOUNG CANNIBALS (LONDON)	MEN AND WOMEN — SIMPLY RED (WEA)
11	WITH OR WITHOUT YOU — U2 (ISLAND)	TRUE BLUE — MADONNA (SIRE)
12	A BOY FROM NOWHERE — TOM JONES (EPIC)	INVISIBLE TOUCH — GENESIS (VIRGIN)
13	SHEILA TAKE A BOW — THE SMITHS (ROUGH TRADE)	ELECTRIC — THE CULT (BEGGARS BANQUET)
14	ANOTHER STEP — KIM WILDE & JUNIOR (MCA)	SILK AND STEEL — FIVE STAR (TENT/RCA)
15	NOTHING'S GONNA STOP US NOW — STARSHIP (GRUNT/RCA)	THE VERY BEST OF HOT CHOCOLATE — HOT CHOCOLATE (RAK)
16	WANTED DEAD OR ALIVE — BON JOVI (VERTIGO/PHONOGRAM)	THE CIRCUS — ERASURE (MUTE)
17	DIAMOND LIGHTS — GLENN & CHRIS (RECORD SHACK)	SIGN 'O' THE TIMES — PRINCE (PAISLEY PARK/WARNER BROS)
18	(SOMETHING INSIDE) SO STRONG — LABI SIFFRE (CHINA)	INTO THE FIRE — BRYAN ADAMS (A&M)
19	ORDINARY DAY — CURIOSITY KILLED THE CAT (MERCURY)	CONTROL — JANET JACKSON (A&M)
20	THE IRISH ROVER — THE POGUES AND THE DUBLINERS (STIFF)	SHE WAS ONLY A GROCER'S DAUGHTER — THE BLOW MONKEYS (RCA)

S I N G L E S US A L B U M S

#	SINGLES	ALBUMS
1	(I JUST) DIED IN YOUR ARMS — CUTTING CREW (VIRGIN)	THE JOSHUA TREE — U2 (ISLAND)
2	WITH OR WITHOUT YOU — U2 (ISLAND)	INTO THE FIRE — BRYAN ADAMS (A&M)
3	LA ISLA BONITA — MADONNA (SIRE/WARNER BROS)	TANGO IN THE NIGHT — FLEETWOOD MAC (WARNER BROS)
4	LOOKING FOR A NEW LOVE — JODY WATLEY (MCA)	LET ME UP (I'VE HAD ENOUGH) — TOM PETTY & THE HEARTBREAKERS (MCA)
5	THE FINER THINGS — STEVE WINWOOD (ISLAND/WARNER BROS)	NEVER LET ME DOWN — DAVID BOWIE (EMI AMERICA)
6	I KNEW YOU WERE WAITING — ARETHA FRANKLIN & GEORGE MICHAEL (ARISTA)	I'M NO ANGEL — GREGG ALLMAN BAND (EPIC)
7	SIGN 'O' THE TIMES — PRINCE (PAISLEY PARK/WARNER BROS)	READY OR NOT — LOU GRAMM (ATLANTIC)
8	DON'T DREAM IT'S OVER — CROWDED HOUSE (CAPITOL)	COME AS YOU ARE — PETER WOLF (EMI AMERICA)
9	BIG LOVE — FLEETWOOD MAC (WARNER BROS)	FROZEN GHOST — FROZEN GHOST (ATLANTIC)
10	HEAT OF THE NIGHT — BRYAN ADAMS (A&M)	WISHES — JON BUTCHER (CAPITOL)
11	WHAT'S GOING ON — CYNDI LAUPER (PORTRAIT/CBS)	BROADCAST — CUTTING CREW (VIRGIN)
12	THE LADY IN RED — CHRIS DE BURGH (A&M)	SLIPPERY WHEN WET — BON JOVI (MERCURY/PG)
13	DOMINOES — ROBBIE NEVIL (MANHATTAN)	BIG LIFE — NIGHT RANGER (CAMEL/MCA)
14	TALK DIRTY TO ME — POISON (ENIGMA/CAPITOL)	UNDER THE VOLCANO — ROCK & HYDE (CAPITOL)
15	NOTHING'S GONNA STOP US NOW — STARSHIP (GRUNT/RCA)	WHITESNAKE — WHITESNAKE (GEFFEN)
16	COME AS YOU ARE — PETER WOLF (EMI AMERICA)	CAN'T HOLD BACK — EDDIE MONEY (COLUMBIA)
17	I KNOW WHAT I LIKE — HUEY LEWIS AND THE NEWS (CHRYSALIS)	MIDNIGHT TO MIDNIGHT — PSYCHEDELIC FURS (COLUMBIA)
18	SERIOUS — DONNA ALLEN (21/ATCO)	ELECTRICITY — CULT (SIRE/WARNER BROS)
19	RIGHT ON TRACK — BREAKFAST CLUB (MCA)	LITTLE AMERICA — LITTLE AMERICA (GEFFEN)
20	NOTHING'S GONNA CHANGE MY LOVE FOR YOU — GLENN MEDEIROS (AMHERST)	AUGUST — ERIC CLAPTON (DUCK/WARNER BROS)

WEEK ENDING MAY 2 1987
S I N G L E S UK A L B U M S

#	SINGLES	ALBUMS
1	LA ISLA BONITA — MADONNA (SIRE)	NOW, THAT'S WHAT I CALL MUSIC 9 — VARIOUS (VIRGIN/EMI/POLYGRAM)
2	CAN'T BE WITH YOU TONIGHT — JUDY BOUCHER (ORBITONE)	INVISIBLE TOUCH — GENESIS (VIRGIN)
3	NOTHING'S GONNA STOP US NOW — STARSHIP (GRUNT/RCA)	F.L.M. — MEL & KIM (SUPREME)
4	THE SLIGHTEST TOUCH — FIVE STAR (TENT/RCA)	RAINDANCING — ALISON MOYET (CBS)
5	LEAN ON ME — CLUB NOUVEAU (KING JAY/WARNER BROS)	RUNNING IN THE FAMILY — LEVEL 42 (POLYDOR)
6	LIVING IN A BOX — LIVING IN A BOX (CHRYSALIS)	NEVER LET ME DOWN — DAVID BOWIE (EMI AMERICA)
7	A BOY FROM NOWHERE — TOM JONES (EPIC)	THE JOSHUA TREE — U2 (ISLAND)
8	IF YOU LET ME STAY — TERENCE TRENT D'ARBY (CBS)	THIS TIME — CULTURE CLUB (VIRGIN)
9	ANOTHER STEP — KIM WILDE & JUNIOR (MCA)	TANGO IN THE NIGHT — FLEETWOOD MAC (WARNER BROS)
10	SHEILA TAKE A BOW — THE SMITHS (ROUGH TRADE)	GRACELAND — PAUL SIMON (WARNER BROS)
11	RESPECTABLE — MEL & KIM (SUPREME)	TRUE BLUE — MADONNA (SIRE)
12	DIAMOND LIGHTS — GLENN & CHRIS (RECORD SHACK)	MEN AND WOMEN — SIMPLY RED (WEA)
13	EVER FALLEN IN LOVE — FINE YOUNG CANNIBALS (LONDON)	MOVE CLOSER — VARIOUS (CBS)
14	TO BE WITH YOU AGAIN — LEVEL 42 (POLYDOR)	SILK AND STEEL — FIVE STAR (TENT/RCA)
15	LET'S WAIT AWHILE — JANET JACKSON (BREAKOUT/A&M USA)	CONTROL — JANET JACKSON (A&M)
16	(SOMETHING INSIDE) SO STRONG — LABI SIFFRE (CHINA)	OUTLAND — SPEAR OF DESTINY (10/VIRGIN)
17	LET IT BE — FERRY AID (SUN/ZEEBRUGGE DISASTER FUND)	ELECTRIC — THE CULT (BEGGARS BANQUET)
18	WITH OR WITHOUT YOU — U2 (ISLAND)	SIGN 'O' THE TIMES — PRINCE (PAISLEY PARK/WARNER BROS)
19	APRIL SKIES — THE JESUS & MARY CHAIN (BLANCO Y NEGRO)	'THE PHANTOM OF THE OPERA' — VARIOUS (POLYDOR)
20	WANTED DEAD OR ALIVE — BON JOVI (VERTIGO/PHONOGRAM)	THE CIRCUS — ERASURE (MUTE)

S I N G L E S US A L B U M S

#	SINGLES	ALBUMS
1	(I JUST) DIED IN YOUR ARMS — CUTTING CREW (VIRGIN)	THE JOSHUA TREE — U2 (ISLAND)
2	WITH OR WITHOUT YOU — U2 (ISLAND)	INTO THE FIRE — BRYAN ADAMS (A&M)
3	LA ISLA BONITA — MADONNA (SIRE/WARNER BROS)	TANGO IN THE NIGHT — FLEETWOOD MAC (WARNER BROS)
4	LOOKING FOR A NEW LOVE — JODY WATLEY (MCA)	LET ME UP (I'VE HAD ENOUGH) — TOM PETTY & THE HEARTBREAKERS (MCA)
5	BIG LOVE — FLEETWOOD MAC (WARNER BROS)	NEVER LET ME DOWN — DAVID BOWIE (EMI AMERICA)
6	HEAT OF THE NIGHT — BRYAN ADAMS (A&M)	I'M NO ANGEL — GREGG ALLMAN BAND (EPIC)
7	THE FINER THINGS — STEVE WINWOOD (ISLAND/WARNER BROS)	READY OR NOT — LOU GRAMM (ATLANTIC)
8	THE LADY IN RED — CHRIS DE BURGH (A&M)	FROZEN GHOST — FROZEN GHOST (ATLANTIC)
9	I KNOW WHAT I LIKE — HUEY LEWIS AND THE NEWS (CHRYSALIS)	COME AS YOU ARE — PETER WOLF (EMI AMERICA)
10	YOU KEEP ME HANGIN' ON — KIM WILDE (MCA)	UNDER THE VOLCANO — ROCK & HYDE (CAPITOL)
11	TALK DIRTY TO ME — POISON (ENIGMA/CAPITOL)	LITTLE AMERICA — LITTLE AMERICA (GEFFEN)
12	DON'T DREAM IT'S OVER — CROWDED HOUSE (CAPITOL)	WHITESNAKE — WHITESNAKE (GEFFEN)
13	SIGN 'O' THE TIMES — PRINCE (PAISLEY PARK/WARNER BROS)	BROADCAST — CUTTING CREW (VIRGIN)
14	RIGHT ON TRACK — BREAKFAST CLUB (MCA)	CAN'T HOLD BACK — EDDIE MONEY (COLUMBIA)
15	WHAT'S GOING ON — CYNDI LAUPER (PORTRAIT/CBS)	SLIPPERY WHEN WET — BON JOVI (MERCURY/PG)
16	I KNEW YOU WERE WAITING — ARETHA FRANKLIN & GEORGE MICHAEL (ARISTA)	WEAPONS OF LOVE — TRUTH (IRS/MCA)
17	ALWAYS — ATLANTIC STARR (WARNER BROS)	ELECTRICITY — CULT (SIRE/WARNER BROS)
18	IF SHE WOULD HAVE BEEN FAITHFUL — CHICAGO (WARNER BROS)	CROWDED HOUSE — CROWDED HOUSE (CAPITOL)
19	NOTHING'S GONNA CHANGE MY LOVE FOR YOU — GLENN MEDEIROS (AMHERST)	WISHES — JON BUTCHER (CAPITOL)
20	WANTED DEAD OR ALIVE — BON JOVI (MERCURY/PG)	AUGUST — ERIC CLAPTON (DUCK/WARNER BROS)

WEEK ENDING MAY 9 1987

S I N G L E S UK A L B U M S

#	Singles	Albums
1	NOTHING'S GONNA STOP US NOW — STARSHIP (GRUNT/RCA)	KEEP YOUR DISTANCE — CURIOSITY KILLED THE CAT (MERCURY)
2	CAN'T BE WITH YOU TONIGHT — JUDY BOUCHER (ORBITONE)	SOLITUDE STANDING — SUZANNE VEGA (A&M)
3	LA ISLA BONITA — MADONNA (SIRE)	RUNNING IN THE FAMILY — LEVEL 42 (POLYDOR)
4	A BOY FROM NOWHERE — TOM JONES (EPIC)	THE JOSHUA TREE — U2 (ISLAND)
5	THE SLIGHTEST TOUCH — FIVE STAR (TENT/RCA)	RAINDANCING — ALISON MOYET (CBS)
6	LIVING IN A BOX — LIVING IN A BOX (CHRYSALIS)	INVISIBLE TOUCH — GENESIS (VIRGIN)
7	(SOMETHING INSIDE) SO STRONG — LABI SIFFRE (CHINA)	NOW, THAT'S WHAT I CALL MUSIC 9 — VARIOUS (VIRGIN/EMI/POLYGRAM)
8	APRIL SKIES — THE JESUS & MARY CHAIN (BLANCO Y NEGRO)	TANGO IN THE NIGHT — FLEETWOOD MAC (WARNER BROS)
9	ANOTHER STEP — KIM WILDE & JUNIOR (MCA)	F.L.M. — MEL & KIM (SUPREME)
10	TO BE WITH YOU AGAIN — LEVEL 42 (POLYDOR)	TRUE BLUE — MADONNA (SIRE)
11	LEAN ON ME — CLUB NOUVEAU (KING JAY/WARNER BROS)	GRACELAND — PAUL SIMON (WARNER BROS)
12	IF YOU LET ME STAY — TERENCE TRENT D'ARBY (CBS)	NEVER LET ME DOWN — DAVID BOWIE (EMI AMERICA)
13	BIG LOVE — FLEETWOOD MAC (WARNER BROS)	SILK AND STEEL — FIVE STAR (TENT/RCA)
14	DIAMOND LIGHTS — GLENN & CHRIS (RECORD SHACK)	CONTROL — JANET JACKSON (A&M)
15	SHEILA TAKE A BOW — THE SMITHS (ROUGH TRADE)	THIS TIME — CULTURE CLUB (VIRGIN)
16	BACK & FORTH — CAMEO (CLUB/PHONOGRAM)	MEN AND WOMEN — SIMPLY RED (WEA)
17	LIL' DEVIL — THE CULT (BEGGARS BANQUET)	MOVE CLOSER — VARIOUS (CBS)
18	RESPECTABLE — MEL & KIM (SUPREME)	OUTLAND — SPEAR OF DESTINY (10/VIRGIN)
19	NEVER TAKE ME ALIVE — SPEAR OF DESTINY (10/VIRGIN)	SO — PETER GABRIEL (VIRGIN)
20	EVER FALLEN IN LOVE — FINE YOUNG CANNIBALS (LONDON)	ELECTRIC — THE CULT (BEGGARS BANQUET)

S I N G L E S US A L B U M S

#	Singles	Albums
1	WITH OR WITHOUT YOU — U2 (ISLAND)	THE JOSHUA TREE — U2 (ISLAND)
2	(I JUST) DIED IN YOUR ARMS — CUTTING CREW (VIRGIN)	LET ME UP (I'VE HAD ENOUGH) — TOM PETTY & THE HEARTBREAKERS (MCA)
3	LOOKING FOR A NEW LOVE — JODY WATLEY (MCA)	TANGO IN THE NIGHT — FLEETWOOD MAC (WARNER BROS)
4	LA ISLA BONITA — MADONNA (SIRE/WARNER BROS)	INTO THE FIRE — BRYAN ADAMS (A&M)
5	BIG LOVE — FLEETWOOD MAC (WARNER BROS)	NEVER LET ME DOWN — DAVID BOWIE (EMI AMERICA)
6	HEAT OF THE NIGHT — BRYAN ADAMS (A&M)	I'M NO ANGEL — GREGG ALLMAN BAND (EPIC)
7	YOU KEEP ME HANGIN' ON — KIM WILDE (MCA)	READY OR NOT — LOU GRAMM (ATLANTIC)
8	THE LADY IN RED — CHRIS DE BURGH (A&M)	FROZEN GHOST — FROZEN GHOST (ATLANTIC)
9	I KNOW WHAT I LIKE — HUEY LEWIS AND THE NEWS (CHRYSALIS)	UNDER THE VOLCANO — ROCK & HYDE (CAPITOL)
10	ALWAYS — ATLANTIC STARR (WARNER BROS)	COME AS YOU ARE — PETER WOLF (EMI AMERICA)
11	TALK DIRTY TO ME — POISON (ENIGMA/CAPITOL)	LITTLE AMERICA — LITTLE AMERICA (GEFFEN)
12	RIGHT ON TRACK — BREAKFAST CLUB (MCA)	WHITESNAKE — WHITESNAKE (GEFFEN)
13	IF SHE WOULD HAVE BEEN FAITHFUL — CHICAGO (WARNER BROS)	CROWDED HOUSE — CROWDED HOUSE (CAPITOL)
14	WANTED DEAD OR ALIVE — BON JOVI (MERCURY/PG)	WEAPONS OF LOVE — TRUTH (IRS/MCA)
15	IN TOO DEEP — GENESIS (ATLANTIC)	ELECTRICITY — CULT (SIRE/WARNER BROS)
16	MEET ME HALF WAY — KENNY LOGGINS (COLUMBIA)	AUGUST — ERIC CLAPTON (DUCK/WARNER BROS)
17	HEAD TO TOE — LISA LISA (COLUMBIA)	STRONG PERSUADER — ROBERT CRAY BAND (MERCURY/PG)
18	IF SHE WOULD HAVE BEEN FAITHFUL — CHICAGO (WARNER BROS) [NOTHING'S GONNA CHANGE MY LOVE FOR YOU — GLENN MEDEIROS (AMHERST)]	SLIPPERY WHEN WET — BON JOVI (MERCURY/PG)
19	THE FINER THINGS — STEVE WINWOOD (ISLAND/WARNER BROS)	WISHES — JON BUTCHER (CAPITOL)
20	DIAMONDS — HERB ALPERT (A&M)	BROADCAST — CUTTING CREW (VIRGIN)

WEEK ENDING MAY 16 1987

S I N G L E S UK A L B U M S

#	Singles	Albums
1	NOTHING'S GONNA STOP US NOW — STARSHIP (GRUNT/RCA)	KEEP YOUR DISTANCE — CURIOSITY KILLED THE CAT (MERCURY)
2	CAN'T BE WITH YOU TONIGHT — JUDY BOUCHER (ORBITONE)	SOLITUDE STANDING — SUZANNE VEGA (A&M)
3	A BOY FROM NOWHERE — TOM JONES (EPIC)	RUNNING IN THE FAMILY — LEVEL 42 (POLYDOR)
4	(SOMETHING INSIDE) SO STRONG — LABI SIFFRE (CHINA)	THE JOSHUA TREE — U2 (ISLAND)
5	LIVING IN A BOX — LIVING IN A BOX (CHRYSALIS)	TANGO IN THE NIGHT — FLEETWOOD MAC (WARNER BROS)
6	ANOTHER STEP — KIM WILDE & JUNIOR (MCA)	NOW, THAT'S WHAT I CALL MUSIC 9 — VARIOUS (VIRGIN/EMI/POLYGRAM)
7	LA ISLA BONITA — MADONNA (SIRE)	INVISIBLE TOUCH — GENESIS (VIRGIN)
8	THE SLIGHTEST TOUCH — FIVE STAR (TENT/RCA)	RAINDANCING — ALISON MOYET (CBS)
9	BIG LOVE — FLEETWOOD MAC (WARNER BROS)	F.L.M. — MEL & KIM (SUPREME)
10	APRIL SKIES — THE JESUS & MARY CHAIN (BLANCO Y NEGRO)	TRUE BLUE — MADONNA (SIRE)
11	LIL' DEVIL — THE CULT (BEGGARS BANQUET)	SO — PETER GABRIEL (VIRGIN)
12	BOOPS (HERE TO GO) — SLY & ROBBIE (FOURTH & BROADWAY/ISLAND)	GRACELAND — PAUL SIMON (WARNER BROS)
13	BACK & FORTH — CAMEO (CLUB/PHONOGRAM)	SILK AND STEEL — FIVE STAR (TENT/RCA)
14	NEVER TAKE ME ALIVE — SPEAR OF DESTINY (10/VIRGIN)	ELECTRIC — THE CULT (BEGGARS BANQUET)
15	TO BE WITH YOU AGAIN — LEVEL 42 (POLYDOR)	MEN AND WOMEN — SIMPLY RED (WEA)
16	STRANGELOVE — DEPECHE MODE (MUTE)	CONTROL — JANET JACKSON (A&M)
17	LEAN ON ME — CLUB NOUVEAU (KING JAY/WARNER BROS)	NEVER LET ME DOWN — DAVID BOWIE (EMI AMERICA)
18	SHATTERED DREAMS — JOHNNY HATES JAZZ (VIRGIN)	OUTLAND — SPEAR OF DESTINY (10/VIRGIN)
19	REAL FASHION REGGAE STYLE — CAREY JOHNSON (OVAL/10/VIRGIN)	MOVE CLOSER — VARIOUS (CBS)
20	IF YOU LET ME STAY — TERENCE TRENT D'ARBY (CBS)	THE CIRCUS — ERASURE (MUTE)

S I N G L E S US A L B U M S

#	Singles	Albums
1	WITH OR WITHOUT YOU — U2 (ISLAND)	THE JOSHUA TREE — U2 (ISLAND)
2	LOOKING FOR A NEW LOVE — JODY WATLEY (MCA)	LET ME UP (I'VE HAD ENOUGH) — TOM PETTY & THE HEARTBREAKERS (MCA)
3	YOU KEEP ME HANGIN' ON — KIM WILDE (MCA)	TANGO IN THE NIGHT — FLEETWOOD MAC (WARNER BROS)
4	BIG LOVE — FLEETWOOD MAC (WARNER BROS)	INTO THE FIRE — BRYAN ADAMS (A&M)
5	(I JUST) DIED IN YOUR ARMS — CUTTING CREW (VIRGIN)	NEVER LET ME DOWN — DAVID BOWIE (EMI AMERICA)
6	ALWAYS — ATLANTIC STARR (WARNER BROS)	I'M NO ANGEL — GREGG ALLMAN BAND (EPIC)
7	THE LADY IN RED — CHRIS DE BURGH (A&M)	FROZEN GHOST — FROZEN GHOST (ATLANTIC)
8	I KNOW WHAT I LIKE — HUEY LEWIS AND THE NEWS (CHRYSALIS)	UNDER THE VOLCANO — ROCK & HYDE (CAPITOL)
9	HEAT OF THE NIGHT — BRYAN ADAMS (A&M)	READY OR NOT — LOU GRAMM (ATLANTIC)
10	IN TOO DEEP — GENESIS (ATLANTIC)	CROWDED HOUSE — CROWDED HOUSE (CAPITOL)
11	RIGHT ON TRACK — BREAKFAST CLUB (MCA)	LITTLE AMERICA — LITTLE AMERICA (GEFFEN)
12	IF SHE WOULD HAVE BEEN FAITHFUL — CHICAGO (WARNER BROS)	WHITESNAKE — WHITESNAKE (GEFFEN)
13	WANTED DEAD OR ALIVE — BON JOVI (MERCURY/PG)	WEAPONS OF LOVE — TRUTH (IRS/MCA)
14	HEAD TO TOE — LISA LISA (COLUMBIA)	COME AS YOU ARE — PETER WOLF (EMI AMERICA)
15	MEET ME HALF WAY — KENNY LOGGINS (COLUMBIA)	STRONG PERSUADER — ROBERT CRAY BAND (MERCURY/PG)
16	LA ISLA BONITA — MADONNA (SIRE/WARNER BROS)	ELECTRICITY — CULT (SIRE/WARNER BROS)
17	DIAMONDS — HERB ALPERT (A&M)	WISHES — JON BUTCHER (CAPITOL)
18	TALK DIRTY TO ME — POISON (ENIGMA/CAPITOL)	SLIPPERY WHEN WET — BON JOVI (MERCURY/PG)
19	NOTHING'S GONNA CHANGE MY LOVE FOR YOU — GLENN MEDEIROS (AMHERST)	BROADCAST — CUTTING CREW (VIRGIN)
20	I WANNA DANCE WITH SOMEBODY — WHITNEY HOUSTON (ARISTA)	MECHANICAL RESONANCE — TESLA (GEFFEN)

WEEK ENDING MAY 23 1987

S I N G L E S UK A L B U M S

#	Singles	Albums
1	NOTHING'S GONNA STOP US NOW — STARSHIP (GRUNT/RCA)	IT'S BETTER TO TRAVEL — SWING OUT SISTER (MERCURY/PHONOGRAM)
2	A BOY FROM NOWHERE — TOM JONES (EPIC)	KEEP YOUR DISTANCE — CURIOSITY KILLED THE CAT (MERCURY)
3	CAN'T BE WITH YOU TONIGHT — JUDY BOUCHER (ORBITONE)	SOLITUDE STANDING — SUZANNE VEGA (A&M)
4	(SOMETHING INSIDE) SO STRONG — LABI SIFFRE (CHINA)	RUNNING IN THE FAMILY — LEVEL 42 (POLYDOR)
5	SHATTERED DREAMS — JOHNNY HATES JAZZ (VIRGIN)	TANGO IN THE NIGHT — FLEETWOOD MAC (WARNER BROS)
6	INCOMMUNICADO — MARILLION (EMI)	SO — PETER GABRIEL (VIRGIN)
7	LIVING IN A BOX — LIVING IN A BOX (CHRYSALIS)	RAINDANCING — ALISON MOYET (CBS)
8	ANOTHER STEP — KIM WILDE & JUNIOR (MCA)	THE JOSHUA TREE — U2 (ISLAND)
9	BIG LOVE — FLEETWOOD MAC (WARNER BROS)	NOW, THAT'S WHAT I CALL MUSIC 9 — VARIOUS (VIRGIN/EMI/POLYGRAM)
10	I WANNA DANCE WITH SOMEBODY — WHITNEY HOUSTON (ARISTA)	F.L.M. — MEL & KIM (SUPREME)
11	BACK & FORTH — CAMEO (CLUB/PHONOGRAM)	INVISIBLE TOUCH — GENESIS (VIRGIN)
12	BOOPS (HERE TO GO) — SLY & ROBBIE (FOURTH & BROADWAY/ISLAND)	TRUE BLUE — MADONNA (SIRE)
13	LIL' DEVIL — THE CULT (BEGGARS BANQUET)	TRIBUTE — OZZY OSBOURNE (EPIC)
14	WISHING I WAS LUCKY — WET WET WET (PHONOGRAM)	MEN AND WOMEN — SIMPLY RED (WEA)
15	THE SLIGHTEST TOUCH — FIVE STAR (TENT/RCA)	ELECTRIC — THE CULT (BEGGARS BANQUET)
16	NEVER TAKE ME ALIVE — SPEAR OF DESTINY (10/VIRGIN)	GRACELAND — PAUL SIMON (WARNER BROS)
17	LA ISLA BONITA — MADONNA (SIRE)	SILK AND STEEL — FIVE STAR (TENT/RCA)
18	HOT SHOT TOTTENHAM! — TOTTENHAM HOTSPUR/CHAS & DAVE (RAINBOW)	CONTROL — JANET JACKSON (A&M)
19	PRIME MOVER — ZODIAC MINDWARP (MERCURY/PHONOGRAM)	OUTLAND — SPEAR OF DESTINY (10/VIRGIN)
20	STRANGELOVE — DEPECHE MODE (MUTE)	THE GREATEST HITS — TOM JONES (TELSTAR)

S I N G L E S US A L B U M S

#	Singles	Albums
1	WITH OR WITHOUT YOU — U2 (ISLAND)	THE JOSHUA TREE — U2 (ISLAND)
2	YOU KEEP ME HANGIN' ON — KIM WILDE (MCA)	LET ME UP (I'VE HAD ENOUGH) — TOM PETTY & THE HEARTBREAKERS (MCA)
3	ALWAYS — ATLANTIC STARR (WARNER BROS)	TANGO IN THE NIGHT — FLEETWOOD MAC (WARNER BROS)
4	IN TOO DEEP — GENESIS (ATLANTIC)	INTO THE FIRE — BRYAN ADAMS (A&M)
5	BIG LOVE — FLEETWOOD MAC (WARNER BROS)	NEVER LET ME DOWN — DAVID BOWIE (EMI AMERICA)
6	HEAD TO TOE — LISA LISA (COLUMBIA)	SOUNDTRACK — BEVERLY HILLS COP II (MCA)
7	LOOKING FOR A NEW LOVE — JODY WATLEY (MCA)	I'M NO ANGEL — GREGG ALLMAN BAND (EPIC)
8	THE LADY IN RED — CHRIS DE BURGH (A&M)	CROWDED HOUSE — CROWDED HOUSE (CAPITOL)
9	WANTED DEAD OR ALIVE — BON JOVI (MERCURY/PG)	WEAPONS OF LOVE — TRUTH (IRS/MCA)
10	I KNOW WHAT I LIKE — HUEY LEWIS AND THE NEWS (CHRYSALIS)	FROZEN GHOST — FROZEN GHOST (ATLANTIC)
11	RIGHT ON TRACK — BREAKFAST CLUB (MCA)	LITTLE AMERICA — LITTLE AMERICA (GEFFEN)
12	IF SHE WOULD HAVE BEEN FAITHFUL — CHICAGO (WARNER BROS)	WHITESNAKE — WHITESNAKE (GEFFEN)
13	DIAMONDS — HERB ALPERT (A&M)	UNDER THE VOLCANO — ROCK & HYDE (CAPITOL)
14	MEET ME HALF WAY — KENNY LOGGINS (COLUMBIA)	COME AS YOU ARE — PETER WOLF (EMI AMERICA)
15	I WANNA DANCE WITH SOMEBODY — WHITNEY HOUSTON (ARISTA)	GYPSY BLOOD — MASON RUFFNER (CBS ASSOCIATED)
16	(I JUST) DIED IN YOUR ARMS — CUTTING CREW (VIRGIN)	SLIPPERY WHEN WET — BON JOVI (MERCURY/PG)
17	HEAT OF THE NIGHT — BRYAN ADAMS (A&M)	WISHES — JON BUTCHER (CAPITOL)
18	SONGBIRD — KENNY G (ARISTA)	READY OR NOT — LOU GRAMM (ATLANTIC)
19	LA ISLA BONITA — MADONNA (SIRE/WARNER BROS)	BROADCAST — CUTTING CREW (VIRGIN)
20	JUST TO SEE HER — SMOKEY ROBINSON (MOTOWN)	MECHANICAL RESONANCE — TESLA (GEFFEN)

WEEK ENDING MAY 30 1987

S I N G L E S UK A L B U M S

#	Singles	Albums
1	NOTHING'S GONNA STOP US NOW — STARSHIP (GRUNT/RCA)	IT'S BETTER TO TRAVEL — SWING OUT SISTER (MERCURY/PHONOGRAM)
2	I WANNA DANCE WITH SOMEBODY — WHITNEY HOUSTON (ARISTA)	SOLITUDE STANDING — SUZANNE VEGA (A&M)
3	HOLD ME NOW — JOHNNY LOGAN (EPIC)	KEEP YOUR DISTANCE — CURIOSITY KILLED THE CAT (MERCURY)
4	A BOY FROM NOWHERE — TOM JONES (EPIC)	TANGO IN THE NIGHT — FLEETWOOD MAC (WARNER BROS)
5	SHATTERED DREAMS — JOHNNY HATES JAZZ (VIRGIN)	THE JOSHUA TREE — U2 (ISLAND)
6	INCOMMUNICADO — MARILLION (EMI)	RUNNING IN THE FAMILY — LEVEL 42 (POLYDOR)
7	JACK MIX II/III — MIRAGE (DEBUT/PASSION)	RAINDANCING — ALISON MOYET (CBS)
8	CAN'T BE WITH YOU TONIGHT — JUDY BOUCHER (ORBITONE)	F.L.M. — MEL & KIM (SUPREME)
9	(SOMETHING INSIDE) SO STRONG — LABI SIFFRE (CHINA)	MEN AND WOMEN — SIMPLY RED (WEA)
10	WISHING I WAS LUCKY — WET WET WET (PHONOGRAM)	SO — PETER GABRIEL (VIRGIN)
11	BACK & FORTH — CAMEO (CLUB/PHONOGRAM)	NOW, THAT'S WHAT I CALL MUSIC 9 — VARIOUS (VIRGIN/EMI/POLYGRAM)
12	BIG LOVE — FLEETWOOD MAC (WARNER BROS)	INVISIBLE TOUCH — GENESIS (VIRGIN)
13	FIVE GET OVER EXCITED — THE HOUSEMARTINS (GO! DISCS)	TRUE BLUE — MADONNA (SIRE)
14	LIVING IN A BOX — LIVING IN A BOX (CHRYSALIS)	GIRLS GIRLS GIRLS — MÖTLEY CRÜE (ELEKTRA)
15	SERIOUS — DONNA ALLEN (PORTRAIT)	SILK AND STEEL — FIVE STAR (TENT/RCA)
16	BORN TO RUN — BRUCE SPRINGSTEEN (CBS)	GRACELAND — PAUL SIMON (WARNER BROS)
17	ANOTHER STEP — KIM WILDE & JUNIOR (MCA)	ELECTRIC — THE CULT (BEGGARS BANQUET)
18	PRIME MOVER — ZODIAC MINDWARP (MERCURY/PHONOGRAM)	LICENSED TO ILL — BEASTIE BOYS (DEF JAM)
19	BOOPS (HERE TO GO) — SLY & ROBBIE (FOURTH & BROADWAY/ISLAND)	THE GREATEST HITS — TOM JONES (TELSTAR)
20	LIL' DEVIL — THE CULT (BEGGARS BANQUET)	THE CIRCUS — ERASURE (MUTE)

S I N G L E S US A L B U M S

#	Singles	Albums
1	YOU KEEP ME HANGIN' ON — KIM WILDE (MCA)	THE JOSHUA TREE — U2 (ISLAND)
2	ALWAYS — ATLANTIC STARR (WARNER BROS)	LET ME UP (I'VE HAD ENOUGH) — TOM PETTY & THE HEARTBREAKERS (MCA)
3	IN TOO DEEP — GENESIS (ATLANTIC)	TANGO IN THE NIGHT — FLEETWOOD MAC (WARNER BROS)
4	HEAD TO TOE — LISA LISA (COLUMBIA)	INTO THE FIRE — BRYAN ADAMS (A&M)
5	WITH OR WITHOUT YOU — U2 (ISLAND)	BAD ANIMALS — HEART (CAPITOL)
6	I WANNA DANCE WITH SOMEBODY — WHITNEY HOUSTON (ARISTA)	SOUNDTRACK — BEVERLY HILLS COP II (MCA)
7	WANTED DEAD OR ALIVE — BON JOVI (MERCURY/PG)	NEVER LET ME DOWN — DAVID BOWIE (EMI AMERICA)
8	DIAMONDS — HERB ALPERT (A&M)	CROWDED HOUSE — CROWDED HOUSE (CAPITOL)
9	MEET ME HALF WAY — KENNY LOGGINS (COLUMBIA)	WEAPONS OF LOVE — TRUTH (IRS/MCA)
10	THE LADY IN RED — CHRIS DE BURGH (A&M)	RICHARD MARX — RICHARD MARX (MANHATTAN)
11	BIG LOVE — FLEETWOOD MAC (WARNER BROS)	I'M NO ANGEL — GREGG ALLMAN BAND (EPIC)
12	IF SHE WOULD HAVE BEEN FAITHFUL — CHICAGO (WARNER BROS)	WHITESNAKE — WHITESNAKE (GEFFEN)
13	RIGHT ON TRACK — BREAKFAST CLUB (MCA)	GYPSY BLOOD — MASON RUFFNER (CBS ASSOCIATED)
14	SONGBIRD — KENNY G (ARISTA)	LITTLE AMERICA — LITTLE AMERICA (GEFFEN)
15	ALONE — HEART (CAPITOL)	SLIPPERY WHEN WET — BON JOVI (MERCURY/PG)
16	JUST TO SEE HER — SMOKEY ROBINSON (MOTOWN)	WISHES — JON BUTCHER (CAPITOL)
17	LOOKING FOR A NEW LOVE — JODY WATLEY (MCA)	SOLITUDE STANDING — SUZANNE VEGA (A&M)
18	LESSONS IN LOVE — LEVEL 42 (POLYDOR/PG)	MECHANICAL RESONANCE — TESLA (GEFFEN)
19	I KNOW WHAT I LIKE — HUEY LEWIS AND THE NEWS (CHRYSALIS)	READY OR NOT — LOU GRAMM (ATLANTIC)
20	DON'T DISTURB THIS GROOVE — SYSTEM (ATLANTIC)	GIRLS, GIRLS, GIRLS — MOTLEY CRUE (ELEKTRA)

WEEK ENDING JUNE 6 1987

S I N G L E S UK A L B U M S

	#	
I WANNA DANCE WITH SOMEBODY — WHITNEY HOUSTON (ARISTA)	1	LIVE IN THE CITY OF LIGHT — SIMPLE MINDS (VIRGIN)
NOTHING'S GONNA STOP US NOW — STARSHIP (GRUNT/RCA)	2	SOLITUDE STANDING — SUZANNE VEGA (A&M)
HOLD ME NOW — JOHNNY LOGAN (EPIC)	3	IT'S BETTER TO TRAVEL — SWING OUT SISTER (MERCURY/PHONOGRAM)
JACK MIX II/III — MIRAGE (DEBUT/PASSION)	4	THE JOSHUA TREE — U2 (ISLAND)
SHATTERED DREAMS — JOHNNY HATES JAZZ (VIRGIN)	5	KEEP YOUR DISTANCE — CURIOSITY KILLED THE CAT (MERCURY)
WISHING I WAS LUCKY — WET WET WET (PHONOGRAM)	6	KISS ME KISS ME KISS ME — THE CURE (FICTION)
VICTIM OF LOVE — ERASURE (MUTE)	7	TANGO IN THE NIGHT — FLEETWOOD MAC (WARNER BROS)
SERIOUS — DONNA ALLEN (PORTRAIT)	8	RAINDANCING — ALISON MOYET (CBS)
A BOY FROM NOWHERE — TOM JONES (EPIC)	9	F.L.M. — MEL & KIM (SUPREME)
GOODBYE STRANGER — PEPSI & SHIRLIE (POLYDOR)	10	RUNNING IN THE FAMILY — LEVEL 42 (POLYDOR)
FIVE GET OVER EXCITED — THE HOUSEMARTINS (GO! DISCS)	11	LICENSED TO ILL — BEASTIE BOYS (DEF JAM)
INCOMMUNICADO — MARILLION (EMI)	12	MEN AND WOMEN — SIMPLY RED (WEA)
I STILL HAVEN'T FOUND WHAT I'M LOOKING FOR — U2 (ISLAND)	13	SO — PETER GABRIEL (VIRGIN)
CAN'T BE WITH YOU TONIGHT — JUDY BOUCHER (ORBITONE)	14	TRUE BLUE — MADONNA (SIRE)
(SOMETHING INSIDE) SO STRONG — LABI SIFFRE (CHINA)	15	INVISIBLE TOUCH — GENESIS (VIRGIN)
NO SLEEP TILL BROOKLYN — BEASTIE BOYS (DEF JAM)	16	NOW, THAT'S WHAT I CALL MUSIC 9 — VARIOUS (VIRGIN/EMI/POLYGRAM)
BACK & FORTH — CAMEO (CLUB/PHONOGRAM)	17	SILK AND STEEL — FIVE STAR (TENT/RCA)
NOTHING'S GONNA STOP ME NOW — SAMANTHA FOX (JIVE)	18	THE CIRCUS — ERASURE (MUTE)
BIG LOVE — FLEETWOOD MAC (WARNER BROS)	19	DANCING ON THE COUCH — GO WEST (CHRYSALIS)
LIVING IN A BOX — LIVING IN A BOX (CHRYSALIS)	20	THE GREATEST HITS — TOM JONES (TELSTAR)

S I N G L E S US A L B U M S

	#	
ALWAYS — ATLANTIC STARR (WARNER BROS)	1	THE JOSHUA TREE — U2 (ISLAND)
YOU KEEP ME HANGIN' ON — KIM WILDE (MCA)	2	LET ME UP (I'VE HAD ENOUGH) — TOM PETTY & THE HEARTBREAKERS (MCA)
IN TOO DEEP — GENESIS (ATLANTIC)	3	TANGO IN THE NIGHT — FLEETWOOD MAC (WARNER BROS)
HEAD TO TOE — LISA LISA (COLUMBIA)	4	BAD ANIMALS — HEART (CAPITOL)
I WANNA DANCE WITH SOMEBODY — WHITNEY HOUSTON (ARISTA)	5	INTO THE FIRE — BRYAN ADAMS (A&M)
DIAMONDS — HERB ALPERT (A&M)	6	SOUNDTRACK — BEVERLY HILLS COP II (MCA)
WANTED DEAD OR ALIVE — BON JOVI (MERCURY/PG)	7	NEVER LET ME DOWN — DAVID BOWIE (EMI AMERICA)
ALONE — HEART (CAPITOL)	8	CROWDED HOUSE — CROWDED HOUSE (CAPITOL)
MEET ME HALF WAY — KENNY LOGGINS (COLUMBIA)	9	RICHARD MARX — RICHARD MARX (MANHATTAN)
SONGBIRD — KENNY G (ARISTA)	10	WEAPONS OF LOVE — TRUTH (IRS/MCA)
WITH OR WITHOUT YOU — U2 (ISLAND)	11	GYPSY BLOOD — MASON RUFFNER (CBS ASSOCIATED)
JUST TO SEE HER — SMOKEY ROBINSON (MOTOWN)	12	WHITESNAKE — WHITESNAKE (GEFFEN)
SHAKEDOWN — BOB SEGER (MCA)	13	EXILES — DAN FOGELBERG (EPIC)
DON'T DISTURB THIS GROOVE — SYSTEM (ATLANTIC)	14	SOLITUDE STANDING — SUZANNE VEGA (A&M)
LESSONS IN LOVE — LEVEL 42 (POLYDOR/PG)	15	WISHES — JON BUTCHER (CAPITOL)
THE LADY IN RED — CHRIS DE BURGH (A&M)	16	I'M NO ANGEL — GREGG ALLMAN BAND (EPIC)
POINT OF NO RETURN — EXPOSE (ARISTA)	17	GIRLS, GIRLS, GIRLS — MOTLEY CRUE (ELEKTRA)
IF SHE WOULD HAVE BEEN FAITHFUL — CHICAGO (WARNER BROS)	18	BROADCAST — CUTTING CREW (VIRGIN)
EVERY LITTLE KISS — BRUCE HORNSBY & THE RANGE (RCA)	19	HARD TIMES IN THE LAND OF PLENTY — OMAR & THE HOWLERS (COLUMBIA)
SOMETHING SO STRONG — CROWDED HOUSE (CAPITOL)	20	FREEDOM-NO COMPROMISE — LITTLE STEVEN (MANHATTAN)

WEEK ENDING JUNE 13 1987

S I N G L E S UK A L B U M S

	#	
I WANNA DANCE WITH SOMEBODY — WHITNEY HOUSTON (ARISTA)	1	WHITNEY — WHITNEY HOUSTON (ARISTA)
HOLD ME NOW — JOHNNY LOGAN (EPIC)	2	LIVE IN THE CITY OF LIGHT — SIMPLE MINDS (VIRGIN)
NOTHING'S GONNA STOP US NOW — STARSHIP (GRUNT/RCA)	3	SGT. PEPPER'S LONELY HEARTS CLUB BAND — THE BEATLES (PARLOPHONE)
I WANT YOUR SEX (RHYTHM 1 LUST) — GEORGE MICHAEL (EPIC)	4	THE JOSHUA TREE — U2 (ISLAND)
JACK MIX II/III — MIRAGE (DEBUT/PASSION)	5	SOLITUDE STANDING — SUZANNE VEGA (A&M)
I STILL HAVEN'T FOUND WHAT I'M LOOKING FOR — U2 (ISLAND)	6	IT'S BETTER TO TRAVEL — SWING OUT SISTER (MERCURY/PHONOGRAM)
SHATTERED DREAMS — JOHNNY HATES JAZZ (VIRGIN)	7	LICENSED TO ILL — BEASTIE BOYS (DEF JAM)
VICTIM OF LOVE — ERASURE (MUTE)	8	KEEP YOUR DISTANCE — CURIOSITY KILLED THE CAT (MERCURY)
GOODBYE STRANGER — PEPSI & SHIRLIE (POLYDOR)	9	TANGO IN THE NIGHT — FLEETWOOD MAC (WARNER BROS)
WISHING I WAS LUCKY — WET WET WET (PHONOGRAM)	10	RAINDANCING — ALISON MOYET (CBS)
NOTHING'S GONNA STOP ME NOW — SAMANTHA FOX (JIVE)	11	MEN AND WOMEN — SIMPLY RED (WEA)
SERIOUS — DONNA ALLEN (PORTRAIT)	12	F.L.M. — MEL & KIM (SUPREME)
STAR TREKKIN' — THE FIRM (BARK)	13	TRUE BLUE — MADONNA (SIRE)
NO SLEEP TILL BROOKLYN — BEASTIE BOYS (DEF JAM)	14	RUNNING IN THE FAMILY — LEVEL 42 (POLYDOR)
YOU'RE THE VOICE — JOHN FARNHAM (WHEATLEY/RCA)	15	THE CIRCUS — ERASURE (MUTE)
IT'S TRICKY — RUN DMC (LONDON)	16	NOW, THAT'S WHAT I CALL MUSIC 9 — VARIOUS (VIRGIN/EMI/POLYGRAM)
UNDER THE BOARDWALK — BRUCE WILLIS (MOTOWN)	17	ATLANTIC SOUL CLASSICS — VARIOUS (ATLANTIC)
LOOKING FOR A NEW LOVE — JODY WATLEY (MCA)	18	KISS ME KISS ME KISS ME — THE CURE (FICTION)
FIVE GET OVER EXCITED — THE HOUSEMARTINS (GO! DISCS)	19	THE GREATEST HITS — TOM JONES (TELSTAR)
A BOY FROM NOWHERE — TOM JONES (EPIC)	20	INVISIBLE TOUCH — GENESIS (VIRGIN)

S I N G L E S US A L B U M S

	#	
HEAD TO TOE — LISA LISA (COLUMBIA)	1	THE JOSHUA TREE — U2 (ISLAND)
I WANNA DANCE WITH SOMEBODY — WHITNEY HOUSTON (ARISTA)	2	BAD ANIMALS — HEART (CAPITOL)
IN TOO DEEP — GENESIS (ATLANTIC)	3	TANGO IN THE NIGHT — FLEETWOOD MAC (WARNER BROS)
ALWAYS — ATLANTIC STARR (WARNER BROS)	4	LET ME UP (I'VE HAD ENOUGH) — TOM PETTY & THE HEARTBREAKERS (MCA)
ALONE — HEART (CAPITOL)	5	INTO THE FIRE — BRYAN ADAMS (A&M)
DIAMONDS — HERB ALPERT (A&M)	6	SOUNDTRACK — BEVERLY HILLS COP II (MCA)
YOU KEEP ME HANGIN' ON — KIM WILDE (MCA)	7	RICHARD MARX — RICHARD MARX (MANHATTAN)
SONGBIRD — KENNY G (ARISTA)	8	NEVER LET ME DOWN — DAVID BOWIE (EMI AMERICA)
SHAKEDOWN — BOB SEGER (MCA)	9	CROWDED HOUSE — CROWDED HOUSE (CAPITOL)
WANTED DEAD OR ALIVE — BON JOVI (MERCURY/PG)	10	SENTIMENTAL HYGIENE — WARREN ZEVON (VIRGIN)
JUST TO SEE HER — SMOKEY ROBINSON (MOTOWN)	11	GYPSY BLOOD — MASON RUFFNER (CBS ASSOCIATED)
DON'T DISTURB THIS GROOVE — SYSTEM (ATLANTIC)	12	WHITESNAKE — WHITESNAKE (GEFFEN)
MEET ME HALF WAY — KENNY LOGGINS (COLUMBIA)	13	EXILES — DAN FOGELBERG (EPIC)
LESSONS IN LOVE — LEVEL 42 (POLYDOR/PG)	14	SOLITUDE STANDING — SUZANNE VEGA (A&M)
POINT OF NO RETURN — EXPOSE (ARISTA)	15	WEAPONS OF LOVE — TRUTH (IRS/MCA)
FUNKY TOWN — PSEUDO ECHO (RCA)	16	GIRLS, GIRLS, GIRLS — MOTLEY CRUE (ELEKTRA)
EVERY LITTLE KISS — BRUCE HORNSBY & THE RANGE (RCA)	17	I'M NO ANGEL — GREGG ALLMAN BAND (EPIC)
SOMETHING SO STRONG — CROWDED HOUSE (CAPITOL)	18	BROADCAST — CUTTING CREW (VIRGIN)
ENDLESS NIGHTS — EDDIE MONEY (COLUMBIA)	19	HARD TIMES IN THE LAND OF PLENTY — OMAR & THE HOWLERS (COLUMBIA)
HEART AND SOUL — T'PAU (VIRGIN)	20	WISHES — JON BUTCHER (CAPITOL)

WEEK ENDING JUNE 20 1987

S I N G L E S UK A L B U M S

#	SINGLES	ALBUMS
1	STAR TREKKIN' — THE FIRM (BARK)	WHITNEY — WHITNEY HOUSTON (ARISTA)
2	I WANNA DANCE WITH SOMEBODY — WHITNEY HOUSTON (ARISTA)	LIVE IN THE CITY OF LIGHT — SIMPLE MINDS (VIRGIN)
3	I WANT YOUR SEX (RHYTHM 1 LUST) — GEORGE MICHAEL (EPIC)	THE JOSHUA TREE — U2 (ISLAND)
4	HOLD ME NOW — JOHNNY LOGAN (EPIC)	SOLITUDE STANDING — SUZANNE VEGA (A&M)
5	NOTHING'S GONNA STOP US NOW — STARSHIP (GRUNT/RCA)	KEEP YOUR DISTANCE — CURIOSITY KILLED THE CAT (MERCURY)
6	UNDER THE BOARDWALK — BRUCE WILLIS (MOTOWN)	SGT. PEPPER'S LONELY HEARTS CLUB BAND — THE BEATLES (PARLOPHONE)
7	I STILL HAVEN'T FOUND WHAT I'M LOOKING FOR — U2 (ISLAND)	LICENSED TO ILL — BEASTIE BOYS (DEF JAM)
8	NOTHING'S GONNA STOP ME NOW — SAMANTHA FOX (JIVE)	IT'S BETTER TO TRAVEL — SWING OUT SISTER (MERCURY/PHONOGRAM)
9	YOU'RE THE VOICE — JOHN FARNHAM (WHEATLEY/RCA)	RAINDANCING — ALISON MOYET (CBS)
10	VICTIM OF LOVE — ERASURE (MUTE)	FRIENDS AND LOVERS — VARIOUS (K-TEL)
11	JACK MIX II/III — MIRAGE (DEBUT/PASSION)	THE CIRCUS — ERASURE (MUTE)
12	GOODBYE STRANGER — PEPSI & SHIRLIE (POLYDOR)	ATLANTIC SOUL CLASSICS — VARIOUS (ATLANTIC)
13	LOOKING FOR A NEW LOVE — JODY WATLEY (MCA)	INVISIBLE TOUCH — GENESIS (VIRGIN)
14	WHEN SMOKEY SINGS — ABC (NEUTRON/PHONOGRAM)	TANGO IN THE NIGHT — FLEETWOOD MAC (WARNER BROS)
15	WISHING I WAS LUCKY — WET WET WET (PHONOGRAM)	MEN AND WOMEN — SIMPLY RED (WEA)
16	IS THIS LOVE — WHITESNAKE (EMI)	RUNNING IN THE FAMILY — LEVEL 42 (POLYDOR)
17	IT'S TRICKY — RUN DMC (LONDON)	NOW, THAT'S WHAT I CALL MUSIC 9 — VARIOUS (VIRGIN/EMI/POLYGRAM)
18	SHATTERED DREAMS — JOHNNY HATES JAZZ (VIRGIN)	THE RETURN OF BRUNO — BRUCE WILLIS (MOTOWN)
19	NO SLEEP TILL BROOKLYN — BEASTIE BOYS (DEF JAM)	F.L.M. — MEL & KIM (SUPREME)
20	IT'S NOT UNUSUAL — TOM JONES (DECCA/LONDON)	TRUE BLUE — MADONNA (SIRE)

S I N G L E S US A L B U M S

#	SINGLES	ALBUMS
1	I WANNA DANCE WITH SOMEBODY — WHITNEY HOUSTON (ARISTA)	THE JOSHUA TREE — U2 (ISLAND)
2	HEAD TO TOE — LISA LISA (COLUMBIA)	TANGO IN THE NIGHT — FLEETWOOD MAC (WARNER BROS)
3	ALONE — HEART (CAPITOL)	BAD ANIMALS — HEART (CAPITOL)
4	IN TOO DEEP — GENESIS (ATLANTIC)	LET ME UP (I'VE HAD ENOUGH) — TOM PETTY & THE HEARTBREAKERS (MCA)
5	SHAKEDOWN — BOB SEGER (MCA)	INTO THE FIRE — BRYAN ADAMS (A&M)
6	SONGBIRD — KENNY G (ARISTA)	RICHARD MARX — RICHARD MARX (MANHATTAN)
7	ALWAYS — ATLANTIC STARR (WARNER BROS)	SOUNDTRACK — BEVERLY HILLS COP II (MCA)
8	DON'T DISTURB THIS GROOVE — SYSTEM (ATLANTIC)	SENTIMENTAL HYGIENE — WARREN ZEVON (VIRGIN)
9	JUST TO SEE HER — SMOKEY ROBINSON (MOTOWN)	NEVER LET ME DOWN — DAVID BOWIE (EMI AMERICA)
10	POINT OF NO RETURN — EXPOSE (ARISTA)	GYPSY BLOOD — MASON RUFFNER (CBS ASSOCIATED)
11	FUNKY TOWN — PSEUDO ECHO (RCA)	WHITESNAKE — WHITESNAKE (GEFFEN)
12	DIAMONDS — HERB ALPERT (A&M)	RADIO K.A.O.S. — ROGER WATERS (COLUMBIA)
13	SOMETHING SO STRONG — CROWDED HOUSE (CAPITOL)	CROWDED HOUSE — CROWDED HOUSE (CAPITOL)
14	EVERY LITTLE KISS — BRUCE HORNSBY & THE RANGE (RCA)	SOLITUDE STANDING — SUZANNE VEGA (A&M)
15	LESSONS IN LOVE — LEVEL 42 (POLYDOR/PG)	BANGIN' — OUTFIELD (COLUMBIA)
16	HEART AND SOUL — T'PAU (VIRGIN)	EXILES — DAN FOGELBERG (EPIC)
17	YOU KEEP ME HANGIN' ON — KIM WILDE (MCA)	GIRLS, GIRLS, GIRLS — MOTLEY CRUE (ELEKTRA)
18	ENDLESS NIGHTS — EDDIE MONEY (COLUMBIA)	HARD TIMES IN THE LAND OF PLENTY — OMAR & THE HOWLERS (COLUMBIA)
19	KISS HIM GOODBYE — NYLONS (OPEN AIR/WINDHAM HILL)	BROADCAST — CUTTING CREW (VIRGIN)
20	I STILL HAVEN'T FOUND WHAT I'M LOOKING FOR — U2 (ISLAND)	I'M NO ANGEL — GREGG ALLMAN BAND (EPIC)

WEEK ENDING JUNE 27 1987

S I N G L E S UK A L B U M S

#	SINGLES	ALBUMS
1	STAR TREKKIN' — THE FIRM (BARK)	WHITNEY — WHITNEY HOUSTON (ARISTA)
2	I WANNA DANCE WITH SOMEBODY — WHITNEY HOUSTON (ARISTA)	THE JOSHUA TREE — U2 (ISLAND)
3	UNDER THE BOARDWALK — BRUCE WILLIS (MOTOWN)	LIVE IN THE CITY OF LIGHT — SIMPLE MINDS (VIRGIN)
4	I WANT YOUR SEX (RHYTHM 1 LUST) — GEORGE MICHAEL (EPIC)	KEEP YOUR DISTANCE — CURIOSITY KILLED THE CAT (MERCURY)
5	IT'S A SIN — PET SHOP BOYS (PARLOPHONE)	SOLITUDE STANDING — SUZANNE VEGA (A&M)
6	HOLD ME NOW — JOHNNY LOGAN (EPIC)	THE RETURN OF BRUNO — BRUCE WILLIS (MOTOWN)
7	YOU'RE THE VOICE — JOHN FARNHAM (WHEATLEY)	SGT. PEPPER'S LONELY HEARTS CLUB BAND — THE BEATLES (PARLOPHONE)
8	NOTHING'S GONNA STOP ME NOW — SAMANTHA FOX (JIVE)	IT'S BETTER TO TRAVEL — SWING OUT SISTER (MERCURY/PHONOGRAM)
9	MISFIT — CURIOSITY KILLED THE CAT (MERCURY)	INVISIBLE TOUCH — GENESIS (VIRGIN)
10	NOTHING'S GONNA STOP US NOW — STARSHIP (GRUNT/RCA)	RAINDANCING — ALISON MOYET (CBS)
11	IS THIS LOVE — WHITESNAKE (EMI)	ATLANTIC SOUL CLASSICS — VARIOUS (ATLANTIC)
12	WHEN SMOKEY SINGS — ABC (NEUTRON/PHONOGRAM)	LICENSED TO ILL — BEASTIE BOYS (DEF JAM)
13	I STILL HAVEN'T FOUND WHAT I'M LOOKING FOR — U2 (ISLAND)	FRIENDS AND LOVERS — VARIOUS (K-TEL)
14	WISHING WELL — TERENCE TRENT D'ARBY (CBS)	THE CIRCUS — ERASURE (MUTE)
15	VICTIM OF LOVE — ERASURE (MUTE)	HIS FINEST COLLECTION — ROGER WHITTAKER (TEMBO/POLYGRAM)
16	LOOKING FOR A NEW LOVE — JODY WATELY (MCA)	THE GREATEST HITS — TOM JONES (TELSTAR)
17	IT'S NOT UNUSUAL — TOM JONES (DECCA/LONDON)	TANGO IN THE NIGHT — FLEETWOOD MAC (WARNER BROS)
18	LET'S DANCE — CHRIS REA (MAGNET)	MEN AND WOMEN — SIMPLY RED (WEA)
19	GOODBYE STRANGER — PEPSI & SHIRLIE (POLYDOR)	NOW, THAT'S WHAT I CALL MUSIC 9 — VARIOUS (VIRGIN/EMI/POLYGRAM)
20	JACK MIX II/III — MIRAGE (DEBUT/PASSION)	GRACELAND — PAUL SIMON (WARNER BROS)

S I N G L E S US A L B U M S

#	SINGLES	ALBUMS
1	I WANNA DANCE WITH SOMEBODY — WHITNEY HOUSTON (ARISTA)	TANGO IN THE NIGHT — FLEETWOOD MAC (WARNER BROS)
2	ALONE — HEART (CAPITOL)	THE JOSHUA TREE — U2 (ISLAND)
3	SHAKEDOWN — BOB SEGER (MCA)	BAD ANIMALS — HEART (CAPITOL)
4	HEAD TO TOE — LISA LISA (COLUMBIA)	LET ME UP (I'VE HAD ENOUGH) — TOM PETTY & THE HEARTBREAKERS (MCA)
5	DON'T DISTURB THIS GROOVE — SYSTEM (ATLANTIC)	INTO THE FIRE — BRYAN ADAMS (A&M)
6	SONGBIRD — KENNY G (ARISTA)	RICHARD MARX — RICHARD MARX (MANHATTAN)
7	POINT OF NO RETURN — EXPOSE (ARISTA)	SAMMY HAGAR — SAMMY HAGAR (GEFFEN)
8	IN TOO DEEP — GENESIS (ATLANTIC)	SOUNDTRACK — BEVERLY HILLS COP II (MCA)
9	FUNKY TOWN — PSEUDO ECHO (RCA)	RADIO K.A.O.S. — ROGER WATERS (COLUMBIA)
10	SOMETHING SO STRONG — CROWDED HOUSE (CAPITOL)	WHITESNAKE — WHITESNAKE (GEFFEN)
11	EVERY LITTLE KISS — BRUCE HORNSBY & THE RANGE (RCA)	SENTIMENTAL HYGIENE — WARREN ZEVON (VIRGIN)
12	I STILL HAVEN'T FOUND WHAT I'M LOOKING FOR — U2 (ISLAND)	SOUNDTRACK — LOST BOYS (ATLANTIC)
13	HEART AND SOUL — T'PAU (VIRGIN)	BANGIN' — OUTFIELD (COLUMBIA)
14	JUST TO SEE HER — SMOKEY ROBINSON (MOTOWN)	SOLITUDE STANDING — SUZANNE VEGA (A&M)
15	ALWAYS — ATLANTIC STARR (WARNER BROS)	ROVER'S RETURN — JOHN WAITE (EMI AMERICA)
16	KISS HIM GOODBYE — NYLONS (OPEN AIR/WINDHAM HILL)	GYPSY BLOOD — MASON RUFFNER (CBS ASSOCIATED)
17	RHYTHM IS GONNA GET YOU — GLORIA ESTEFAN & MIAMI SOUND MACHINE (EPIC)	HARD TIMES IN THE LAND OF PLENTY — OMAR & THE HOWLERS (COLUMBIA)
18	GIRLS, GIRLS, GIRLS — MOTLEY CRUE (ELEKTRA)	NEVER LET ME DOWN — DAVID BOWIE (EMI AMERICA)
19	ENDLESS NIGHTS — EDDIE MONEY (COLUMBIA)	GIRLS, GIRLS, GIRLS — MOTLEY CRUE (ELEKTRA)
20	I WANT YOUR SEX (RHYTHM 1 LUST) — GEORGE MICHAEL (COLUMBIA)	5 TO 1 — TOM KIMMEL (MERCURY/PG)

WEEK ENDING JULY 4 1987
S I N G L E S UK A L B U M S

#	SINGLES	ALBUMS
1	IT'S A SIN — PET SHOP BOYS (PARLOPHONE)	WHITNEY — WHITNEY HOUSTON (ARISTA)
2	STAR TREKKIN' — THE FIRM (BARK)	CLUTCHING AT STRAWS — MARILLION (EMI)
3	UNDER THE BOARDWALK — BRUCE WILLIS (MOTOWN)	THE JOSHUA TREE — U2 (ISLAND)
4	I WANNA DANCE WITH SOMEBODY — WHITNEY HOUSTON (ARISTA)	KEEP YOUR DISTANCE — CURIOSITY KILLED THE CAT (MERCURY)
5	WISHING WELL — TERENCE TRENT D'ARBY (CBS)	LIVE IN THE CITY OF LIGHT — SIMPLE MINDS (VIRGIN)
6	YOU'RE THE VOICE — JOHN FARNHAM (WHEATLEY/RCA)	THE RETURN OF BRUNO — BRUCE WILLIS (MOTOWN)
7	MISFIT — CURIOSITY KILLED THE CAT (MERCURY)	SOLITUDE STANDING — SUZANNE VEGA (A&M)
8	I WANT YOUR SEX (RHYTHM 1 LUST) — GEORGE MICHAEL (EPIC)	INVISIBLE TOUCH — GENESIS (VIRGIN)
9	IS THIS LOVE — WHITESNAKE (EMI)	ATLANTIC SOUL CLASSICS — VARIOUS (ATLANTIC)
10	MY PRETTY ONE — CLIFF RICHARD (EMI)	IT'S BETTER TO TRAVEL — SWING OUT SISTER (MERCURY/PHONOGRAM)
11	WHEN SMOKEY SINGS — ABC (NEUTRON/PHONOGRAM)	HITS REVIVAL — VARIOUS (K-TEL)
12	LET'S DANCE — CHRIS REA (MAGNET)	THE CIRCUS — ERASURE (MUTE)
13	HOLD ME NOW — JOHNNY LOGAN (EPIC)	LICENSED TO ILL — BEASTIE BOYS (DEF JAM)
14	NOTHING'S GONNA STOP ME NOW — SAMANTHA FOX (JIVE)	NEVER LET ME DOWN — DAVID BOWIE (EMI AMERICA)
15	NOTHING'S GONNA STOP US NOW — STARSHIP (GRUNT/RCA)	FRIENDS AND LOVERS — VARIOUS (K-TEL)
16	ALWAYS — ATLANTIC STARR (WARNER BROS)	RAINDANCING — ALISON MOYET (CBS)
17	THE LIVING DAYLIGHTS — A-HA (WARNER BROS)	THE HOLIDAY ALBUM — VARIOUS (CBS)
18	COMIN' ON STRONG — BROKEN ENGLISH (EMI)	SGT. PEPPER'S LONELY HEARTS CLUB BAND — THE BEATLES (PARLOPHONE)
19	PROMISED YOU A MIRACLE — SIMPLE MINDS (VIRGIN)	TANGO IN THE NIGHT — FLEETWOOD MAC (WARNER BROS)
20	IF I WAS YOUR GIRLFRIEND — PRINCE (PAISLEY PARK/WARNER BROS)	NOW, THAT'S WHAT I CALL MUSIC 9 — VARIOUS (VIRGIN/EMI/POLYGRAM)

S I N G L E S US A L B U M S

#	SINGLES	ALBUMS
1	I WANNA DANCE WITH SOMEBODY — WHITNEY HOUSTON (ARISTA)	SAMMY HAGAR — SAMMY HAGAR (GEFFEN)
2	ALONE — HEART (CAPITOL)	BAD ANIMALS — HEART (CAPITOL)
3	SHAKEDOWN — BOB SEGER (MCA)	INTO THE FIRE — BRYAN ADAMS (A&M)
4	DON'T DISTURB THIS GROOVE — SYSTEM (ATLANTIC)	TANGO IN THE NIGHT — FLEETWOOD MAC (WARNER BROS)
5	POINT OF NO RETURN — EXPOSE (ARISTA)	LET ME UP (I'VE HAD ENOUGH) — TOM PETTY & THE HEARTBREAKERS (MCA)
6	FUNKY TOWN — PSEUDO ECHO (RCA)	THE JOSHUA TREE — U2 (ISLAND)
7	I STILL HAVEN'T FOUND WHAT I'M LOOKING FOR — U2 (ISLAND)	RICHARD MARX — RICHARD MARX (MANHATTAN)
8	SOMETHING SO STRONG — CROWDED HOUSE (CAPITOL)	GOT ANY GUM? — JOE WALSH (FULL MOON/WARNER BROS)
9	SONGBIRD — KENNY G (ARISTA)	SOUNDTRACK — LOST BOYS (ATLANTIC)
10	HEART AND SOUL — T'PAU (VIRGIN)	WHITESNAKE — WHITESNAKE (GEFFEN)
11	EVERY LITTLE KISS — BRUCE HORNSBY & THE RANGE (RCA)	RADIO K.A.O.S. — ROGER WATERS (COLUMBIA)
12	RHYTHM IS GONNA GET YOU — GLORIA ESTEFAN & MIAMI SOUND MACHINE (EPIC)	ROVER'S RETURN — JOHN WAITE (EMI AMERICA)
13	KISS HIM GOODBYE — NYLONS (OPEN AIR/WINDHAM HILL)	BANGIN' — OUTFIELD (COLUMBIA)
14	GIRLS, GIRLS, GIRLS — MOTLEY CRUE (ELEKTRA)	HOT NUMBER — FABULOUS THUNDERBIRDS (CBS ASSOCIATED)
15	CROSS MY BROKEN HEART — JETS (MCA)	NO PROTECTION — STARSHIP (GRUNT/RCA)
16	I WANT YOUR SEX (RHYTHM 1 LUST) — GEORGE MICHAEL (COLUMBIA)	SOLITUDE STANDING — SUZANNE VEGA (A&M)
17	HEAD TO TOE — LISA LISA (COLUMBIA)	HARD TIMES IN THE LAND OF PLENTY — OMAR & THE HOWLERS (COLUMBIA)
18	JUST TO SEE HER — SMOKEY ROBINSON (MOTOWN)	LIFE — NEIL YOUNG & CRAZY HORSE (GEFFEN)
19	IN TOO DEEP — GENESIS (ATLANTIC)	SENTIMENTAL HYGIENE — WARREN ZEVON (VIRGIN)
20	HAPPY — SURFACE (COLUMBIA)	5 TO 1 — TOM KIMMEL (MERCURY/PG)

WEEK ENDING JULY 11 1987
S I N G L E S UK A L B U M S

#	SINGLES	ALBUMS
1	IT'S A SIN — PET SHOP BOYS (PARLOPHONE)	WHITNEY — WHITNEY HOUSTON (ARISTA)
2	UNDER THE BOARDWALK — BRUCE WILLIS (MOTOWN)	THE JOSHUA TREE — U2 (ISLAND)
3	STAR TREKKIN' — THE FIRM (BARK)	INVISIBLE TOUCH — GENESIS (VIRGIN)
4	WISHING WELL — TERENCE TRENT D'ARBY (CBS)	THE RETURN OF BRUNO — BRUCE WILLIS (MOTOWN)
5	THE LIVING DAYLIGHTS — A-HA (WARNER BROS)	LIVE IN THE CITY OF LIGHT — SIMPLE MINDS (VIRGIN)
6	MY PRETTY ONE — CLIFF RICHARD (EMI)	KEEP YOUR DISTANCE — CURIOSITY KILLED THE CAT (MERCURY)
7	ALWAYS — ATLANTIC STARR (WARNER BROS)	CLUTCHING AT STRAWS — MARILLION (EMI)
8	I WANNA DANCE WITH SOMEBODY — WHITNEY HOUSTON (ARISTA)	CONTROL — JANET JACKSON (A&M)
9	YOU'RE THE VOICE — JOHN FARNHAM (WHEATLEY/RCA)	ATLANTIC SOUL CLASSICS — VARIOUS (ATLANTIC)
10	MISFIT — CURIOSITY KILLED THE CAT (MERCURY)	HITS REVIVAL — VARIOUS (K-TEL)
11	IS THIS LOVE — WHITESNAKE (EMI)	SOLITUDE STANDING — SUZANNE VEGA (A&M)
12	SWEETEST SMILE — BLACK (A&M)	IT'S BETTER TO TRAVEL — SWING OUT SISTER (MERCURY/PHONOGRAM)
13	LET'S DANCE — CHRIS REA (MAGNET)	THE HOLIDAY ALBUM — VARIOUS (CBS)
14	WHEN SMOKEY SINGS — ABC (NEUTRON/PHONOGRAM)	LICENSED TO ILL — BEASTIE BOYS (DEF JAM)
15	ALONE — HEART (CAPITOL)	BAD ANIMALS — HEART (CAPITOL)
16	F.L.M. — MEL & KIM (SUPREME)	THE CIRCUS — ERASURE (MUTE)
17	SWEET SIXTEEN — BILLY IDOL (CHRYSALIS)	F.L.M. — MEL & KIM (SUPREME)
18	COMIN' ON STRONG — BROKEN ENGLISH (EMI)	TRUE BLUE — MADONNA (SIRE)
19	I WANT YOUR SEX (RHYTHM 1 LUST) — GEORGE MICHAEL (EPIC)	TANGO IN THE NIGHT — FLEETWOOD MAC (WARNER BROS)
20	HOLD ME NOW — JOHNNY LOGAN (EPIC)	SO — PETER GABRIEL (VIRGIN)

S I N G L E S US A L B U M S

#	SINGLES	ALBUMS
1	ALONE — HEART (CAPITOL)	SAMMY HAGAR — SAMMY HAGAR (GEFFEN)
2	SHAKEDOWN — BOB SEGER (MCA)	IN THE DARK — GRATEFUL DEAD (ARISTA)
3	I WANNA DANCE WITH SOMEBODY — WHITNEY HOUSTON (ARISTA)	BAD ANIMALS — HEART (CAPITOL)
4	I STILL HAVEN'T FOUND WHAT I'M LOOKING FOR — U2 (ISLAND)	INTO THE FIRE — BRYAN ADAMS (A&M)
5	DON'T DISTURB THIS GROOVE — SYSTEM (ATLANTIC)	TANGO IN THE NIGHT — FLEETWOOD MAC (WARNER BROS)
6	POINT OF NO RETURN — EXPOSE (ARISTA)	RICHARD MARX — RICHARD MARX (MANHATTAN)
7	HEART AND SOUL — T'PAU (VIRGIN)	SOUNDTRACK — LOST BOYS (ATLANTIC)
8	SOMETHING SO STRONG — CROWDED HOUSE (CAPITOL)	GOT ANY GUM? — JOE WALSH (FULL MOON/WARNER BROS)
9	FUNKY TOWN — PSEUDO ECHO (RCA)	THE JOSHUA TREE — U2 (ISLAND)
10	RHYTHM IS GONNA GET YOU — GLORIA ESTEFAN & MIAMI SOUND MACHINE (EPIC)	WHITESNAKE — WHITESNAKE (GEFFEN)
11	KISS HIM GOODBYE — NYLONS (OPEN AIR/WINDHAM HILL)	LET ME UP (I'VE HAD ENOUGH) — TOM PETTY & THE HEARTBREAKERS (MCA)
12	CROSS MY BROKEN HEART — JETS (MCA)	ROVER'S RETURN — JOHN WAITE (EMI AMERICA)
13	I WANT YOUR SEX (RHYTHM 1 LUST) — GEORGE MICHAEL (COLUMBIA)	BANGIN' — OUTFIELD (COLUMBIA)
14	GIRLS, GIRLS, GIRLS — MOTLEY CRUE (ELEKTRA)	HOT NUMBER — FABULOUS THUNDERBIRDS (CBS ASSOCIATED)
15	SONGBIRD — KENNY G (ARISTA)	NO PROTECTION — STARSHIP (GRUNT/RCA)
16	LUKA — SUZANNE VEGA (A&M)	RADIO K.A.O.S. — ROGER WATERS (COLUMBIA)
17	HAPPY — SURFACE (COLUMBIA)	HARD TIMES IN THE LAND OF PLENTY — OMAR & THE HOWLERS (COLUMBIA)
18	THE PLEASURE PRINCIPLE — JANET JACKSON (A&M)	LIFE — NEIL YOUNG & CRAZY HORSE (GEFFEN)
19	WOT'S IT TO YA — ROBBIE NEVIL (MANHATTAN)	AFTER DARK — CRUZADOS (ARISTA)
20	BACK IN THE HIGH LIFE AGAIN — STEVE WINWOOD (ISLAND/WARNER BROS)	5 TO 1 — TOM KIMMEL (MERCURY/PG)

WEEK ENDING JULY 18 1987

SINGLES UK

#	Title	Artist (Label)
1	IT'S A SIN	PET SHOP BOYS (PARLOPHONE)
2	UNDER THE BOARDWALK	BRUCE WILLIS (MOTOWN)
3	WHO'S THAT GIRL	MADONNA (SIRE)
4	WISHING WELL	TERENCE TRENT D'ARBY (CBS)
5	ALWAYS	ATLANTIC STARR (WARNER BROS)
6	THE LIVING DAYLIGHTS	A-HA (WARNER BROS)
7	F.L.M.	MEL & KIM (SUPREME)
8	SWEETEST SMILE	BLACK (A&M)
9	ALONE	HEART (CAPITOL)
10	STAR TREKKIN'	THE FIRM (BARK)
11	MY PRETTY ONE	CLIFF RICHARD (EMI)
12	I WANNA DANCE WITH SOMEBODY	WHITNEY HOUSTON (ARISTA)
13	A LITTLE BOOGIE WOOGIE	SHAKIN' STEVENS (EPIC)
14	JIVE TALKIN'	BOOGIE BOX HIGH (HARDBACK)
15	(YOUR LOVE KEEPS LIFTING ME) HIGHER & HIGHER	JACKIE WILSON (SMP)
16	MISFIT	CURIOSITY KILLED THE CAT (MERCURY)
17	YOU'RE THE VOICE	JOHN FARNHAM (WHEATLEY/RCA)
18	SWEET SIXTEEN	BILLY IDOL (CHRYSALIS)
19	IS THIS LOVE	WHITESNAKE (EMI)
20	LET'S DANCE	CHRIS REA (MAGNET)

ALBUMS UK

#	Title	Artist (Label)
1	WHITNEY	WHITNEY HOUSTON (ARISTA)
2	THE JOSHUA TREE	U2 (ISLAND)
3	INVISIBLE TOUCH	GENESIS (VIRGIN)
4	ECHO & THE BUNNYMEN	ECHO & THE BUNNYMEN (WEA)
5	THE RETURN OF BRUNO	BRUCE WILLIS (MOTOWN)
6	KEEP YOUR DISTANCE	CURIOSITY KILLED THE CAT (MERCURY)
7	LIVE IN THE CITY OF LIGHT	SIMPLE MINDS (VIRGIN)
8	CONTROL	JANET JACKSON (A&M)
9	THE ISLAND STORY	VARIOUS (ISLAND)
10	ATLANTIC SOUL CLASSICS	VARIOUS (ATLANTIC)
11	F.L.M.	MEL & KIM (SUPREME)
12	CLUTCHING AT STRAWS	MARILLION (EMI)
13	HITS REVIVAL	VARIOUS (K-TEL)
14	IT'S BETTER TO TRAVEL	SWING OUT SISTER (MERCURY/PHONOGRAM)
15	BAD ANIMALS	HEART (CAPITOL)
16	SIXTIES MIX	VARIOUS (STYLUS)
17	SOLITUDE STANDING	SUZANNE VEGA (A&M)
18	J.-MICHEL JARRE IN CONCERT LYON/HOUSTON	JEAN-MICHEL JARRE (DREYFUS/POLYDOR)
19	TRUE BLUE	MADONNA (SIRE)
20	TANGO IN THE NIGHT	FLEETWOOD MAC (WARNER BROS)

SINGLES US

#	Title	Artist (Label)
1	ALONE	HEART (CAPITOL)
2	SHAKEDOWN	BOB SEGER (MCA)
3	I STILL HAVEN'T FOUND WHAT I'M LOOKING FOR	U2 (ISLAND)
4	HEART AND SOUL	T'PAU (VIRGIN)
5	I WANNA DANCE WITH SOMEBODY	WHITNEY HOUSTON (ARISTA)
6	RHYTHM IS GONNA GET YOU	GLORIA ESTEFAN & MIAMI SOUND MACHINE (EPIC)
7	LUKA	SUZANNE VEGA (A&M)
8	CROSS MY BROKEN HEART	JETS (MCA)
9	SOMETHING SO STRONG	CROWDED HOUSE (CAPITOL)
10	I WANT YOUR SEX (RHYTHM 1 LUST)	GEORGE MICHAEL (COLUMBIA)
11	DON'T DISTURB THIS GROOVE	SYSTEM (ATLANTIC)
12	KISS HIM GOODBYE	NYLONS (OPEN AIR/WINDHAM HILL)
13	BACK IN THE HIGH LIFE AGAIN	STEVE WINWOOD (ISLAND/WARNER BROS)
14	WHO'S THAT GIRL	MADONNA (SIRE/WARNER BROS)
15	THE PLEASURE PRINCIPLE	JANET JACKSON (A&M)
16	WOT'S IT TO YA	ROBBIE NEVIL (MANHATTAN)
17	HAPPY	SURFACE (COLUMBIA)
18	POINT OF NO RETURN	EXPOSE (ARISTA)
19	GIRLS, GIRLS, GIRLS	MOTLEY CRUE (ELEKTRA)
20	DON'T MEAN NOTHING	RICHARD MARX (MANHATTAN)

ALBUMS US

#	Title	Artist (Label)
1	IN THE DARK	GRATEFUL DEAD (ARISTA)
2	SAMMY HAGAR	SAMMY HAGAR (GEFFEN)
3	BAD ANIMALS	HEART (CAPITOL)
4	TANGO IN THE NIGHT	FLEETWOOD MAC (WARNER BROS)
5	SOUNDTRACK	LOST BOYS (ATLANTIC)
6	WHITESNAKE	WHITESNAKE (GEFFEN)
7	INTO THE FIRE	BRYAN ADAMS (A&M)
8	ROVER'S RETURN	JOHN WAITE (EMI AMERICA)
9	GOT ANY GUM?	JOE WALSH (FULL MOON/WARNER BROS)
10	NO PROTECTION	STARSHIP (GRUNT/RCA)
11	HOT NUMBER	FABULOUS THUNDERBIRDS (CBS ASSOCIATED)
12	LET ME UP (I'VE HAD ENOUGH)	TOM PETTY & THE HEARTBREAKERS (MCA)
13	BANGIN'	OUTFIELD (COLUMBIA)
14	ONE WAY HOME	HOOTERS (COLUMBIA)
15	THE JOSHUA TREE	U2 (ISLAND)
16	RICHARD MARX	RICHARD MARX (MANHATTAN)
17	AFTER DARK	CRUZADOS (ARISTA)
18	RADIO K.A.O.S.	ROGER WATERS (COLUMBIA)
19	LIFE	NEIL YOUNG & CRAZY HORSE (GEFFEN)
20	5 TO 1	TOM KIMMEL (MERCURY/PG)

WEEK ENDING JULY 25 1987

SINGLES UK

#	Title	Artist (Label)
1	WHO'S THAT GIRL	MADONNA (SIRE)
2	IT'S A SIN	PET SHOP BOYS (PARLOPHONE)
3	ALWAYS	ATLANTIC STARR (WARNER BROS)
4	UNDER THE BOARDWALK	BRUCE WILLIS (MOTOWN)
5	LA BAMBA	LOS LOBOS (SLASH/FFRR/LONDON)
6	ALONE	HEART (CAPITOL)
7	F.L.M.	MEL & KIM (SUPREME)
8	WISHING WELL	TERENCE TRENT D'ARBY (CBS)
9	SWEETEST SMILE	BLACK (A&M)
10	JIVE TALKIN'	BOOGIE BOX HIGH (HARDBACK)
11	THE LIVING DAYLIGHTS	A-HA (WARNER BROS)
12	JUST DON'T WANT TO BE LONELY	FREDDIE McGREGOR (GERMAIN)
13	A LITTLE BOOGIE WOOGIE	SHAKIN' STEVENS (EPIC)
14	STAR TREKKIN'	THE FIRM (BARK)
15	I HEARD A RUMOUR	BANANARAMA (LONDON)
16	MY PRETTY ONE	CLIFF RICHARD (EMI)
17	LABOUR OF LOVE	HUE & CRY (CIRCA/VIRGIN)
18	I WANNA DANCE WITH SOMEBODY	WHITNEY HOUSTON (ARISTA)
19	(YOUR LOVE KEEPS LIFTING ME) HIGHER & HIGHER	JACKIE WILSON (SMP)
20	SHE'S ON IT	BEASTIE BOYS (DEF JAM)

ALBUMS UK

#	Title	Artist (Label)
1	INTRODUCING THE HARDLINE ACCORDING TO . . .	TERENCE TRENT D'ARBY (CBS)
2	HITS 6	VARIOUS (CBS/WEA/BMG)
3	WHITNEY	WHITNEY HOUSTON (ARISTA)
4	THE JOSHUA TREE	U2 (ISLAND)
5	INVISIBLE TOUCH	GENESIS (VIRGIN)
6	THE RETURN OF BRUNO	BRUCE WILLIS (MOTOWN)
7	F.L.M.	MEL & KIM (SUPREME)
8	KEEP YOUR DISTANCE	CURIOSITY KILLED THE CAT (MERCURY)
9	BAD ANIMALS	HEART (CAPITOL)
10	SIXTIES MIX	VARIOUS (STYLUS)
11	LIVE IN THE CITY OF LIGHT	SIMPLE MINDS (VIRGIN)
12	THE ISLAND STORY	VARIOUS (ISLAND)
13	IT'S BETTER TO TRAVEL	SWING OUT SISTER (MERCURY/PHONOGRAM)
14	TRUE BLUE	MADONNA (SIRE)
15	ATLANTIC SOUL CLASSICS	VARIOUS (ATLANTIC)
16	CONTROL	JANET JACKSON (A&M)
17	SOLITUDE STANDING	SUZANNE VEGA (A&M)
18	ECHO & THE BUNNYMEN	ECHO & THE BUNNYMEN (WEA)
19	LICENSED TO ILL	BEASTIE BOYS (DEF JAM)
20	J.-MICHEL JARRE IN CONCERT LYON/HOUSTON	JEAN-MICHEL JARRE (DREYFUS/POLYDOR)

SINGLES US

#	Title	Artist (Label)
1	SHAKEDOWN	BOB SEGER (MCA)
2	I STILL HAVEN'T FOUND WHAT I'M LOOKING FOR	U2 (ISLAND)
3	ALONE	HEART (CAPITOL)
4	HEART AND SOUL	T'PAU (VIRGIN)
5	LUKA	SUZANNE VEGA (A&M)
6	RHYTHM IS GONNA GET YOU	GLORIA ESTEFAN & MIAMI SOUND MACHINE (EPIC)
7	CROSS MY BROKEN HEART	JETS (MCA)
8	WHO'S THAT GIRL	MADONNA (SIRE/WARNER BROS)
9	I WANT YOUR SEX (RHYTHM 1 LUST)	GEORGE MICHAEL (COLUMBIA)
10	BACK IN THE HIGH LIFE AGAIN	STEVE WINWOOD (ISLAND/WARNER BROS)
11	THE PLEASURE PRINCIPLE	JANET JACKSON (A&M)
12	DON'T MEAN NOTHING	RICHARD MARX (MANHATTAN)
13	WOT'S IT TO YA	ROBBIE NEVIL (MANHATTAN)
14	ROCK STEADY	WHISPERS (SOLAR/CAPITOL)
15	LA BAMBA	LOS LOBOS (SLASH/WARNER BROS)
16	ONLY IN MY DREAMS	DEBBIE GIBSON (ATLANTIC)
17	I WANNA DANCE WITH SOMEBODY	WHITNEY HOUSTON (ARISTA)
18	I'D STILL SAY YES	KLYMAXX (CONSTELLATION/MCA)
19	SEVEN WONDERS	FLEETWOOD MAC (WARNER BROS)
20	HAPPY	SURFACE (COLUMBIA)

ALBUMS US

#	Title	Artist (Label)
1	IN THE DARK	GRATEFUL DEAD (ARISTA)
2	SAMMY HAGAR	SAMMY HAGAR (GEFFEN)
3	BAD ANIMALS	HEART (CAPITOL)
4	TANGO IN THE NIGHT	FLEETWOOD MAC (WARNER BROS)
5	SOUNDTRACK	LOST BOYS (ATLANTIC)
6	WHITESNAKE	WHITESNAKE (GEFFEN)
7	ONE WAY HOME	HOOTERS (COLUMBIA)
8	ROVER'S RETURN	JOHN WAITE (EMI AMERICA)
9	NO PROTECTION	STARSHIP (GRUNT/RCA)
10	HOT NUMBER	FABULOUS THUNDERBIRDS (CBS ASSOCIATED)
11	BANGIN'	OUTFIELD (COLUMBIA)
12	LET ME UP (I'VE HAD ENOUGH)	TOM PETTY & THE HEARTBREAKERS (MCA)
13	THE JOSHUA TREE	U2 (ISLAND)
14	AFTER DARK	CRUZADOS (ARISTA)
15	GOT ANY GUM?	JOE WALSH (FULL MOON/WARNER BROS)
16	INTO THE FIRE	BRYAN ADAMS (A&M)
17	RADIO K.A.O.S.	ROGER WATERS (COLUMBIA)
18	RICHARD MARX	RICHARD MARX (MANHATTAN)
19	ONCE BITTEN	GREAT WHITE (CAPITOL)
20	5 TO 1	TOM KIMMEL (MERCURY/PG)

MUSIC REFERENCE

RECORD COMPANIES

• **A&M Records**
136-140 New Kings Road, London
SW6 4LZ. Tel: (01) 736 3311 Tx: 916342
Labels: A&M, Breakout, Windham Hill

• **Abstract Sounds**
10 Tiverton Road, London NW10 3HL
Tel: (01) 969 4018
Labels: Abstract Dance, Abstract Records,
TIM

• **Ace Records**
48-50 Steele Road, London NW10
Tel: (01) 453 1311 Tx: 893805 Acerec
Labels: Ace, Big Beat, Bluesville, Boplicity,
Cascade, Contemporary, Debut, Del Rio,
Fantasy, Globestyle, Impact, Jazzland,
Kent, Milestone, Moodsville, Offbeat,
Prestige, Riverside, Stax, Swingville

• **Arista Records**
3 Cavendish Square, London W1
Tel: (01) 580 5566 Tx: 298933
Labels: Arista

• **Backs Cartel**
St Mary's Works, St Mary's Plain,
Norwich NR3 3AF. Tel: (0603) 626221
Labels: Backs, Criminal Damage, Empire,
Frank, Grunt-Grunt-A-Go-Go, Kick, Power
Of Voice, Pure Trash, Ready To Eat,
Re-elect The President, Shellfish, Shelter,
Small Wonder, Soul Supply, Vinyl Drip

• **Bam-Caruso Records**
9 Ridgemont Road, St Albans, Herts
Tel: (0727) 32109
Labels: Bam-Caruso

• **BBC Records**
Woodlands, 80 Wood Lane, London W12
OTT. Tel: (01) 576 0202 Tx: 934678
Labels: Artium, BBC Records

• **Beggar's Banquet**
17-19 Alma Road, London SW18
Tel: (01) 870 9912 Tx: 915733
Labels: Beggar's Banquet, Coda, 4AD

• **Carrere Records**
PRT House, Bennett Street,
London W4 2AH
Tel: (01) 995 3031
Labels: Carrere

• **CBS Records**
17-19 Soho Square, London W1
Tel: (01) 734 8181 Tx: 24203
Labels: Blue Sky, Cameo, Caribou, CBS,
Def Jam, Diamond, Epic, Monument,
Portrait, Reformation, Tabu

• **Charly Records**
156-166 Ilderton Road, London SE15
1NT. Tel: (01) 639 8603/6 Tx: 8953184
Labels: Affinity, Atlantis, Caliente, Charly,
Decal, Goldband, New Cross, Sun, Topline

• **Cherry Red Records**
53 Kensington Gardens Square, London W2
4BA. Tel: (01) 229 8854 Tx: 943763 Chr
Labels: Anagram, Cherry Red, El, Time
Stood Still, Virginia, Zebra

• **Chrysalis**
12 Stratford Place, London W1N 9AF
Tel: (01) 408 2355 Tx: 21753
Labels: Big Time, China, Chrysalis,
Cooltempo, Ensign, Go! Discs, MAM,
2-Tone

• **Conifer Records**
Horton Road, West Drayton, Middlesex
UB7 8JL. Tel: (0895) 447707 Tx: 27492
Labels: Cambra, Conifer, DRG, EMI France/
Germany/Holland/Italy/Sweden,
Entertainers, Happy Days, Masters, MFP
France, Moss Music, Muse, RCA Germany,
Saville, Starjazz, Sunnyside

• **Creation Records**
83 Clerkenwell Road, London EC1R 5AR
Tel: (01) 831 7132
Labels: Creation, Elevation

• **Creole Records**
91-93 High Street, Harlesden, London
NW10. Tel: (01) 965 9223 Tx: 28905
Labels: Blast From The Past, Cactus,
Creole, Creole Classics, Dynamic, Ecstasy,
909, Replay, Review, Winner

• **Decca International**
1 Rockley Road, London W14 0DL
Tel: (01) 743 9111 Tx: 23533
Labels: Decca, Deram, Threshold

• **Demon Records**
Canal House, Stars Estate,

Transport Avenue, Brentford,
Middlesex TW8 0QP
Tel: (01) 847 2481 Tx: 894666
Labels: Demon, Edsel, HDH, Hi, Imp,
Vebvals, Zippo

• **DEP International**
92 Fazeley Street, Digbeth, Birmingham
B5 5RD. Tel: (021) 643 1321 Tx: 339447
Depint
Labels: DEP International

• **DJM Records**
James House, Salisbury Place, Upper
Montagu Street, London W1H 1FJ
Tel: (01) 486 5838 Tx: 27135
Labels: DJM

• **EG Records**
63 Kings Road, London SW3 4NT
Tel: (01) 730 2162 Tx: 919205
Labels: Editions EG, EG Records

• **EMI Records**
20 Manchester Square, London W1A 1ES
Tel: (01) 486 4488 Tx: 22643
Labels: Blue Note, Capitol, Columbia, EMI,
Harvest, HMV, Manhattan, Parlophone,
Philadelphia International, RAK, Zonophone

• **Factory Communications**
86 Palatine Road, Manchester 20
Tel: (061) 434 3876 Tx: 669009 Facman
Labels: Factory Records

• **Fast Forward**
21a Alva Street, Edinburgh EH2 4PS
Tel: (031) 226 4616
Labels: Disposable, DDT, 53rd And 3rd

• **Flicknife**
1st Floor, The Metrostore, 5/10 Eastman
Road, The Vale, London W3 7YG
Tel: (01) 743 9412
Labels: Flicknife

• **FM Revolver**
152 Goldthorn Hill, Penn, Wolverhampton
WV2 3JA. Tel: (0902) 345345 Tx: 335419
Rockson G
Labels: FM, FM Dance, Heavy Metal
Worldwide, Revolver, Revolver Jazzmasters

• **Go! Discs**

Go! Mansions, 8 Wendell Road, London W12. Tel: (01) 743 3845/3919
Labels: Go! Discs

• **Greensleeves Records**
Unit 7, Goldhawk Industrial Estate, 2a Brackenbury Road, London W6
Tel: (01) 749 3277/8 Tx: 8955504
Labels: Greensleeves, Ras, UK Bubblers, Unit 7

• **Hannibal Records**
PO Box 742, London W11 3LZ
Tel: (01) 727 7480 Tx: 8950511 Oneoneg
Labels: Hannibal

• **Illuminated Productions**
46 Carter Lane, London EC4
Tel: (01) 236 6668
Labels: Illuminated Records

• **(IRS) International Recording Syndicate**
5 Sherwood Street, London W1B 7RA
Tel: (01) 437 9797 Tx: 299338 Mcarec G
Labels: Illegal, IRS

• **Island Records**
22 St Peter's Square, London W6 9NW
Tel: (01) 741 1511 Tx: 934541
Labels: Antilles, Fourth & Broadway, Mango, Mother, Taxi, ZTT

• **K-Tel International**
K-Tel House, 620 Western Avenue, London W3 0TU. Tel: (01) 992 8055 Tx: 934195
Labels: K-Tel, Lotus

• **London Records**
15 St George Street, London W1. Tel: (01) 491 4600 Tx: 261583 Polygn G
Labels: London, Slash

• **Magnet Records**
Magnet House, 22 York Street, London W1H 1ED. Tel: (01) 486 8151 Tx: 25537
Labels: Magnet, Magnetic Dance

• **MCA Records**
72-74 Brewer Street, London W1
Tel: (01) 437 9797 Tx: 23158
Labels: MCA

• **Music For Nations**
8 Carnaby Street, London W1 1PG
Tel: (01) 437 4688 Tx: 296217
Labels: Food For Thought, Fun After All, Music For Nations, Rough Justice, Under One Flag

• **Music For Pleasure**
1-3 Uxbridge Road, Hayes, Middlesex UB4 0SY. Tel: (01) 561 8722 Tx: 934614
Labels: Classics For Pleasure, Eminence, Fame, Golden Age, Hour Of, Listen For Pleasure, Music For Pleasure

• **Mute Records**
429 Harrow Road, London W10 4RE
Tel: (01) 969 8866 Tx: 268623
Labels: Blast First, Mute, Product Inc., Rhythm King

• **Neat Records**
71 High Street, East Wallsend, Tyne and Wear NE28 7RJ. Tel: (091) 262 4999
Tx: 537681 Alwrld
Labels: Completely Different, Floating World, Neat

• **Nine Mile Records**
Lower Avenue, Leamington Spa, Warwickshire. Tel: (0926) 881292.
Labels: Chapter 22, Cooking Vinyl,

Crammed Discs, Dojo, Fire, Glass, Moksha, One Little Indian, Red Flame, Ron Johnson, Wire

• **Old Gold Records**
Unit 1, Langhedge Lane Industrial Estate, Edmonton N18 2TQ. Tel: (01) 884 2220
Tx: 264597 OldGol G
Labels: Decades, Old Gold, Start

• **Oval Records**
11 Liston Road, London SW4. Tel: (01) 622 0111 Tx: 946240 Cweasy G Ref. 19017005
Labels: Oval

• **People Unite**
50.52 King Street, Southall, Middlesex
Tel: (01) 574 1718
Labels: People Unite

• **Phonogram Ltd**
50 New Bond Street, London W1Y 9HA
Tel: (01) 491 4600 Tx: 261583
Labels: Club, Fontana, Mercury, Neutron, Phillips, Phonogram, Rocket, Vertigo

• **Pickwick International**
The Hyde Industrial Estate, The Hyde, London NW9 6JU. Tel: (01) 200 7000
Tx: 922170
Labels: Camden, Contour, Ditto, Hallmark, IMP Red, Pickwick, Spot

• **Polydor**
19 Upper Brook Street, London W1A 1BG
Tel: (01) 499 8686 Tx: 261583
Labels: MGM, Polydor, RSO, Urban, Verve, Wonderland

• **President Records**
Broadmead House, 21 Panton Street, London SW1 4DR. Tel: (01) 839 4672/5
Tx: 24158 Kassmu G
Labels: Bulldog, Energy, Enterprise, Joy, Max's Kansas City, New World, President, Rhapsody, Seville, Spiral, TBG

• **Probe Plus**
8-12 Rainford Gardens, Liverpool 2
Tel: (051) 236 6591
Labels: The Ark, Fat Wallet, Fend For Yourself, Galaxy, Moral Burro, Mother Africa, Snow Company, Swell Kitchen

• **PRT Records**
PRT House, Bennett Street, London W4 2AH. Tel: (01) 995 3031
Labels: PRT

• **RCA/Ariola Records**
1 Bedford Avenue, London WC1
Tel: (01) 636 8311 Tx: 21349
Labels: Gordy, Inevitable, Morocco, Motown, Planet, Prelude, RCA, Victor, Salsoul, Tent, Total Experience

• **Red Rhino Records**
The Grainstore, 74 Eldon Street, York. Tel: (0904) 611656 Fax: (0904) 644190
Labels: Agit-Prop, All Or Nothing, American Activities, Batfish Inc., Black Lagoon, Dead Man's Curve, Dossier, Ediesta, Fundamental, In-Tape, Kaleidoscope Sounds, Media Burn, Medium Cool, Native, Play It Again Sam, Reception, Red Rhino, Roir UK, RRE, Ruska, Sever, Sharp, Sin, Skysaw, Sterile, Tanz, Technical, Uglyman, Volume, White Line

• **Revolver Records**
The Old Malt House, Little Ann Street, Bristol 2. Tel: (0272) 541291/4
Labels: Antar, Bam Caruso, C.O.R., Disorder, Disque Afrique, Earache, Five

Hours Back, Get Ahead, Head, Heartland, ID, Manic Ears, Noise UK, One Big Guitar, RDL, Remorse, SS20, Subway, WOMAD, World Grant, Zap

• **Rocket Record Company**
51 Holland Street, London W8 7JB
Tel: (01) 938 1741 Tx: 265870
Labels: Rocket

• **Rough Trade Records**
61-71 Collier Street, London N1
Tel: (01) 833 2133/2561/3 Tx: 299579
Labels: All The Madmen, Alternative Tentacles, Bad, Big Life/Society, Burning Rome, Celluloid, Creation, Disc Chevalier, Dreamworld, Flying Nun, Fon, Food, Homestead, Hot, Lazy, Midnight, Nervous, NER, Own Up, Pink, Raw TV, Reflex, Rough Trade, Side Effects, Stuff, Sweatbox, Temple, Third Mind, United Dairies, Very Mouth, Vindaloo

• **See For Miles**
PO Box 238, Maidenhead, Berks SL6 2NE
Tel: (0628) 39790 or (01) 398 6143
Labels: See For Miles

• **Siren Records**
61-63 Portobello Road, London W11 3DD
Tel: (01) 221 7535 Tx: 295417 Siren G
Labels: Siren

• **Some Bizzare**
166 New Cavendish Street, London W1M 7LJ. Tel: (01) 631 3140 Tx: 8951182
Gecoms G
Labels: Some Bizzare

• **Sonet Records**
121 Ledbury Road, London W11
Tel: (01) 229 7267 Tx: 25793
Labels: Gramavision, Red Stripe, Sonet, Stone, Titanic

• **Stiff Records**
111 Talbot Road, London W11. Tel: (01) 221 5101 Tx: 297314
Labels: Bluebird, Stiff

• **Ten Records**
101-109 Ladbroke Grove, London W11 1PG. Tel: (01) 221 8585 Tx: 25593
Labels: MDM, Ten

• **Virgin Records**
Kensal House, 533-579 Harrow Road, London W10. Tel: (01) 968 6688
Tx: 22542
Labels: Charisma, Circa, EG, Foundry, Linn, Red Eye, Venture, Virgin, Zarjazz

• **WEA Records**
20 Broadwick Street, London W1V 2BH
Tel: (01) 434 3232 Tx: 261425
Labels: Asylum, Atco, Atlantic, blanco y negro, Cotillion, Duck, Elektra, Geffen, Korova, Megaforce, Nonesuch, Paisley Park, Q-West, Real, Reprise, Sire, Valentino, Warner Bros, WEA Int

• **Zomba Productions**
Zomba House, 165-167 Willesden High Road, London NW10 2SG
Tel: (01) 459 8899 Tx: 237316 Zomba
Labels: Jive, Jive Afrika, Jive Electro, Lifestyle

• **ZTT Records**
111 Talbot Road, London W11
Tel: (01) 221 5101 Tx: 297314 Sarm G
Labels: ZTT

LABELS

Affinity — Charly
Agit-Prop — Red Rhino
All Or Nothing — Red Rhino
All The Madmen — Rough Trade
Alternative Tentacles — Rough Trade
American Activities — Red Rhino
Anagram — Cherry Red
Antar — Revolver
Antilles — Island
Artium — BBC
Asylum — WEA
Atco — WEA
Atlantic — WEA
Atlantis — Charly

Bad — Rough Trade
Batfish Inc — Red Rhino
Big Beat — Ace
Big Life/Society — Rough Trade
Big Time — Chrysalis
Black Lagoon — Red Rhino
blanco y negro — WEA
Blast First — Mute
Blast From The Past — Creole
Blue Note — EMI
Blue Sky — CBS
Bluebird — Stiff
Bluesville — Ace
Boplicity — Ace
Breakout — A&M
Bulldog — President
Burning Rome — Rough Trade

Cactus — Creole
Caliente — Charly
Cambra — Conifer
Camden — Pickwick
Cameo — CBS
Capitol — EMI
Caribou — CBS
Cascade — Ace
Celluloid — Rough Trade
Chapter 22 — Nine Mile
Charisma — Virgin
China — Chrysalis
Circa — Virgin
Classics For Pleasure — Music For Pleasure
Club — Phonogram
Coda — Beggar's Banquet
Columbia — EMI
Completely Different — Neat
Contemporary — Ace
Contour — Pickwick
Cool Tempo — Chrysalis
Cooking Vinyl — Nine Mile
C.O.R — Revolver
Cotillion — WEA
Crammed Discs — Nine Mile
Criminal Damage — Backs
Crown — Ace

DDT — Fast Forward
Deadman's Curve — Red Rhino
Debut — Ace
Decades — Old Gold
Decal — Charly
Def Jam — CBS
Del Rio — Ace
Deram — Decca
Disc Chevalier — Rough Trade
Disorder — Revolver
Disposable — Fast Forward
Disque Afrique — Revolver
Ditto — Pickwick
Dojo — Nine Mile
Dossier — Red Rhino
Dreamworld — Rough Trade

DRG — Conifer
Duck — WEA
Dynamic — Creole

Earache — Revolver
Ecstasy — Creole
Ediesta — Red Rhino
Edsel — Demon
El — Cherry Red
Elektra — WEA
Elevation — Creation
EMI France — Conifer
EMI Germany — Conifer
EMI Holland — Conifer
EMI Italy — Conifer
EMI Sweden — Conifer
Eminence — Music For Pleasure
Empire — Backs
Energy — President
Ensign — Chrysalis
Enterprise — President
Entertainers — Conifer
Epic — CBS

Fame — Music For Pleasure
Fantasy — Ace
Fat Wallet — Probe Plus
Fend For Yourself — Probe Plus
53rd And 3rd — Fast Forward
Fire — Nine Mile
Five Hours Back — Revolver
Floating World — Neat
Flying Nun — Rough Trade
Fon — Rough Trade
Fontana — Phonogram
Food — Rough Trade
Food For Thought — Music For Nations
Foundry — Virgin
4AD — Beggar's Banquet
Fourth And Broadway — Island
Frank — Backs
Fun After All — Music For Nations
Fundamental — Red Rhino

Galaxy — Probe Plus
Geffen — WEA
Get Ahead — Revolver
Glass — Nine Mile
Globestyle — Ace
Goldband — Charly
Golden Age — Music For Pleasure
Gordy — RCA/Ariola
Gramavision — Sonet
Grunt-Grunt-A-Go-Go — Backs

Hallmark — Pickwick
Happy Days — Conifer
Harvest — EMI
Head — Revolver
Heartland — Revolver
HDH — Demon
Heavy Metal Worldwide — FM Revolver
Hi — Demon
HMV — EMI
Homestead — Rough Trade
Hot — Rough Trade
Hour Of — Music For Pleasure

Ice — RCA/Ariola
ID — Revolver
Illegal — IRS
Imp — Demon
IMP Red — Pickwick
Impact — Ace
Inevitable — RCA/Ariola
In-Tape — Red Rhino

Jazzland — Ace
Jive — Zomba
Joy — President

Kaleidoscope Sounds — Red Rhino
Kent — Ace
Kick — Backs
Korova — WEA

Lazy — Rough Trade
Lifestyle — Zomba
Linn — Virgin
Listen For Pleasure — Music For Pleasure
Lotus — K-Tel

Magnetic Dance — Magnet
MAM — Chrysalis
Mango — Island
Manhattan — EMI
Manic Ears — Revolver
Masters — Conifer
Max's Kansas City — President
MDM — Ten
Media Burn — Red Rhino
Medium Cool — Red Rhino
Megaforce — WEA
Mercury — Phonogram
MFP France — Conifer
MGM — Polydor
Midnight — Rough Trade
Milestone — Ace
Moksha — Nine Mile
Monument — CBS
Moodsville — Ace
Moral Burro — Probe Plus
Morocco — RCA/Ariola
Moss Music — Conifer
Mother — Island
Mother Africa — Probe Plus
Motown — RCA/Ariola
Muse — Conifer

Native — Red Rhino
Neutron — Phonogram
Nervous — Rough Trade
NER — Rough Trade
New Cross — Charly
New World — President
909 — Creole
Noise UK — Revolver
Nonesuch — WEA

Off Beat — Ace
One Big Guitar — Revolver
One Little Indian — Nine Mile
Own Up — Rough Trade

Paisley Park — WEA
Parlophone — EMI
Philadelphia International — EMI
Phillips — Phonogram
Pink — Rough Trade
Planet — RCA/Ariola
Play It Again Sam — Red Rhino
Portrait — CBS
Power Of Voice — Backs
Prelude — RCA/Ariola
Prestige — Ace
Product Inc — Mute
Pure Trash — Backs

Q-West — WEA

RAK — EMI
Ras — Greensleeves
Raw TV — Rough Trade
RCA Germany — Conifer
RDL — Revolver

Ready To Eat — Backs
Real — WEA
Reception — Red Rhino
Red Eye — Virgin
Red Flame — Nine Mile
Red Stripe — Sonet
Re-elect The President — Backs
Reflex — Rough Trade
Reformation — CBS
Remorse — Revolver
Replay — Creole
Reprise — WEA
Review — Creole
Revolver — FM Revolver
Rhapsody — President
Rhythm King — Mute
Riverside — Ace
Rocket — Phonogram
Roir UK — Red Rhino
Ron Johnson — Nine Mile
Rough Justice — Music For Nations
RRE — Red Rhino
RSO — Polydor
Ruska — Red Rhino

Salsoul — RCA/Ariola
Saville — Conifer
Sever — Red Rhino
Seville — President
Sharp — Red Rhino
Shellfish — Backs
Shelter — Backs
Side Effects — Rough Trade
Sin — Red Rhino
Sire — WEA

Skysaw — Red Rhino
Slash — London
Small Wonder — Backs
Snow Company — Probe Plus
Soul Supply — Backs
Spiral — President
Spot — Pickwick
SS20 — Revolver
Starjazz — Conifer
Start — Old Gold
Stax — Ace
Sterile — Red Rhino
Stone — Sonet
Stuff — Rough Trade
Subway — Revolver
Sun — Charly
Sunnyside — Conifer
Sweatbox — Rough Trade
Swell Kitchen — Probe Plus
Swingville — Ace

Tabu — CBS
Tanz — Red Rhino
Taxi — Island
TBG — President
Technical — Red Rhino
Temple — Rough Trade
Tent — RCA/Ariola
The Ark — Probe Plus
Third Mind — Rough Trade
Threshold — Decca
TIM — Abstract
Time Stood Still — Abstract
Titanic — Sonet
Topline — Charly

Total Experience — RCA/Ariola
2-Tone — Chrysalis

Uglyman — Red Rhino
UK Bubblers — Greensleeves
Under One Flag — Music For Nations
Unit 7 — Greensleeves
United Dairies — Rough Trade
Urban — Polydor

Valentino — WEA
Venture — Virgin
Verbals — Demon
Vertigo — Phonogram
Verve — Polydor
Very Mouth — Rough Trade
Vindaloo — Rough Trade
Vinyl Drip — Backs
Virginia — Cherry Red
Volume — Red Rhino

Warner Bros — WEA
White Line — Red Rhino
Windham Hill — A&M
Winner — Creole
Wire — Nine Mile
WOMAD — Revolver
Wonderland — Polydor
World Grant — Revolver

Zap — Revolver
Zarjazz — Virgin
Zebra — Cherry Red
Zippo — Demon
Zonophone — EMI
ZTT — Island

MUSIC PUBLISHERS

● **Albion Music**
See Complete Music

● **All Boys Music**
4-7 The Vineyard, Sanctuary Street, London
SE1. Tel: (01) 403 0007

● **Ambassador Music**
22 Denmark Street, London WC2
Tel: (01) 836 5996

● **APB Music**
28 Ivor Place, London NW1. Tel: (01) 723
9269

● **ATV Music**
See SBK Songs

● **Barn Publishing**
12 Thayer Street, London W1
Tel: (01) 935 8323 Tx: 22787 Thayer G

● **Belsize Music**
2nd Floor, 24 Baker Street, London W1
Tel: (01) 935 2076 Tx: 23840

● **Black Sheep Music**
Fulmer Gardens House, Fulmer, Bucks
Tel: (02816) 2143/2109 Tx: 849208

● **Blue Mountain Music**
334-336 King Street, London W6 0RA
Tel: (01) 846 9566 Tx: 934541

● **Bocu Music**
1 Wyndham Yard, Wyndham Place, London
W1H 1AR. Tel: (01) 402 7433/5
Tx: 298976

● **Margaret Brace Copyright Bureau**
4a Newman Passage, London W1A 4QD
Tel: (01) 580 7118

● **Brampton Music**
9 Carnaby Street, London W1. Tel: (01) 437
1958

● **Burlington Music**
129 Park Street, London W1. Tel: (01) 499
0067 Tx: 268403

● **Carlin Music**
14 New Burlington Street, London W1X
2LR. Tel: (01) 734 3251 Tx: 267 488

● **CBS Songs**
See SBK Songs

● **Chappell Music**
129 Park Street, London W1Y 3FA
Tel: (01) 629 7600 Tx: 268403

● **Charisma Music**
Russell Chambers, Covent Garden, London
WC2. Tel: (01) 240 9891

● **Charly Publishing**
155-166 Ilderton Road, London SE15
Tel: (01) 732 5647 Tx: 8953184

● **Chelsea Music Publishing**
184-186 Regent Street, London W1R
5DR. Tel: (01) 439 7731 Tx: 27557

● **Chrysalis Music**
12 Stratford Place, London W1N 9AF
Tel: (01) 408 2355 Tx: 21753

● **Complete Music**
49-53 Kensington Gardens Square, London
W2 4BA. Tel: (01) 229 8854
Tx: 943763 Chr

● **Creole Music**
91-93 High Street, Harlesden, London

NW10. Tel: (01) 965 9223 Tx: 296133

● **Eaton Music**
8 West Eaton Place, London SW1X 8LS
Tel: (01) 235 9046 Tx: 296133

● **EG Music**
63a King's Road, London SW3 4NT
Tel: (01) 730 2162 Tx: 919205

● **EMI Music Publishing**
138-140 Charing Cross Road, London
WC2H 0LD. Tel: (01) 836 6699
Tx: 269189 Emi Pub G

● **Empire Music**
27 Queensdale Place, London W11. Tel:
(01) 602 5031.

● **Faber Music**
3 Queen Square, London WC1N 3AU
Tel: (01) 278 6881 Tx: 299633

● **Filmtrax**
7-9 Greenland Place, London NW1. Tel: (01)
482 4979

● **Noel Gay Music**
24 Denmark Street, London WC2H 8NJ
Tel: (01) 836 3941 Tx: 21760

● **Go! Discs Music**
Go! Mansions, 8 Wendell Road, London
W12. Tel: (01) 743 3845/3919

● **Handle Music**
1 Derby Street, London W1. Tel: (01) 493
9637 Tx: 892756

● **Heath Levy Music**
184/186 Regent Street, London W1. Tel:
(01) 439 7731

- **Hit And Run/Cleofine Music**
81-83 Walton Street, London SW3 2HP. Tel: (01) 581 0261

- **Illegal Music**
194 Kensington Park Road, London W11. Tel: (01) 727 0734

- **Intersong Music**
129 Park Street, London W1Y 3FA
Tel: (01) 499 0067 Tx: 268403

- **Island Music**
Media House, 334-336 King Street
London W6 0RA. Tel: (01) 846 9141
Tx: 934541

- **Dick James Music**
James House, Salisbury Place, Upper
Montagu Street, London W1. Tel: (01) 486 5838

- **Jobete Music**
Tudor House, 35 Gresse Street, London
W1P 1PN. Tel: (01) 631 0380
Tx: 8811658 G

- **Kassner Associated Publishers**
21 Panton Street, London SW1
Tel: (01) 839 4672 Tx: 24158

- **Leosong Copyright Service**
4a Newman Passage, London W1
Tel: (01) 580 7118 Tx: 268048

- **Magnet Music**
22 York Street, London W1H 1FD
Tel: (01) 486 8151 Tx: 25537

- **Bill Martin Music**
11th Floor, Alembic House, 93 Albert
Embankment, London SE1 7TY
Tel: (01) 582 7622

- **Mautoglade**
22 Denmark Street, London WC2. Tel: (01) 836 5996

- **MCA Music**
139 Piccadilly, London W1V 9FH
Tel: (01) 629 7211 Tx: 22219

- **Minder Music**
22 Bristol Gardens, London W9 2JQ
Tel: (01) 289 7281 Tx: 923421 Wemsec G

- **Mood Music**
35-37 Parkgate Road, London SW11. Tel: (01) 228 4000

- **Morrison Leahy Music**
Flat 3, 1 Hyde Park Place, London W2
2LH. Tel: (01) 402 9238 Tx: 266589 Mlm G

- **MPL Communications**
1 Soho Square, London W1V 6BQ
Tel: (01) 439 6621 Tx: 21294

- **Neptune Music**
31 Old Burlington Street, London W1X
1LB. Tel: (01) 437 2066/7 Tx: 8954748

- **Oval Music**
11 Liston Road, London SW4
Tel: (01) 622 0111 Tx: 946240 Cweasy G
Ref. 19017005

- **Pattern Music**
22 Denmark Street, London WC2
Tel: (01) 836 5996

- **Perfect Songs**
111 Talbot Road, London W11. Tel: (01) 221 5101

- **Pink Floyd Music Publishers**
27 Noel Street, London W1V 3RD
Tel: (01) 734 6892 Tx: 28905 Ref. 907

- **Plangent Visions**
27 Noel Street, London W1V 3RD
Tel: (01) 734 6892

- **Point Music**
Studio 5, The Royal Victoria Patriotic
Building, Trinity Road, London SW18
Tel: (01) 871 4155 Tx: 265871 Monres G
Attn. DGS1483

- **PolyGram Music**
45 Berkeley Square, London W1. Tel: (01) 493 8800

- **RAK Publishing**
42-48 Charlbert Street, London NW8 7BU
Tel: (01) 586 2012 Tx: 299501

- **RCA Music**
3 Cavendish Square, London W1
Tel: (01) 580 5566 Tx: 298933

- **The Really Useful Company**
20 Greek Street, London W1V 5LF
Tel: (01) 734 2114 Tx: 8953151

- **Red Bus Music**
Red Bus House, 48 Broadley Terrace,
London NW1. Tel: (01) 258 0324/8 Telex: 25873 Red Bus

- **Reformation Music**
Suite 7, 3rd Floor, 89 Great Portland Street,
London W1. Tel: (01) 580 4007

- **Renegade Music**
145 Oxford Street, London W1. Tel: (01) 437 2777

- **Riva Music**
114 Wardour Street, London W1
Tel: (01) 734 3481 Tx: 28781 Glass G

- **Rock City Music**
Shepperton Studio Centre, Shepperton,
Middlesex. Tel: (09328) 66531/2

- **Rock Music**
27 Noel Street, London W1V 3RD
Tel: (01) 734 6892

- **Rondor Music**
Rondor House, 10a Parsons Green,
London SW6 4TW. Tel: (01) 731 4161/5

- **St Anne's Music**
Kennedy House, 31 Stamford Street,
Altrincham, Cheshire WA14 1ES
Tel: (061) 941 5151 Tx: 666255

- **SBK Songs**
3-5 Rathbone Place, London W1V SDG. Tel: (01) 637 5831

- **Sonet Music Publishing**
121 Ledbury Road, London W11 2AQ
Tel: (01) 229 7267 Tx: 25793

- **Sound Diagrams**
21 Atholl Crescent, Edinburgh, EH3 8HQ
Tel: (031) 229 8946 Tx: 265871 Monref G

- **Southern Music Publishing**
8 Denmark Street, London WC2H 8LT. Tel: (01) 836 4524 Tx: 23557

- **10 Music**
Advance House, 101-109 Ladbrokr Grove,
London W11 1PG. Tel: (01) 221 8585

- **Tritec Music**
32 Marshall Street, London W1. Tel: (01) 439 7100

- **Virgin Music Publishers**
Advance House, 101-109 Ladbroke Grove,
London W11 1PG. Tel: (01) 229 1282

- **Warner Brothers Music**
17 Berners Street, London W1P 3DD
Tel: (01) 637 3771 Tx: 25522

- **Westminster Music**
19-20 Poland Street, London W1V 3DC
Tel: 734 8121 Tx: 22701

- **Zomba Music**
165-167 Willesden High Road, London
NW10. Tel: (01) 459 8899

INDEPENDENT DISTRIBUTORS

- **Arabesque Ltd**
Swan Centre, Fisher's Lane, London W4
1RX. Tel: (01) 747 0365 Tx: 291908

- **Backs Cartel**
St Mary's Works, St Mary's Plain, Norwich
Tel: (0603) 626221

- **Caroline Exports**
56 Standard Road, London NW10
Tel: (01) 961 2919 Tx: 22164

- **Conifer Records**
Horton Road, West Drayton, Middlesex
UB7 8LJ. Tel: (0895) 447707 Tx: 27492

- **Counterpoint Distribution**
Wharf Road, London E15 2SU
Tel: (01) 555 4321 Tx: 8951427

- **Discovery Records**
107 Broad Street, Beechingstoke, Pewsey,
Wilts. Tel: (067285) 406

- **Electronic Synthesizer Sound Projects (ESSP)**
The Sound House, PO Box 37B, East
Molesey, Surrey. Tel: (01) 979 9997/
577 5818

- **Fast Forward**
21a Alva Road, Edinburgh EH2 4PS
Tel: (031) 226 4616

- **S. Gold and Son**
Gold House, 69 Flempton Road, Leyton,
London E10 7NL. Tel: (01) 539 3600
Tx: 894793

- **Greensleeves Records**
Unit 7, Goldhawk Industrial Estate, 2a
Brackenbury Road, London W6
Tel: (01) 749 3277/8 Tx: 8955504

- **Hotshot Records**
29 St Michael's Road, Headingley, Leeds, Yorkshire. Tel: (0532) 742106

- **Jazz Horizons**
103 London Road, Sawbridgeworth, Herts CM1 9JJ. Tel: (0279) 724572

- **Jazz Music**
7 Kildare Road, Swinton, Manchester M27 3AB. Tel: (061) 794 3525

- **Jungle Records**
24 Gaskin Street, London N1 2RY
Tel: (01) 359 8444 Tx: 896559
Gecoms G Attn. Jungle

- **Lasgo Exports**
Unit 2, Chapman's Park Industrial Estate, 378-388 High Road, Willesden, London NW10 2DY. Tel: (01) 459 8800 Tx: 22111 Lasgo G

- **Lightning Distribution**
Bashley Road, London NW10 6SD
Tel: (01) 965 5555 Tx: 927813 Larrec

- **New Roots**
61-71 Collier Street, London N1. Tel: (01) 833 2133 Tx: 299579

- **Nine Mile Distribution**
Lower Avenue, Leamington Spa, Warwickshire. Tel: (0926) 881292

- **Oldies Unlimited**
Dukes Way, St George's, Telford, Shropshire. Tel: (0952) 616911 Tx: 35493

- **Pickwick International**
The Hyde Industrial Estate, The Hyde, London NW9 6JU. Tel: (01) 200 7000
Tx: 922170

- **Pinnacle Records**
Unit 2, Orpington Trading Estate, Sevenoaks Way, Orpington, Kent BR5 3FR. Tel: (0689) 70622 Tx: 929053

- **Pizza Express Music Distribution**
29 Romilly Street, London W1
Tel: (01) 734 6112 Tx: 27950 Ref. 3396

- **Probe Plus**
8-12 Rainford Gardens, Liverpool 2
Tel: (051) 236 6591

- **PRT Distribution**
105 Bond Road, Mitcham, Surrey CR4 3UT. Tel: (01) 648 7000

- **Recommended Distribution**
387 Wandsworth Road, London SW8
Tel: (01) 622 8834 Tx: 8813271 Gecoms G

- **Red Lightnin' Records**
The White House, North Lopham, Diss, Norfolk Tel: (0379) 88693

- **Red Rhino Distribution**
The Coach House, Fetter Lane, York YO1 1EM. Tel: (0904) 641415 or 27828

- **Revolver Distribution**
The Old Malt House, Little Ann Street, Bristol 2. Tel: (0272) 541291/4

- **Rose Records**
3 Ellington Street, London N7 8PP
Tel: (01) 609 8288 Tx: 268048

- **Ross Record Distribution**
29 Main Street, Turriff, Aberdeenshire
Tel: (0888) 62403

- **Rough Trade Distribution**
61-71 Collier Street, London N1
Tel: (01) 833 2133 Tx: 299579

- **Spartan Records**
London Road, Wembley, Middlesex HA9 7HQ. Tel: (01) 903 4753 Tx: 923175

- **Wynd-up Records**
Turntable House, Guinness Road Trading Estate, Trafford Park, Manchester
Tel: (061) 872 0170 Tx: 635363

- **World Service**
61-71 Collier Street, London N1. Tel: (01) 833 2133 Tx: 299579

MUSIC MAGAZINES

- **Beatles Monthly**
43 St Mary's Road, Ealing, London W5 5RQ. Tel: (01) 579 1082

Beatlemania resurrected; monthly, 48pp; £1.25; circ. n/a

- **Blitz**
1 Lower James Street, London W1
Tel: (01) 734 8311/3

A stylish multi-media extravaganza; monthly; 116pp; £1.00; circ. 60,000

- **Blues and Rhythm**
18 Maxwelton Close, London NW7 3NA
Tel: (01) 906 0986

Blues, R&B, gospel, vintage, soul, cajun, tex-mex, news, updates, and latest albums; monthly (except January and August) in first fortnight; 36pp; £1.25; circ. 2,000

- **Blues and Soul**
153 Praed Street, London W2
Tel: (01) 402 6869

Covers all black music and dance music (except reggae); fortnightly; 48pp; £0.80; circ. 41,600

- **Brum Beat**
195 Hagley Road, Edgbaston, Birmingham B16 6UT. Tel: (021) 454 7020

The Birmingham and West Midlands scene; monthly; 16pp; free; circ. 40,000

- **Country Music People**
78 Grovelands Road, St Paul's Cray, Orpington, Kent. Tel: (01) 309 7606

Covers all country music; monthly; 42pp; £0.90; circ. 12,000 worldwide

- **Disco and Club Trade International**
410 St John Street, London EC1
Tel: (01) 278 3591/6 Tx: 24637 Wigmor

Trade magazine for discos, clubs, pubs etc; monthly; 86pp; £1.00; circ. 25,000

- **Echoes**
Rococco House, 283 City Road, London EC1 1LA. Tel: (01) 253 6662/4

Covers all black music, especially funk, soul and reggae; every Wednesday; 24pp; £0.50; circ. 25,000

- **Electronics and Music Maker**
Alexander House, 1 Milton Road, Cambridge CB4 1UY. Tel: (0223) 313722

Interviews and reviews of new equipment, for musicians and studio technicians; monthly; 112pp; £1.20; circ. 20,500

- **Elvis Monthly**
41-47 Derby Road, Heanor, Derbyshire DE7 7QH. Tel: (0773) 712460

Elvis, Elvis . . . and more Elvis, monthly, last Tuesday; 56pp; £0.95; circ. 25,000

- **Elvisly Yours**
107 Shoreditch High Street, London E1
Tel: (01) 739 2001

As above; bi-monthly; 32pp; £1.50; circ. n/a

- **The Face**
The Old Laundry, Ossington Buildings, Off Moxon Street, London W1. Tel: (01) 935 8232

The magazine by which others are judged – the gazette of style in the UK; monthly, third Thursday; 116pp; £0.90p; circ. 92,000 worldwide

- **Folk Roots**
PO Box 73, Farnham, Surrey GU9 7UN
Tel: (0252) 724638

Across the board, traditional and modern folk from the UK, US, and around the world, plus blues, tex-mex, African, etc; monthly; third Thursday; 60pp; £1.20; circ. 12,000

- **Guitarist**
Alexander House, 1 Milton Road, Cambridge CB4 1UY. Tel: (0223) 313722

For guitarists! Lots of interviews, reviews of new equipment; monthly, second Thursday; 72pp; £1.20; circ. 21,000

- **Home and Studio Recording**
Alexander House, 1 Milton Road, Cambridge CB4 1UY. Tel: (0223) 313722

For anyone interested in music recording and how to do it; monthly, third Thursday; 80pp; £1.20; circ. 18,500

- **Home Keyboard Review**
Alexander House, 1 Milton Road, Cambridge CB4 1UY. Tel: (0223) 313722

For the domestic keyboard player; monthly, third Thursday; 64pp; £0.90; circ. 16,000

- **i-D**
27-29 Macklin Street, London WC2
Tel: (01) 430 0871

Music of all descriptions, as well as fashion and features; monthly, third Tuesday; 100pp; £1.00; circ. 47,000

- **International Country Music News**
18 Burley Rise, Kegworth, Derby DE8 2DZ
Tel: (05097) 3224

British and American country music; monthly, fourth Thursday; 24pp; £0.50; circ. 25,000

• International Musician and Recording World
PO Box 381, Mill Harbour, London E14
Tel: (01) 987 5090 Tx: 24676 Norshl G

Everything the modern musician needs to know about equipment, recordings, production, etc; monthly, in the last week; 148pp; £1.95; circ. 24,000

• Jazz Journal International
35 Great Russell Street, London WC1 3PP
Tel: (01) 580 7244

Jazz enthusiasts' and record collectors' magazine; monthly, last Friday; 40pp; £1.20; circ. 11,500

• Kerrang!
Greater London House, Hampstead Road, London NW1. Tel: (01) 387 6611

Heavy metal and heavy rock; fortnightly, Thursdays; 56pp; £0.85; circ. 90,000 worldwide

• Mega Metal Kerrang!
Greater London House, Hampstead Road, London NW1 Tel: (01) 387 6611

Heavy, heavy metal; quarterly; 52pp; £1.25; circ. 45,000

• Melody Maker
Berkshire House, 168-173 High Holborn, London WC1. Tel: (01) 379 3581

Music, trouble and fun for the older 'teenager'; every Wednesday; 52pp; £0.50; circ. 61,000

• Music Week
Greater London House, Hampstead Road, London NW1. Tel: (01) 387 6611

Music trade magazine for record companies and retailers; every Wednesday; 36pp; £1.50; circ. 13,500

• New Kommotion
3 Bowrons Avenue, Wembley, Middlesex
Tel: (01) 902 6417

Fifties rockabilly and rock 'n' roll for record collectors; quarterly; 50pp; £1.20; circ. 3,000

• NME (New Musical Express)
Commonwealth House, 1-19 New Oxford Street, London WC1.
Tel: (01) 404 0700

"What? You'll only give us twelve words to describe NME? It's *outrageous*!!!" – the editor; every Wednesday; 56pp; £0.50; circ. 105,000

• No. 1
Commonwealth House, 1-19 New Oxford Street, London WC1. Tel: (01) 404 0700

Teenage magazine covering the whole range of pop music; every Wednesday; 48pp; £0.45; circ. 171,000

• Now Dig This
69 Quarry Lane, Simonside, South Shields, Tyne and Wear. Tel: (0632) 563213

Fifties US rock 'n' roll, roots; monthly, first week; 40pp; £1.25; circ. 2,000

• One Two Testing/Zig Zag
PO Box 381, Mill Harbour, London E14
Tel: (01) 987 5090 Tx: 24676 Norshl G

Instrument reviews, interviews, and features for the younger musician; monthly, third week; 100pp; £1.40; circ. 12,000

• Q
42 Great Portland Street, London W1N 5AH. Tel: (01) 637 9181

A modern guide to music and more with features and reviews of albums, CDs, videos, books, films, etc; monthly; 100pp; £1.10; circ. n/a

• Record Collector
43 St Mary's Road, London W5
Tel: (01) 579 1082

All kinds of music from the fifties to the present, with discographies of major artists, features etc for the serious record collector; monthly; 116pp; £1.20; circ. 25,000

• Rhythm
Alexander House, 1 Milton Road, Cambridge CB4 1UY. Tel: (0223) 313722

For drummers and drummer programmers. Interviews and reviews of new equipment; monthly; 72pp; £1.00; circ. 18,000

• RM (Record Mirror)
Greater London House, Hampstead Road, London NW1. Tel: (01) 387 6611

Concentrates on up-and-coming bands, all types of music for the younger person; every Thursday; 48pp; £0.55; circ. 63,000

• Sky
Rex House, 4-12 Lower Regent Street, London SW1 4PE. Tel: (01) 839 7799

Glossy, colour music, style and related issues magazine; fortnightly, Wednesdays; 76pp; £0.65; circ. n/a

• Smash Hits
Lisa House, 52-55 Carnaby Street, London W1. Tel: (01) 437 8050

Chart hits, news and features for teenagers; "the biggest-selling music magazine in the world"; fortnightly, Wednesdays; 68pp; £0.45; circ. 515,000

• Sounds
Greater London House, Hampstead Road, London NW1. Tel: (01) 387 6611

Broad-based rock magazine for the under 25's; every Wednesday; 52pp; £0.55; circ. 77,000

• Studio Sound and Broadcast Engineering
Link House, Dingwall Avenue, Croydon CR9 2TA. Tel: (01) 686 2599

Trade magazine for recording engineers, record producers, etc; monthly, second Friday; 140pp; £1.50 (free for professionals); circ. 16,000 worldwide

• Swing 51
41 Bushey Road, Sutton, Surrey SM1 1QR

Roots, rock and beyond . . . reviews of folk, ethnic, and rock music worldwide; every six months; 60pp; £1.50; circ. 1,500

• The Wire
Unit G/H 115 Cleveland Street, London W1P 5PN. Tel: (01) 580 7522

Jazz, improvised and new music etc; monthly, first week; 56pp; £1.20; circ. 15,000

MUSIC RELATED ASSOCIATIONS

• American Society of Composers, Authors, and Publishers (ASCAP)
Suite 9, 52 Haymarket, London SW1Y 4RP. Tel: (01) 930 1121 Tx: 25833

• Association of Professional Recording Studios
23 Chestnut Avenue, Chorleywood, Herts WD3 4HA. Tel: (0923) 772907

• British Academy of Songwriters, Composers and Authors
148 Charing Cross Road, London WC2H 0LB. Tel: (01) 240 2823/4

• The British Library National Sound Archive
29 Exhibition Road, London SW7 2AS
Tel: (01) 589 6603/4

• British Music Information Centre
10 Stratford Place, London W1N 9AE
Tel: (01) 499 8567

• British Phonographic Industry
4th Floor, Roxburghe House, 273/287 Regent Street, London W1R 7PB
Tel: (01) 629 8642

• British Tape Industry Association
7-15 Lansdowne Road, Croydon CR9 2PL
Tel: (01) 688 4422 Tx: 917857 Binder G

• Composers Guild of Great Britain
10 Stratford Place, London W1N 9AE
Tel: (01) 499 4795

• Country Music Association
Suite 3, 52 Haymarket, London SW1Y 4RP. Tel: (01) 930 2445/6 Tx: 25833

• International Federation of Phonogram and Videogram Producers
54 Regent Street, London W1R 5PJ
Tel: (01) 434 3521 Tx: 919044 IFPI G

• International Jazz Federation
13 Foulser Road, London SW17 8UE
Tel: (01) 767 2213

• Jazz Centre Society
5 Dryden Street, London WC2E 9NW
Tel: (01) 240 2430

• London Musicians' Collective
42a Gloucester Avenue, London NW1
Tel: (01) 722 0456

● **Mechanical Copyright Protection Society**
Elgar House, 41 Streatham High Road, London SW16 1ER. Tel: (01) 769 4400

● **Media Research and Information Bureau (MRIB)**
12 Manchester Mews, London W1M 5PJ
Tel: (01) 935 0346 Tx: 946240 Cweasy G

● **Music Publishers Association**
7th Floor, 103 Kingsway, London WC2B 6QX. Tel: (01) 831 7591

● **Musicians Benevolent Fund**
16 Ogle Street, London W1P 7LG
Tel: (01) 636 4481

● **Musicians' Union**
60-62 Clapham Road, London SW9 0JJ
Tel: (01) 582 5566 Tx: 881 4691

● **Performing Rights Society**
29-33 Berners Street, London W1P 4AA
Tel: (01) 580 5544 Tx: 892678

● **Record Labels Register**
202 Finchley Road, London NW3 6BL
Tel: (01) 794 0461 Tx: 261712

● **Royal Society of Musicians of Great Britain**
10 Stratford Place, London W1N 9AE
Tel: (01) 629 6137

● **Society for the Promotion of New Music**
10 Stratford Place, London W1N 9AE
Tel: (01) 491 8111

● **Variety Club of Great Britain**
32 Welbeck Street, London W1M 7PG
Tel: (01) 935 4466

US MUSIC REFERENCE

RECORD COMPANIES

● **A&M Records**
1416 North LaBrea Avenue, Hollywood, CA 90068. Tel: (213) 469 2411 Tx: 691282
and
New York Office:
595 Madison Avenue, New York, NY 10022. Tel: (212) 826 0477
Tx: 961105
Labels: A&M

● **Arista Records**
6 West 57th Street, New York, NY 10019
Tel: (212) 489 7400 Tx: 666282
Labels: Arista

● **Atlantic Recording Corp**
75 Rockerfeller Plaza, New York, NY 10019. Tel: (212) 484 6000 Tx: 424602
and
LA office:
9229 Sunset Boulevard, Los Angeles, CA 90069. Tel: (213) 205 7450 Tx: 4720852
Labels: Atco, Atlantic, Cotillion, Elektra, Sire, 21

● **Bearsville Records**
PO Box 135, Bearsville, NY 12409
Tel: (914) 679 7303 Tx: 5102470848
Bearson G
Labels: Bearsville

● **The Benson Co**
365 Great Circle Road, Nashville, TN 37228. Tel: (615) 259 9111
Labels: !Alarma!, Greentree, Heartwarming, Impact, Lifeline, NewPax, Onyx, Paragon

● **Biograph Records**
16 River Street, Chatham, NY 12037
Tel: (518) 392 3400/1
Labels: Biograph, Center, Dawn, Historical, Melodeon, Waterfall

● **Bomp Records**
2702 San Fernando Road, Los Angeles, CA 99065. Tel: (213) 227 4141
Labels: Bomp, Voxx

● **Buddha Records**
1790 Broadway, New York, NY 10019
Tel: (212) 582 6900 Tx: 422573
Labels: Buddha, Roulette, Streetwise, Sunnyview, Sutra

● **Capitol/EMI Records**
1750 Vine Street, Hollywood, CA 90028
Tel: (213) 462 6252 Tx: 674051
and
New York Office:
1370 Avenue of the Americas, New York, NY 10019. Tel: (212) 757 7470
Labels: Blue Note, Capitol, EMI-America, Manhattan

● **CBS Records**
51 West 52nd Street, New York, NY 10019
Tel: (212) 975 4321 Tx: 220561
and
LA office:
1801 Century Park West, Los Angeles, CA 90067. Tel: (213) 556 4700
Labels: CBS, Columbia, Epic

● **Celluloid Records**
330 Hudson Street, New York, NY 10013
Tel: (212) 751 8310 Tx: 669253 Cell
Labels: Celluloid, OAO

● **Chrysalis Records**
645 Madison Avenue, New York, NY 10022. Tel: (212) 758 3555 Tx: 971860
Labels: China, Chrysalis

● **Cream Records**
13107 Ventura Boulevard, Suite 102, Studio City, CA 91604. Tel: (818) 905 6344 Tx: 182693 Shelby
Labels: Cream, Hi

● **Def Jam Records**
594 Broadway (8th Floor), New York, NY 10012. Tel: (212) 925 0169

● **DJ International Records**
727 W. Randolph St, Chicago, Illinois 60606
Tel: (312) 559 1845

Enigma Records
1750 East Holly Avenue, PO Box 2428, El Segundo, CA 90245. Tel: (213) 640 6869 Tx: 503809
Labels: Attune, Enigma, Metal Blade, Pink Dust, Restless

Fantasy Records
2600 10th Street, Berkeley, CA 94710 Tel: (415) 549 2500 Tx: 171312 Universal Berk
Labels: Contemporary, Fantasy, Galaxy, Goodtime, Jazz, Milestone, Prestige, Riverside, Stax

Flying Fish Records
1304, West Schubert Street, Chicago, IL 60614. Tel: (312) 528 5455 Tx: 297175
Labels: Flying Fish

Folkways Records
632 Broadway, New York, NY 10012 Tel: (212) 777 6606 Tx: 220883 Tour
Labels: Folkways

415 Records
PO Box 14563, San Francisco, CA 94114 Tel: (415) 621 3415
Labels: 415

Geffen Records
9130 Sunset Boulevard, Los Angeles, CA 90069. Tel: (213) 278 9010 Tx: 295854
and
New York office:
75 Rockerfeller Plaza, New York, NY 10019. Tel: (212) 474 7170 Tx: 424602
Labels: Geffen

Hannibal Records
3575 Cahuenga Boulevard West, Suite 470, Los Angeles, CA 90068 Tel: (213) 850 5660
Labels: Hannibal

Homestead Records
PO Box 570, Rockville Ctr, New York 11571. Tel: (516) 764 6200

Island Records
14 East 4th Street, New York, NY 10012 Tel: (212) 477 8000 Tx: 7105815292
Labels: Antilles, 4th and Broadway, Island, Mango

Jem Records
3619 Kennedy Road, South Plainfield, NJ 07080. Tel: (201) 753 6100 Tx: 275297 Jemur
and
West Coast office:
18629 Topham Street, Reseda, CA 91335 Tel: (213) 996 6754 Tx: 674851 Jemrec wstreda

Labels: Audion, Coda, Editions EG, EG, EG Classics, Jem, Landscape, Ode, Passport, PVC, Visa

MCA Records
100 Universal City Plaza, Universal City, CA 91608. Tel: (818) 777 1000
and
New York office:
445 Park Avenue, 6th Floor, New York, NY 10022. Tel: (212) 759 7500
Labels: Chess, Dot, Impulse, MCA, Zebra

Motown Records
6255 Sunset Boulevard, Los Angeles, CA 90028. Tel: (213) 468 3500 Tx: 4720916
Labels: Gordy, Motown, Tamla

PolyGram Records
810 Seventh Avenue, New York, NY 10019. Tel: (212) 333 8000 Tx: 620985
and
LA office:
8335 Sunset Boulevard, Los Angeles, CA 90069. Tel: (213) 656 3003
Labels: Casablanca, Mercury, Polydor

Profile Records
740 Broadway (7th Floor), New York, NY 10003. Tel: (212) 529 2600

Ralph Records
109 Minna Street, Suite 391, San Francisco, CA 94105. Tel: (415) 543 4085
Labels: Ralph

RCA/Ariola Records
1133 Avenue of the Americas, New York, NY 10036. Tel: (212) 930 4000
Tx: 234367
and
LA office:
6363 Sunset Boulevard, Hollywood, CA 90028. Tel: (213) 468 4000
Tx: 234367 Attn. Hollywood
Labels: RCA

Reachout International Records
611 Broadway, Suite 725, New York, NY 10012. Tel: (212) 477 0563
Labels: Reachout

Rhino Records
1201 Olympic Boulevard, Santa Monica, CA 90404. Tel: (213) 450 6323
Tx: 4972305
Labels: Rhino

Rough Trade Inc
326 Sixth Street, San Francisco, CA 94103. Tel: (415) 621 4045
Tx: 6771141
Labels: Factory-US, Pitch Attempt, Rough Trade, Silo

Rounder Records
1 Camp Street, Cambridge, MA 02142 Tel: (617) 354 0700 Tx: 921724
Labels: Daring, Fretless, Heartbeat, Philo, Rounder, Varrick

Shanachie Records
1 Hollywood Avenue, Ho-Ho-Kus, NJ 07423. Tel: (201) 445 5561 Tx: 247352
Labels: Herwin, Meadow Lark, Morning Star, Shanachie

Slash Records
7381 Beverly Boulevard, Los Angeles, CA 90036. Tel: (213) 937 4660
Labels: Slash

Sugar Hill Records
96 West Street, Englewood, NJ 07631. Tel: (201) 569 5170 Tx: 429762
Labels: Sugar Hill

Tommy Boy Records
1747 First Avenue, New York, NY 10128 Tel: (212) 722 2211 Tx: 6971684 Funk
Labels: Tommy Boy

Touch And Go Records
PO Box 25520, Chicago, Illinois 60625 Tel: (312) 463 4446

Trax Records
932 W. 38th Place, Chicago, Illinois 60629 Tel: (312) 247 3033

Vanguard Records
71 West 23rd Street, New York, NY 10010 Tel: (212) 255 7732 Tx: 469150
Labels: Terra, Vanguard

Warner Brothers Records
3300 Warner Boulevard, Burbank, CA 91510. Tel: (818) 846 9090
Tx: 698512
and
New York office:
3 East 54th Street, New York, NY 10022 Tel: (212) 702 0318 Tx: 7105815718
Labels: Warner Brothers, Warner Nashville

Wax Trax Records
2445 N. Lincoln Ave, Chicago, Illinois 60614 Tel: (312) 528 8753 Tx: 5106003326

Windham Hill Records
PO Box 9388, Stanford, CA 94305 Tel: (415) 329 0647
Labels: Windham Hill

LABELS

!Alarma! — Benson
Antilles — Island
Atco — Atlantic
Attune — Enigma
Audion — Jem
Blue Note — Capitol/EMI
Casablanca — PolyGram
Center — Biograph
Chess — MCA
China — Chrysalis
Coda — Jem
Columbia — CBS
Contemporary — Fantasy
Cotillion — Atlantic

Daring — Rounder
Dawn — Biograph
Dot — MCA
Editions EG — Jem
EG — Jem
Electra — Atlantic
EMI America — Capitol/EMI
Epic — CBS
Factory US — Rough Trade
4th and Broadway — Island
Fretless — Rounder
Galaxy — Fantasy
Goodtime Jazz — Fantasy
Gordy — Motown

Greentree — Benson
Heartbeat — Rounder
Heartwarming — Benson
Herwin — Shanachie
Hi — Cream
Historical — Biograph
Impact — Benson
Impulse — MCA
Landscape — Jem
Lifeline — Benson
Mango — Island
Manhattan — Capitol/EMI
Meadow Lark — Shanachie
Melodeon — Biograph

Mercury — PolyGram
Metal Blade — Enigma
Milestone — Fantasy
Morning Star — Shanachie
NewPax — Benson
Ode — Jem
Onyx — Benson
Paragon — Benson
Passport — Jem
Philo — Rounder
Pink Dust — Enigma

Pitch Attempt — Rough Trade
Polydor — PolyGram
Prestige — Fantasy
PVC — Jem
Restless — Enigma
Riverside — Fantasy
Roulette — Buddha
Silo — Rough Trade
Stax — Fantasy
Streetwise — Buddha
Sunnyview — Buddha

Sutra — Buddha
Tamla — Motown
Terra — Vanguard
21 — Atlantic
Varrick — Rounder
Visa — Jem
Voxx — Bomp
Waterfall — Biograph
Zebra — MCA

MUSIC PUBLISHERS

• Abkco Music
1700 Broadway, 41st Floor, New York,
NY 10019. Tel: (212) 399 0300
Tx: 234874

• Acuff-Rose Publications
2510 Franklin Road, Nashville, TN 37204
Tel: (615) 385 3031 Tx: 554366

• April/Blackwood Music
49 East 52nd Street, New York, NY 10022
Tel: (212) 975 4886 Tx: 220561

• Augsburg Publishing
426 South Fifth Street, Minneapolis,
MN 55415. Tel: (612) 330 3300

• Beserkely
2054 University Avenue, Suite 400,
Berkeley, CA 94704. Tel: (415) 848 6701

• Big Music
10 George Street, Wallingford, CT 06492
Tel: (203) 269 4465

• Big Seven Music
1790 Broadway, 18th Floor, New York,
NY 10019. Tel: (212) 582 4267
Tx: 422573

• Bourne Co
437 Fifth Avenue, New York, NY 10016
Tel: (212) 679 3700

• Buddha Music
1790 Broadway, New York, NY 10019
Tel: (212) 582 6900 Tx: 422573

• Bug Music
6777 Hollywood Boulevard, 9th Floor,
Hollywood, CA 90028. Tel: (213) 466 4352
Tx: 9103213926

• Cameron Organisation
822 Hillgrove Avenue, Western Springs,
IL 60558. Tel: (312) 246 8222

• CBS Songs
49 East 52nd Street, New York, NY 10022
Tel: (212) 975 4886 Tx: 960213

• Chappell/Intersong Music
810 Seventh Avenue, 32nd Floor, New
York, NY 10019. Tel: (212) 399 6910
Tx: 421749

• Chrysalis Music Group
645 Madison Avenue, New York, NY
10022. Tel: (212) 758 3555 Tx: 971860

• Cotillion Music
75 Rockerfeller Plaza, New York, NY
10019. Tel: (212) 484 8132 Tx: 424602

• Crazy Cajun Music
5626 Brock Street, Houston, TX 77023
Tel: (713) 926 4431

• Cream Publishing
13107 Ventura Boulevard, Suite 102,
Studio City, CA 91604. Tel: (818) 905 6344

• Entertainment Company Music
1700 Broadway, 41st Floor, New York, NY
10019. Tel: (212) 265 2600 Tx: 6972989

• Evansongs
1790 Broadway, New York, NY 10019
Tel: (212) 765 8450 Tx: 125609 Espnyk

• Famous Music
1 Gulf and Western Plaza, New York, NY
10023. Tel: (212) 333 3433 Tx: 235260

• Carl Fisher Inc
62 Cooper Square, New York, NY 10003
Tel: (212) 777 0900 Tx: 4774129

• Flying Fish Music
1304 West Schubert Street, Chicago IL
60614. Tel: (312) 528 5455 Tx: 297175

• Al Gallico Music
344 East 49th Street, New York,
NY 10017. Tel: (212) 355 5980

• Garrett Music
4121 Radford Avenue, Studio City,
CA 91604. Tel: (818) 506 8964

• Glad Music
3409 Brinkman Street, Houston, TX 77018
Tel: (713) 861 3630

• Graph Music
34 Ratterman Road, Woodstock, New York,
NY 12498. Tel: (914) 679 2458

• Al Green Music
PO Box 456, Millington, TN 38053
Tel: (901) 794 6220

• Hilaria Music
315 West Gorham Street, Madison,
W1 53703. Tel: (608) 251 2644

• Home Grown Music
4412 Whitsett Avenue, Studio City,
CA 91604. Tel: (818) 763 6323

• House of Cash
700 Johnny Cash Parkway,
Hendersonville, TN 37075
Tel: (615) 824 5110

• Hudson Bay Music
1619 Broadway 11th Floor, New York,
NY 10019. Tel: (212) 489 8170 Tx: 62932

• Intersong Music
6255 Sunset Boulevard, Suite 1904,
Hollywood, CA 90028. Tel: (213) 469 5141
Tx: 4991128

• Island Music
6525 Sunset Boulevard, 2nd Floor,
Hollywood, CA 90028. Tel: (213) 469 1285
Tx: 691223
Ackeelsa

• Jobete Music
6255 Sunset Boulevard, Hollywood,
CA 90028. Tel: (213) 468 3500

• Largo Music
425 Park Avenue, New York, NY 10022
Tel: (212) 371 9400 Tx: 8389487

• Laurie Publishing
450 Livingston Street, Norwood,
NJ 07648. Tel: (201) 767 5551

•Hal Leonard Publishing
PO Box 13809, Milwaukee WI 53213
Tel: (414) 774 3630 Tx: 26668

• Marsaint Music
3809 Clematis Avenue, New Orleans,
LA 70122. Tel: (504) 949 8386

• MCA Music
70 Universal City Plaza, Suite 425,
Universal City CA 91608
Tel: (818) 777 4550 Tx: 677053 Universal
City

• Ivan Mogull Music
625 Madison Avenue, New York, NY
10022. Tel: (212) 355 5636 Tx: 236973

• Neil Music
8400 Sunset Boulevard, Suite 4a, Los
Angeles, CA 90069. Tel: (213) 656 2614
Tx: 5106000877

• Pale Pachyderm Publishing
566 Folsom Street, San Francisco,
CA 94105. Tel: (415) 543 8248

• Peer-Southern Organisation
1740 Broadway, New York, NY 10019
Tel: (212) 265 3910 Tx: 424361

• The Richmond Organisation (TRO)
10 Columbus Circle, New York, NY 10019
Tel: (212) 765 9889 Tx: 429359

• Rough Trade
326 Sixth Avenue, San Francisco, CA
94103. Tel: (415) 621 4045
Tx: 6771141

• Screen Gems — EMI Music
6920 Sunset Boulevard, Hollywood, CA
90028. Tel: (213) 469 8371

• Paul Simon Music
1619 Broadway, Room 500, New York,
NY 10019. Tel: (212) 541 7571
Tx: 645 491

- **Special Rider Music**
PO Box 860, Cooper Station, New York,
NY 10276. Tel: (212) 473 5900
Tx: 661139

- **TRO**
See the Richmond Organisation

- **20th Century-Fox Music**
PO Box 900, Beverly Hills, CA 90213
Tel: (213) 203 1487 Tx: 674895

- **Warner Brothers Music**
9000 Sunset Boulevard, The Penthouse
Suite, Los Angeles, CA 90069. Tel: (213)
273 3323 Tx: 9104902598

- **Welk Music**
1299 Ocean Avenue, Suite 800, Santa
Monica, CA 90401. Tel: (213) 870 1582

- **Word Music**
PO Box 2790, Waco, TX 76796. Tel: (817)
772 7650 Tx: 530642

- **WPN Music**
10 Swirl Lane, Levittown, NY 11756
Tel: (516) 796 3698

DISTRIBUTORS/IMPORTERS

- **Abbey Road Record Distributors**
1721 Newport Circle, Santa Ana,
CA 92705. Tel : (714) 546 7177

- **All South Distribution**
1037 Broadway, New Orleans, LA 70118
Tel: (504) 861 2906

- **ARC Distributing Corp**
580 Reading Road, Cincinnati, OH 45202
Tel: (513) 381 4237

- **Associated Distributors**
3803 North 36th Avenue, Phoenix,
AZ 85019. Tel: (602) 278 5584

- **Rick Ballard Imports**
PO Box 24854, Oakland, CA 94623
Tel: (415) 832 1277

- **Bayside Record Distribution**
10341 San Pablo Avenue, El Cerrito,
CA 94530. Tel: (415) 525 4996

- **California Record Distributors**
1242 Los Angeles Street, Glendale,
CA 91204. Tel: (818) 246 8228

- **Dutch East India Trading**
81 North Forest Avenue, Rockville Center,
NY 11570 Tel: (516) 764 6200

- **Goldenrod Distribution**
5505 Delta River Drive, Lansing, MI 48906
Tel: (517) 323 4325

- **Greenworld Distribution**
20445 Gramercy Place, Torrance, CA
90501. Tel: (213) 533 8075 Tx: 4720103

- **Important Record Distribution**
149-03 Guy R. Brewer Boulevard, Jamaica,
NY 11434. Tel: (718) 995 9200

- **Jem Record Distribution**
3619 Kennedy Road, South Plainfield,
NJ 07080 Tel: (201) 753 6100
and
West Coast office:
18629 Topham Street, Reseda, CA 91335
Tel: (213) 996 6754

- **MS Distributing Co**
1050 Arthur Avenue, Elk Grove Village,
IL 60007. Tel: (312) 364 2888

- **Music Town Record Distributors**
830 Glastonbury Road, Suite 614,
Nashville, TN 37217. Tel: (615) 327 4538

- **Rough Trade**
326 Sixth Street, San Francisco, CA
94103. Tel: (415) 621 4045 Tx: 6771141

- **Rounder Distribution**
1 Camp Street, Cambridge, MA 02142
Tel: (617) 345 0700 Tx: 921724

- **SDA Distribution**
1109 Xerxes Avenue South, Minneapolis,
MN 55405. Tel: (612) 0590

- **Sounds Good Import Co**
3355 West El Segundo Avenue,
Hawthorne, CA 90250. Tel: (213) 973
8800 Tx: 4990518

- **Southern Cross Record
Distributors**
1200 Newell Hill Place, Suite 302, Walnut
Creek, CA 94596. Tel: (415) 945 1855

- **Spring Arbor Distribution**
10885 Textile Road, Belleville, MI 48111
Tel: (313) 481 0900

- **Systematic Record Distributors**
1331 Fulsom Street, San Francisco, CA
94103. Tel: (415) 431 9377

- **Twin Cities Imports**
1451 University Avenue, St Paul, MN
55104. Tel: (612) 645 0227 Tx: 4940057

- **Universal Record Distribution**
919 North Broad Street, Philadelphia, PA
19123. Tel: (215) 232 3333

MUSIC RELATED ASSOCIATIONS

- **Academy of Country Music**
6255 Sunset Boulevard, Suite 915,
Hollywood, CA 90028. Tel: (213) 462 2351

- **American Federation of Musicians**
1501 Broadway, Suite 600, New York,
NY 10036. Tel: (212) 869 1330

- **ASCAP**
1 Lincoln Plaza, New York, NY 10023
Tel: (212) 585 3050 Tx: 7105812084

- **Association of Independent Music
Publishers**
c/o Harrison Music, 6253 Hollywood
Boulevard, Hollywood, CA 90028
Tel: (213) 466 3834

- **Black Music Association**
1500 Locust Street, Suite 1905,
Philadelphia, PA 19102
Tel: (215) 545 8600

- **BMI**
320 West 57th Street, New York, NY
10019. Tel: (212) 586 2000 Tx: 127823

- **Country Music Association**
7 Music Circle North, Nashville, TN 37202
Tel: (615) 244 2840 Tx: 786528

- **Jazz Composers' Orchestra
Association**
500 Broadway, New York, NY 10012
Tel: (212) 925 2121 Tx: 291524

- **National Academy of Recording
Arts and Sciences**
303 North Gen Oaks Boulevard, Suite 140,
Burbank, CA 91502. Tel: (818) 843 8233

- **National Association of
Independent Record Distributors**
c/o Richman Brothers Records,
6935 Airport Highway Lane, Pennsauken,
NJ 08109. Tel: (609) 665 8085

- **National Association of Music
Merchants**
5240 Avenida Encinas, Carlsbad,
CA 92008. Tel: (619) 438 8001

- **Recording Industry Association of
America**
888 Seventh Avenue, New York,
NY 10106. Tel: (212) 765 4330

- **SESAC**
10 Columbus Circle, 13th Floor, New York,
NY 10019. Tel: (212) 586 3450

- **Songwriters Guild of America**
276 5th Avenue, Room 306, New York,
NY 10001. Tel: (212) 686 6820

- **American Songwriter**
5065 Lebanon Road, Old Hickory,
Tennessee 37138. Tel: (615) 754 5200
Pop, R&B, country music, geared to the
professional and amateur songwriter; bi-monthly;
32pp; $2.25; circ: 5,000 subscription only

- **BAM**
5951 Canning Street, Oakland, CA 94609
Tel: (415) 652 3810
and
1800 North Highland, Suite 220,
Hollywood CA 90028. Tel: (213) 467 7878
Covers US and international bands with the
emphasis of commercial successes from
mainstream rock to pop and progressive; also has
features on up-and-coming bands (California
edition covers mainly Californian artists);
national ed. bi-monthly, California ed. fortnightly;
64pp; national ed. $1.95, California ed. free; circ:
125,000 (each)

- **Billboard**
1515 Broadway, New York, NY 10036
Tel: (212) 764 7300
Trade magazine covering most of the areas of rock
music, also sells to the punter on the street; every
Tuesday; 80pp; $3.50; circ: 48,000

- **Boston Rock**
1318 Beacon Street, Suite 7, Brooklyme,
MA 02146. Tel: (617) 734 7043
Alternative arts and lifestyle magazine, covering
local and national underground acts as well as
imports; monthly; 32pp; free in MA, $1.50 outside
MA; circ: 30,000

- **Cash Box**
330 West 58th Street, New York,
NY 10019 Tel: (212) 586 2640
Trade magazine covering rock, pop, jazz, black
contemporary and dance music; every Monday;
50pp; $3,50; circ: n/a

- **Circus**
419 Park Avenue South, New York,
NY 10016. Tel: (212) 685 5050
Hard rock and heavy metal superstars; monthly,
last week; 90pp; $1.95/£1.50; circ: n/a

- **CMJ New Music Report**
834 Willis Avenue, Albertson, NY 11507
Tel: (516) 248 9600
Magazine covering progressive rock, jazz, folk,
country, reggae, selling primarily to younger
musicians and record industry execs; 50% charts,
50% features; fortnightly; 60pp; $6.00; circ: 14,000

- **Country News**
5065 Lebanon Road, Old Hickory,
Tennessee 37138. Tel: (615) 754 5200
The latest country industry news for fans as well as
record executives; monthly; 24pp; $1.50;
circ: 160,000 subscription only

- **Country Rhythms**
5065 Lebanon Road, Old Hickory,
Tennessee 37138. Tel: (615) 754 5200
Features and interviews with prominent country
artists; monthly; 56pp; $2.50; circ: 120,000

- **Country Songs Round-up**
Charlton Buildings, Division Street, Derby,
CT 06418. Tel: (203) 735 3381
Lyrics of country music Top 40, reviews, features;
monthly; 58pp; $1.75; circ: n/a

- **Country Sounds**
700 East State Street, Iola, WI 54990
Tel: (715) 445 2214
Country record collectors' magazine; monthly;
60pp; $1.95; circ: n/a

- **CREEM**
210 South Woodward Avenue,
Birmingham, MI 48011
Tel: (313) 642 8833
Eclectic magazine that credits its readers with a
sense of humour and the second longest-running
US music magazine after *Rolling Stone*; monthly;
66pp; $2.25; circ: c. 100,000

- **Down Beat**
180 West Park Avenue, Elmhurst,
IL 60126. Tel: (312) 941 2030
Jazz magazine for contemporary musicians, also
covering rock, blues and contemporary classical
instrumentalists; monthly; 62pp; $1.75/£2.00;
circ: 95,000

- **Flipside**
PO Box 363, Whittier, CA 90608
Hardcore punk fanzine; irregular monthly;
nothing else known

- **Frets**
20625 Lazaneo, Cupertino, CA 95014
Tel: (408) 446 1105
Folk, classical, and bluegrass for acoustic stringed
instrument players; monthly; 68pp; $1.95; circ:
70,000

- **Goldmine**
700 East State Street, Iola, WI 54990
Tel: (715) 445 2214
Eclectic record collectors' magazine from hard rock
to folk and country; fortnightly; 90pp; $1.95; circ:
15,000

- **Guitar Player**
20605 Lazaneo, Cupertino, CA 95014
Tel: (408) 446 1105
Guitar magazine written by musicians for
musicians, rock, jazz, classical; monthly; 156pp;
$2.95; circ: 170,000

- **Guitar World**
1115 Broadway, 8th Floor, New York,
NY 10010. Tel: (212) 807 7100
Covers all kinds of guitar-based music, rock, jazz,
blues, etc, except classical; bi-monthly; 102pp;
$2.95; circ: 160,000

- **Hard Rock**
475 Park Avenue South, New York,
NY 10016. Tel: (212) 689 2830
Mainstream hard rock, hardcore and metal; lots of
interviews and regular features; monthly; 80pp;
$2.25/£1.45; circ: 200,000 worldwide

- **High Fidelity**
825 Seventh Avenue, New York,
NY 10019. Tel: (212) 887 8337
Reviews of the latest hi-fi equipment along with
some features on pop and classical releases;
monthly; 86pp; $2.25; circ: 350,000

- **Hit Parader**
Charlton Building, Division Street, Derby
CT 06148. Tel: (203) 735 5381
and
New York office:
441 Lexington Avenue, Suite 808,
New York, NY 10017. Tel: (212) 370 0986
Looks at hard rock and heavy metal superstars,
interviews, features etc for the teenager; monthly;
82pp; $2.25/£1.50; circ: 100,000

- **Illinois Entertainer**
PO Box 356, Mount Prospect, IL 60056
Tel: (312) 298 9333
Entertainment magazine covering the music scene
(among other things) in Illinois; monthly; 90pp; free
in record stores, etc; circ: 80,000

- **International Musician and
Recording World**
1075 Easton Avenue, Suite 1, Tower 2,
Somerset, NJ 08873. Tel: (201) 249 1600
Spans all types of contemporary music from pop,
rock to avant-garde ethnic. Reviews latest
equipment and releases primarily for musicians
and recording executives, but also for the listener;
monthly; 64pp; $2.50; circ: 65,000

- **Jazz Times**
8055 13th Street, Silver Springs,
MD 20910. Tel: (301) 558 4114
Straight-ahead traditional jazz, trade and fan
magazine; news, reviews, artist profiles, listings of
radio airplay; monthly; 28pp; $1.50; circ: 58,000

- **Keyboard**
20605 Lazaneo, Cupertino, CA 95014
Tel: (408) 446 1105
Features on equipment, techniques and artists, for
keyboard players; monthly; 140pp; $2.50/£2.00;
circ: 85,000

- **Living Blues**
The Center for the Study of Southern
Culture, University of Mississippi,
University, MS 38677. Tel: (601) 232 5993
Blues news, interviews, and record reviews; bi-monthly; 48pp; $3.00; circ: 5,000

- **Musician**
31 Commercial Street, Gloucester,
MA 01930. Tel: (617) 281 3110
and
New York office:
1515 Broadway, New York, NY 10036
Tel: (212) 764 7300
Up-market serious magazine covering the entire
spectrum of the music-making process, creative
and technological, for the professional and
dedicated amateur; monthly; 116pp; $2.50/£1.50;
circ: 116,000

- **Radio and Records**
1930 Century Park West, Los Angeles,
CA 90067. Tel: (213) 553 4330
Radio and record industry magazine with lots of
charts regular features on US radio, news, etc;
every Friday; 96pp; $5.00; circ: n/a

- **Rock & Soul**
Charlton Building, Division Street, Derby,
CT 06418. Tel: (203) 735 3381
and
New York office:
441 Lexington Avenue, Suite 808,
New York, NY 10017. Tel: (212) 370 0986
Glossy magazine covering commercial black
music, with news hotline, profiles, reviews;
monthly; 50pp; $1.75; circ: 80,000

- **Rocket**
Charlton Building, Division Street, Derby,
CT 06418. Tel: (203) 735 3381
New superstar magazine; monthly; 50pp $1.95;
circ: n/a

The Rocket
2322 Second Avenue, Seattle, WA 98121
Tel: (206) 587 4001
Sardonic entertainments magazine covering local
and national acts, music, arts, politics, cartoons
and gossip columns; monthly; 38pp; $2.00;
circ: 65,000

Rockpool Newsletter
83 Leonard Street, 2nd Floor, New York, NY
10013. Tel: (212) 219 0777
An alternative look at hip black music and new
wave dance, playlists and charts from club DJs and
US college radio scene; fortnightly; 30pp; $1.75;
circ: 2,000

Rolling Stone
745 Fifth Avenue, New York, NY 10151
Tel: (212) 758 3800
The magazine for young American adults; much
more than just a music magazine: looks at politics,
popular culture, etc etc; a national institution;
fortnightly; 100pp; $1.95/£1.90; circ: 1,000,000
worldwide

Song Hits
Charlton Building, Division Street, Derby
CT 06418. Tel: (203) 735 3381
Song lyrics, concert and album reviews of Top 40
rock, soul and country musicians; for teenage girls;
monthly; 66pp; $1.95; circ: 160,000

Spin
1965 Broadway, New York, NY 10023
Tel: (212) 496 6100
A zany, humorous look at established, new, and
underground acts; news and reviews from
mainstream rock to ethnic sounds; also looks at
topical issues of youth culture; monthly; 82pp;
$2.00; circ: 15,000

Star Hits
25 W. 39th Street, New York, NY 10018
Tel: (212) 302 2626
Glossy teenage girls' magazine styled after the
British *Smash Hits*; interviews and features on
commercial successes; monthly; 64pp; $1.95; circ:
163,000

WAM
PO Box 356, Mount Prospect, IL 60056
Tel: (312) 298 9333
Entertainment magazine covering the music scene
in Wisconsin; monthly; 60pp; free at record stores,
etc; circ: 30,000

WAVELENGTH
PO Box 15667, New Orleans, LA 707175
Tel: (504) 895 2342
New Orleans jazz, R&B, blues, cajun, etc and local
culture; reviews independently released records;
monthly; 40pp; free in LA, $1.50 outside LA;
circ: 30,000